Consumer Behavior
and
Marketing Action

Henry Assael

New York University

Kent Publishing Company
Boston, Massachusetts
A Division of Wadsworth, Inc.

To Alyce, Shaun, and Brenda

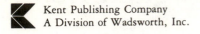 Kent Publishing Company
A Division of Wadsworth, Inc.

Production Editor: Nancy Phinney
Text Designer: Armen Kojoyian
Cover Designer: Steve Snider
Production Coordinator: Linda Card

Printed in the United States of America
3 4 5 6 7 8 9 — 85 84 83 82

Library of Congress Cataloging in Publication Data

Assael, Henry.
    Consumer behavior and marketing action.

Includes bibliographical references and index.
    1. Consumers.   2. Consumers—Examination, questions, etc.   3. Motivation research (Marketing)
4. Motivation research (Marketing)—Examinations, questions, etc.   I. Title.
HC79.C6A87   658.8′342   80–27898
ISBN 0–534–00958–1

ACKNOWLEDGMENTS

Figures. Page 60: Figure 3–4, reprinted with permission from Charles E. Merrill Publishing Co. *Page 69:* Figure 3–6, reprinted with permission from Elsevier North-Holland, Inc. *Page 117:* Figure 5–5, by permission of Estée Lauder, Inc. *Page 222:* Figure 9–6, reprinted with permission from the American Marketing Association. *Page 279:* Figure 11–1, ad for L'Oreal Radiance by permission of Mingo-Jones Advertising, Inc. Ad for Dark & Lovely by permission of Lockhard & Pettus, Inc., Advertising & Public Relations. *Page 298:* Figure 12–2, reprinted by permission of Amway Corporation. *Page 578:* Figure 23–1, reprinted with permission from Jagdish N. Sheth.
Tables. Page 65: Table 3–1, reprinted with permission from the *Journal of Marketing Research.* Page 89: Table 4–2, reprinted with permission of the American Marketing Association. *Page 90:* Table 4–3, reprinted with permission from the *Journal of Marketing Research. Page 158:* Table 7–1, reprinted with permission of the American Marketing Association. *Page 227:* Table 9–2, reprinted with permission from the American Marketing Association. *Page 566:* Table 22–3, reprinted with permission from *European Research.*

Contents

Six

Consumer Perceptions and Marketing Strategy

134

Seven

Consumer Attitudes and Needs

154

Eight

Attitude Change Strategies

188

Nine

Demographics
208

Ten

Psychographic Characteristics
232

Part Three

Environmental Influences
on Consumer Behavior
261

Eleven

Cultural Influences
262

Twelve

Social Class Influences

294

Thirteen

Reference Group Influences

316

Fourteen

Family Decision Making

340

Part Four
Applications
445

ix

Glossary
602

Name Index
620

Subject Index
627

Preface

The motivation for writing this book was to link consumer behavior concepts to strategic applications. At the time that the book was initiated, the author had been teaching consumer behavior for over ten years and had been a consultant to marketing firms for an even longer period. He felt that texts in consumer behavior did not provide students with the important link between concept and application. Comments of many students bore this out. The statement that "My consumer behavior course seemed like a rehash of my social psych course" was all too frequent.

The lack of an applications perspective to consumer behavior was a function of a natural process of growth. Consumer behavior was not fully developed as a separate social science. The field had to rely on concepts and empirical tools of other social sciences. As a result, the focus on marketing applications was lacking. Attitudinal, perceptual, social, and personality theories and constructs were borrowed from psychology and sociology without the necessary adaptation to the more applied, day-to-day considerations of consumer purchase behavior.

The strategic orientation of this book does not diminish the importance placed on a conceptual foundation. The first three sections of the book establish such a foundation within a strategic context. The fourth is devoted specifically to behavioral applications related to product, promotional, price, and place considerations. The book is organized around the consumer decision process (Part I). The purchase decision is a function of the individual consumer (Part II), the consumer's environment (Part III), and marketing influences (Part IV).

The process of consumer decision making is the logical starting point for a book on consumer behavior since it provides an integrated view of consumer choice and introduces many of the concepts that are considered in more detail in the individual consumer and environmental sections. Three types of consumer choice processes are considered: (1) complex decision making, (2) habit, and (3) low involvement decision making. The distinction between decision making and habit is fairly standard. But the distinction is also made between high and low involvement decision processes. A chapter is devoted to the latter. Low involvement decision making has not previously been treated in a consumer behavior text. The lack of attention to low involvement decision processes is surprising since so much of consumer behavior can be described as low involvement.

Part II deals with the cognitive consumer variables—needs, attitudes, and perceptions—and the descriptive consumer characteristics—demographics, personality, and life-style. The attitudinal chapter describes in detail multi-attribute models of attitude structure. Both chapters on perceptions and attitudes have succeeding chapters that focus on strategic applications. In the case of perceptions, the chapter deals with the strategic implications of processes of selective perception and perceptual organization. In the case of attitudes, the chapter deals with strategies of attitude change based on the multiattribute models described previously—namely, strategies to change brand beliefs and values. The chapters on demographics and life-style present examples of the utilization of these variables from some proprietary industry studies.

Part III first deals with the broadest influences on consumer behavior—culture and social class. The focus then shifts to a more specific level with chapters on reference group influences and family decision making. The next two chapters deal with group communications. One describes word-of-mouth communications within groups and the process of opinion leadership. The other considers communications across groups through a process of diffusion of products and ideas.

The section on the environment concludes with a chapter on situational determinants. The purchase and consumption situation must be considered part of the consumer's environment. In fact, it may be the determining environmental factor since many brands are purchased on a situation-specific basis. This is another important area that has received little attention in consumer behavior texts and in the marketing literature.

Part IV is a basic departure from conventional consumer behavior texts. It links behavioral concepts to each component of marketing strategy. The initial chapter deals with market segmentation and product positioning, and thus emphasizes the identification of market opportunity. Subsequent chapters deal with specific components of the marketing plan—advertising, in-store stimuli, personal selling, and price. But, the focus is not managerial; it is faithfully behavioral. In each chapter the strategic material is linked to a behavioral component. Thus, market segmentation considers definition of consumer groups by needs, descriptive characteristics, and response predispositions. Advertising is discussed within the framework of a basic communications model and consumer information processing. Store influences are examined in terms of consumer shopping types and shopping behavior and within the context of a model of store choice. The section on pricing considers the consumer's awareness of and sensitivity to prices. Personal selling deals with the behavioral interactions involved in the consumer-salesperson dyad. Much of the material in Part IV is based on proprietary industry studies.

Up to this point, the book deals with consumer behavior. Another type of behavior that has not been treated in other consumer behavior texts is organizational buyer behavior. A chapter on industrial buying is essential, considering the fact that over half the economic activity in America is represented by the industrial purchaser. The book concludes by reviewing the consumer movement, consumer rights, and marketing's responsibility to the consumer.

Comprehensive questions at the end of each chapter can be used for class discussion and provide a sufficient basis for integrating much of the chapter content. Utilizing the discussion questions permits constant student involvement. In addition, each chapter has several comprehensive research assignments that can be reasonably implemented by students. A glossary of terms at the back of the book should be of assistance to students.

Writing the book has been an educational experience. It has convinced the author that consumer behavior exists in its own right as a social discipline. Moreover, the orientation of the book suggests that consumer behavior can be studied and taught in an applications framework that is linked to marketing management and strategy. If this were not the case, one would have to question the place of consumer behavior in a business school curriculum. Fortunately, the link between concept and application can be established.

Henry Assael
New York City
March 1981

Acknowledgments

Many people have helped in the preparation of this text. Special thanks are due to three colleagues for their valuable assistance and advice: Rich Lutz at UCLA, Mike Houston at the University of Wisconsin, and Bill Locander at the University of Houston. The orientation and perspective of the book are a reflection of their input.

Thanks are also due to Dave McEttrick, senior editor at Kent, for being a faithful adherent to the manuscript. Dave provided much needed support and his insights into the field of consumer behavior were most helpful. It is rare to find an editor so involved. Nancy Phinney, production editor at Kent, was invaluable in editing and organizing the book. Her efforts ensured an accurate rendering of the book. Michael Paladini, editorial secretary, also assisted in the final stages of production.

John Gettel and his staff at the manuscript center at New York University's Graduate School of Business Administration spent many hours preparing the manuscript. Their faithful assistance is acknowledged. Special thanks also go to Suzanne Diaz for pulling together many of the administrative details in the final months of manuscript preparation. The author's research assistant, Lynn Davis, was also extremely helpful in this regard.

Finally, sincere thanks are due to Alyce Assael, not just for being my wife, but for being a true colleague in this effort. Her reading of the chapters and her many suggestions proved invaluable.

ONE

Introduction

Focus of Chapter

Sales determine profits, and consumer actions determine sales. Yet, only in the last twenty years has marketing management become concerned with studying consumer behavior. Why? Until recently, marketing management was satisfied with evaluating sales results only: it did not consider the needs and motives leading to consumer behavior.

Today, the marketing manager's concern with "why" has brought a new, more efficient focus to marketing products. It has caused marketing management to analyze the factors that influence the choice of a particular brand. Now marketing managers are concerned about delivering product benefits, changing brand attitudes, and influencing consumer perceptions. Marketing management realizes that marketing plans must be based on the psychological and social forces that are likely to condition consumer behavior — that is, what goes on inside the consumer's head.

This introductory chapter establishes a managerial orientation to the study of consumer behavior. Why the study of consumer behavior is important will be considered and the organization of the book will be reviewed.

A HISTORICAL PERSPECTIVE

The widespread use of behavioral research to further the goals of marketing management dates to the emergence of the marketing concept in the post–Korean War buyers' market. The **marketing concept*** states that all

*All terms in boldface type are defined in the glossary at the back of the book.

strategies must be based on known consumer needs. Marketers must first identify the benefits consumers want from certain products and then gear marketing strategies accordingly.

The marketing concept seems so logical today that one may wonder why marketers did not turn to it sooner. There are two reasons. First, marketing institutions were not sufficiently developed before 1950 to accept the marketing concept. Behavioral research was in its infancy. Moreover, advertising and distributive facilities were more suited to the mass-production and mass-marketing strategies of that time. The implementation of the marketing concept requires a diversity of facilities for promoting and distributing products that meet the needs of smaller and more diverse market segments. This diversity in marketing institutions did not exist before 1950. The emphasis was on economies of scale in production and marketing. Coca-Cola was a one-product company; Chevrolet had only one model.

The second reason the marketing concept was not accepted until the 1950s is that prior to that time there was no economic necessity to do so. There was little purchasing power during the depression to spur an interest in consumer behavior. During World War II and immediately thereafter, scarcities were prevalent. There was no competitive pressure to find out consumers' motives or to adjust product offerings to consumer needs. Manufacturers could sell what they made.

The end of the Korean War in 1953 changed all this. The conversion to peacetime production was rapid and efficient. Different marketers brought out similar lines of refrigerators, ovens, and cars. But now they found consumers reluctant to buy. Many consumers were not in the market to buy because they had foreseen scarcities and had purchased durables at the onset of the Korean War. Others had become more selective in their purchasing habits after two major wars and a depression. Consumers became reluctant buyers. For the first time, supply exceeded demand and inventories built up in the face of consumer purchasing power. The economy experienced its first true buyers' market.

Some marketers reacted by intensifying the old strategies: Push the existing line, heighten selling efforts, repeat selling themes, and push excess inventories on unwilling distributors and dealers. Others reacted with more foresight by recognizing that the right combination of product benefits would induce reluctant consumers to purchase. These manufacturers researched the market to identify consumer needs and develop products to fit these needs. This newer approach resulted in an expanded set of product offerings. It also caused advertising strategy to shift from the repetitive campaigns designed to maintain brand awareness to more creative, diverse campaigns designed to communicate product benefits.

Marketers began talking in behavioral terms. A product must deliver a set of consumer benefits and must be positioned to meet the needs of a defined segment of consumers. Advertising's goals are to communicate symbols and images that show how the brand meets consumer needs, to create a favorable attitude towards the brand, and to induce trial. Reinforcing favorable experiences in consumers' minds is needed to influence people to repurchase.

The shift from a logistical, sales orientation to a more behavioral orientation did not occur overnight. It is still going on today. It has changed the nature of marketing operations by:

- *providing a spur to behavioral research.* Marketers are now more likely to define consumer needs in consumer terms. Coffee might be described by its richness, brewed flavor, or strength.

- *encouraging quantification of the qualitative factors that influence consumers to purchase.* What percentage of consumers want a stronger or weaker coffee? What percentage see a certain brand as strong?

- *emphasizing market segmentation.* Consumers with similar needs and behavior are grouped into segments. One segment of the coffee market that is dissatisfied with existing decaffeinated coffee might want a richly brewed coffee that allows sleep; another segment might want coffee to serve to guests.

- *emphasizing product positioning to meet consumer needs.* Products are developed and advertised to fill a specific place in the market relative to consumer needs. Objectives are developed to achieve product uniqueness relative to competition and to communicate product benefits to defined market segments.

- *creating greater selectivity in advertising and personal selling.* Messages must communicate to defined segments. Emphasis is now on selective marketing rather than mass marketing.

- *creating more selective media and distributive outlets.* There are now more specialized magazines, greater uses of direct mail, and more specialty wholesalers and retailers.

In summary, the acceptance of the marketing concept means that marketing management has recognized that the determinants of consumer behavior have a direct bearing on the formulation of marketing strategies. The process of consumer decision making must therefore be studied, and behavioral sciences such as psychology and sociology contribute to understanding consumer behavior.

Figure 1–1 portrays this shift from a sales to a consumer behavior orientation by describing the role of marketing research for a hypothetical company, National Soups, in 1950 and in 1980. The nature of research in 1980 demonstrates the understanding that feedback from the consumer is central to evaluating new product opportunities.

FIGURE 1–1   A Marketing Manager's View of Consumer Behavior: 1950 Versus 1980 The following memos between the marketing manager and the marketing research director of National Soups, a hypothetical company that produces condensed soup, represent two separate points in time. (In 1950, the company did not have a marketing research director. The individual in charge of research was the director of sales research.)

1950

TO: Director of Sales Research

FROM: Marketing Manager

DATE: October 25, 1950

SUBJECT: Introduction of new soup concentrate

What are your plans to obtain information from industry and consumer sources that might indicate the sales performance of the new soup concentrate after introduction?

TO: Marketing Manager

FROM: Director of Sales Research

DATE: October 28, 1950

SUBJECT: Plans to obtain information on new soup concentrate

The most important advantage of the new concentrate as communicated by our laboratory people is that it loses less flavor in processing. On this basis I feel the prospects of success are good, but we cannot proceed on my judgment alone. Therefore, I plan to utilize the following sources of information:

- sales figures on the introduction of a similar concentrate by a competitor;
- feedback from our sales representatives on attitudes of wholesalers and chain food buyers; (Do they think the product will sell? Are they willing to give the product adequate shelf space?)
- blind taste tests with our employees (our product versus competitor's product);
- blind taste tests on our panel of housewives, known as taste experts, to provide a check against the results from our employee tests.

1980

TO: Marketing Research Director

FROM: Marketing Manager

DATE: October 25, 1980

SUBJECT: Introduction of new soup concentrate

What are your plans to obtain information from the consumer on acceptability of the new soup concentrate prior to launch?

TO: Marketing Manager

FROM: Marketing Research Director

DATE: October 28, 1980

SUBJECT: Research plans for new soup concentrate

Based on our prior meeting with the advertising group and the VP of marketing, the basic positioning relies on two benefits: (1) similarity to homemade soup due to the addition of more vegetables and natural ingredients and (2) greater nutrition. The research plan calls for the following:

1. **depth interviews** with four or five small groups of canned soup users to discuss occasions for purchasing canned soups, canned soups versus homemade soups, and the benefits associated with canned soups. From these interviews a **vocabulary of consumer benefits** will be identified. This might provide some indication of the importance of natural ingredients and nutrition. This research should provide an indication of the types of needs that lead to the purchase of one brand over another.

2. a **product concept test** to evaluate several alternative positionings for the product. Should homemade be the primary appeal and nutrition secondary or vice versa? Three or four alternative descriptions will be provided to the consumer and the products will be rated utilizing the need vocabulary defined in step 1. This test will be conducted on 200 to 300 consumers.

    The concept test will identify consumers that consider nutrition and natural ingredients most important. The key questions are what are the characteristics of this target group and what positioning (**product concept**) do they prefer most.

3. an in-home **product use test** to evaluate the product in use. Consumers will try the new product for one week and their regular soup for one week on a rotated basis. The products will be rated utilizing the same need vocabulary identified in the depth interviews. Results of the in-home test would provide further refinement of the definition of the target segments and the positioning of the product. The in-home test would also indicate if consumers felt the product delivered the promised benefits.

    By the way, I suggest we terminate the expert taste panel the company has been using for over thirty years. Results from the taste panel frequently contradict findings from the concept and in-home use tests. My feeling is that in-home use tests are more reliable as a measure of consumer perceptions and attitudes towards brand offerings and as an indication of future purchase intent.

4. **test marketing** the product in key cities and then projecting sales results on a national basis, assuming results from the concept and in-home use tests are positive.

    Once the product is in test market for about six months I suggest conducting a survey of consumers to determine their reactions to the product. The survey would determine:

- product characteristics consumers perceive our brand to have versus competition (salty, spicy, too watery);
- product benefits consumers perceive our brand to have versus competition (nutritious, economical, good for the family);
- attitudes towards our brand versus competition (prefer first, second, third);
- future buying intentions;
- life-style and demographic characteristics of respondents;
- advertising recall for our brand versus competition.

This survey would provide us with a basis for assessing our marketing strategy by focusing on the key to our success or failure — the consumer. Specifically, it would allow us to:

- identify the market segments most likely to buy our brand;
- evaluate the positioning of the product to these target segments;
- assess our strengths and weaknesses relative to competition;
- measure the effects of specific components of our marketing strategy (price, advertising, in-store displays).

I have outlined a fairly comprehensive research plan. It will be costly, but I believe we must first assess market opportunity by determining consumer needs relative to our brand offering (steps 1–3) and then by evaluating the consumer's reaction to our marketing plan (step 4).

STRATEGIC APPLICATIONS OF CONSUMER BEHAVIOR

A marketing manager faces two important tasks : (1) identifying new opportunities in the marketplace and (2) evaluating the strengths and weaknesses of existing brand offerings. The fulfillment of these tasks requires information about the determinants of consumer behavior — consumers' needs, perceptions, attitudes, and intentions.

Marketing management requires information on the consumer in order to:

- define and segment the market,
- plan marketing strategies,
- evaluate marketing strategies,
- assess future customer behavior.

Defining and Segmenting the Market

Assume the research steps proposed in Figure 1–1 are undertaken to investigate another product category — disposable diapers. A company producing paper products has substantial excess capacity and wants to determine if disposable diapers are an area of opportunity. The company has acquired the rights to a new disposable diaper product with an improved fastener.

The company conducts some preliminary research and identifies a segment of users that emphasize the importance of fastening convenience and rate their current brand as unsatisfactory on this point. Further, the manufacturer finds that users in this group tend to be higher income suburbanites with smaller families of one or two children.

The company has successfully identified a market segment for its product that is based on an unmet need. Defining such segments is essential for these reasons:

1. Marketing management cannot deal with individual consumers; it must divide consumers into segments to identify opportunity.
2. These segments define consumers with common needs and/or perceptions of the existing offerings, thereby identifying marketing opportunity.

3. These defined segments can provide management with important criteria for *planning* and *evaluating* marketing strategies.

Planning Marketing Strategies

Next, the company initiates a product concept test as described in Figure 1–1. The reaction to the idea of an improved fastener is positive and the company proceeds to manufacture a limited number of test products. A small sample of disposable diaper users are then asked to use the new product. The company is interested in identifying consumers who rate the diapers positively and who express a definite interest in buying them. The company finds that consumers who intend to buy emphasize fastening ability and rate the test product better than their current brand on both fastening and absorbency. Therefore, the product is positioned correctly to meet the needs of the target segment.

This information is used to guide the marketing plan for the product. Since the test product is rated highest on fastening and absorbency, it is logical to emphasize these benefits in the promotional campaign. Media should be selected to reach the target group. The consumers emphasizing fastening ability are defined as high-income suburbanites. Therefore, the company will advertise in magazines or on TV programs that most likely reach this group.

Evaluating Marketing Strategies

Based on product test results, the company decides to first introduce the product on a limited scale in test markets and to then introduce it on a national scale if sales goals are met. Once the product is marketed nationally, the company will again survey disposable diaper users to determine needs, perceptions, and attitudes towards the product. The objective is to determine the effectiveness of marketing strategy for the product. The survey will seek to answer the following types of questions:

- Are the needs of the target group being met by the product?
- Are users' perceptions of the product consistent with the advertising message?
- Is the message reaching the target group?
- Is the product being purchased by the target group?
- Are the attitudes of users of the product positive enough to induce repeat purchasing behavior?

With the information gathered from these questions management will be able to evaluate the product positioning strategy, advertising plan, and media strategy. A negative answer to any of the questions above may require changing promotional or media directions, adjusting product characteristics, or possibly taking the product off the market.

Assessing Future Customer Behavior

If needs, perceptions, or attitudes are closely related to buying intentions, then these characteristics can predict what the consumer will do. In the concept and product tests, parents emphasizing fastening convenience and rating their current brand poorly on fastening are more likely to say they will buy the new brand. Changed consumer perceptions of the product from good to poor on fastening may forecast a decrease in purchasing.

There have been numerous attempts to utilize brand perceptions and attitudes to predict subsequent purchasing behavior. The value of such predictions is that they assist management in estimating future sales potential or changes in sales. These studies have one common principle: Changes in brand perceptions or attitudes will influence future purchases.

Strategic Applications Summarized

What goes on in the consumer's mind affects the planning of new marketing strategies and the evaluation of existing strategies. The development of new marketing strategies is influenced in the following ways:

1. Marketing opportunity is identified by unmet needs.
2. New products are developed and positioned to meet these needs.
3. Successful positioning depends on consumer perceptions of the new product.
4. Advertising strategy is based on communicating benefits that consumers desire.
5. Media strategy is guided by the demographic characteristics of a target segment of consumers.
6. Consumer purchase intent depends on the degree to which consumers associate the brand's characteristics to their needs.

The success or failure of existing strategies depends on whether:

1. needs have been met by the product;
2. consumers perceive the brand in the manner intended by the advertising message;
3. attitudes toward the brand are positive;
4. needs, perceptions, and attitudes lead the consumer to remain loyal to the brand.

THE ORGANIZATION OF THIS BOOK

The premise of this book is that marketing strategies must be based on the determinants of consumer behavior. In Figure 1–2 a simple model of consumer behavior is shown, which incorporates the interaction between the marketer and the consumer. The central component of the model is consumer decision making — that is, the process of perceiving and evaluating brand information, considering brand alternatives relative to the consumer's needs, and deciding on a brand.

Three factors influence the consumer's decision making. The first factor is the individual consumer. Brand choice is influenced by the consumer's needs, perceptions of brand characteristics, and attitudes toward brand alternatives. In addition, brand choice is influenced by the consumer's demographic, lifestyle, and personality characteristics.

The other factors — environmental influences and marketing strategies —

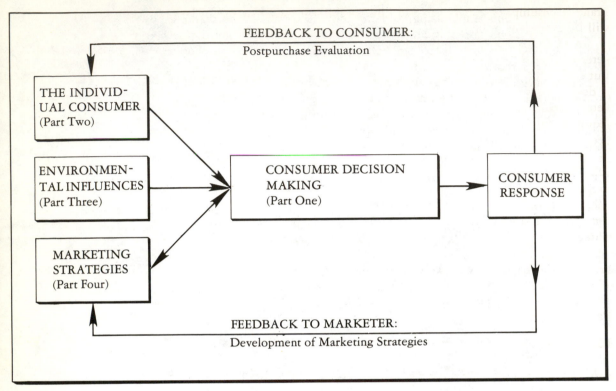

FIGURE 1–2   A Simple Model of Consumer Behavior

directly affect the consumer and influence the consumer's purchase behavior. The consumer's purchasing environment is represented by social influences (friends, family members, reference groups), culture (the norms of society, the influences of religious or ethnic subcultures), social class (the broad socioeconomic group to which the consumer belongs), and situational factors (the situation for which a product is purchased; e.g., buying a car for business or family purposes).

Marketing strategy, the third factor, represents variables within the control of the marketer that attempt to inform and influence the consumer. These variables — product, price, advertising, and distribution — may be regarded as stimuli perceived and evaluated by the consumer in the process of brand choice. The marketer must obtain information from the consumer to evaluate marketing opportunity *prior* to allocating marketing resources. This requirement is represented by the double arrow between marketing strategy and consumer decision making in Figure 1–2. Marketing research provides information to marketing organizations on consumer needs, attitudes, and characteristics. Marketing strategies are then developed and directed to the consumer.

Once the consumer has made a decision, postpurchase evaluation, represented as feedback to the individual consumer, takes place. In the process of evaluation, the consumer will learn from the experience and may change his or her pattern of acquiring information, evaluating brands, and selecting a brand. Consumption experience will directly influence whether the consumer will buy the same brand again.

A feedback loop also leads back to the marketing organization. The marketer will track consumer responses in the form of market share and sales data. But such information does not tell the marketer why the consumer purchased; it does not provide information on the strengths and weaknesses of the marketer's brand relative to competition. Therefore, marketing research is also required at this step to reformulate marketing strategy to better meet consumer needs.

The model in Figure 1–2 is an oversimplified representation of consumer behavior. The purpose of this book is to consider the components of the model in detail, particularly consumer behavior applications to marketing strategy. Each section of the book considers a portion of the model. Part One reviews consumer decision making. Part Two considers the individual consumer. Part Three covers the environmental factors influencing behavior. Part Four focuses on the applications of consumer behavior principles to marketing strategy and provides the major focus for the book by linking consumer behavior to marketing strategy. Each of these sections is described in more detail below.

Part One: Consumer Decision Making

The process by which consumers make purchasing decisions must be understood in order to develop strategic applications. Consumer decision making is not a singular process. Deciding to buy a car is a different process than deciding to buy toothpaste. Figure 1–3 presents a typology of consumer decision making based on two dimensions: First, the extent of decision making, and second, the degree of involvement in the purchase.

The first dimension distinguishes between decision making and habit. Decisions can be made based on a cognitive process of information search and evaluation of brand alternatives. On the other hand, little or no decision making may take place when the consumer is satisfied with a particular brand and purchases it consistently. The second dimension provides a distinction between high versus low involvement purchases. **High involvement purchases** are purchases that are important to the consumer. Such purchases are closely tied to the consumer's ego and self-image. They also involve some risk to the consumer — financial risk (highly priced items), social risk (products important to the peer group), or psychological risk (the wrong decision might cause some concern and anxiety). In such cases, it is worth the consumer's time and energies to consider product alternatives more carefully. Therefore, a complex process of decision making is more likely for high involvement purchases.

Low involvement purchases represent purchases that are not important to the consumer. Financial, social, and psychological risks are not nearly as great. In such cases, it may not be worth the consumer's time and effort to search for information about brands and to consider a wide range of alternatives. Therefore, a low involvement purchase generally entails a limited process of decision making

Decision making versus habit and low involvement versus high involvement produce four types of consumer purchase processes. The first process occurs when involvement is high and decision making is complex. In

	HIGH INVOLVEMENT PURCHASE DECISION	LOW INVOLVEMENT PURCHASE DECISION
DECISION MAKING (Information Search, Consideration of Brand Alternatives)	COMPLEX DECISION MAKING (autos, major appliances) Chapter 2	IMPULSE PURCHASING (cereals) Chapter 4
HABIT (Little or No Information Search, Consideration of Only One Brand)	BRAND LOYALTY (cigarettes, perfume) Chapter 3	INERTIA (canned vegetables, paper towels) Chapter 4

FIGURE 1–3 Consumer Decision Making (Part One)

such cases, consumers actively search for information to evaluate and consider alternative brands by applying specific criteria such as gas mileage, styling, durability, and service. The subject of **complex decision making** is particularly important since it introduces many of the key behavioral concepts relevant to the development of marketing strategy.

Such a process of complex decision making will not occur every time the consumer purchases a brand. When choice is repetitive, the consumer learns from past experience and buys the brand that seems most satisfactory. As a result, brand loyalty, the second consumer purchase process, may develop based on past experiences. Brand loyalty is a method of simplifying the decision process since information search and brand evaluation are limited or nonexistent. There is a saving of the consumer's time and effort.

Figure 1–3 also illustrates two types of consumer purchase processes where the consumer is not involved with the product. First, a decision in a low involvement condition is likely to be characterized by **impulse purchasing** (upper right-hand box). Brands are not likely to differ significantly and consumers may not take the time and effort to search for information and evaluate alternatives. As a result, decisions are likely to be made within the store. Also, when involvement is low, consumers are more likely to switch brands out of boredom and in a search for variety.[1] Risks are minimal and there is less commitment to a particular brand.

Second, low involvement may lead to buying the same brand, not because of loyalty, but because of **inertia** (lower right-hand box). Robertson states that under low involvement conditions "brand loyalty may reflect only the convenience inherent in repetitive behavior rather than commitment to the brand purchased."[2] The consumer is not buying the same brand over and over out of strong preferences but because the brand is satisfactory and it is not worth the time and trouble to search for an alternative. Under such conditions, the consumer is more likely to select a satisfactory rather than an optimal brand.

Part Two: The Individual Consumer

Central to an understanding of consumer behavior is the manner in which the individual consumer influences the decision process. The consumer's role in the decision process is presented in Figure 1–4.

The first influence on consumer choice is stimuli. Stimuli represent information perceived by the consumer. The three broad types of stimuli are **marketing, social,** and **environmental.**

The second and central influence on consumer choice is the consumer. The consumer is represented by thought variables and characteristics. **Consumer thought variables** refer to the cognitive processes involved in decision making. The three types of thought variables are perceptions of a brand's characteristics,

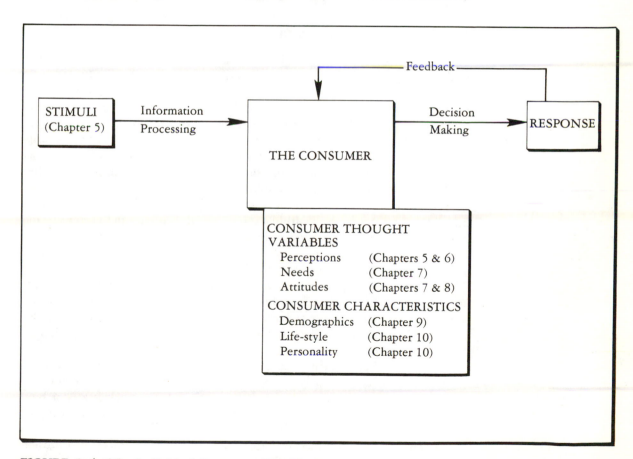

FIGURE 1–4 The Individual Consumer (Part Two)

needs for or benefits from the brand, and attitudes towards the brand. **Consumer characteristics** are represented by the demographic, life-style, and personality characteristics of the consumer.

The marketing manager wishes to know whether consumer characteristics influence behavior. This knowledge can be used to try to influence behavior. If users of disposable diapers tend to be higher income, better educated suburbanites, advertising messages can be designed to appeal to this group. Media that are most likely to be read or seen by this target group will be selected. If heavy users of analgesics tend to be compulsive, this knowledge can guide the advertiser in developing appeals to the compulsive personality. An appeal could suggest a strict routine in using analgesics and could portray the benefits received by regular and systematic use.

The third influence on consumer choice, consumer response, is the end result of the consumer's decision process and is an integral consideration throughout the book. Consumer response most frequently refers to brand choice, but there are other facets of consumer response; for example, choice of a product category (light beer), choice of a store (purchase of a refrigerator in a department store), or choice of a particular stimulus (a decision to read a magazine or to listen to a salesperson to get information).

Part Three: Environmental Influences

Figure 1–4 accounts for only the internal influences on consumer behavior; that is, the consumer's characteristics and state of mind. As seen in Figure 1–5, the consumer is also affected by **environmental variables** — culture, social class, face-to-face groups, and situational factors. The consumer's needs, perceptions, and attitudes are affected by these external forces.

Culture refers to widely shared norms and patterns of behavior of a large group of people. A generally accepted norm in American society is the emphasis on slimness as a sign of vitality and success. The consequent emphasis on diet foods is a cultural influence.

Social class represents broader groupings based on income, education, and occupation. Individuals within a certain social class tend to live in the same areas and have similar purchasing patterns. The influence of social class is based on the acceptance of certain norms derived from power, money, and prestige rather than any direct and personalized small-group influence.

Face-to-face groups are important sources of information and influence for the consumer. Such groups are called **reference groups** because they provide consumers with a means of comparing and evaluating their own brand attitudes and purchasing behavior. The group that is most likely to influence purchasing behavior is the family.

An essential component of face-to-face group influence is communication. One friend tells another that a certain brand of cold tablets is more effective than another. One business associate tells another that a stock is a poor buy. Such influence is by word-of-mouth communication. The individual who influences the consumer is referred to as the **opinion leader**.

Communication also occurs across groups through a process of diffusion of information on new products. The individual most likely to buy new products

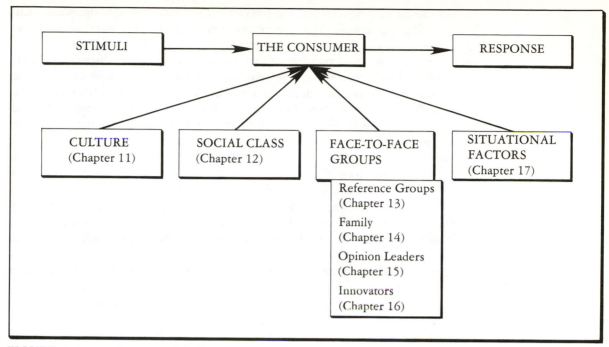

FIGURE 1–5   Environmental Influences (Part Three)

and to influence others to buy is known as the **innovator.** The acceptance of new products across groups is particularly important to the marketer since new product development directly influences the firm's profit position.

The final environmental variable to be considered in Part Three is the usage situation. When asked whether a certain beverage, perfume, or automobile is preferred, it would be quite logical for the consumer to say, "It depends on the situation." Preferences for coffee brands have been shown to vary depending on situations such as "when alone," "feeling sleepy," or "after I wake up in the morning."[3] Preferences for snack products have also varied markedly depending on whether they are purchased for parties, for afternoon snacks, or for bedtime snacks.[4] Interestingly, **situational variables** have been largely ignored in consumer research on the mistaken assumption that consumer preference for brands is uniform regardless of the situation. Such an assumption ignores an essential component of the consumer's purchasing environment.

Part Four: Applications of Consumer Behavior to Marketing Strategies

The strategic applications of consumer behavior principles are the key focus of this book. Figure 1–6 portrays the link between marketing strategy and consumer behavior. The two components represented, the strategic component and the behavioral component, constantly interact in that consumer behavior conditions marketing strategy and marketing strategy influences consumer behavior

The strategic component includes the definition of marketing opportunity and the development of the marketing plan. The definition of marketing opportunity requires market segmentation and product positioning. Market segmentation involves the identification of target markets based on consumer needs. For example, the prospective marketer of the new disposable diaper might define three benefit segments as consumers who emphasize fastening convenience, absorbency, and economy. Since the product's major benefit is improved fastening ability, the company would gear its marketing strategy to consumers who emphasize fastening convenience. Market segmentation can also be based on consumer behavior. For example, the prospective marketer might identify the demographic or life-style characteristics of the loyal purchaser of Pampers or Kimbies. Product positioning requires communication of product benefits to meet the defined needs of one or more segments.

Information on market opportunity provides guidelines for the development of the marketing plan. Each component of the marketing plan is linked to a particular facet of consumer behavior. Advertising is evaluated by the manner in which consumers perceive, interpret, and retain marketing communications. The behavioral component of advertising is therefore **consumer information processing.** Sales promotion and in-store stimuli are evaluated by the manner in which consumers react to store advertising, price promotions, in-store displays, and the store environment. The behavioral component of in-store marketing strategies is logically in-store shopping behavior. Personal selling is evaluated by sales strategies and the nature of the consumer-salesperson interaction. Pricing strategies are evaluated by the consumer's sensitivity and reaction to price levels (i.e., consumer pricing behavior). Figure 1–6 suggests that the evaluation of any component of the marketing plan must be based on some aspect of consumer behavior. Each of these links between strategy and behavior is treated in Part Four.

Figure 1–6 cites one other type of behavior that is important to marketers — organizational buyer behavior. The **organizational buyer** does not buy for personal-end use, but rather to satisfy some organizational need. Examples are industrial purchasers who buy products as input into manufacturing processes, and institutional purchasers who buy for organizations such as hospitals and schools. The needs, decision processes, and behavior of the organizational buyer are sufficiently different from the consumer buyer to warrant separate consideration. The most important differences are the technical complexity of organizational buying, the likelihood of negotiation, and the frequency of group decision making in the industrial purchase decision.

The book concludes by considering the broad question of consumer rights and marketing's responsibilities to the consumer. Activities on the part of consumer groups to guarantee the provision of adequate product information, product choice, and product safety have come to be known as **consumerism.** Recently, consumerist concerns have been expanded to include the integrity of the environment, energy conservation, and the protection of disadvantaged consumers from unfair business practices. In many cases, marketers have acted responsibly by developing codes to ensure that advertising will not be deceptive and that products will be safe and

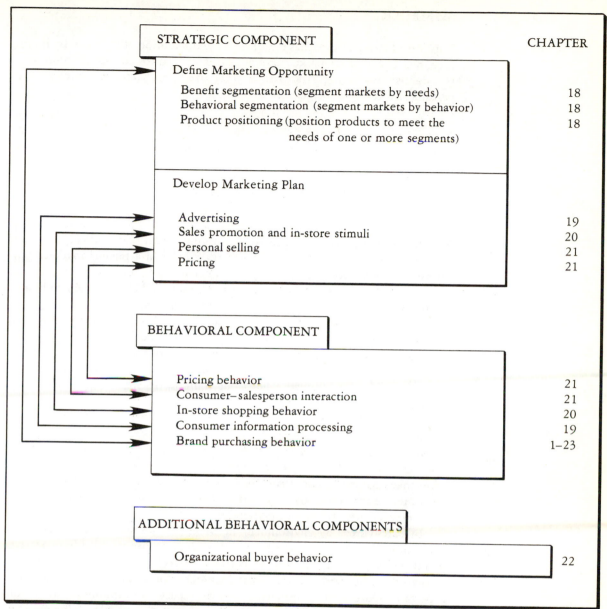

	CHAPTER
STRATEGIC COMPONENT	
Define Marketing Opportunity	
Benefit segmentation (segment markets by needs)	18
Behavioral segmentation (segment markets by behavior)	18
Product positioning (position products to meet the needs of one or more segments)	18
Develop Marketing Plan	
Advertising	19
Sales promotion and in-store stimuli	20
Personal selling	21
Pricing	21
BEHAVIORAL COMPONENT	
Pricing behavior	21
Consumer–salesperson interaction	21
In-store shopping behavior	20
Consumer information processing	19
Brand purchasing behavior	1–23
ADDITIONAL BEHAVIORAL COMPONENTS	
Organizational buyer behavior	22

FIGURE 1–6   Applications of Consumer Behavior to Marketing Strategies (Part Four)

perform adequately. Some marketing organizations have also begun programs to educate consumers regarding alternative product choices. It is likely that marketing organizations will continue to be monitored by private organizations and by legislation to insure that the consumer is offered reasonable product quality at fair prices.

SUMMARY

This introductory chapter has established the orientation of the book by linking consumer behavior to marketing strategy. The need for consumer information to establish marketing strategies is recognized. Such consumer information permits marketing management to:

- define and segment markets;
- position new products and reposition existing products;
- develop advertising, price, and in-store stimuli;
- evaluate marketing strategies;
- assess future customer behavior.

A historical perspective shows that a consumer orientation developed out of economic necessity in the 1950s. With the advent of a buyers' market, marketing managers needed to identify consumer needs in a competitive environment and gear marketing strategies accordingly. A better understanding of consumer needs, perceptions, attitudes, and intentions became necessary.

Much of this chapter is devoted to describing the organization of the book, which is outlined in the model in Figure 1–2. The model has four components: consumer decision making and the three elements that influence consumer decision making — (1) the individual consumer, (2) environmental influences, and (3) marketing strategies. These four components make up the four parts of the book.

Part One describes the types of consumer decision making — complex decision making, habit, and high and low involvement decision making.

In Part Two the individual consumer's needs, brand perceptions, and attitudes are considered. They are referred to as consumer thought variables since they involve a cognitive assessment of brands and products by the consumer. Part Two also examines the consumer's characteristics — demographics, life-styles, and personality.

In Part Three the environment in which the consumer makes decisions is considered. Culture provides the broadest environmental perspective. Social class also influences consumer behavior. Face-to-face groups, particularly the family and the consumer's peer group, are the most important sources of information and influence. Communications within face-to-face groups take place by word-of-mouth and are influenced by opinion leaders. Communications between groups take place through a process of diffusion of information and are influenced by innovators. Situational factors describing when, where, and why a product is purchased or consumed represent another set of environmental influences.

Part Four provides the link between consumer behavior concepts and marketing strategies. Figure 1–6 illustrates this linkage. Behavioral applications are covered in the areas of market segmentation, product positioning, advertising, pricing, in-store environment, and consumer-salesperson interaction. Organizational buyer behavior is also considered.

A concluding chapter considers the consumer's right to information, product safety, and product satisfaction, and the marketer's responsibility to insure that these rights are obtained.

The next three chapters provide an important framework for considering the applications of these theories to marketing policies. They examine the process of consumer decision making in detail, thereby identifying the elements in consumer decisions that are most likely to influence marketing strategies.

QUESTIONS

1. A vice-president of marketing for a large beer company often states that sales is the ultimate criterion of marketing effectiveness and, as such, one must look primarily at the relationship between marketing stimuli (price, advertising, deals, coupons) and sales.
   - What arguments could you as director of marketing research present in support of behavioral research to counter this view?

2. What do the differences in orientation imply at National Soups in 1950 and 1980 for (a) marketing research, (b) product positioning, and (c) market segmentation?

3. Could the research steps outlined in testing the new disposable diaper also be used as a prototype in testing the following?
   a) a new analgesic that can be taken without water
   b) a high potency vitamin for children
   c) a video disc recorder

4. The 1950s and 1960s are regarded as a time when the marketing concept and a consumer orientation were widely accepted. What trends might occur in the 1980s and 1990s? For example:
   - What impact might energy shortages and conservation have on acceptance of the marketing concept?
   - Will there be changes in consumer proprieties (e.g., performance vs. style; value and quality vs. lower price; nutrition vs. taste)? If so, will marketing organizations adjust to these changes?

5. The distinction made in Figure 1–3 between decision making and habit is fairly commonplace. Less common are the distinctions made between (1) decision making and impulse purchasing and (2) brand loyalty and inertia.
   - Do all purchases of a new brand or switches from one brand to another involve a process of information search and brand evaluation?
   - Do all repeat purchases of a brand reflect brand loyalty?

6. Is there a meaningful distinction between purchase behavior and consumption behavior? What are the implications of the distinction for the following?
   a) the introduction of a nutritionally oriented cereal
   b) the introduction of a new electric foot massager
   c) automobile advertising

7. In most cases, marketing studies are concerned with brand or product choice. But

in some cases, the focus may more appropriately be on store choice or even on the choice of media.

- Under what conditions might store choice be more influential than brand or product characteristics in the consumer's final decision?
- Under what circumstances might the media environment (types of magazines, TV shows, radio programs) be more influential than brand characteristics in the consumer's final choice?

8. Even brand choice is not simply defined. Under what circumstances are each of the following measures most likely to be relevant for the marketing manager?
   a) selection of a brand
   b) frequency of purchase
   c) brand loyalty based on repeat purchase behavior
   d) number of times the brand has been purchased with coupons or on deal
   e) number of times the brand has been purchased with another product.

9. Could a large marketing organization (Lever Brothers, American Can, RCA) use Figure 1–6 as a guide in the development of a marketing information system?

RESEARCH ASSIGNMENTS

Attempt to trace the development of a marketing concept and evolution of a behavioral orientation for a large manufacturer of consumer packaged goods. Do so by tracing references to the company in business periodicals and, when possible, by interviewing company executives who have been with the company in marketing for twenty years or more.

- What has been the change in marketing research procedures, particularly in regard to (a) product testing, (b) advertising evaluation, (c) in-store testing, and (d) utilization of concepts of market segmentation and product positioning?
- What changes have occurred in the organization of the research function?
- Do the changes in the company reflect the changes for National Soups in Figure 1–1?

NOTES

1. M. Venkatesan, "Cognitive Consistency and Novelty Seeking," in Scott Ward and Thomas S. Robertson eds., *Consumer Behavior: Theoretical Sources* (Englewood Cliffs, N.J.: Prentice-Hall Inc, 1973), pp. 354–384.
2. Thomas S. Robertson, "Low-Commitment Consumer Behavior," *Journal of Advertising Research* 16 (April 1976): 20.
3. Russell W. Belk, "Situational Variables and Consumer Behavior," *Journal of Consumer Research* 2 (December 1975): 162.
4. Private communication based on study by a large food company.

PART ONE

Consumer Decision Making

Part One of the book recognizes that consumers make different types of decisions. There is a distinction between complex decision making and habit, just as there is between high involvement decisions and low involvement decisions. In Chapters 2–4 each type of decision making is reviewed.

TWO

Complex Decision Making

Focus of Chapter

This chapter presents a model of complex decision making. A detailed example of a family deciding on the purchase of a new car will be used to describe the process of complex decision making. The next chapter will distinguish between complex decision making and habit by describing behavior that involves little information search and brand evaluation. The process of complex decision making includes many important behavioral concepts. For example, since complex decision making involves active search, consumer information processing must be introduced. Since complex decision making involves risk, perceived risk must be considered. Since complex decision making involves perceptions of brand characteristics and formation of brand attitudes, the hierarchy of effects or sequence from perception to purchase behavior must be studied. In this way Chapter Two sets the stage for many of the concepts that follow. Before describing this model of complex decision making, Chapter Two begins with a consideration of decision making models and their purposes, advantages, and limitations.

THE IMPORTANCE OF A CONSUMER MODEL

A model of consumer decision making describes a sequence of factors that lead to purchase behavior and hypothesizes the relationship of these factors to behavior and to each other. But why a model of consumer decision making? Why should management be interested in a sequence of steps leading to purchase behavior? There are at least five reasons: 23

The Limitations of
a Consumer Model

1. *A model encourages a total and integrative view of the process of consumer behavior.* Consumer behavior is dependent on a multiplicity of factors (multivariate relationships). Segmenting the car market into younger versus older purchasers would not be sufficient to guide advertising, media, and product development. It would be more relevant to identify a segment as young singles who emphasize mobility and view a Honda as economical and a stepping stone to a higher priced car.

Management has recently begun to analyze consumer behavior in more multivariate terms. In order to do this, management needs some integrative framework to relate consumer thought variables to behavior and to each other. This is exactly what a model of consumer behavior attempts to do.

2. *A model helps identify areas of information necessary for making marketing decisions.* If brand awareness and brand attitudes are associated with behavior, then these would be key variables to evaluate advertising effectiveness.

3. *A model encourages quantification of these variables.* Relationships like the one between attitude and behavior must be demonstrated in a statistically reliable manner.

4. *A model provides a basis for segmenting markets.* If a model hypothesizes that life-style factors are likely to influence consumer choice, then life-style variables should be collected in a survey and related to behavior. If there is a relationship, then these variables should be used to identify consumer segments; for instance, sociable versus stay-at-home types, or do-it-yourself versus buy-it types.

5. *A model provides a basis for developing marketing strategies.* If perceptions of a brand are related to behavior, then reinforcing positive perceptions or changing negative perceptions might strengthen the brand's market position.

THE LIMITATIONS OF A CONSUMER MODEL

The usefulness of a consumer model to marketing management is limited for several reasons.

1. *A model of consumer behavior identifies only the most common elements in decision making.* The same model cannot be equally applied to buying cereals and coffee. Management requires an understanding of specific markets and particular consumer segments. Management receives only general guidance from models and must orient these models to specific markets. Key attitudes in the cereal market may relate to nutrition, weight watching, or appeal for the whole family. For coffee, the important attitudes may relate more to taste, flavor, and stimulation. In one case, the orientation is more toward health, in the other toward pleasure. A model cannot point this out, but it can help management associate attitudes with such key elements as needs and purchase intent.

2. *The components of a model may not be equally important for all product categories.* Some may not even apply. For example, the level of information regarding product attributes is going to be more important in purchasing a stereo set than a portable radio. Brand attitudes may be more important in influencing the purchase of cereals than of frozen vegetables.

3. *The components of a model may not be equally important for all usage situations.* The purchase of a car for business use may produce a very different decision compared to the purchase of a car for family use. The number of alternatives

may be much more restricted in buying a car for business reasons. Moreover, the criteria of selection may be very different. Once again, a general model cannot identify these differences.

4. *A model is going to vary among individuals in the same market.* Evaluating alternative brands in a product category is going to be more important for those who like to switch brands than it is for those who are more likely to stay loyal to one brand. Acquiring product information is going to be more important for consumers who like to buy new products than it is for those who tend to reduce risk by buying established brands.

5. *All purchase decisions are not equally complex.* The purchase of a new car or stereo is more complex than the purchase of frozen orange juice. In buying a car, the consumer will carefully evaluate a number of alternatives, search for information, and assess the features of each make. The consumer may buy a brand of frozen orange juice by habit.

These limitations do not restrict the use of decision-making models. They merely point to the fact that models must be adapted to particular circumstances. Adaptation from the general model to specific markets requires research that will define those needs, perceptions, and attitudes most likely to influence the consumer's choice of particular brands. The general model is essential in defining the important variables in the consumer decision process.

A MODEL OF COMPLEX DECISION MAKING

Students of decision making have identified five phases in the decision process: (1) problem recognition, (2) search for information, (3) evaluation of alternatives, (4) choice, and (5) outcome of the choice.[1] These steps can be translated into the steps involved in the process of complex decision making as follows: (1) need arousal, (2) consumer information processing, (3) brand evaluation, (4) purchase, and (5) postpurchase evaluation. A model of complex decision making which includes these five steps is presented in Figure 2–1. In brief, the model presents a process of complex decision making as follows:

1. *Need arousal.* A consumer begins with a particular state of mind that represents existing perceptions of and attitudes toward brands known to the consumer. For example, a consumer aware of various makes of cameras might regard Nikon as having a higher quality lens and a better facility for changing lenses than alternative makes. Attitude toward the brand is favorable and if the consumer were to buy at this time a Nikon would be purchased

The consumer becomes aware of various new features in cameras such as automatic lens settings and automatic rewind. The consumer is also aware that several friends have purchased cameras with these newer features (stimulus exposure). As a result, the consumer considers the possibility of buying a camera (need arousal).

2. *Consumer information processing.* The immediate result of need arousal is a greater consciousness of information about the product. Consumers are more likely to take notice of ads for products they are evaluating. Although Nikon is the favored brand, our consumer is also considering an Olympus and a Pentax. An ad for Canon is seen on television (perception of stimulus) and, as a result, Canon is also considered (change in consumer's state of mind by introducing a new brand and developing an attitude toward that brand).

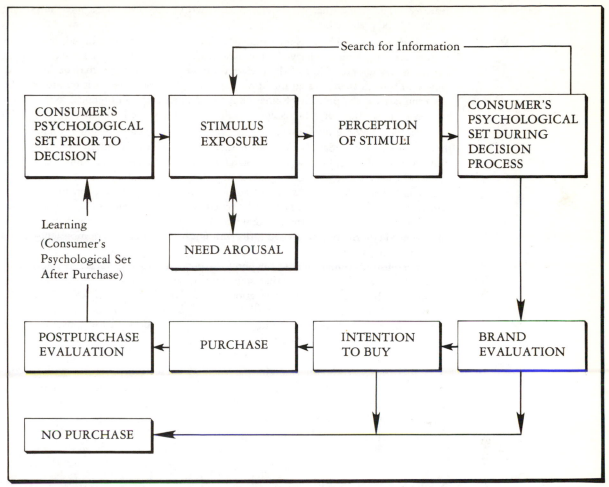

FIGURE 2–1 A Model of Complex Decision Making

At this point, the consumer decides there is not sufficient information for a choice and undertakes an active search for additional information. Various magazines such as *Popular Photography* and *Modern Photography* are read and the findings in *Consumer Reports* are reviewed. In addition, the consumer visits a camera dealer and examines the four brands at first hand to determine models, options, and prices.

3. *Brand evaluation.* Brand evaluation takes place in concert with information processing. But as the consumer collects more information, he or she comes closer to a decision. To evaluate alternative brands, the consumer establishes certain evaluative criteria (the two most important criteria for our consumer are the quality of the lens and the price). Each brand is judged on these criteria (Nikon has a higher quality lens, Canon a lower price). If two brands are equal on the most important criteria, a secondary criterion will be used to decide (do both Nikon and Canon have an automatic exposure feature?). The brand that comes closest to meeting the consumer's most important needs will be preferred.

   4. *Purchase.*   The consumer intends to buy the most preferred brand, but various factors may intervene to delay the purchase (lack of funds, additional information on other makes, unavailability of the preferred brand). The consumer may decide not to buy even though there was an intention to purchase. In fact, the decision process may be terminated at any point. (Information is too confusing and ambiguous, so the easiest option is not to buy; or, brands do not sufficiently meet need criteria).

   5. *Postpurchase evaluation.*   After a purchase, the consumer will evaluate the brand's performance. Satisfaction will reinforce the consumer's judgment and increase the probability of repurchase of the brand in the future. Dissatisfaction will lead to a reassessment of the consumer's choice and decrease the likelihood of repurchase of the brand. Dissatisfaction may also lead to a change in future decision making. The same sources of information may not be relied on (several friends may have suggested the chosen brand, causing the consumer to doubt the reliability of their judgments); or, the need criteria may be revised (price will not be one of the most important criteria in future purchases).

   Dissonant information after the purchase (poor performance, negative information about the chosen brand from other sources) may lead to an attempt to reduce such **dissonance** by ignoring such information or perceiving it selectively (the camera may be bulky and hard to handle, but it's worth the effort). Regardless of the outcome, postpurchase evaluation is a learning process that feeds back to the consumer and is stored as information for future reference.

   In the remainder of this chapter each of these five processes will be considered in more detail in order to introduce some of the important behavioral concepts that will appear in later chapters. The model of complex decision making will be illustrated by another example, a family purchasing an automobile during a period of increased energy costs.

NEED AROUSAL

Need arousal is outlined in Figure 2–2. The consumer's state of mind is described as the **psychological set** towards the prospective purchase — that is, his or her needs relative to the product category and his or her attitudes towards various brands. The psychological set is represented at a given point in time, prior to decision making. It will change during decision making as new information is processed, resulting in new needs and attitudes.

   The consumer's needs and attitudes at a given point in time are a function of various input variables (listed in Figure 2–2). These include the consumer's characteristics; motivations; past experiences with brands; environmental influences; and, of course, past marketing stimuli (product, price, promotion, and in-store strategies directed to the consumer).

Input Variables

Consider the following example. Mr. and Mrs. Goodfriend (hereafter Mr. and Mrs. G) and their two young children live in a middle-class, suburban neighborhood of a large metropolitan area. They are a one-car family and have owned

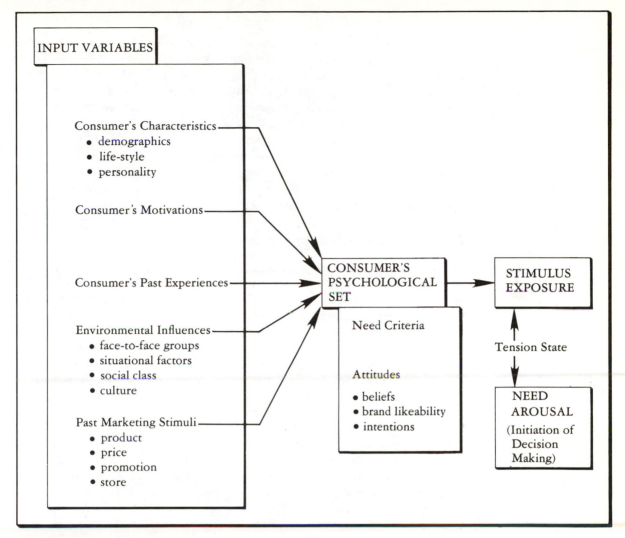

FIGURE 2–2 Need Arousal

Note: The solid arrows in this and in other representations of models of consumer decision making represent the hypothesized direction of causation. Thus, the various input variables influence the consumer's psychological set. Similarly, stimulus exposure influences need arousal, and need arousal influences stimulus exposure (as represented by a double arrow) since the nature of needs influence the stimuli the consumer selects. Dotted arrows further define a given variable. For instance, the consumer's psychological set is composed of needs and attitudes, the latter represented by brand beliefs, brand likability, and purchase intentions.

three different Oldsmobiles in the last ten years, purchasing a new one about every three years.

Past Experiences

Mr. and Mrs. G emphasize comfort, smoothness of ride, and service dependability. Almost every day they use their car and it has served them well, based on the need criteria they emphasize in purchasing a car.

Consumer's Characteristics

Consumer needs and attitudes towards brands are partially conditioned by the consumer's characteristics — the **demographics, life-style,** and **personality** of the consumer. Income will affect the type of car purchased — compact, standard, or luxury. Age, marital status, and number of children may affect the class — sports car, sedan, or station wagon. Life-style may affect the particular make. A socially oriented, outer directed couple may want a car that impresses others and may stress styling and size of car. A family that travels a lot may emphasize comfort at the expense of styling. Even personality has an influence. The power-oriented, aggressive individual may want a car with a great deal of acceleration. The compulsive individual may stress regular service needs and the alleviation of anxieties by better warranty terms.

Consumer's Motivations

The influence of personality on brand choice raises the question of consumer **motivations.** Individuals develop patterns of behavior that become ingrained in one's personality as motives. Motives are general predispositions that direct behavior toward attaining certain desired objectives. Common motives may include factors such as taste, possession, economy, curiosity, dominance, pleasure, and imitation. These motives are not specific to any product. Economy or possession could apply equally well to buying a car or a record album.

Motives may directly affect the specific need criteria used in evaluating brands. If Mr. G is motivated by status, then two important need criteria will be the size and styling of the car. If economy is an important motive, the most important need criteria may be gas mileage, service costs, and initial price.

Abraham Maslow developed a theory based on a **hierarchy of motives.**[2] Five levels of motives are specified from lowest to highest order. According to Maslow, an individual will satisfy the lowest motivational level first. Once satisfied, a new and higher order motive will emerge to generate behavior. Thus, it is the dissatisfied needs that lead to action. The five levels of motives from lowest to highest are:

1. physiological (food, water, shelter, sex);
2. safety (protection, security, stability);
3. social (affection, friendship, acceptance);
4. ego (prestige, success, self-esteem);
5. self-actualization (self-fulfillment).

In advanced economies, most consumers' physiological and safety needs have been met. Yet according to Maslow, few people satisfy their social and ego needs to move to the fifth level — self-actualization. Therefore, the most important motivating forces in purchase behavior are social and ego needs. This is true even for relatively mundane products such as detergents, as seen by advertising that relates detergents to social benefits and potential social ostracism ("ring around the collar").

Many products are purchased and used in a social setting. The purchase of a car is frequently a family decision. As such, each member of the family influences the decision. Neighbors and business associates may also be important sources of information and influence. It is clear that cultural norms and values affect attitudes toward the automobile. The automobile is the prime means of transportation in the United States, but it is also a prime means of socialization and a representation of socioeconomic status.

Past Marketing Stimuli

Past information about brand characteristics and prices will affect beliefs and brand attitudes. Such information is obtained from advertising, in-store stimuli, and sales representatives.

Consumer's Psychological Set

In the context of consumer decision making, the consumer's psychological set is directed to brand, product, and store evaluations. The psychological set is made up of four components: need criteria; beliefs about the brands, products, or stores; likeability of the brands, products, or stores; and intentions. The assumption is that these components operate in sequence: needs are formulated, beliefs are formed about the brand, attitudes are developed toward the brand, and the consumer finally forms an action predisposition. This sequence has been referred to as a **hierarchy of effects** model of consumer decision making since it stipulates the sequence of cognitive stages that the consumer goes through in reaching a tendency to act.[3]

Need Criteria

Need criteria are the factors that consumers consider important in deciding on one brand over another. Mr. and Mrs. G's most important criteria are durability and economy. But other criteria may be relevant such as roominess, styling, safety, and road performance. The need criteria are generally benefits consumers expect from the brand. These benefits are directed to goal objects (physical attributes of the product). Thus, the goal objects used to evaluate economy may be gas mileage and service costs; the goal objects used to evaluate durability may be the expected life of the car and the resale price.

Brand Attitudes

Beliefs, brand likeability, and intentions form the consumer's **attitudinal structure**. Ray refers to consumer attitudes in terms of a tri-component model representing these three factors.[4]

Beliefs are the cognitive components of attitudes, representing the characteristics a brand is believed to have. Mr. G sees the Oldsmobile as providing durability and comfort, but has his doubts about economy based on its reported gas mileage. Mrs. G finds the car convenient and easy to drive, but is also concerned about economy. Consumers attribute characteristics to brands whether they have used them or not. Based on advertising and comments from friends, Mrs. G suggests they look into a Toyota Celica since she feels it is nicely styled, provides comfort, and gives good gas economy.

Brand likeability or preference is the affective component of attitudes and represents the favorable or unfavorable disposition toward the object. The key question is whether the beliefs about the object conform to the consumer's needs. If so, then the consumer will rate the brand favorably. Before the energy crisis, Mr. G's primary need criteria were durability and comfort. On this basis, the Oldsmobile was the preferred make (affective component) since it had the characteristics (cognitive component) that best met Mr. G's needs. As a result, Mr. G intended to buy the car again (action tendency), but the gas crisis changed the ground rules by substantially increasing the importance of what, up to that point, was a relatively secondary consideration — gas mileage and economy.

Arousal of Needs

As a result of the gas crisis, Mr. and Mrs. G's need priorities are realigned and the psychological set changed. The new information represents a set of stimuli that create a tension state because Mr. G is no longer satisfied with the performance of his current make. Need arousal is the result.

Decision making can be initiated by external forces such as marketing stimuli (a new product or additional information about an existing product) or environmental influences (seeing a friend use a product, information about the economy, a shift in cultural norms away from usage of certain products). Decision making can also be initiated by stimuli internal to the consumer (an out-of-stock situation, a poor product performance, or, more basically, physical needs such as hunger and thirst). Mr. and Mrs. G were motivated to consider a new car by internal as well as external stimuli. Mr. G learned that the Oldsmobile would need a transmission overhaul in the next six months. This fact in addition to increased gas prices caused the initiation of decision making.

Given need arousal, a state of tension will occur that energizes the consumer to search for information relevant to the decision. Figure 2–2 shows an interaction between need arousal and stimulus exposure. New stimuli create need arousal, and need arousal results in a heightened awareness of relevant stimuli.

CONSUMER INFORMATION PROCESSING

Consumer information processing involves the exposure to, organization of, and search for information. These processes are represented in Figure 2–3. In order to influence the consumer's psychological set, stimuli must gain the consumer's attention, be comprehended, and must be retained in the consumer's memory for a certain period of time. As will be seen in Chapter Four, information processing in low involvement conditions may be quite different. Consumers could become aware of a stimulus with little interpretation or comprehension, and the stimulus could still influence behavior.

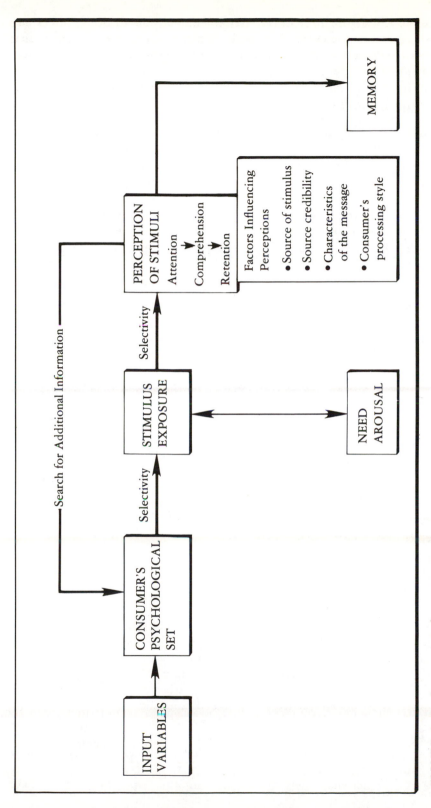

FIGURE 2-2 Consumer Information Processing

As seen in Figure 2–3, various factors influence the degree of attention, comprehension, and retention such as the nature of the source, the credibility of the source, the nature of the message, and the consumer's style of processing information.

Stimulus Exposure

The consumer's exposure to stimuli is selective. People tend to choose friends who support their views, reinforce their egos, and parallel their life-styles. They seek out commercials that support recent purchases in an attempt to justify them. They also tune out when information is presented that conflicts with their needs or beliefs. The cigarette smoker may not see the Surgeon General's warning on a pack of cigarettes or may conveniently switch stations if an antismoking commerical appears.

Therefore, stimulus exposure is a selective process that is directed by the need to (1) reinforce existing brand attitudes and perceptions, and (2) seek additional information.

Another cause for selectivity is the avoidance of clutter. Consumers are exposed to thousands of marketing stimuli every day. It would be impossible to notice them all. Therefore, it is necessary to pick and choose. One of the best examples of selective exposure occurred during the first Super Bowl game between the Green Bay Packers and the Kansas City Chiefs. During halftime, the water pressure in Kansas City fell to its lowest level on record — a testament to the propensity of football fans to catch up on their needs in between halves!

Perception of Stimuli

Through perceptions consumers organize and interpret stimuli to make sense of them. Stimuli are more likely to be perceived when they:

- conform to consumers' past experiences;
- conform to consumers' current beliefs about a brand;
- are not too complex;
- are believable;
- relate to a set of current needs;
- do not produce excessive fears and anxieties.

It is clear that perceptions of stimuli, as well as exposure to stimuli, are selective. Ads that reinforce the consumer's predispositions are more likely to be noticed and retained. Ads or other communications that contradict past experiences and current beliefs about a brand are more likely to be dismissed or interpreted in such a way as to conform to current beliefs. Mrs. G recently encountered a friend who related a series of bad experiences about an Oldsmobile that she finally sold. Mrs. G's reaction was to attribute her friend's experience to chance. By refusing to relate negative information to her own set of experiences, Mrs. G avoided conflict in her psychological set. This balanced state is a desirable one which most people attempt to achieve — namely, a state that lacks conflict and avoids contradictory information. Mrs. G might have also followed another strategy, one of dismissing the information altogether by judging her friend much too finicky and critical when it came to cars.

Perceptions go through three distinct phases once the consumer is exposed to the stimulus: attention, comprehension, and retention. Selectivity will take place in each phase. A fourth phase — memory — represents information storage.

Attention

Attention is the process of taking note of a stimulus or certain portions of the stimulus. Attention will be selective since consumers are more likely to notice that portion of a stimulus relevant to their needs and in conformity with their experiences.

Comprehension

Comprehension is selective since consumers are more likely to interpret a message to agree with their beliefs. The same ad may be interpreted differently by two consumers because of differences in beliefs, attitudes, and experiences regarding the product being advertised.

Mr. G's interpretation of various messages is selective because he accepts certain stimuli and discounts others. Claims of economy cars with low gas mileage were generally accepted, although Mr. G did not believe an ad by one manufacturer that claimed mileage of over forty miles per gallon. Claims regarding comfort were generally discounted because Mr. G strongly believed that economy cars cannot be that comfortable.

Retention

A message may be noticed, interpreted, and quickly forgotten. Messages that are most relevant to consumers' needs are more likely to be remembered. In the process of initial information search, Mr. and Mrs. G decide to seriously consider an economy car as a replacement for the Oldsmobile. They retain two types of information; first, the types of economy cars on the market (brand awareness); and second, the alternative features of these makes (brand beliefs).

Memory

Information that is retained will be stored in the consumer's memory. **Memory** is composed of past information and experiences and new information provided by marketing and environmental stimuli. The new information will be used in the decision process and may change beliefs about the brand, evaluation, and, ultimately, behavior. Once stored in memory, information can then be recalled for future use.

Search for Additional Information

Consumers may not be satisfied with the amount and quality of information available to make an adequate decision. In such cases, they will engage in an active search for additional information. Such a search is most likely when the consumer:

- feels that alternative brands being considered are inadequate;
- has insufficient information regarding the characteristics of the brands under consideration;
- receives information from friends or media sources that conflicts with past experiences and current information;
- is close to deciding on a particular brand and would like some confirmation of expectations regarding its performance.

Studies have shown that consumers do not engage in extensive information search unless they consider the time and cost of such a search worth the benefits gained from additional information. One study found that when consumers were presented with information on sixteen alternative brands, they used only 2 percent of the information available in making a decision.[5] Another study found that one-half of all consumers studied visited only one store or showroom when buying cars and major appliances.[6] A limited search does not necessarily reflect undue casualness on the part of the consumer; it merely may mean that the consumer felt sufficient information was already obtained at the time of purchase.

About two weeks after deciding on the purchase of a new car, Mr. and Mrs. G visited several showrooms. Figures were obtained from dealers on gas mileage, service costs, and resale value of various makes of cars. Mrs. G took several copies of *Consumer Reports* out of the library to determine ratings of various makes from an impartial source. On occasion, they asked friends who owned one of the makes under consideration about their experiences. On the basis of this information search, Mr. and Mrs. G narrowed their choice down to four cars — the Toyota Celica, the Audi Fox, the VW Dasher, and the Oldsmobile.

Figure 2–3 shows that the search for additional information feeds back to the consumer's psychological set since additional information may change brand attitudes and stimulate further search. This illustrates the dynamic nature of the consumer decision-making process. The components of information processing and brand evaluation are not discrete but occur on an ongoing basis until a final decision is reached.

Factors Influencing Perceptions

Four factors affect attention, comprehension, and retention. The first factor is the source of the stimulus. Marketing studies generally agree that advertising through the mass media is important in providing information about a brand or product, but that personal sources (friends and relatives) are most important in influencing the purchasing decision.[7]

The editorial content of mass media is also likely to influence stimulus perception. An identical ad for a car in *Playboy* and in *Cosmopolitan* is likely to induce quite different reactions.[8]

Source credibility is the second factor that influences perceptions. The greater the believability of the source, the greater the likelihood the message will be perceived and retained.[9] Both Mr. and Mrs. G place greater credibility in *Consumer Reports* than in the judgment of a car salesperson because of the impartiality of the source.

The third factor is the characteristics of the message. One issue regarding the character of advertising messages is whether they should be one-sided or two-sided. Several studies lend support to the conclusion that under certain conditions, an advertising message presenting an opposing view and then refuting it is more effective than a one-sided message.[10] Such advertising presents consumers who are favorably disposed toward the brand with arguments to counter competitive claims.[11] **Comparative advertising** — that is, advertising that names a competitor — is an example of a two-sided message. Other studies believe that two-sided messages confuse the consumer and create more awareness of the competitor's brand.[12] Mr. G notices an ad for the VW Dasher that cites more expensive makes of cars. Since he is looking for a rationale to consider an economy rather than a luxury car, he appreciates the ad's arguments for not buying a larger car.

A fourth factor influencing stimulus perception is the consumer's processing style. Consumers differ by the rules they use to organize information. Some consumers might evaluate information by product attributes, comparing each brand's gas mileage, durability, and safety. Others might evaluate the VW Dasher with all the relevant need criteria and then evaluate the Toyota Celica with all the relevant criteria. Evidence from marketing studies suggests that it is easier to organize information by attributes than by brand.[13] This means that consumers evaluate alternative brands by comparing each brand, using the most important need criteria to do so.

BRAND EVALUATION

The process of brand evaluation is illustrated in Figure 2–4. The search for additional information will result in changes in the consumer's psychological set. New brands will be considered, criteria used to evaluate brands may change, or beliefs about the characteristics of brands may change. Past and current information will be used to associate brand offerings with consumer needs. Association of brands with consumer needs will result in the development of expectations for each brand. The brand producing the highest expectation of satisfaction of consumer needs will be the preferred brand.

Changes in the Psychological Set

Perception of marketing, social, and environmental stimuli will cause changes in the consumer's psychological set. Any of the following changes may occur:

- *Changes in current information.* The consumer might become aware of a new brand or of changes in the features of existing brands.

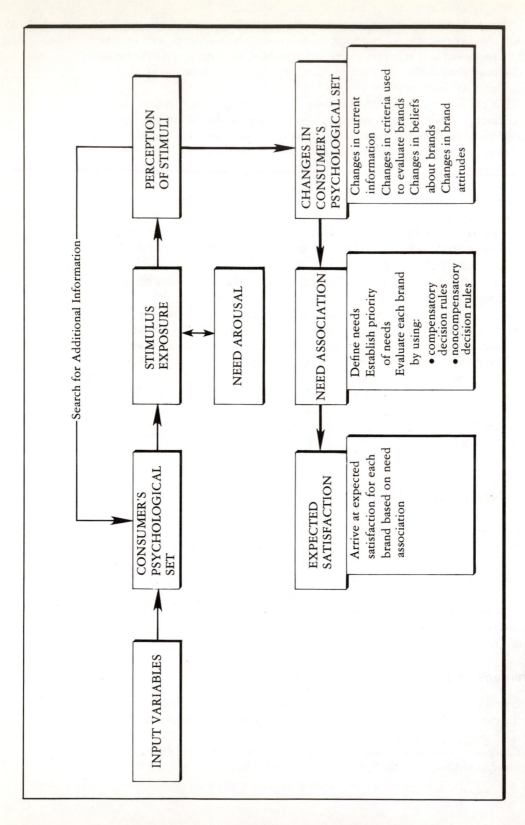

FIGURE 2-4 Brand Evaluation

- *Changes in criteria used to evaluate brands.* This could occur in two ways:

    1. A new need is recognized that was not previously instrumental in selection. (Mr. G did not consider gas mileage in evaluating alternative makes until fuel costs began to rise.)

    2. The priority of needs changes. (Comfort and styling decreased in importance, and economy and service increased.)

- *Changes in beliefs about brands.* New information may cause consumers to change beliefs about features of existing brands. At one time, Nestlé advertised Nescafe as having large, dark granules. Not only did this advertising introduce a new need criterion, it changed the image of the brand because consumers began to notice this physical attribute.

- *Changes in brand attitudes.* Brand attitudes may change as a result of changing needs or new information. In Mr. G's case, attitudes toward an Oldsmobile became more negative due to greater emphasis on economy and less emphasis on comfort and styling.

Fig. 2–4 may be deceiving in that changes in the psychological set appear to take place at a given point in time. This is not the case. The consumer's mental set is constantly changing because of continual exposure to new stimuli. Although the model may appear static, consumer perceptions, needs, and attitudes influence purchase behavior in a continuous and dynamic way.

Need Association

The process of need association requires relating a brand's characteristics to consumer needs. In order to establish the relationship of brand alternatives to consumer needs, a consumer must have a defined set of needs ordered by importance. In Mr. and Mrs. G's case, the ordering they agree to is economy (gas mileage and operating costs); service dependability; durability (life of car); comfort; safety; and styling. Mr. and Mrs. G evaluate the four makes they are considering based on each of these need criteria. Greater weight is given to needs regarded as most important, but the other needs are included in assessing the relative merits of each car.

This evaluative procedure is known as a compensatory method of evaluation because a negative rating on one criterion can be made up by a positive rating on another. Thus, even though the Oldsmobile obtains poorer gas mileage than the Toyota and Audi, rating it much cheaper to service and operate and rating it more highly on comfort and styling allow the possibility of choosing the Oldsmobile over the other makes. The alternative to this procedure is a noncompensatory method of evaluation. For example, gas mileage could be such a dominant concern that any car that does not achieve a certain minimum performance in gas mileage might be eliminated from consideration, regardless of how highly it is rated on other criteria. Thus, consumers may use different decision rules in evaluating brands.[14]

A Compensatory Model for Brand Evaluation

A **compensatory model** assumes that consumers evaluate each brand across all need criteria. Such an approach requires rating specific needs from most to least important and evaluating the characteristics of each brand by need. The brand that is rated closest to consumer needs is preferred. In effect, the compensatory model assumes the consumer is saying, "These are my needs and this is what I expect to get if I buy the brand."

Table 2–1 presents hypothetical ratings for Mr. G's needs and brand evaluations. Four need criteria are presented. Economy is the most important (a rating of 10 on a 10-point scale), followed closely by service dependability and performance. Styling is relatively unimportant (a rating of 2).

Next, the consumer determines the degree to which each brand being considered meets these needs. This evaluation requires rating the brands on goal objects associated with the four need criteria. The goal objects used to evaluate brands on service dependability are quality and speed of repairs. The Dasher and Celica do best on gas mileage (ratings of 9 and 8), the Dasher scores best on service costs, and the Oldsmobile is rated highest on quality of repairs, performance, and styling.

The decision-making rule involves weighting the brand ratings by the needs and then summing across the need criteria. On this basis, the Dasher is selected despite the fact it does not do as well as the Oldsmobile on service dependability, performance, and styling. Poorer evaluations on these criteria are compensated by better evaluations on the most important criterion, economy.

The procedure described by the compensatory model is not meant to be a literal description of the decision process. Consumers do not actually compute importance weights and brand ratings in an empirical manner, but they do:

1. determine the brands under consideration;
2. define their needs and order them by importance;
3. evaluate brands to determine the degree to which they meet these needs;
4. select that brand that will best meet the more important needs.

A Noncompensatory Model for Evaluating Expected Satisfaction

A **noncompensatory model** assumes that consumers rate brands by one attribute at a time rather than evaluating each brand across all attributes. Table 2–2 presents an example of a noncompensatory model. The four cars are first evaluated on gas mileage. Any brand that dominates on this criterion is selected. If two or more brands are equal or close to equal, then a second criterion is used to evaluate the brands.

Table 2–2 shows that Mr. G eliminated the Oldsmobile and Audi Fox in the first step based on gas mileage. The next most important criterion was then used to evaluate the two remaining brands, the Dasher and Celica. Using service cost as a criterion, the Celica was eliminated and the Dasher selected. The Dasher was selected based on two evaluative criteria.

Both the compensatory and noncompensatory models describe a **multiattribute** approach to decision making. That is, consumers use more than one

TABLE 2–1   Evaluation of Alternative Brands: Compensatory Model

Need	Importance of Need (10-pt. scale)	Goal Object	Make	Evaluation of Make on Goal Objects (10-pt. scale)	Contribution[a] to Expected Satisfaction
ECONOMY	10	GAS MILEAGE	Olds	2	20
			Dasher	9	90
			Celica	8	80
			Fox	5	50
		SERVICE COSTS	Olds	4	40
			Dasher	8	80
			Celica	4	40
			Fox	5	50
SERVICE DEPEND- ABILITY	8	QUALITY OF REPAIRS	Olds	8	64
			Dasher	7	56
			Celica	4	32
			Fox	5	40
		SPEED OF RE- PAIRS	Olds	8	64
			Dasher	8	64
			Celica	6	48
			Fox	8	64
PERFORM- ANCE	8	SMOOTH RIDE	Olds	10	80
			Dasher	8	64
			Celica	5	40
			Fox	8	64
		PICKUP	Olds	10	80
			Dasher	7	56
			Celica	6	48
			Fox	7	56
STYLING	2	EXTERIOR	Olds	10	20
			Dasher	4	8
			Celica	4	8
			Fox	6	12
		INTERIOR	Olds	9	18
			Dasher	7	14
			Celica	5	10
			Fox	7	14
TOTAL EXPECTED SATISFACTION FOR EACH BRAND:			Olds		386
			Dasher		432
			Celica		306
			Fox		350

[a] Contribution to expected satisfaction is derived by multiplying importance weight by brand rating, and adding across the goal objects.

TABLE 2–2   Evaluation of Alternative Brands: Noncompensatory Model

Evaluative Criterion	Brand	Evaluation of Brand on Criterion (10-pt. scale)
Gas mileage	Olds	2 (Eliminated)
	Dasher	9
	Celica	8
	Fox	5 (Eliminated)
Service costs	Dasher	8
	Celica	4 (Eliminated)

attribute to determine the preferred brand, but in using a noncompensatory approach, they are likely to evaluate alternative brands one attribute at a time rather than examining several attributes simultaneously.[15] One study found that subjects had difficulty in considering more than two attributes simultaneously. The result is that many consumers are more likely to use the noncompensatory decision-making rules in Table 2–2 rather than the compensatory rules in Table 2–1.[16]

These findings suggest that consumers follow a principle of parsimony in brand evaluation: Use the smallest number of criteria consistent with a satisfactory evaluation of brand alternatives. Rather than evaluate brands on a broad set of characteristics, consumers may be more likely to accept or reject brands on one or two criteria and then move to secondary criteria when necessary.

PURCHASE AND POSTPURCHASE EVALUATION

The outcome of brand evaluation is an intention to buy (or not to buy). The final sequence in complex decision making involves purchasing the intended brand, evaluating the brand during consumption, and storing this information in the psychological set. These steps are outlined in Figure 2–5.

Intention to Buy

Once brands are evaluated the consumer intends to purchase the brand achieving the highest level of expected satisfaction. Purchasing in complex decision making is not likely to be immediate. Mr. G may not have decided what dealer to buy a Dasher from. He may still have some shopping to do to obtain the best trade-in value on his present car, and he may have to obtain financing. Therefore, a period of time will ensue before the car is purchased. In order to purchase, certain instrumental actions must take place; namely, selecting a store, determining when to purchase, physically transporting oneself to the point of purchase, and, as in the case of an automobile purchase, arranging for financing. Moreover, additional decisions may have to be made. For instance,

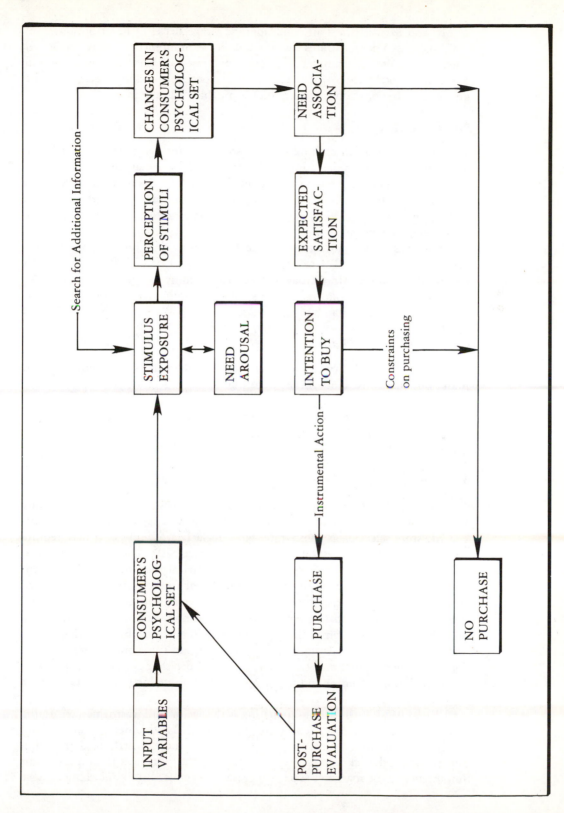

FIGURE 2–5   The Complete Model of Complex Decision Making

do Mr. and Mrs. G want air conditioning, a tape deck, or other options?

Figure 2–5 demonstrates that the link between intention to buy and actual purchase requires instrumental action. The time lag between intention and purchase is likely to be greater in complex decision making because of the greater number of actions required for a purchase to take place.

No Purchase

The consumer decision-making model also recognizes that a decision might be made to not buy or to delay purchase. Mr. and Mrs. G may decide not to buy a new car because they estimate that, in the long run, it would be cheaper to fix up the old car, despite rising gasoline costs. Or, having evaluated the various makes, they may decide to wait and see if some additional options may be introduced in next year's models.

Figure 2–5 demonstrates that the decision-making process may be terminated at any stage. For example, during the process of information search or brand evaluation, Mr. G may feel that an economy car just would not meet his needs for comfort. Information on smaller cars might have merely reinforced his liking for larger, standard-sized cars.

Constraints on Purchasing

There is also a possibility the consumer might make a decision to buy a certain brand but that constraints might lead to unforeseen delays or to a decision not to purchase. Unavailability of the brand, a change in price, or information about a new brand may cause the consumer to delay or change the purchase decision. Such outside constraints, represented in Figure 2–5, result in a decision not to buy or in a delay in the purchase decision.

Purchase

In order to purchase, certain instrumental actions must be undertaken to ensure that the consumer is at the place of purchase at an appropriate time. In this regard, store selection is most important. In fact, store selection may require a decision-making process of its own (see Chapter 20). The store decision in the purchase of a suit or dress may be more critical than the brand decision. The physical act of purchasing is more important in the purchase of packaged (convenience) goods because the decision is sometimes made in the store, and the decision and purchase process are almost simultaneous. A consumer in a supermarket may be reminded of a need for canned peas by just glancing at the shelf. There are no strong brand loyalties; two or three brands are examined for price, ingredients, and brand name; and, a decision is made. Prior advertising had minimal effect and the complete decision-making process takes place in the store.

Paradoxically, the act of purchasing is the easiest and least time-consuming part of Mr. and Mrs. G's decision-making process. Having decided on a brand, selected the options, and arranged for financing, there is little to do but sign the papers and pick up the car. Of course, the purchase is of paramount importance to the marketer since it represents revenue. But of more importance from the standpoint of developing future marketing strategies is (1) what influenced them to buy and (2) will they be satisfied after the purchase.

Postpurchase Evaluation

Once the product is purchased, the consumer will evaluate its performance in the process of consumption. It is important to distinguish between purchase and consumption. First, the product may be purchased by one person and consumed by another. The consumer, not the purchaser, determines product satisfaction. Second, the purchase depends on consumer expectations of the degree to which brands are likely to satisfy needs. Consumption will determine whether these expectations are confirmed. Third, postpurchase evaluation determines whether the brand is likely to be repurchased. An important maxim in marketing is that, in most cases, success depends not on the first purchase but on repurchase. It is unlikely that any brand can survive over time without some degree of loyalty. Lack of satisfaction will lead to negative word-of-mouth communication and inhibit sales.

Satisfaction Versus Dissatisfaction

Satisfaction occurs when consumer expectations are met or exceeded, leading to reinforcement of the purchase decision. Such reinforcement is represented in Figure 2–5 as input from postpurchase evaluation to the consumer's psychological set. Satisfaction reinforces positive attitudes toward the brand, leading to a more positive action tendency and a greater likelihood that the same brand will be purchased again. Dissatisfaction has the opposite results — negative brand attitudes and a decrease in the likelihood of purchasing.

Postpurchase Dissonance

In addition to satisfaction or dissatisfaction, a third possibility is that the consumer may attempt to rationalize the decision when expectations are not met. In many cases, decisions are made involving two or more close alternatives. The decision could have gone either way. Having made the decision, the consumer may feel insecure, particularly if substantial financial or social risks are involved. Any negative information about the chosen product will cause **postpurchase dissonance**; that is, conflict resulting from two contradictory beliefs.

Assume in Mr. and Mrs. G's decision-making process that the Oldsmobile was a close second to the Dasher. The likelihood of postpurchase dissonance increases. The financial risks of purchasing the car make dissonance even more likely. There are also the social risks of buying a car that may not conform to the norms of friends and neighbors, and there is the psychological risk that the wrong decision may have been made.

Shortly after the purchase, Mr. G meets a friend who relates some negative experiences with her Dasher — lower than expected gas mileage, mechanical failures. Mr. G also learns that Oldsmobile will be coming out with a smaller, more economical car next year. This information produces postpurchase doubt since Mr. G feels perhaps he should have delayed the purchase. Such doubt is psychologically uncomfortable. The tendency is to reduce doubt by confirming the purchase. This can be done by:

1. ignoring the dissonant information;
2. selectively interpreting the information by saying that any make will have an occasional lemon;
3. lowering the level of prior expectations by saying that even if there are a few problems with the car, it still is an acceptable choice.

In each case, dissonance is reduced.[17]

Now assume that after six months, Mr. G finds that gas mileage is about 20 percent lower than dealer and advertised claims and that service costs are somewhat higher than expected. In other respects (styling, comfort, performance), the car meets expectations. The theory of postpurchase dissonance says that Mr. G will focus on the positive performance and tend to dismiss or rationalize the negative performance. Such an evaluation conforms to **assimilation theory** since conflict between performance and prior expectations is reduced. The evaluation of the product remains positive.

But if there is a great disparity between prior expectations and performance, a **contrast** effect is likely to take place — recognizing and magnifying poor performance.[18] Thus, if the Dasher's gas mileage is half of that claimed in the advertising, it is unlikely that Mr. G would focus solely on the positive aspects of performance. Extreme dissatisfaction would be more likely, leading to negative attitudes toward the selected brand and a reduction in the probability the brand would be considered the next time.

The description of complex decision making has focussed on the individual consumer. The complexities of group decision making were not emphasized in this chapter. For example, what occurs when a husband and wife have different objectives, different sources of information, or different preferences? What is the nature of word-of-mouth influence from friends and relatives in the decision process? What is the impact of differing roles such as influencer, information gatherer, purchasing agent, decision maker, and consumer in the process of group decision making? These considerations will be incorporated into the model of complex decision making in Chapters 13–16.

SUMMARY

The purpose of this chapter is to present a comprehensive model of complex decision making. Such a model provides an integrative framework since it presents many of the concepts to be covered in other sections of the book.

The general model of decision making has several phases:

1. *Need arousal* initiates a decision process. A consumer's needs may be stimulated by receiving new information about brands, economic conditions, advertising claims, or simply by recognizing an out-of-stock situation. Needs, brand attitudes, and preferences already exist prior to need arousal. These factors are known as the consumer's

psychological set. In addition, the consumer's life-style, demographic, and personality characteristics are likely to influence the purchase decision.

2. *Consumer information processing* involves a search for and organization of information from various sources. Information processing is selective since consumers choose information that is: (1) most relevant to their needs and (2) likely to conform to their beliefs and attitudes. Processing of information involves a series of steps — exposure, attention, comprehension, and retention.

3. In the process of ***brand evaluation,*** a consumer will evaluate the characteristics of various brands and choose the brand that is most likely to fulfill the consumer's needs. Two models of brand evaluation are described. The compensatory model assumes the consumer will evaluate each brand alternative across a number of need criteria and that a poor rating on one criterion can be counterbalanced by a good rating on another. The noncompensatory model recognizes that if a brand is evaluated poorly on one very important criterion, this may be sufficient to exclude it from further consideration.

4. Once the consumer has made a purchase, *postpurchase evaluation* will occur. If performance has met the consumer's prior expectations, the consumer is likely to be satisfied with the product. If not, dissatisfaction will occur, reducing the probability the same brand will be repurchased. In some cases where the consumer had difficulty making up his or her mind, dissonance is likely. Dissonance or postpurchase conflict results from doubts about the decision. Since dissonance is not a desirable state, the consumer may seek to reduce dissonance by ignoring negative information or by seeking out positive information about the brand.

The next chapter shifts the focus from complex decision making to habit.

QUESTIONS

1. A large auto manufacturer conducted a survey of recent car purchasers to determine needs in buying a new car, determine how the company's makes are perceived, and evaluate possible new product offerings. The specific types of information collected by the company can be classified into information dealing with each of the four stages of the decision-making model, namely:
   A. Need arousal
       1) consumer thought variables
       2) consumer characteristics
   B. Information processing
       1) exposure to marketing stimuli
       2) perceptions of marketing stimuli
   C. Evaluation of alternative brands of cars
   D. Purchase and postpurchase evaluation
   • Specify the types of information the auto manufacturer might collect from consumers for each of the four stages described above.
   • Specify the strategic applications of such information.
2. Use the model of complex decision making in this chapter to describe the steps in the decision-making process for the following cases:
   • a businessman considering the adoption of a new picture phone for communication between branches of his firm;

- a family considering the purchase of a videodisc machine;
- a consumer considering the purchase of a headache remedy that is advertised as stronger and more effective.

3. What are the implications for marketing strategy based on your description of the decision-making process for each of the three cases in question 2, particularly implications (where applicable) for (a) market segmentation, (b) product positioning, (c) advertising, (d) pricing, (e) distribution, and (f) new product development?

4. What are the limitations of the model of complex decision making in deriving strategic implications?

5. What differences in the decision-making process might exist in the following situations?
   - Mr. and Mrs. G (a) have never purchased a car before, (b) are in the lower income group, and (c) are buying a car for business purposes.
   - There had been no energy crisis.

6. This chapter described three factors that may change a consumer's predisposition to buy a brand: (a) a change in needs, (b) a change in the perceptions of a brand, and (c) a change in the attitudes toward a brand.
   - Which of these changes is a marketer most likely to influence? Why?
   - Under what circumstances is a marketer more likely to influence one of these changes than another?

7. Of what use might the model of complex decision making be to a marketing manager in the following situations?
   - Folger's introduces its coffee line in the East.
   - Mead-Johnson attempts to reposition Metracal from a medically oriented diet drink to a line of tasty and nutritious diet food products.
   - A company introduces the better fastening disposable diaper described in Chapter One.
   - Remington introduces a new electric razor directed primarily to black men.

8. What differences exist in the decision-making process for a product category (buying a new washing machine or not) versus a brand (having decided on purchasing a washing machine, then selecting a brand)?

9. In some cases, consumers buy almost immediately after reaching a decision. In other cases, there might be a time gap between intention and purchase.
   - What are the implications of such a gap for advertising and selling strategies?

RESEARCH ASSIGNMENTS

1. Select an electronics product that costs over a hundred dollars (a CB radio, stereo equipment, telephone answering machine). Then conduct depth interviews with consumers who have purchased the item within the last year or are currently considering purchasing.*

   * Many of the research assignments proposed in the book will involve conducting depth interviews. **Depth interviews** are unstructured interviews designed to provide the re-

- Describe the decision-making process for both the decision to buy the product and the particular brand to be purchased.
- Does the decision-making process conform to the model in Chapter 2?
- What are the implications of the decision-making process for (a) market segmentation, (b) product positioning, and (c) advertising strategy?

2. Now select an electronics product that costs under fifty dollars (headphones, transistor radio, portable calculator). Conduct depth interviews with consumers who have purchased the item within the last year or are currently considering purchasing.

- How does the decision-making process differ from that described in the first assignment?
- What are the implications of the decision-making process for (a) market segmentation, (b) product positioning, and (c) advertising strategy?

NOTES

1. See John Dewey, *How We Think* (New York: Heath, 1910), and Orville Brim, et al., *Personality and Decision Processes* (Stanford, Calif.: Stanford University Press, 1962).
2. Abraham H. Maslow, *Motivation and Personality* (New York: Harper & Row, 1954).
3. R. Lavidge and Gary A. Steiner, "A Model for Predictive Measurements of Advertising Effectiveness," *Journal of Marketing* 25 (Oct. 1961): 59–62, and Michael L. Ray, "Marketing Communication and the Hierarchy of Effects," in P. Clarke, ed, *New Models for Mass Communication Research* (Beverly Hills, Calif.: Sage Publications, 1973), pp. 147–175.
4. Michael L. Ray, "Attitudes in Consumer Behavior," in Leon G. Schiffman and Leslie L. Kanuk, *Consumer Behavior* (Englewood Cliffs, N.J.: Prentice-Hall Inc., 1978), pp. 150–154.
5. Jacob Jacoby et al., "Pre-Purchase Information Acquisition," in Beverlee B. Anderson, ed, *Advances in Consumer Research*, vol. 3 (Atlanta: Association for Consumer Research, 1975), pp. 306–314.
6. Joseph W. Newman and Richard Staelin, "Prepurchase Information Seeking for New Cars and Major Household Appliances," *Journal of Marketing Research* 9 (August 1972): 249–257.
7. For example, see Thomas S. Robertson, *Innovative Behavior and Communications* (New York: Holt, Rinehart and Winston, Inc. 1971), and Joseph W. Newman and Richard Staelin, "Information Sources of Durable Goods," *Journal of Advertising Research* 13 (April 1973): 19–29.
8. For an example of media effects see David A. Aaker and Phillip K. Brown, "Evaluating Vehicle Source Effects," *Journal of Advertising Research* 12 (August 1972): 11–16.
9. G. Miller and J. Basehart, "Source Trustworthiness, Opinionated Statements, and Response to Persuasive Communication," *Speech Monographs* 36 (1969), pp. 1–7. Also for an example of source credibility see Samuel Craig and John M. McCann, "Assessing Communication Effects on Energy Conservation," *Journal of Consumer Research* 5 (September 1978): 82–88.
10. See Robert B. Settle and Linda L. Golden, "Attribution Theory and Advertiser Credibility," *Journal of Marketing Research* 11 (May 1974): 181–185, and Alan G. Sawyer, "The Effects of Repetition of Refutational and Supportive Advertising Appeals," *Journal of Marketing Research* 10 (February 1973): 23–33.
11. George J. Szybillo and Richard Heslin, "Resistance to Persuasion: Inoculation Theory in a Mar-

searcher with general insights into the motives and behavior of consumers. They can be conducted with individual consumers, or the researcher can bring a group of five to ten consumers together for a group discussion (known as focused group interviews). In both cases, the researcher does not ask specific questions. Rather, he or she acts as a moderator or passive listener. The researcher may develop a list of areas to be covered in the discussion and may steer the conversation to these topics. Generally, focused group interviews tend to be more insightful and productive because of the stimulation of group interaction. At the end of a series of depth interviews, the researcher should have developed sufficient hypotheses regarding consumer behavior to permit the formulation of a more structured and empirically based research design.

48   keting Context," *Journal of Marketing Research,* 10 (November 1973): 23–33.

12. "The Effects of Comparative Television Advertising That Names Competing Brands," Ogilvy & Mather Research, New York (private report).

13. J. Edward Russo and Barbara A. Dosher, "Dimensional Evaluation: A Heuristic for Binary Choice" (working paper, University of California, San Diego, 1975).

14. For a good review of compensatory and noncompensatory models see William L. Wilkie and Edgar A. Pessemier, "Issues in Marketing's Use of Multi-Attribute Attitude Models," *Journal of Marketing Research* 10 (November 1973): 435–438.

15. See James R. Bettman and Jacob Jacoby "Patterns of Processing in Consumer Information Acquisition," in Beverlee B. Anderson, ed, *Advances in Consumer Research,* vol. 3 (Atlanta: Association for Consumer Research, 1976), pp. 315–320,

and Amos Tversky, "Elimination by Aspects: A Theory of Choice," *Psychological Review* 79 (July 1972): 281–299.

16. Russo and Dosher, "Dimensional Evaluation," 1975.

17. For a review of the literature on postpurchase dissonance see William H. Cummings and M. Venkatesan, "Cognitive Dissonance and Consumer Behavior: A Review of the Evidence," in Mary Jane Schlinger (ed)., *Advances in Consumer Research, Vol. 2* (Ann Arbor: Association for Consumer Research, 1975), pp. 21–31.

18. For a description of assimilation versus contrast theories see Rolph E. Anderson, "Consumer Dissatisfaction: The Effect of Disconfirmed Expectancy on Perceived Product Performance," *Journal of Marketing Research* 10 (February 1973): 38–44.

THREE

Habit, Learning and Decision Making

Focus of Chapter

This chapter describes the opposite of complex decision making — habit. Prior satisfaction with a brand may lead to repeat purchases and eventually to purchases based on **habit.** The consumer may find little need for information search and for evaluation of brand alternatives. Recognizing a need will lead directly to a purchase. Therefore, habit is a way of ensuring satisfaction based on past experience and of simplifying decision making by reducing the need for information search and brand evaluation.

In this chapter, the process of habitual purchasing will be described. Understanding the process requires understanding the principles of consumer **learning** since learning theory focuses on the conditions that produce consistent behavior over time.

Habit and learning lead to **brand loyalty,** that is, commitment to a certain brand because of prior **reinforcement** (satisfaction as a result of product usage). Brand loyalty is the result of involvement on the part of the consumer. Complex decision making was required at one time to select a brand. Satisfaction with the brand's performance leads to the establishment of favorable attitudes and to repurchase over time.

The next section will describe the process of habitual purchase behavior, its characteristics and importance to the consumer. Learning theories will then be described and brand loyalty considered as an outcome of consumer learning.

A Model of Habitual Purchasing Behavior

A model showing the process of habitual purchasing behavior is presented in Figure 3–1. The consumer has settled on a regular brand (for example, Crest toothpaste) based on past experience and has become a loyal purchaser. This is reflected in the consumer's psychological set by confirmed beliefs about the brand and a strong positive attitude toward the brand. Need arousal is limited primarily to a reminder of the need to purchase (the consumer is out of stock) or to simple internal stimuli such as hunger or thirst. Consumer information processing is limited or nonexistent. Stimulus perception is presented as a shaded box in Figure 3–1 because it is not necessarily part of the process. Advertising or word-of-mouth communications operate to reinforce the consumer's belief about the brand. The consumer is likely to see advertising for Crest and competitive brands. But beliefs about Crest remain unchanged and a positive attitude toward the brand is maintained.

The process of need association is also presented as a shaded box because the consumer may continue to evaluate Crest relative to other brands. The cavity prevention properties, price, and other characteristics of Crest may still be evaluated relative to Gleem, Colgate, and other brands, but such evaluation is of limited scope.

The more likely circumstance is that need arousal will lead directly to intention to buy. Being out of the brand may be sufficient reason to add Crest to the shopping list. Or perhaps the loyal consumer will be reminded by seeing Crest on the store shelf. After purchase, the toothpaste will undergo postpurchase evaluation. The consumer expects the same satisfaction from the brand as previously. A consistent experience with the brand will occur since prepackaged products generally ensure standardization. Satisfaction will confirm existing beliefs and attitudes, and a high probability of repurchasing will be maintained.

There is also the possibility that the product will not meet expectations. The loyal cigarette smoker finds his regular brand suddenly harsh; a box of cereal is half empty when purchased; a reformulation of a brand of toothpaste produces a taste the consumer does not like. The link between product usage and positive rewards is broken and causes the consumer to consider alternative brands. The result is the initiation of decision making.

Other factors besides dissatisfaction may cause the consumer to change from habit to complex decision making. For instance, a new product comes on the market, the consumer becomes aware of it and considers purchasing. Information search and brand evaluation result. Or, additional information may cause a change in needs resulting in decision making. For example, information on the negative effects of smoking might cause a smoker to reassess the favored brand in terms of tar and nicotine content. The possibilities are represented by the line between perception of stimuli and revert to decision making in Figure 3–1.

It is also possible that boredom with a brand may prompt the consumer to look for something new. Howard and Sheth state that at times consumers

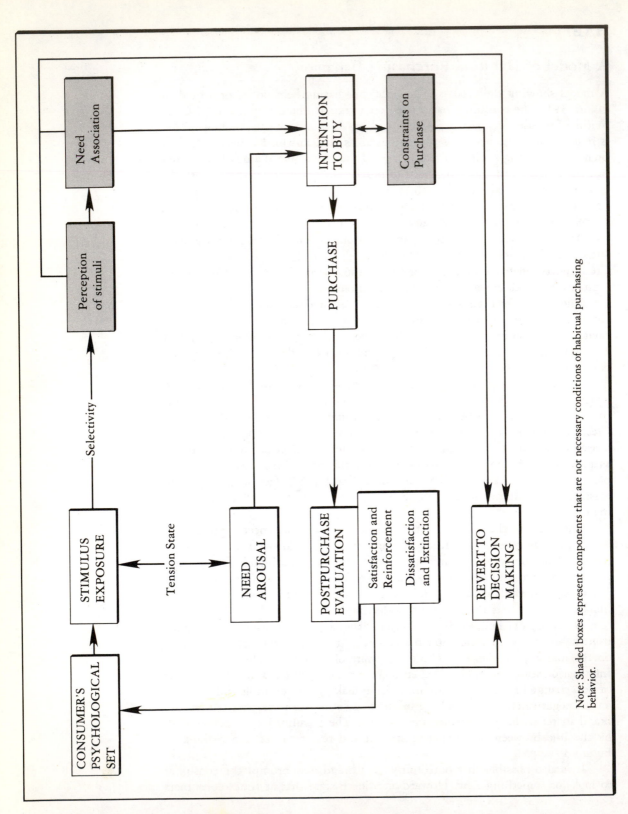

Note: Shaded boxes represent components that are not necessary conditions of habitual purchasing behavior.

FIGURE 3–1 A Model of Habitual Purchasing Behavior

> The buyer, after attaining routinization of his decision process, may find himself in too simple a situation. He is likely to feel monotony or boredom associated with such repetitive decision making . . . . He feels a need to complicate his buying situation by considering new brands.[1]

The result, again, is a move away from habit to more complex decision making.

Finally, certain constraints on purchasing may exist once the consumer decides to buy. The store may be out of the consumer's preferred brand. The consumer goes to another store and buys a less preferred brand. The consumer may be satisfied with the brand and will consider it in the future, necessitating decision making.

Another constraint on purchasing is a change in price. A reduction in price of a less preferred brand, or an increase in price of the regular brand may cause the consumer to consider alternatives. The sharp increase in coffee prices in the mid-1970s caused many habitual coffee drinkers to switch to tea. Some coffee drinkers permanently reduced their consumption of coffee. Others began drinking more instant coffee. In all these cases, a habitual purchase became more complex because of the need for information on alternatives to higher priced coffees.

Habit and Information Seeking

Habit can be defined as a limitation or absence of (1) information seeking and (2) evaluation of alternative choices. Several studies have examined the relationship between habit and information seeking. Newman and Werbel developed a categorization of habitual purchasing based on information seeking and the number of alternative choices considered.[2] Their classification is presented in Figure 3–2. Habit requires the consideration of only the favored brand and no information seeking (condition 1). Two other conditions approach habit: (a) a consideration of only the favored brand but some brand-related information seeking (condition 2); and (b) a consideration of other brands but no information seeking (condition 3). Thus, it would be possible to consider only Crest but to examine information on other brands as well (condition 2) or to consider Crest, Gleem, and Colgate but not to seek out any additional information about these brands (condition 3). More complex decision making would be identified by a consideration of more than one brand and/or brand-related information seeking (conditions 4–8).

This scheme was used to analyze the purchase of major appliances. One would assume the incidence of habit would be very low for major appliances since they are infrequently purchased and are relatively high in financial and psychological risk. Newman and Werbel found that 15 percent of the purchases could be characterized as habit (condition 1 in Figure 3–2) and another 12 percent as approaching habit (conditions 2 and 3). Therefore, over one-fourth of the purchases of major appliances are routinized despite the potential risks.

In another study, Sheth and Venkatesan confirmed the association between habit and information seeking.[3] They found that as decision making became

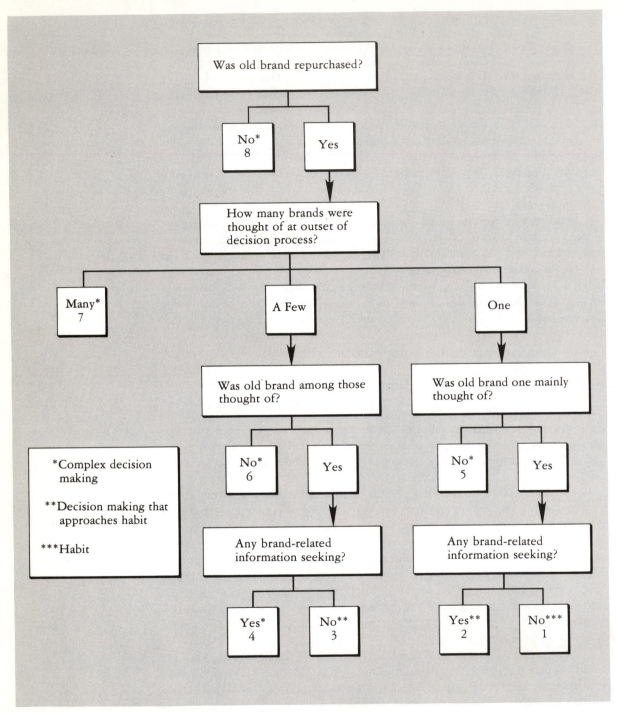

FIGURE 3–2   A Classification of Habitual Purchasing Behavior

Source: Adapted from Joseph W. Newman and Richard A. Werbel, "Multivariate Analysis of Brand Loyalty for Major Household Appliances," *Journal of Marketing Research* 10 (November 1973): 405. Reprinted with permission from the *Journal of Marketing Research.*

more routinized, information seeking from informal sources (such as friends and family) decreased, as well as the amount of time for considering alternatives.

The Functions of Habit

Purchasing by habit provides two important benefits to the consumer. First, it reduces risk; second, it facilitates decision making. Habit is a means of reducing purchase risk when involvement is high. Buying a well-known brand time and again reduces the risk of product failure and financial loss. Buying a popular brand also reduces the risk of being overly individualistic. Several studies cite brand loyalty as a means of reducing risk. Roselius questioned consumers on various means used to reduce purchase risk. Brand loyalty and buying a well-known brand were mentioned most frequently.[4] Sheth and Venkatesan asked female college students to evaluate hair sprays (a relatively high risk item for them). The lower the information seeking and prepurchase deliberation, the lower the perceived risk.[5]

Habit also facilitates shopping behavior by minimizing the necessity for information search. Most consumers seek to minimize search behavior because of the time and energy involved. The functional nature of habit is best illustrated in supermarket shopping. A typical shopping list may easily include twenty items or more. Consider the amount of time the consumer would spend in the process of prepurchase deliberation or in-store selection if each item required an examination of brand alternatives.

Habit is most likely to be used as a means of minimizing risk for high involvement items and minimizing information search and brand deliberation for low involvement items. When consumers regard certain products as relatively unimportant, they may purchase by habit simply to avoid the nonmonetary costs (time and energy) of brand evaluation.

Strategic Implications of Habit Versus Complex Decision Making

Complex decision making and habit are two extremes of a continuum. In between is what might be described as limited decision making. The top of Figure 3–3 presents complex decision making, limited decision making, and habit on a continuum based on the probability of repurchase. Products bought by habit tend to be purchased more frequently, providing a greater opportunity for positive reinforcement and brand loyalty. With each successive purchase of the same brand, the chances of buying again increase until there is a high probability the consumer will continue to repurchase. As the probability of repurchasing increases, the time spent on information search and prepurchase deliberation decreases as shown on the bottom of Figure 3–3.

It is important for marketing management to identify the position of a brand on the continuum from habit to complex decision making. The strategic implications of the position on this continuum apply to every facet of marketing strategy as follows:

Probability of
Purchasing Same
Brand Again

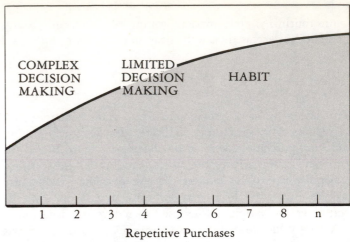

Time Spent in
Prepurchase
Information
Search

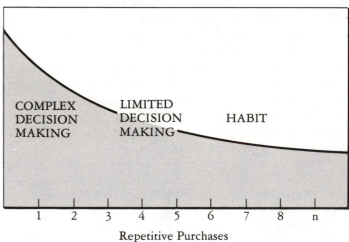

FIGURE 3–3 As the Probability of Purchasing the Same Brand Increases, the Amount of Information Search and Prepurchase Deliberation Decreases

Distribution

Brands purchased by habit should be distributed intensively because they are more likely to be high turnover, low margin items. Widespread distribution has an important reminder effect on the consumer purchasing by habit. The classic example is Hershey's sole reliance, until recently, on intensive distribution rather than on advertising to promote its chocolate products. Products characterized by complex decision making are not purchased as frequently and are more likely to be distributed selectively or exclusively.

Product

Products purchased by complex decision making, primarily appliances and durables, tend to be of a higher level of technical complexity. Personal selling is more important for these products and service is more likely to be required. Products purchased by habit are generally packaged goods involving few service requirements and little direct selling.

The nature of advertising and promotions also differs by the position of the product on the continuum from habit to complex decision making. Products with a high incidence of habitual purchases are more likely to use advertising for a reminder effect. Frequency is relatively more important than selectivity. Markets characterized by complex decision making are more likely to use advertising to convey information as an aid to decision making. In-store stimuli will also be more important for products purchased by habit. Given the importance of the reminder effect, displays and shelf position become important vehicles to induce purchasing. In contrast, complex decision making requires promotions that will stimulate prepurchase deliberation. Advertising and personal sources of information (friends and salespersons) will be relied on.

Pricing

Pricing policies are also likely to differ. When brands are purchased by habit, frequently the only way a competitor can get a brand-loyal consumer to try an alternative brand is to introduce a deal or special sale. Another method of inducing trial among brand loyalists is to provide free samples in the hope the loyal consumer will consider the alternative brand. Utilizing deals or free samples is less effective in complex decision making because the risks of buying based on price alone may be too great. In addition, the marketer's costs of offering free samples or price deals for specialty items may be prohibitive.

HABIT AND CONSUMER LEARNING

The development of habit is closely related to consumer learning. Implicit in habitual purchasing is the assumption that consumers learn from past experience and that future behavior is conditioned by such learning processes. In fact, learning can be defined as a change in behavior occurring as a result of past experience.

Certain concepts in learning theory such as contiguity, reinforcement, and extinction are relevant to understanding habit. These concepts have grown out of the **behaviorist** tradition in psychology as reflected by two learning theories: classical conditioning and instrumental conditioning. **Classical conditioning** explains behavior based on repetitive stimuli and the establishment of a close association (**contiguity**) between a secondary stimulus (picture of cowboy in a Marlboro ad) and the primary stimulus (need for a cigarette). **Instrumental conditioning** views behavior as a function of the consumer's actions (purchase behavior) and the consumer's assessment of the degree of satisfaction obtained from the action. Satisfaction leads to reinforcement and to an increase in the probability of repurchasing.

Other learning concepts are derived from the **cognitive school of psychology**. The cognitive school views learning more as problem-solving behavior and tends to emphasize changes in the consumer's psychological set (formation of beliefs about brands, changes in attitudes, relation of brand attitudes to needs). In this respect, the cognitive school more closely describes learning within a framework of complex decision making. But the concepts are relevant to habit since complex decision making may lead to habit given satisfaction over a period of time. These three schools of learning may therefore be represented as:

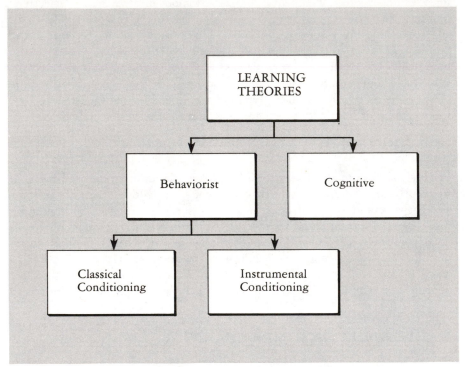

Their relevance to marketing will be considered next.[6]

Classical Conditioning

In classical conditioning, a stimulus is paired with another stimulus that already elicits a particular response. The need for a smoke is a **primary** or **unconditioned stimulus** that will result in the smoker reaching for a cigarette and lighting up (response). An effective advertising campaign may link a symbol to the need for a smoke. The best example is one of the most effective media campaigns in history — the Marlboro cowboy. The campaign succeeded in establishing a link between the cowboy and Marlboro based on (1) repetition, (2) contiguity (cowboy always related to Marlboro), and (3) the power of the stimulus (cowboy conveys strength, quiet security, masculinity). The Marlboro-cowboy association is a **secondary** or **conditioned stimulus** because conditioning is required to learn the association between cowboy and smoking. The individual who already smokes Marlboro may substitute the secondary stimulus for the primary stimulus. That is, the cowboy may remind the consumer of the need for having a cigarette. For the smoker who does not smoke Marlboro, repetition and association of the cowboy with smoking may result in trial of the brand.

Theories of classical conditioning[7] are reflected in Pavlov's famous experiments.[8] Pavlov reasoned that since his dogs salivated (response) at the sight of food (unconditioned stimulus) a neutral stimulus such as a bell could also cause the dogs to salivate if the bell was closely associated with the unconditioned stimulus. After a number of trials, the dogs learned the connection between bell and food and salivated when they heard the bell, even in the absence of food. These associations are represented in Figure 3–4. The association between the conditioned and unconditioned stimulus is represented as a dotted line because it is a learned association. The association between conditioned stimulus and response is also learned. The two key concepts are repetition and contiguity. The conditioned stimulus must be frequently repeated in close contiguity to the unconditioned stimulus to establish the association with response.

Principles of classical conditioning are of limited usefulness in marketing because of the required link between the conditioned stimulus and response. Such a link requires automatic response behavior. The assumption is that the Marlboro cowboy will cause a smoker to light up with no cognitive processes. Such automatic responses are unlikely (although not impossible) because advertising is not a powerful enough vehicle of communication to create the strength of association established by Pavlov.

Classical conditioning is of more relevance to marketing in terms of the possibility of establishing associations between symbols and brand names by repetition and contiguity. But, even here, the emphasis on repetition has decreased since the 1950s. Before then, jingles and themes were repeated frequently in radio commercials. The advent of television lent a new dimension to advertising by providing more variability through the video component. In addition, a more consumer-oriented approach to advertising resulted in emphasis on variations in advertisements directed to particular segments. A mass advertising approach based on a single repeated theme was not as viable a strategy.

The shift in advertising emphasis away from classical conditioning also implied a shift towards principles of cognitive learning. Measures of recall are still used in evaluating ads to determine whether basic brand associations have been established. But measures of attitude change (changes in brand beliefs, preferences, and intention as a result of advertising) are used in addition to measures of recall as criteria for advertising effectiveness. This means that criteria of effectiveness have shifted from measures of association (e.g., recall) to measures of changes in the consumer's psychological set (e.g., attitude change).

Instrumental Conditioning

Instrumental conditioning also requires developing a link between a stimulus and response. In **instrumental conditioning**, the individual determines the response that provides the greatest satisfaction. No previous stimulus-response connection is required. In classical conditioning, the unconditioned stimulus is already linked to a response. The difference can best be illustrated by a hypothetical experiment. Assume Pavlov had provided his dogs with two levers;

CLASSICAL CONDITIONING

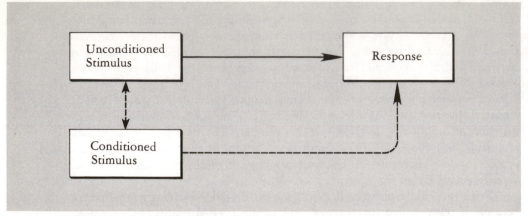

Emphasis: Association through repetition and contiguity

INSTRUMENTAL CONDITIONING

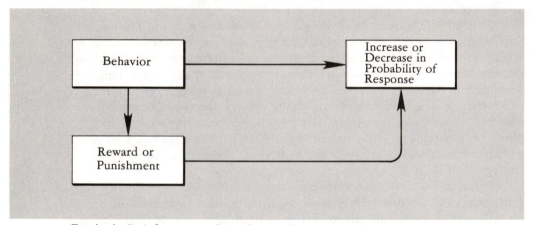

Emphasis: Reinforcement; dependence of outcome on learner's actions

COGNITIVE LEARNING THEORY

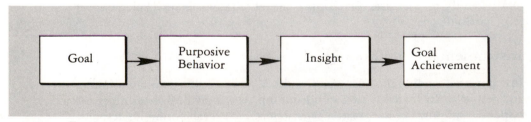

Emphasis: Problem solving; understanding relationships

FIGURE 3–4 Summary of Three Learning Theories

Source: Adapted from Kenneth E. Runyon, *Consumer Behavior and the Practice of Marketing* (Columbus, Ohio: Charles E. Merrill, 1977), p. 212.

one when pushed would produce food, the other a shock. The dogs would quickly learn to press the lever with food and avoid the lever producing a shock. Learning occurs because the same act is repeatedly rewarded or reinforced.

The foremost proponent of instrumental conditioning is B.F. Skinner. In Skinner's experiments, the subject is free to act in a variety of ways.[9] The consequences of the act (degree of satisfaction or dissatisfaction) will influence future behavior. These associations are summarized in Figure 3–4. Behavior results in an evaluation of degree of reward or punishment obtained from the behavior. Reward will increase the probability of repeating the behavior; punishment will decrease that probability.

Reinforcement

The process of instrumental conditioning comes closer to describing the formation of habit in consumer purchasing. The consumer has control over his or her purchasing behavior. Current behavior influences brand evaluations and future behavior. Continuous reinforcement (repeated satisfaction) resulting from product usage increases the probability the same brand will be purchased. Eventually, the probability of buying the same brand is high enough that information search and brand evaluation decrease. The curve in Figure 3–3 reflects this process. Initially, a decision process takes place, but with continuous reinforcement the probability of buying the same brand on repetitive purchase occasions increases until a habit is established. This curve may be regarded as a **learning curve** since it reflects the definition of learning, namely, changes in the probability of behavior as a result of past experience.

The role of reinforcement in producing a habit is illustrated in a study by Bennett and Mandell.[10] They asked a sample of recent car purchasers to recall the cars they had purchased in the past and to determine the amount of information seeking in the most recent purchase. They found that information seeking did not decrease with the number of car purchases made in the past. Yet, information seeking did decrease if the same car was purchased repetitively. In other words, past experience alone will not reduce information seeking. Information seeking is reduced only by past experience that is reinforced. Therefore, a necessary condition for the formation of habit is reinforcement of past purchase behavior.

In another study, Carey et al. sought to create reinforcement artificially by calling customers of a jewelry store and thanking them for their patronage. Sales among customers who did not receive the call were unchanged, whereas sales among the test group increased substantially.[11]

Extinction and Forgetting

Theories of instrumental conditioning also formulate the events that may lead a consumer to cease buying by habit. If a consumer is no longer satisfied with the product, then a process of **extinction** takes place — that is, the elimination of the link between stimulus and expected reward. Extinction will lead to rapid decrease in the probability that the same brand will be repurchased.

Forgetting differs from extinction. **Forgetting** occurs when the stimulus is no longer repeated or perceived. Lack of use of a product or elimination of an advertising campaign can result in forgetting. At the turn of the century, Sapolio soap was on a par with Ivory as a leading brand. The demise of the company began when it decided that the brand was so well known that a reduction in advertising was warranted. A process of extinction did not occur — the brand still satisfied consumers. The lack of repetition resulted in forgetting and a long-term decline in sales until the product was taken off the market. Another cause of forgetting is competitive advertising, causing interference with receipt of the message. Advertising clutter may create confusion in the consumer's mind and weaken the link between stimulus and reward.

Marketers can combat forgetting by repetition, but repetition, in and of itself, is of limited use since the same ad, time and again, may merely irritate the consumer. Simply maintaining the level of advertising expenditures relative to competition is generally sufficient to avoid any serious forgetting on the part of the consumer. Of more direct relevance is avoiding a process of extinction. Lack of sufficient reward can mean the quick end of any brand. The most important vehicle for avoiding extinction is proper product positioning. If the product can deliver sufficient benefits to a defined target group, then reinforcement is assured. The company will have a core of loyal consumers insuring the brand's long-term survival.

Figure 3–5 presents learning curves that reflect processes of reinforcement, extinction, and forgetting. Reinforcement increases the probability of repurchase, extinction quickly decreases that probability, and forgetting results in a longer term decline. The importance of these concepts is illustrated by a recent decision by the Federal Trade Commission to force Listerine to undertake corrective advertising to counter its long advertised claim that the brand helps stop colds. The FTC could have merely requested a cessation of the claim, but it chose corrective advertising because of the cumulative effects of past reinforcement. Since the campaign had run for many years, wear out would be slow and positive association between stimulus and response would continue. In other words, the consumer would be on the forgetting portion of the curve. Corrective advertising would force extinction between the stimulus and any deceptive reward. As *Ad Age* reported, "The FTC said it believed it had ample evidence to demonstrate that the effects of Listerine advertising will carry over into future consumer buying decisions unless corrective advertising is implemented."[12]

In a similar situation, the FTC chose not to force Ocean Spray to correct the impression that cranapple juice has more vitamins than apple juice. The FTC was satisfied with having Ocean Spray cease advertising the claim. One possible reason for the difference in the two cases is that Listerine advertising was shown for a significantly longer period and forgetting would have been more drawn out than for cranapple juice.

Importance of Instrumental Conditioning in Marketing

Instrumental conditioning is important in marketing because the theory focuses on reinforcement. Simply stated, consumers will repurchase when they are

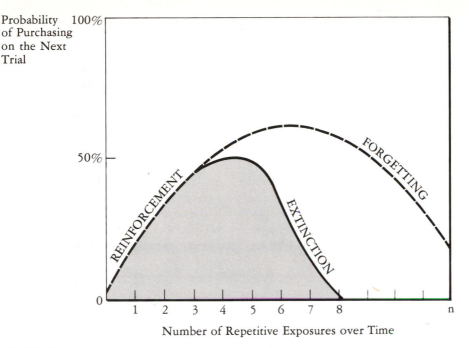

Probability 100%
of Purchasing
on the Next
Trial

50%

0

1 2 3 4 5 6 7 8 n

Number of Repetitive Exposures over Time

FIGURE 3–5 Reinforcement, Extinction, and Forgetting

satisfied. Therefore, the objective of all marketing strategy should be to reinforce the consumer through product satisfaction. This thesis is the very basis of the marketing concept — develop marketing strategies based on known consumer needs. Only in this manner can a brand achieve repeat purchases and a core of loyal users.

Cognitive Learning Theory

Cognitive psychologists view learning as a problem-solving process rather than the development of connections between stimulus and response. Learning is a cognitive process of perceiving stimuli, associating stimuli to needs, evaluating alternative brands, and assessing whether expectations have been met. Learning is equated to a process of complex decision making because of the emphasis on problem solving.

Markin compares the cognitive orientation to learning with the behaviorist orientation as follows:

> The behaviorist is inclined to ask, "What has the subject learned to do?" The cognitivist, on the other hand, would be inclined to ask, "How has the subject learned to perceive the situation?" The cognitivist is interested in examining a learning situation in terms of such factors as motivation, the perceived goals, the overall nature of the situation, and the beliefs, values and personality of the subject — in short, the entire range of the subject's psychological field. The cognitivist, as opposed to the behaviorist, contends that consumers do not respond simply to stimuli but instead act on beliefs, express attitudes, and strive toward goals.[13]

In other words, cognitive theory emphasizes the thought process involved in consumer learning; classical and instrumental conditioning emphasize the results based on the stimulus associations.

Cognitive learning theory is an outgrowth of the experiments of Kohler on apes.[14] In one experiment, a chimpanzee was placed in a cage with several boxes, and bananas were hung from the roof. After trying to reach the food and failing, the chimp solved the problem by placing a box under the bananas. Learning was not a result of contiguity between stimulus and response or reinforcement; it was the result of insight. Kohler's approach to learning is presented in Figure 3–4 as recognition of a goal, purposive behavior to achieve the goal, insight as to a solution, and goal achievement. Reinforcement is a recognized part of cognitive learning since there must be an awareness of goal achievement for learning to take place. But the nature of the goal is understood from the beginning and the reward is anticipated (e.g., eating the bananas). In instrumental conditioning, the reward is not apparent until after behavior takes place.

Market Learning by New Residents

Cognitive learning is especially relevant in understanding how consumers learn about innovations or in understanding how new residents learn about product alternatives.

This approach is reflected in two studies of the purchasing patterns of recent residents of a community. Andreasen and Durkson studied the purchasing patterns of three groups of housewives; those who had been living in the Philadelphia area less than three months, one and a half to two years, and three years or more.[15] They reasoned that for national brands there would be little difference between the three groups. But for local brands, the longer a family lived in the area, the closer brand awareness and purchasing would be to that of established residents. This meant that those living in the area one and a half to two years should be closer to the purchase patterns of the established residents than families living in the area three months or less. Results confirmed the hypothesis. The longer a family lived in the area the more the family was aware of local brands. Awareness levels for those living in the area one and a half to two years were closer to established residents. Some of the figures for local and regional brands are presented in Table 3–1.[16]

Andreasen and Durkson identified learning tasks in a new market environment as (1) brand identification, (2) brand evaluation, and (3) establishment of regular behavioral patterns with respect to the evaluated brands. This perspective clearly reflects a cognitive orientation to learning.

In a related study, Sheth examined the purchasing patterns of a panel of foreign students to determine the nature of learning in a new environment.[17] He found that cognitive processes such as information gathering through imitative behavior (buying same brand as one's best friend) and generalization (generalizing from product experiences in the home country) were instrumental in the development of habit among foreign students.

TABLE 3–1 Brand Awareness Levels   65

Brand Loyalty

| Brand | New Movers | Brand Awareness Levels | |
		Living in Area 1½ to 2 Years	Established Residents
Horn & Hardart coffee	5%	17%	33%
Atlantic gasoline	32%	49%	65%
Hudson facial tissues	17%	32%	37%
Abbot's milk	17%	28%	55%

Source: Adapted from Alan R. Andreasen and Peter G. Durkson, "Market Learning of New Residents," *Journal of Marketing Research* 10 (May 1968): 170.

BRAND LOYALTY

There is a close link between habit, learning, and brand loyalty. **Brand loyalty** represents a favorable attitude toward and consistent purchase of a single brand over time. As such, it is a reflection of habitual purchasing since brand loyalty requires less information seeking and brand evaluation. Sheth summarized this link: "Intuitively, learning seems very relevant as a conceptual explanation of brand loyalty. Both learning and brand loyalty are processes which are manifested over a period of time, and in both cases, there arises a habitual course of action which is dominant in a given situation."[18]

Two approaches to the study of brand loyalty have dominated marketing literature. The first approach, an instrumental conditioning approach, views consistent purchasing of one brand over time as an indication of brand loyalty. Repeat purchasing behavior is assumed to reflect reinforcement and a strong stimulus-to-response link. Research that takes this approach uses probabilistic (stochastic) models of consumer learning to estimate the probability of a consumer buying the same brand again, given a number of past purchases of that brand. The shape of the learning curve in Figure 3–3 determines this probability. Thus, ten consecutive purchases of Minute Maid frozen orange juice means a 92 percent probability the consumer will buy the same brand again on the next purchase. This is a **stochastic model** rather than a deterministic model of consumer behavior since it does not predict one specific course of action. Rather, the prediction is always in probability terms. **Deterministic models** would predict a particular course of action based on the input variables such as consumer characteristics, brand attitudes, and consumer needs. The models of complex decision making in the previous chapter and of habit in this chapter (Figure 3–1) are examples of deterministic models.

The second approach to the study of brand loyalty is based on cognitive theories. Some researchers believe that behavior alone does not reflect brand loyalty. Loyalty implies a commitment to a brand that may not be reflected by just measuring continuous behavior. A family may buy a particular brand because it is the lowest priced brand on the market. A slight increase in price may cause the family to shift to another brand. In this case, continuous purchasing does not reflect reinforcement or loyalty. The stimulus (product) and reward links are not strong. Some attitudinal measure combined with a behavioral measure is required to identify true loyalty.

The differences between a behavioral and a cognitive orientation in defining brand loyalty and habit are best illustrated by the statements of two researchers. Tucker takes a strong behavioral position:

> No consideration should be given to what the subject thinks or what goes on in his central nervous system; his behavior is the full statement of what brand loyalty is.[19]

Jacoby takes a clear cognitive position:

> To exhibit brand loyalty implies repeat purchasing behavior based on cognitive, affective, evaluative and predispositional factors — the classical primary components of an attitude.[20]

> Brand loyalty is a function of psychological (decision-making, evaluative) processes.[21]

In this discussion behavioral (instrumental conditioning) and attitudinal (cognitive) approaches to understanding brand loyalty will be considered.

A Behavioral Approach to Brand Loyalty

Researchers using a behavioral measure of brand loyalty generally rely on **consumer panel data**. A consumer panel is a sample of consumers that record their purchases for a wide range of goods (brand purchased, store in which bought, price paid, whether bought on deal). These records are then mailed to a research organization that tabulates data by brand. Such data permit the researcher to trace the consumer's pattern of brand purchases over time.

Behavioral Measures of Loyalty

Behavioral measures have defined loyalty by the sequence of purchases (purchased brand A five times in a row) and/or the proportion of purchases (brand A represents 80 percent of all purchases of frozen orange juice). In one of the earliest studies in this area, Brown defined brand loyalty as five purchases in a row of the same brand. He analyzed a panel of consumers for frequently purchased items such as coffee, orange juice, soap, and margarine and found that loyalty of the families studied varied from 12 percent to 73 percent, depending on the product.[22] Tucker defined loyalty as three purchases in a row.[23] Lawrence defined loyalty to a new brand as four purchases in a row.[24]

These varying definitions illustrate the fact that no consistent measure of behavioral loyalty has been accepted in consumer research. Blattberg and Sen used proportion of purchases rather than sequence as the behavioral measure of loyalty.[25] They identified four types of loyalty segments:

High national brand loyal. This segment is highly loyal to one national brand. Over 90 percent of all purchases are devoted to this brand.

- *National brand loyal.* Most purchases are devoted to one national brand, but degree of loyalty is not as high as 90 percent of all purchases.
- *Private label loyal.* Consumers in this segment are loyal to a private brand. Since the private brand can be purchased only in one type of store, brand loyalty is linked to store loyalty. Further, since private brands are priced lower than national brands, this consumer is price sensitive and may switch to another brand given any price increase of the private label brand.
- *Last purchase loyal.* Consumers in this segment buy one brand on successive occasions, switch to another and buy that several times, switch to another, etc.

Blattberg and Sen identified brand loyal consumers in each of these four segments. Their study presents a more realistic approach to behavioral measures of loyalty since it recognizes that loyalty is a multidimensional concept and that consumers can be segmented by type of loyalty.

Stochastic Models of Brand Loyalty

A natural extension of learning theories based on concepts of instrumental conditioning is the development of stochastic models of brand choice. Lawrence states the link between stochastic models and instrumental conditioning: "Such models make explicit the underlying assumption (of learning theory): Learning takes place as stimulus elements are progressively conditioned to a particular response under influence of a reward."[26] In relying on past purchase behavior to predict future behavior, the assumption is that repeat purchasing reflects satisfaction and increases the probability the brand will be purchased again.

It is beyond the scope of this book to consider the detailed and mathematically complex models of brand choice developed in marketing.[27] The stochastic models most frequently referred to are linear learning models[28] and Markov models.[29] Both approaches can be regarded as applications of instrumental conditioning theory.

Limitations of Behavioral Measures of Loyalty

Several limitations of a strictly behavioral approach to identifying brand loyalty should be recognized. First, measurement of loyalty based on past behavior may be misleading. Consider the consumer who buys one brand of coffee for personal consumption, another brand for the spouse, and occasionally a third, higher priced brand to have around the house for guests. The purchase sequence would not indicate loyalty; yet, the consumer may be highly loyal to the preferred brand.

Second, consumer purchases may not reflect a reinforcement learning process. Lawrence studied the sequence of purchases after a consumer switched out of his or her regular brand.[30] He found four patterns of purchasing:

- reversion (switching back to the original brand)
- conversion (remaining loyal to the new brand)
- vacillation (characterized by random switching between brands)
- experimentation (characterized by further systematic trial of other brands)

Only the reversion and conversion patterns would conform to instrumental conditioning since, in both cases, previous purchase is clearly increasing or decreasing the probability of buying the same brand again. But, for vacillation and experimentation no specific sequence is established, making it difficult to predict future behavior based on past purchases. Yet, Lawrence found that over 50 percent of the consumers studied conformed to a pattern of vacillation or experimentation.

Third, brand loyalty is not just a function of past behavior. It is a multidimensional concept which must incorporate the consumer's commitment toward the brand. The very term loyalty implies commitment rather than just repetitive behavior, suggesting the need for a cognitive as well as a behavioral view of loyalty.

A Cognitive Approach to Brand Loyalty

Some of the limitations of a strictly behavioral approach in measuring brand loyalty are overcome when loyalty includes both attitudes and behavior. Day states that in order to be truly loyal, the consumer must hold a favorable attitude toward the brand in addition to purchasing it repeatedly.[31] Day recognizes that consumers might continue to buy the same brand because other brands are not readily available, a brand offers a long series of price deals, or inertia may cause the consumer to repurchase. Day defines these conditions as spurious loyalty because they do not reflect commitment.

Wind states that consumers who are spuriously loyal to a brand are vulnerable to switching to another brand.[32] Wind's conception of loyalty is presented in Figure 3–6. Consumers who like a brand and buy it regularly are identified as loyal (upper left-hand box). Consumers who buy the brand regularly but are indifferent to it or dislike it are vulnerable to switching to a competitive brand (upper right-hand box). Conversely, consumers who do not buy the company's brand but like it are vulnerable to switching from a competitive brand to the company's brand.

Evidence suggests that utilizing both the attitudinal and behavioral components provides a more powerful definition of brand loyalty. In his study, Day found that when he attempted to predict brand loyalty, the predictive power of the model using both attitude and behavior measures was almost twice as good as the model using behavior alone.[33] Furthermore, if the behavioral measure alone was used, over 70 percent of the sample would have been defined as brand loyal. Adding the attitudinal component reduced the proportion of brand loyal consumers to under 50 percent. In other words, defining loyalty based only on repeat purchasing overstates the degree of loyalty.

The Brand Loyal Consumer

A number of studies have attempted to define the characteristics of a brand loyal consumer. These studies have uniformly found that there is no general, brand loyal consumer; that is, a consumer who tends to be loyal regardless of product category. Brand loyalty is product-specific. Consumers will be loyal to brands in one category based on strong commitment and will portray little loyalty to brands in other categories.

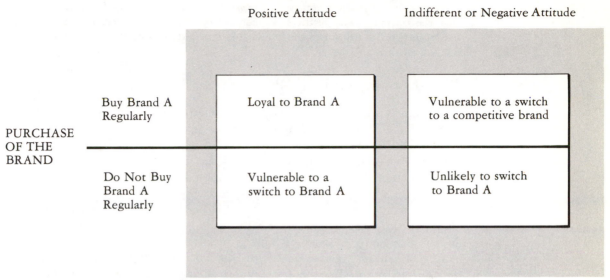

FIGURE 3–6 **Defining Brand Loyalty by Attitudes and Behavior**
Source: Adapted from Yoram Wind, "Brand Loyalty and Vulnerability," in Arch G. Woodside, Jagdish N. Sheth, and Peter D. Bennett, *Consumer and Industrial Buying Behavior* (New York: North-Holland, Inc., 1977), p. 314.

Despite the product-specific nature of brand loyalty, some generalizations can be made regarding the characteristics of those who tend to be brand loyal. Earlier studies based on behavioral measures of loyalty found few relationships between loyalty and consumers' demographic and personality characteristics.[34] More recent studies using attitudinal measures of loyalty found some relationship to consumer characteristics. These findings can be summarized as follows:

1. *Brand loyal consumers are more likely to be influenced by reference groups.* One study found that the preferred brand tended to be the brand chosen by the informal group leader.[35] Another found that the loyal consumer for a particular brand of coffee was more interested in status than the nonloyal consumer.[36]

2. *The loyal consumer tends to be more self-confident in his or her choice.* Both Day[37] and Carman[38] found this relationship to be true in separate studies of consumer packaged goods.

3. *The brand loyal consumer tends to be in the higher income group.*[39] This effect is explained as a result of a need on the part of low income consumers to be more careful shoppers. High income buyers can be more casual about shopping.

Other studies contradict this and find that high income consumers are more likely to engage in comparison shopping and are thus less predisposed to be loyal.[40] These findings illustrate the difficulty in equating demographic characteristics to loyalty. It is likely that high income consumers are more likely to be loyal for certain categories (probably convenience goods because it may not be worth their effort to shop for alternatives) and less likely to be loyal for other categories (probably specialty goods since they are more likely to be knowledgeable about brand and price alternatives.)

4. Brand loyal consumers are more likely to perceive a higher level of risk in the purchase and use repeat purchasing of a single brand as a means of reducing risk.[41]

5. The brand loyal consumer is more likely to be store loyal.   Carman states that the consumer who restricts the number of stores visited thereby restricts the opportunity to be disloyal to the brands sold in the store. Therefore, "store loyalty is a regulator of brand loyalty."[42]

Brand Loyalty and Involvement

The cognitive definition of brand loyalty means that loyalty represents commitment and, therefore, a high degree of involvement with the purchase. Loyalty and commitment are likely to occur when the brand is an important source of self-identification. In such cases, any change in the positioning or in the perception of the image of the preferred brand is likely to change preferences.

Spurious brand loyalty — that is, repeat purchasing of a brand without commitment — represents habitual purchasing with a low level of involvement. In this case, the consumer has no strong opinions or feelings about the brand. Purchasing is based on what is most familiar to the consumer. Information search and brand evaluation are not worth the time and effort required. Repeat purchase of a brand does not represent commitment; it merely represents acceptance.

SUMMARY

Habit, consumer learning, and brand loyalty are closely linked concepts. Habitual purchasing behavior is the result of consumer learning from reinforcement. Consumers will repeatedly buy what satisfies them best. This leads to brand loyalty.

A model representing habitual purchasing behavior is presented. Need arousal leads directly to an intention to buy, a subsequent purchase, and a process of postpurchase evaluation. Information search and brand evaluation are minimal.

Habit serves two important functions. It reduces risk for high involvement purchases and saves time and energy for low involvement products.

Concepts of learning are necessary to understand habit. The distinction is made between behavioral and cognitive approaches to learning. Behaviorist learning focuses on the stimuli that affect behavior and on behavior itself. Cognitive learning focuses on problem solving and emphasizes the consumer thought variables that influence the process of learning. Within the behavioral school, the distinction is also made between classical and instrumental conditioning. Classical conditioning explains behavior based on the establishment of a close association between a primary and secondary stimulus. Instrumental conditioning views behavior as a function of the consumer's actions. Satisfaction leads to reinforcement and to an increase in the probability of repurchasing.

The different learning theories are also reflected in differing views of what constitutes brand loyalty. An instrumental conditioning approach suggests that consistent purchase of a brand is a reflection of brand loyalty. The cognitive school believes that behavior is an insufficient measure of loyalty. Attitudinal commitment to the brand is required as well. The cognitive school views consistent purchase of a brand without commitment as spurious loyalty or buying by inertia. The cognitive theorist links true brand loyalty with brand involvement.

The next chapter focuses on the low involvement conditions that encourage spurious loyalty and inertia, as distinct from a high level of involvement identified with brand loyalty.

Questions

QUESTIONS

1. Why are cigarettes frequently cited as the type of product characterized by habitual purchasing behavior? What other product categories are likely to be purchased by habit? What do they have in common?

2. If habit is based on reinforcement and an increased likelihood of buying the same product, why have certain dominant brands, once purchased by habit, become extinct or experienced a substantial loss in market share (e.g., Sapolio soap, L&M cigarettes, Kolynos toothpaste)?

3. This chapter suggests that boredom and desire for variety may result in a change from habit to decision making.
   - Is this more likely for certain product categories than others?
   - Is this more likely for certain consumers than others? That is, is there a "stick with it" type as opposed to a "novelty seeker type"?

4. Habit serves two different purposes for high and low involvement situations.
   - What are they?
   - Can you cite examples of habit in a high involvement situation? In a low involvement situation?

5. The implication in this chapter is that the emphasis in advertising strategy has shifted from an adherence to classical learning theory before 1950 to an adherence to cognitive theories of learning after 1950.
   - How would such a shift be reflected in advertising strategy?
   - Do you agree that such a shift has taken place in advertising in the last thirty years?

6. What are the differing implications of classical and instrumental conditioning in the development of advertising strategies?

7. As a member of the Federal Trade Commission, what principles of conditioning would you use in deciding whether a company engaging in misleading advertising should either correct its advertising or simply stop it? Assuming corrective advertising was ordered, what principles of conditioning would you use to determine if this action had the desired effects?

8. A good example of the operation of cognitive learning is to determine how new residents in a community learn about new products not available in their previous community.
   - What evidence might demonstrate that a process of learning is taking place among new residents of a community?

9. A brand manager for a brand with frequent deals and coupons assumes that consumers who repeatedly buy the brand are loyal purchasers.

- What are the dangers of such an assumption?
- What marketing errors might result in (a) advertising strategy, (b) pricing, and (c) in-store promotions?

RESEARCH ASSIGNMENTS

1. Develop a measure of brand loyalty using either a behavioral or cognitive approach. Interview a sample of from thirty to fifty consumers of a frequently purchased, packaged product (coffee, toothpaste, frozen orange juice). Identify those who are loyal to a brand versus those who are not. Are there any differences between the two groups in terms of:

- demographic characteristics;
- importance placed on need criteria in selecting brands;
- brand attitudes;
- advertising recall; and
- price paid?

What are the implications of the differences between loyalists and nonloyalists for:

- attempts at increasing the number of loyal users;
- product positioning; and
- utilization of deals and coupons?

2. Develop a measure of loyalty incorporating both behavior and brand attitudes. Interview a sample of consumers of a frequently purchased packaged good. Distinguish between true loyalists and those who buy regularly out of inertia.

- What are the differences between the two groups based on the same criteria as in assignment 1 above?
- Based on your findings, should marketers try to influence consumers who buy their brand out of inertia to become truly loyal? What are the advantages and disadvantages of such a strategy?
- What other marketing implications emerge based on your findings?

NOTES

1. John A. Howard and Jagdish Sheth, *The Theory of Buyer Behavior* (New York: John Wiley & Sons, 1969), pp. 27–28.
2. Joseph W. Newman and Richard A. Werbel, "Multivariate Analysis of Brand Loyalty for Major Household Appliances," *Journal of Marketing Research* 10 (November 1973): 404–409.
3. Jagdish N. Sheth and M. Venkatesan, "Risk-Reduction Processes In Repetitive Consumer Behavior," *Journal of Marketing Research* 3 (August 1968): 307–311.
4. Ted Roselius, "Consumer Rankings of Risk Reduction Methods," *Journal of Marketing* 35 (January 1971): 56–61.

5. Sheth and Venkatesan, "Risk Reduction Processes."
6. For a good summary of these three learning theories see Michael L. Ray and Peter H. Webb, "Three Learning Theory Traditions and Their Application in Marketing," in Ronald C. Curhan ed., *Combined Proceedings of the American Marketing Association,* Series No. 36 (1974), pp. 100–103.
7. E.L. Thorndike, *The Psychology of Learning* (New York: Teacher's College, 1913); and J.B. Watson and R. Rayner, "Conditioned Emotional Reactions," *Journal of Experimental Psychology* 3 (1920): 1–14.
8. Ivan Pavlov, *Conditioned Reflexes. An Investigation of the Physiological Activity of the Cerebral Cortex,* G.V. Anrep, ed., (London: Oxford University Press, 1927).
9. B.F. Skinner, *The Behavior of Organisms: An Experimental Analysis* (New York: Appleton-Century-Crofts, 1938).
10. Peter D. Bennett and Robert M. Mandel, "Prepurchase Information Seeking Behavior of New Car Purchasers — The Learning Hypothesis," *Journal of Marketing Research* 6 (November 1969): 430–433.
11. J. Ronald Carey et al., "A Test of Positive Reinforcement of Customers," *Journal of Marketing* 40 (October 1976): 98–100.
12. *Advertising Age,* September 13, 1976, p. 124.
13. Rom J. Markin, Jr. *Consumer Behavior, A Cognitive Orientation* (New York: Macmillan Publishing Co. Inc, 1974), p. 239.
14. Wolfgang Kohler, *The Mentality of Apes* (New York: Harcourt Brace & World, 1925).
15. Alan R. Andreasen and Peter G. Durson, "Market Learning of New Residents," *Journal of Marketing Research* 5 (May 1968): 166–176.
16. Ibid., p. 170.
17. Jagdish N. Sheth, "How Adults Learn Brand Preference," *Journal of Advertising Research* 8 (September 1968): 25–36.
18. Ibid., p. 26.
19. W. T. Tucker, "The Development of Brand Loyalty," *Journal of Marketing Research* 1 (August 1964): 32.
20. Jacob Jacoby, "A Model of Multi-Brand Loyalty," *Journal of Advertising Research* 11 (June 1971): 26.
21. Jacob Jacoby and David B. Kyner, "Brand Loyalty vs. Repeat Purchasing Behavior," *Journal of Marketing Research* 10 (February 1973): 2.
22. George Brown, "Brand Loyalty — Fact or Fiction?" *Advertising Age* (June 19, 1952): 53–55; (June 30, 1952): 45–47; (August 11, 1952): 56–58; (September 1, 1952): 80–82; (October 6, 1952): 82–86; (December 1, 1952): 76–79; (January 25, 1953): 32–35.
23. Tucker, "The Development of Brand Loyalty."
24. Raymond J. Lawrence, "Patterns of Buyer Behavior: Time for a New Approach?" *Journal of Marketing Research* 6 (May 1969): 137–144.
25. Robert C. Blattberg and Subrata K. Sen, "Market Segments and Stochastic Brand Choice Models," *Journal of Marketing Research* 13 (February 1976): 34–45.
26. Lawrence, "Patterns of Buyer Behavior," p. 137.
27. For an excellent overview of stochastic models and their application to the analysis of brand choice see Frank M. Bass, "The Theory of Stochastic Preference and Brand Switching," *Journal of Marketing Research* 11 (February 1974): 1–20.
28. Alfred A. Kuehn, "Consumer Brand Choice as a Learning Process," *Journal of Advertising Research* 2 (December 1962): 10–17.
29. See for example refinements in Markov models by Benjamin Lipstein, "A Mathematical Model of Consumer Behavior," *Journal of Marketing Research* 2 (August 1965): 259–265; and Donald G. Morrison, "Testing Brand-Switching Models," *Journal of Marketing Research* 3 (November 1966): 401–409.
30. Lawrence, "Patterns of Buyer Behavior."
31. George S. Day, "A Two-Dimensional Concept of Brand Loyalty," *Journal of Advertising Research* 9 (September 1969): 29–36.
32. Yoram Wind, "Brand Loyalty and Vulnerability," in Arch G. Woodside, Jagdish N. Sheth and Peter D. Bennett, eds., *Consumer and Industrial Buying Behavior* (New York: North-Holland Inc., 1977), pp. 313–319.
33. Day, "A Two-Dimensional Concept."
34. See *Are There Consumer Types?* (New York: Advertising Research Foundation, 1964); and Ronald E. Frank, William F. Massy, and Thomas M. Lodahl, "Purchasing Behavior and Personal Attributes," *Journal of Advertising Research* 9 (December 1969): 15–24.
35. James E. Stafford, "Effect of Group Influences on Consumer Brand Preferences," *Journal of Marketing Research* 3 (February 1966): 68–75.
36. James M. Carman, "Correlates of Brand Loyalty: Some Positive Results," *Journal of Marketing Research* 7 (February 1970): 67–76.
37. Day, "A Two-Dimensional Concept."
38. Carman, "Correlates of Brand Loyalty."
39. William A. Chance and Norman D. French, "An Exploratory Investigation of Brand Switching," *Journal of Marketing Research* 9 (May 1972): 226–229; and Carman, "Correlates of Brand Loyalty."
40. See for example Arieh Goldman, "The Shopping Style Explanation for Store Loyalty," *Journal of Retailing* 53 (Winter 1977–78): 33–46; and Fred D. Reynolds, William R. Darden, and Warren S. Martin, "Developing an Image of the Store-Loyal Customer," *Journal of Retailing* 50 (Winter 1974–75): 73–84.
41. Roselius, "Consumer Rankings"; and Sheth and Venkatesan, "Risk-Reduction Processes."
42. Carman, "Correlates of Brand Loyalty."

FOUR

Low Involvement Decision Making

Focus of Chapter

Most marketing studies have been devoted to situations requiring complex decision making or brand loyalty. Such situations assume the consumer is involved in the purchase. But, most purchase decisions are low in consumer involvement.[1] A low involvement purchase is one where the consumer does not consider the product sufficiently important to his or her belief system and does not strongly identify with the product.

In this chapter purchase decisions where the consumer is not highly involved will be considered. The importance of a low involvement perspective will be considered first. Then, consumer decisions will be classified by level of product involvement. The theoretical basis for low involvement purchase behavior will be described based on a theory of passive learning. Strategic implications in high versus low involvement situations will then be considered, with special emphasis on advertising strategy.

THE IMPORTANCE OF A LOW INVOLVEMENT PERSPECTIVE

Kassarjian effectively makes the case that most purchase decisions are better described by low involvement conditions:

Subjects just do not care much about products; they are unimportant to them. Although issues such as racial equality, wars and the draft may stir them up, products do not. Hence, the emerging conclusion must be that true attitudes about these items most likely do not exist for many subjects. Bicycles, colas, and toothpaste generally do not have attitudes associated with them. To claim that attitudes about these products do exist is to claim that subjects "give a damn" about them. [Most] subjects do not.[2]

There is support for Kassarjian's low involvement perspective in a study conducted by Hupfer and Gardner.[3] They asked college students to rate twenty issues and twenty products on a 7-point scale from very important (7) to not important at all (1). Not surprisingly, the issues were rated much more important than the products. Some of the relative ratings are listed below:

Product or Issue	Rating
the draft	6.71
Vietnam War	6.28
world peace	6.17
automobiles	4.52
houses	4.17
beer	3.00
coffee	2.61
fraternity membership	2.38
toothpaste	1.95
bicycles	1.39
facial tissues	1.19

Although some of the products were rated relatively higher (automobiles and houses), it is apparent that in most cases, the product categories were relatively unimportant. Product choice is simply not one of the most important concerns in most consumers' lives.

Involvement and the Hierarchy of Effects

Given the prominence of low involvement purchasing, why has marketing focused on complex decision making and brand loyalty? There are two reasons. First, it is easier to influence the consumer when the marketer assumes there is a cognitive process of brand evaluation. Product benefits can be directed to target segments in an attempt to change brand attitudes. Advertising strategies can be geared initially to creating brand awareness, then brand interest, brand commitment, and eventually brand loyalty.

Second, the process of complex decision making assumes a hierarchy of effects that stipulates that consumers first form brand beliefs (the cognitive component of attitudes), then evaluate brands (the affective component), and then make a purchase decision (the behavioral component). This hierarchy conforms well to the dominant view in cognitive psychology that consumers think before they act. The beliefs/evaluation/behavior hierarchy has dominated marketing thought since consumer behavior became an integrated field of study.

The Low Involvement Hierarchy

The traditional model of belief/evaluation/behavior does a poor job in describing low involvement decisions. Using an extreme example, when a consumer purchases table salt, it is unlikely that a process of information search will be initiated to determine brand characteristics. Nor is it likely the consumer will evaluate alternative brands to identify the most favored brand.

Rather than searching for information, the consumer will receive information passively. The consumer sits in front of the television and sees an advertisement for Morton Salt. Stifling a yawn, the consumer is thinking about anything but salt. The advertisement is not really perceived in the sense of being comprehended. It is just seen and a few bits and pieces of information are stored in the consumer's mind without any active cognitive process. Lastovicka refers to this process as information "catching" rather than information "seeking."[4]

The consumer buys the brand (Morton Salt) when the need arises primarily because of familiarity. Repetitive advertising produces this familiarity. Seeing the brand on the shelf and associating the name with the advertising may be a sufficient stimulus to purchase. Under these conditions, an attitude toward the brand is not formed. There is no favorable or unfavorable reaction to the brand. The consumer regards the brand as relatively neutral since it is not associated with any important benefits tied to self-identification.

Relatively weak attitudes toward the brand may develop if, for example, a new feature such as a convenient spout is introduced (favorable evaluation) or if the brand performs poorly (sticks to the container producing an unfavorable reaction). But these attitudes develop after the purchase, not before. Therefore, the hierarchy of effects for low involvement products is quite different from the high involvement case.[5]

Low Involvement Hierarchy
1. Brand beliefs are formed first by *passive* learning.
2. A purchase decision is then made.
3. The brand may or may not be evaluated afterwards.

High Involvement Hierarchy
1. Brand beliefs are formed first by *active* learning.
2. Brands are then evaluated.
3. A purchase decision is made.

FOUR TYPES OF CONSUMER BEHAVIOR

The high involvement hierarchy — beliefs/evaluation/behavior — represents the model of complex decision making described in Chapter Two. As noted, both the process of complex decision making and the formation of brand loyalty assume an involved consumer who sees sufficient differences between brands to warrant an active process of brand evaluation. The example described above is exactly the reverse — low involvement and few differences between brands. The two remaining conditions — (1) high involvement and few brand differences and (2) low involvement and significant brand differences — also describe purchasing situations. The four types of consumer behavior are summarized below.[6]

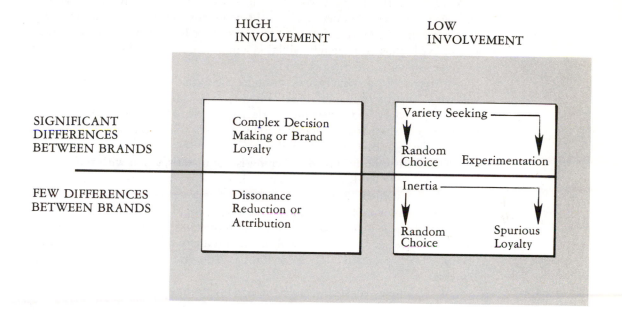

Complex Decision Making and Brand Loyalty

The upper left-hand box represents the complex decision making/brand loyalty continuum covered in the previous two chapters.

Inertia

The lower right-hand box represents the Morton Salt example — low involvement and few differences between brands. Under these conditions, consumers will either choose a brand at random (pick the first brand of salt they see) or will develop spurious loyalty (repeatedly buy Morton because it is familiar, thus avoiding a decision process). In both cases, the governing principle is **inertia** — a passive process of information processing, a passive process of brand choice, and little or no brand evaluation.

Complex decision making, brand loyalty, and inertia probably represent the most frequent cases of consumer choice in the marketplace. Given the dominance of low involvement products, inertia is probably much more common than most marketing managers would like to admit. The product manager or advertiser is trying to make the relatively undifferentiated low involvement product as different from competition as possible. The assumption governing most attempts to create product differences is that the consumer does notice, comprehend, and care.

Variety Seeking

The two remaining cases occur less frequently but, still, should be understood by marketers because the cases involve different strategic implications. **Variety seeking** is described by low consumer involvement and significant, perceived differences between brands (upper right-hand box). This situation is clearly different from the Morton Salt example since there is some basis for evaluating alternative brands. Yet, brand evaluation will not be extensive because consumer involvement with the product is low.

Variety seeking is likely to occur under these conditions since the consumer will try a diversity of brands. There is little psychological or social involvement with the product and, therefore, little risk in switching to another brand. Furthermore, the basis for brand switching exists since there are distinct differences between brands.

The motivation for brand switching is not dissatisfaction with the current brand. Since the level of involvement is low, the consumer is not likely to be seriously dissatisfied. Rather, the motivation is a desire for change, a search for novelty. Venkatesan recognized that variety-seeking behavior may be the result of routinized choice and boredom with the familiar.[7] Given the repetitive nature of advertising for low involvement products and the mundane nature of many such products, variety seeking is a logical expression of consumer boredom.

For example, consider cookies, a low involvement product having differences between brands. It is unlikely that the consumer will develop a strong preference for a brand. A switch in brands may be made on a random basis by purchasing the first brand seen in the supermarket. There may also be a conscious attempt at experimentation (buying a variety of brands on a sequential basis). In each case, the purchase is made without brand evaluation and with no change in brand attitudes. The chosen brand will be evaluated in the process of consumption. Variety seeking, therefore, conforms to the low involvement hierarchy described previously — brand beliefs/behavior/evaluation.

Dissonance Reduction or Attribution

The fourth type of behavior — high consumer involvement with few perceived differences between brands (lower left-hand box) — is best described by dissonance theory. As noted in Chapter Two, dissonance is a state of postpurchase conflict created by contradictory beliefs.[8] If the consumer is involved in the purchase decision and sees little difference between the characteristics of several brand alternatives, then postpurchase dissonance is likely to result regardless of the brand chosen. Since the brands are so similar, the first contradictory piece of information the consumer receives about the chosen brand results in the feeling that the other brand should have been purchased.

A good example is carpets. Although differences do exist between brands of carpets, most consumers do not know the nature or importance of these differences and are likely to regard all carpeting within a given price range as similar. The purchase of a carpet is an involving decision. It is a high-priced item that relates to self-identification (furnishing the home). Yet, the consumer has little basis for brand evaluation. Under these circumstances, the consumer may rely on information supplied by a salesperson or on opinions of friends and relatives.

Two or three relatively equal brands of carpeting are considered. A brand of carpeting is chosen without any firm beliefs about its relative merits compared to other brands. Once chosen, the consumer will attempt to justify the choice by seeking out positive information and by ignoring negative information about the brand. The process of information search and brand evaluation occurs *after* behavior. The hierarchy of effects in the case of dissonance would therefore be:

1. Behavior occurs first.
2. Brand beliefs are formed to support the chosen brand.
3. The brand is favorably evaluated.

An alternative explanation to the behavior/beliefs/evaluation hierarchy is provided by attribution theory. **Attribution theory** states that a consumer will attribute certain motives to his or her actions after the fact. Bem provides a direct example of attribution: In asking a consumer who frequently eats brown bread to evaluate the product, the answer might be "Since I am always eating it, I guess I like it."[9] Similarly, the purchaser of a brand of carpet might say, "Since I bought it, it must be pretty good." In this case, there are no prior beliefs or evaluation. Brand beliefs and evaluation occur after the purchase and are attributed to the behavior. The end result is the same as dissonance theory — a behavior/beliefs/evaluation sequence.

The Four Hierarchies Summarized

Figure 4–1 summarizes the four types of behavior. In each case the behavioral model, the underlying theory, and the decision process are listed. High involvement and significant differences between brands describes the traditional beliefs/evaluation/behavior hierarchy. The decision-making process involves complex decision making or brand loyalty. The underlying theory is one of cognitive learning by problem solving.

The high involvement/few brand differences condition describes a behavior/beliefs/evaluation hierarchy. The underlying theories are dissonance or attribution; the behavioral pattern involves dissonance reduction or attribution based on behavior.

The two low involvement conditions describe the development first of brand beliefs and then behavior. Where significant brand differences exist, brand evaluation is likely. In both cases, the underlying theory is one of passive learning. There is little information processing. Information is retained because of repetition and is remembered only when the purchasing situation arises. Brands are frequently purchased because they are familiar. Brand switching may occur for the sake of variety rather than dissatisfaction. Repetitive purchase of a single brand is likely to reflect inertia rather than brand loyalty.

	HIGH INVOLVEMENT	LOW INVOLVEMENT

SIGNIFICANT DIFFERENCES BETWEEN BRANDS	MODEL
	  Beliefs
	  Evaluation
	  Behavior
	
	THEORY
	  Cognitive Learning
	
	DECISION PROCESS
	  Complex Decision Making or Brand Loyalty
		MODEL
		  Beliefs
		  Behavior
		  Evaluation
		
		THEORY
		  Low Involvement Decision Making
		
		DECISION PROCESS
		  Variety Seeking

FEW DIFFERENCES BETWEEN BRANDS	MODEL
	  Behavior
	  Beliefs
	  Evaluation
	
	THEORY
	  Dissonance or Attribution Theory
	
	DECISION PROCESS
	  Dissonance Reduction or Attribution
		MODEL
		  Beliefs
		  Behavior
		
		THEORY
		  Low Involvement Decision Making
		
		DECISION PROCESS
		  Inertia

FIGURE 4–1   A Classification of Four Types of Consumer Behavior

Marketing Implications of the Four Behavioral Models

A number of important marketing implications arise based on the four behavioral processes described above.

Complex Decision Making Versus Dissonance

Assuming there is a high level of involvement, strategic implications will differ depending on whether the consumer sees significant differences between brands.

If there are significant differences, the role of advertising is to inform consumers of the relative advantages of the company's brand. Product positioning to meet the needs of a defined segment of consumers becomes critical.

In the absence of perceived brand differences, the role of advertising is to influence and to reassure the consumer once the choice is made. Such reassurance is essential since a state of postpurchase dissonance will cause the consumer to seek support for the choice. Informational advertising is not as important since there are fewer brand differences to be advertised.

High Involvement Versus Low Involvement

Different implications also emerge depending on the level of involvement. In the low involvement case, the role of advertising is to create awareness and familiarity through repetition.[10] Since, in most cases, the consumer could not care less and is probably paying a minimal amount of attention, a small number of points should be emphasized in the advertising. Symbols that can be positively identified with the brand should be used. These principles apply concepts of classical conditioning. Repetition is required to create contiguity between advertising symbols and brand use. A picture of a cold bottle of Coke may be all that is required to serve as a reminder and cause the consumer to purchase.

In the high involvement case, advertising seeks to go beyond creating awareness. It seeks to influence the consumer by communicating a persuasive message. Repetition is not the key; the content of the message is the key. Messages are likely to be more complex and varied and are likely to deal more directly with desired product benefits.

There are also different implications for price and promotional strategies. When the consumer is not involved with the product, prepurchase evaluation is minimal. Brand choice is frequently made in the store. Therefore, in-store conditions become much more important for low involvement products. The brand at the eye level position or the one with the largest shelf space may be purchased simply because of the reminder effect. In-store displays may also encourage purchases.

Another important strategic implication is the greater facility of inducing trial of low involvement products.[11] The consumer is not strongly committed to the chosen brand. Therefore, a decrease in price or a coupon offer may be sufficient to induce a brand switch. Attempts at inducing trial are particularly important for low involvement products since a favorable attitude toward the brand may be formed after the purchase. A consumer may try a free sample of toothpaste, like the taste, and purchase it. The consumer is not seeking to maximize satisfaction. Continued purchasing of the toothpaste may occur because the brand is adequate.[12] Information search and further brand evaluation are not warranted. Due to inertia, trial may be sufficient to induce continued purchasing.

What strategies can the marketer employ to encourage trial under low involvement conditions? Free samples, deals and coupons, joint promotions with other products, in-store displays, and intensive distribution can be employed. These are strategies that are unlikely to induce trial under high involvement conditions because of the consumer's commitment to the brand. A price deal or coupons may not provide sufficient incentive for a switch because of brand loyalty. The brand-loyal consumer is too price inelastic to be influenced by short-term price deals and coupon offers. Trial under high involvement conditions can be encouraged only by demonstrating product benefits relevant to consumer needs. Trial is induced under low involvement conditions primarily through price and promotional strategies; under high involvement conditions trial is induced through strategies of product positioning.

The remainder of this chapter will focus on low involvement decision making by considering the conceptual basis for a theory of low involvement consumer behavior and by describing studies of low involvement decision-making processes.

A THEORY OF LOW INVOLVEMENT CONSUMER BEHAVIOR

A better understanding of the nature of low involvement choice has evolved in marketing based on two theories: the theory of passive learning developed by Krugman[13] and the theory of social judgment developed by Sherif.[14]

Krugman's Theory of Passive Learning

Much of the work on low involvement consumer behavior is based on Krugman's perspective of television as an uninvolving medium. Krugman sought an answer to why television advertising produced high levels of brand recall yet little change in attitudes toward brands. He hypothesized that television is a low involvement medium that results in **passive learning**. The viewer is in a relaxed state and does not pay attention to the message. In this low involvement environment, the viewer does not link the message to his or her needs, brand beliefs, and past experiences (as is assumed in the high involvement case). Information is retained on a random basis because of repetition of the message. As a result, a respondent can show a high level of recall for a particular television advertisement, but the advertisement has little influence on brand attitudes.

Why is television a low involvement medium? Because as Krugman states:

- Television advertising is animate while the viewer is inanimate (passive).
- The pace of viewing is out of the viewer's control and there is little opportunity for reflection and making connections.[15]

In contrast, print media (magazines and newspapers) are high involvement media because the advertising is inanimate while the reader is animate. The pace of exposure is within the reader's control since the reader has more opportunity to reflect on the advertising.

Krugman predicts that television would be more effective for low involvement cases and print advertising for high involvement cases. This view was confirmed in a study by Grass and Wallace.[16] They found that for unmotivated consumers television was more effective in conveying a message than print ads were. For motivated consumers, print ads were somewhat more effective. Krug-

TABLE 4–1   The High Involvement, Active Consumer Versus the Low
Involvement, Passive Consumer

Traditional, High Involvement View of an Active Consumer	Newer, Low Involvement View of a Passive Consumer
1. Consumers are information processors.	1. Consumers learn information at random.
2. Consumers are information seekers.	2. Consumers are information gatherers.
3. Consumers represent an active audience for advertising. As a result, the effect of advertising on the consumer is *weak*.	3. Consumers represent a passive audience for advertising. As a result, the effect of advertising on the consumer is *strong*.
4. Consumers evaluate brands before buying.	4. Consumers buy first. If they do evaluate brands, it is done after the purchase.
5. Consumers seek to maximize expected satisfaction. As a result, consumers compare brands to see which provide the most *benefits* related to needs and buy based on multiattribute comparisons of brands.	5. Consumers seek some acceptable level of satisfaction. As a result, consumers buy the brand least likely to give them *problems* and buy based on a few attributes. Familiarity is the key.
6. Personality and life-style characteristics are related to consumer behavior because the product is closely tied to the consumer's identity and belief system.	6. Personality and life-style characteristics are not related to consumer behavior because the product is not closely tied to the consumer's identity and belief system.
7. Reference groups influence consumer behavior because of the importance of the product to group norms and values.	7. Reference groups exert little influence on product choice because products are unlikely to be related to group norms and values.

man summarizes his view of television by saying "the public lets down its guard to the repetitive commercial use of television . . . it easily changes its ways of perceiving products and brands and its purchasing behavior without thinking very much about it at the time of TV exposure."[17] In other words, beliefs about a brand can change leading to a purchase decision with very little thought and deliberation involved.

Implications for Consumer Behavior

Krugman's view of a passive consumer has literally stood many of the traditional behavioral concepts in marketing on their head. Table 4–1 lists the traditional behavioral concepts associated with an involved, active consumer and the parallel concept for an uninvolved, passive consumer.

The traditional view holds that:

1. *Consumers are information processors.* The involved consumer is viewed as processing information in a cognitive manner by going through stages of awareness, comprehension, and retention. Krugman views the uninvolved consumer as learning from repetitive advertising, much as children learn nonsense syllables, by just picking up random stimuli and retaining them. A study by Hollander and Jacoby confirms Krugman's view of nonsense learning. They overlayed the audio portion of one com-

mercial on the video portion of another, producing a nonsense TV commercial. Recall of the nonsense commercial was higher than the recall of the normal commercial.[18]

This research suggests a distraction hypothesis.[19] That is, when the consumer is uninvolved and the message is uninteresting (the typical case for TV advertising), distraction may actually increase message awareness.

2. *Consumers are information seekers.* The high involvement consumer is regarded as an information seeker, actively searching for information from alternative sources and engaging in shopping behavior. In the low involvement case, the consumer is an information catcher, that is, a passive receiver of information.

The limited amount of information search for most consumer products is demonstrated in studies that show that many consumers typically visit one store[20] and consider only one brand.[21]

3. *Consumers represent an active audience for advertising.* The active audience view is tied to the assumption that the consumer is an involved information seeker with strongly held brand attitudes. Under such conditions, the consumer is likely to resist advertising that does not conform to prior beliefs (selective perception). This view logically leads to the conclusion that advertising is a relatively weak vehicle for changing people's minds and is better suited to confirming current beliefs. Bauer summarizes the active audience view in describing advertising as a "most difficult business . . . Typical communication experiments, including advertising tests, show that only a few percentages of the people exposed to the communication ever change their mind on anything important."[22] But, advertising generally deals with unimportant matters. Under these conditions, advertising may be a much more effective medium for inducing purchasing behavior. In Krugman's view, exposure in and of itself is persuasive and may lead to purchasing without the intervening step of comprehension. Therefore, when the consumer is passive and the message relatively unimportant, advertising may be a more powerful medium than is assumed in the active audience view.

4. *Consumers evaluate brands before buying.* The traditional view holds that consumers evaluate alternative brands before purchasing. Krugman states that the uninvolved consumer may buy just due to a reminder effect. The connection between a need and the brand is frequently made in the store due to a lack of prepurchase deliberation.

5. *Consumers seek to maximize expected satisfaction.* The active consumer seeks to maximize the satisfaction expected from a brand by going through an extensive process of brand evaluation. Complex decision making involves a comparison of brand characteristics with consumer needs. Various brand attributes are compared and the brand that best meets the consumer's needs is selected.

The low involvement case neither assumes the consumer seeks to maximize brand satisfaction nor does it assume that consumers seek out particular benefits. A consumer buying plastic wrap does not seek to maximize satisfaction by searching for the best brand. The energy required in such a search is not worth the expected benefits. The consumer will buy a wrap that performs acceptably. In finding an acceptable wrap, the consumer will not evaluate alternative benefits such as strength, protection, etc. He or she is more likely to select the wrap that is least likely to shred, least likely to stick together, and least likely to come apart once wrapped. In other words, the perspective is not on benefit maximization; it is on problem minimization. Furthermore, the consumer will not evaluate plastic wraps on a number of alternative attributes. The wrap that is most familiar may be the one that will be purchased.

This view of satisfying rather than optimizing and of being oriented to problem minimization rather than to benefit maximization has important implications for marketing strategy. The marketing concept states that all marketing strategies should be directed to known consumer wants. If the low involvement view of a passive problem-oriented consumer is correct, then the marketing concept should be modified to convey that all marketing strategies should be directed to known consumer wants in the high involvement case and to known consumer problems in the low involvement case. Taking a high involvement view, a toothpaste might be positioned to provide whiter teeth (benefit maximization); but taking a low involvement view, a toothpaste might be better positioned to prevent cavities (problem minimization). Given the effectiveness of Crest in positioning itself based on cavity prevention, it would appear that some marketers intuitively recognize the importance of a problem rather than a benefit orientation for low involvement products.

6. *Personality and life-style characteristics are related to consumer behavior.* The traditional view assumes that the personality and life-style characteristics of the consumer will be related to the purchase decision. Brand purchases may be related to compulsiveness, sociability, dominance, etc. Such relationships are assumed to exist because a high level of involvement assumes the product is important to the consumer's belief system and self-identity. Since self-identity is reflected in the consumer's personality and life-style, it makes sense to relate these characteristics to products with high consumer involvement.

However, there is no reason to assume that personality and life-style characteristics are related to behavior for the passive, uninvolved consumer. Most products purchased by consumers are not central to their beliefs or closely identified with self-identity. As Kassarjian says:

> Personality variables may be related to racial prejudice, suicide, violent crimes, or the selection of a spouse. But turning to unimportant, uninvolving, low-commitment consumer products such as brands of beer, chewing gum, t-shirts, and magazine exposure, the correlations [of personality to behavior] are extremely low.[23]

7. *Reference groups influence consumer behavior.* The involved consumer is more likely to be influenced by reference groups because a high involvement product is more likely to reflect the norms and values of the group. Products such as automobiles, homes, and stereo sets are visible and have important status connotations.

A study by Cocanougher and Bruce found that reference groups have little impact for low commitment products.[24] Products such as salt, toothpaste, paper towels, and plastic wrap have little visibility and are not relevant to group norms. Kassarjian again provides a good quote for the low involvement case: "We doubt very much that there are many consumers in the world that ask the advice of Mrs. Olson on whether or not to buy Folger's coffee with mountain grown beans."[25] Given the relative lack of importance of reference groups for low involvement products, much of the advertising portraying social approval in the use of products such as floor wax or room deodorizers may be misplaced. The more relevant approach may be to portray the problems such products can eliminate.

Sherif's Social Judgment Theory

A second theory that sheds additional light on the passive, uninvolved consumer is Sherif's theory of social judgment. Sherif describes an individual's position on an issue based on the individual's involvement with the issue.[26] Sherif operationalizes this concept of involvement by identifying a latitude of acceptance (the positions the individual accepts), a latitude of rejection (positions the individual rejects), and a latitude of noncommitment (positions toward which the individual is neutral). A highly involved individual having a definite opinion about the issue would accept very few positions and reject a wide number of positions (narrow latitude of acceptance and wide latitude of rejection). An uninvolved individual would find more positions acceptable (wide latitude of acceptance) or would have no opinion about the issue (wide latitude of noncommitment).

For a highly involved individual, a message that is agreed with (latitude of acceptance) will be interpreted more positively than it actually is. This reaction represents an **assimilation effect**. A message that the individual disagrees with (latitude of rejection) will be interpreted more negatively than it actually is. This reaction represents a **contrast effect**. Therefore, the highly involved individual is more likely to perceive messages selectively based on his or her preconceptions and biases. The uninvolved individual is less likely to distort the message, and an assimilation or contrast effect is less likely to occur.

Translated into marketing terms, Sherif's theory predicts that the active, involved consumer would find many brands unacceptable, while the less involved consumer would find many brands acceptable. Furthermore, the involved consumer would be more attentive to advertising messages and more likely to interpret these messages in line with current attitudes and previous experiences. The less involved consumer would be less attentive to advertising messages and more likely to accept them. There would be less thought in reacting to these messages and, therefore, less likelihood of selective perception.

Sherif's theory conforms well to Krugman's concept of passive learning and provides more insight into the passive consumer. Uninvolved consumers are willing to consider a wider number of brands because of a lack of commitment to one or several brands. But they do not search for alternatives. Given a lack of commitment, they are less willing to spend time interpreting advertising messages and evaluating brands. As a result, advertising is perceived with little cognitive activity and brands are purchased in the easiest way possible — by purchasing the most familiar brand and buying the same brand repetitively.

Applications of Sherif's Theory to Marketing

Rothschild and Houston extend Sherif's theory to predict that the highly involved consumer will use more attributes in evaluating brands, while the less involved consumer will use fewer attributes.[27] This assumption makes sense since the more involved consumer goes through a more extensive process of brand evaluation and is more likely to operate on the principle of maximizing expected benefits. Thus, more attributes are required in evaluation. On this basis, Rothschild and Houston conceptualize the high versus low involvement case as follows:

	High Involvement	*Low Involvement*
Number of Attributes Used in Brand Evaluation	Many	Few
Latitude of Acceptance	Narrow (Fewer brands considered)	Wide (More brands considered)

In the high involvement case, fewer brands will be evaluated using many attributes. In the low involvement case, more brands will be evaluated using few attributes.

Since more attributes will be used in the high involvement case, then a multiattribute view of brand evaluation is more relevant. More specifically, Rothschild and Houston say that a compensatory method of brand evaluation is more likely — that is, consumers will evaluate the alternative brands on many attributes; better performance on one attribute will outweigh poorer performance on another. In contrast, a noncompensatory process is likely to occur in the low involvement case. Since there are few attributes used in evaluation, poor performance on one attribute may be sufficient to knock the brand out of contention.

To use the example of Mr. and Mrs. G in Chapter Two — if Mr. and Mrs. G are highly involved with the purchase of the car, they will have quickly narrowed their choice down to a few brands and use a large number of attributes to evaluate each brand (see Table 2–1). If they are not as involved with the purchase, they will consider a large number of brands and use a smaller number of attributes to evaluate each brand (see Table 2–2).

Rothschild and Houston went on to apply Sherif's measures of involvement to political rather than consumer choice.[28] They identified two types of political choices: a presidential election (high involvement) and a state assembly race (low involvement). They found the latitude of acceptance of issues was narrower for the presidential race and the number of issues used to evaluate the candidates was greater than in the state assembly race. These findings conform to the matrix presented above.

Lastovicka and Gardner found a similar set of relationships.[29] They determined the number of car makes that respondents accepted, rejected, and were neutral to. On this basis, respondents were classified into low, medium, and high involvement individuals. The cognitive structure for the low involvement group was simpler — a simpler set of decision rules was used in evaluating brands. Although not tested directly, these results support the theory that fewer attributes and simpler noncompensatory rules are used in evaluating brands in the low involvement case.

STUDIES OF LOW INVOLVEMENT
DECISION MAKING

This section will be short since there have been few studies in marketing focusing on low versus high involvement decisions. Given the fact that the majority of product decisions are not involving to the consumer, the lack of research in this area probably represents the most glaring gap in the consumer behavior field today. Practitioners are unlikely to take a low involvement view of their product because of a vested interest in viewing their market as involved. An active consumer is more easily researched and appealed to. Krugman's view that the passive consumer is one that pays little attention to advertising or brands, that retains advertising messages almost in a random fashion, and that purchases with little deliberation may be abhorrent to many marketers. Tyebjee notes the reluctance of product and advertising managers to consider a passive consumer:

> These individuals [product and advertising managers] spend a major part of their waking hours thinking about their brand. Therefore when they evaluate the advertising strategy, they do so as highly involved individuals, unlike the target consumer. Highly cluttered, complex advertising copy is often a result of agency and brand group decision makers who are unable to view the product from the perspective of the [uninvolved] consumer.[30]

Academicians are more willing to accept the view of a passive consumer, but this view has only recently gained prominence. It will be some time before a body of research can be developed on the passive consumer. The few studies that have dealt specifically with involvement have selected politics rather than consumer choice as the subject. For example, Swinyard and Coney hypothesized that advertising would be more effective in a low involvement political race than in a high involvement race.[31] Two political races were studied; a high involvement race (for U.S. senator) and a low involvement race (for county treasurer). Some consumers received advertising for the senatorial race but no advertising for the local race; others received the opposite. Combinations of personal contact and direct mail were used in advertising.

Advertising for the local race was found to be more effective than for the senatorial race. The intention to vote in the local race went from 5 percent for those receiving no advertising messages to 25 percent for those receiving four advertising messages. The intention to vote in the senatorial race was the same regardless of the number of messages received. Despite the increase in voting intentions in the local race, attitudes toward the candidates remained unchanged. This finding tends to confirm the low involvement hierarchy — voters in a local race are exposed to political messages, develop an intention to vote, and then determine their attitudes toward the candidate after he or she is elected.

Two studies of involvement in consumer choice can be cited. In one study Lastovicka and Gardner asked respondents to agree or disagree with various statements about fourteen product categories.[32] The statements were indicators of involvement with the product: for example, "I use this product to help express the 'I' and 'me' within myself," (a measure of product importance in self-identification); "If my preferred brand in this product class is not available at the store, it makes little difference to me if I must choose another brand" (an indication of low involvement). Responses to the statements were analyzed by a statistical technique known as factor analysis.

Factor analysis will group together items that are highly correlated. For example, consumers tended to associate blue jeans, autos, hi-fi speakers, and beer with statements such as "the product expresses the 'I' and 'me' within myself." Therefore, these items appear in the same factor (Table 4–2). The higher the positive number associated with a product in the table, the more strongly the product is associated with the factor. Thus, automobiles are most strongly related to self-identity since they scored highest on the involvement factor.

TABLE 4–2   Positioning Product Categories by Level of Involvement

Products	I Low Involvement	II High Involvement	III Special Interest
light bulb	.384	−.202	.142
facial tissue	.486	−.032	−.088
blanket	.285	.131	.082
toothbrush	.420	.047	−.046
suntan preparation	.278	.066	.067
soap	.452	.032	−.082
blue jeans	.100	.435	.010
automobile	−.067	.648	−.039
hi-fi speakers	−.046	.406	.162
beer	.137	.345	−.067
sleeping bag	−.046	.019	.565
screwdriver	.190	−.133	.336
canvas tent	−.032	−.029	.588
athletic shoes	−.008	.122	.373

Source: John L. Lastovicka and David M. Gardner "Components of Involvement," in John C. Maloney and Bernard Silverman, eds., *Attitude Research Plays for High Stakes* (Chicago: American Marketing Association, 1979), p. 65.

The analysis produced three groups of products. Products with high numbers in the first column represent low involvement products. The low involvement products are (in order): facial tissue, soap, toothbrush, light bulb, blanket, and suntan preparation. These items represent everyday products that are not important and are not expressions of self-identity.

The second column is composed of high involvement products, namely: automobile, blue jeans, hi-fi speakers, and beer. These are also everyday products, but they are expressions of the life-styles and identities of college students in the study. Thus, beer and blue jeans are viewed as high involvement items for college students; but for a sample of middle-aged business executives they may be uninvolving.

The third column represents special interest items that are not represented by commitment or importance (sleeping bags, athletic shoes, etc.). Therefore, they do not fit into the high/low involvement continuum.

A second marketing study of involvement was conducted by Cohen and Houston.[33] They selected two brands, Crest and Colgate, because they represent a low involvement product category, are relatively undifferentiated, and advertise the same product benefit. These brands are therefore a good example of purchasing by inertia. Regular Colgate users, regular Crest users, and users of other brands were asked to rate both Crest and Colgate on five brand attributes. Table 4–3 shows that Colgate users and Crest users saw their own brand as superior to the other on all five attributes. Users of other brands saw practically no difference between Crest and Colgate. (A plus (+) score means Colgate was rated as better than Crest; a minus (−) score means Crest was rated better than Colgate).

TABLE 4–3   Brand Ratings for a Low Involvement Product Category

Attribute	Brand	Difference Score[a]
Decay and cavity	Colgate users	+2.40
	Crest users	−3.59
	Users of other brands	−.46
Taste	Colgate users	+2.63
	Crest users	−2.76
	Users of other brands	−.28
Breath freshness	Colgate users	+2.73
	Crest users	−1.96
	Users of other brands	−.41
Appearance and whiteness	Colgate users	+1.80
	Crest users	−1.89
	Users of other brands	−.23
Low price	Colgate users	+.63
	Crest users	−1.80
	Users of other brands	−.38

Source: Adapted from Joel B. Cohen and Michael J. Houston, "Cognitive Consequences of Brand Loyalty," *Journal of Marketing Research* 9 (February 1972): 98.
[a]Plus (+) score means Colgate preferred to Crest; minus (−) score means Crest preferred to Colgate.

Cohen and Houston conclude that the value of considering additional information for toothpaste is low. Therefore, rather than considering additional information, the consumer minimizes time and effort by justifying the purchase of the regular brand. The result is that attitudes conform to past purchases so as to avoid brand evaluation. Consistent purchasing of the favored brand does not represent brand loyalty; it represents inertia.

Although the three studies cited above shed some light on the nature of low involvement behavior, the lack of adequate research in the area remains. It is an area that will receive more attention in the future.

STRATEGIC ISSUES IN LOW INVOLVEMENT DECISION MAKING

Several strategic issues dealing with low involvement decision making remain to be considered, namely:

- Should marketers attempt to get consumers more involved with a low involvement product? If so, how?
- Given low involvement, should marketers attempt to shift consumers from a pattern of repetitive buying which reflects inertia to variety-seeking behavior?
- Should the strategies and basic perspective of advertising differ in the low versus high involvement case? If so, in what way?

- Should markets be segmented by the consumer's degree of involvement so that different strategies are directed to the high involvement and low involvement consumer for a particular product category?

Shift Consumers from Low to High Involvement?

It would make sense for a marketer to try to get the consumer to be more involved in a product. Since involvement means commitment, there is a greater likelihood the consumer will remain loyal to the marketer's brand in the face of competitive activity. Rothschild says, "The notion of changing low-involvement individuals to high-involvement individuals is an appealing one, for here the consumer would be less subject to the appeals of competitive advertising, promotional and pricing strategies and more likely to retain information."[34] What strategies can the marketer use to involve the consumer with the product?

1. *Linking the product to some involving issue.* Rothschild uses Sherif's theory in citing one strategy as an attempt to widen the latitude of competitive brands that are rejected. This can be done by linking the advertised brand to an involving issue.[35] Crest linked an uninvolving product (toothpaste) to an involving issue (cavity prevention) by introducing fluoride. Other examples of linking low involvement products with high involvement issues are relating orange juice to a health attribute such as vitamin C or relating cigarettes to tar and nicotine content.

2. *Linking the product to some involving personal situation.* Another strategy is to associate a low involvement product with some involving situation through advertising. Tyebjee suggests relating the product to an activity the consumer is engaged in.[36] He cites examples such as a coffee commercial at wake-up time, automobile products advertised on drive-time radio, sleep aids on nighttime television shows. In each case, involvement with the product increases because of the relevance of the situation.

3. *Linking the product to involving advertising.* A third strategy is to create involvement with the advertising in the hope that some link will be established with the product. Lutz says that just because "some products may be inherently low in involvement, their advertising need not be."[37] He cites two types of ads that may create involvement. An ego defensive ad would help consumers defend themselves against inadequacy (e.g., Marlboro smokers are masculine). A value expressive advertisement expresses the consumer's central values and beliefs (e.g., Pepsi drinkers think young). Both these ads are involving, yet deal with relatively uninvolving product categories.

4. *Changing the importance of product benefits.* A more difficult strategy would be to try to change the importance consumers attach to product benefits directly. Boyd et al. cite one example of this strategy: "An airline company which noted that 'on schedule' was not given a high saliency rating might seek to increase the rating of this product class characteristic provided that it felt that its 'on schedule' performance was better than that of its competitors."[38] This strategy is more difficult than linking the product with involving situations or issues because it seeks to *change* consumer need priorities. The airline company must now convince consumers of the importance of scheduling through advertising.

5. *Introducing an important characteristic in the product.* Boyd et al. also cite the possibility of introducing an attribute into a product that had not been considered important or that did not previously exist.[39] Examples are the use of additives in gasoline, adding minerals to cereals, and introducing automatic rewinds in cameras.

These five strategies would assist the marketer in creating more product involvement on the part of the consumer. But involvement is relative. Creating greater involvement for toothpaste or facial tissue does not mean that the consumer is likely to engage in complex decision making when brands are being evaluated. It means that some moderate amount of cognitive activity may be stimulated through advertising and product policies.

Shift Consumers from Inertia to Variety Seeking?

Given a condition of low involvement, another question is whether marketers should encourage consumers to switch brands in a search for variety or to stay with the same brand based on familiarity and a simplification of product search.

An obvious answer to this question is that if the brand is a market leader, it should encourage inertia; if it is a lesser known brand, it should encourage variety seeking. In a low involvement situation the market leader may be purchased because of familiarity. In such conditions, the marketer should use advertising as a reminder. In-store conditions would also be important to maintain brand familiarity. The market leader would seek the dominant shelf space in the store to keep the brand in front of the consumer. A less familiar brand would attempt to encourage variety seeking by using deals, lower prices, coupons, and free samples to encourage trial. The objective is to induce consumers to switch brands and gain wider experience. Sherif's theory would support this view. In a low involvement condition, the consumer has a wide latitude of acceptance suggesting a greater willingness to try a diversity of brands.

Campbell's Soup is a good example of a market leader in a low involvement category. Campbell's strategy has consistently been to advertise frequently to maintain familiarity and to dominate shelf space within the store. Other canned soups have occasionally been introduced. Competitors' strategies have reflected attempts to induce trial by lower prices, free samples, and appeals to variety in advertising, but Campbell's high frequency advertising campaigns and in-store dominance have made entry into the canned soup market difficult.

Is a Different Advertising Strategy Needed for Low Involvement Products?

The theories of Krugman and Sherif strongly suggest that advertising strategy should be very different for a low involvement product compared to a high involvement product. Differences in advertising approaches, as reflected in these theories, suggest that for low involvement products:

1. *Advertising should focus on a few key points rather than a broad based information campaign.* Where there is little interest, there is limited ability to process and assimilate information. A proper campaign in the low involvement case therefore "utilizes short messages emphasizing a few key points."[40]

2. *Advertising dollars should be spent in a campaign of high repetition and should use short duration messages.*[41] As Krugman notes, repetition is necessary to gain exposure, even though processing the message may be minimal. High repetition and short messages encourage passive learning and ensure brand familiarity.

3. There is considerable leeway in the advertising messages acceptable to the consumer.[42]   According to Sherif, the latitude of acceptance of message content is greater in the low involvement case. This means that most advertising messages for low involvement products will be acceptable to consumers. A high latitude of acceptance also means that consumers are less likely to shut out messages from competitive brands in an attempt to justify the purchase of the chosen brand.

4. Visual components are more important in influencing behavior.[43]   Since consumers are not involved, learn passively, and forget quickly, it is important to keep the product visually in front of the consumer. This means that in-store displays and packaging are important communications tools. It also means that television advertising is more likely to be effective than print because of the active visual component in television commercials.

5. Symbols and imagery should be used to develop a strong association with the brand.   Since learning is fostered by repetition, it is important to develop favorable stimuli associated with the brand. Simply advertising the brand name again is an unacceptable means of ensuring familiarity. So a symbol such as an individual, a scene, or a phrase is repeated to serve as a substitute for the brand and also to maintain some minimum amount of interest. Given the lack of substantial product differences for low involvement products, advertising, therefore, becomes a means of competitive differentiation. As Tyebjee states, "Communication differentiation rather than product differentiation is the strategic role of the sales proposition of low involvement advertising."[44]

6. Television rather than print media should be the primary vehicle for communication.   If less product information is required, a low involvement medium such as television is more suitable. This is because television does not encourage an evaluation of the content of the communication. Print media are more suitable if the audience is active in seeking information and evaluating it.

Based on the differences between high and low involvement products, the answer to the original question must be a definite yes. Different advertising strategies should be employed for low compared to high involvement products.

Should Markets Be Segmented by Degree of Consumer Involvement?

The concept of involvement is consumer related, not product related. Involvement is defined in terms of the consumer's evaluation of the importance of and identity with the product. Therefore, although most consumers may have a relatively low degree of involvement with toothpaste, some consumers may be more highly involved with the product category.

Since involvement can be measured on the individual consumer level, markets can be segmented by the degree of consumer involvement with the product. Purchasers of toothpaste can be categorized as high, medium, and low involvement consumers. Given this fact, should marketing strategies for a given product category be differentiated by the degree of consumer involvement? Should one set of strategies be directed to involved consumers and another set of strategies to uninvolved consumers?

Tyebjee believes that strategies should differ for high and low involvement segments of a particular product. He says:

The high involvement segment would require product differentiation, copy strategy stressing product benefits, allocation of advertising budgets to print media and recognition of personal influence as a factor in the decision process. . . . On the other hand, the low involvement segment implies communication differentiation as opposed to product differentiation, copy strategy stressing brand name, avoiding print media in favor of broadcast media, and low instances of word-of-mouth influence.[45]

In other words, differences in strategy should be directed to high and low involvement segments for the same product.

A good example is cereal, ordinarily regarded as a low involvement product, but to parents concerned with nutritional benefits for young children, the product can be regarded as in a high involvement category. A high involvement segment would be receptive to advertising about nutritional information. It would be willing to read copy in magazines about the relative benefits of one cereal versus another. It would not be swayed by deals or coupons. It would find information on the package important. The low involvement segment would not take the time to read about nutritional information on the package or ads. It might switch brands based on price appeals. It would be more likely to buy a more familiar brand. It would be more likely to buy on impulse in the store.

Therefore, advertising, price, and in-store promotional strategies will have very different effects depending on the degree of consumer involvement with the product category. In short, where it is possible to identify a high versus low involvement segment, marketers should consider differentiating their strategies accordingly.

Having focused on low involvement decision making in this chapter, much of the rest of the book will consider behavioral concepts and strategic applications that assume an active and involved consumer. This focus should not be interpreted as meaning that low involvement decisions are unimportant in marketing. This chapter has strongly stated the importance of the topic to marketers. Rather, the focus on an involved consumer merely reflects the current state of knowledge in marketing and the current state of emphasis among marketing practitioners.

SUMMARY

This chapter introduces an important determinant of both consumer behavior and marketing strategy — the degree of consumer involvement with the product. Consumers are involved when they consider the product as important and as a reflection of their self-image and belief system. Most of the behavioral literature and many marketing managers assume the consumer to be highly involved when, in reality, the consumer may be uninvolved with the product.

Four types of consumer behavior are identified, based on two dimensions — differences in features between brands and level of consumer involvement:

1a. *Complex decision making and brand loyalty* require a high level of involvement on the part of the consumer and sufficient differences between brands to sustain this involvement. Consumers form beliefs about brands, evaluate them, and choose. This think-before-you-act model conforms to a traditional hierarchy of effects.

2. *Dissonance reduction* assumes a high level of involvement but the consumer sees few differences between the brands being considered. Since there is no firm basis for deciding on one brand or the other, dissonance or postpurchase doubt is likely to arise.

3. *Variety seeking* assumes a low level of involvement yet assumes differences between brands. Given the low level of involvement, there is little risk in switching to another brand; given the differences between brands, there may be reasons for such a switch.

4. *Inertia* assumes a low level of involvement and assumes few differences between brands. The consumer has found a reasonably satisfactory brand and will stick with it. Brand switching may be induced by price deals and coupons.

Two theories are presented as a basis for understanding low involvement decision making. Krugman's theory of passive learning suggests that when the consumer is not involved, he or she does not cognitively evaluate advertising messages. Exposure to advertising could occur without recall and comprehension. Sherif's theory of social judgment suggests that in conditions of low involvement, consumers are willing to consider many brands, yet few attributes are likely to be used in evaluating brands. Based on these theories, a profile of the low involvement consumer is developed (see Table 4–1).

The remainder of the chapter is devoted to considering the strategic implications of low involvement decision making. Several important strategic questions are raised:

- Should marketers attempt to get consumers more involved with low involvement products?
- Should advertising strategies differ for low involvement versus high involvement situations?
- Should markets be segmented by the consumer's degree of involvement?

In each case, the answer to these questions is yes.

QUESTIONS

1. This chapter suggests that many consumers are not involved with the brand purchased and that decisions are frequently made based on inertia.
   - If this is true, why do most marketing strategies assume an involved consumer?
   - Why is it hard for a marketing manager to accept that most consumers might not be involved in the purchase of the company's brand?
2. What are the differences in the reasons for brand switching in a high versus a low involvement purchase situation?

   What are the differences in the reasons for brand loyalty in a high versus a low involvement purchasing situation?

3. A consumer in the market for a refrigerator has difficulty in deciding between three brands with very similar features and at about the same price. The consumer finally decides on a brand based on the strong recommendation of the store salesperson. Having made a purchase, the consumer then begins to evaluate the chosen brand compared to other brands and experiences some doubt about the choice.

   - Explain the consumer's process of choice and postpurchase evaluation based on dissonance theory and attribution theory.
   - What would be the implication for a marketing strategy designed to eliminate postpurchase doubts based on dissonance theory and attribution theory?

4. (a) Design a general marketing strategy for a new brand of paper towel that is positioned as more economical because it has more sheets at the same price, yet has the same level of quality as other towels. (In most cases, consumers would regard paper towels as a low involvement product category.)

   (b) Now assume the same manufacturer has identified a segment of the paper towel market that is more involved with the product because the segment recognizes many usage situations that require a high quality towel. The company decides to introduce a heavier weight/high quality towel to this involved segment. How would marketing strategy differ from the strategy for the brand in question 4a?

5. Develop a profile of the involved consumer for paper towels (the segment in question 4b) versus the uninvolved consumer (the segment in question 4a). Use Table 4–1 as a basis for profiling these two segments.

6. Discuss the two arguments that (1) advertising is a weak communications medium because of consumer involvement resulting in selective exposure (the active audience view) versus (2) advertising is a strong communications medium because of a lack of consumer involvement resulting in retention of the message with little cognitive activity (the passive audience view).

   - What is the predominant view in advertising today? Why?
   - Can you cite advertising examples that tend to support recognition on the part of advertisers of a passive audience?

7. Pick a low involvement product category. Assume you are introducing a new brand in this category. Devise a strategy for attempting to create higher involvement with the brand by utilizing the five strategies for shifting consumers from low to high involvement.

8. Is it realistic to develop separate brand and marketing strategies for high and low involvement segments of a product category?

9. Decision making in high involvement conditions is more likely to follow principles of *optimizing*. Decision making in low involvement conditions is more likely to follow principles of *satisfying*. Explain.

RESEARCH ASSIGNMENTS

Select what you regard as a high involvement and a low involvement product category. Develop a means of measuring degree of consumer involvement for these two product categories based on a consumer's rating of (1) the importance of the product, and (2) the degree to which the product reflects self-identity. Then interview a small sample of consumers applying this measure.

- Was your assumption correct? That is, are significantly more consumers involved in what you identify as the high involvement category compared to the low?

- Categorize the sample into those above and below average on level of involvement for each product category. Are there differences in characteristics between those more and less involved by:

  (a) brand regularly purchased,
  (b) average price paid,
  (c) frequency of use,
  (d) advertising exposure, and
  (e) need criteria considered important in buying?

- Do your findings conform to the theories of Krugman and Sherif?

NOTES

1. There are two excellent reviews of the current state of knowledge on low involvement consumer behavior. See John C. Maloney and Bernard Silverman, eds., *Attitude Research Plays for High Stakes* (Chicago: American Marketing Association, 1979); and William L. Wilkie, ed., *Advances in Consumer Research,* vol. 6 (Ann Arbor: Association for Consumer Research, 1979), pp. 174–199.

2. Harold H. Kassarjian and Waltraud M. Kassarjian, "Attitudes Under Low Commitment Conditions," in John C. Maloney and Bernard Silverman, eds., *Attitude Research Plays for High Stakes* (Chicago: American Marketing Association, 1979), p. 8.

3. Nancy T. Hupfer and David M. Gardner, "Differential Involvement With Products and Issues: An Exploratory Study," in David M. Gardner, ed., *Proceedings of the 2nd Annual Conference of the Association for Consumer Research* (College Park, Md.: Association for Consumer Research, 1971), pp. 262–269.

4. John L. Lastovicka, "Questioning the Concept of Involvement Defined Product Classes," in William L. Wilkie, ed., *Advances in Consumer Research,* vol. 6 (Ann Arbor: Association for Consumer Research, 1979), pp. 174–179.

5. See Michael L. Rothschild, "Advertising Strategies for High and Low Involvement Situations," in Maloney and Silverman, eds., *Attitude Research Plays for High Stakes,* pp. 74–93.

6. For a similar four-part classification, see F. Stewart DeBruicker, "An Appraisal of Low-Involvement Consumer Information Processing," in Maloney and Silverman, eds., *Attitude Research Plays for High Stakes,* p. 124.

7. M. Venkatesan, "Cognitive Consistency and Novelty Seeking," in Scott Ward and Thomas S. Robertson, eds., *Consumer Behavior: Theoretical Sources* (Englewood Cliffs, N.J.: Prentice-Hall Inc., 1973), p. 377.

8. See E. Aronson, "The Theory of Cognitive Dissonance," in L. Berkowitz, ed., *Advances in Experimental Social Psychology,* vol. 4 (New York: Academic Press, 1969), Chapter 1.

9. D. Bem, "Attitudes as Self-Descriptions: Another Look at the Attitude-Behavior Link," in A. Greenwald, T. Brock, and T. Ostrom, eds., *Psychological Foundations of Attitudes* (New York: Academic Press, 1968).

10. Rothschild, "Advertising Strategies," p. 84.

11. Thomas S. Robertson, "Low-Commitment Consumer Behavior," *Journal of Advertising Research* 16 (April 1976): 23; and Henry Assael, "The Conceptualization of a Construct of Variety Seeking Behavior," New York University, Graduate School of Business Administration, Working Paper series #79–43, May 1979, p. 5.

12. Peter L. Wright, "The Choice of a Choice Strategy: Simplifying vs. Optimizing," faculty working paper No. 163, Department of Business Administration, University of Illinois, 1974.

13. Herbert E. Krugman, "The Impact of Television Advertising: Learning Without Involvement," *Public Opinion Quarterly* 29 (Fall 1965): 349–356.

14. C.W. Sherif, M. Sherif and R.W. Nebergall, *Attitude and Attitude Change* (Philadelphia: Saunders, 1965).

15. Herbert E. Krugman, "The Measurement of Advertising Involvement," *Public Opinion Quarterly* 30 (Winter 1966): 584–585.

98

16. Robert C. Grass and Wallace H. Wallace, "Advertising Communication: Print Vs. TV," *Journal of Advertising Research* 14 (October 1974): 19–23.
17. Krugman, "The Impact of Television Advertising," p. 354.
18. Stephen W. Hollander and Jacob Jacoby, "Recall of Crazy, Mixed-Up TV Commercials," *Journal of Advertising Research* 13 (June 1973): 39–42.
19. G.A. Haaland and M. Venkatesan, "Resistance to Persuasive Communications: Examination of the Distraction Hypotheses," *Journal of Personality and Social Psychology* 9 (1968): 167–170.
20. W.P. Dommermuth, "The Shopping Matrix and Marketing Strategy," *Journal of Marketing Research* 2 (May 1965): 128–132; and Joseph W. Newman and Richard Staelin, "Prepurchase Information Seeking for New Cars and Major Household Appliances," *Journal of Marketing Research* 9 (August 1972): 249–257.
21. Newman and Staelin, "Prepurchase Information Seeking."
22. R.A. Bauer, "The Obstinate Audience," *American Psychologist* 19 (May 1964): 319–328.
23. Kassarjian and Kassarjian, "Attitudes Under Low Commitment Conditions," p. 10.
24. A. Benton Cocanougher and Grady Bruce, "Socially Distant Reference Groups and Consumer Aspirations," *Journal of Marketing Research* 8 (August 1971): 378–381.
25. Kassarjian and Kassarjian, "Attitudes," p. 11.
26. Sherif, Sherif, and Nebergall, *Attitude and Attitude Change;* and M. Sherif and C.E. Hovland, *Social Judgment* (New Haven: Yale University Press, 1964).
27. Michael L. Rothschild and Michael J. Houston, "The Consumer Involvement Matrix: Some Preliminary Findings," in Barnett A. Greenberg and Danny N. Bellenger, *Proceedings of the American Marketing Association Educators' Conference,* Series #41 (1977), pp. 95–98.
28. Ibid.
29. John L. Lastovicka and David M. Gardner, "Low Involvement Versus High Involvement Cognitive Structures," in H. Keith Hunt, ed., *Advances in Consumer Research,* vol. 5 (Ann Arbor: Association for Consumer Research, 1978), pp. 87–92.
30. Tyzoon T. Tyebjee, "Refinement of the Involvement Concept: An Advertising Planning Point of View," in Maloney and Silverman, eds., p. 106.
31. William R. Swinyard and Kenneth A. Coney, "Promotional Effects on a High- Versus Low-Involvement Electorate," *Journal of Consumer Research* 5 (June 1978): 41–48.
32. John L. Lastovicka and David M. Gardner, "Components of Involvement," in Maloney and Silverman, eds., pp. 53–73.
33. Joel B. Cohen and Michael J. Houston, "Cognitive Consequences of Brand Loyalty," *Journal of Marketing Research* 9 (February 1972): 97–99.
34. Rothschild, "Advertising Strategies," p. 87.
35. Ibid.
36. Tyebjee, "Refinement of the Involvement Concept," p. 100.
37. Richard J. Lutz, "A Functional Theory Framework for Designing and Pretesting Advertising Themes," in Maloney and Silverman, eds., p. 47.
38. Harper W. Boyd, Jr., Michael L. Ray and Edward C. Strong, "An Attitudinal Framework for Advertising Strategy," *Journal of Marketing* 36 (April 1972): 31.
39. Ibid.
40. Rothschild, "Advertising Strategies," p. 84.
41. Ibid.
42. Ibid., p. 85.
43. Ibid., p. 86.
44. Tyebjee, "Refinement," p. 97.
45. Ibid., p. 108.

PART TWO

The Individual Consumer

In Part Two the focus is on the role of the individual consumer in the purchasing process. Chapters 5–8 are concerned with the consumer's thought variables—namely, perceptions, attitudes, and needs. The thought variables are central to consumer behavior since they affect the development of product and promotional strategies. In Chapters 9–10 the second component representing the consumer is described—the consumer's demographic, life-style, and personality characteristics. These factors are important in describing the consumer and segmenting consumer markets.

FIVE

Consumer Perceptions and Marketing Stimuli

Focus of Chapter

One of the key ways to a successful marketing strategy is to develop product and promotional stimuli that consumers will perceive as relevant to their needs. Chapter 2 described consumer perception as the selection, organization, and interpretation of marketing and environmental stimuli. In this chapter, consumer perception will be considered in more detail.

The way consumers perceive marketing and environmental stimuli depends on how these stimuli are selected and organized. Selection and organization of marketing stimuli represents **information process-**

ing. Consumer information processing will be described in Chapter 19 in the applied context of marketing communications and advertising. Chapter 5 will concentrate on the processes of selecting and organizing marketing stimuli.

Two factors influence the selection and organization of marketing stimuli. The first is the stimulus itself; the second is the characteristics of the individual consumer. The latter part of this chapter will be concerned with the effects of marketing stimuli and consumer characteristics on consumer perceptions.

CONSUMER PERCEPTIONS

The model of complex decision making identified four steps in information processing—exposure to information, attention, comprehension, and retention of information in memory. Figure 5–1 is a more detailed model of these stages.

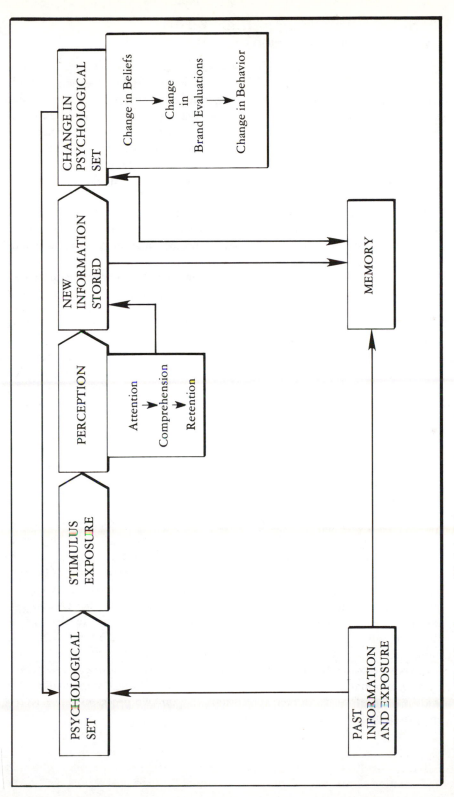

FIGURE 5–1 A High Involvement Model of Consumer Perceptions

Information Processing in High Versus Low Involvement Decisions

The model in Figure 5–1 is more descriptive of consumers who are involved in the decision. The model shows the traditional hierarchy of effects in both perception (exposure first, then attention, comprehension, and retention) and in decision making (beliefs precede brand evaluation which precedes behavioral intentions and behavior). The traditional hierarchy therefore assumes that once the consumer is exposed to a stimulus, the consumer will be attentive to the message and take the time to interpret it. Having thought about the message, the consumer is more likely to use the information in evaluating alternative brands.

Information processing in the low involvement case is a different matter. Information can be stored in the memory without going through a sequence involving attention and comprehension.[1] Exposure in itself may be sufficient for information to be retained.

A model of information processing in the low involvement case is presented in Figure 5–2. In this case, exposure to a marketing stimulus may be sufficient for retention and storage. For instance, the consumer seeing an advertisement for Bounty paper towels may remember two things—the brand name and its theme, "the better picker upper." But the theme is almost like a series of nonsense syllables and has little immediate meaning, although eventually it may sink in that Bounty is more absorbent. The message is not comprehended or interpreted, yet it is stored in the memory. The next time the consumer goes to the store, seeing Bounty on the shelf may evoke an association with "the better picker upper" and may remind the consumer of a need to purchase paper towels. But the process of brand evaluation has not taken place prior to the purchase.

Selectivity and Organization of Information

Selectivity and organization represent the basic processes underlying consumer perceptions. Information processing in both the high and low involvement cases requires that consumers selectively choose marketing stimuli. In the high involvement case, consumers will selectively choose information that (1) helps them evaluate brands that meet their needs (the informational or perceptual vigilence component of selectivity), and (2) conforms to their beliefs and predispositions (the emotional or perceptual defense component). In the low involvement case, consumers will selectively screen out most information in an attempt to avoid cognitive activity and informational clutter.

Exposure to multiple sources of information also requires consumers to organize information into a meaningful whole if it is to be comprehended and acted on. Therefore, consumer perceptions rely on two processes: (1) selective perception, and (2) perceptual organization.

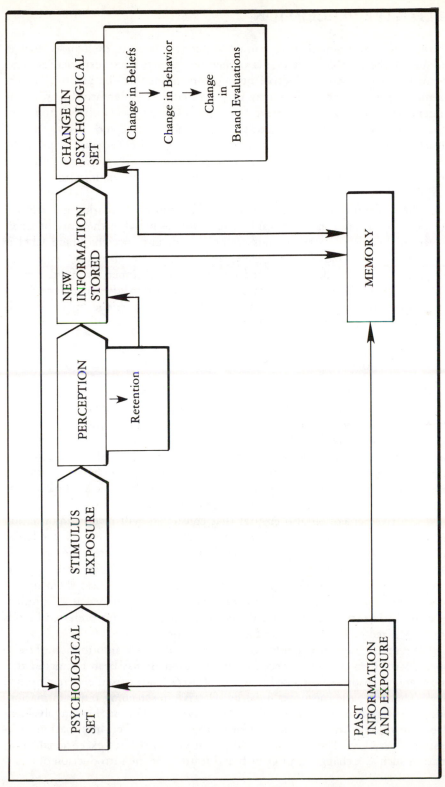

FIGURE 5–2   A Low Involvement Model of Consumer Perceptions

Consumers perceive marketing stimuli selectively because each individual is unique in the combination of his or her needs, attitudes, experiences, and personal characteristics. **Selective perception** means that the identical advertisement, package, or product may be perceived very differently by two consumers. One consumer may believe a claim that Clorox gets clothes whiter than other bleaches; another may regard such a claim as untrue and believe that all bleaches are the same. One consumer may perceive higher gasoline prices as a legitimate means of underwriting increased domestic exploration and production costs; another may perceive higher prices as exploitation of the consumer.

There is sufficient evidence of selective perception of marketing stimuli. For example, many consumers cannot discriminate between the taste or smell of various brands when the brands are unlabeled, but once the brand label is seen, strong taste and quality preferences are voiced. Consumers cannot distinguish objective reality as defined by the physical properties of the brand. Their perception is based on the associations derived from advertising and social communications. These associations are likely to conform to the current knowledge and past experiences of the consumer.

The Functions of Selective Perception

Consumers sometimes distort information to conform to their beliefs and attitudes. This is referred to as **perceptual defense** since it operates to protect the individual from threatening or contradictory stimuli. For example, the cigarette smoker may avoid antismoking advertisements or play down their importance. Accepting the message may mean recognizing that the smoker's actions are detrimental to his or her health. The recent purchaser of a poorly insulated home may ignore unexpectedly high fuel bills or rationalize the situation by saying fuel costs are rising for everyone.

Selective perception also ensures that consumers will receive information most relevant to their needs and to brand evaluation. This process is referred to as **perceptual vigilance.** Several studies have demonstrated the operation of perceptual vigilance. In one classic study, poor children overestimated the size of coins more than wealthy children did because they valued them more.[2] Given their needs, the poor children were more aware of money as a stimulus. In a marketing study Spence and Engel found that names for preferred brands are recognized faster than names for other brands.[3]

Perceptual vigilance guides consumers to necessary information. It also operates to filter out any unnecessary information. It has been estimated that the average consumer is exposed to from 300 to 600 advertisements in a normal day.[4] Therefore, the consumer must be selective in screening out information. Such a filtering process becomes particularly important in low involvement decision making. In these circumstances, the time spent on information processing is very low. The consumer will pay attention only to exceptional information such as a change in price or brand features or the introduction of a new brand. Information processing occurs, therefore, by exception. Little attention will be paid to frequently repeated and expected stimuli. Attention is only devoted to unexpected stimuli.

107

Selective Perception

Conditions Likely to Produce Perceptual Vigilance

Perceptual vigilance is a function of the consumer's needs. The desire to fulfill certain needs leads the consumer to select stimuli and pay attention to them.

Perceptual vigilance will therefore be determined by the consumer's need structure. The consumer who places the greatest importance on gas mileage will take more notice of advertisements providing information on gas mileage. Generally, the greater the intensity of need, the greater the perceptual vigilance. But, as noted, perceptual vigilance is also greater when the intensity of needs are low. Under such conditions the consumer screens out most information. Therefore, it is likely that perceptual vigilance will be greatest when consumer involvement is either very high or very low. This relationship is illustrated in Figure 5–3. Under conditions of high involvement, information unrelated to needs will be screened out. Under conditions of low involvement, routine and expected information will be screened out.

Conditions Likely to Produce Perceptual Defense

Whereas perceptual vigilance is a function of the necessity to screen out unnecessary information, perceptual defense is the result of a desire for consistency. The desire to avoid conflicting and contradictory messages leads the consumer to avoid or misinterpret potentially relevant information.

Certain conditions are likely to produce greater perceptual defense:

1. *The stronger the beliefs and attitudes regarding a brand, the greater the likelihood of perceptual defense.* In terms of Sherif's social judgment theory, firmly held beliefs reflect a narrow latitude of acceptance.[5] This means that messages in agreement with the consumer's beliefs will be accepted and distorted in the direction of those beliefs. Messages that do not conform to the consumer's strongly held beliefs will be rejected and distorted to contrast with the consumer's opinions.

2. *The greater the consistency of experience, the greater the likelihood of perceptual defense.* Consumers strongly loyal to a certain brand are likely to reject any information that contradicts positive brand experiences. A consumer loyal to a certain brand of cigarettes is told it has one of the highest tar and nicotine contents on the market. The consumer may ignore the information or may rationalize the situation by saying he has been smoking the brand since he was a teenager and is in excellent health.

3. *The greater the anxiety produced by a stimulus, the greater the likelihood of perceptual defense.* Maintaining perceptual equilibrium may lead the consumer to avoid stimuli that produce fears and anxieties. Stuteville refers to three other strategies, all examples of distortion.[6] One strategy is simply to say, "That can't happen to me." In reality, what the consumer is saying is that bad breath does not always lead to social ostracism or that smoking does not always lead to death and that he or she is likely to be one of the exceptions. A second strategy is to deny the validity of the message (There is no experimental proof that smoking causes cancer.). A third strategy is to selectively perceive the positive elements of an anxiety-producing message. The

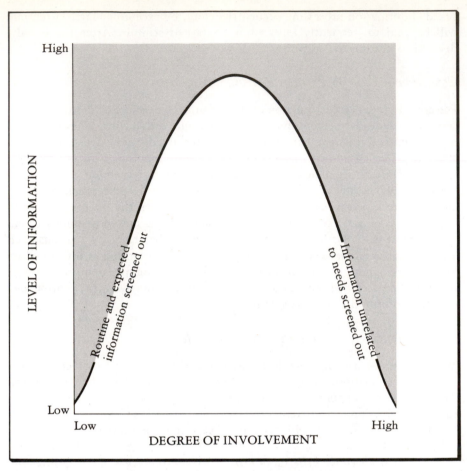

FIGURE 5–3   Degree of Involvement and Perceptual Vigilance

use of cowboys or young and vigorous adults in cigarette advertisements is a means of reassuring smokers that smoking does not lead to negative results.

   4. The greater the level of postpurchase dissonance, the greater the likelihood of perceptual defense.   When consumers receive contradictory messages after having made a purchase, they will try to increase the certainty they have made the right choice by selectively searching for positive information about the brand and ignoring negative information. Another strategy of perceptual defense is to minimize the importance of the action by reducing expectations after the fact. In a study of attitudes towards smoking, Kassarjian and Cohen report that significantly more smokers minimized the importance of health compared to nonsmokers by statements such as, "Lots of things are a hazard."[7] Smokers find it easier to justify smoking by reducing concerns about health.

Perceptual Equilibrium

The underlying principle in the operation of selective perception is that consumers seek consistency between the information they receive about a brand and their prior beliefs about that brand. Such consistency ensures that the consumer's psychological set is in equilibrium. Thus, when consumers choose information consistent with prior beliefs, or interpret information to conform to these beliefs, they are processing information to ensure a **perceptual equilibrium.**

The cognitive theories cited in the previous chapters conform well to principles of selective perception and perceptual equilibrium. Sherif's **social judgment theory** states that consumers process information to ensure consistency by either rejecting contradictory information (contrast) or by interpreting acceptable information to more closely fit in with their views (assimilation.)[8] Heider's **balance theory** states that when information about an object conflicts with the consumer's belief, balance will be achieved by changing one's opinion about the object, the source of information, or to some degree both.[9] The result is a balance in beliefs about the information and the object. (For example, if a close friend expresses the view that your favorite camera takes poor pictures, you can doubt the credibility of your friend as a source of information about cameras, form a more negative attitude toward your favorite camera, or do a little bit of both to obtain balance between information and object.) **Cognitive dissonance theory** states that when postpurchase conflict arises, consumers will seek balance in the psychological set by seeking supporting information or by distorting contradictory information. Each of these theories results in consistency between consumers' perceptions of marketing stimuli and their beliefs and attitudes.

The Process of Selective Perception

The drive to consistency and perceptual equilibrium results in selectivity at each stage of the perceptual process—exposure, attention, comprehension, and retention.

1. *Selective exposure.* Sufficient evidence exists to demonstrate **selective exposure** since people's beliefs influence what they choose to listen to or read. Surlin and Gordon found that people are more likely to be exposed to political messages for their favorite candidates.[10] Paletz et al. found that an audience for an anti-Vietnam-War movie had almost uniformly antiwar sentiments to begin with.[11] In the marketing sphere Engel determined that new car purchasers had greater recall and interest in advertising for their own cars.[12] Ehrlich et al. found that recent car buyers preferred to select advertising for the cars purchased.[13]

2. *Selective attention.* **Selective attention** results in greater awareness of supportive information and avoidance of contradictory information. Brehm asked respondents to rate several products and then choose one as a gift.[14] Before leaving, they were given a research report citing the good and bad characteristics of each product. Respondents focused attention on the positive characteristics of the selected product and the negative characteristics of the rejected product.

3. *Selective comprehension.* **Selective comprehension** involves interpreting discrepant information so that it is consistent with beliefs and attitudes. Kassarjian and Cohen reported that 80 percent of nonsmokers believed the link between smoking and lung cancer was proven; yet only 52 percent of heavy smokers accepted the link.[15]

4. *Selective retention.* The key question is what information is retained in memory to influence future behavior. Most advertising has a quick wear-out effect as consumers sort out what is meaningful and what is not. Bogart reports that many respondents could not identify a commercial they saw less than two minutes before.

Among those who did identify the advertisement, recall of commercial content leveled off to 12 percent or less.[16] Information that is relevant to the decision and/or conforms to existing beliefs and attitudes is most likely to be **selectively retained.**

Perceptual Disequilibrium

The emphasis on selective perception may make it appear that consumers always seek out information consistent with their beliefs and interpret information to conform to their beliefs and attitudes. If this were the case, there would be no opportunity to assess conflicting information.

Disequilibrium Before the Purchase

Several factors limit the operation of perceptual defense and consistency. When conflicting information is received before the purchase is made, Mills notes, there is less pressure to ignore such information.[17] Even if beliefs and attitudes are strong, the consumer is more likely to listen since the commitment has not yet been made. Therefore, it is psychologically easier to accept contradictory information. Further, such information may be revealing and may help the consumer make the right decision. On the other hand, once the decision has been made, contradictory information is likely to be ignored to maintain perceptual equilibrium.

Consumers sometimes purposefully seek out disequilibrium because of boredom. They may search for complex and contradictory information just to maintain product interest. As Maddi notes, "Novelty, unexpectedness, change and complexity are pursued because they are inherently satisfying."[18] Such a search for novelty and complexity is more likely to occur in low involvement decisions because the risk of switching brands is less.

Disequilibrium After the Purchase

Although perceptual defense is more likely to occur once the purchase is made, consumers will also accept discrepant information about a selected product. If they did not, it would mean that every time a consumer was dissatisfied, some attempt would be made to rationalize the purchase.

Learning theory suggests that when a brand does not meet expectations, the consumer learns from the experience and adjusts beliefs and attitudes accordingly. The result is a reduction in the probability of repurchase. Thus, perceptual disequilibrium must occur during the sometimes painful process of reappraising the original decision. Even though 80 percent of nonsmokers accepted the link between smoking and cancer, over half the heavy smokers also accepted this link. These smokers must, therefore, be in a state of perceptual disequilibrium since their actions are contradicting their beliefs in an important sphere of their lives—their health. In such cases, the consumer may accept dissonant information and seek to change behavior to conform to the information rather than to change the information to conform to prior behavior.

Although there may appear to be a conflict between learning theory (adjust behavior to past experience) and dissonance theory (adjust experience to past behavior), this is not the case. Either theory is more likely to be relevant depending on the risk perceived in the situation, the degree of involvement, and the propensity of the consumer to accept complex and ambiguous situations. In fact, Festinger—the originator of the theory of cognitive dissonance—points out that in cases where consumers are very dissatisfied with their original decision, a reverse process of perceptual defense may take place. Consumers may actually seek out negative information to facilitate changing future behavior.[19] A new car purchaser totally dissatisfied with the car might seek information from friends to confirm his or her experience. Such confirmation will make it easier to trade in the car earlier. In this case, perceptual disequilibrium will facilitate subsequent behavior change.

PERCEPTUAL ORGANIZATION

Given the fact that the typical consumer may be exposed to from 300 to 600 commercials a day, it is apparent that some form of organization of disparate, and at times conflicting, stimuli is necessary. Two basic principles help consumers organize marketing information.

The first principle involves a tendency to place information into logical categories. **Categorization** helps the consumer process known information quickly and efficiently. (E.g., "This is another ad for Bounty. I know what they are going to say, so I don't have to pay much attention.") Categorization also helps the consumer classify new information. (E.g., "This is an ad for a new breakfast food that is probably like Carnation Slender.") In categorizing new information, the consumer tends to generalize from past experience. Thus, the information that a new product is a breakfast food designed to provide nutritional benefits will cause the consumer to perceive the advertisement in the same context as all past experiences with nutritional breakfast foods. Nutritional breakfast foods, therefore, become a product category into which various brands can be slotted.

The second principle of organization is that of **integration**. This principle states that various stimuli will be perceived as an organized whole. Such an organization of stimuli simplifies information processing and provides an integrated meaning for the stimuli. These principles have been derived from **Gestalt psychology**. (Gestalt is roughly translated from German as total configuration or whole pattern.) Principles of Gestalt psychology directly apply to marketing strategy since they provide a framework for interpreting advertising messages as an integrated whole. The picture, the layout, the headline, and the location in a magazine, for example, are not disparate elements but interact to produce an overall reaction to the advertisement and to the brand. Similarly, the advertising campaign, price level, distribution outlet, and brand characteristics are not disparate elements of the marketing plan. They are viewed in concert and produce an overall brand image. In short, the whole is greater than the sum of the parts.

These two elements of perceptual organization—categorization and integration—will be considered.

Perceptual Categorization

Marketers seek to facilitate the process of perceptual categorization. They want to make sure the consumer recognizes a brand as part of a product class, but they do not want their brand to be a direct duplicate of other brands. The process of product positioning attempts to establish both product categorization and product uniqueness. Recently, a manufacturer introduced a new artificial bacon product under the name Lean Strips. Both the package and the contents clearly placed the product within the category of bacon, although the name itself may have caused some initial confusion. The manufacturer did not want the product to appear as another brand of bacon, so the emphasis was placed on lack of fat and on nutritional benefits. The marketing plan succeeded in positioning the product within the bacon category, yet the positioning was sufficiently distinct to provide a unique set of consumer benefits.

Runyon cites an example of a new product that would appear to be easily categorized on the surface, but that failed because differences with the parent category were not made clear.[20] Monsanto introduced a product called Starch-Eze, a starch concentrate that had to be diluted and only had to be used every ten or twelve washings. The product was advertised as a starch and the name implied it was easy to use. Consumers categorized it as another brand of starch and used it frequently. The result was a cardboard shirt.

Day recognizes the importance of categorization. He states, "Once a new object is placed in an existing category, it becomes the focus of the existing repertory of behaviors which are appropriate to the overall category."[21] The problem with Starch-Eze was that the object was placed in the traditional category of starch; the existing repertory of behaviors required using the product frequently and resulted in the product's failure.

The process of categorization involves a series of steps starting with a preliminary judgment about a product and ending with a definite categorization of the product. Bruner identifies four stages in the categorization process:[22]

1. *Primitive categorization.* This is the consumer's first snap judgment concerning the nature of the stimulus. Perhaps a consumer's first exposure to Lean Strips was a quick glance in a supermarket. The initial reaction might have been that Lean Strips is a quick energy breakfast food for weight watchers.

2. *Cue search.* The object is now examined more closely and a larger number of informational sources are examined to help the consumer categorize the object. A glance at Lean Strips in a second trip to the supermarket causes the consumer to realize that it is labeled as an artificial meat product and looks like bacon. The consumer notices that the package emphasizes lack of fat and less calories. Some confusion still exists. Is the product an artificial bacon product, some kind of meat substitute, or something else? The consumer is interested and is receptive to more information.

3. *Confirmation check.* The consumer obtains additional information and with some certainty categorizes the object. As a result, the consumer need not seek out sources any longer to determine the nature of the product. The consumer has seen the first Lean Strips commercial on television which directly compares the product to bacon and emphasizes the advantages of it having less fat, fewer calories, and greater nutrition. The product looks like bacon. And, a friend used the product as a bacon substitute and liked it.

4. *Confirmation Completion.* This stage represents the final categorization. Once the product is categorized, additional exploratory search for information is no longer necessary. The consumer's mind is made up and any stimuli that are contrary to the final categorization are likely to be ignored. Our consumer decides to try Lean Strips. This first actual contact with the product confirms the information obtained from secondary stimuli. The product does indeed look like bacon. The consumer tries the product and finds it a suitable bacon substitute but not as fat-free as expected. As a result, the consumer prefers bacon to Lean Strips. But, Lean Strips is clearly categorized as a bacon substitute.

If this categorization is common to many consumers, then the company has succeeded in positioning Lean Strips as a bacon substitute but has not established a sufficient level of product uniqueness to ensure that the product is seen as fat-free and nutritious. More product development may then be required to reduce the fat content even further.

Perceptual Integration

The principles of perceptual integration are based on Gestalt psychologists' basic hypothesis that people organize perceptions to form a complete picture of an object. **Perception** is a process of forming many disparate stimuli into an organized whole. The picture on a television screen is a good example. In actuality, it is made up of thousands of tiny dots, but we integrate these dots into a cohesive whole so that there is little difference between the picture on the screen and the real world.

An illustration of the importance of principles of perceptual integration in marketing is the formation by consumers of images of brands, products, stores, or companies. Another set of applications of these principles deals with the interpretation of advertising messages based on the configuration of stimuli in the message.

The most important principles of perceptual integration are those of closure, grouping, and context.

Closure

Closure refers to a perceiver's tendency to fill in the missing elements when a stimulus is incomplete. Consumers have a desire to form a complete picture and derive a certain amount of satisfaction in completing a message on their own. The most obvious implication is to provide the consumer with an incomplete advertising message and to let the consumer fill it in. Presumably, this may increase attention to and recall of the message. A study by Heimbach and Jacoby somewhat confirms this assumption.[23] They presented one group of consumers with a complete commercial and another group with a commercial cut at the end. The incomplete commercial generated 34 percent more recall than the complete version.

A number of examples of the use of closure in advertising can be cited. A number of years back, Kellogg showed its company name in billboard advertising with the last *g* cut off by the right boundary of the billboard.[24] The desire to produce closure generated attention to the ad. Salem cigarettes used the theme: "You can take Salem out of the country, *but* you can't take the country out of Salem." The first line was then repeated and the advertisement closed with *but*. The expectation was the consumer would complete the second line. The desire for closure involved the consumer with the advertisement and resulted in a successful campaign.

Grouping

Consumers are more likely to perceive a variety of information as chunks rather than as separate units. They integrate various bits and pieces of information into organized wholes. Chunking or **grouping information** permits consumers to evaluate one brand over another based on a variety of attributes and the overall image. Various principles of grouping have emerged from Gestalt psychology, namely, proximity, similarity, and continuity. These principles of grouping are represented in Figure 5–4.

The tendency to group stimuli by **proximity** means that one object will be associated with another based on its closeness to that object. The twelve dots in Figure 5–4 are seen as three columns of four dots rather than four rows of three dots because of their proximity. Most advertising uses principles of proximity by associating the product with positive symbols and imagery that is close to the product. Consider the two advertisements for the same product in Figure 5–5 which were published in the same issue of *Vogue* just a few pages apart. Both attempt to establish an association with the product by proximity. The Cinnabar advertisement associates the products with a sense of luxury and elegance, the products being grouped in the lower right hand side of the ad. The Charlie advertisement associates the products with a very different scene, one of carefree abandon, the products being positioned in the lower right. Proximity has established two individual images.

Consumers also group products by **similarity**. Stereotyping often reflects grouping by similarity — for example, all men with long hair and beards are anti-establishment. The eight squares and four circles in Figure 5–4 are grouped in three sets because of their similarity — two sets of four squares and one set of four circles. The Cinnabar advertisement in Figure 5–5 demonstrates a principle of grouping by similarity. The tendency is to group the products together because of proximity and similarity in name and color. The intention is to view the set of products as an integrated whole.

Consumers also group stimuli into continuous and uninterrupted forms rather than into discontinuous contours. The dots in the third part of Figure 5–4 are more likely to be seen as an arrow projecting to the right than as columns of dots. Principles of **continuity** suggest that the basic flow of the sales message should be continuous. Similarly, not only should the products in a retail store be grouped by similarity of merchandise, but also the change from one sales station to the next should be reasonably continuous.

Context

Consumers will tend to perceive an object by the **context** in which it is shown. The setting of an advertisement will influence the perception of a product. The

GROUPING

Proximity

Similarity

Continuity

CONTEXT

Figure and
Ground

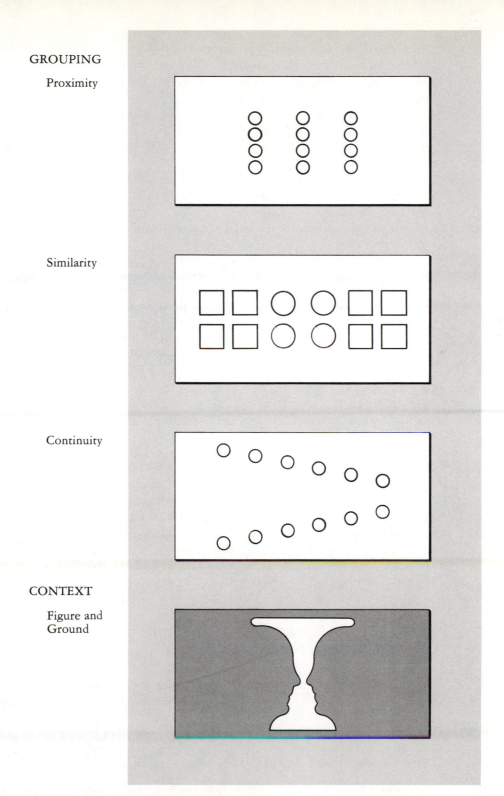

FIGURE 5–4   Principles of Organization

two perfume advertisements in Figure 5–5 utilize a very different positioning based on the setting in which the product is placed. The identical advertisement may also be perceived quite differently in two different media. For example, Fuchs placed identical advertisements in high prestige magazines *(Harper's, New Yorker)* and in low prestige magazines *(True, Detective).* Not surprisingly, he found that consumers rated advertisements in the high prestige magazines much higher.[25] Therefore, the media context will directly influence the perception of the ad.

The purchase situation will also identify the context in which a stimulus is perceived. An advertisement for a new nutritional cereal will be seen in one context by the single person who buys cereal as an occasional midmorning snack and in quite a different context by the parent with two young children who buys cereal for the family.

The most important principle of context is **figure and ground.** Gestalt psychologists state that in organizing stimuli into wholes, individuals will distinguish stimuli that are prominent (the figure which is generally in the foreground) from stimuli that are less prominent (the ground or background). The determination of what part of the whole is the figure and what part is ground will greatly affect the way stimuli are perceived.

The lower part of Figure 5–4 illustrates the principle of figure and ground. The picture can be seen as a goblet (figure) with a black background or as two profiles (figure) with a white background. Advertisers seek to ensure that the product is the figure and the setting is the background. In both perfume advertisements the product is placed in the foreground and the setting is in the background.

The danger of confusing figure and ground is illustrated in a famous series of commercials run a number of years ago for Piels beer. Bert and Harry Piels (played by the comedians Bob and Ray) were used in a cartoon format. The intention was that Bert and Harry would be the setting (ground) to sell the beer (figure). So much attention was focused on Bert and Harry that the reverse occurred. They became the figure and the product was lost in the background. Although recall for the advertisements was very high, the commercials were not selling the product. The principle is that advertising should clearly specify what is figure and what is ground.

EFFECTS OF MARKETING STIMULI ON CONSUMER PERCEPTIONS

In the remainder of this chapter, the two primary influences on consumer perceptions of a stimulus will be considered: the characteristics of the stimulus and the characteristics of the consumer. The two most important stimuli influencing consumer behavior are marketing and environmental stimuli. This section will review the effects of marketing stimuli on consumer perceptions. Environmental stimuli will be considered in Part Three.

FIGURE 5–5 Use of Principles of Proximity and Context in Advertising

Marketing Stimuli

Marketing stimuli are any communications or physical stimuli (such as the product or package) that are designed to influence the consumer. Communications designed to influence consumer behavior are **secondary stimuli** that either represent the product through words, pictures, and symbolism, or through other stimuli associated with the product (price, store in which purchased, effect of salesperson). The product and its components (package, contents, physical properties) are the **primary stimuli.**

Constant exposure to secondary marketing stimuli is a requisite to survival in a competitive market. But, continuous advertising would not be profitable unless enough consumers were to buy again. Therefore, the ultimate determinant of future consumer actions is experience with the primary stimulus, the product. At times, manufacturers attempt to introduce such product experience prior to a purchase through the use of free samples. Offering samples is an attempt to provide direct product experience to the consumer at no risk prior to market introduction. However, use of the product as a direct stimulus in attempting to influence the consumer to buy is the exception. The dominant element in marketing strategy is communications about the product.

The key requirement in communicating secondary stimuli to the consumer is the development of a product concept. A **product concept** is a bundle of product benefits that can be directed to the needs of a defined group of consumers through symbolism and imagery. The product concept represents the organization of the secondary stimuli into a coordinated product position that can be more easily directed to consumers. For example, Nestlé positioned its freeze-dried coffee entry, Taster's Choice, as providing the benefits of instant coffee with the taste and aroma of regular coffee. Given this basic concept, the secondary stimuli were geared to the intended positioning. The brand name implied taste and the advertising demonstrated the taste benefits of a good instant coffee for the man of the family. Even the shape of the jar was tested. It was determined that a deep square jar would provide more of an image of hefty taste and masculinity compared to the traditional circular jar. Definition of the product concept must therefore precede development of the secondary stimuli in the marketing plan.

Stimulus Factors Affecting Perception

A number of characteristics of advertising and other marketing stimuli will affect the likelihood of the message being perceived. These characteristics can be divided into structural elements (size, shape, position, color) and sensory elements (smell, feel, taste). The structural elements have implications primarily for print advertising; the sensory elements primarily for direct product experience.

Structural Factors

A number of findings have emerged from studies of print advertising in the following areas:

- *Size.* The larger the size of the advertisement, the greater the likelihood it will be perceived. The impact increases in proportion to the square root of the increase in space. That is, if an advertisement's size is increased four-fold, awareness will double.[26]
- *Position.* There will be greater awareness of advertisements in the first 10 percent of the pages of a magazine. Beyond this point, position has little effect.[27] In addition, the upper half of a printed page produces more attention than the lower half. But there is little difference if an advertisement is on the left- or right-hand page.[28]
- *Color.* Generally, color advertisements produce more attention than black and white ones. But there is some question whether color is worth the additional cost. One study suggests not.[29] In addition, if most advertisements are in color, it may be advantageous to have a black and white ad because of the contrast effect.
- *Contrast.* Contrast is likely to produce attention. The picture of a product on a stark white background may produce attention. But, it may not ensure comprehension and retention. Contrast is also used in television commercials to attract attention by sometimes increasing volume during commercials.
- *Novelty.* Novelty is another attention-getting device. An ad for Mobil for energy conservation features the word *imagination* with each letter in the word presented as a visual illustration. But, novelty does not ensure communication of the message.

Sensory Factors

Sensory factors will also affect the way an object is perceived. In one study two fragrances were added to the same facial tissue. Consumers perceived one facial tissue as elegant and expensive, while they regarded the other as a product to use in the kitchen.[30] Taste is another sensory factor that will condition perception of the object. A strong coffee will produce one image of a brand, a weak coffee quite another. The feel of certain products will also influence perceptions. Consumers frequently judge carpets or clothing by the feel of the material. Softness is considered a desirable attribute in many paper products. The well-advertised theme "Don't squeeze the Charmin" suggests the importance of feel.

Other common elements in the marketing plan also have sensory components. Color has sensory connotations. One study found that the color of bread was more important in determining consumer perceptions than were price or nutritional information.[31] Another example of the use of color is the fact that Frank Perdue takes advantage of northeasterners' association of yellow-skinned chicken with succulence.[32] He uses marigold petals and corn in the feed to produce yellower chickens. This is one reason why Perdue's share of market in New York City went from 1 percent to 20 percent in ten years.

Even the voice of an announcer on a commercial may influence perceptions due to sensory qualities. Prusmack produced three identical advertisements with three different announcers.[33] One announcer's voice was educated and smooth, another's was more aggressive, the third announcer's voice was in-between. He tested the three commercials on a group of adults going back to college. The commercial with the first announcer scored highest on believability and likeability. Prusmack concludes, "It is the perception of what they (the respondents) have seen or heard that is just as important, if not more important, than the actual words."[34]

Stimulus Discrimination

One of the basic questions regarding the effect of marketing stimuli on perceptions is whether the consumer can discriminate between differences in stimuli. Does the consumer perceive differences between brands in taste, in feel, in price, in the shape of the package?

The ability to discriminate between stimuli is learned. Generally, frequent users of a product are better able to discriminate small differences in product characteristics between brands. But, in most cases, sensory discrimination of physical differences between brands is small. As a result, marketers rely on advertising to convey brand differences that physical characteristics alone would not impart. They attempt to create a brand image that will convince consumers one brand is better than another.

Marketing experiments support the fact that most consumers do not differentiate products based only on taste or other sensory factors. Consumers perceive brands selectively based on advertising, price, and other marketing stimuli.

A test by Allison and Uhl found that brand image rather than taste criteria was the basis for discriminating between beers. Consumers were given three brands of unlabeled beer, one of which was the brand they drank most often.[35] They were then asked to rate the beers on an overall basis from excellent to poor and on specific characteristics such as aroma, aftertaste, body, and carbonation. The results showed that consumers did not discriminate between the three brands. Ratings of all the brands tested were similar, and no beer scored significantly higher on any of the taste criteria such as aroma and body. Moreover, there was little evidence that consumers could identify their regular brand. The same brands were then presented to the consumers labeled and they were again asked to rate the brands. In this case there were significant differences between brands. The consumer's regular brand was rated significantly higher than others. Allison and Uhl conclude that "the physical product differences had little to do with the various brands' relative success."[36] Rather, the brand image produced differences in preferences and taste perceptions. Tests of taste discrimination for soft drinks and cigarettes have confirmed these findings.[37]

Other studies have found that many consumers *can* tell the difference between beers. A replication of the Allison and Uhl experiment found that beer drinkers can distinguish among brands based on taste and aroma alone, without reference to brand labels.[38] And, another study estimated that 40 percent to 50 percent of beer drinkers can reliably tell the difference in taste between beers.[39] But even in these cases, beer drinkers do not agree on what tastes better. One beer expert concluded, "It is extremely difficult to separate the actual taste stimulation from the marketing and psychology of the beer and what a consumer feels he or she should like."[40]

In reviewing the evidence on taste discrimination, Myers and Reynolds reached a similar conclusion:

> Since many types of consumer products are nearly or wholly indistinguishable on the basis of sensory processes, they must be distinguished on the basis of something else. The consumer must have something to hang his perceptual hat on. The "something else" which serves to distinguish such

products is often the product image that is created by the manufacturer. On the other hand, because the consumer likes to *believe* he can discriminate among brands, advertising encourages him with themes that stress "the difference you can *taste*."[41]

Advertising is therefore the key ingredient in creating discrimination between brands. There is a constant attempt to impart uniqueness. But a perceived difference is not enough. The difference must be related to need. In many cases such differences will be based on imagery rather than physical characteristics. At times, physical characteristics are emphasized in the advertising. Cigarettes are advertised as being lower in tar and nicotine, longer, mentholated, etc. But as one cigarette executive noted, sensory discrimination is minimal. Consumer perceptions frequently reflect a playback of advertising themes.[42]

The Just Noticeable Difference

A basic principle of stimulus discrimination is that a differential threshold exists in comparing two stimuli. The consumer will not be able to detect any difference between stimuli below his or her **differential threshold.** The differential threshold therefore represents the **just noticeable difference** (j.n.d.). For example, if a private label detergent is three cents below the consumer's regular brand, the consumer may not notice the difference. A difference of five cents also may not be noticed. But, if the private label brand is ten cents below the regular brand, the consumer will notice the difference. Therefore, ten cents is the differential threshold or j.n.d. for this consumer.

Weber's Law

Marketers sometimes seek to make changes in marketing stimuli that will not be noticed (a decrease in package size or an increase in price). A good example of the need to change a marketing stimulus without notice is the periodic updating of existing packaging. Morton Salt has subtly changed the hemline and style of the girl on the package to relate to the contemporary scene.[43] Most consumers would not notice these changes because they are below the j.n.d. Similarly, Campbell's Soup, Heinz Ketchup and Ivory Soap have all changed their packaging subtly over the years so that a change from one package to the next is not detectable. Figure 5–6 illustrates the packaging changes for Ivory Soap over a seventy year period. A single change would be below the j.n.d. for most consumers, but the overall difference in packaging is easily detectable.

Of even more direct application to marketing strategy is the need to differentiate a brand from competition so that it will be noticed. In this case, the marketer seeks to develop product characteristics and advertising messages that are easily detectable (e.g., differences in size, taste, color, ingredients, etc.).

Since most consumers cannot detect relatively small changes in price, package size, or physical characteristics of a product, a relevant question for marketers is what degree of change is required for consumers to take notice. A principle developed by two German physiologists over a hundred years ago, known as **Weber's law,** provides some insight into this question. Weber's law

FIGURE 5–6 Changes in Packaging Below the Just Noticeable Difference

Source: Walter P. Margulies, "Design Changes Reflect Switches in Consumer, Retail Graphics," *Advertising Age,* February 12, 1972, p. 12.
Reprinted with permission from the February 12, 1972 issue of *Advertising Age.* Copyright 1972 by Crain Communication, Inc.

says that that stronger the initial stimulus, the greater the change required for the stimulus to be seen as different. Translated in marketing terms, this would mean that the higher the price, the greater the change in price required for the consumer to take notice. Price would have to increase more significantly to be noticed for a five-hundred-dollar stereo set compared to a fifty-dollar tape recorder. Moreover, Weber's law says that the increase in the difference required to reach the differential threshold (the j.n.d.) is constant. This means that if price had to increase by a minimum of five dollars to be noticed for a fifty-dollar tape recorder, then it would have to increase by a minimum of fifty dollars to be noticed for a five-hundred-dollar stereo set. In both cases, the j.n.d. is 10 percent.

Weber's law can be stated as

$$k = \frac{\Delta I}{I}$$

where:

I = the original stimulus level (e.g., a $50.00 tape recorder)
ΔI = the change required to be noticed (the j.n.d. of $5.00)
k = the constant increase or decrease required for the stimulus to be noticed. (In the above example $k = 10\%$.)

The Federal Trade Commission implicitly recognized the nature of Weber's law when it required that the Surgeon General's warning on possible effects of cigarette smoking had to appear in print advertising.[44] The bigger the ad, the bigger the type had to be in order to be noticed. If the type fell below the specifications set by the FTC, it might fall below the j.n.d. for many consumers, and the warning would not be perceived.

Britt cites the use of Weber's law in ensuring that a change in a brand's characteristics will be detected.[45] For instance, Weber's law could indicate the required increase in length of a cigarette, increase in sweetness of a soft drink, or alteration in size or weight of a package to be noticed.

Perhaps the most direct applications of Weber's law are in regard to price. One important implication is that the higher the original price of an item, the greater the markdown required to increase sales. The required markdown on a designer suit would be greater than on a regular suit. Another implication is that as prices increase, each subsequent price increase will not be noticed as much. The best example is the increasing price of gasoline after 1973. Assume that a consumer paying thirty cents a gallon for regular gasoline in 1973 noticed a three cent a gallon increase in price. As prices went up to seventy cents a gallon, this meant that the next jump to be noticed would be seventy-seven cents. As prices went up to a dollar a gallon, the next jump to be noticed would be $1.10, etc. Thus, as price goes up, consumers become less sensitive to further increases.

Weber's law seems to contradict a basic principle in economics that higher prices will result in greater price sensitivity and in a decrease in quantity consumed. However, the experience of the 1970s suggests that Weber might be right and many economists wrong. The level of stimulus discrimination to prices seems to have remained constant, meaning that the consumers are willing to pay more as prices increase.

Subliminal Perceptions

The differential threshold was identified as the minimum difference between two stimuli that can be detected. Thus, a consumer may be able to tell the difference between two cordials of 40 proof and 60 proof, but if the difference between the two is smaller, it will not be detected (60–40, or 20 proof, is the j.n.d.). There is also an **absolute threshold** below which the consumer cannot detect the stimulus at all. Thus, a consumer can detect alcohol in a cordial that is 10 proof, but below that no alcoholic content can be detected in the beverage. Therefore, the differential threshold is 20 proof and the absolute threshold is 10 proof.

One of the major controversies regarding consumer perceptions is whether consumers can actually perceive marketing stimuli below their absolute threshold. The term **subliminal perception** means perception of a stimulus below the conscious level. (The conscious level is referred to as the *limen;* thus perception below the conscious level is subliminal or below the absolute threshold.) It may seem contradictory that a consumer can perceive a message below the minimum level of perception, but experiments conducted in the 1950s suggest that exposure may actually occur without attention and comprehension. That is, the consumer does not see the message, but it registers.

Vicary conducted a test in which two messages, "Eat Popcorn" and "Drink Coca-Cola" were shown in a movie theater at $1/3000$ of a second (well below the absolute threshold) at intervals of every five seconds.[46] Popcorn sales in the theater increased by 58 percent and Coca-Cola sales by 18 percent compared to periods in which there was no subliminal advertising (e.g., advertising was below the absolute threshold). These results immediately raised serious ethical questions since consumers could be influenced by messages without their approval or knowledge. The possible use of subliminal advertising generated a great deal of controversy, but the controversy proved shallow since there was little proof that subliminal advertising influenced consumer actions.

Subsequent attempts to replicate Vicary's findings did not succeed. The Federal Communications Commission took an immediate interest in the implications of subliminal advertising but could not confirm the conclusion that subliminal advertising influences the receiver's responses.[47]

The conclusion of two noted social scientists is that there is

> no scientific evidence that subliminal stimulation can initiate subsequent action, to say nothing of commercially or politically significant action. And there is nothing to suggest that such action can be produced against the subject's will, or more effectively than through normal, recognized messages.[48]

Therefore, subliminal advertising has only proved that exposure can occur without perception.

Stimulus Generalization

Consumers not only learn to discriminate between stimuli, they learn to generalize from one similar stimulus to another. The process of **stimulus generalization** is closely tied to classical conditioning. Two stimuli are seen as similar (contiguous) and the effects of one can therefore be substituted for the effects of the other, much as the bell was substituted for food in Pavlov's experiments. The dogs were generalizing from food to bell.

Discrimination allows consumers to judge brands selectively and to make evaluative judgments about preferences for one brand or another. Generalization allows consumers to simplify the process of evaluation because they do not have to make a separate judgment for each stimulus. Brand loyalty is a form of stimulus generalization. The consumer assumes that positive past experiences with the brand will be repeated. Therefore, a separate judgment is not required with each purchase. Perceptual categorization is also a form of stimulus generalization. As new products are introduced, consumers generalize from past experience to categorize them. When the automobile was first introduced at the turn of the century, it was called the horseless carriage. People generalized from their experience with the best known mode of transportation, the horse and carriage.

It may appear that marketers seek to avoid generalization since they are attempting to distinguish their brands from competition, but, in some cases, generalization may be a conscious and productive strategy. Heinz uses a strategy of generalization by advertising "57 varieties." The hope is that a positive experience with one of the company's brands will be generalized to other brands. This policy of family branding is also followed by General Electric. On the other hand, Procter and Gamble purposefully avoids a policy of generalization, preferring to position each brand without reference to the company name.

Strategies of generalization are also used in positioning brands to compete with the market leader. A brand may be introduced with the same basic benefits but at a lower price or in a larger package. The hope is that the consumer will generalize the known benefits of the leading brand to the new entry and thus accept it. Some private brands use a principle of generalization by making their package look as similar as possible to the leading brand in the category. The hope is that the consumer will generalize from the positive association with the leading brand to the private brand. Some of the more obvious attempts at such stimulus generalization are presented in Figure 5–7.

Some attempts at generalization have backfired. Crest became the leading toothpaste because of the association between fluorides and cavity prevention. Colgate introduced fluoride to capture part of the decay prevention segment, but when Colgate began advertising its toothpaste as a fluoride that prevents cavities, many consumer confused it with Crest. Thus, Colgate was advertising for Crest as well as Colgate.

FIGURE 5–7   Examples of Stimulus Generalization in Packaging
Source: "Checkout-Counter Lookalikes," *Money,* May 1976, p. 71.

INDIVIDUAL DIFFERENCES IN PERCEPTION

As noted in the beginning of this chapter, two consumers may perceive an identical stimulus very differently. If the stimulus does not influence perceptions, then something else must. That something else is the individual consumer. There are three characteristics of the consumer that will influence the nature of perceptions. First, the perceptual abilities of the consumer; second, his or her perceptual style; third, perceptual predispositions.

Perceptual Abilities

We all have different abilities to perceive stimuli. Three components of perceptual abilities are differences in the threshold level (the j.n.d.), in the adaptation level, and in the attention span.

Consumers will differ in their ability to detect variations in light, sound, smell, or texture based on their **threshold level.** Some consumers are much more sensitive to these sensory stimuli than others. Arthur D. Little, a management consulting firm, has identified expert taste-testers for products such as cigarettes and coffee, whose level of sensory discrimination is much greater than the average consumer's since they can detect subtle differences in coffee or cigarette blends. These expert taste-testers are used to evaluate various test products and to screen out potential losers. The attributes used by expert taste-testers to judge these blends are quite different from those used by regular consumers. For example, in testing cigarette blends certain characteristics (such as green and woody) are evaluated. These characteristics are relatively meaningless to consumers with less sensory discrimination. Once the best prospective blends are identified, they are then tested on consumers in standard taste tests. In these cases, consumers are asked to evaluate attributes that are more readily understood, such as harsh or leaving no aftertaste.

Another component of perceptual abilities is **adaptation level.** Adaptation refers to the process of adjusting to a frequently repeated stimulus so that it is no longer noticed. An individual walking into an air-conditioned room, a kitchen full of fragrances, or a noisy party will not notice these stimuli after a period of time. Similarly, a consumer will take little notice of frequently repeated advertisements or familiar products on the supermarket shelf. They are taken for granted.

Consumers differ in their level of adaptation. Some consumers tune out more quickly than others. Certain consumers have a tendency to be much more aware of the facets of information and communication, even of repeated stimuli. Given the advertiser's desire to gain attention and maintain distinctiveness, the objectives of the typical advertising campaign are to decrease the level of adaptation by introducing attention-getting features. Novelty, humor, contrast, and movement are all stimulus effects that may gain attention and reduce adaptation. The most effective means of reducing the adaptation level, however, is to ensure that the message is directed to consumer needs and communicates the benefits consumers desire.

Another perceptual component that differs between individuals is **attention span,** that is, the number of items that can be perceived at any given time. The attention span for most individuals is relatively narrow. The average span for adults is about seven items (interestingly, phone numbers have seven digits). The time in which attention can be held is also short. This may be one reason why thirty-second commercials are most prominent. The obvious implications for advertisers is to keep the message short with just a few, basic themes.

Both the concepts of adaptation level and attention span would conform well to a theory of passive learning. If Krugman is right and most viewers watch commercials in a passive and tuned-out state, a low attention span and a relatively high level of adaptation to frequently repeated commercials could be the cause.

Perceptual Style

Consumers also differ in how they process information. As noted, consumers tend to process information by organizing it into chunks so that it can be viewed as an organized whole. A brand image or a store image is an information chunk. Consumers differ in their propensity to process information by chunks. Several studies have found that consumers can be divided into those that tend to process information by chunk versus those that process information by discrete pieces.[49]

Another element of perceptul style is the willingness of consumers to consider new information — complex and ambiguous information and information that may contradict their beliefs. In each case, such information will create some disequilibrium in the psychological set. Therefore, the question is the degree to which a consumer can adapt to a state of perceptual disequilibrium. Kelman and Cohler identify two types of consumers in this regard — sharpeners and levelers.[50] Sharpeners actively look for new information and tend to be more comfortable with contradictory information. They are more likely to notice differences between messages and between product characteristics. Levelers seek a greater degree of simplicity in information processing. They shun ambiguous and complex information and are more likely to seek a state of perceptual equilibrium.

There is some evidence that sharpeners have a lower level of anxiety, a higher level of self-esteem, and a higher level of coping behavior.[51] Consumers with these traits may be more willing to accept complex and contradictory information because they are more self-confident in their abilities to process such information.

Perceptual Predispositions

A consumer's needs, attitudes, and past experiences will affect the manner in which stimuli are perceived. Since needs directly influence perceptions, the apparent implication for marketing strategy is to directly appeal to existing needs rather than attempt to change these needs. If advertising conforms to a consumer's predispositions, the message is more likely to be perceived.

THE MEASUREMENT OF CONSUMER PERCEPTIONS

The foregoing discussion assumes that consumer perceptions can be measured. Measurement is a necessary prerequisite to evaluation of the impact of consumer perceptions on subsequent behavior. Therefore, marketers must be able to measure exposure, attention, comprehension, and retention of marketing information. A recent study evaluating the effectiveness of advertising for a leading petroleum company provides a good summary of measurement of consumer perceptions at each stage of information processing. The study was conducted in 1974, a time of heightened awareness of and concern with potential energy shortages. The purposes of the study were to:

1. Determine degree of advertising awareness for the company's brand and for competitive brands;
2. Assess the effects of advertising awareness on brand and company image;
3. Determine the most effective media for reaching the energy conscious consumer.

The survey was conducted among a random sample of 2,000 households with automobiles. The various stages of information processing were measured as follows:

General Media Exposure

1. Readership of sixteen magazines (if read and numbers of issues read or looked through in the past six months)
2. Viewing of nine news-related TV shows
3. Number of hours spent watching TV

Specific Advertising Exposure

The consumer recalled the location of a particular advertisement.

Awareness

1. General advertising awareness was determined by asking, "What brands of gasoline have you seen or heard advertised in the last several months?"

2. Specific recall of advertising themes was obtained by the following: "Please tell me everything you can recall that was said or shown in the advertising for (the brand)."

Comprehension

Comprehension was determined by assessing the effects of advertising awareness on corporate and brand image. Respondents were asked to associate advertising themes to five leading brands of gasoline. Some of the themes were:

- helps keep the engine clean
- helps reduce air pollution
- helps car's performance
- reduces engine knock

Respondents were divided into those who were aware of the company's advertising and those who were not. Brand image was then determined for the two groups. The hypothesis was that image of the brand among those who were aware would conform more closely to the content of the advertising. If so, this would demonstrate that those aware of the advertising were more likely to accept and *retain* the message.

SUMMARY

A product's success depends largely on the way consumers perceive the product and the marketing stimuli designed to promote the product. This chapter considered consumer perceptions. Consumers process information from marketing organizations in a series of steps — exposure to the marketing stimuli, attention, comprehension, and retention.

Selectivity and organization are the two basic processes underlying consumer preceptions. Selective perception serves two purposes. One, it guides consumers in selecting information that is relevant and in screening out information that is not relevant to their needs. This is known as perceptual vigilance. Two, consumers tend to select information that conforms to their beliefs and predispositions about brands, products, and companies. This function is known as perceptual defense.

Perceptual vigilance and perceptual defense operate because consumers seek consistency between the information they receive and their needs, attitudes, and postpurchase behavior. Such consistency ensures that the consumer's psychological set is in balance (perceptual equilibrium). But, a state of conflict can occur (perceptual disequilibrium), especially if the product does not meet prior expectations.

The organization of marketing stimuli also depends on two processes, categorization and integration. Categorization simplifies information processing by permitting consumers to classify brands into product categories. Integration permits consumers to perceive many different stimuli and organize them into a cohesive whole. Consumers form images of brands, stores, or companies by perceiving information from many sources and by forming an overall impression. Consumers are able to integrate information by processes of closure, grouping, similarity, continuity, and context.

The chapter also considered the marketing stimuli that affect consumer perceptions of brands. These stimuli were classified into the primary stimulus — the product — and the secondary stimuli — symbols, imagery, and information representing the product.

A key question is the degree to which consumers can discriminate between marketing stimuli. Marketers attempt to create such discrimination by informing consumers about the advantages of their brand relative to competitors'. But a number of studies have raised doubts about the ability of consumers to discriminate between brands on sensory factors such as taste and smell.

At times, consumers will generalize from one similar stimulus to another. Marketers use strategies of stimulus generalization in family branding and in attempts to duplicate market leaders.

The chapter concludes by recognizing that consumers differ in their ability to perceive marketing stimuli. Some consumers may have a more refined innate ability to detect differences in stimuli than others. Consumers may also differ in the manner in which information is processed.

The next chapter focuses on the strategic implications of the processes of consumer perceptions.

QUESTIONS

1. What is the distinction between perceptual vigilance and perceptual defense? Which is most likely to operate in the following cases?
   a) organizational buying behavior
   b) a consumer buying the same brand of frozen orange juice because of inertia
   c) a consumer buying the same perfume because of brand loyalty

2. The chapter cites two conflicting possibilities when postpurchase doubts arise: (1) learning theory suggests the consumer will adjust behavior to the dissonant information and will reduce the likelihood of buying the same brand again; and (2) dissonance theory suggests the consumer will adjust the dissonant information to behavior by avoiding negative information or looking for positive information. This reaction might increase the probability of buying the same brand again.
   • When is the consumer more likely to react in accordance with dissonance rather than learning theory?

3. Categorization is an important requirement when consumers perceive brand information.
   • Can you cite any examples when consumers did not categorize a product as it was intended by the manufacturer, leading to product failure?
   • Can you cite examples when the product was not categorized as intended, leading to new and unforeseen uses and an expanded market?

4. What are the implications of principles of *proximity* and *similarity* for (a) product line policies and (b) in-store product organization?

5. What are the implications of principles of *context* for (a) media selection, (b) advertising layout, and (c) positioning brands to specific usage situations?

6. Some researchers would argue it is not relevant to measure brand perceptions of consumers who have never tried the brand. They feel the success of a brand is based on repeat purchase, and, therefore, consumers who have never tried the brand should not be in a position to influence marketing strategy. Should perceptions of consumers who have never tried a brand be determined?

7. Can you cite applications of the differential threshold to changes in (a) package size and (b) advertising duration and intensity?

8. Some studies have shown that sensory perceptions (taste, smell, etc.) play a minimal role in the selection of major national brands in such categories as tea, coffee, cigarettes, perfumes, etc.

   • What are the implications of this finding for the development of product specifications for these product categories?

   • What are the implications for advertising and product positioning?

   • Under what conditions are consumers more likely to discriminate between brands?

9. What are the implications of the concept of stimulus discrimination for (a) Folger's introducing its coffee in the eastern market and (b) Cadillac introducing a medium-sized car?

10. What are the implications of the concept of stimulus generalization for (a) The Xerox Corp. trying to avoid the generic use of its name for all copying equipment and (b) Lever Brothers entering the hair care market?

RESEARCH ASSIGNMENTS

1. Pick two closely competing brands in two product categories: a high involvement category (e.g., cars) and a low involvement category (e.g., toothpaste). Identify a number of consumers who own or regularly use each brand. Ask consumers to rate the two competing brands (their own and the close competitor) on a number of need criteria (e.g., for cars it might be economy, durability, style, etc). If consumers perceive brands selectively, they are likely to rate their own brand much higher than the competitive brand. Further, this is more likely for the high involvement category compared to the low involvement category.

   • Based on your findings, is this true? That is, (1) are brand ratings for the consumer's own brand much higher than that of the competitive brand and (2) are the differences in ratings between the regular and competitive brand greater for the high involvement product category?

   • Do consumers rate their own brand much higher on certain attributes but not on others?

   • Do these differences reflect a process of selective perception?

2. Test the ability of consumers to discriminate between the taste of alternative brands in one of the following product categories: soft drinks, coffee, tea. Run the following experiment:

   Identify three leading brands in the category. Then select an equal number of respondents who select one of the three brands as their regular brand. Ask each respondent to taste the three brands without identifying them. (Make sure to rotate the order of tasting.) Then ask the respondent to identify his or her preferred brand. (Make sure the brands tested are in the same class for the product; for example, colas or uncolas for soft drinks, regular or instant for coffee.) On the basis of chance, one would expect one-third correct identification.

   • Was the proportion of correct identification significantly greater than chance?

   • Were those who correctly identified their preferred brand different from those who did not? Were they more frequent users of the category? Did they use a certain brand?

NOTES

1. Herbert E. Krugman, "Memory Without Recall, Exposure With Perception," *Journal of Advertising Research* 17 (August 1977): 7–12.
2. Jerome Bruner and Cecil C. Goodman, "Value and Need as Organizing Factors in Perception," *Journal of Abnormal and Social Psychology* 42 (1947): 33–44.
3. Homer E. Spence and James F. Engel, "The Impact of Brand Preference on the Perception of Brand Names: A Laboratory Analysis," in David T. Kollat, Roger D. Blackwell, and James F. Engel, eds., *Research in Consumer Behavior* (New York: Holt, Rinehart and Winston Inc., 1970), pp. 61–70.
4. Steuart Henderson Britt, Stephen C. Adams, and Alan S. Miller, "How Many Advertising Exposures Per Day?"*Journal of Advertising Research* 12 (December 1972): 3–10.
5. M. Sherif and C. E. Hovland, *Social Judgment* (New Haven: Yale University Press, 1964).
6. John R. Stuteville, "Psychic Defense Against High Fear Appeals: A Key Marketing Variable," *Journal of Marketing* 34 (April 1970): 39–45.
7. Harold H. Kassarjian and Joel B. Cohen, "Cognitive Dissonance and Consumer Behavior," *California Management Review* 8 (Fall 1965): 55–64.
8. Sherif and Hovland, *Social Judgment.*
9. Fritz Heider, *The Psychology of Interpersonal Relations* (New York: John Wiley and Sons, Inc., 1958).
10. Stuart H. Surlin and Thomas F. Gordon, "Selective Exposure and Retention of Political Advertising," *Journal of Advertising* 5 (Winter 1976): 32–37.
11. David L. Paletz et al., "Selective Exposure: The Potential Boomerang Effect," *Journal of Communication* 22 (March 1972): 48–53.
12. James Engel, "Are Automobile Purchasers Dissonant Consumers," *Journal of Marketing* 27 (April 1963): 55–58.
13. Danuta Ehrlich et al., "Post-Decision Exposure to Relevant Information," *Journal of Abnormal and Social Psychology* 54 (January 1957): 98–102.
14. J. E. Brehm, "Post-Decision Changes in the Desirability of Alternatives," *Journal of Abnormal and Social Psychology* 52 (July 1956): 384–389.
15. Kassarjian and Cohen, "Cognitive Dissonance and Consumer Behavior."
16. Leo Bogart, *Strategy and Advertising* (New York: Harcourt Brace Jovanovich, 1967), Chapter 5.
17. Judson Mills, "Avoidance of Dissonant Information," *Journal of Personality and Social Psychology* 2 (1965): 589–593.
18. Salvatore R. Maddi, "The Pursuit of Consistency and Variety," in R. P. Abelson, ed., *Theories of Cognitive Consistency: A Sourcebook* (Skokie, Ill: Rand McNally & Co., 1968), pp. 267–274.
19. Leon Festinger, *A Theory of Cognitive Dissonance* (Stanford, Calif.: Stanford University Press, 1957).
20. Kenneth E. Runyon, *Consumer Behavior and the Practice of Marketing* (Columbus, Ohio: Charles E. Merrill Publishing Co., 1977), pp. 302–303.
21. George S. Day, "Theories of Attitude Structure and Change," in Scott Ward and Thomas S. Robertson, eds., *Consumer Behavior: Theoretical Sources* (Englewood Cliffs, N.J.: Prentice-Hall, Inc., 1973), p. 341.
22. Jerome S. Bruner, "On Perceptual Readiness," *The Psychological Review* 64 (1957): 123–152.
23. James T. Heimbach and Jacob Jacoby, "The Zeigarnik Effect in Advertising," in M. Venkatesan, ed., *Proceedings, 3rd Annual Conference, Association for Consumer Research* (1972), pp. 746–758.
24. James H. Myers and William H. Reynolds, *Consumer Behavior and Marketing Management* (Boston: Houghton Mifflin Co., 1967), p. 21.
25. Douglas A. Fuchs, "Two Source Effects in Magazine Advertising," *Journal of Marketing Research* I (August 1964): 59–62.
26. R. Barton, *Advertising Media* (New York: McGraw-Hill, 1964), p. 109.
27. "Position in Newspaper Advertising: 2," *Media/Scope,* March 1963, pp. 76–82.
28. Ibid.
29. J. W. Rosberg, "How Does Color, Size Affect Ad Readership," *Industrial Marketing* 41 (May 1956): 54–57.
30. William Copulsky and Katherine Marton, "Sensory Cues," *Product Marketing* (January 1977): 31–34.
31. Robert A. Peterson, "Consumer Perceptions as a Function of Product Color, Price and Nutrition Labeling," in William D. Perreault, Jr., ed., *Advances in Consumer Research* 4 (Atlanta: Association for Consumer Research, 1977), pp. 61–63.
32. Copulsky and Marton, "Sensory Cues", p. 84.
33. A. Jon Prusmack, "Consumer Perceptions — Can They Be Measured?" *Advertising Age,* September 18, 1978, p. 84.
34. Ibid.
35. R. I. Allison and K. P. Uhl, "Influence of Beer Brand Identification on Taste Perception," *Journal of Marketing Research* 1 (August 1964): 36–39.
36. Ibid., p. 39.
37. R. W. Husband and J. Godfrey, "An Experimental Study of Cigarette Identification," *Journal of Applied Psychology* 18 (1934): 220–251; and N. H. Pronko and J. W. Bowles, "Identification of Cola Beverages," *Journal of Applied Psychology,* first study, 32 (1948): 304–312; second study, 32 (1948): 559–564; third study, 33 (1949): 605–608.
38. G. A. Mauser, "Allison and Uhl Revisited: The Effects of Taste and Brand Name on Perceptions and Preferences," in William L. Willkie, ed., *Advances in Consumer Research* 6 (Ann Arbor: Association for Consumer Research, 1979), pp. 161–165.
39. Copulsky and Marton, "Sensory Cues", p. 31.
40. Ibid., p. 32.
41. Myers and Reynolds, *Consumer Behavior and Marketing Management,* p. 19.
42. Private communication.

43. Walter R. Margulies, "Design Changes Reflect Switches in Consumer, Retail Graphics," *Advertising Age,* February 14, 1972, pp. 41–42.

44. John Revett, "FTC Threatens Big Fines for Undersized Cigarette Warnings," *Advertising Age,* March 17, 1975, p. 1.

45. Steuart Henderson Britt, "How Weber's Law Can be Applied to Marketing," *Business Horizons* 13 (February 1975):21–29.

46. See H. Brean, "What Hidden Sell is All About," *Life,* March 31, 1958, pp. 104–114.

47. "Subliminal Ad Okay If It Sells: FCC Peers into Subliminal Picture on TV," *Advertising Age,* 1957.

48. Bernard Berelson and Gary A. Steiner, *Human Behavior: An Inventory of Scientific Findings* (New York: Harcourt, Brace & World, Inc., 1964), p. 95.

49. See Jacob Jacoby, Robert W. Chestnut and William A. Fisher, "A Behavioral Process Approach to Information Acquisition in Nondurable Purchasing," *Journal of Marketing Research* 15 (November 1978): 532–544; and J. Edward Russo and Barbara A. Dosher, "Dimensional Evaluation: A Heuristic for Binary Choice," working paper, University of California, San Diego, 1975.

50. H. C. Kelman and Jonas Cohler, "Reactions to Persuasive Communications as a Function of Cognitive Needs and Styles," Paper read at the Thirtieth Annual Meeting of the Eastern Psychological Association, Atlantic City.

51. Michael L. Ray and William L. Wilkie, "Fear: The Potential of an Appeal Neglected by Marketing," *Journal of Marketing* 34 (January 1970): 54–62.

SIX

Consumer Perceptions and Marketing Strategy

Focus of Chapter

The manner in which consumers select and organize marketing stimuli directly affects marketing strategy. The consumer's image of a brand represents a composite of the organization of brand perceptions. Similarly, price, store, and corporate images represent the sum total of perceptions of various marketing stimuli. The selectivity consumers exercise in picking and choosing marketing stimuli will also have strategic implications. Marketers want to ensure that consumers will be influenced by advertising and in-store promotions. Selective avoidance of such information means the message is not reaching the consumer.

In this chapter, the strategic applications of consumer perceptual processes will be considered. Selective perception and perceptual organization, the two basic processes of consumer perception, will be considered from a strategic perspective, particularly the implications for advertising strategy. The chapter concludes by shifting the focus from the consumer's perception of the product to the consumer's perception of the purchasing process. The key concept here is perceived risk — that is, the degree of risk the consumer associates with the purchase.

SELECTIVE PERCEPTION AND MARKETING STRATEGY

Selective perception helps the consumer deal with complex and ambiguous stimuli so as to conform to the consumer's predispositions, avoid anxiety-producing stimuli, and maintain perceptual equilibrium after the purchase by avoiding contradictory information and seeking supportive information. Each of these functions has important ramifications for marketing stragegy.

Stimulus Ambiguity

A consumer will seek to interpret an ambiguous message to conform to current beliefs and past experiences. For consumers who do not hold strong beliefs about the brand, an ambiguous message is more likely to be accepted and will be interpreted to conform to the consumer's needs. If the message is too explicit, the consumer has little room for projecting and the marketer may be unnecessarily restricting the potential market. The addition of a moderate amount of ambiguity introduces symbolism and imagery that can mean different things to different people. Such ambiguity may be particularly effective in low involvement conditions since the latitude of acceptance is greater. When the consumer is highly involved in the purchase, a clear-cut statement of the manner in which the product can fulfill needs may be more effective. An unstructured message may not be processed because it does not contribute to the information the consumer is seeking. Whether ambiguous messages should be introduced into advertising campaigns depends on principles of perceptual vigilance and perceptual defense.

Perceptual Vigilance

Marketers should be explicit in their advertising if the product's benefits are clear-cut and the product is targeted to a well-defined segment — for example, salt-free baby foods directed to the well-educated, health conscious mother.[1] In such cases, the informational content of the advertisement dominates and ambiguity is held to a minimum. Industrial advertising tends to be less ambiguous because it is more heavily balanced toward informational content than toward symbolism. The operating principle is perceptual vigilance. The consumer is seeking information directed to his or her needs and avoids unnecessary information.

A good example of an unambiguous advertisement with straightforward informational content is the one at the bottom of Figure 6–1. The advertisement refers to one basic benefit directed to drivers concerned with gas economy. This is a high involvement area. The information is clear and readily perceived by consumers interested in this benefit. It is also easily filtered out by those who do not believe that the type of oil affects gas economy or by those who simply are not concerned with gas economy.

Perceptual Defense

A moderate amount of ambiguity permits a process of perceptual defense since the consumer can more easily project into the advertisement whatever is desired. Where benefits are not as clear-cut and are not targeted to a specific segment, the use of symbolism and imagery may effectively allow the consumer to project his or her needs. The Lenox China and Crystal advertisement at the top of Figure 6–1 illustrates this well. The purpose of the advertisement is to

By permission of Lenox China, Inc.

FIGURE 6–1 An Example of an Unambiguous Advertisement and an Ambiguous Advertisement

By permission of Mobil Oil Corp.

provide a medium to enhance the female ego by projecting almost any motive into the advertisement. The theme "Live the Legend" and the imagery can mean many different things to different women. The consumer can selectively perceive what is desired with a minimum of informational content.

Some ambiguity, therefore, permits different segments of a market to selectively perceive a message in line with their needs. But some informational content is necessary, otherwise product benefits may not be conveyed and the message not understood. The Lenox advertisement is clearly conveying a message of quality and luxury. Excessive ambiguity will cause the consumer to screen out the message because of difficulty in understanding it or relating to it. Possibly the symbolism might be so remote as to have no meaning. An example is the case of a lower priced beer attempting to establish a quality image by using a fox hunt as a setting.

Anxiety-Producing Stimuli and Fear Appeals

Maintaining perceptual equilibrium may require the avoidance of stimuli that produce fear and anxieties. Consumers will exert perceptual defense by avoiding such stimuli (selective exposure) or interpreting them so as to reduce the impact of any anxiety-producing message (selective perception).

In the past, advertisers have used fear appeals to demonstrate the possible consequences of product ownership or lack of it. A number of years ago, a cooperative campaign among clothing manufacturers showed a daughter concerned with the appearance of her father (see Figure 6–2). She asks her mother, "Couldn't Daddy stay upstairs when Jim comes?" The advertisement is addressed to the man of the house and concludes, "Dress Right — you can't afford not to." A campaign for an insurance company demonstrated potential family hardships brought on by the death of the wage earner which were due to inadequate insurance. A small West Coast airline tried to bring the fear of flying into the open by using advertising copy that joked about these fears.

Public service advertising has also used fear appeals. Initially, the American Cancer Society demonstrated the harmful effects of smoking with appeals from terminal cancer patients. High school students have seen the results of careless driving in detailed scenes of car crashes and victims crippled for life.

All of these campaigns were ineffective for one reason: The potential results were so stark that they were ignored or dismissed. A natural process of perceptual defense operated to dismiss the message. Acceptance of these messages meant facing the possibility of job loss or death because of the individual's action or inaction. Avoidance of such anxiety-producing information is illustrated in a Federal Trade Commission report which found that the average number of cigarettes consumed did not change after health warnings became public.[2]

Fear appeals do not always produce avoidance behavior. In some cases they might be very effective in conveying a message. McGuire suggests that when the level of a consumer's concern is low to begin with, fear appeals might be effective.[3] An appeal to fear based on social ostracism for having bad breath might be effective because the level of anxiety concerning bad breath may not be that high. On the other hand, fear appeals concerning the results of cigarette smoking deal with death, not social ostracism. What is feared in this case is

FIGURE 6–2   Example of an Appeal to Fear
Reprinted by permission of Men's Fashion Association of America.

harm to the physical self, not to the social image.[4] The result is selective perception through avoidance.

Fear appeals are also more likely to succeed when the consumer has a choice. Fear appeals may influence nonsmokers to stay away from cigarettes or light smokers to quit. But they will not be successful in influencing the behavior of addictive smokers. Nor are they likely to be successful in influencing teenagers who are under heavy peer group pressure to smoke. These teenagers may feel they have no choice but to conform to group norms.

The degree of anxiety produced by a fear related message is not only a function of the stimulus; it is also a function of the consumer's characteristics. One consumer may perceive the purchase of mouthwash as being a relatively high anxiety situation because of self-consciousness about breath. A fear appeal may not be effective for this consumer because he or she may not be able to face embarrassment in a social situation. The result is stimulus avoidance. A more effective campaign for such a consumer is to portray the positive benefits of usage (fresh, clean breath; social popularity) rather than the negative consequences of lack of usage. Ray and Wilkie suggest that individuals with a lower level of anxiety and a higher level of self-esteem are better able to cope with fear appeals because they will consider these messages less threatening.[5] Fear appeals will be more readily accepted by this group without strategies of perceptual defense.

Seeking Supportive Information

As noted in previous chapters, the perception of contradictory information after an important purchase is psychologically uncomfortable for the consumer, producing a state of dissonance. Marketers attempt to reduce dissonance for their brands and increase dissonance for competitive brands. They can reduce dissonance by providing the consumer with supportive information after the purchase.

The potential effectiveness of such a strategy was demonstrated in a study of new car purchasers.[6] Two groups of new car purchasers were selected after the sale was made but before delivery. In one group (the experimental group) salespersons telephoned purchasers twice before delivery and provided positive information about the car. Purchasers in the second group (the control group) received no such information between sale and delivery. About 6 percent of those who received no positive information backed out of the purchase, whereas only 2.5 percent of those receiving the positive sales pitch backed out. Providing positive information before delivery succeeded in reducing the cancellation rate for new cars by more than one half. This suggests that there is a role for advertising and personal selling in reducing dissonance after the purchase, as well as in influencing the consumer before the purchase.

Marketers might also seek to create dissonance among purchasers of competitive products through comparative advertising. Doubts may be raised concerning product quality and performance. The advertisement for the Volkswagen Dasher raises the question of whether the cost of a Mercedes or other luxury car is worth it when the same comfort and performance can be obtained with a Volkswagen. Such an advertisement may well create some doubt in the mind of the recent purchaser of a luxury car and cause a reappraisal of performance.

Combating Selective Perception

The marketer naturally seeks to avoid perceptual processes by which consumers screen out the company's advertisements or misinterpret them. How can a marketer combat selective exposure and perception? One approach is to use rewards, contests, and premiums to try to induce consumers to read the material in print advertisements. This strategy could combat the very low readership of print advertisements (generally less than 20 percent of those who notice print advertisements read the copy). Direct mail may be particularly effective in reaching consumer segments that can be identified by location or zip code. Coupled with a national advertising campaign, the direct communication may generate sufficient interest to take notice of advertising for a new product or repositioning of an existing product.

Sometimes consumers may be avoiding the medium rather than the advertisement. If this is so, the obvious implication is to broaden the range of media used to ensure the advertisement will be seen, even at the risk of increasing the cost of reaching a prospective consumer. Aaker and Myers cite an even more indirect approach at increasing advertising exposure — by reaching opinion leaders for the product category and relying on them to communicate information through word of mouth.[7] But attempts at identifying and influencing opinion leaders for specific categories have not been successful.

Marketers can also seek to combat selective comprehension that misinterprets the advertising. One simple strategy is to use advertising dollars to direct communications to those who are most likely to comprehend and accept the message. A marketing survey may identify certain consumers who emphasize the benefits advertised by the brand and have a favorable attitude toward it. For example, Carnation may identify a segment who emphasizes weight watching and nutrition and who has favorable attitudes toward Carnation Slender. Assume that 40 percent of the consumers in this group do not buy Carnation Slender. It would be more efficient to advertise to this 40 percent who do not buy but are favorable to the product, than to the much larger group who do not buy and are not favorable to the product.

Another strategy to combat misinterpretation of the advertisement is to try to reinforce learning after initial exposure. The package could be used to provide additional information that is not in the advertisement and to correct any possible miscomprehension of the advertisement. A related strategy is to use "hang-tags" on products in stores to reinforce the message in the advertisement. Engel et al. report on the experience of a trade association that found people were miscomprehending its messages in public meetings.[8] The association developed an attractive and well-designed brochure that restated the oral message in an attempt to combat misinterpretation. Similarly, many salespersons for industrial products will provide leave-behind material to reinforce the sales presentation and provide information in writing to avoid any misunderstanding of company offerings, prices, or policies.

All of these strategies are designed to ensure that the message gets through and is understood.

PERCEPTUAL ORGANIZATION AND MARKETING STRATEGY

Consumers tend to organize marketing information into images of brands, products, stores, and companies. An image is a total perception of the object that is formed by processing information from various sources over time. Gestalt psychology suggests that forming an image is a natural process of developing a total perception of the object. An important objective of marketing strategy is to try to influence the manner in which a brand, price level, store, or company is perceived. Marketers are therefore constantly trying to influence consumers' images.

Brand Image

Brand images represent the overall perception of the brand and are formed from information about the brand and past experience. The image of a brand is related to attitudes (beliefs about and preferences for the brand). Consumers with more positive images of the brand are more likely to purchase it. Therefore, a major purpose of advertising strategy is to develop a positive brand image. As one writer states, "Not only is the development of the product perception [i.e., brand image] the basis for early prognostication of success, but it constitutes the control for the entire product development program. . . ."[9]

The impact of brand image on preferences for brands was demonstrated in the previous chapter. Various studies were cited showing that consumers could not discriminate brands based on taste alone, but when the brand was identified, strong preferences developed. The brand's image resulted in brand preferences; the physical properties of the brand did not. The features attributed to these brands are generally consistent with the advertising claims made for the brand. This suggests that advertising can develop brand images for relatively undifferentiated products.

A change in a single component of the brand may totally change the image of a commonplace product. An example of how the alteration of a single component of a brand can change brand image is provided by Martineau. He states:

> When Procter & Gamble introduced Cheer with adequate advertising proclaiming it as "good for tough-job washing," it was just another detergent going no particular place in sales. . . . Then it was given a blue color, and in the housewife's mind it acquired a completely different character, making it seemingly capable of functional wonders totally uncalled for by anything in the mere color. Thereupon it became a tremendous national success.[10]

This example supports the Gestalt notion that the organized whole, as represented by brand image, is more than the sum of its parts.

An example of the possible negative consequences of a change in brand is provided by White.[11] Sugar coating was added to a well-known cereal and tested on consumers. Reaction to the brand was not just a matter of liking or not liking presweetening. The whole perception of the brand changed, suggesting that while the brand might gain a new market segment, it may alienate its loyal users. White concludes that the perception of product values by consumers is an "indivisible whole or *gestalt* because it is triggered by product advantages."[12]

The key ingredient in influencing a consumer's brand image is the positioning of the product. Marketers try to position their brands to meet the needs of defined consumer segments. They do so by developing a product concept that can communicate the desired benefits through advertising and by utilizing media that will reach the target segment.

When Schweppes first came on the market in the United States, it could have been positioned as a soft drink or as a mixer. Positioning it as a mixer guided the promotional direction. The use of Commander Whitehead as the dapper Englishman referring to "Schweppervescence" produced an image of prestige for a product category that might otherwise be regarded as commonplace. This positioning also required selecting media for an older, more conservative, and more upscale group compared to the media that would have been required if the product was positioned as a soft drink.

Considering the tremendous investment in new product introductions, research on new product concepts is extremely important. Careful screening of alternative concepts must be undertaken to determine the brand image they convey. A good example of the evaluation of alternative positionings is the testing of various concepts by General Foods that eventually led to the introduction of Gainesburgers. In early 1960, General Foods' Post Division was examining alternative positionings for its new intermediate moisture dog food requiring no refrigeration. The decision had been made that the product would be shaped like a patty and packaged in cellophane containers for ease of storage. But the positioning of the product, advertising direction, price, and brand name had not been decided.[13]

General Foods could have positioned Gainesburgers as:

- A complete dog diet positioned against canned foods;
- A high nutrition supplement;
- A group of several product variations based on the dog's age;
- A new and unique concept in dog feeding positioned independently of existing canned dog foods.

The selection of one of these four positionings would determine the direction of subsequent marketing strategy. This point was emphasized by the advertising agency, Young and Rubicam, in a memo to General Foods' management:

> In absolute terms, there is no such thing as a "best" name, or a "best" package, or a "best" price, etc. The measure of "best" in these brand dimensions is the extent to which the available name, package, price, etc. alternatives most successfully support or harmonize with the agreed upon brand strategy (brand positioning). Consequently, what is "best" for one strategic opportunity might very possibly be wrong for every other brand position.

General Foods ultimately chose to position the dog food as a unique concept independent of canned dog foods based on Young and Rubicam's reasoning:

The size, form, general appearance and nonperishable nature of the product argue strongly in favor of a position which consciously and boldly attempts to dissociate itself from the established order of dog foods on the market — a position in its own right. Different in formulation, it is also different in intent.[14]

This positioning provided guidelines for advertising, packaging, and in-store promotions. Specifically, it meant:

1. A campaign directed at both canned and dry segments of the market;
2. Promotional appeals designed to create consumer wants or needs rather than tap those already in existence;
3. Reliance on one brand rather than on several "flanker" brands;
4. Selection of a brand name that would emphasize the new patty concept.

This example shows that all aspects of the marketing strategy will depend on product positioning. The importance of positioning is highlighted by the fact that inability to communicate new product concepts is one of the prime reasons cited by marketing management for a high failure rate in new product introductions.[15] Given the importance of brand image and positioning strategies in influencing consumer choice, Chapter 18 will further explore applications of product positioning.

Price Image

Perceptions of price will directly affect brand image. Numerous studies have shown that consumers associate higher price with higher quality.[16] This is especially true where product performance criteria may be lacking. Barring knowledge of product specifications, the purchaser of a stereo set or a rug may assume that higher price means better quality. There have been cases where brands could have been introduced at lower prices and would have met the investment criteria of marketers, but a fear of low quality perception resulted in introduction at a higher price.

One study found a strong relationship between price and quality for certain products and not for others.[17] Seven product categories were tested. Consumers were given a choice of three brands for each product category. The brands were identical in all respects except price. Respondents tended to pick the highest priced brand for stereos and tennis rackets, but not for toothpaste, suntan lotion, or coffee. Stereos and tennis rackets were the two products perceived as having the highest quality variation between brands. In the absence of product information, higher price connotes higher quality only if the consumer feels there is sufficient quality difference between brands. Suntan lotion, coffee, and toothpaste were seen as too standardized for a price quality image to apply.

Manufacturers attempt to create price inelasticity even if their brands are relatively undifferentiated. Bleach is a standardized product, yet Clorox's advertising campaign was successful in convincing many consumers that the brand is more effective, permitting Clorox to be sold for a few cents more than most other bleaches. Effectiveness in developing a strong brand image created a price quality association for a relatively undifferentiated brand.

Store Image

Consumers also develop store images based on advertising, merchandise in the store, opinions of friends and relatives, and shopping experiences. Store image will directly influence brand image. The identical product will be perceived quite differently in Woolco or Penney's compared to Nieman-Marcus or Bloomingdale's. In one study, four identical samples of carpet were given to consumers to evaluate.[18] Each sample was labeled with a higher or lower price and a more or less prestigious store. The samples with the higher price and from the more prestigious store were rated significantly higher on quality than samples with a low price from a prestigious store, or samples with a high price from a less prestigious store. In other words, the combination of a positive store *and* price image produced a positive brand image.

Consumers will tend to equate a store image and a brand image for private brands. Perceptions of a line of Sears major appliances will be governed by perceptions of the store. Perceptions of national brands sold on an exclusive franchise basis will also be closely tied to perceptions of the store. Automobile manufacturers attempt to exert control over their dealers in matters of showroom appearance and behavior of sales personnel. At times, dealers — as independent business persons — have resisted such control. The manufacturers' position is that having spent millions of dollars on product development and advertising, they want to ensure that the store's image will reinforce the positive brand image they are trying to create.

Corporate Image

Consumers also organize the variety of information about companies and experiences with a company's products into corporate images. Companies spend millions of dollars to improve their image with the public for several reasons. First, a positive corporate image will reinforce positive perceptions of the company's products. Such a link between corporate and brand image is particularly important when the brand name is closely associated with the company. General Electric will advertise itself as innovative and forward looking in the hope that the association will carry over to its brands. Such advertising is not as important for Procter and Gamble because the company does not link the brand closely to the corporate name.

Companies also seek to maintain a favorable image regarding public issues that may directly affect the consumer. The oil companies have engaged in heavy advertising to combat any negative image as a result of rapidly increasing gasoline prices. For example, Mobil has cited its developmental efforts in solar energy, coal-derived methanol, and petroleum exploration.

Myers and Reynolds equate corporate image to Gestalt concepts of figure and ground.[19] If a company's image is neutral, it is unlikely to affect brand image and becomes ground. If it is either positive or negative, it becomes figure and will determine the brand image. In this regard, a company's credibility will influence the impact of corporate advertising. The consumer who regards the oil companies as exploitative is unlikely to accept the message in the Mobil advertisement. The consumer who views gas prices as the result of foreign influences and inflation will be more receptive to the message.

Image of the Purchasing Process

So far, the focus in this chapter has been on consumer perceptions of marketing stimuli and the organization of these perceptions into brand, store, and company images. Consumers also develop perceptions of the purchasing process. For some consumers, the decision to buy a new car may be anxiety producing and may be perceived as a potentially risky decision. For others, it may be viewed as a relatively routine process with little risk. Once again, the basic concept is one of organization of stimuli. Consumers will view a decision as risky or not, depending on past experiences with the product and current information about the product.

The risk perceived in purchasing is a particularly important influence on consumer choice. The subject of perceived risk has direct strategic ramifications.

PERCEIVED RISK IN THE PURCHASING PROCESS

Consumers may be uncertain about the outcome of a choice between brands and may be concerned about the consequences of a poor decision. Therefore, two components of **perceived risk** are (1) uncertainty about the decision, and (2) the potential consequences of the decision.

Marketers often seek to gain competitive advantage by reducing the consumer's risk of purchasing their brand. Guarantees and warranties on major appliances and automobiles reduce the consumer's financial risk. Risks associated with the purchase of new products are high because of lack of information and prior experience. Many manufacturers offer free samples to provide experience. Risks for certain over-the-counter drugs are seen as high because of concern with health and possible side effects. Approval of the product by some government or private testing agency is often advertised as a means of reducing perceived risk. In all these cases, marketers attempt to reduce risks by (1) lowering the consequences of a loss — for example, by a warranty, or (2) increasing the certainty of the outcome — for example, by free samples or government testing.

Factors Associated with Perceived Risk

A number of factors are likely to increase the risk the consumer perceives in purchasing. Perceived risk is likely to be greater when:

- there is little information about the product category.
- there is little experience with brands in the product category.
- the product is technologically complex.
- the consumer has little self-confidence in evaluating brands.
- there are variations in quality between brands.
- the price is high.
- the purchase is important to the consumer.[20]

For example, consider the introduction of video-discs — that is, visual transcriptions on records or cartridges that can be played on television sets. As video-disc equipment is marketed, perceived risk in purchasing will be generally high because most of the above criteria will be met. Since the product category is completely new, there is little information by which to evaluate alternatives and little experience with brands in the product category. Moreover, the product is technologically complex, making evaluation more difficult. As a result, consumer confidence in selecting one brand over another is low. Furthermore, there is substantial variation between brands because several different systems are being introduced. The high price will also contribute to perceived risk. Finally, the purchase is probably important to the consumer because it represents a totally new concept in home entertainment.

Perceived risk is also likely to exist in the purchase of existing products. Consumer self-confidence in purchasing products such as cameras, stereo equipment, and carpeting has been low because the consumer lacks knowledge of the criteria by which to judge variations between brands and price. In an attempt to reduce risk consumers tend to rely on sources of information with a high degree of credibility, such as friends who have purchased the brand, or on impartial sources, such as *Consumer Reports*.

Types of Risk

The consumer faces various types of risk in purchasing decisions. These can be classified as financial, social, psychological, and performance risks.

Financial Risk

The degree of financial risk is a function of the consumer's marginal utility of money. The consumer that has saved for four years to buy a high priced car runs a much greater risk than the individual who can buy the same car out of discretionary income every two years. Financial risk is also associated with technological risk. Products that are technologically complex cost more and run a greater risk of failure, thus incurring the potential expense of repairs as well as the initial cost of the item.

Social Risk

Individuals are concerned about what others think; this concern is manifested in the risk that a purchase may not meet the standards of an important reference group. Visible items such as clothing, appliances, automobiles, and household furnishings are particularly subject to social risk. The purchase of cosmetics, deodorants, and mouthwash are subject to social risk because of fear that they may not work in enhancing attractiveness and social acceptability.

Psychological Risk

Consumers purchase some products to conform to their own self-image. Clothes, automobiles, or personal services may be selected for self-enhancement purposes.

The risk is that once the product is purchased, it may not be seen as conforming to the individual's self-concept. The suit does not look quite right; the automobile just does not have the right feel in driving; the favorite vacation spot was a little too noisy this year.

Performance Risk

There is some risk of product failure with almost any product purchased. Performance risk will be seen as greater when (1) the product is technically complex and (2) product performance is related to health and safety. Products such as cars, stereo sets, televisions, and large appliances involve a greater risk of product failure simply because a greater number of parts can misperform. Some products are dangerous to health or safety when they do not perform correctly: faulty brakes, a defective oil burner, a drug with unforeseen side effects, etc.

Consumer Predisposition to Take Risks

Certain consumers are more likely to take risks than others. The degree of risk taking depends on the consumer's personality and economic resources. The most obvious type of risk-taking behavior is the purchase of a new product before it is well established. Consumers who purchased an air conditioner, color TV, or stereo when they were first available incurred a substantially greater risk than those who purchased later. Such risk-taking behavior has been found to be associated with a number of consumer characteristics such as upward social mobility, higher income, and a greater need for achievement, change, and dominance.[21]

Popielarz associated risk taking with Type I and Type II errors in statistics.[22] A Type I error involves taking action when no action is warranted (an actual loss); whereas, a Type II error involves taking no action when action is warranted (an opportunity loss). The high risk taker is more willing to make a Type I error. He or she is risking subsequent product failure in an attempt to achieve maximum enjoyment in the purchase of a new product. The low risk taker is unwilling to incur a Type I error and would prefer to minimize the possibility of product failure by waiting until the product is established. Borrowing a line from Shakespeare, the high risk taker may agree, "Tis better to have loved and lost than never to have loved at all," while the low risk taker would probably say, "Tis better not to have loved at all than to risk the possibility of rejection." Popielarz tested this relationship and found that consumers with a higher propensity for a Type I error were more willing to incur the risk of new product failure.

Schiffman examined the risk predispositions in buying a new food product among elderly consumers.[23] He measured predisposition toward a Type I or Type II error by asking "Who is a wiser consumer: (1) a person who tries a new food product which turns out to have a poor taste or (2) a person who does not try a new food product and later learns it has a good taste?" He also measured the willingness to incur the risk of buying immediately by asking, "Do you prefer to: (1) try a new food product when it first comes out, or (2) wait and learn how good it is before trying it?"

These two measures were related to adoption by households of a new salt substitute. Consumers predisposed toward a Type I error (based on the first question) and those who were early adopters (based on the second question) were more likely to have tried the new product.

Strategies of Risk Reduction

Both marketers and consumers engage in strategies to reduce risk perceived in the purchasing process. These strategies are categorized in Table 6–1 into (1) strategies marketers use to reduce the consumer's risk and (2) strategies consumers initiate to reduce risk.

Marketer Controlled Strategies

Marketers can reassure consumers prior to purchasing by either reducing the consequences of product failure or by increasing the certainty that the product will perform adequately. Reducing the consequences of failure for the consumer can be accomplished by offering warranties, money-back guarantees, and liberal return policies for defective merchandise (see Table 6–1). Offering products at lower prices or in smaller packages minimizes the consumer's risk in trying a product for the first time.

Marketers can also attempt to increase the certainty of the purchase outcome. Endorsements by experts might assure consumers of the certainty of product performance for product categories when purchase self-confidence is low. Free samples give the consumer the opportunity to try new products before a purchase commitment. The most common strategy to increase certainty is that of the marketer conveying sufficient information to provide the consumer with a sound basis for choice. Technical specifications on performance, complete labeling of ingredients, nutritional information, and unit pricing are all means of providing the consumer with more information to better judge product performance. A key question is whether manufacturers will provide such information voluntarily without pressure from government agencies such as the Federal Trade Commission.

Consumer Initiated Strategies

The most common means of reducing the consequence of product failure is to buy the lowest priced item or the smallest size (see Table 6–1). Another strategy is to reduce the level of expectation before making the purchase. A purchaser who decides that cars are a necessary evil that inevitably produce mechanical failures and repair bills is not going to be terribly disappointed if his or her car does not perform well; he or she expects it. Although the financial and performance risk may not have been reduced, the psychological and social risks have been eliminated.

Brand loyalty is a common means of reducing risk because the consumer knows what to expect from the product based on past experience. The best way to avoid the possibility of dissatisfaction is to stay with a reasonably acceptable alternative. This is apparent in industrial, as well as in consumer, buying behavior. Risk reduction frequently results in staying loyal to the same vendor

TABLE 6–1 Methods of Reducing Risk

Marketer Controlled Strategies

Reduce the consequences of failure by:

- offering better or longer warranties;
- offering money-back guarantees;
- offering liberal return policies;
- offering a low priced alternative;
- offering a small package size.

Increase the certainty of the purchase outcome by:

- providing free samples for new products;
- providing endorsements by experts;
- providing government or private testing;
- providing complete performance information;
- providing complete ingredient information.

Consumer Initiated Strategies

Reduce the consequences of failure by:

- buying a lower priced brand;
- buying smaller amounts;
- reducing the expectations regarding performance before the purchase.

Increase the certainty of the purchase outcome by:

- buying the same brand;
- buying a popular brand;
- seeking additional information;
- having greater prepurchase deliberation (e.g., comparison shopping).

---

for years, even though other sources of supply may be less costly. The perceived risk of change by the purchasing agent involves new associations and greater uncertainty.

Buying the most popular brand is also a safe strategy. A consumer may spend a few cents more for an analgesic or vitamin produced by a well-known company. There may be some cost savings in buying a private brand or a brand produced by a lesser known manufacturer, but the perceived safety risks may be too high. Similarly, given a lack of information, purchasing the most popular brand is the best means of increasing the certainty of the outcome. Consumers purchasing appliances, television sets, or stereos may lack confidence in comparing brands. Claims that a certain brand is the largest seller or a leading brand may be attempts to influence prospective buyers by assuring them that millions of fellow consumers cannot be wrong.

The alternative to playing it safe is to seek out additional information. A consumer that perceives social risk in buying a suit or dress may seek the opinion of friends and relatives before making a decision. An individual who sees performance risk in purchasing a car will seek information from impersonal sources such as *Consumer Reports*.

Perceived risk may encourage more extensive prepurchase deliberation, but certain consumers may not be predisposed to take the time and make the effort required for extensive information search or comparison shopping. Buying the most popular brand or remaining loyal to a given brand may provide greater savings in time but possibly at a higher cost.

Several studies have examined consumer risk reduction strategies. Roselius asked housewives to rate eleven different strategies for reducing financial, psychological, and performance risk. Brand loyalty and buying a well-known brand were rated highest in reducing all types of risk. Free samples and comparison shopping were also considered effective in reducing financial and psychological risks.[24]

Sheth and Venkatesan studied consumer risk reduction strategies in selecting a hair spray.[25] Two groups were formed: a high risk group which was told it could select a hair spray from relatively unknown brands and a low risk group which was told it could select a hair spray from nationally advertised brands. Information seeking and prepurchase deliberation were significantly greater for the high risk group. Further, the high risk group tended to rely more on personal sources for information compared to the low risk group.

SUMMARY

Consumer perceptions of brands impact directly on marketing strategy. In this chapter, the two processes of consumer perception — selective perception and perceptual organization — are considered from a strategic perspective.

Selective perception provides at least three guidelines for advertising strategy. First, the process of selectivity suggests that, at times, advertisers may wish to introduce a certain amount of ambiguity in their communications to permit advertisements to have different meaning to different consumers. Second, selectivity sometimes causes consumers to avoid anxiety-producing stimuli such as fear appeals. Consumers have rejected such appeals as a threat because they would rather not think about the intended message. Fear appeals may be more successful if the degree of anxiety is moderate rather than great.

Third, selective perception may cause consumers to justify a purchase despite negative information about a brand. The strategic implication is to give the consumer support that justifies the consumer's decision after the purchase through advertising or direct mail.

The principles of perceptual organization also have strategic applications. Consumers organize marketing information into images of brands, price, stores, and companies. The brand's image has the most direct impact on purchase behavior. To positively influence brand image marketers try to position their product by developing product concepts that communicate the desired benefits. Marketers try to create a price image by establishing a price/quality association, even for relatively standardized brands. The store image will also influence the brand image, particularly for brands that are distributed selectively. The corporate image affects purchasing behavior, particularly for family brands that are tied to the company name.

The chapter concludes by considering the consumer's perception of the purchasing process. Consumers frequently perceive risk in purchasing a product for two reasons: (1) they experience uncertainty of the outcome of the purchase and (2) they are concerned about the consequences of the decision. Both marketers and consumers attempt to reduce risk by various strategies that increase certainty about performance and/or decrease the possibility of the product's not fulfilling expectations.

The next chapter shifts the focus on the individual consumer from the process of perception to the nature of consumer needs and attitudes.

QUESTIONS

1. Can you cite examples of advertising campaigns that have sought to introduce some degree of ambiguity?

2. Assume the Department of Energy introduces a campaign to conserve energy based on fear related appeals (dependence on foreign oil, necessity for gas rationing, etc.).
   - Is such a campaign likely to be successful? Why or why not?

3. The introduction of video-discs will involve two competitive systems: one introduced by RCA, the other by MCA. A consumer buying one system may easily experience postpurchase doubts, thinking perhaps the other should have been purchased.
   - What strategies would you recommend for either RCA or MCA to attempt to reduce postpurchase dissonance among consumers who bought their system?

4. The focus in this and the previous chapter has been on selective perceptions by consumers of marketing stimuli. But, do marketers sometimes perceive consumers selectively? That is, do they sometimes seek out information to confirm their own marketing strategies?
   - Cite examples of selective perceptions of consumers on the part of (a) marketers, (b) retailers, and (c) salespeople.

5. The statement is made that "a change in a single component of a brand may totally change the image of a commonplace product."
   - Can you cite an example of a change in a brand producing a positive influence on the brand's image?
   - A change in a brand may be made to attract a new or broader segment of the market, but in so doing alienate another more important segment of users. Can you cite an example of such a change resulting in negative consequences on the brand image?

6. Why are certain companies that do not sell directly to the final consumer (e.g., U.S. Steel) concerned with the corporate image they project to the consuming public?

7. Should the marketer introducing a new, high priced product purposefully aim the initial introductory effort to risk takers? What are the pros and cons of such a strategy?

8. What strategies have you used to (1) reduce the consequences of failure and (2) increase the certainty of the outcome in (a) buying a car and (b) selecting a business school?

9. Is there a general risk taker across product categories? If so, what are the likely characteristics of the general risk taker?

RESEARCH ASSIGNMENTS

1. Select two advertising campaigns that are informationally oriented and two that rely on symbolism and imagery and can be regarded as more ambiguous. Then select a sample of consumers and measure (a) unaided advertising awareness for the four brands and (b) awareness of key points in the advertising message.

   - Was awareness of the informationally oriented campaign more accurate than that of the more ambiguous campaign?

   - Were consumers more likely to project themes and messages not actually in the ads into the more ambiguous communications? If so, what was the nature of these projections?

   - Did you detect any misperception or misinterpretation of the advertising messages? Did these misperceptions reflect perceptual defense?

2. Some studies have compared perceived risk across product categories. For example, Jacoby and Kaplan studied the risk perceived by college students in the purchase of twelve product categories such as cars, life insurance, color TV sets, clothing items, and pharmaceutical products.* Based on the references in this chapter, develop a measure of perceived risk which incorporates measures about (1) the uncertainty of product performance and (2) the consequences of a product not meeting consumer expectations. Also measure the respondent's self-confidence in selecting a brand in the product category. Select a sample of college students and apply the measure of perceived risk and self-confidence to four or five product categories.

   - What are the variations in perceived risk between product categories?

   - What are the variations in perceived risk between students? That is, do certain individuals see less risk than others (i.e., risk-takers). If so, are there any differences in characteristics (e.g., frequency of use of the product categories, brands purchased, needs emphasized) between those who tend to see more risk versus those who tend to see less risk?

* Jacob Jacoby and Leon B. Kaplan, "The Components of Perceived Risk," in M. Venkatesan, ed., *Proceedings of the Third Annual Conference of the Association for Consumer Research* (1972), pp. 382–393.

1. "Baby's Business," *Newsweek,* March 21, 1977, p. 72.

2. "Study Finds Nonsmokers Living 2 Years More by Heeding Alerts," *New York Times,* September 22, 1979, p. 6.

3. W.J. McGuire, *Effectiveness of Appeals In Advertising* (New York: Advertising Research Foundation, 1963).

4. John R. Stuteville, "Psychic Defense Against High Fear Appeals: A Key Marketing Variable," *Journal of Marketing* 34 (April 1970): 39–45.

5. Michael L. Ray and William Wilkie, "Fear: The Potential of an Appeal Neglected by Marketing," *Journal of Marketing* 34. (January 1970): 54–62.

6. James H. Donnelly, Jr. and John M. Ivancevich, "Post-Purchase Reinforcement and Back-Out Behavior," *Journal of Marketing Research* 7 (August 1970): 399–400.

7. David A. Aaker and John G. Myers, *Advertising Management* (Englewood Cliffs, N.J.: Prentice-Hall, 1975), p. 280.

8. James F. Engel, Roger D. Blackwell, and David T. Kollat, *Consumer Behavior,* 3rd ed. (Hinsdale, Ill.: The Dryden Press, 1978), p. 359.

9. Milton I. Brand, "What Is a New Product?" in Milton I. Brand and Alfred Gruber, eds., *The Professionals Look at New Products,* Michigan Business Papers #30, Bureau of Business Research, University of Michigan, 1969, p. 11.

10. Pierre Martineau, *Motivation in Advertising* (New York: McGraw-Hill, 1957), p. 114.

11. Irving S. White, "The Perception of Value in Products," in Joseph W. Newman, ed., *On Knowing the Consumer* (New York: John Wiley & Sons, 1966), p. 94.

12. Ibid., p. 93.

13. Intercollegiate Clearing House, *General Foods — Post Division (B),* Harvard Business School, 1964, pp. 1–40.

14. Ibid., p. 15.

15. Brand, "What Is a New Product?"

16. See Douglas J. McConnell, "Effect of Pricing on Perception of Product Quality," *Journal of Applied Psychology* 52 (August 1968): 331–334; and Folke Olander, "The Influence of Price on the Consumer's Evaluation of Products and Purchases," in B. Taylor and G. Wills, eds., *Pricing Strategy* (Staples Press, 1969), pp. 50–69.

17. Zarrell V. Lambert, "Product Perception: An Important Variable in Pricing Strategy," *Journal of Marketing* 34 (October 1970): 68–71.

18. Ben M. Enis and James E. Stafford, "Consumers' Perception of Product Quality as a Function of Various Informational Inputs," in Phillip R. McDonald, ed., *Marketing Involvement in Society and the Economy,* Proceedings, American Marketing Association, series no. 30 (1969), pp. 340–344.

19. James H. Myers and William H. Reynolds, *Consumer Behavior and Marketing Management* (Boston: Houghton Mifflin Company, 1967), p. 31.

20. James R. Bettman, "Perceived Risk and its Components: A Model and Empirical Test," *Journal of Marketing Research* 10 (May 1973): 184–190.

21. Thomas S. Robertson, "The Touch-Tone Telephone: Diffusion of an Innovation," in Roger D. Blackwell, James F. Engel, and David T. Kollat, *Cases in Consumer Behavior* (New York: Holt, Rinehart & Winston, 1969), pp. 274–297.

22. Donald T. Popielarz, "An Exploration of Perceived Risk and Willingness to Try New Products," *Journal of Marketing Research* 4 (November 1967): 368–372.

23. Leon G. Schiffman, " Perceived Risk in New Product Trial by Elderly Consumers," *Journal of Marketing Research* 9 (February 1972): 106–108.

24. Ted Roselius, "Consumer Rankings of Risk Reduction Methods," *Journal of Marketing* 35 (January 1971): 56–61.

25. Jagdish N. Sheth and M. Venkatesan, "Risk-Reduction Processes in Repetitive Consumer Behavior," *Journal of Marketing Research* 5 (August 1968): 307–310.

SEVEN

Consumer Attitudes and Needs

FOCUS OF CHAPTER

Attitudes and needs are an important influence on consumer behavior. In this chapter, brand attitudes and consumer needs are examined from the consumer's and the marketing manager's perspectives. The nature, function, and development of brand attitudes and the components of consumer needs are described. Research that establishes a relation between brand attitudes and purchasing behavior is cited. Also, attitude structure models, particularly multiattribute models, are given. These models provide a basis by which marketers can identify consumer needs, evaluate a brand's strength or weakness on relevant product attributes, and develop guidelines for advertising and product positioning. The relationship between attitudes, needs, and marketing strategies is a consistent theme throughout this chapter.

THE NATURE OF ATTITUDES AND NEEDS

The most frequently used definition of attitudes was formulated by Gordon Allport almost fifty years ago. He wrote, "Attitudes are learned predispositions to respond to an object or class of objects in a consistently favorable or unfavorable way."[1] **Attitudes** toward brands are consumers' tendencies to evaluate brands in a consistently favorable or unfavorable way. This evaluation is based on past experience with a brand, current information, and environmental influences. The model of complex decision making referred to attitudes as a central component of the consumer's psychological set and one of the two thought variables.

The other thought variable is needs. **Needs** are directed toward achieving specific goals. Attitudes make it possible to evaluate alternative brands; needs direct the consumer to one brand or another.

Multidimensional Nature

Recently, the definition of attitudes has been extended from a one-dimensional measure (brand A being evaluated on an overall basis from poor to excellent) to a multidimensional concept. Marketers recognize that consumers do not evaluate a brand as good or bad alone; they judge brands on a number of evaluative dimensions. A consumer may formulate three needs in purchasing a cereal: nutrition, weight watching, and natural ingredients. These needs are translated into evaluative attributes, like vitamin content, number of calories, and whole-bran content. Attitudes toward brands will depend on the degree to which brands have these attributes and on the value which is placed on these attributes.

The degree to which a brand has the attributes wanted by a consumer is called **perceived instrumentality** (e.g., the extent to which a certain brand of cereal is instrumental in achieving nutrition, weight control, or natural ingredients). The value placed on each attribute depends on the consumer's emphasis on each attribute. Both value and instrumentality determine whether the consumer is satisfied by the attribute. Therefore, the consumer's attitude toward a brand depends on the instrumentality of the brand in achieving certain needs and on the value of these needs. This newer multidimensional definition of attitudes[2] is the basis of many of the multiattribute models considered later in this chapter. **Multiattribute models** measure attitudes on a multidimensional basis by determining how consumers evaluate brands across product attributes (e.g., consumers would rate cereals on good taste, freshness, opening convenience, etc.). The sum of these ratings weighted by the value which is placed on each attribute would represent the consumer's attitude toward the brand.

The validity of a multidimensional definition of attitudes is demonstrated in a study by Woodside et al.[3] Brand attitudes were measured on a multidimensional basis by product attributes and on a one-dimensional basis by obtaining a simple, overall evaluation of the brand. It was found that the multiattribute measure of brand attitudes was significantly more related to consumer behavior than the single measure.

ATTITUDES AND THE DEVELOPMENT OF MARKETING STRATEGY

Consumer needs are defined to identify market opportunity. But why should marketers also be interested in defining and measuring attitudes toward their brands? Because attitudes can help predict consumer behavior, describe consumer segments, and evelute marketing strategies.

Predict Consumer Behavior

Underlying attitude measurement is the assumption that attitudes are related to behavior. The more a consumer favors a brand, the greater the likelihood he or she will purchase it. Attitudes are a measure of inclinations to purchase. Therefore, a positive trend in an attitude forecasts an increase in sales.

Describe Consumer Segments

Identifying both needs and attitudes can be useful in describing consumer segments. Segments are frequently based on need criteria. For example, in the cereal market, certain consumers primarily emphasize nutrition, others good taste, price, or caloric content. A company introducing a new cereal wants to target its promotions toward one or two of these segments depending on the positioning strategy. A brand emphasizing vitamin content would direct its marketing effort primarily to the nutrition segment and secondarily to weight watchers. A brand emphasizing low calories would do the reverse.

Consumer segments can also be described in terms of brand attitudes. Certain consumers may favorably view a brand yet not purchase it because of a high price, lack of availability, or loyalty to another brand. These consumers are what Wind refers to as the vulnerable segment; that is, they are vulnerable to the company's promotional influences due to positive attitudes toward the brand.[4] Identifying the demographic characteristics of this segment may permit the company to use media most likely to reach this group. Research into their needs may permit development of more effective promotional and product positioning strategies.

Evaluate Marketing Strategies

As a diagnostic consumer measure, brand attitudes are used in evaluating:

- new product concepts;
- products in test markets prior to launch;
- product effectiveness over time;
- advertising messages prior to introduction; and,
- advertising effectiveness over time.

Attitudes are critical in evaluating alternative positionings for **new product concepts.** For example, a Picturephone could be positioned as a more cost-effective substitute for sales trips, a more accurate means of communication, or a means of ensuring dependable communications. The proper positioning depends on the needs of a defined target group and how it rates the various key product attributes like speed, precision, or control. A new product concept must be rated on key evaluative criteria using a multiattribute approach. The marketer will then try to position the product to be rated favorably on the criteria important to the target group.

Similarly, products must be rated on these same evaluative criteria when they are introduced into a **test market** prior to launch, as well as when they have been on the market for some time. Evaluating a description of a Picturephone is different from evaluating the product in use. Marketers must determine if the product has successfully delivered on the key criteria. The product's evaluation may also change over time as customers' needs change and new products enter the market. Periodic reassessments of product attitudes are essential.

Attitudes also are important in evaluating the *effectiveness of advertising messages*. Television commercials and print ads are frequently judged by how large and how favorable an attitude shift they produce. Brand attitudes are measured before and after exposure to a commercial in a controlled environment. Overall changes in attitudes as well as changes in specific criteria related to product positioning are used to evaluate the commercials' effectiveness.

Attitudes are also used in evaluating *advertising campaigns over time* in order to determine whether attitudes are being maintained, or whether an increasing number of consumers are shifting brand attitudes favorably or unfavorably. Advertising campaigns may have attitude change as a specific objective. Cadillac's introduction of a medium-sized car required careful tracking by the company to determine whether such a change would alienate its core market by weakening associations with prestige. The ad campaign required a modification of beliefs (Cadillac is no longer a large car) without creation of an unfavorable shift in attitudes (Cadillac still represents prestige and luxury).

In considering the role of attitudes in developing marketing strategies one point to remember is that attitudes are more effective in evaluating high involvement products. For low involvement products, a highly favorable, strongly held attitude may not be a necessary condition for purchase.

ATTITUDE RESEARCH BEFORE AND AFTER 1970

This chapter emphasizes a multiattribute approach in measuring attitudes. Multiattribute models gained prominence in marketing after 1970. Before then, the focus was more on the relationship between attitudes and behavior. Attitudes were defined in a one-dimensional manner. Marketers tried to relate attitudes to behavior to demonstrate their predictive powers. The results were mixed. Marketers came to realize that attitudes influenced behavior under certain conditions only. If they were to have diagnostic value in influencing strategy, attitudes had to be measured multidimensionally.

The realization that attitudes may not influence behavior was largely the result of Festinger's work in cognitive dissonance[5] and Krugman's work in passive learning.[6] Both theories tended to downplay the importance of attitudes as a determinant of future behavior. Attitudes could result from previous behavior as well as influence future behavior. After 1970, the work of Rosenberg[7] and Fishbein[8] came into increasing prominence in marketing. Both saw attitudes as the result of a process by which consumers evaluated brands on a number of criteria linked to consumer needs. This multiattribute approach was well suited to the needs of marketers since they had long recognized that consumers evaluate brands on specific attributes.

As a result, the primary focus was on determining the structure of attitudes. Attitudes were regarded as multidimensional and were thought to be more relevant for high involvement products and for products where the choice criteria were more apparent.

Later sections of this chapter will describe the emphasis on the attitude-to-behavior link prior to 1970 and the emphasis on multiattribute models after 1970. Before considering these two streams of consumer research, it is important to understand the functions that attitudes serve and how attitudes develop.

FUNCTIONS OF ATTITUDES

Understanding the **functions of attitudes** requires understanding how they serve the individual. Daniel Katz classified attitudes[9] into these four functions:

1. the utilitarian function;
2. the value-expressive function;
3. the ego-defensive function; and,
4. the organization of knowledge function.

The Utilitarian Function

As a utilitarian function, attitudes serve to guide consumers in achieving desired needs. For example, if a consumer considers safety and immediate relief the most important criteria in selecting an analgesic, the consumer will be directed to brands that fulfill these needs. In the utilitarian role, attitudes will also direct consumers away from brands unlikely to fulfill their needs.

Lutz notes that media advertising is consistent with the utilitarian function by featuring performance characteristics.[10] In Table 7–1 he summarizes examples of advertising's use of each function. The theme "Crest whitens teeth" is an example of the utilitarian function. If a consumer values white teeth, then the appeal serves to enhance the utility of the brand.

The Value-Expressive Function

Attitudes express a self-concept and value system. The self-image of an individual purchasing a sports car, for example, may be of a hard driving, domineering person who likes to gain the upper hand. Aggressiveness may manifest

TABLE 7–1 Advertising Directed Toward the Four Attitude Functions

Function	Advertising Message
Utilitarian	"Crest whitens teeth."
Value-expressive	"Pepsi drinkers think young."
Ego-defensive	"Marlboro smokers are masculine."
Organization of knowledge	"Pringles potato chips are different."

Source: Adapted from Richard J. Lutz, "A Functional Theory Framework for Designing and Pretesting Advertising Themes" in John C. Maloney and Bernard Silverman, eds., *Attitude Research Plays for High Stakes* (Chicago: American Marketing Association, 1979), p. 43.

itself in purchasing a car that fits this image. Likewise, the individual who adopts an organizational code of conformity and dresses in a conservative manner has accepted the values of conservatism and wealth as expressions of success.

Advertisers often appeal to the value-expressive nature of attitudes by implying that use or purchase of a certain item will lead to self-enhancement, achievement, or independence. In this manner, advertisers are appealing to a large segment who value these self-expressive traits. An example of an ad serving a value-expressive function is "Pepsi drinkers think young." To the extent that youth is highly valued, the theme serves a value-expressive function.

The Ego-Defensive Function

Attitudes protect the ego from anxieties and threats. Many products, like mouthwashes, are purchased to avoid anxiety-producing situations. Most individuals use mouthwashes to avoid bad breath rather than to cure it. Advertising capitalizes on the fears of social ostracism by demonstrating greater social acceptance through use of certain products. As a result, consumers develop positive attitudes toward brands associated with social acceptance, confidence, and sexual desirability.

Advertising appeals to the ego-defensive nature of attitudes by demonstrating the benefits of product usage or the risks of nonusage. An example of an ego-defensive ad in Table 7–1 is the implication that "Marlboro smokers are masculine." Marlboro ads may appeal to men who value masculinity and wish to demonstrate it through product purchases.

The Organization of Knowledge Function

Attitudes organize the mass of information consumers are exposed to daily and help set up standards on which to judge the information. The consumer sorts all the messages, ignoring the less relevant information in favor of other information more relevant to his or her needs. The organization of knowledge function reduces uncertainty and confusion. Advertising that provides information about new brands or new characteristics of existing brands is valuable for the information it provides. The advertisement "Pringles potato chips are different" is an expression of the knowledge function if it provides information on the relative merit of Pringles compared to other brands.

In summary, attitudes do have different functions. The function that is served will affect the individual's overall evaluation of an object.[11] For example, two individuals having equally favorable attitudes toward Bayer aspirin will vary markedly in the nature of these attitudes depending on whether they reflect a utilitarian function (Bayer provides quick relief) or an ego-defensive function (The more I take aspirin, the more likely I am to draw attention to myself.)

ATTITUDE DEVELOPMENT

Attitudes develop over time through a learning process that is affected by family influences, peer group influences, information and experience, and personality.

Family Influences

The family is an important influence on purchase decisions. Regardless of the tendency to rebel in the teenage years, there is a high correlation between the attitudes of parents and their children. As Bennett and Kassarjian have said; "Attitudes toward personal hygiene, preferences for food items, attitudes toward boiled vegetables or fried food, and beliefs about the medicinal value of chicken soup are similarly acquired [from parents]."[12]

This influence is demonstrated in some advertising themes. For instance, Johnson and Johnson has advertised its baby powder by portraying a mother using it on her daughter's wedding day and tearfully reminiscing about its earlier use. Parental influence is especially apparent in attitudes toward candy. If candy was used as a punishment or reward in childhood, in later years adults have subconscious guilt feelings about eating candy.[13] Some advertising tries to alleviate guilt feelings by making positive associations with candy.

Peer Group Influences

Many studies have shown pervasive group influence on purchasing behavior. Katz and Lazarsfeld found peer groups are much more likely to influence attitudes and purchasing behavior than is advertising.[14] Coleman found that socially integrated doctors who valued peer group norms accepted a new drug faster.[15] Arndt found socially integrated consumers accepted a new coffee product sooner.[16] In each study, product attitudes were influenced by group norms. Advertising demonstrates the beneficial aspects of conforming to group standards by associating a brand's image with social acceptability.

Information and Experience

Past experiences influence brand attitudes. According to learning theory, such experiences condition future behavior. But, brand loyalty will quickly end if the brand does not peform sufficiently. Therefore, information is also an important attitude determinant. Knowing that a product has a newer, faster acting formula may induce a consumer to switch.

Personality

The consumer's personality affects attitudes. Traits such as aggression, extroversion, submissiveness, or authoritarianism may influence attitudes toward brands and products. Contrary to the norms of the peer group, an aggressive consumer may buy an expensive sports car to manifest aggression by driving a car with speed and pickup. In such a case, attitudes toward the car are a function of personality rather than group influence.

ATTITUDE COMPONENTS

As previously mentioned, three components establish consumer attitudes. These components are (a) **beliefs** (the cognitive component); (b) brand evaluation (the affective component); and, (c) the tendency to act (the behavioral component). Each component will be looked at in more detail.

Beliefs

What consumers believe about a brand becomes the characteristics they ascribe to the brand. There are two types of beliefs: informational beliefs and evaluative beliefs. Informational beliefs are associated with product attributes (e.g., gas mileage or horsepower). Evaluative beliefs are associated with product benefits (e.g., economy, roominess). Benefits are a basis for defining opportunity (is there a segment emphasizing nutrition? what is its size?); for positioning a new product (can a new beverage be introduced to appeal to this segment?); and, for developing advertising strategy (what symbols, ideas, and messages will communicate nutrition for the whole family?).

Through marketing research, marketers develop a vocabulary of product attributes and benefits similar to the vocabulary developed by a large food company for a beverage (see Table 7–2).

These vocabularies are based on the results of a series of **depth interviews** with consumers. Once a vocabulary of product attributes and benefits is established, it is included in a questionnaire and a consumer survey is conducted in which respondents are asked to rate brands utilizing the vocabulary. Thus, a study of soft drinks may involve asking consumers to rate various brands on the criteria listed in Table 7–2.

Brand Evaluation

The second attitude component represents the consumer's overall evaluation of the brand. Beliefs about a brand are multidimensional because they represent the various brand attributes the consumer perceives. In contrast to this, the affective dimension is one-dimensional. A consumer's overall evaluation of a brand can be measured by rating it from poor to excellent or from prefer least to prefer most.

Ordinarily, when attitudes are referred to without further elaboration, it is the affective component that is being referred to. Research attempting to link attitudes to behavior generally relied on a one-dimensional measure representing the affective component. It was only after 1970, when the multiattribute models started to be applied, that the measurement of beliefs assumed a more important role in attitude research.

TABLE 7–2 Vocabulary of Brand Beliefs for a Beverage Product

Product Attributes	*Product Benefits*
caloric content	good at mealtimes
vitamin content	refreshing
natural ingredients	good for the whole family
sweetness	gives a lift
bitterness	thirst quenching
aftertaste	restores energy
carbonation	nutritional

Tendency to Act

The third attitude component is the consumer's predisposition to act toward an object, and this is generally measured in terms of intention to buy. Measuring buying intent is particularly important in developing marketing strategy. Marketing managers frequently test the components of the marketing mix — alternative product concepts, ads, packages, or brand names — to determine what most effectively influences purchase behavior. Tests of these alternatives are conducted under artificially controlled circumstances which try to hold all factors constant except the alternative marketing stimuli being tested. Consumers viewing alternative ads or trying alternative product formulations are asked about their intentions to buy. The alternative producing the highest buying intent is regarded as the best choice. In the absence of actual buying behavior, management relies on the closest substitute to determine the effectiveness of the components of the marketing mix.

The Relationship Between the Components

In the traditional hierarchy of effects, beliefs influence brand evaluations which then influence behavior. As was noted in Chapter 4, this traditional association is more likely to be true under conditions involving complex or high involvement decision making. The traditional hierarchy is more relevant to attitude research because it is assumed that attitudes (as measured by beliefs and brand evaluations) influence behavior — an assumption then incorporated into strategy formulation. If consumers act according to the traditional hierarchy, management then must identify the beliefs most likely to influence brand evaluations and behavior.

Alpert refers to beliefs that influence subsequent steps in the hierarchy as **determinant** since they determine preference and purchase behavior.[17] He uses the following example:

> Both owners and nonowners of, say, Buicks probably hold comparable opinions about the car's safety, but differ in opinions about handling ability, appearance, and other traits. Thus, it would make more sense to promote the latter attributes rather than safety, which probably strikes most people as being equally present in most cars and, therefore, is not used as a basis of selection.[18]

As an example of the importance of determinant beliefs, assume a company tests a new hair conditioner concept and finds that practically everyone rates the brand high on "leaves hair clean," but only those who are likely to buy rate the brand high on "manageability." Leaves hair clean is not a determinant belief, but manageability is since it is likely to influence brand evaluations and behavior. The company now produces the product on a limited basis and conducts a product test. The brand is no longer rated high on manageability because when it was used, women did not find the brand made their hair more manageable. The link between belief and preference for a determinant attribute — manageability — has been broken. The actual product failed to deliver the promise of manageability which was made in the concept description.

The brand is sent back to research and development in an attempt to improve manageability. After modification, further use tests show the revised product is rated higher on manageability as well as on overall preference. The brand is now introduced into test markets and data are gathered on brand attitudes among users and nonusers. The survey shows that users rate the brand significantly higher on the key determinant attribute — manageability. The decision is then made to go national and base the advertising campaign on this benefit.

This example supports the traditional hierarchy: Beliefs about the brand (defined by the determinant attribute) influence the overall evaluation of the brand which then influences choice. There is sufficient evidence in marketing studies to suggest that such a belief/evaluation/behavior link exists and is important enough to justify the attention marketers pay to attitudes.[19]

Consistency Between the Components

Research supports the idea that there is a consistency between beliefs, brand evaluations, and behavior. This theory is known in psychology as **balance** or **consistency theory.** This theory maintains that the evaluation of an object is a function of consistently held beliefs about the object. The belief that the new hair conditioner is manageable is consistent with a favorable evaluation of the brand.

According to Rosenberg, when beliefs and evaluations are not in balance, such "affective-cognitive inconsistency is reduced or eliminated [through a] general attitude reorganization."[20] Such a reorganization will occur in one of two ways: a change in beliefs will lead to a change in brand evaluation, or a change in brand evaluation will lead to a change in beliefs.

Continuing with the example above, a loyal user of the new hair conditioner is told by a friend it makes her hair greasy. This information is inconsistent with the user's beliefs. If the user accepts the new information, her feelings toward the brand will become increasingly negative and she will be less likely to buy it again. This would conform to Rosenberg's first proposition — a change in beliefs leads to a change in brand evaluations. A second proposition suggests that a change in brand evaluations leads to a change in beliefs about the brand. The purchaser of the new hair conditioner receives a raise and now goes to a hair dresser regularly. She becomes indifferent to the new hair conditioner and, as a result, no longer sees it as the best means of obtaining manageability and a better set. In this case, changes in evaluation and behavior preceded changes in beliefs.

The principles of balance and equilibrium need not apply to every purchasing situation. A consumer may buy a new brand out of boredom. The consumer's beliefs do not change, yet his or her behavior changes due to a search for variety. This type of behavior is much harder for the marketing manager to evaluate. There is little diagnostic information to go on if consumers switch brands for the sake of variety alone. Only when belief/evaluation/behavior links can be established can the implications for marketing strategy be direct.

NEED COMPONENTS

Overall brand evaluation does not just depend on brand beliefs. It depends on beliefs that are related to consumer needs. In other words, the belief that Pepsi is a light soft drink is unlikely to influence the overall evaluation of the brand or subsequent behavior if the consumer does not care if a soft drink is light or heavy. Therefore, brand attitudes must be considered in conjunction with consumer needs. The traditional hierarchy of effects can be restated as shown in Figure 7–1. The relationship between brand beliefs and consumer needs will determine the favorable or unfavorable evaluation of the brand; the brand's evaluation will then determine the action tendency.

Consumer needs are made up of two components: *direction* and *intensity*. Direction refers to the nature of the need. On a continuum from mild to strong, some consumers may prefer a mild coffee, some a moderately strong coffee, others a very strong coffee. Intensity refers to the importance of needs to the individual. The degree to which a coffee is strong or mild may be a critical attribute for one individual but relatively unimportant for another. If a consumer defines direction of need as a strong coffee, if he or she considers this an

FIGURE 7–1   A Traditional Hierarchy of Effects

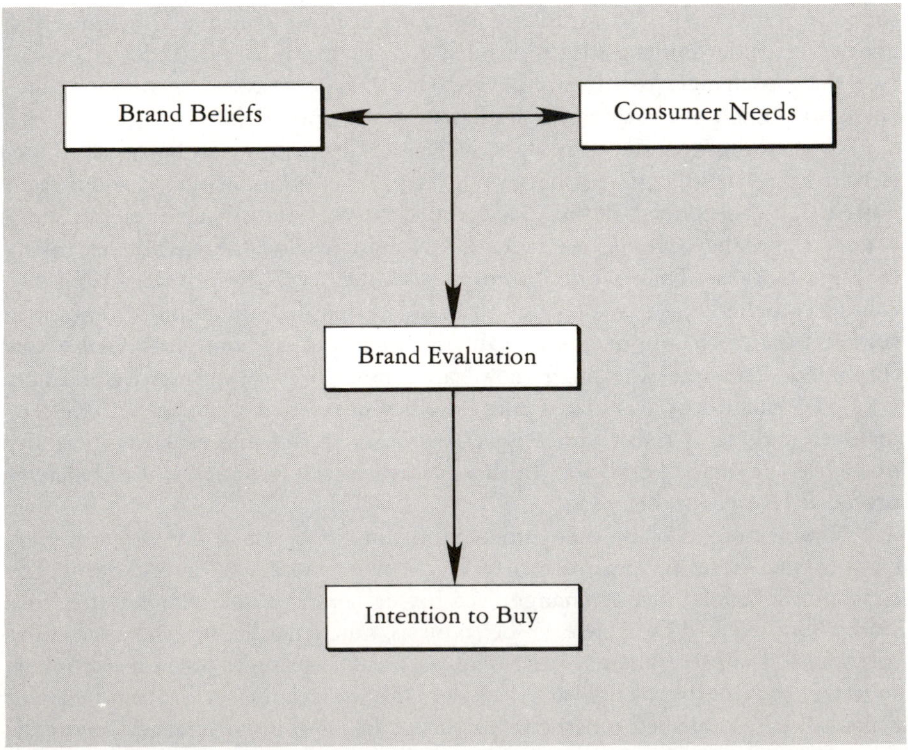

important need, and if he or she perceives a given brand as strong, that brand will probably be preferred over other alternatives. If another individual also wants a strong coffee but rates this need relatively unimportant, a coffee that is seen as strong will not necessarily be preferred.

ATTITUDE AND NEED MEASUREMENT

The components of attitudes and needs must be measured in a reliable manner if they are to form the basis for marketing strategies. However, it is a difficult task since these are qualitative variables. The general approach is to develop rating scales so consumers can identify the degree to which they think a brand has a certain attribute or the degree to which they like or dislike a brand.

In measuring attitudes and needs, it is essential to identify the particular component being measured: beliefs, evaluation, or intention in the case of attitudes and direction or intensity in the case of needs. Table 7–3 presents each need and attitude component and uses a rating scale to measure that component as an illustration. The measurement of attitudes toward cola brands is used as the example. Various brands of cola may be rated on characteristics such as degree of carbonation, sweetness, strength, etc. Typically from ten to twenty attributes will be identified in in-depth interviews. Scales such as those listed in Table 7–3 will then be used to measure brand attributes in a survey questionnaire.

Beliefs

Three alternative belief measures are presented in Table 7–3. The first measure rates brand attributes on a probability basis. The likelihood of a brand having a certain attribute is rated on a seven-point scale from improbable to probable. The second measure represents a scaling device known as the **semantic differential.** The semantic differential utilizes bipolar adjectives on a seven-point scale. A brand of cola would be rated on any one of the seven positions from carbonated to noncarbonated, depending on the consumer's belief about the level of carbonation in the brand. The third scale measures beliefs based on the accuracy of the description. Consumers are asked to rate brand attributes from "describes the brand very well" to "does not describe the brand at all."

Each of these three rating scales approaches the measurement of beliefs in a different way, suggesting that there is no standard measure of attitudes. The method chosen depends on the multiattribute model selected as the model of consumer behavior. The semantic differential (b_2) is the most widely used attitudinal scale because it is easy to construct and administer and is relevant to marketing strategy. It is actionable to position a brand on a continuum from "strong" to "weak" or from "suitable for guests" to "not suitable for guests." Marketers can quickly determine the image of their brand depending on how consumers position it on the various bipolar adjectives. The measurement of beliefs on a probability basis (b_1) or on the basis of accuracy of description (b_3) is more indirect and harder to apply to positioning strategies.

Evaluation

The evaluative or affective attitude component can also be measured in various ways. Table 7–3 suggests two ways, based on likeability of a brand (seven-point scale from "I like it very much" to "I don't like it at all") or on favorability (from very favorable to very unfavorable). A third possibility is to rank the order of preference for various brands. The most preferred would be rated "1", the second most preferred "2," etc. The **rank of order of preference** is a non-metric scale. The values have ordinal meaning in the sense of "better than" or

TABLE 7–3   Measures of Attitude and Need Components

Attitude Components

Brand Beliefs (b)

b_1:   Brand A is a highly carbonated cola.

Improbable   —— —— —— —— —— —— ——   Probable

Brand A is a sweet cola.

Improbable   —— —— —— —— —— —— ——   Probable

b_2: *Rate Brand A by the following characteristics:*

Highly
carbonated   —— —— —— —— —— —— ——   Not carbonated

Sweet   —— —— —— —— —— —— ——   Not sweet

b_3: *Indicate how well Brand A is described by the following characteristics:*

Brand A is a highly carbonated cola.

Describes very   Does not
well   —— —— —— —— —— —— ——   describe at all

Brand A is a sweet cola.

Describes very   Does not
well   —— —— —— —— —— —— ——   describe at all

Overall Evaluation (A)

A_1: *Rate Brand A as follows:*

In general, I   In general, I
like it very   don't like it at
much   —— —— —— —— —— —— ——   all

A_2:

Very favorable   —— —— —— —— —— —— ——   Very unfavorable

A_3: *Which of the following brands do you prefer most? Which of the brands do you prefer second? Third, etc.?*

Intention to Buy (BI)

What is the likelihood you will buy this brand the next time you purchase cola?

Definitely will buy	——	Probably will not buy ——
Probably will buy	——	Definitely will not buy ——
Might buy	——	

TABLE 7–3 (cont.)

167

Need Components

Value or Direction Component (a)

a_1: *Indicate how you would evaluate the following:*

A highly carbonated cola

Good ——— ——— ——— ——— ——— ——— ——— Bad

A sweet cola

Good ——— ——— ——— ——— ——— ——— ——— Bad

a_2: *Indicate the degree of satisfaction you would get from the following:*

A highly carbonated cola

Very satisfied ——— ——— ——— ——— ——— ——— ——— Very dissatisfied

A sweet cola

Very satisfied ——— ——— ——— ——— ——— ——— ——— Very dissatisfied

a_3: *Think about your ideal brand of cola and rate it on the characteristics listed below.*

Highly carbonated ——— ——— ——— ——— ——— ——— ——— Not carbonated

Sweet ——— ——— ——— ——— ——— ——— ——— Not sweet

Intensity or Importance (I)

Rate each of the following characteristics based on how important they are in determining your selection of a brand of cola.

Right degree of carbonation

Very important ——— ——— ——— ——— ——— ——— ——— Not important at all

Right level of sweetness

Very important ——— ——— ——— ——— ——— ——— ——— Not important at all

Note: More than one brand would be evaluated in the typical consumer study. This example shows only two attributes. Ordinarily, a vocabulary of attributes would be presented ranging from ten to twenty attributes.

"more than." They do not have metric meaning in the sense that "1" is equidistant to "2," and "2" is equidistant to "3." The previous scales are assumed to be metric since they have equal intervals.

Another technique used to measure preference is the **constant sum scale.** For example, consumers are asked to assume they will be given ten free bottles of cola and can select any combination of brands they want. The degree to which a brand is selected is a measure of preference. The scale is referred to as a constant sum scale since the value must always add to the same number—in this case, ten. The constant sum scale is a ratio scale since there is a zero value. Thus, a consumer who picks eight cans of 7-Up and two cans of Pepsi has picked four times as much of one as the other. The ability to make ratio statements is a valuable asset to a scale. Whether it can be said that this consumer prefers 7-Up four times as much as Pepsi is open to question.

The constant sum scale, semantic differential, and rank order of preference represent the three major categories of scales. The constant sum scale has ratio properties, the semantic differential is an equal interval scale, and the rank order of preference is an ordinal scale.

Intention

Intention to buy is typically measured on a five-point scale from "definitely will buy" to "definitely will not buy." In this case, there is a description next to each position on the scale indicating its meaning. The first position (definitely will buy) is referred to as *top box*. Marketers closely watch the percentage of consumers rating a new entry in the top box because studies have shown a close relationship between this percentage rating and subsequent trial.

Needs

The three scales shown to rate the value component of needs attempt to determine what the consumer wants. The first scale asks consumers to rate each attribute from good to bad, the second from very satisfied to very dissatisfied. Attributes that are rated as good or satisfying are those which the consumer values. The third rating scale asks the consumer to visualize an ideal cola. A semantic differential scale is used to rate the ideal brand as if it were an actual brand. The rating of the ideal brand reflects the direction of consumer needs. Thus, a consumer's ideal cola may be a slightly carbonated cola that is very sweet. If so, the consumer would rate the ideal cola close to the middle on carbonation and on the extreme left on sweetness.

Consumers may also be asked to rate the importance of each of the attributes on a scale from "very important" to "not important at all." The combination of both value and importance identifies attributes that are most actionable for the marketer.

THE RELATIONSHIP OF ATTITUDES TO BEHAVIOR

The rest of this chapter will be concerned with (1) research that attempts to link attitudes to behavior (this research was the major thrust of attitude research prior to 1970) and (2) the development of multiattribute models of attitude structure (this has been the thrust of attitude research since 1970).

Evidence of a Relationship Between Attitudes and Behavior

Two types of studies have attempted to establish a relationship between attitudes and behavior. First, studies done at a particular point in time demonstrate such a relationship, but because the measures of attitude and behavior were taken at the same time, the researcher does not know if attitudes influenced subsequent behavior or vice versa. Second, studies done over time can show whether changes in a consumer's attitudes are related to *subsequent* changes in behavior. In both types of studies, attitudes tend to be measured on a one-dimensional basis by measures such as A_1–A_3 in Table 7–3.

One of the most extensive studies of the relationship between attitudes and behavior was conducted by Achenbaum. The same consumers were interviewed in three different time periods regarding their attitudes toward and consumption of nineteen brands in seven product categories.[21] Since the same consumers were reinterviewed, attitudes in time 1 could be related to behavior in time 2; attitudes in time 2 could be related to behavior in time 3.

Figure 7–2 shows a clear relationship between attitudes and behavior for four categories (see Figure 7–2, left) and for all nineteen brands (see Figure 7–2, right). Averaging all nineteen brands, 58 percent of those rating a brand as excellent actually used the brand. The percentage of users quickly declines as attitudes become less favorable. Only 23 percent of those rating brands as very good were users and no one rating a brand as poor was a user. A more interesting relationship is the one between attitude change and subsequent behavior. Among brand users who improved their attitude toward the brand, 80 percent continued to use the brand;[22] yet, among users who became substantially more negative toward the brand, less than 30 percent continued to use the brand.

Achenbaum also found a strong relationship between changes in beliefs, overall evaluation of the brand, and changes in a brand's market share.[23] For example, a 4 percent increase in the rating of a brand on economy (a belief) was followed by a 2.5 percent increase in the overall rating of the brand (evaluation) and a 5 percent increase in the brand's share of users (behavior). The Achenbaum study supports a hierarchy of effects since beliefs influence overall brand evaluations which, in turn, influence behavior.

Another study supporting the relationship between attitudes and behavior was conducted by Assael and Day.[24] They analyzed the relationship between changes in attitudes and subsequent market share for analgesics, deodorants, and instant coffee. Measures of attitudes and awareness were related to subsequent market share for thirteen brands over a two-year period. Assael and Day found strong relationships between awareness and market share and between attitudes and market share for many of the brands studied. An important outcome of this study was the conclusion that a tracking system to measure consumer attitudes over time by a series of surveys would be a worthwhile expenditure for many companies. Such a system provides a basis for evaluating the strengths and weaknesses of a company's brands and can be utilized to predict future market share.

The Relationship Between Intention to Buy and Behavior

Studies linking attitudes to behavior frequently measure intention to buy rather than actual behavior. Researchers assume intention to buy is related to subsequent behavior and thus use intention to buy to evaluate alternative new product concepts and advertising themes.

The relationship between intention and subsequent behavior should be confirmed if purchase intention is to be regarded as a valid measure of action tendency. Such a relationship has been established by a number of studies. Banks conducted two sets of interviews.[25] The first determined preferences and

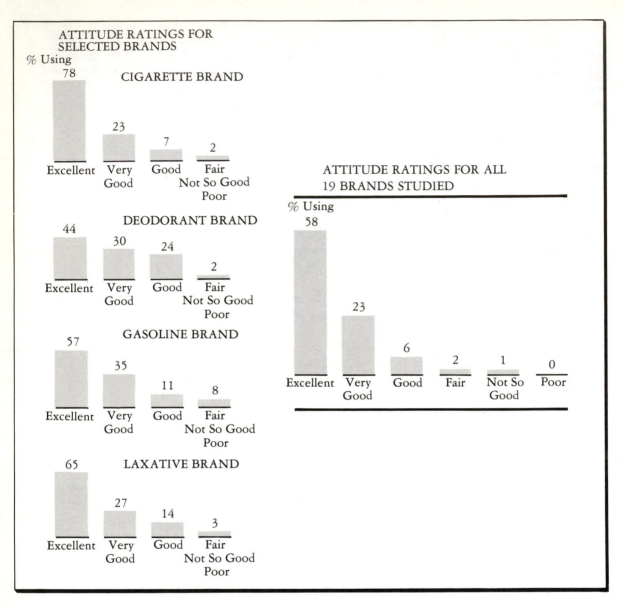

ATTITUDE RATINGS FOR
SELECTED BRANDS

% Using

CIGARETTE BRAND

78 Excellent
23 Very Good
7 Good
2 Fair Not So Good Poor

DEODORANT BRAND

44 Excellent
30 Very Good
24 Good
2 Fair Not So Good Poor

GASOLINE BRAND

57 Excellent
35 Very Good
11 Good
8 Fair Not So Good Poor

LAXATIVE BRAND

65 Excellent
27 Very Good
14 Good
3 Fair Not So Good Poor

ATTITUDE RATINGS FOR ALL
19 BRANDS STUDIED

% Using

58 Excellent
23 Very Good
6 Good
2 Fair
1 Not So Good
0 Poor

FIGURE 7–2   The Relationship Between Attitudes and Usage

Source: Selected brands study from Alvin A. Achenbaum, "Knowledge is a Thing Called Measurement." In Lee Adler and Irving Crespi, eds., *Attitude Research at Sea* (New York: American Marketing Association, 1966), p. 113.

Reprinted with permission from the American Marketing Association.

Nineteen-brand summary from Alvin A. Achenbaum, "Advertising Doesn't Manipulate Consumers," *Journal of Advertising Research* 12 (April 1972): 7.

Reprinted from the *Journal of Advertising Research.* © Copyright 1972 by the Advertising Research Foundation.

intentions for seven product categories; the second, conducted three weeks later, determined actual purchase behavior. Of the respondents who said they would buy a particular brand, 62 percent actually purchased it. Among those who did not intend to buy, 28 percent purchased it. The greatest fulfillment rate occurred for coffee and scouring cleanser. The lowest fulfillment rate was for ice cream, reflecting the impulse nature of ice cream purchases.

The most extensive confirmation of the relationship between intentions and purchase is provided by the Survey Research Center at the University of Michigan. George Katona, former director of the Center, reported on the close relationship between intentions and behavior for automobiles.[26] Among those who said they planned to or may buy a new car, 63 percent bought in the next year. Among those who did not intend to buy, 29 percent purchased a new car. These fulfillment rates are almost identical to those in Banks's study. The average purchase rate across a number of diverse products appears to be around 60 percent for intenders and 30 percent for nonintenders.

Factor Inhibiting the Relationship Between Attitudes and Behavior

Positive attitudes do not always lead to a purchase. Several conditions may cause a lack of association between attitudes and behavior. As seen in Chapter 4, attitudes are less likely to be related to behavior for low involvement product categories. In addition, several market conditions may affect the relationship between attitudes and behavior. One factor is price. An increase in the price of the favored brand may cause the consumer to switch with no change in attitudes. Another factor is availability. The unavailability of the preferred brand may lead to the purchase of a less preferred brand with no change in attitudes.

Another factor inhibiting the relationship between attitudes and behavior is the repurchase cycle. A consumer is more likely to fulfill purchase intentions when the purchase cycle is short. The University of Michigan study interviewed consumers to determine actual car purchases one year after determining intentions. Many factors can intervene in the space of a year to change intentions, such as a change in needs, economic circumstances, or alternatives available. In such cases, intentions may change as a result of short-term changes in the marketing environment.

THE RELATIONSHIP OF BEHAVIOR TO ATTITUDES

Not only do attitudes influence behavior; behavior can influence subsequent attitudes. Chapter 4 presented two conditions when behavior influences attitudes: during cognitive dissonance and during passive learning. A third condition when behavior can influence attitudes is when there is a **disconfirmation of expectations**.

Theories of cognitive dissonance, passive learning, and disconfirmation of expectations have reduced the importance of attitudinal research in the study of consumer behavior since these theories show that attitude change is not a necessary condition for a change in purchasing behavior. Each of these three conditions will be discussed here.

Cognitive Dissonance

According to dissonance theory, attitudes change to conform to previous behavior, thus reducing postpurchase conflict. Several studies have confirmed these relationships.

In one study, Knox and Inkster interviewed bettors at a racetrack before bets on a horse were made.[27] On the average, bettors gave the horse little better than a fair chance of winning. The researchers then interviewed the same bettors after the bet was made but before the race. Predictions about the performance of the horse became substantially more positive after the decision was made. Thus it was felt bettors sought to reduce the potential for postdecisional conflict by enhancing the evaluation of the chosen alternative.

In a study of two household cleaning products, Ginter found that attitudes both before and after the purchase were related to brand selection, but the postdecision attitude change was greater.[28] Consumers tended to rate the brand closer to the ideal after the purchase was made. These findings indicate that consumers may tend to reinforce their decision after the fact.

Passive Learning

The theory of passive learning provides another basis for downplaying the importance of attitudes as determinants of behavior.[29] As we have seen, under conditions of low involvement a change in attitude is not necessary to influence a change in behavior. The awareness of a new brand may be sufficient reason to switch in a search for variety. Attitudes toward the new brand may be formed after usage.

Disconfirmation of Expectations

When expectations regarding product performance are not met, consumers may develop more negative attitudes toward the product after the purchase. According to **assimilation/contrast theories,** when the consumer is only slightly disappointed, attitudes will adjust to expectations since the experience is accepted and assimilated. When the consumer is very disappointed, however, a negative change in attitudes is likely to occur after the purchase and this change may be exaggerated.

MULTIATTRIBUTE MODELS OF CONSUMER ATTITUDES

Earlier attempts to relate brand attitudes to consumer behavior did not consider that attitudes toward a brand are determined by reactions to a variety of brand attributes. Product positioning by marketers requires identification of needs across a variety of dimensions (nutrition, convenience, taste, etc). Therefore, the identification of brand attitudes to ensure need satisfaction and product positioning require what is known as a multiattribute approach. As Wilkie and Pessemier state:

> The potential advantage of multiattribute models over the simpler "overall affect" approach [the earlier approaches cited above] is in gaining understanding of attitudinal structure. *Diagnosis* of brand strengths and weaknesses on relevant product attributes can then be used to suggest specific changes in a brand and its marketing support.[30]

In other words, multiattribute models provide marketers with the ability to diagnose the strengths and weaknesses of their brands relative to the competition by determining how consumers evaluate the brand alternatives on determinant attributes.

Various multiattribute models have been applied to marketing.[31] The models all have one thing in common: they regard attitudes as a function of consumer beliefs about the attributes of a brand. Most of these models also weight beliefs by the value or importance of the attributes to the consumer. For example, the consumer who regards Pepsi as a strongly carbonated, sweet cola and who places a high value on a strongly carbonated, sweet cola will buy Pepsi. This formulation is similar to Rosenberg's model that was cited earlier since:

Attitudes toward an object (A_o) = the sum of beliefs about the object on various attributes (b_i) times the value placed on each attribute (a_i)

These models also have one other element in common: they are compensatory. That is, the weakness of a brand on one attribute can be compensated by the strength on another (thus the necessity of a summation sign in each of the models). All the attributes are summed to determine the favorability or unfavorability of the attitude toward the brand.

Using a simple example, assume two colas are rated on two attributes as follows:

Brand A	Strong carbonation	___ ___ ___ ___ ___ X ___	Weak carbonation
Brand B	Strong carbonation	___ X ___ ___ ___ ___ ___	Weak carbonation
Brand A	Sweet	___ ___ X ___ ___ ___ ___	Not sweet
Brand B	Sweet	___ ___ ___ ___ ___ X ___	Not sweet

Consumers are then asked to rate the value of the two attributes as follows:

Indicate how satisfied you would be:

With a strongly carbonated cola

Very satisfied __X__ _____ _____ _____ _____ _____ _____ Very dissatisfied

With a sweet cola

Very satisfied _____ ___X___ _____ _____ _____ _____ _____ Very dissastisfied

This consumer wants a strongly carbonated, sweet cola. Brand B is preferred over Brand A because it is more carbonated, even though it is less sweet. In other words, the carbonation of Brand B *compensated* for its lack of sweetness, producing a positive attitude and a preference for Brand B over Brand A.

A Normative Multiattribute Model

The multiattribute models accept a traditional hierarchy in which beliefs about a product and the values placed on these beliefs (the $b_i a_i$ factor cited above) result in an overall evaluation of the brand (A_o) that, in turn, results in a positive or negative intention to buy (BI) and that, ultimately, results in behavior (B). The typical multiattribute model is shown in Figure 7–3.

Stated algebraically, the model is represented as

$$B = BI = A_o = \sum_{i=1}^{N} b_{oi} a_i$$

where:

N = the number of attributes

i = one attribute

o = the object being evaluated (a brand)

b_{oi} = beliefs about the brand on attribute i (e.g., brand A is a sweet cola)

a_i = the value placed on attribute i (e.g., the degree of sweetness of a cola is an important criterion in evaluating alternative brands)

Σ = a summation sign representing the necessity to sum all the attributes used in evaluating the brand (b_{oi}) weighted by the value of each attribute (a_i) so as • to obtain an overall attitude toward the brand (A_o).

The models to be described all agree that brand beliefs (b_i) and consumer needs (a_i) are only relevant if they affect behavior (B). This fact is the key point for marketers. If consumers rating Pepsi as a sweet cola are no more likely to buy Pepsi than those consumers rating it as not sweet, then the attribute sweet-not sweet is not a determinant in the formulation of marketing strategy. In short, the multiattribute models all recognize that they must deal only with the determinant attributes. The models differ in their definition of the value (a_i) component and in the emphasis placed on this component. These five multiattribute models will be briefly described:

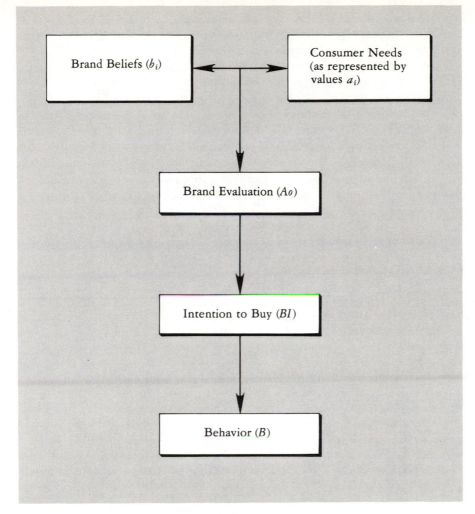

FIGURE 7–3 A Typical Multiattribute Model

1.   beliefs/evaluation model[32]
2.   beliefs/importance model
3.   ideal point model
4.   beliefs only model
5.   extended beliefs/evaluation model[33]

Evidence will then be cited regarding the relationship of each of these models to overall attitudes and to behavior.

Beliefs/Evaluation Model

According to the **beliefs/evaluation model,** an attitude toward a brand depends on the probability that the brand has some attribute and on the evaluative aspects of that attribute (does the consumer regard the attribute as good or bad?). The formula for this model duplicates the normative model, except that in the beliefs/evaluation model beliefs are measured in terms of the probability of a brand having certain attributes. The measures in Table 7–3 that would be used by this model are b_1 for the belief component and a_1 for the value (e.g., needs) component.

This model, first formulated by Fishbein, received wide application in marketing after 1970 because it became apparent to marketers that the model provided a framework for analyzing brands based on the attributes consumers use to evaluate brands. The attributes most related to overall brand evaluation and brand intentions could be identified and marketing strategy could be developed accordingly. Specifically, the Fishbein model allows marketers to:

1. *Identify the strengths and weaknesses of the company's brand in relation to the competition.*   Example: The belief component may show that Bayer is seen as a weaker analgesic than Anacin.

2. *Identify the needs of segments of the market based on the value component.*   Consumers who emphasize strength and quick action would require a different marketing strategy than consumers who emphasize no side effects. Bayer may be in a weak position in marketing to the former segment and in a stronger position in the latter segment.

3. *Identify the determinant attributes for strategic purposes.*   The belief component may show that no side effects, strength, and immediate relief do differentiate brand attitudes and are determinant. Therefore, marketing strategies would be based on these criteria in an attempt to gain a competitive advantage.

4. *Identify new product opportunities.*   The value component may show that a number of consumers consider no side effects *and* immediate relief as desirable attributes. Yet, there is no single brand that delivers both these attributes (as determined by the belief component). Such a finding strongly suggests an important market opportunity to introduce a brand to meet this combination of needs.

Since the time that Fishbein's model became widely known in marketing, researchers have sought to formulate alternative multiattribute models in an attempt to develop measures that are more specifically related to marketers' needs. These researchers recognized that Fishbein's model was not developed with consumer behavior in mind. The use of a probability scale to measure brand attributes proved cumbersome to use in marketing research studies and simpler scales were more widely used as a measure of beliefs (e.g., scale b_2 in Table 7–3 rather than scale b_1). The value component also gave way to a measure of importance (Scale I in Table 7–3 rather than scale a_1 or a_2) because it was felt that importance was a more operational measure to identify consumer needs than value. As a result, a beliefs/importance model was developed.

Beliefs/Importance Model

The **beliefs/importance model** was first proposed by Bass and Talarzyk.[34] They stated that the overall evaluation of a brand is a function of beliefs about the attributes possessed by a brand (b_i) weighted by the importance of each attribute (I); so that,

$$A_o = \sum_{i=1}^{N} b_{oi} I_i$$

The advantage of the beliefs/importance model is that the scales required are easier to administer in a consumer survey than the beliefs/evaluation model. But the key question is whether the model is superior to the beliefs/evaluation model for explaining attitudes and behavior. Recent evidence comparing the two models is mixed. Bettman et al. found that consumers tend to evaluate brands along the lines of the beliefs/evaluation model rather than the beliefs/ importance model.[35]

On the other hand, when Mazis and Ahtola compared the two models for three product categories, they found that the beliefs/importance model was more related to behavioral intention than the Fishbein model.[36] These conflicting results merely demonstrate the fact that one model may perform better under certain conditions than another, depending on the types of products studied, the nature of the consumer, and so on.

Ideal Point Model

Another multiattribute model developed by researchers, the **ideal point model,** is an offshoot of the beliefs/importance model. It seeks to determine the consumer's ideal brand by asking consumers to rate their ideal on various attributes (see measure a_3 in Table 7–3). For example, consumers may be asked to rate their ideal coffee on strength, flavor, etc. This would indicate the direction of needs. They would then be asked to rate various brands of coffee on the same attributes by using measure b_2 in Table 7–3. The closer the brand is to the ideal, the stronger its position is. Thus, if the ideal is a moderately strong, dark coffee and Yuban is seen as a moderately strong, dark coffee, it will be preferred. One additional component of the model is that each attribute is weighted by importance (measure I in Table 7–3).

A hypothetical example of the use of the ideal point model for a particular consumer is illustrated in Table 7–4. The consumer is asked to rate Coca Cola (C), Pepsi (P), and the ideal cola (Id). Importance ratings for each attribute are on the right. The consumer's ideal is a strongly carbonated, sweet, thirst-quenching, refreshing cola. The two most important needs are carbonation and sweetness. Even though Pepsi is closer to the ideal on three of the five characteristics, the prediction is that the consumer will buy Coke since it is closer to the ideal on the two most important attributes.

Simply stated, the model says, "This is what I want" (ratings of the ideal brand) and "This is what I think I am going to get" (brand ratings). The brand that best satisfies consumer needs on the most important attributes is the brand that will be selected.

The model is appealing in its potential applications for assessing brands and identifying need segments. Although it has been used more widely in the commercial sphere, it has not been reported widely or compared to other

TABLE 7–4   Ratings of a Respondent's Ideal Cola Versus Coke and Pepsi

Id = Ideal C = Coke P = Pepsi							IMPORTANCE RATINGS 7 = Very important 1 = Not important at all	
Strongly carbonated	Id	C			P		Weakly carbonated	7
Thirst quenching	Id	P		C			Not thirst quenching	3
Refreshing	Id	P	C				Not refreshing	2
Sweet		Id			C	P	Not sweet	6
Good at mealtimes		C	P	Id			Not good at mealtimes	1

multiattribute models. An application of the model is reported by Lehmann in a study of TV shows.[37] He asked respondents to rate their ideal TV show on attributes such as action, suspense, and humor. Respondents then rated twenty TV shows on these attributes. Lehmann found that the closer a TV show is to the ideal, the more likely the consumer will watch the show.

Beliefs Only Model

Another multiattribute model developed by researchers is the **beliefs only model.** This model was developed when the beliefs/importance model was being tested and researchers found that the ratings on the importance of attributes were not related to brand attitudes. In other words, using the cola example, if Coke is the preferred cola, the only factor related to this preference is the evaluation of Coke's attributes, not the importance of these attributes. That Coke is satisfactory on carbonation more likely determines its evaluation and selection than the importance of carbonation does.

The beliefs only model was first proposed by Sheth and Talarzyk.[38] In a study of six consumer goods, they found that satisfaction ratings on specific attributes of each brand (taste, price, nutrition, package) were related to the overall evaluation of the brand. There was little relationship, though, between the importance assigned to each attribute and brand evaluations. Sheth and Talarzyk concluded that the brand's attributes, rather than the importance of these attributes, should be emphasized in advertising and product concept formulations. In keeping with this, it would be more appropriate to advertise a Remington electric razor as providing a closer shave (an attribute of the brand) rather than to convince the consumer that having a closer shave will achieve social or business goals and, therefore, that a Remington should be purchased (an appeal to the value importance of the attribute).

Appeals based on brand attributes are more likely to be successful because such appeals attempt to offer consumers what they want. Appeals based on value importance attempt to reorganize the priority of needs, a much more difficult task. It is easier to get people to switch from larger cars to compacts than it is to get them to ride mass transit. A compact car appeals to a specific attribute — economy. Convincing consumers to ride mass transit involves decreasing the value of mobility and convenience and increasing the value of energy conservation. Such a change in priorities is a more difficult task.

Some research supports beliefs, alone, as the key influence on brand evaluations and behavior.[39] Other research, however, supports including the importance term in the model as a signficant contributor to brand evaluations and behavior.[40] Once again, the best attitudinal model seems to depend on what and whom are being tested.

Extended Beliefs/Evaluation Model

The ambiguous results obtained from the multiattribute models described above prompted Fishbein and others to reassess the beliefs/evaluation model in an attempt to make it more relevant to consumer behavior. Fishbein offered several modifications of his model in an attempt to explain the formation of brand attitudes and purchase intentions.[41]

The most important modification was in the measure of attitudes. Fishbein proposed that the appropriate attitudes measurement is based on the act of purchasing a brand, (A_{act}), not on the brand itself, (A_o). That is, from the marketer's standpoint, it is more meaningful to evaluate a consumer's attitude toward purchasing (or consuming) than it is to evaluate the consumer's attitude toward a product per se. It is the act of purchasing and, ultimately, consuming the product that determines satisfaction. Measuring the attitude toward the act of purchasing and consuming involves the consumer more directly in the evaluation of that brand. Moreover, the attitude toward the object may not be a valid basis for gauging attitudes. Someone may have a very positive attitude toward a Rolls Royce but the attitude toward purchasing may be negative because of price constraints. In Fishbein's words:

> Even though I may have a positive attitude toward Brand X I might not have a positive attitude toward buying Brand X, and according to behavioral decision theory, it is this latter attitude that should be related to buying behavior. For example, a woman might believe that "high pile" carpeting is "warm," "comfortable," "luxurious," and "prestigious," and since she positively evaluates those attributes, she is likely to have a positive attitude toward "high pile carpeting." However, what do you think the consequences of buying high pile carpeting are for that woman if she has two dogs, a cat, and three children under nine?[42]

Fishbein therefore concludes that the attitude toward the act of purchasing or consuming a brand should be measured (based on A_{act}), not the attitude toward the brand itself (A_o).

Second, given the mixed results of applying the beliefs/evaluation model to brand attitudes, Fishbein concluded that other elements must also influence attitudes. He therefore introduced social influences into his model since family and peer group norms play such an important part in shaping attitudes. Two social elements were introduced: normative beliefs and the motivation to comply. Normative beliefs may be represented by the following measure:

My family thinks I

| should buy | | should not |
| Brand X | — — — — — — — | buy Brand X |

The motivation to comply could be measured by the following scale:

I want to do		I do not want
what my family		to do what my
thinks I should		family thinks
do regarding		I should do
Brand X	— — — — — — —	regarding Brand X

The **extended beliefs/evaluation model** has been applied extensively in recent years and has generally been found to predict intentions and behavior better than the original model. In a review of many of these studies, Ryan and Bonfield concluded that attitudes toward purchasing a brand were more highly correlated with behavior than were attitudes toward the brand itself.[43] Wilson et al. measured intentions and behavior for toothpaste purchases using the original and extended Fishbein model.[44] They also found that attitudes toward the purchase of a brand were more closely related to behavior than were attitudes toward the brand. Thus, it is more relevant to ask consumers whether their teeth will get whiter if they use Ultra-Brite than it is to ask if they think Ultra-Brite whitens teeth.

Noncompensatory Models of Attitude Structure

All of the five multiattribute models described assume that consumers evaluate brands across a number of different attributes and then determine the most preferred brand by summing across these attributes. Such an evaluation process may in fact be too complex for many consumer packaged goods.[45] Consumers may evaluate brands on two or three key attributes and eliminate brands if they are not adequate on any one attribute. Such a decision rule is a significant time-saver compared to the complex evaluation processes assumed in multiattribute models.

Simpler attitude structure models do not assume a compensatory process of evaluation since a brand can be eliminated due to a deficiency in one attribute (sort of a "one strike and you're out" model). Therefore, noncompensatory models may represent a more accurate description of the way consumers process information to evaluate brand alternatives for certain products. Three types of noncompensatory models have been described: conjunctive models, disjunctive models, and lexicographic models.[46]

According to the **conjunctive model,** a consumer will consider a brand only if it meets acceptable standards on key attributes. Table 7–5 presents an example. Four toothpaste brands are evaluated on three key attributes. A seven-point scale is used, seven representing a high level of satisfaction with the brand's performance on the attribute, and one representing a high level of dissatisfaction. Using a conjunctive model, the consumer immediately elimi-nates Ultra-Brite because of a low rating on decay prevention and eliminates Crest because of a low rating on whitens teeth. The choice is then between Gleem and Colgate. If decay prevention is more important than whitens teeth, Gleem will be selected. If it is the reverse, Colgate will be selected.

In a **disjunctive model** one or two attributes stand out as the selection criteria. Assume that whitens teeth is the dominant attribute. This means that Crest and Gleem will be immediately eliminated. Colgate will then be selected because of a higher rating than Ultra-Brite on other criteria.

A **lexicographic model** assumes that all the attributes are used in stepwise fashion. Brands are evaluated on the most important attribute first. If there is a tie, then they are evaluated on the second most important attribute, etc. In the example in Table 7–5, assume the brands are first evaluated on decay prevention, then taste, and then whitens teeth. This time, Gleem and Crest are considered for purchase since they score highest on decay prevention. Since they are tied, the criterion for selection now becomes taste, and Gleem is selected on this basis.

TABLE 7–5   Examples of Noncompensatory Attitude Models

Sample Ratings of Four Brands of Toothpaste

7 = highly satisfied with the brand's performance on the attribute
1 = highly dissatisfied with the brand's performance on the attribute

	Ultra-Brite	*Gleem*	*Crest*	*Colgate*
Decay Prevention	2	7	7	4
Taste	6	6	4	6
Whitens Teeth	7	5	2	7

Conjunctive Model

- Ultra-Brite is eliminated because of poor performance on decay prevention.
- Crest is eliminated because of poor performance on whitens teeth.
- Select between Gleem and Colgate.

Disjunctive Model

- Whitens teeth is assumed to be the dominant attribute.
- Crest and Gleem are eliminated because of poorer performance compared to Ultra-Brite and Colgate.

Lexicographic Model

- The most important attributes are assumed to be (1) decay prevention, (2) taste, and (3) whitens teeth.
- The selection is between Gleem and Crest because of better performance on decay prevention. Since these two brands are tied, move on to taste.
- Select Gleem on taste because of better performance than Crest. No need to move on to next criterion (whitens teeth).

The noncompensatory models require consumers to process information by attribute across brands. The compensatory models require consumers to process information by brand across attributes. Since brand evaluations are simpler in noncompensatory models, it is likely that consumers follow these rules in evaluating low involvement brands. The compensatory models more accurately describe brand evaluations for high involvement products in complex decision making. Despite the importance of low involvement purchasing behavior, little has been done in marketing to assess the relevance of noncompensatory models and their ability to predict brand evaluations and subsequent behavior.

SUMMARY

This chapter focuses on the most important consumer thought variables — attitudes and needs. Attitudes are predispositions toward specific products causing consumers to respond favorably or unfavorably toward them. Needs are forces directed toward achieving certain goals that result in accepting or rejecting a product. Brand attitudes are important to marketers because they: (a) influence the consumer's behavior, (b) enable marketers to define attitudinal segments toward which strategies can be directed, and (c) help marketers evaluate strategies.

Brand attitudes are composed of beliefs about a brand, an overall evaluation of the brand, and an action tendency. Needs are represented by their direction and importance. A refinement of the hierarchy of effects states that only those beliefs about a brand that reflect important consumer needs will influence brand evaluation and behavior.

Two very distinct streams of attitudinal research in consumer behavior are defined. Prior to 1970 most research focused on showing that brand attitudes were related to consumer behavior. Attitudes were identified one-dimensionally by determining the overall favorability to a brand. Various studies showed that brand attitudes were related to brand choice, but there were problems in relying on a simple association of a one-dimensional measure of attitudes with behavior.

As a result, after 1970, attitudinal research began to focus more on multiattribute models of consumer attitudes. These models are used in diagnosing a brand's strengths and weaknesses on relevant product attributes and provide a more complete set of guidelines for product positioning and promotional strategy. Five multiattribute models are described. In each case the model emphasizes a different component of attitude or interprets beliefs and values in a different manner. A revision of these models suggests that the appropriate measure of attitudes should be toward purchasing or using the brand, not toward the brand itself. Thus, for example, one should measure the attitude toward purchasing a Rolls Royce (which may be negative) not the attitude toward the Rolls (which may be positive).

A distinction is made between compensatory and noncompensatory models of attitude structure. Multiattribute models are compensatory since a brand's weakness on one attribute can be compensated for by strength on another. The three noncompensatory models described assume that consumers might evaluate brands on the one or two most important attributes. Noncompensatory models are more relevant for low involvement products since it is not worth the consumer's time to process information across a large number of attributes.

This chapter has been concerned with a description of the role of needs and attitudes in influencing consumer behavior. The next chapter will focus on the strategic applications of attitudes, particularly strategies for attitude change.

QUESTIONS

1. Two manufacturers of men's clothing launch a national advertising campaign. One directs the campaign to value-expressive attitudes toward men's clothing. The other directs advertising to ego-defensive attitudes.
   - What may be the resultant differences in the two campaigns?
   - To what types of consumers would each ad appeal?
2. What is the importance of the distinction between product attributes and product benefits for a) developing a product concept for a new snack food item and b) introducing a new low tar cigarette?
3. What is the relevance of the distinction between the evaluative and the belief components of attitudes for positioning a new, artificial bacon product that is leaner than regular bacon?
4. Some analysts have argued that the concept of an ideal brand is artificial and is not really a reflection of brand preferences. Others feel the ideal helps consumers conceptualize their needs and should be used in attitudinal research.
   - What is your position?
   - Is it easier to conceptualize an ideal brand for certain product categories compared to others? What products and why?
5. The Assael and Day study suggests that an ongoing marketing information system designed to track changes in attitudes may benefit management.
   - Of what use would a system that tracks consumer attitudes be for (a) new product development and (b) evaluating advertising effectiveness?
6. The ideal point model is cited as one way to measure the relationship between consumer needs, brand attitudes, and brand preferences.
   - How can the model be used to (a) position new brands and (b) identify the target group for a new brand?
7. Consider the statement, "Consumer attitudes toward the act of using or purchasing a brand are more closely related to behavior than are consumer attitudes toward the brand itself." Assume you are considering repositioning a breakfast food so that it will also appeal to the snack market.
   - What are the implications of the statement for repositioning strategy?
8. Some findings suggest that beliefs about the attributes of a brand are more closely related to brand choice than the value placed on these attributes.
   - If this is true, what implications would it have on an advertising campaign for (a) solar energy devices, (b) dental care clinics, and (c) a new diet food?
9. What are the marketing strategy implications of using compensatory versus noncompensatory rules in evaluating brands?

10. Are certain consumers more likely to use compensatory rules and others noncompensatory rules? If so, what do you think are the characteristics of consumers more likely to use compensatory rules? noncompensatory rules?

RESEARCH ASSIGNMENTS

1. According to the theory of cognitive dissonance, recent purchasers of important items such as cars or appliances are more likely to have positive attitudes toward their brands than those who have owned the brand for a longer period of time. The reason is that once a purchase is made, recent purchasers are likely to seek out positive information about the brand to reinforce the choice that they have made.

    Test this hypothesis by selecting both recent purchasers of a major durable good (car, stereo set, microwave oven) and consumers who have owned the item for a longer period of time. Measure: (1) beliefs about the brand utilizing a vocabulary of need criteria and (2) overall attitude toward the brand.

    • Do recent purchasers have more positive attitudes?

    • Are there differences in beliefs about brands between recent purchasers and long-time owners?

    • What are the strategic implications of your findings, particularly for (a) advertising and (b) service policies?

2. Select a particular brand to study (preferably a consumer packaged good). You would like to evaluate the strengths and weaknesses of the brand relative to the competition. In order to do so, you decide to utilize the ideal point, multiattribute model.

    Conduct a number of depth interviews with consumers to develop a vocabulary of attributes that consumers use in evaluating brands. Then construct scales (see Table 7–3) to measure (1) the consumer's ideal product based on the vocabulary of attributes; (2) beliefs about the brand under study and two or three other key competitive brands; and (3) the importance of each attribute. Select a sample of users of the product category so that at least one-third of your sample uses the brand under study.

    • What are the brand's strengths and weaknesses based on a comparison of the brand to (1) the ideal and (2) the competitive brands?

    • How do brand ratings differ between users and nonusers of the brand?

    • What are the implications of your findings for (1) possible repositioning strategies for the brand; (2) identification of unmet needs; and (3) formulation of new product concepts to meet consumer needs?

3. Some marketers feel that a significant proportion of consumers develop images of brands based on the advertising rather than on product experience. If this is true, then one would expect beliefs about brands to reflect advertising themes. Select a product category where different advertising themes can be associated with brands (analgesics, airlines, paper towels). Construct a vocabulary of product attributes. Include the advertising themes in the vocabulary. Then ask consumers to rate the brands in the product category utilizing the vocabulary.

- Are brands rated higher on criteria used in the brand's advertising?
- Do both heavy and light users of the product category rate brands in accordance with the advertising themes? Do both users and nonusers of the brand?

NOTES

1. Gordon W. Allport, "Attitudes," in C.A. Murchinson, ed., *A Handbook of Social Psychology* (Worcester, Mass.: Clark University Press, 1935), pp. 798–844.
2. Milton J. Rosenberg, "Cognitive Structure and Attitudinal Affect," *Journal of Abnormal and Social Psychology* 53 (November 1956): 367–372.
3. Arch G. Woodside, James D. Clokey, and Joan M. Combes, "Similarities and Differences of Generalized Brand Attitudes, Behavioral Intentions, and Reported Behavior," in Mary Jane Schlinger, ed., *Advances in Consumer Research*, vol. 2 (Ann Arbor: Association for Consumer Research, 1975), pp. 335–344.
4. Yoram Wind, "Brand Loyalty and Vulnerability," in Arch G. Woodside, Jagdish N. Sheth and Peter D. Bennett, eds., *Consumer and Industrial Buying Behavior* (New York: North-Holland Inc., 1977), pp. 313–319.
5. Leon Festinger, *A Theory of Cognitive Dissonance* (New York: Harper and Row, 1957).
6. Herbert E. Krugman, "The Impact of Television Advertising: Learning Without Involvement," *Public Opinion Quarterly* 29 (Fall 1965): 349–356.
7. Rosenberg, "Cognitive Structure and Attitudinal Affect."
8. Martin Fishbein, "A Behavior Theory Approach to the Relations Between Beliefs About an Object and the Attitude Towards the Object," in Martin Fishbein, ed., *Readings in Attitude Theory and Measurement* (New York: John Wiley & Sons, 1967), pp. 389–400.
9. Daniel Katz, "The Functional Approach to the Study of Attitudes," *Public Opinion Quarterly* 24 (Summer 1960): 163–204.
10. Richard J. Lutz, "A Functional Theory Framework for Designing and Pretesting Advertising Themes," *Attitude Research Plays for High Stakes* (Chicago: American Marketing Association, 1979), pp. 37–49.
11. William B. Locander and W. Austin Spivey, "A Functional Approach to Attitude Measurement," *Journal of Marketing Research* 15 (November 1978): 576–587.
12. Peter D. Bennett and Harold H. Kassarjian, *Consumer Behavior* (Englewood Cliffs, N.J.: Prentice-Hall Inc., 1972), p. 81.
13. Intercollegiate Clearing House Case; *Young and Rubicam (A)* (Cambridge, Mass.: Harvard Graduate School of Business Administration, 1957).
14. Elihu Katz and Paul F. Lazarsfeld, *Personal Influence* (New York: The Free Press, 1955).
15. James S. Coleman, Elihu Katz, and Herbert Menzel, *Medical Innovation: A Diffusion Study* (New York: Bobbs-Merrill, 1966).
16. Johan Arndt, "Role of Product-Related Conversations in the Diffusion of a New Product," *Journal of Marketing Research* 4 (August 1967): 291–295.
17. Mark I. Alpert, "Identification of Determinant Attributes: A Comparison of Methods," *Journal of Marketing Research* 8 (May 1971): 184–191.
18. Ibid., p. 184.
19. See Richard J. Lutz, "An Experimental Investigation of Causal Relations Among Cognitions, Affect, and Behavioral Intentions," *Journal of Consumer Research* 3 (March 1977): 197–208.
20. Milton J. Rosenberg, "Inconsistency Arousal and Reduction in Attitude Change," in D.T. Kollat, R.B. Blackwell, and J.F. Engel, eds., *Research in Consumer Behavior* (New York: Holt, Rinehart and Winston, 1970), p. 277.
21. Alvin A. Achenbaum, "Advertising Doesn't Manipulate Consumers," *Journal of Advertising Research* 12 (April 1972): 3–13; and Alvin A. Achenbaum, "Knowledge Is a Thing Called Measurement," in Lee Adler and Irving Crespi, eds., *Attitude Research at Sea* (New York: American Marketing Association, 1966), pp. 111–126.
22. Achenbaum, "Advertising Doesn't Manipulate Consumers," p. 7.
23. Achenbaum, "Knowledge Is a Thing Called Measurement," p. 115.
24. Henry Assael and George S. Day, "Attitudes and Awareness as Predictors of Market Share," *Journal of Advertising Research* 8 (December 1968): 3–10.
25. Seymour Banks, "The Relationship Between Preference and Purchase of Brands," *Journal of Marketing* 15 (October 1950): 145–157.
26. George Katona, *The Powerful Consumer* (New York: McGraw-Hill Book Co., 1960), pp. 80–83.
27. Robert E. Knox and James A. Inkster, "Post-Decision Dissonance at Post Time," *Journal of Personality and Social Psychology* 8 (1968): 319–323.
28. James L. Ginter, "An Experimental Investigation of Attitude Change and Choice of a New Brand," *Journal of Marketing Research* 11 (February 1974): 30–40.
29. Krugman, "The Impact of Television Advertising."
30. William L. Wilkie and Edgar A. Pessemier,

186   "Issues in Marketing's Use of Multi-Attribute Attitude Models," *Journal of Marketing Research* 10 (November 1973): 428.

31. For a good review of multiattribute models see Wilkie and Pessemier, "Issues"; and Richard J. Lutz and James R. Bettman, "Multiattribute Models in Marketing: A Bicentennial Review," in Arch G. Woodside, Jagdish N. Sheth, and Peter D. Bennett, eds., *Consumer and Industrial Buying Behavior* (New York: North-Holland, 1977), pp. 137–149.

32. Martin Fishbein, "An Investigation of the Relationships Between Beliefs About an Object and the Attitude Toward that Object," *Human Relations* 16 (1963): 233–240.

33. Martin Fishbein, "Attitudes and the Prediction of Behavior," in Martin Fishbein, ed., *Readings in Attitude Theory and Measurement* (New York: John Wiley and Sons Inc, 1967), pp. 477–492.

34. Frank M. Bass and W. Wayne Talarzyk, "An Attitude Model for the Study of Brand Preference," *Journal of Marketing Research* 9 (February 1972): 93–96.

35. James R. Bettman, Noel Capon, and Richard J. Lutz, "Cognitive Algebra in Multi-Attribute Attitude Models," *Journal of Marketing Research* 12 (May 1975): 151–164.

36. Michael B. Mazis and Olli T. Ahtola, "A Comparison of Four Multi-Attribute Models in the Prediction of Consumer Attitudes," *Journal of Consumer Research* 2 (June 1975): 38–52.

37. Donald R. Lehmann, "Television Show Preference: Application of a Choice Model," *Journal of Marketing Research* 8 (February 1971): 47–55.

38. Jagdish N. Sheth and W. Wayne Talarzyk, "Perceived Instrumentality and Value Importance as Determinants of Attitudes," *Journal of Marketing Research* 9 (February 1972): 6–9.

39. Ibid.; see also Jagdish N. Sheth, "Brand Profiles From Beliefs and Importances," *Journal of Advertising Research* 13 (February 1973): 37–42.

40. Frank M. Bass and William L. Wilkie, "A Comparative Analysis of Attitudinal Predictions of Brand Preference," *Journal of Marketing Research* 10 (August 1973): 262–269; and David E. Weddle and James R. Bettman, "Marketing Underground: An Investigation of Fishbein's Behavioral Intention Model," in Scott Ward and Peter Wright, eds., *Advances in Consumer Research,* vol. 1 (Urbana, Ill.: Association for Consumer Research, 1973), pp. 310–318.

41. Fishbein, "Attitudes and the Prediction of Behavior."

42. Martin Fishbein, "Some Comments on the Use of 'Models' in Advertising Research," in *Proceedings: Seminar on Translating Advanced Advertising Theories Into Research Reality* (Amsterdam, The Netherlands: European Society of Marketing Research, 1971), p. 301.

43. Michael J. Ryan and E.H. Bonfield, "The Fishbein Extended Model and Consumer Behavior," *Journal of Consumer Research* 2 (September 1975): 118–136.

44. David T. Wilson, H. Lee Matthews, and James W. Harvey, "An Empirical Test of the Fishbein Behavioral Intention Model," *Journal of Consumer Research* 1 (March 1975): 39–48.

45. Masao Nakanishi and James R. Bettman, "Attitude Models Revisited: An Individual Level Analysis," *Journal of Consumer Research* 1 (December 1974): 20–21.

46. For a description of noncompensatory attitude models see Wilkie and Pessemier, "Issues," p. 437. For one of the few marketing studies utilizing these models see Albert V. Bruno and Albert R. Wildt, "Toward Understanding Attitude Structure: A Study of the Complimentarity of Multi-Attribute Attitude Models," *Journal of Consumer Research* 2 (September 1975): 137–145.

EIGHT

Attitude Change Strategies

Focus of Chapter

The foregoing consideration of needs and attitudes has assumed two types of strategies. In one strategy, the needs and attitudes of consumers are determined. Products are then developed to meet existing needs, and promotional policy is guided by existing attitudes. This is an *adaptive* strategy in that the marketer is swimming with the tide.

The second strategy is a *change* strategy. To increase sales the marketer decides that an attempt will be made to change the consumer's priorities of needs and/or the consumer's brand attitudes. It can be unequivocally stated that an adaptive strategy is more likely to be successful than a change strategy for the simple reason that it is easier to reinforce existing needs and attitudes than to change them.

This chapter will show how consumer needs and attitudes are used to develop attitude adaptation and attitude change strategies. Existing attitudes are reinforced or changed primarily through advertising. Therefore, prior to considering strategic attitude applications, it is necessary to understand how marketing stimuli are communicated. The next section will present a basic model of communications. The remainder of the chapter will then utilize this model in considering strategies of attitude adaptation and attitude change.

THE COMMUNICATION MODEL

Any type of communication requires a source, a message, a means of transmitting the message, and a receiver. A basic communication model is presented in Figure 8–1. The source determines the need for a message. For instance, a

189

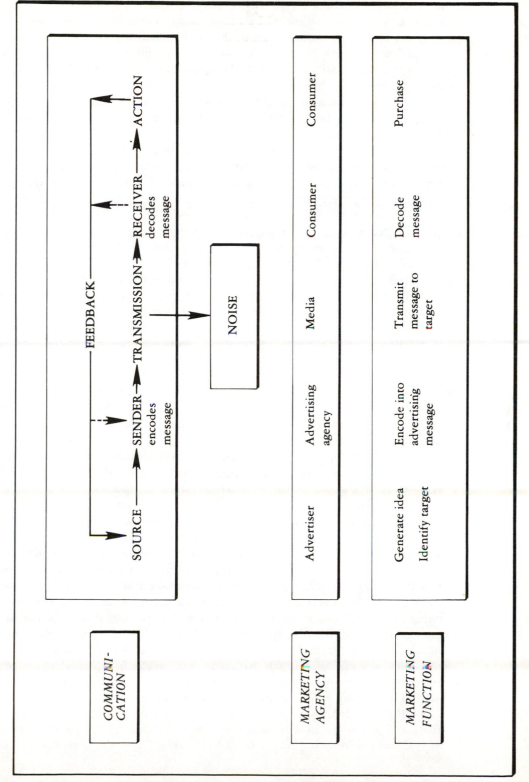

FIGURE 8–1 A Communication Model

manufacturer develops a new instant coffee with chicory and determines the need for an advertising campaign to inform consumers of the benefits of the product. The manufacturer asks its advertising agency to develop a series of messages to inform consumers about the product and to persuade them to buy it based on its taste benefits. The manufacturer informs the agency of the product's characteristics, benefits, and proposed target segments which are most likely to buy it.

In chapter 5 the advertising message was described as a marketing stimulus designed to create brand awareness and persuade the consumer to buy. In communications, the process of developing the marketing stimulus is known as **encoding.** Based on the information supplied by the manufacturer, the advertising agency translates the manufacturer's communications objectives into a form that can be communicated to the public. Encoding requires that the product's benefits are communicated by a series of symbols (a picture of the product and/or some object positively associated with the product such as a hot cup of coffee) and imagery (a husband and wife around the breakfast table). A good advertising campaign uses symbols and imagery that successfully communicate the product's benefits to the consumer.

After developing an advertising campaign acceptable to the marketer, the advertising agency selects the media to transmit the message to the target consumer. In a good advertising campaign the message will reach the intended receiver. A natural outgrowth of the communications process is **noise** — that is, interference with message transmission. Noise can occur due to competitive clutter resulting from the large number of messages directed to the consumer. Interference with the communications process can also occur, however, at the encoding or decoding phases of communications. Perhaps the agency did not adequately convey the idea that chicory produces a mild yet distinctive taste, or perhaps the message was not directed to instant coffee drinkers interested in a milder coffee.

In the next step, the consumer (receiver) decodes the message. In Chapter 5 **decoding** was described as information processing in which consumers are exposed to and aware of the message and then comprehend and retain its meaning so the information can be used at some future time. There are key questions involved in decoding: Does the consumer accept the message? Will the message lead to the last step — action? The purpose of marketing communications is to influence the consumer to act. Therefore, consumer purchasing behavior is the critical variable in assessing the effectiveness of communications.

Evaluating the effectiveness of the communication is represented by a feedback loop from action to the source of the communication and the advertising agency. Of course the manufacturer will track sales results for the new brand, but it is difficult to tie purchasing actions directly to marketing communications since so many other factors influence purchasing behavior.

Difficulties in relating advertising to sales results have caused researchers to evaluate advertising effectiveness by studying the consumer's decoding process and purchasing action. Advertising messages can be evaluated by the level of recall (attention), by interpretation of the advertising message (comprehension), and by changes in attitudes toward the brand (influence). The importance of evaluating advertising effectiveness in the decoding stage is represented by a dotted line from decoding back to the source and transmitter in the feedback loop.

The presentation of the communications model sets the stage for considering the role of attitudes in marketing communications. Communication is important enough to warrant more detailed consideration. Chapter 19 will consider the relation of the communications model to consumer information processing and consumer purchasing behavior within the applied framework of advertising strategies.

ATTITUDES AND NEEDS IN ADAPTIVE STRATEGIES

Advertising is more effective when it is in keeping rather than in conflict with attitudes and needs. It is for this reason, for example, that advertising for diet drinks has been successful, whereas advertising for men's hats and overcoats has not. Diet drinks and diet foods follow the trend emphasizing slimness and youth. Men's hats and overcoats are symbols of age and conservatism. The greater success of adaptive strategies also makes it easier to position a new product than to reposition an existing product. Metrecal's attempt to reposition itself from a medicinal food substitute to an energy-giving food product failed. A change from distribution in drug stores to supermarkets did not rescue the brand. In contrast, when products such as freeze-dried coffees or diet drinks were first introduced, they were successful because they met the needs of identified market segments.

Needs and attitudes influence behavior using adaptive strategies in the following ways:

1. They define opportunities in the marketplace based on unmet needs.
2. They position new products to meet these needs.
3. They attract new users for existing products by emphasizing positive attitudes in advertising.
4. They reinforce positive brand attitudes among existing users through advertising.

Defining Unmet Needs and Positioning New Products

In introducing a new product, one of the first steps must be the identification of a need. Needs constitute the evaluative criteria by which brands are judged; therefore, consumers should be asked to rate the value of various attributes or the position of an ideal brand on these attributes (see measures a_1 to a_3 in Table 7–3). These ratings are a measure of needs. Then consumers should be grouped by similarity of needs, and product strategies should be directed to these groups.

An adaptive strategy for a large telecommunications company is illustrated in Table 8–1 and Figure 8–2. The company is interested in evaluating the market for a Picturephone (visual telephone). They develop a vocabulary of communications needs (precision, speed, directness, service, multiple usages, etc.) and then survey business organizations responsible for communications.

TABLE 8–1   Segmenting Organizations by Similarity of Communications Needs

Need Segment Defined as	Efficiency	Service/Economy	Flexibility	Risk Reduction
Common Needs of Segment (Needs Considered Most Important)	Precision Speed Directness Documentation	Service Maintenance Durability Dependability Economy	Multiple Usage Multiple Channel Nonverbal Communications	Privacy Control No Interference
Identification of Characteristics	New Centralized	Small Retail Older	Large Service Decentralized	Large Manufacture
Concept Evaluation: Ratings of Picturephone	Average	Average	High	Low

These organizations are asked to determine their most important needs, and the potential users are then divided into four groups based on a similarity of needs. These groups are referred to as **benefit segments.** The groups are identified as stressing efficiency, service/economy, flexibility, and risk reduction (see Table 8–1). Further, the distinctive organizational characteristics of each of the four segments are identified. For example, the service/economy segment may be composed of smaller older companies in retail trade.

The concept of the Picturephone is now ready to be introduced to the organizations that were interviewed. The flexibility segment is thought to be the prime target segment for the product. How is the Picturephone seen by this segment? Are their needs met? The analysis in Figure 8–2 shows how various ways of communicating are rated by companies in the flexibility segment. The telegram, mailgram, and mail are similar and meet the needs for privacy. The telex meets the needs for speed and precision. The Picturephone meets the needs for multiple communications, multiple usage, and nonverbal communications, apparently meeting the most important needs of the flexibility segment. Thus, the expectations that the flexibility segment is the prime market for the Picturephone have been confirmed.

Since the flexibility segment is composed of large service organizations that are decentralized (banks, sales organizations, large law firms), the company now has some guidance in defining the primary target market. The next step is to produce a few prototypes of the Picturephone for product testing. Some large service organizations are asked to try it and then rate it in relation to other modes of communication. The ratings of the Picturephone in the use test are about the same as in the concept test. (This is shown in Figure 8–2 as "Picturephone in product test.") The benefits described in the product concept were delivered when the product was used.

This is an example of an adaptive strategy because the product met the existing needs. In fact, some new needs and attitudinal dimensions may be created since a new component is being added to telecommunications — visual communications. Moreover, if needs associated with the Picturephone had not been strong, the producers would have needed to change the priority of needs,

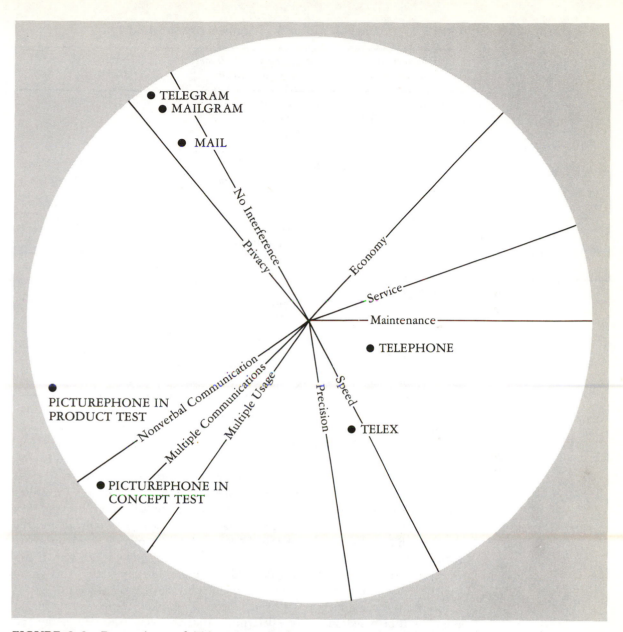

FIGURE 8–2 Perceptions of Telecommunications Alternatives Among the Flexibility Segment

using a more difficult, costly strategy. More than likely, in that case, the product would have been dropped.

Attracting and Reinforcing Users

If the product is already on the market, management will seek to keep existing users and to attract new users through its advertising. An adaptive advertising strategy emphasizes the positive beliefs about a brand. Table 8–2 describes

TABLE 8–2   Common Attitudes of Segment Toward Iced Tea

Percent of Iced Tea Users	Common Attitudes of Segment	Percent of Iced Tea Used
Segment 1. 17%	Restores energy. Year-round drink.	36%
Segment 2. 15%	Restores energy. Is not a year-round drink.	12%
Segment 3. 38%	Does not restore energy. Easy to prepare.	36%
Segment 4. 30%	Does not restore energy. Is not easy to prepare.	16%

Source: Adapted from Henry Assael, "Segmenting Markets by Group Purchasing Behavior: An Application of the AID Technique." *Journal of Marketing Research* 7 (May 1970): 157.
Reprinted with permission from the American Marketing Association.

an analysis by a manufacturer who wishes to direct advertising to the heavy users of iced tea. A study of drinkers of iced tea found that the most concentrated usage group consisted of those who viewed iced tea as a way of restoring energy and as a good year-round drink.[1] This group represents 17 percent of the market but accounts for 36 percent of the volume of iced tea used. Clearly, "restores energy" and "good year-round drink" are determinant attributes[2] because they are directly related to the volume of usage. The marketer would define the demographic characteristics of this 17 percent of the market (they are more likely to live in the South, have two or more children, be better educated) and direct advertising toward them. Each advertising dollar directed to this group will be twice as effective as spending it on the total market since this group consumes twice as much as the average iced tea drinker. Moreover, the major theme will be based on the two determinant attributes — restores energy and good year-round drink.

The least concentrated group is made up of consumers who rate iced tea low on restores energy and easy to prepare. Members of this group represent 30 percent of the market but only 16 percent of consumption. One may argue that changing their beliefs about iced tea to a drink that provides energy would be a good expenditure of resources since they would then behave more like heavy iced tea drinkers. This could be true, but it would entail more risks than the adaptive strategy of appealing to the heavy user group. There is no assurance attitudes can be changed. Appealing to existing attitudes assures their reinforcement. Moreover, if the attitude that iced tea does not restore energy is a strong one, there is little chance advertising will change it.

CHANGING ATTITUDES AND NEEDS

Though strategies of attitude change are harder to implement than strategies of attitude reinforcement, they are a valid basis for allocating marketing resources. In fact, a significant portion of advertising expenditures is devoted to changing brand attitudes and preferences by providing additional information and persuasive appeals. An important fact to consider is the strength of attitudes or the degree of attitude modification needed for a change to take place.

The basic assumption in most advertising conforms to the traditional hierarchy of effects: a change in beliefs about a brand will lead to a change in preference and a subsequent change in behavior. It is in this way that advertising can induce nonusers of the product category, users of competitive brands, or former users to become users of the company's brand. The question marketers must ask, however, is "Under what conditions should changes in attitudes be attempted?"

Principles of Attitude Change

A number of conditions reflecting the product category, market environment, and nature of the consumer may make it easier to produce changes in needs and attitudes through marketing strategies. These principles of attitude change consider changing the components of attitudes (beliefs, evaluation, and behavioral intent) and the components of needs (direction and intensity).

1. *Attitudes are easier to change than needs.*   Marketers could seek to change consumer needs or they could seek to change attitudes toward a brand within a given set of needs. For instance, a manufacturer of analgesics produces a brand that consumers regard as significantly stronger and as providing more immediate relief. Yet, most consumers want a mild, safe brand that is recommended by doctors. The manufacturer could try to convince consumers that analgesics are nonprescription items that do not need a doctor's recommendation, that safety should be of no concern, and that a stronger product is perfectly acceptable. Or, the manufacturer could tone down the emphasis on strength in the advertising, still emphasize quick relief, and point out the safety of the product based on FDA approval. The latter strategy is going to be more effective than the former because the marketer is operating within the existing priorities of the consumer.

Needs are more enduring, ingrained, and internalized than attitudes. Moreover, some needs are harder to change than others. Needs that reflect cultural values and a social orientation instilled from childhood are deep-seated and almost impossible to change by advertising. Marketers of men's hats could seek to change consumers' priorities regarding youth and vigor and attempt to bring back the old-time values to get men to wear hats more often. Or they could attempt to change consumers' attitudes toward hats by introducing sporty and casual varieties that emphasize existing needs. The latter strategy would be more effective because there is no attempt to change deep-seated needs.

2. *Brand beliefs are easier to change than brand evaluations.*   The traditional hierarchy of effects states that a change in beliefs precedes a change in brand evaluations that precedes a change in behavior. Therefore, changing beliefs should be easier than

changing brand evaluations, and changing beliefs and evaluations should be easier than changing behavior. The information that a brand of aspirin has a new pain-killing formulation will change beliefs about the brand, but the evaluation of the brand will not necessarily change unless killing pain happens to be a high priority need. Most advertising implicitly follows the principle that beliefs are easier to change because advertising generally communicates the attributes of a brand.

3. Brand beliefs and evaluations are easier to change than behavior. A marketer may be able to change consumers' beliefs about a product or bring about a more favorable evaluation, yet, it is possible there may be no change at all in behavior. Attempts can be made to short-circuit beliefs by offering lower prices or deals on products, but such strategies are unlikely to work for high involvement products. The consumer will be more skeptical of lower priced brands of cars, refrigerators, or cameras because of a link between price and quality.

Strategies to change behavior without changing attitudes are more likely to work for low involvement goods because there is less risk associated with the purchase. A typical example of this is a consumer who buys a brand of soap only because it is on sale. Furthermore, repetitious advertising may cause the consumer to remember a brand while in the store.[3] A purchase may result just from the reminder effect with no change in brand attitudes.

4. The intensity of needs is easier to change than the direction of needs. Assume a particular coffee drinker does not consider the strength of the coffee to be an important attribute in brand evaluation. However, if asked, the consumer states that he or she prefers a weaker coffee. It is possible, through advertising, to convince the consumer that the strength of the coffee directly influences taste and aroma and is therefore an important consideration. Changing the nature of a consumer's needs by trying to convince the consumer that a strong coffee provides better taste is more difficult since it may contradict a long held response that favors weaker coffee.

5. Weak attitudes are easier to change. If preference for a brand is not particularly strong the latitude of acceptance for new brands will be greater. On the other hand, an individual who strongly favors a particular brand cannot be readily converted to a competing brand. In this case the latitude of acceptance is narrow and the consumer is likely to reject most claims about the competing brand.

6. Attitudes held by consumers with less confidence in their brand evaluations are easier to change. If a consumer is unsure in his or her evaluation of a brand, the consumer will be more receptive to the informational content of advertising and more subject to attitude change. A consumer in the market for a color TV set may favor a brand based on the reception seen in a friend's home or in a showroom, but may have few evaluative criteria on which to make a decision. Up to this point, there is little to go by in evaluating specific product attributes. If a manufacturer then advertises a brand with certain features, such as finer color tuning, better color hold, or more contrast, this may induce a change in preference in the consumer. The advertiser has in effect supplied a set of evaluative criteria for the consumer.

Confusion about the criteria can also cause the consumer to lack self-confidence in making a decision. A number of years ago the Carpet Institute hired a research firm to study the purchasing process for rugs and carpets. This is what was found:

> There is a great deal of confusion and misconception about the characteristics, features and terminology in carpeting. Even the terms rug vs. carpet, the type of rug construction vs. company names are confused. It would seem on the surface that too wide a variety of features are pressed upon the housewife with her rather simple needs in floor covering.[4]

Consumers' lack of self-confidence in purchasing rugs and carpets was manifested by their reluctant reliance on salespeople and their failure to refer to literature on the care and construction of carpeting. The study concluded that "most of the attitudes measured in this study were found to be unrelated to buying behavior."

In a case like this, consumers would be receptive to a brand that emphasized a few key product attributes. The key strategy would be to change beliefs about the product category and to capitalize on these attitudinal changes by associating them with the manufacturer's brand name.

7. *Attitudes are easier to change when information is ambiguous.* If consumers are faced with conflicting claims about competitive products or with highly technical information which they cannot assess, then clarifying information is sought which may produce attitude change. When information is highly ambiguous, any clarifying information can cause a change in cognitions on key evaluative criteria. Lipstein, in a study, equated a high level of informational ambiguity to high anxiety in purchasing and found that high informational ambiguity and purchase anxiety consistently produced greater attitude change over a wide variety of products.[5]

8. *Attitudes are easier to change when there is a low level of ego involvement.* The greater the individual's self-identification with the product, the greater the difficulty there will be in changing attitudes about the product. Values associated with the consumer's self-image are likely to be reinforced by friends and neighbors creating an even higher level of ego involvement with the product.

Sherif's theory of social judgment supports this.[6] Given a high level of involvement with a product, messages will be accepted only if they agree with the individual's beliefs. Such a prediction conforms to consistency theory.[7] Discrepant information will be screened out by a process of selective perception.

9. *Attitudes are easier to change when they are not in balance.* According to Rosenberg, attitudes that do not conform to each other will change to achieve balance.[8] Heider's balance theory states that when two beliefs conflict, one or both of the conflicting beliefs will change to come into balance.[9] An individual may have a positive attitude toward large cars, but also be strongly in favor of energy conservation. The imbalance in these beliefs will produce tension leading to a change in one or both attitudes. Recognizing that large cars waste energy, either the consumer's attitude toward large cars will become more negative, the attitude toward energy conservation will be rationalized to include maintaining a large car, or both beliefs will change to achieve a balance. The consumer in this situation would be receptive to advertising for compact cars that permits the maintenance of a belief in energy conservation as a goal. Just as likely, however, is the possibility that the consumer may also be influenced by statements of friends valuing larger cars for comfort and status. In either case, beliefs about large cars and energy conservation have to be modified to achieve a balance.

10. *Attitudes are easier to change when the object is new.* For new and innovative products such as the Picturephone or video-discs, current preconceptions can be more readily changed than can those for existing products such as the telephone or television.

STRATEGIES FOR ATTITUDE CHANGE PRIOR TO PURCHASE

Marketers may attempt to change consumers' attitudes before purchases are made in an attempt to induce them to try a certain brand. Marketers may also attempt to change attitudes after a purchase to counter dissonant information about the brand and to minimize any negative experiences (disconfirmation of expectations) that may result.

The multiattribute models described in the previous chapter provide the best framework for considering strategies of attitude change *before* a purchase because these models accept the traditional hierarchy of effects theory that assumes behavior is the end result. Two other models can be taken into consideration when planning strategies of attitude change before a purchase. These are Katz's *functional theory of attitudes* and Sherif's *social judgment theory,* both of which are oriented to communications effects.

On the other hand, dissonance theory, attribution theory, and the theory of passive learning are best used in strategies for attitude change *after* a purchase because these theories recognize that behavior may change with little change in attitudes and that attitude change may be the result of a change in behavior.

Multiattribute Models and Attitude Change

In the basic multiattribute model, brand beliefs (the b_i component) and consumer needs (as measured by the value placed on these beliefs — the a_i component) influence the overall evaluation of the brand (A_o) which, in turn, influences behavioral intent (BI) and, ultimately, behavior (B).

On this basis, four strategies can be considered to influence behavior based on the multiattribute models:

1. Change needs (a change in an a_i component)
2. Change beliefs (a change in a b_i component)
3. Change the overall evaluation of the brand (a change in A_o)
4. Change behavioral intentions (a change in BI) or behavior (a change in B)

These strategies for change are briefly considered below.

1. Change the direction and/or intensity of needs. This strategy requires convincing consumers to reassess the value of a particular attribute — for example, convincing the consumer that bad taste is a good quality in mouthwash. Any attempt to change needs must rely on prior research showing that a certain segment of the market would be receptive to such a change. For example, the packaging component of many products is rarely the most important criterion in selection. Pringles introduced potato chips in a new cylindrical container as a means of preserving freshness. Such a strategy can be successful only if the company has done prior research to demonstrate that the importance of the package could be increased through advertising and through an association established between the package and freshness. The warning against attempting to change deep-seated social and cultural needs bears repeating. Needs may be changed regarding sugar content in cereals or packaging in potato chips, but it is doubtful that advertising could influence a change in needs regarding transportation, leisure, or weight watching.

2. Change beliefs. By far the most common strategy is one that attempts to change the beliefs about brands through product and advertising strategies. In this case, the marketer must convince the consumer that the product has certain positive attributes either by changing product features, by attempting to change product perceptions, or both (e.g., change beliefs that Cadillac gets poor gas mileage). The important point is to ensure that the beliefs being changed will induce favorable changes in brand evaluations and the intention to buy (the belief Cadillac gets better gas mileage will increase the likelihood of buying).

Features taken for granted cannot be the basis for attitude change. For example, advertising good taste for a ground coffee cannot be a basis for changing beliefs about a brand because all ground roast coffees are expected to have good taste. In a sense, the attribute of taste is an entry card into the market and should be used as a secondary theme just to remind consumers that the coffee is acceptable in this regard. Primary themes may revolve around flavor or perkiness.

On the other hand, taste could be a determinant attribute for decaffeinated coffee since consumers do not always expect a decaffeinated coffee to be good tasting. In a sense, consumers are trading better taste for benefits such as less stomach irritation or the ability to sleep. As noted previously, Sanka attempted to change beliefs about the brand from a medicinal coffee to a more flavorful coffee. In a 1959 survey taken by Sanka's advertising agency, one of the basic findings was that "people regarded Sanka more as a medicine than as a flavorful beverage."[10] In view of this survey, "the decision was made to emphasize flavor even more strongly. The development of the 'land of origin' advertising campaign followed." This campaign emphasized the flavor aspects of the brand — for example, the idea that Sanka has 100 percent pure coffee flavor. A survey taken in 1961 revealed that the beliefs about the brand remained the same. "Coffee servers in 1961 continued to view instant Sanka as they had in 1959, namely as a coffee for older people, for women, . . . expensive, weak, as a coffee that cannot stimulate, is never harmful, and has slightly poor flavor."[11] In fact, the percentage of those accepting the brand as flavorful declined slightly. The company could not change beliefs over a two-year period. Yet, over a longer period of time, there was movement toward a more flavorful perception of the brand, indicating that changes in beliefs required a prolonged period to be implemented.

The two strategies described above — a change in needs and a change in beliefs — were both tested by Lutz by introducing a fictitious laundry soap to consumers in a test situation.[12] After describing the brand to consumers, they were given an article in *Consumer Reports* to read that was designed to change their beliefs about the brand. A second message attempted to change their values by convincing them that high sudsiness was not a valuable attribute. Lutz found that a change in beliefs resulted in a change in the overall evaluation of the brand, but an attempted change in values (needs) was not closely related to any change in the evaluation of the brand. This finding conforms to the principle that changing beliefs about a brand (the b_i element) holds more promise than does attempting to change the value of these beliefs (the a_i element).

3. *Change brand evaluations.* Marketers also try to affect evaluations directly without specific reference to product attributes. This shortcut strategy may involve associating a positive mood with product usage. For example, a beer ad might show a group of men drinking the brand in a happy environment after winning some hectic athletic event. If the consumer accepts the association of product use with success, then a favorable evaluation has been established with little reference to product attributes. To a degree, many cosmetic companies try to induce a mood in advertising, perhaps one of mystery, romanticism, or social success, and associate this mood with product use. This type of advertising could change the evaluation of a brand if the mood created is sufficient to differentiate the brand from others. In most cases, differentiation by mood alone is insufficient and some reference must be made to product attributes like scent, strength, or packaging.

4. *Change intentions to buy or behavior.* Another change strategy is to induce a consumer to purchase a brand for which there may be no strong preference — that is, to induce attitude-discrepant behavior. The assumption is that if there is some

inducement to try a brand that is not preferred (possibly by lowering the price or by offering a deal or a coupon), then the individual may change attitudes to conform to behavior.

For example, suppose an individual purchases an analgesic because there is a five-cents-off deal. Assume there is little difference in effectiveness between the regular brand and the new brand. In order to justify the purchase, the consumer views the new brand as having provided immediate relief and therefore decides to buy it again, even when the price returns to normal. This strategy makes use of the theory of cognitive dissonance. According to Festinger, the magnitude of such inducements to switch should not be large; otherwise the consumer could always say the only reason for a brand switch was the obvious price difference.[13] The tendency would then be to switch back to the regular brand when the price of the less preferred brand returns to normal. However, if the difference is a relatively small price change, but one sufficient to cause a saving, the consumer will have to find some reason other than price to justify the purchase.

Functional Theory and Attitude Change

Another model that has implications for strategies of attitude change prior to purchase is Katz's functional theory of attitudes.[14] As noted in the previous chapter, Katz believes that there are four functions served by attitudes: a utilitarian function, a knowledge function, a value expressive function, and an ego defensive function. Marketing strategies can attempt to change attitudes serving each of these functions.

Changing Attitudes Through the Utilitarian Function

One way of influencing a positive change in brand attitudes is to show that the product can solve a utilitarian goal the consumer may not have previously considered. For example, Arm & Hammer began advertising various utilitarian uses of baking soda in an attempt to increase sales. Quoting from the Arm & Hammer package, the product will:

- brighten smiles (pour soda into your hand and brush with wet toothbrush);
- provide indigestion relief (half a teaspoon in 1/2 glass of water and feel the burp of relief);
- clean and sweeten (fill sink with solution of 3 tbsps. to quart of water to clean coffee and tea pots, thermos jugs, etc.);
- remove sour smells and stains (open container and leave in refrigerator or freezer);
- refresh baths (one cupful into bath cleans off oils and perspiration and will leave your skin feeling smooth, clean, and fresh).

This is quite an array of uses for a traditional cooking and baking product. These uses may induce a favorable change in a consumer's attitude toward the brand because they satisfy a utilitarian function.

Changing Attitudes Through the Knowledge Function

The knowledge function organizes and classifies information, thus facilitating the consumer's information-processing task. It is important for marketers to provide a clear and unambiguous positioning for their product to ensure favorable attitudes. Day states this need clearly:

> New product marketers are acutely conscious of [the need to] generally avoid positioning a new product where it defies easy categorization. A better strategy is to demonstrate that the new product fits into several existing categories at the same time and thus delivers additional benefits.[15]

A good example of a clear and unambiguous positioning is Carnation Instant Breakfast. The company clearly positioned the product as a breakfast food directed to nutritionally oriented consumers who did not have time to prepare a traditional breakfast. Information was provided on the nutritional value and caloric content of the product. Had the product tried to reach a broader market with a more ambiguous positioning, it might have failed. For instance, an alternative strategy might have been to position it as a nutritional pick-me-up at any time of the day. Although this positioning may be directed to a greater number of usage situations, it would be more likely to confuse the consumer. The product could have been seen as a breakfast food, a nutritional snack, or a dietary supplement. Such an ambiguous positioning might have led to a less favorable evaluation of the brand.

Changing Attitudes Through the Value Expressive Function

Advertising that attempts to influence the value expressive function confronts deep-seated, personal values that are difficult to change. For example, advertising retirement communities by extolling the virtues of getting older would be a poor campaign. Rather, advertising should accept the predominant value orientation on youth and vigor by emphasizing the physical activities and facilities provided by these communities which help one stay young. The clear principle is that advertising should accept deep-seated values rather than attempt to change them.

Changing Attitudes Through the Ego Defensive Function

Research has consistently shown that the more ego defensive the attitude is, the less subject it is to outside influence. The individual who is an avid reader of a particular magazine that reflects his or her self-image, life-style and interests, is unlikely to accept any discrepant information from competitive magazines. Here again, the principle is that advertising should accept and adapt to ego defensive attitudes rather than try to change them.

Social Judgment Theory and Attitude Change

Sherif's theory of social judgment provides direct implications for strategies of attitude change.[16] Two strategies cited above — to change beliefs about a brand or to change the value associated with these beliefs — require that the consumer accept the advertising message. Sherif's theory predicts that if the change suggested by advertising is too extreme, the message will be rejected (a contrast effect), because the message will fall into the consumer's latitude of rejection.

If the message suggests moderate changes, then it will be accepted (assimilation) because it is within the consumer's latitude of acceptance.

The more involved the consumer is, the less likely it is that the message proposing a change in beliefs or values will be accepted. But, as noted in Chapter 4, consumers are not highly involved with most product categories. Therefore, advertising suggesting moderate changes in beliefs or values is likely to be accepted.

For example, the introduction by Cadillac of a medium sized car was acceptable to most Cadillac owners because it did not represent an extreme change in beliefs. There was an attempt to associate the medium sized Cadillac with the same traditional values of comfort and status as the larger model. Had Cadillac attempted to introduce a compact car to compete with the VW, Toyota, or Datsun, this change would have fallen outside the latitude of acceptance of most Cadillac owners and would have resulted in a negative change in attitudes toward the car (contrast effect).

There is some evidence that messages attempting to change beliefs and values that are extreme, but not extreme enough to bring about rejection of the message, may create curiosity and lead to product trial.[17] Introduction of a highly styled refrigerator (different color and design, possibly even different shape) would represent an extreme change in beliefs for a standard product. Yet, the change may not be extreme enough to be rejected outright, especially since it does not threaten basic values or self-identification. An arousal of curiosity, a visit to a store to see the product, and, in some cases, a purchase may result.

STRATEGIES FOR ATTITUDE CHANGE AFTER A PURCHASE

Marketers may seek to change brand attitudes after, as well as before, a purchase. Such a strategy may attempt to counter competitive advertising that is creating doubts in the consumer's mind about the purchase (dissonance) or may attempt to counteract negative experiences with the product. As noted, three theories provide strategy implications for attitude change after the purchase: dissonance theory, attribution theory, and the theory of passive learning. These theories were described in Chapter 4 and will be briefly reviewed here within the context of attitude change strategies.

Dissonance Theory

Dissonance theory suggests marketers should seek to reduce dissonance by supplying consumers with positive information about the brand after the purchase. Runyon cites five strategies to provide supporting information after the purchase and thus to reduce dissonance:

1. Provide additional product information and suggestions for product care and maintenance through brochures or advertising.
2. Provide warranties and guaranties to reduce postpurchase doubt.

3. Ensure good service and immediate follow-up on complaints to provide postpurchase support.

4. Advertise reliable product quality and performance to reassure recent purchasers of product satisfaction.

5. Follow up after the purchase with direct contacts to make sure the customer understands how to use the product and to ensure satisfaction.[18]

All these strategies are relevant for high risk, high involvement product categories. They are designed to counteract any negative attitude toward the product due to postpurchase doubts.

Attribution Theory

Attribution theory suggests that the consumer will seek some reason for the purchase after the fact.[19] Such behavioral attributions are most likely to occur when the product has been purchased with little evaluation of brand alternatives. The reason ascribed to the purchase is essentially an afterthought resulting in a change in attitudes as a result of the behavior.

If this is true, then attribution theory implies that advertisers should supply consumers reasons for the purchase after they have bought. For example, a consumer buys brown eggs in a supermarket because they are cheaper. The consumer reads an article that says brown eggs are more nourishing and less likely to crack. A friend asks the consumer, "Why in the world did you buy brown eggs?" and the consumer answers, "Because they are more nourishing and less likely to crack." The appropriate marketing strategy for low involvement products with few differences is, therefore, to demonstrate potentially significant product differences after the purchase. Such differences provide the consumer with a reason for buying again. In the above case, the consumer has an adequate reason to buy brown eggs again.

Passive Learning and Postpurchase Attitude Change

Krugman's passive learning theory states that consumers learn about brands with little involvement and purchase with little evaluation of alternative brands.[20] Attitudes are more likely to be formed after, rather than before, a purchase.

Krugman's theory is most relevant for providing strategies to increase the level of consumer involvement after the purchase. Marketers seek to increase involvement with their brand since the higher the level of commitment, the greater the likelihood that true, rather than spurious, brand loyalty will result. Chapter 4 cited the following strategies for increasing involvement:

1. Link the product to an involving issue.
2. Link the product to an involving personal situation.
3. Create involving advertising.
4. Increase the importance of a product attribute.
5. Introduce a new and important attribute to the product.

Given a greater level of involvement, a more favorable attitude toward the product will result. As in dissonance and attribution theories, such a favorable shift in attitude will follow behavior.

SUMMARY

This chapter describes marketing strategies that adapt to existing needs and attitudes and those that attempt to change these needs and attitudes. To illustrate these strategies, a basic communications model is used. Communications require generating an idea, encoding it, and transmitting it to the consumer. Then the message must be decoded by the consumer and acted on.

Adaptive strategies are likely to be more successful than change strategies because it is difficult to change consumer needs and beliefs, especially if they are strongly held. Adaptive strategies aim to:

- identify unmet needs;
- position products to meet existing needs;
- identify those segments of the market that have positive attitudes toward the brand but who are not purchasers, and try to convince them to buy;
- identify those segments of the market that have positive attitudes and who are purchasers, and reinforce these positive attitudes.

Although strategies of attitude change are harder to implement than strategies of attitude reinforcement, they should be considered. Attitudes are easier to change when:

- attitudes are weakly held;
- the consumer is less confident in evaluating brands;
- information is ambiguous;
- attitudes conflict with each other;
- there is a low level of involvement.

Various strategies of attitude change are considered based on the components of needs and attitudes. The marketer may attempt to change consumer needs, change consumer beliefs about a brand, change the overall evaluation of the brand, or change behavior directly without attempting to change attitudes.

Functional theory also provides guidelines for strategies to change utilitarian, value expressive, and ego defensive attitudes, as well as to change attitudes by providing knowledge.

Marketers may also seek to change attitudes toward a brand after, as well as before, a purchase. Three theories provide strategic guidelines. Dissonance theory suggests that advertisers should provide consumers with positive information after the purchase to reduce dissonance. Attribution theory suggests that marketers supply consumers with a reason for purchasing after the fact.

The theory of passive learning suggests that inertia can be translated into brand loyalty by increasing the commitment to the brand.

Whereas the last four chapters were concerned with consumer thought variables, the next two chapters will be concerned with consumer characteristics — namely, demographics, life-style, and personality.

QUESTIONS

1. Marketers can position new products to fit existing needs (an adaptive strategy) as illustrated by the Picturephone example. If the telecommunications company producing the Picturephone found that visual communication was relatively unimportant, one option would be to try to change the need criteria by demonstrating the importance of visual communication to businesses through an advertising campaign.
   - What are the pros and cons of such a strategy?
   - Under what circumstances is such a strategy most likely to succeed?

2. A producer of ready-to-eat cereals conducts a survey and finds that consumers who rate the company's brand high on nutrition are more likely to buy it. These consumers tend to be younger and more affluent. The advertising manager decides to direct a major portion of the advertising budget to nonusers (older, less affluent consumers) to try to convince them of the cereal's nutritional content. He reasons there will be a higher payoff in attempting to change attitudes of nonusers than in reinforcing attitudes of users.
   - What are the pros and cons of this argument?

3. What problems may the Department of Transportation face in mounting an advertising campaign to induce people to switch from automobiles to mass transit? What other forms of communication and influence may be more persuasive than advertising. Why?

4. When Cadillac introduced a medium sized car, it could have developed an *adaptive* or a *change* strategy in communicating this basic change in their line.
   - What focus could advertising have taken in following a change strategy? In following an adaptive strategy?

5. The statement was made that "the intensity of a consumer's needs is easier to change than the direction of needs." As an example, it is easier to convince consumers to reduce the intake of sugar in colas than it is to try to get them to like sugarless colas.
   - What are the implications of the statement for marketing a new and more effective mouthwash?

6. A manufacturer of high priced stereo components finds that attitudes toward the company's line of products are very positive, but many stereo purchasers are uncertain of the criteria to use in selecting components and, therefore, reduce risk by buying the lowest priced or the best known brand. The company would like to increase the consumer's confidence in the purchase process. By doing so, it believes it will increase the likelihood consumers will buy its products.

- What strategies can the company use to increase self-confidence in the purchasing process?

7. Consider this statement: Attitudes are easier to change when there is a low level of ego involvement.
   - In view of this statement, why might it be particularly hard to change attitudes toward a consumer's regular perfume, baby food, and clothing store?

8. Marketers can attempt to change beliefs about competitive brands as well as change beliefs about their own brand.
   - Can you cite examples of such a strategy?
   - What might be the danger of pursuing such a strategy?

9. Consumers who switch to a brand because its price is *somewhat lower* than their regular brand are more likely to develop favorable attitudes toward the new brand than if the brand is sold at a *much lower* price.
   - Why is this true?
   - Does this finding suggest that marketers should moderate price decreases?

RESEARCH ASSIGNMENTS

1. Principles of attitude change suggest that attitudes are easier to change when consumers are less confident in their evaluations of a brand. Pick a product category and ask consumers to rate three of the leading brands on (1) an overall basis, and (2) a vocabulary of product attributes. Also, ask consumers to (3) rate their degree of confidence in making judgments about brands in the category, and (4) rate the degree to which they think the product is important to them.

   Then present consumers with ads for each of the three brands in a dummy magazine format. Have consumers rate the brands once again on an overall basis and on the vocabulary of product attributes.
   - Do overall brand ratings for those with less confidence in their brand evaluations shift more than those with a greater degree of confidence?
   - Do ratings shift in the direction of the advertised claims?
   - Attitude theory also suggests that those who rate the product category as less important are more likely to change attitudes. Do your findings support this?

2. Marketers sometimes seek to induce a behavior change without appeals to attitudes by offering brands at a lower price. The theory of cognitive dissonance would predict that if the consumer bought a brand other than the regular brand at a much lower price, the attitude toward the brand would be more negative than if the brand was bought at a price only slightly lower than the regular brand.
   - Select a heavily dealed product category such as coffee, paper towels, or detergents. Identify a sample of consumers who recently bought a brand other than their regular brand on a price deal or by coupon. Determine attitudes for the brand purchased.
   - Does your data confirm the hypothesis that the greater the price differential between the regular and the dealed brand, the more negative the attitude toward the brand purchased on deal?

1. Henry Assael, "Segmenting Markets by Group Purchasing Behavior: An Application of the AID Technique," *Journal of Marketing Research* 7 (May 1970): 153–158.

2. Mark I. Alpert, "Identification of Determinant Attributes: A Comparison of Methods," *Journal of Marketing Research* 8 (May 1971): 184–191.

3. Herbert E. Krugman, "The Measurement of Advertising Involvement," *Public Opinion Quarterly* 30 (Winter 1966): 584–585.

4. Neil H. Borden and Martin V. Marshall, *Advertising Management: Text and Cases* (Homewood, Ill.: Richard D. Irwin, 1959), p. 126.

5. Benjamin Lipstein, "Anxiety, Risk and Uncertainty in Advertising Effectiveness Measurements," in Lee Adler and Irving Crespi, eds., *Attitude Research on the Rocks* (Chicago: American Marketing Association, 1968), pp. 11–27.

6. M. Sherif and C.E. Hovland, *Social Judgment* (New Haven: Yale University Press, 1964).

7. See S. Feldman, ed., *Cognitive Consistency: Motivational Antecedents and Behavioral Consequents* (New York: Academic Press, Inc., 1966).

8. Milton J. Rosenberg, "Inconsistency Arousal and Reduction in Attitude Change," in D. T. Kollat, R.B. Blackwell, and J.F. Engel, eds., *Research in Consumer Behavior* (New York: Holt, Rinehart and Winston, 1970), pp. 271–286.

9. Fritz Heider, *The Psychology of Interpersonal Relations* (New York: John Wiley and Sons, Inc., 1958).

10. Joseph W. Newman, *Marketing Management and Information* (Homewood, Ill.: Richard D. Irwin, 1967), p. 211, Sanka Case (B).

11. Ibid., p. 217.

12. Richard J. Lutz, "Changing Brand Attitudes Through Modification of Cognitive Structures," *Journal of Consumer Research* 1 (March 1975): 49–59.

13. Leon Festinger, *A Theory of Cognitive Dissonance* (New York: Harper and Row, 1957).

14. Daniel Katz, "The Functional Approach to the Study of Attitudes," *Public Opinion Quarterly* 24 (Summer 1960): 163–204.

15. George S. Day, "Theories of Attitude Structure and Change," in Scott Ward and Thomas S. Robertson, eds., *Consumer Behavior: Theoretical Sources* (Englewood Cliffs, N.J.: Prentice-Hall, Inc., 1973), p. 341.

16. Sherif and Hovland, *Social Judgment*.

17. John C. Maloney, "Is Advertising Believability Really Important?" *Journal of Marketing,* 27 (October 1963): 1–8.

18. Kenneth E. Runyon, *Consumer Behavior and the Practice of Marketing* (Columbus, Ohio: Charles E. Merrill Publishing Co., 1977), p. 287.

19. D. Bem, "Attitudes as Self-Descriptions: Another Look at the Attitude-Behavior Link," in A. Greenwald, T. Brock and T. Ostrom, eds., *Psychological Foundations of Attitudes* (New York: Academic Press, 1968). For applications of attribution theory to consumer behavior, see Bobby Calder, "When Attitudes Follow Behavior — A Self-Perception/Dissonance Interpretation of Low Involvement," in John C. Maloney and Bernard Silverman, eds., *Attitude Research Plays for High Stakes* (Chicago: American Marketing Association, 1979), pp. 25–36.

20. Herbert E. Krugman, "The Impact of Television Advertising: Learning Without Involvement," *Public Opinion Quarterly* 29 (Fall 1965): 349–356.

NINE

Demographics

Focus of Chapter

During the 1976 presidential campaign, Jimmy Carter assigned Joseph Califano to study the pressures affecting the American family. Califano's report summarized three significant changes:[1]

1. The proportion of working women dramatically increased;
2. The divorce rate increased to the point where two out of five marriages in the United States end in divorce;
3. Residential mobility rates revealed the average American moves fourteen times in his or her lifetime, and 20 percent of the American population moves each year.

These changes, plus the changing age and educational makeup of the U.S. market, are the most major demographic shifts influencing marketing strategies.

This chapter will consider these demographic shifts. The marketing applications of demographics will be evaluated — namely, the use of demographics to guide media planning, segment markets, and identify targets for new products. Since the following chapter will review the other two key consumer descriptors, life-styles and personality, this chapter will begin by showing the importance of demographic, life-style and personality variables in developing marketing strategies. A discussion of demographic trends will then follow.

THE IMPORTANCE OF CONSUMER CHARACTERISTICS IN MARKETING STRATEGY

Demographics

The demographic profile of the American consumer is changing significantly. The proportion of working women has increased dramatically, the birth rate continues to decline, and the median age is increasing. These demographic changes cause significant shifts in consumer attitudes and purchasing behavior. Consider the following:

- Levi Strauss, the jeans maker whose ads with psychedelic and sexual overtones were the commercial embodiment of the youthful culture of the 1960s, has made subtle changes in its pitch. The company now promotes sportswear with a fuller cut, for that 1965 college boy who can no longer squeeze into his size 30 Levis.[2]

- Faced with declining sales of baby food, the Gerber Products Company has diversified and now makes such products as vaporizers and shampoo. It is also testing adult foods such as catsup and peanut spreads as well as single serving foods for the elderly. As it is, company officials privately estimate that as much as 10 percent of its baby food is actually consumed by the elderly.[3]

- The FM rock radio stations that emerged in the 1960s are still thriving, but the sponsors are selling condominium apartments and suburban homes as well as phonograph records and acne remedies.[4]

- Avon, the largest manufacturer of costume jewelry, is purchasing Tiffany, one of the most expensive jewelry stores. Why this least likely of all mergers? *The New York Times* reported that "Avon has seen its door-to-door cosmetics operations suffer as American women began to join the work force in greater numbers and thus were not at home when the Avon sales representatives came calling."[5] The company began directing its fragrances to younger, more affluent working women. It has also adjusted to the increased proportion of working women by allowing its representatives to call at nights and weekends and at offices.[6] The purchase of Tiffany provides a more direct source to working women who "want to spend and want to go out more and look better when they do."[7]

- Pepsi Cola acquired Pizza Hut to take advantage of the trend toward eating at fast food establishments. *Business Week* reports that shifting demographics is the primary reason for the acquisition. "Pizza Hut, Pepsi feels, is positioned to catch the members of the post-World-War-II baby boom as they enter their 30s and 40s."[8] This is the hamburger and coke generation that finds fast foods more acceptable.

Marketers are interested in both the long-term demographic trends cited above and the more particular demographic profile of their customers. When marketers ask who their customers are, they frequently refer to the age, income, and regional makeup of customers buying their brand.

For example, consider a large manufacturer of packaged foods that identifies a group of heavy snackers concerned with calories and nutrition. The company decides to position its brand of potato chips as a natural snack to appeal to this target segment. Can media be selected to direct advertising specifically to the target segment? Or does advertising have to be directed to a more general market? The answer depends on whether the target group differs from the general population by demographic characteristics. Is the target group older, younger, higher or lower income, in certain occupational groups? If demographics identify the target group, more effective media can be selected to reach this group.

Life-Style and Personality Characteristics

More recently, marketers have begun to describe their customers in psychographic terms (life-style and personality characteristics). These variables provide a richer description of the consumer than just demographics. Psychographics aid in product positioning and in setting the tone of advertising messages. The snack food company introducing the new brand of potato chips would want to advertise the brand as a natural snack and as low in calories. But, should the potato chip be positioned in a family setting, at a party, at a beach scene, or while watching a football game? The life-style characteristics of the target group will provide guidelines for advertisers — whether the group tends to be cosmopolitan, isolates, socializers, etc. Again, the assumption is that the group differs in its life-style characteristics from the population as a whole. If not, no guidelines can emerge.

Personality characteristics may also guide advertising and product directions. Does the target group tend to be compulsive, anxious? If so, perhaps the advertising should suggest the opportunity to continue snacking without the anxieties associated with preservatives and calories.

Consumer Characteristics Versus
Needs and Attitudes

The distinction between consumer needs and attitudes (described in previous chapters) and consumer characteristics is important. Needs and attitudes are product-specific whereas consumer characteristics are generalized. A need or attitude must be related to a particular brand or product. Advertising the need for a lift may be relevant for coffee but not for soap suds. A demographic characteristic such as age or a life-style characteristic such as home orientation is relevant for coffee *and* soap suds.

Attitudes and needs are more subjective and harder to formulate and measure. Consumer characteristics are more objective, standardized, and measurable, especially demographics. As a result, demographics are the most widely used consumer descriptors. Age is age; income is income. But standardization is also a weakness. There is more reason to believe that attitudes and needs will be related to consumer behavior because these variables have been defined with the product in mind. There is less reason to believe that demographics will be related to consumer behavior. If there are no demographic differences between brand users and the general population, the marketer loses the ability to selectively choose media and distribution strategies and must use more diffuse and costly marketing methods. Despite these shortcomings, demographics and psychographics are important as consumer descriptors.

Consumer needs, attitudes, and perceptions are only half the input required by the marketer to make sound decisions. The importance of the other half — demographics and psychographics — is summarized by one marketing expert as follows:

> Every customer list [i.e., group] has identifiable demographic and psychographic characteristics. Each list has a profile. The marketer who really doesn't know who his customer is — a startlingly large number don't — is really flying blind.

> The products [customers] will buy are a condition of age, education, marital status, and income. Likewise the propensity to buy is a condition of lifestyle . . .

> What type of vacations do your customers take? What type of entertainment do they enjoy? Do they prefer books to movies, or vice versa? Are they outdoor people or indoor people? Life-style characteristics provide "road signs" to product desires.[9]

THE CHANGING DEMOGRAPHIC TRENDS OF AMERICAN CONSUMERS

Marketers have tracked changes in demography because of the long-range implications for marketing strategy. Diversification by Gerbers, Avon, and Pepsi are examples. In this section the general demographic trends impacting on marketing strategies will be considered. The next section will discuss the more specific utilization of demographic characteristics to segment markets.

Increases in the Proportion of Working Women

The proportion of working wives increased from 24 percent in 1950 to 46 percent in 1976 (see Figure 9–1).[10] By 1978, more than 50 percent of women with children held jobs outside the home.[11] The point has been reached where more women are working than not.

What are the results of this remarkable shift? For one thing, family purchasing roles are changing. The woman may no longer be the purchasing agent for most family household needs. She may not even be the prime homemaker. Today, 46 percent of husbands shop for groceries and 24 percent cook.[12] Furthermore, the husband can no longer be considered the prime decision maker for high expenditure items. The general manager for marketing research at Armstrong Cork says, "Women who feel they are bringing in a significant portion of the family income will make the decision to buy a new kitchen floor, for example, on their own, without their husbands along."[13] The result has been a blurring of traditional definitions of household purchasing roles. Today, it would be shortsighted for a marketer conducting a survey of paper towels, disposable diapers, or frozen foods to restrict the sample to the "woman of the house." In the early 1970s this would have been the rule.

Having more women in the work force also means less time for shopping and greater emphasis on product benefits such as speed and convenience. Stuart

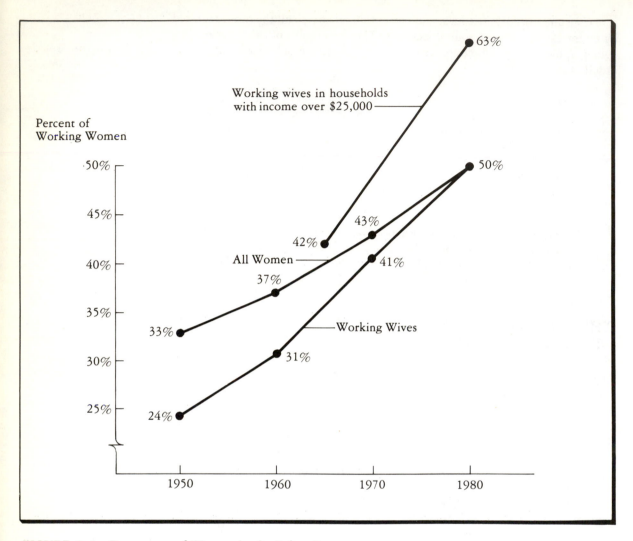

FIGURE 9–1   Percentage of Women in the Labor Force

Sources: U.S. Department of Labor and *Business Week,* Feb. 20, 1978, p. 80.
    Reprinted with permission from *Business Week,* Feb. 20, 1978.

D. Watson, chairman of the board of Heublein, believes that since working wives will have less time to shop, brand names will become increasingly more important. There will be less willingness to experiment with unknown products.[14] Working wives may be more brand loyal as a result of a lack of time for decision making rather than as a result of inherent product benefits (i.e., spurious rather than true brand loyalty). The emphasis on time-saving benefits has also been extended to services. One investment counselor sees a growth in financial services to accommodate working couples with little time to devote to money planning.[15]

The most apparent result of this emphasis on time is the increasing popularity of fast food establishments. *Ad Age* reports:

Working mothers do not have as much time to devote to preparing meals —
meals which they can pick up in a matter of minutes at a fast food restaurant.
With a second salary in hand, families have a greater disposable income
and they are spending a good deal of it on food not cooked at home.[16]

The result is that 75 percent of American families eat out at least once a week;
families with working wives average 7.4 meals out per week.[17]

The potential losers in the fast food trend are food companies and food
stores. They have begun to adjust rapidly. Food stores have adapted by selling
fast foods and installing carryout food counters. An increasing number are
introducing sit-down restaurants in or near the store. A&P's Price and Pride
Burger Bistros is an example. The food companies are introducing fast food
products. Many have their own fast food chains — for example, Pillsbury,
General Mills, General Foods, Quaker Oats, CPC International, and Pepsi.
Traditional food lines have been adapted to the trend. Campbell's Chunky
Soups are advertised as the perfect light meal which even a husband can fix for
his working wife.[18]

Another effect of the greater proportion of working women is increased
affluence among two-income families. In 1976, 63 percent of the families with
incomes over $25,000 had a working husband and wife compared to only 42
percent in 1967 (see Figure 9–1). The result is greater discretionary income
and expenditures on luxury goods.

The recognition of working women as an important demographic segment
of the American market has led to the introduction of a number of magazines
to this group. In 1978 McCall's began *Working Mother*. *Working Woman* has been
on the newsstands since 1976 (see Figure 9–2). *Enterprising Women* introduced
a preview issue in the Fall of 1979. *Working Woman* and *Working Mother* appeal
to advertisers who promote products and services to working women —convenience goods, cosmetics, panty hose, luggage, and cars. To demonstrate the
degree of segmentation, *Working Woman* is geared to the upwardly mobile, more
affluent, chic woman executive, whereas *Working Mother* is directed to the special
problems of working mothers.[19] *Enterprising Women* is directed to the financial
concerns of working women and provides financial news and advice. Advertising
in this magazine is geared primarily to financial services.

A more subtle implication of the growth of the number of working women
is the recognition of a change in their psychological profile — greater independence, freedom, and self-assurance. A 1976 study of women's attitudes
toward fragrances suggested a "shift in emphasis from perfume used to support
confidence to perfume demonstrating confidence."[20] The shift in positioning
was implemented to place greater emphasis on the needs of working women.

Changing Family Composition

The American family is becoming a smaller and less cohesive unit. Since 1960
the divorce rate has increased sharply while marriages have decreased (see Figure
9–3). In 1976 there were 2.1 million marriages in the United States and 1.1
million divorces.[21] The birthrate is also decreasing dramatically. In 1976 the
birthrate was 65.7 births per 1,000 women of childbearing age — a rate lower
than the Depression low of 75.8 in 1936.[22] At the peak of the postwar baby

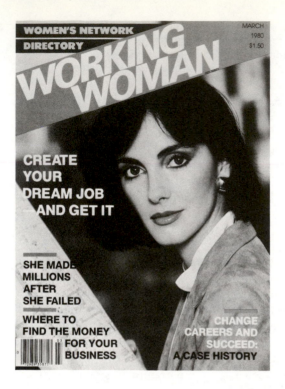

FIGURE 9–2 Magazines Directed to the Working Woman

By permission of McCall's *Working Mother.*

By permission of *Working Woman.* HAL Publications, Inc. 1980. Cover designed by Susan Niles. Photograph by Ron Nicolaysen.

boom in 1957, the birthrate was about twice as great as in 1976 — 122.7 per thousand (see Figure 9–4).

Fewer marriages and births have resulted in a greater proportion of single- and two-member households. In 1950 only 11 percent of all households in the United States were single. By 1975 that figure almost doubled to 20 percent.[23] In 1977 the Census Bureau was reporting more one- and two-member households than multiple-person units.[24] The Califano report touched on the fragmentation of the American household by referring to the fact that in 1900 50 percent of all households in Boston consisted of at least one adult relative other than parents. In 1976 the comparable figure was 4 percent.[25] The extended family has virtually disappeared from the American scene.

What are the implications of more singles and smaller families? No children probably means more discretionary income. The director of corporate planning at General Mills says that "the trend to smaller families will free more discretionary income for such goods as games and clothing."[26] In fact, greater affluence may be related to smaller families. A study by the Rand Corporation links the twenty-year decline in the birthrate to increasingly higher wages available to women.[27] As a result, marketers have come to view singles and young couples as an increasingly profitable segment. Cosmetics, travel, leisure products, investment, and banking services are being advertised more heavily to this group.

Media are also being targeted to singles and younger couples. In 1969 Meredith Corporation, publishers of *Better Homes and Gardens*, introduced *Apartment Life*. The magazine editor comments:

> The audience does not necessarily have to be living in apartments. Rather, the emphasis is on the word *Life* because the individual who leads a certain kind of life is our target. These individuals are apt to be young (60 percent of the magazine's readers are 18 to 34), well educated, earning more than $15,000 a year, and living either alone or as unmarried couples.[28]

In 1977 *Your Place* was introduced by McCall Publishing and targeted to the same segment. The advertising director of *Your Place* expects manufacturers to rethink traditional approaches to the prospective target. He points out, "Volkswagen is already trying to sell station wagons to single women by advertising 'I bought a wagon out of wedlock.' "[29] Primary advertisers in both *Apartment Life* and *Your Place* are liquor, car, cigarette, and home furnishings companies. Recent topics include getting landlords to live up to contracts and a survey on living together without getting married. The editor of *Apartment Life* summarizes the marketing implications of the increasing proportion of one- and two-member households in the following way: "I think we've gone a long way toward convincing people that there's a whole new kind of life-style out there that calls for new editorial and advertising approaches."[30]

Changing Age Compositions

Two groups are accounting for a greater proportion of the American population. The 25–34-year-old group has increased by 22 percent from 1974 to 1980 compared to an overall population increase of only 5 percent. This growth is a result of the post-World-War-II baby boom. And, the 65 and over group has

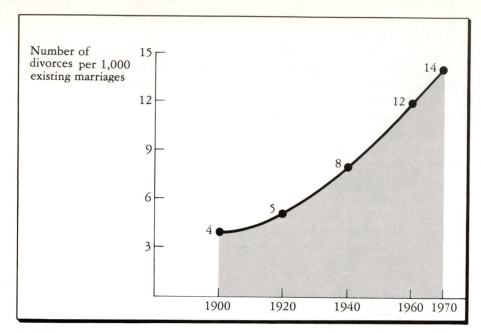

FIGURE 9–3   Rate of Divorce in the United State

Source: Adapted from K. Davis. "The American in Relation to Demographic Change," in C. Westoff and R. Parke, Jr., eds., *U.S. Commission on Population Growth and the American Future, Vol. 1, Demographic Aspects of Population Growth* (Washington, D.C.: U.S. Government Printing Office, 1972), Table 8.

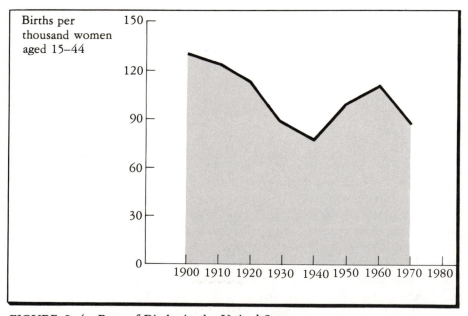

FIGURE 9–4   Rate of Births in the United States

Source: U.S. Bureau of the Census, *Historical Statistics of the United States, Colonial Times to 1970, Bicentennial Edition,* part 2. (Washington, D.C.: Government Printing Office, 1976), Tables B5–10.

increased by 12 percent in the same period compared to the 5 percent growth in overall population (see Figure 9–5.)[31]

The 25–34-year olds represent an important target for marketers. Numerically, they are the largest age segment, tend to be more mobile, and are better educated. Further, they are the first generation of adults to have been brought up with convenience foods, fast foods, and television. In 1978 the postwar babies headed 7.5 million of the nation's 73 million households and the proportion will increase as this group becomes older. *Ad Age* says:

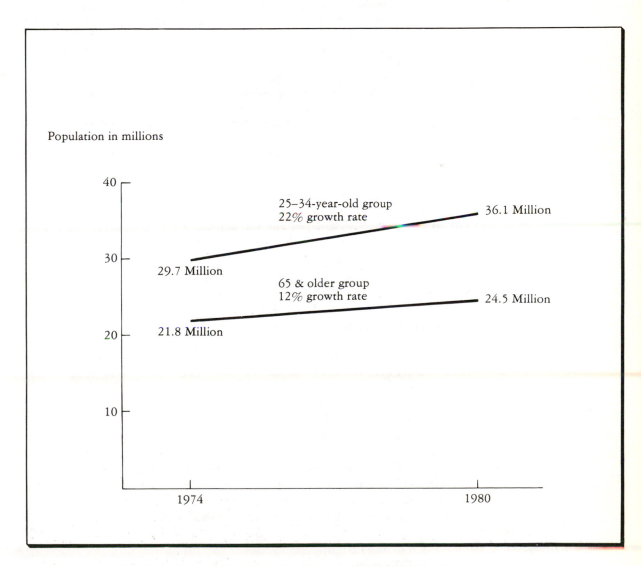

FIGURE 9–5 Two Age Groups Representing Greatest Growth Rate

Source: U.S. Department of Commerce figures, from *Consumer Behavior,* Third Edition, by James F. Engel, Roger D. Blackwell, and David T. Kollat, p. 50. Copyright © 1978 by The Dryden Press, a division of Holt, Rinehart and Winston, Publishers, Hinsdale, Illinois. Reprinted by permission of Holt, Rinehart and Winston.

This group tends to buy with more regard to what it wants than to cost, and buys its food the day it's eaten. It's also a group that doesn't want to spend more than half an hour on the average in preparing a meal. Not surprisingly, this is the segment of the population most inclined to eat out.[32]

A report by A.C. Nielsen further explores the implications of marketing to this segment:

> The fast growing segment of young adults has been within sight and sound of television almost since the day they were born and has been exposed to tens of thousands of commercial messages for virtually every consumer product being marketed. Does this make them more or less susceptible to commercial messages delivered by television?
>
> No one has provided a definitive answer to this question yet, but this is a fact of life; and since this unique group is and will continue to be important buyers of most every product sold for some years to come, it must be seriously considered in terms of product advertising and promotion.
>
> Further, will their priorities, as they get older, fall within the general framework of their parents or be markedly different? If so, what will the differences be and how will they be expressed?[33]

The 65 and over segment will also become more important. It represented 10 percent of the total population in 1977 but is projected to be 17 percent by 2030. Further, the median age of Americans will have climbed from 28 to 37 in the same period.[34] As a result, demand should increase for retirement homes, medical care, recreational facilities, and entertainment to suit the needs of the elderly. This group's buying power is likely to increase with rises in pensions and social security, despite the limits of a fixed income in inflationary periods.

Increasing Mobility

With one-fifth of the American population moving each year, more Americans are becoming exposed to a wider variety of brands, products, and retail stores. Mobility produces brand switching since the brands that families are loyal to in their old location may not be available in their new location. Even national brands may be susceptible to brand switching by movers since promotional effort and loyalty rates vary greatly from one region to another.

New residents are likely to go through a process of learning about brand and store alternatives. Marketers have largely ignored the effects of greater mobility on brand purchases. It may be wise to study differences in reactions to deals, promotions, and advertising between new and old residents. New residents may be a market segment to be appealed to by direct mail or special promotions to increase the learning rate of local brands and store alternatives.

Regional Trends

The most common demographic characteristic used in analyzing purchasing behavior is region. Marketers traditionally break out sales results by sales territories and metropolitan area. Therefore, changes in population distributions will have important effects on allocation of marketing effort.

The most significant regional change in the last thirty years has been the growth of the suburbs. The suburban population grew from 21 percent of the total population in 1950 to 45 percent in 1980.[35] This growth has been achieved at the expense of rural areas and, to a lesser degree, central cities. But, demographers predict a shift back to less populated areas as suburban density increases and suburbs become incorporated into larger metropolitan areas.

Marketers have become more sensitive to the importance of geographic analysis with the increasing use of in-store promotions and direct mail to influence consumers. The introduction of the Universal Product Code (UPC) permits marketers to analyze sales in smaller geographic areas. UPC data will become more widely used as stores begin to read sales by computerized scanners. Once UPC data is available nationally (projected to be by 1985), marketers can identify sales by store and by brand. This will permit management to relate in-store conditions to sales results — for example, a manufacturer could find that in-store displays work best in chain stores in suburban areas. Such a finding would permit in-store promotions to be geared regionally to sales results.

USING DEMOGRAPHICS IN DEVELOPING MARKETING STRATEGY

The growth of the older market or the increasing proportion of working women does not mean every marketer seeks to appeal to these segments. Marketers use demographics in a more specific sense — to describe and better understand existing and potential users of their products. Such information provides guidelines for market segmentation, media selection, and new product development.

Using Demographics to Describe and Understand Consumers

The consumer's demographic characteristics underlie his or her attitudes and purchase behavior. One marketer believes that "demographic segmentation is the indirect measurement of something else — needs and attitudes that buyers of a product category have in common."[36] The relation between demographics and attitudes provides a basis for describing and understanding consumer behavior.

As an example, GTE Sylvania completed a study in 1976 designed to evaluate the position of their product within the color TV market. One objective was to describe purchasers of Sylvania versus purchasers of competitive makes. Specific comparisons were made of Sylvania versus Magnavox purchasers, Sylvania versus Sony, etc. Table 9–1 presents results of a comparison of Sylvania and Sony purchasers. It shows the demographic characteristics of consumers most likely to buy Sylvania, relative to Sony. For example, whereas 42 out of 100 purchasers buy a Sylvania, among nonurban residents 64 out of 100 buy a Sylvania. Therefore, if a consumer lives in a nonurban area, there is a 52 percent greater likelihood of buying a Sylvania compared to the average pur-

TABLE 9–1 Demographic Characteristics That Distinguish Sylvania from Sony Purchasers

Demographic Characteristics	(1) Percent Who Purchased	(2) Percent of Sample Represented by Demographic Group	(3) Percent of All Sylvania Purchases Represented by Demographic Group	Index of Revenue Leverage for Sylvania Versus Sony (col. 3 ÷ col. 2)
Total Sample	41.8%	100%	100%	100
Occupation				
Unskilled Laborer or Housewife	65.2	10	16	160
Skilled Labor and Miscellaneous	43.8	49	52	106
Professional/Manager/ Sales	31.9	41	32	78
Urban/Nonurban				
Nonurban	63.5	20	30	150
Urban	36.5	80	70	87
Income				
Less than $10,000	58.5	20	28	140
$10,000–$20,000	42.5	57	58	102
Over $20,000	27.1	23	15	65
Education				
Elementary School or Less	58.1	23	32	139
Some High School or More	36.4	77	68	88
Household Composition				
Family with Children	51.3	41	50	122
No Children	35.0	59	50	85
Region				
East/Central/South	46.1	80	88	110
West	23.8	20	12	60

By permission of General Telephone & Electronics

chaser (63.5 percent of those owning among nonurban residents compared to 41.8 percent among all consumers). The greater sales leverage that Sylvania has relative to Sony in nonurban areas is represented as an index of revenue leverage of 152. This means that if Sylvania directs its marketing resources to nonurban areas, the effectiveness of dollar expenditures directed against Sony will be one-and-one-half times more effective than in other areas. This advantage is also demonstrated by the fact that nonurban residents accounted for 20 percent of the sample but 30 percent of all Sylvania purchasers.

To summarize Table 9–1, Sylvania is significantly stronger than Sony among lower income consumers who are less educated and unskilled. It is apparent that Sylvania must gear its product line to higher socioeconomic consumers if it is to make inroads against Sony. Such a strategy does not necessarily imply moving into higher quality, higher priced lines since Sylvania is strong in the higher priced market ($500 or more). Competitive advantage may be gained by developing appeals and product features geared to the needs of the higher income market without alienating the lower income market. Therefore, a follow-up study designed to ascertain differences in needs and attitudes of higher versus lower income groups might be warranted.

In another study, the Oldsmobile division of General Motors identified the demographic characteristics of purchasers of its new diesel car compared to buyers of the conventional gas powered version.[37] The study found that, on average, buyers of the diesel are more likely to:

- be males (93 percent of diesel buyers were males compared to 85 percent who buy the conventional Olds models);
- have a higher income level (an average of $35,000 for owners of the Olds diesel compared to $30,000 for owners of the conventional models);
- be more mechanically inclined ("Even though they don't plan to work on the engine, they're fascinated by the mechanics of it," said David Van Peursen, head of the Oldsmobile marketing division. "If he has a diesel in his garage he's also likely to have a microwave oven in the kitchen and a digital watch on his wrist.");
- keep the car longer (five years for the diesel compared to three years for owners of the conventional model);
- do more highway driving, presumably to take advantage of the diesel's better fuel economy.

This profile suggests:

- Upscale media (media directed to higher socioeconomic groups) should be used to reach prospective purchasers of the Olds diesel;
- Advertising should concentrate on the utilitarian benefits of the car in more technical terms to appeal to the mechanically inclined buyer;
- The target market should be consumers who emphasize durability and economy. Appeals should be directed to this group.

Using Demographics to Identify
Brand or Product Segments

Marketers also use demographics to identify a target group for their brand or product categories. A demographic characterization of a brand's target group has important implications for media selection, advertising, and product development.

An example of the use of demographics for market segmentation is a survey conducted by a leading manufacturer of hand lotion to determine the characteristics of buyers of one of its national brands.[38] Those users who said the brand was their usual brand were characterized as the user group. Brand users were then distinguished from nonusers by demographics so as to provide the company with guidelines for selecting media and developing advertising strategies. The results are presented in Figure 9–6.

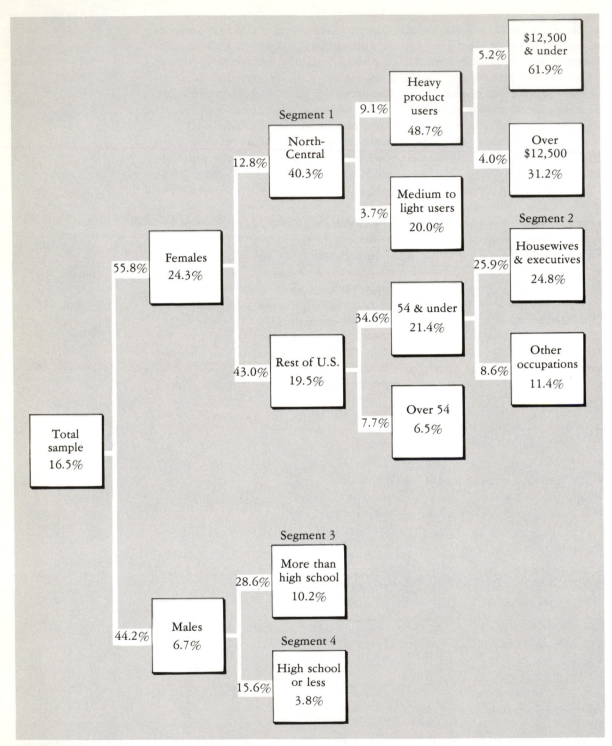

FIGURE 9–6 Socioeconomic Segmentation by Usual Purchasers of Brand X

Source: Henry Assael, "Segmenting Markets by Group Purchasing Behavior." *Journal of Marketing Research* (May 1970):154.

A multivariate computer program known as AID (**Automatic Interaction Detector**) was used to develop segments by brand usage. The program selected consumer characteristics that best distinguish brand users from nonusers. The sample was composed of hand lotion users. Among this group 16.5 percent are users of the brand. Among females 24.3 percent are users compared to 6.7 percent for males. Logically, sex is the most important criterion in distinguishing users from nonusers.

The program then examined the female subgroup to determine additional characteristics that distinguish users from nonusers. Among females living in the north central states 40.3 percent are users, whereas among females living in the rest of the United States only 19.5 percent are users.

Continuing in this iterative fashion, the program identifies the segment most likely to use the brand. The segment is defined as females living in the north central states who are heavy lotion users and are in the lower income group (top right-hand box in Figure 9–6). Within this segment 61.9 percent use the brand. This compares to only 16.5 percent brand usage for the total sample. Thus, the most profitable segment is almost four times as likely to use the brand as the average consumer. On the other hand, those least likely to use the brand are less educated males. Within this group (bottommost box in Figure 9–6) only 3.8 percent are users.

How can a marketer use the information in Figure 9–6? The first question that arises is whether the segment is sufficiently large for marketing purposes. The most profitable segment — females in the north central states in the lower income group — represents only 5.2 percent of the sample. This in itself would not constitute a group large enough to direct advertising and marketing effort. Although this segment is only 5.2 percent of all consumers, it is a much larger proportion of users. This makes it potentially profitable to appeal to this group.

But, the company felt this segment was too small and decided to broaden its definition of the target segment to females in the north central states. Within this group 40.3 percent are brand users. Appeals would therefore be directed to 59.7 percent of the females in the north central region who are not brand users. On this basis, four behavioral segments emerge, two with high potential and two with low potential. The segments are listed below with key behavioral information for each group:

	Demographic Characteristics	Percent of Segment Buying	Percent of All Users	Percent of All Consumers in the Segment
Segment 1	Females in the north central region	40.3	31.3	12.8
Segment 2	Females in rest of U.S. aged 54 & under who are housewives or executives	24.8	38.4	25.9
Segment 3	Males with more than high school education	10.2	11.5	28.6
Segment 4	Males with high school education or less	3.8	3.5	15.6

Note: All others not included in these four segments = 17.1 percent of all lotion users.

The company would want to direct its resources to the first two segments, utilizing female oriented media with heavier concentrations in the north central region and/or to younger and middle-aged housewives or executives. But the demographic information may not provide sufficient guidance for advertising. Therefore, it would be relevant to determine whether segments 1 and 2 differ from other consumers on advertising recall, brand attitudes, and benefits. This information is presented below as an extension of the demographic analysis:

	Percent Recalling Brand's Advertising	Percent Rating Brand Mild	Percent Who Say Mild Is Very Important	Percent Rating Brand Not Greasy	Percent Who Say Not Greasy Is Very Important
All consumers	12	60	40	59	35
Segment 1	52	90	52	85	36
Segment 2	48	88	58	60	56

The data show that half of the consumers in the two key female segments recall advertising for the brand. Interestingly, almost as many consumers in the second segment as in the first recall advertising about the brand despite the fact that far fewer women in the second segment are users. Therefore, an increase in advertising effort directed to the second segment may not be the solution. Rather, it may be a question of determining whether the second segment has different needs. Both segments emphasize mildness and see the brand as mild. This attitude is a strong point for the brand. But, segment 2 does not rate the brand as highly on "not greasy" as did segment 1. Yet, segment 2 puts much more emphasis on "not greasy." Therefore, the implication may be to advertise the brand as both mild and not greasy to segment 2, in the hope that a significant proportion of women in that segment who are not current users will try the brand.

The study demonstrates that segmentation by demographic criteria provides marketers with a basis for defining a target market. Yet, demographics are not enough. Once the demographic characteristics of a target group have been defined, their needs and brand perceptions must also be determined for promotional direction.

Using Demographics to Guide Media Planning

Demographics have been widely used in selecting media that have a higher probability of reaching a defined target group. An example is a study performed for a stereo manufacturer to identify demographic characteristics of their higher priced compact stereo market and to select media most likely to reach this market. A national representative sample of 2,000 stereo owners showed the following:

- Skilled workers were more than twice as likely to prefer higher priced compacts compared to other consumers. The professional/managerial group were more likely to prefer components.

- Suburban dwellers were twice as likely as city dwellers to prefer higher priced compacts.
- Respondents with income of $25,000 and over were one-and-one-half times as likely to prefer high priced compacts as others were.

Given this profile of the target group, what media can best reach it?

Sixteen magazines were analyzed using Simmons data. Simmons is a syndicated service that surveys respondents to determine magazine readership, TV viewing, and product-purchasing behavior. The demographic profile of readers of particular magazines and viewers of certain TV shows can be determined. Simmons data make it possible to link the demographic profile of the magazine reader to that of the target market. The cost of reaching 1,000 target consumers can then be computed for each magazine. The purpose of the analysis was to evaluate the sixteen magazines to determine the cost of reaching the three primary target groups (skilled workers, suburbanites, and higher income consumers). Assume we wish to determine the cost of utilizing *Time* magazine to reach 1,000 consumers with income of $25,000 and over. Based on 1975 data, the computation would be:

Percent of *Time* Readers with an Income of $25,000 and over		Total Circulation		Number of *Time* Readers with an Income of $25,000 and over
10.3%	×	20.25 Million	=	2.1 Million

Cost of Full Page Black & White Ad in *Time* Magazine		Number of *Time* Readers with an Income $25,000 and Over (in thousands)		Cost of Reaching 1,000 Readers with an Income of $25,000 and Over
$24,000	÷	2,100	=	$11.43

Similarly, the cost of reaching 1,000 suburbanites using *Time* was $2.79 and the cost of reaching 1,000 skilled workers was $3.96. The average cost per thousand for *Time* across all three groups would be $6.06.

Results for the four best magazine buys are presented below:

	Average Cost per Thousand of Reaching the Three Target Segments	*Average Audience Across the Three Target Segments (in millions)*
1. *Time*	$6.06	4.4
2. *Newsweek*	6.75	2.7
3. *Esquire*	7.24	1.5
4. *Sports Illustrated*	7.36	2.3

In addition to magazines, sixty-seven nighttime TV shows were analyzed. An average outreach to the prospect group was computed for each show. The top four shows were:

	Average Outreach to the Three Demographic Target Groups
1. "The Tonite Show"	35.9%
2. "NFL Monday Night Football"	33.2%
3. "CBS Sunday Night Movie"	30.4%
4. "Love American Style"	26.4%

The key criterion in developing these media guidelines was the definition of the target group by demographic characteristics. This provided the facility for matching the media's demographic profile to the demographic profile of the target group.

Another study identified the demographic characteristics of heavy users of ten consumer packaged goods.[39] The demographic profiles of heavy versus light buyers are presented in Table 9–2. For example, lightest buyers of catsup were single consumers or older, married households with no children at home. Average usage rates of these two segments ranged from .74 to 1.82 bottles over a two-month period. Heavy buyers were households with three or more children with the male head under 50. Average consumption for this segment ranged from 2.73 to 5.79 bottles. The ratio of the highest to the lowest rate of consumption was 7.8 (5.79/.74). This is an index of the degree to which a household's demographic characteristics discriminate rate of usage.

Once usage rates are established by demographic segments, a particular medium's effectiveness in reaching the heaviest users can be determined. The medium's effectiveness can be determined by multiplying a medium's outreach to the target segment by the segment's usage rate.

For example, assume 200,000 readers of *Newsweek* have the same demographic profile as the heavy purchaser of Brand X (heavy users purchase an average of two units per month). Another 200,000 readers have the same demographic profile as medium purchasers with an average purchase rate of one unit per month, and 100,000 readers conform to the light purchaser profile with an average usage rate of one-half unit. Then *Newsweek* is reaching a target segment with a potential of 650,000 purchasing units (200,000 × 2 + 200,000 × 1 + 100,000 × ½). If a full-page black and white ad in *Newsweek* costs $25,000, it would then cost $38.45 to reach a potential 1,000 purchasing units ($25,000/650).

This is an improvement over the selection procedures cited in the stereo study on two counts. First, media are selected by weighting the purchase rate of each segment rather than by relying on the identification of just one segment such as the heaviest users. Second, media are selected based on a combination of demographics (heaviest purchasers of frozen orange juice are middle aged, have a higher income, and are better educated) rather than on one demographic characteristic at a time.

TABLE 9-2   Demographic Profile of Light Versus Heavy Buyers for Ten Products

Product	Description		Mean consumption rate ranges		Ratio of highest to lowest rate
	Light buyers	*Heavy buyers*	*Light buyers*	*Heavy buyers*	
Catsup	Unmarried or married over age 50 without children	Under 50, 3 or more children	.74–1.82	2.73–5.79	7.8
Frozen orange juice	Under 35 or over 65, income less than $10,000, not college grads, 2 or less children	College grads, income over $10,000, between 35 & 65	1.12–2.24	3.53–9.00	8.0
Pancake mix	Some college, 2 or less children	3 or more children, high school or less ed.	.48–.52	1.10–1.51	3.3
Candy bars	Under 35, no children	35 or over, 3 or more children	1.01–4.31	6.56–22.29	21.9
Cake mix	Not married or under 35, no children, income under $10,000, T.V. less than 3½ hrs.	35 or over, 3 or more children, income over $10,000	.55–1.10	2.22–3.80	6.9
Beer	Under 25 or over 50, college ed., nonprofessional, T.V. less than 2 hrs.	Between 25 & 50, not college grad., T.V. more than 3½ hrs.	0–12.33	17.26–40.30	
Cream shampoo	Income less than $8,000, at least some college, less than 5 children	Income $10,000 or over with high school or less ed.	.16–35	.44–.87	5.5
Hair spray	Over 65, under $8,000 income	Under 65, over $10,000 income, not college grad.	0–.41	.52–1.68	
Toothpaste	Over 50, less than 3 children, income less than $8,000	Under 50, 3 or more children, over $10,000 income	1.41–2.01	2.22–4.39	3.1
Mouthwash	Under 35 or over 65, less than $8,000 income, some college	Between 35 & 65, income over $8,000, high school or less ed.	.46–.85	.93–1.17	2.5

Source: Frank M. Bass, Douglas J. Tigert and Ronald T. Lonsdale, "Market Segmentation: Group Versus Individual Behavior." *Journal of Marketing Research* 5 (August 1968): 267.

Identifying Demographic Targets for a New Product

In 1972, a large food manufacturer began testing a new concept — low calorie breakfast strips designed as a substitute for bacon. They interviewed 600 respondents in four markets to determine the reaction to the product concept. The basic purpose of the study was to identify the segment of the market most likely to buy based on their demographic and psychographic characteristics. Once the respondents reacted to the concept, the product was given to those who had eaten bacon within the previous year *and* who said they would definitely or probably buy the new product.

Two demographic segments were most likely to buy: (1) older (55 years and over), less educated respondents and (2) middle-aged respondents, also less educated, with one or more teenagers in the household. The older segment was more likely to emphasize cholesterol content and health related concerns; the middle-aged segment, calories and nutrition. This finding suggested the product should be positioned to the older market based on a primary health benefit (easier to digest, low in cholesterol) with a secondary appeal to dieting and nutritional benefits. Appeals to the middle-aged market should be the reverse.

In addition to positioning implications, the demographic analysis identified the primary target groups for media purposes. Relative weights would have to be given to the two segments based on purchase potential and media priorities would have to be established by the ability of print or TV advertising to reach potential customers.

SUMMARY

The consumer's demographic characteristics are important in developing marketing strategies since they provide guidelines for identifying prospective consumers and selecting media. Demographics are general rather than product-specific characteristics and marketers frequently describe users and prospect groups in demographic terms. Therefore, it is important to track changes in demographic characteristics that may have an impact on marketing strategies.

This chapter considers a number of such changes, namely:

1. Increases in the proportion of working women;
2. Changes in family composition such as increases in the divorce rate; decreases in the birthrate approaching zero population growth; the virtual extinction of the extended family; and a consequent increase in single and unmarried households;
3. Changing age compositions represented by an increase in the 25–34-year-old group as a result of the postwar baby boom and the 65 and over segment;
4. Increasing mobility resulting in one-fifth of the American population moving once a year;
5. Regional trends such as the growth of the suburbs.

The impact of these changes on marketing is also considered. For example, the increase in the proportion of working women has resulted in changing purchasing and consumption roles within the family, less time for shopping, an increase in brand loyalty, and greater patronage of fast food establishments.

The second half of the chapter considers the use of demographics in developing marketing strategy. Demographics are most frequently used for two purposes: first, to describe segments of brand users or prospective users and, second, to use these descriptions as criteria to select media. This process ensures that media will be directed to current and prospective brand users, but demographics can also help guide the establishment of targets for new products and set the tone of advertising based on the identification of the target group.

QUESTIONS

1. What are the implications of the increase in the proportion of working women for (a) advertising strategy, (b) in-store promotions, (c) product development, and (d) media selection?

2. What are the marketing implications of the increasingly high divorce rate in the United States?

3. What are the marketing implications of the decreasing birthrate in the United States?

4. Consumers in the 25–34-year-old group have been referred to as the "TV generation" and the "disposable generation."
   - Does this group differ from their parents in terms of (a) consumption patterns, (b) information processing, and (c) need priorities?

5. The increasing rate of mobility is likely to have the greatest impact on regional and local brands.
   - Should marketers direct special appeals to new residents? How?
   - What changes might take place in information processing for new residents in a community?

6. What is the significance of the availability of scanner data derived from the Universal Product Code for evaluation of in-store promotions? Identification of target segments?

7. What guidelines does Table 9–1 provide Sylvania for (a) advertising strategy, and (b) product strategy?

8. What are the limitations of using demographics for media selection? What are the alternatives to developing guidelines for selecting media if demographics are not related to usage?

9. The chapter suggests using demographics to define users of a brand or product category, and to direct marketing strategies accordingly. Should demographics also be used to identify a prospect group (i.e., nonusers who have a greater potential for usage)? Cite an example of the use of demographics for this purpose.

RESEARCH ASSIGNMENTS

1. A study by a large electronics firm determined the demographic characteristics of purchasers of various types of color TV sets (table-top models, portables and consoles). Purchasers of tabletop models were most likely to be (a) in the higher

income group ($25,000 and over); (b) better educated (college education); and (c) in professional or managerial occupations.

- Try to obtain a copy of a Simmons Report or some other readership service (it is alright if the report is somewhat dated). Analyze ten or twelve magazines to determine their relative efficiency in reaching the three target groups identified above. Use the analysis procedures described on pp. 225–226 as a guide.
- If data are also available for TV shows, do the same analysis for a selected number of shows as well.

2. Identify owners or users of two closely competing brands for a consumer packaged good and an appliance. (Identify at least twenty users or owners per brand). Then determine their demographic characteristics.

- Are there any significant differences between the demographic characteristics of users of the two packaged goods brands? The two durable goods brands?
- Demographic differences are more likely to occur for durable goods than packaged goods because durables are more likely to vary in price and product characteristics. Did your findings confirm this? Were demographic differences greater between owners of the two durable brands compared to users of the two packaged goods brands?

NOTES

1. Joseph A. Califano, Jr., *American Families: Trends, Pressures and Recommendations,* preliminary report to Gov. Jimmy Carter, Sept. 17, 1976 (mimeographed).
2. "New Population Trends Transforming U.S.," *The New York Times,* Feb. 6, 1977, p. 1.
3. Ibid., p. 42.
4. Ibid.
5. "Avon Plans to Take Over Tiffany for $104 Million," *The New York Times,* Nov. 22, 1978, pp. D1 and D4.
6. "Avon Seeks Diversity in Tiffany Merger Bid," *Advertising Age,* Nov. 27, 1978, p. 94.
7. Ibid., p. 94.
8. "Pepsi Takes on the Champ," *Business Week,* June 12, 1978, p. 97.
9. "Customer Profile is the Key to What They Will Buy," *Advertising Age,* Oct. 9, 1978, p. 75.
10. U.S. Department of Labor; and *The Nielsen Researcher,* No. 2, 1978, a publication of the A.C. Nielsen Co.
11. "Supermarkets Fight Fast Food Challenge," *Advertising Age,* Oct. 30, 1978, p. 30.
12. "Eating Habits Force Changes in Marketing," *Advertising Age,* Oct. 30, 1978, p. 65.
13. "The Upward Mobility Two Incomes Can Buy," *Business Week,* Feb. 20, 1978, p. 84.
14. Ibid.
15. Ibid., p. 85.
16. *Advertising Age,* Oct. 30, 1978, p. 30.
17. Ibid., p. 65.
18. Ibid., pp. 30 and 34.

19. "Reaching Working Women," *The New York Times,* Nov. 9, 1978.
20. "Marketing Emphasis," *Product Marketing,* Dec. 1977, p. 43.
21. *The Nielsen Researcher.*
22. *The New York Times,* Feb. 6, 1977, p. 42.
23. *The Nielsen Researcher.*
24. "Bidding for an Elusive Market," *Business Week,* Nov. 7, 1977, p. 72.
25. Califano, *American Families.*
26. *The New York Times,* Feb. 6, 1977, p. 42.
27. *Business Week,* Feb. 20, 1978, p. 85.
28. *Business Week,* Nov. 7, 1977, p. 72.
29. Ibid.
30. Ibid.
31. U.S. Department of Commerce.
32. *Advertising Age,* Oct. 30, 1978, p. 27.
33. *The Nielsen Researcher.*
34. *The New York Times,* Feb. 6, 1977, p. 42.
35. *The Nielsen Researcher.*
36. "You Can Reach Some of the People Some of the . . ." *Product Marketing,* April, 1978, p. 32.
37. "Who Buys a G.M. Diesel Car?" *The New York Times,* Nov. 9, 1978, p. D7.
38. Henry Assael, "Segmenting Markets by Group Purchasing Behavior," *Journal of Marketing Research* 7 (May 1970): 153–158.
39. Frank M. Bass, Douglas J. Tigert, and Ronald T. Lonsdale, "Market Segmentation: Group Versus Individual Behavior," *Journal of Marketing Research* 5 (August 1968):264–270.

TEN

Psychographic Characteristics

Focus of Chapter

Compared to demographics, the psychological makeup of the consumer provides a richer basis for marketers in understanding consumer behavior. Recently, marketers have relied on the measurement of psychographic characteristics. **Psychographics** are consumer psychological characteristics that can be quantified. They are represented by two classes of variables: **life-style** and **personality.**

This chapter will first focus on the nature of life-style variables and the need for developing an inventory of life-style characteristics. Strategic applications of life-style variables will be presented. Personality variables will be described in the context of various personality theories. The chapter will conclude by considering the use of personality characteristics in the development of marketing strategies.

LIFE-STYLE

A **life-style** is broadly defined as a mode of living that is identified by how people spend their time (*activities*;) their *interests* in terms of what they consider important in their environment; and their *opinions* of themselves and the world around them. Specific elements of activities, interests, and opinions are:[1]

Activities	Interests	Opinions
work	family	themselves
hobbies	home	social issues
social events	job	politics
vacation	community	business
entertainment	recreation	economics
club membership	fashion	education
community	food	products
shopping	media	future
sports	achievements	culture

Changes in life-styles have paralleled changes in demographic characteristcs. In the United States, the preponderance of single and two-member households, the increase in the number of working women, and the virtual extinction of the extended family have meant a shift away from more traditional and conservative values.

The women's movement has challenged traditional male roles. Sexual mores have become more liberated and an unmarried couple's living together no longer implies "living in sin." The focus of younger consumers has increasingly shifted away from accepting family and peer group norms to more independent thinking. The desire to do what is best for oneself has also caused basic doubts about the traditional work ethic, resulting in a greater emphasis on informality and leisure.

Florence Skelly, executive vice president of Yankelovich, Skelly, and White, sums up these changes as follows:

> Under the old consumer values system, possessions, children, earning power and status were viewed as the essentials for a successful stance in life. Under the new system, however, the focus is on self rather than family, sex roles are blurred, childlessness is not considered a taboo, and individualism is an asset. Women can seek careers and nondomestic success goals to achieve self-fulfillment.[2]

This shift to a newer, more liberated value system and life-style is reflected in consumers' purchasing behavior: There are more expenditures on services, leisure products, and time-saving conveniences. Marketers seeking to take advantage of these trends must define and measure their target segments in life-style terms.

Development of a Life-Style Inventory

Life-style characteristics differ from demographics in that they must be constructed deductively, based on the researcher's objectives. There are no fixed definitions like age, income, or occupation. Activity, interest, and opinion (AIO) inventories have been constructed to empirically measure life-style components. Such inventories are developed by first formulating a large number of questions regarding consumer AIO's and by then selecting a smaller number of questions that most representatively define consumer segments. As an example, Wells and Tigert formulated 300 AIO statements and asked respondents to agree or disagree with each on a six-point scale.[3] One typical statement was: "When I set my mind to do something, I can really do it." Another was: "I usually keep my home very neat and clean." These items were then reduced to a smaller number of life-style dimensions by **factor analysis.** Some of the results are presented in Table 10–1. The factor analysis reduced the 300 items to twenty-two life-style dimensions. The analysis showed that, based on responses to the 300 statements, certain consumers could be described as price conscious, fashion conscious, child oriented, etc. The factor analysis showed that those who agreed with the statement "I shop a lot for specials" also tended to agree with the statements "I find myself checking prices," "I watch advertisements for sales," and "A person can save a lot by shopping for bargains." Those who tended to agree with these statements were described as price conscious. Generally, those who agreed with one of the statements under each of the twenty-two headings in Table 10–1 agreed with the other statements in that category, and those who disagreed with one tended to disagree with the others.

These twenty-two life-style dimensions were then used in the same manner as demographics to describe and understand consumer behavior. For instance, users of eye makeup tended to agree with the items defining fashion consciousness, whereas nonusers did not. The heavy user of shortening liked housekeeping, was more child oriented, and tended to be a homebody compared to the nonuser.

TABLE 10–1   Sample Life-Style Categories Based on Perceived Activities, Interests, and Opinions

Price Conscious

I shop a lot for "specials".

I find myself checking the prices in the grocery store even for small items.

I usually watch the advertisements for announcements of sales.

A person can save a lot of money by shopping around for bargains.

Fashion Conscious

I usually have one or more outfits that are of the very latest style.

When I must choose between the two I usually dress for fashion, not for comfort.

An important part of my life and activities is dressing smartly.

I often try the latest hairdo styles when they change.

Child Oriented

When my children are ill in bed I drop most everything else in order to see to their comfort.

My children are the most important thing in my life.

I try to arrange my home for my children's convenience.

I take a lot of time and effort to teach my children good habits.

Compulsive Housekeeper

I don't like to see children's toys lying about.

I usually keep my house very neat and clean.

I am uncomfortable when my house is not completely clean.

Our days seem to follow a definite routine such as eating meals at a regular time, etc.

Dislikes Housekeeping

I must admit I really don't like household chores.

I find cleaning my house an unpleasant task.

I enjoy most forms of housework. (Reverse scored)

My idea of housekeeping is "once over lightly."

Sewer

I like to sew and frequently do.

I often make my own or my children's clothes.

You can save a lot of money by making your own clothes.

I would like to know how to sew like an expert.

TABLE 10–1 (cont.)

Homebody

I would rather spend a quiet evening at home than go out to a party.

I like parties where there is lots of music and talk. (Reverse scored)

I would rather go to a sporting event than a dance.

I am a homebody.

Community Minded

I am an active member of more than one service organization.

I do volunteer work for a hospital or service organization on a fairly regular basis.

I like to work on community projects.

I have personally worked in a political campaign or for a candidate or an issue.

Credit User

I buy many things with a credit card or a charge card.

I like to pay cash for everything I buy. (Reverse scored)

It is good to have charge accounts.

To buy anything, other than a house or a car, on credit is unwise. (Reverse scored)

Sports Spectator

I like to watch or listen to baseball or football games.

I usually read the sports page in the daily paper.

I thoroughly enjoy conversations about sports.

I would rather go to a sporting event than a dance.

Cook

I love to cook.

I am a good cook.

I love to bake and frequently do.

I am interested in spices and seasonings.

Self-Confident

I think I have more self-confidence than most people.

I am more independent than most people.

I think I have a lot of personal ability.

I like to be considered a leader.

Self-Designated Opinion Leader

My friends or neighbors often come to me for advice.

I sometimes influence what my friends buy.

People come to me more often than I go to them for information about brands.

Information Seeker

I often seek out the advice of my friends regarding which brand to buy.

I spend a lot of time talking with my friends about products and brands.

My neighbors or friends usually give me good advice on what brands to buy in the grocery store.

New Brand Tryer

When I see a new brand on the shelf I often buy it just to see what it's like.

I often try new brands before my friends and neighbors do.

I like to try new and different things.

Satisfied with Finances

Our family income is high enough to satisfy nearly all our important desires.

No matter how fast our income goes up we never seem to get ahead. (Reverse scored)

I wish we had a lot more money. (Reverse scored)

Canned Food User

I depend on canned food for at least one meal a day.

I couldn't get along without canned foods.

Things just don't taste right if they come out of a can. (Reverse scored)

Dieter

During the warm weather I drink low calorie soft drinks several times a week.

I buy more low calorie foods than the average housewife.

I have used Metrecal or other diet foods at least one meal a day.

Financial Optimist

I will probably have more money to spend next year than I have now.

Five years from now the family income will probably be a lot higher than it is now.

Wrapper

Food should never be left in the refrigerator uncovered.

Leftovers should be wrapped before being put into the refrigerator.

Wide Horizons

I'd like to spend a year in London or Paris.

I would like to take a trip around the world.

Arts Enthusiast

I enjoy going through an art gallery.

I enjoy going to concerts.

I like ballet.

Source: William D. Wells and Douglas J. Tigert, "Activities, Interests and Opinions," *Journal of Advertising Research* 11 (August 1971): 35.

Reprinted from the *Journal of Advertising Research* © 1971, by the Advertising Research Foundation.

Uses of Life-Style Characteristics in Marketing Strategy

Life-style characteristics have been used with increasing frequency to identify market segments, reposition products through advertising, develop media guidelines, and define targets for new products. Each aspect will be looked at further in this discussion.

Market Segmentation

A study by a leading food manufacturer provides an example of how life-style characteristics are used in segmenting markets. The company (to be referred to as Great Snacks) studied the life-style characterists of snack food purchasers. The objective was to define segments by similarity in (1) life-style characteristics and (2) needs for snack foods. On this basis, the company could determine the appeal of existing brands for each life-style segment and identify new product concepts that may meet the needs of these segments. Also, implications for positioning new products and repositioning existing products were expected to emerge.

Personal interviews were conducted with a representative sample of 1,500 snack food users. The data presented in Table 10–2 are representative of the findings from the study. The first step was to group snackers together by life-style characteristics and benefits sought in snack foods. Statements pertaining to life-style characteristics such as "I am concerned about the snacks my family eats," "I am physically active," "I go out with friends frequently" and "I often discuss snack food products with others" were used. These statements were both product-specific (concern about snacks consumed by family) and general (physical activity). Benefits sought in snack foods were also identified such as "low in calories," "good value," "good to serve guests," etc. Consumer groups were developed by a computer program known as **cluster analysis.** The program's objectives were to group respondents together by similarity in their responses (in this case, similarity in their ratings of life-styles and needs), so there was greatest similarity within groups and greatest differences between groups. (Statistically, the program minimized within-group variance and maximized between-group variance.)

The cluster program produced six snacking segments by similarity in life-styles and needs. The first row in Table 10–2 presents the life-style characteristics of each segment; the second row, the snacking benefits sought by each segment. The first segment is called nutritional snackers because respondents in this group expressed health related concerns, both for themselves and their families. They wanted a nutritious and natural snack with no artificial ingredients. They also tended to be self-confident and controlled, agreeing with statements such as "I like doing things myself to ensure it's done correctly" and "I feel like I am in control of myself."

The next step was to determine the snacking behavior of each of the six segments. Segment 1, the nutritional snackers, tended to snack on fruits, vegetables, and cheese. They were lighter snackers. The final step was to

TABLE 10–2 Life-Style Segmentation of the Snack Food Market

	Nutritional Snackers	Weight Watchers	Guilty Snackers	Party Snackers	Indiscriminate Snackers	Economical Snackers
Percent of Snackers	22%	14%	9%	15%	15%	18%
Life-Style Characteristics	Self-assured Controlled	Outdoor types Influential Venturesome	High anxiety Isolate	Sociable	Hedonistic	Self-assured Price oriented
Benefits Sought	Nutritious No artificial ingredients Natural snack	Low calorie Quick energy	Low calorie Good tasting	Good to serve guests Proud to serve Goes well with beverage	Good tasting Satisfies hunger	Low price Best value
Consumption Level of Snacks	Light	Light	Heavy	Average	Heavy	Average
Type of Snacks Usually Eaten	Fruits Vegetables Cheese	Yogurt Vegetables	Yogurt Cookies Crackers Candy	Nuts Potato chips Crackers Pretzels	Candy Ice cream Cookies Potato chips Pretzels Popcorn	No specific products
Demographics	Better educated Have younger children	Younger Single	Younger or older Females Lower socioeconomic group	Middle aged Nonurban	Teens	Larger families Better educated

determine the demographic characteristics that distinguished one segment from another. Nutritional snackers had a higher proportion of better educated consumers and families with younger children.

Briefly reviewing the other segments, there were two low calorie groups. Weight watchers were outdoor types that emphasized quick energy and fewer calories. They tended to be the younger, upwardly mobile adults who viewed themselves as influential. They were also venturesome, being more likely to buy new products. They differed from the other low calorie group, the guilty snackers, in several respects. Guilty snackers emphasized hedonistic qualities such as good taste, whereas the weight watchers tended to emphasize energy. Guilty snackers were relatively heavy snackers. They felt that they were overeating and that snacking was in conflict with their desire to lose weight. They snacked on yogurt, but also on cookies, crackers, and candy. Weight watchers had no guilt. They were lighter snackers and restricted snacking to low calorie products like yogurt and vegetables. As a reflection of their concern about snacking, the guilty snackers tended to be highly anxious and more isolate, agreeing with such statements as "I get easily upset when things go wrong," "I watch a lot of TV," and "I do not go out very frequently." They also were more likely to be females and to be in the lower socioeconomic group.

The indiscriminate snackers were also hedonistically oriented, agreeing with statements such as "When I get a craving for a snack, I must have one right away" or "I'm not fussy about what I eat as long as it tastes good." They were similar to the guilty snackers in that they snacked heavily. They ate cookies, candy, desserts, and chip type snacks, but were not guilty about snacking. They emphasized good taste and satisfaction.

Party snackers tended to be more sociable and in agreement with statements such as "I have more friends than most people" and "I usually eat snacks when with company." They emphasized the sociable benefits such as "good to serve guests" and "proud to serve." They were average snackers, but were more likely to buy nuts, potato chips, and pretzels, which were products in Great Snack's lines.

The last group was price oriented. They tended to comparison shop and were fairly self-assured in their outlook. Being the second largest segment, the economical snackers are an important part of the snack-food market. They are average snackers, not being identified with any particular snacking category. They are more likely to be better educated and have larger families.

These psychographic segments provide important marketing implications for snack food companies. Great Snack's primary interest was in nuts and chip type snacks since the company has a line of products in both categories. The most profitable segments for nuts and chip type snacks are the party snackers, indiscriminate snackers, and guilty snackers. Great Snacks should continue to appeal to these segments, but advertising to appeal to each segment may be very different. For example, products should be presented in socially oriented situations to appeal to party snackers; appeals to the guilty snacker should be more serious and oriented toward the alleviation of anxiety in snacking; and, given the hedonistic bent of indiscriminate snackers, the appeals to this segment should be oriented to taste and pleasure.

The media used to reach each type of snacker will also differ since the demographic profiles of the three segments are so different. To reach the guilty snacker, media should be selected that have a higher proportion of readers or viewers who are female and in the lower socioeconomic groups. Appeals to party snackers should utilize magazines that are socially oriented and that have a higher proportion of readership in the middle-aged groups. Appeals to the indiscriminate snacker should utilize media oriented toward teens.

There may also be packaging implications. Products directed to the party snackers and indiscriminate snackers may be packaged more colorfully than the products directed toward guilty snackers. Products directed toward nutritional snackers and weight watchers should have nutritional information placed in a prominent position on the package.

More important are the implications for new product development. Great Snacks may wish to introduce products geared toward the two segments in which it is particularly weak — nutritional snackers and weight watchers. These two groups represent over one-third of all snackers. A single product line could be developed to appeal to both segments given the similarity in nutritional and low calorie benefits. For example, Great Snacks may consider positioning a new brand of potato chips or popcorn as a natural snack with no artificial ingredients to appeal to nutritional snackers. Advertising to this group would be more informationally oriented, emphasizing utilitarian appeals directed toward better educated, self-assured consumers.

Great Snacks also may consider the development of a low calorie, dry roasted nut product to appeal primarily to the weight watchers and secondarily to the guilty snackers. Since weight watchers are more venturesome, such a new product may have some appeal. Appeals can be made to energy and fitness in the context of outdoor activities. Although such a context is unlikely to appeal to the guilty snacker, there may be some spillover to this group.

Advertising and Product Positioning

Life-style profiles have been the basis for repositioning existing brands. They have provided copywriters with a picture of the consumer by suggesting the consumer's needs and social roles, thus facilitating the communications process. One advertising agency executive has said:

> For the creative person, life-style data provide a richer and more lifelike picture of the target consumer than do demographics. This enables the writer or artist to have in his own mind a better idea of the type of person he is trying to communicate with about the product. This picture also gives the creative person clues about what may or may not be appropriate to the life-style of the target consumer. This has implications for the setting of the advertising, the type and appearance of the characters, the nature of the music and artwork, whether or not fantasy can be used, and so on.[4]

As an example of the use of life-styles in advertising the following situation may be considered. Before 1969 Schlitz was running an effective campaign based on the theme "When you're out of Schlitz, you're out of beer." The company felt the campaign was wearing out and a search began for a new approach. After several unsuccessful attempts to come up with something new, the creative director began to make the rounds of taverns to meet some heavy beer drinkers. Based on this informal life-style research, the director concluded the heavy beer drinker is a dreamer, a wisher, a guy who is not making it and probably never will. Results from a life-style study (see Table 10–3) confirmed this view.[5] Based on this portrait, it was decided that ads should appeal to the heavy beer drinker's sense of masculinity, hedonism, and fantasy.[6]

In another case, life-style was used in repositioning the Ford Pinto. Introductory Pinto advertising portrayed the car as "carefree, small [and] romantic."[7] Yet, after the introduction of the car, research revealed Pinto purchasers to be practical, utilitarian, and unaffected by the status and romantic concepts about cars. As a result, the Pinto was repositioned as "the epitome

TABLE 10–3   Psychographic Characteristics of Heavy Beer Drinkers

	% Agreement				% Agreement		
	Non-Users	Light Users	Heavy Users		Non-Users	Light Users	Heavy Users
He is self-indulgent, enjoys himself and likes risks				*He likes sports and a physical orientation*			
I like to play poker	18	37	41	I would like to be a pro football player	10	15	21
I like to take chances	27	32	44	I like bowling	32	36	42
I would rather spend a quiet evening at home than go out to a party	67	53	44	I usually read the sports page	47	48	59
If I had my way, I would own a convertible	7	11	15	I would do better than average in a fist fight	17	26	32
I smoke too much	29	40	42	I like war stories	33	37	45
If I had to choose I would rather have a color TV than a new refrigerator	25	33	38	*He rejects old fashioned institutions and moral guidelines*			
He rejects responsibility and is a bit impulsive				I go to church regularly	57	37	31
				Movies should be censored	67	46	43
I like to work on community projects	24	18	14	I have old fashioned tastes and habits	69	56	48
I have helped collect money for the Red Cross or United Fund	41	32	24	There is too much emphasis on sex today	71	59	53
I'm not very good at saving money	20	29	38	*—and has a very masculine view*			
				Beer is a real man's drink	9	16	44
I find myself checking prices, even for small items	51	42	40	*Playboy* is one of my favorite magazines	11	21	28
				I am a girl watcher	33	47	54
				Men should not do the dishes	18	26	38
				Men are smarter than women	22	27	31

Source: Joseph T. Plummer, "Life-Style and Advertising: Case Studies," in Fred C. Allvine, ed., *Combined Proceedings, 1971 Spring and Fall Conference,* (Chicago: American Marketing Association, 1972), p. 294.
Reprinted with permission from the American Marketing Association.

of function, exemplifying basic economical transportation, trading on Ford's heritage of the Model A."[8]

Media Guidelines

Life-style profiles suggest the appropriate media to appeal to a target segment and the appropriate advertising content for the media. Tigert reported on a study of TV viewing in Canada in which the life-style characteristics of viewers of two types of programs — fantasy-comedy shows and talk shows — were determined.

Viewers of fantasy-comedy shows had a strong traditional and conservative orientation, were concerned about cleanliness in the home, tended to see life as a personal and financial defeat and were price conscious. Viewers of talk shows had a strong interest in new products, had a need for excitement in their lives and expressed a strong interest in fashion and personal appearance. Tigert drew the following implications based on these profiles:

1.   The fantasy-comedy shows represent viable media for all types of home-cleaning products from disinfectants to air fresheners to liquid cleaners. And the appeals in the copy should be hard hitting attacks on germs and dirt.

2.   The fantasy-comedy shows represent viable media for all types of proprietary drugs such as deodorants, mouthwashes, and vitamins.

3.   The talk shows represent viable media for many types of *new* products. These shows are a must during the introductory phase.

4.   The talk shows represent viable media for women's cosmetics, fashions, and grooming aids.[9]

Profiling New Product Users

Chapter 9 cited a study aimed at evaluating a low fat artificial bacon product. Respondents in the study were given a twenty-six-item life-style inventory in order to obtain a psychographic profile of potential purchasers. Those consumers who said they were likely to buy were most concerned with nutrition and health. They were more likely to (a) avoid cholesterol, (b) watch their weight, (c) take annual physicals, and (d) shop in health food stores.

Potential purchasers were also more outgoing since they were more likely to eat out and to go to concerts. In addition, they expressed a greater willingness to try new products.

The psychographic profile confirmed the product's positioning to a nutrition oriented segment. The profile also suggested that advertising should be oriented to a cosmopolitan segment. Given the willingness to try something new, the life-style profile indicated good prospects for initial trial as long as the product delivered the promised benefits.

Buyer Profiles by Life-Style

Another approach to using life-style descriptors for segmentation purpose is to describe consumers by their *buying activities* rather than by their *personal activities*. The reasoning for doing this is that the set of products that individuals buy provides insights into their needs and attitudes. Rather than rely on life-style inventories, this approach requires identifying a large number of purchases and determining purchasing patterns. On this basis, an individual may be described as a dieter, a self-medicator, a baker, or a well-groomed consumer. These descriptions can then be used to identify heavy or light users of a certain brand, owners or nonowners, loyalists or brand switchers, etc. For example, Alpert and Gatty obtained data on purchases of eighty products from a sample of male respondents.[10] These items were factor analyzed producing sixteen factors (see Table 10–4). For instance, Factor 2, labeled the "car-conscious man", identified a heavy purchaser of car wax, motor oil, antifreeze, and gasoline. Alpert and Gatty used the sixteen descriptors in Table 10–4 to identify a heavy versus a light beer-drinking segment and to identify users of two brands of beer. The heavy beer drinker was identified as: a hard drinker; an outdoorsman; a photographer; a cosmopolitan traveler; a hard driving man; a deodorized male; and a cough and cold conscious male. Based on activities and interests, this profile closely conforms to the previous description of the heavy beer drinker as masculine and hedonistic.

Wells examined purchases of 104 product categories and identified the following types of consumers by purchase activity: wrappers and savers (heavy purchasers of plastic bags, wraps, foil, etc.); dieters; canned food purchasers; slatherers (mustard, catsup, mayonnaise buyers); bakers; polishers; self-medicators; and germ haters.[11] Although Wells did not relate these categories to specific brands purchased, such descriptors can provide important insights in understanding the types of individuals purchasing brands and identifying heavy versus light brand users.

PERSONALITY

An individual's personality represents another set of characteristics that can be used to describe consumer segments. Personality is more deep-seated than life-style since personalilty variables reflect consistent, enduring patterns of behavior. Given these patterns, it can be assumed that personality variables should be related to purchase behavior.

Such an assumption is reasonable, but the results of relating personality variables to purchase behavior have been equivocal. Most studies have shown a weak relationship between personality variables like aggression, responsibility or dependence, and purchase behavior. The primary reason for this is that marketers have used personality inventories borrowed directly from psychology. These inventories were constructed to examine behavioral predispositions such as self-deprecation, authoritarianism, or neuroticism, which are not closely related to marketing. There is no reason to believe that measures divorced from a consumer's behavior will be a fruitful basis for describing target segments.

The Importance of Personality Characteristics

Like life-style characteristics, personality characteristics can be valuable guides to a copywriter. For example, knowing that users of a brand of analgesics are more likely to be compulsive led one company to shift their advertising cam-

Factors and Variables	Factor Loading	Factors and Variables	Factor Loading
Factor I: The Hard Drinker		**Factor VIII: The Well-Groomed Man**	
Rye whisky	.61	Hair tonic	.56
Canadian whisky	.62	After-shave lotion	.53
Bourbon	.60	Hair shampoo	.65
Scotch	.49	Mouthwash	.47
Gin	.62	**Factor IX: The Cough- and Cold-Conscious Man**	
Vodka	.59		
Highball mixers	.72	Cold tablets	.64
Beer	.65	Cough drops	.68
Factor II: The Car-Conscious Man		Throat lozenges	.71
Car wax and polish	.55	**Factor X: The Man with the Photographic Memory**	
Motor oil	.77		
Antifreeze	.76	Unexposed movie film	.60
Miles driven	.78	Flash pictures taken	.85
Gasoline	.87	Pictures taken without flashbulbs	.84
Factor III: The Candy Consumer		**Factor XI: The Liquor and Wine Connoisseur**	
Candy bars	.70		
Packaged hard candies	.72	Rum	.57
Chewing gum	.63	Brandy	.67
Factor IV: The Cosmopolitan Traveler		Liqueurs	.66
Plane trips in past year	.67	Domestic wine	.53
Car rental in past year	.68	Imported wine	.68
Gas credit cards	.50	**Factor XII: The Old Man**	
Other credit cards	.50	Hats	.48
Foreign trips last year	.54	Denture cream	.55
Factor V: The Electric Shaver		**Factor XIII: The Hard-Driving Man**	
Pre-shave lotion	.69	Miles driven in town	.83
Electric shaver	.82	Miles driven on highways	.81
Factor VI: The Cigar and Pipe Smoker		**Factor XIV: The Cocktail Drinker**	
Small cigars	.71	Bottled cocktails	.81
Cigarillos	.75	Cocktail mixers	.73
Regular cigars	.67	**Factor XV: The Regular Shaver**	
Pipe tobacco	.57	Regular double-edged blades	.77
Factor VII: The Dress-Conscious Man		Stainless steel double-edged blades	.67
Suits	.54	**Factor XVI: The Deodorized Male**	
Shoes	.67	Roll-on deodorant	.80
Dress shirts	.70	Spray deodorant	.67
Sport shirts	.65		

Source: Lewis Alpert and Ronald Gatty, "Product Positioning by Behavioral Life-Styles," *Journal of Marketing* 33 (April 1969): 67.

Reprinted with permission from the *Journal of Marketing*.

paign to present the product in an orderly setting which described a fixed routine. Another company found that an important segment of saccharine users tended to be compliant and accepting of guidance from others — especially medical experts, in an attempt to lose weight. This pointed to product positioning that suggested an easy-way-out approach to dieting.

Personality characteristics may also be a basis for product positioning. One segment of the market may diet primarily because of adherence to group norms and seek the path of least resistance. Another group may diet to draw attention to themselves and may go to certain lengths to ensure their actions are conspicuous — for instance, using several types of diet products rather than one. A company may follow a strategy of introducing several products directed to the latter group, whereas the former segment may desire one product for dieting, such as a simple diet pill.

Personality Theories

The personality measures used to describe markets depend on the personality theory the researcher feels is most relevant. Empirical personality measures have been used in marketing based on three theories: trait theory, social theory, and self-concept theory. A fourth school, the psychoanalytic school, is not empirically based, but has been sufficiently important in consumer behavior research to deserve attention here.

Trait Theory

Trait theory has been the most widely used basis for measuring personality because it is the most empirical. **Trait theory** states that personality is composed of a set of traits that describe general response predispositions. Trait theorists construct personality inventories in the same manner that life-style inventories are constructed. Respondents are asked to respond to many items, perhaps agreeing or disagreeing with certain statements or expressing likes or dislikes for certain situations or types of people. These items are then factor analyzed and a relatively small number of personality dimensions are produced that represent some of the original questions.

The most frequently used inventory in marketing has been the Edwards Personal Preference Schedule (EPPS). This measures the fourteen items described in Table 10–5. Other frequently used inventories are the Gordon Personal Profile which measures items such as ascendency, responsibility, emotional stability, and sociability; and the Thurstone Temperament Schedule which measures items such as dominance, stability, and impulsiveness. The reason these inventories are widely used is that they contain personality traits that are not too abstract and can be easily hypothesized to relate to purchasing behavior. Most importantly, identifying certain traits among a segment of the market can provide operational guidelines for directing product and promotional strategies. Other personality inventories tend to be more remote in their marketing implications.

Applications of Trait Theory. A number of studies have used personality traits to segment markets. In one of the earliest applications of personality

TABLE 10–5 Personality Variables in the Edwards Personal Preference Schedule

Achievement:	To rival and surpass others; to do one's best; to desire prestige, accomplishment, ambition, success
Compliance:	To accept leadership; to follow willingly; to let others make decisions; submission, deference, conformity
Order:	To have things arranged; to be organized; to be clean; tidiness, neatness, organization
Exhibition:	To be the center of attention; to have others notice you; to make an impression on others; vanity and self-dramatization
Autonomy:	To seek freedom; to resist influence; to defy authority and coercion; independence and freedom
Affiliation:	To form friendships and associations; to participate in groups; to do things with others; affiliation and companionship
Analysis:	To understand others; to examine motives; to analyze your own behavior; understanding and introspection
Dependence:	To seek aid; to be helped by others; to be guided and advised; helplessness
Self-Deprecation:	To feel inferior to others; to accept blame; to accept punishment; masochism and shame
Assistance:	To help others; to be sympathetic; to protect others; helpfulness and support
Change:	To do new things; to do different things; to change daily routine; variety and novelty
Endurance:	To stick at a task; to work hard at a job; to complete anything undertaken; persistence and toil
Heterosexuality:	Willingness to talk about sex, to be attracted to the opposite sex, to go out with the opposite sex; love and desire
Aggression:	To attack, assault, or injure; to belittle, harm, blame, punish; sadism and violence

Source: Adapted from Allen L. Edwards, *Edwards Personal Preference Schedule Manual* (New York: Psychological Corp., 1957).

Reprinted with permission from the Psychological Corp.

inventories, Evans used the Edwards Personal Preference Schedule to identify Ford versus Chevrolet owners.[12] Ford owners appeared to be more self-centered and domineering. Chevrolet owners tended toward group affiliation and independence. One may infer from this that power-oriented themes can be more successfully directed to Ford owners whereas social-like themes can be more effective in appealing to Chevrolet owners. These relationships were only marginally significant, and the overall association of personality variables with behavior was weak. In fact, Evans found that demographic variables were more closely related to differences between Ford and Chevrolet owners than personality characteristics. However, personality characteristics such as affiliation and dominance could guide advertising directions.

Westfall also used personality variables to segment the automobile market.[13] He applied the Thurstone Temperament Schedule and found no differences between owners of standard and compact cars, but found convertible owners to differ significantly in being more active, vigorous, and impulsive. On this basis, advertising appeals for convertibles would be directed to active, carefree individuals.

In a study of smoking behavior it was found that personality characteristics measured by the Edwards Personal Preference Schedule discriminated between heavy smokers, average smokers, and nonsmokers.[14] Heavy smokers scored higher on heterosexuality, aggression, and achievement, and lower on order and compliance. Heavy smokers, it was found, are more likely to be oriented toward power and competitiveness and may be more influenced by sexual themes and symbols. They are not as compulsive or submissive as the nonsmoker. Given this emphasis on power and competitiveness, it is not surprising that one of the most successful cigarette commercials was the Marlboro cowboy commercial.

Despite these findings, in most cases the association between personality traits and behavior has been a weak one. There are three ways to improve the use of multitrait personality inventories, like the Edwards Personal Preference Schedule, in order to describe consumer behavior. First, personality may be a moderating influence on behavior. If other variables are taken into account, personality may be more closely related to behavior. Second, researchers must develop logical hypotheses about the relationship between personality and behavior. Multitrait inventories tend to be more of a shotgun approach. When specific traits are hypothesized beforehand, their relationship to behavior is stronger. Third, multitrait inventories were not developed to describe consumer behavior and should not be expected to explain behavior. When personality inventories have been designed specifically for marketing purposes, they have been more successful in explaining consumer behavior. Let us consider each of these improvements further.

Personality as a Moderating Variable. Brody and Cunningham examined the relationship between personality and behavior based on the individual's perceived risk and self-confidence in purchasing. They associated traits from the EPPS with purchases of coffee brands and found personality traits to be more closely related to behavior in high risk situations where the individual is confident of the purchase.[15]

Peterson related personality traits from the EPPS to male and female purchasers of flared pants.[16] Males who scored high on exhibition were more likely to own flared pants. Females who scored high on affiliation and change and lower on deference were more likely to own flared pants (see Table 10–5 for definitions of these traits.) These traits suggest use of a segmented positioning strategy by sex — an exhibitionist appeal to males and an innovative, venturesome appeal to females. Had personality associations been developed for the total sample without regard to sex, the results would have been misleading.

These two studies suggest that interactions are likely between demographics, life-style, and personality variables. For instance, aggression may be associated with heavy smoking only among those with an active life-style; or affiliation may be associated with more frequent purchase of highly styled clothes only for women.

Use of Single Traits to Explain Behavior. Jacoby criticized the use of multitrait personality inventories because investigators did not select "specific personality traits based on theoretically derived hypotheses."[17] He hypothesized that consumers who buy new products are less likely to be dogmatic (i.e. narrow-minded, risk-averse, and threatened). He asked sixty young women to select one of five items in a product category. One of the items was more innovative (Virginia Slims was placed next to four older cigarette brands). Respondents lower in dogmatism were considerably more likely to select new brands. A replication of Jacoby's study among men came up with the same results.[18]

Low dogmatics tend to act on their independent evaluation of message content while high dogmatics rely more on authority figures, peer groups, and cultural norms for influence. Therefore, in appealing to those most likely to buy new products, advertising should "focus on product attributes rather than [on] emphasizing irrelevant ego or social factors."[19]

Personality Inventories Developed for Marketing. Perhaps the most important reason for the difficulty in relating personality to consumer behavior is that multitrait inventories were not originally designed to discriminate marketing behavior. Kassarjian states the problem as follows:

> Instruments originally intended to measure gross personality characteristics such as sociability, emotional stability, introversion, or neuroticism have been used to make predictions of the chosen brand of toothpaste or cigarettes. The variables that lead to the assassination of a president, confinement in a mental hospital, or suicide may not be identical to those that lead to the purchase of a washing machine, a pair of shoes, or chewing gum. Clearly, if unequivocal results are to emerge, consumer behavior researchers must develop their own definitions and design their own instruments to measure the personality variables that go into the purchase decision. . . .[20]

There have been few attempts to develop tailor-made personality inventories for marketing studies. In an early application, Gottleib hypothesized that compulsive and punitive consumers would be more frequent users of antacids.[21] Compulsiveness and punitiveness were measured by agreement or disagreement with a set of predetermined statements such as:

- I like to set up a schedule for my activities and then stick to it (compulsiveness).
- I never seem to be able to throw things away (compulsiveness).
- People learn a great deal from suffering (punitiveness).
- Discipline is the single most important factor in building children's character (punitiveness).

As expected, high compulsives tended to consume more antacids, but punitive respondents tended to consume less. Based on these results, the advertising for the brand under study emphasized a specific routine and regimen to appeal to the compulsive segment. Furthermore, it was not necessary to make the product taste bad to appeal to the punitive segment.

Personality

In a more recent study, Young described the development of a personality inventory to discriminate the use of a cosmetic product (see Table 10–6).[22] Although personality variables are not generally product-specific, the traits in Table 10–6 were selected because of their relevance to cosmetic purchases. Not surprisingly, Young found these traits to be a sound basis for segmenting the cosmetic market. It is unfortunate that so few studies have demonstrated such a product-specific approach to developing personality measures.

Psychoanalytic Theory

Freud's **psychoanalytic theory** stresses the unconscious nature of personality, in which behavior is related to the stresses between the ego, id, and superego. The manifestations of these conflicts in childhood (particularly the sexual drive) determine the adult personality and frequently influence behavior in a manner the adult is not aware of.

The emphasis on unconscious motives and repressed needs results in a nonempirical approach to personality. Marketers applying Freud's theories felt that unconscious motives could be determined only by indirect methods. Two techniques were derived from psychoanalytic theory and applied to marketing — depth interviews and projective techniques.

Depth interviews were designed to determine deep-seated or repressed motives that could not be elicited in structured surveys. Consumers were encouraged to talk freely in an unstructured interview, and responses were inter-

TABLE 10–6   Psychographic Dimensions: Cosmetic Study

Narcissism:	Tendency to be preoccupied with the details of one's personal appearance
Appearance Conscious:	Emphasis on the social importance of looking properly groomed
Exhibitionism:	Tendency toward self-display and attention seeking
Impulsive:	Tendency to act in a carefree, impetuous and unreflective manner
Order:	Tendency to be compulsively neat and live by rules and schedules
Fantasied Achievement:	Measure of narcissistic aspiration for distinction and personal recognition
Capacity for Status:	Measure of the personal qualities and attributes that underline and lead to status
Dominant:	Need to be superior to others by being in control and in the forefront
Sociable:	Need for informal, friendly, agreeable relationship with others
Active:	Need to be on the go, doing things, achieving goals set out for oneself
Cheerful:	Tendency to feel bright, cheerful and optimistic about life
Deference:	Tendency to submit to opinions and preferences of others perceived as superior
Subjective:	Tendency toward naive, superstitious and generally immature thinking

Source: Shirley Young, "The Dynamics of Measuring Unchange," in Russell I. Haley, ed., *Attitude Research in Transition,* (Chicago: American Marketing Association, 1972), p. 62.
Reprinted with permission from the American Marketing Association.

preted carefully to reveal motives and potential purchase inhibitions.

Projective techniques were designed to determine motives that are difficult to express or identify. Rather than ask consumers direct questions they might not have been able to answer, consumers were given a situation, a cartoon, or a set of words and asked to respond. Consumers were projecting to a less involving situation, thus facilitating expressions of feelings and concerns about products.

In one famous experiment, Haire used a projective technique in the late 1940s to uncover why women were reluctant to purchase instant coffee when it was first introduced.[23] He constructed two shopping lists that were identical, except that one included regular coffee and the other instant coffee. Housewives were then asked to project the type of woman most likely to have developed each shopping list. The housewife who included instant coffee in the list was characterized as lazy and a poor planner. These findings demonstrated that many women had a deep-seated fear of buying products like instant coffee or instant cake mixes out of a concern that their husbands would feel they were avoiding their traditional role as homemakers. As a result of the study, instant coffee was advertised in a family setting portraying the husband's approval. A replication of the study today would produce very different results since this traditional view of a woman's role is not as widespread. The study is a classic example of a psychoanalytically oriented approach to the determination of consumer motives.

This psychoanalytical approach came to be called **motivational research.** It was subject to much criticism when it was first introduced in the 1950s because of its lack of empiricism and its use of indirect methods to determine consumer motives. In fact, there was some question as to whether deep-seated motives could or should be influenced by advertising. Nonetheless, motivational research did provide the methodological contributions cited above and did produce actionable findings such as the following:

• Men dislike air travel because of posthumous guilt (the anticipation of leaving a wife a widow).

• Candy consumption is a source of guilt because of childhood associations with reward and punishment.

• Giving blood is sometimes resisted by men because it is associated with a loss of potency.

• Power tools provide men with a feeling of omnipotence and manliness.

• Consumers resist using plastic wraps because of a lack of control over the product.

Even though the psychoanalytic approach is not empirical, it has contributed to the development of psychographic research. In the mid-1950s motivational researchers were the first to argue that consumers are "complex, devious, difficult to understand and driven by mighty forces of which they are unaware."[24] Before the advent of motivational research, the state of advertising and marketing research was described as

a vast wasteland of percentages. The marketing manager who wanted to know why people ate the competitor's cornflakes was told "32 percent of the respondents said taste, 21 percent said flavor, 15 percent said texture, 10 percent said price, and 22 percent said don't know or no answer." The copywriter who wanted to know his audience was told "32.4 years old, 12.62 years of schooling, 90 percent married with 2.1 children."

To this desert Motivational Research brought people. . . . For the first time research brought the marketing manager and the copywriter face to face with an audience or a group of customers instead of a bunch of decimals. The marketing manager and the copywriter thought they were aided in their task of communication.[25]

As a result of this orientation toward people, marketers sought to quantify the personality variables which the motivational researchers were dealing with. Thus, psychographic research can be said to be a direct descendent of psychoanalytic theory and motivational research.

Social Theory

A number of Freud's disciples shifted from his view of personality in two respects. First, social variables rather than biological drives are most important in personality development. Second, conscious motives are more important than unconscious motives. Behavior is most frequently directed to known needs and wants.

Karen Horney's theory, an example of this social orientation, is relevant to marketing. Horney postulated that personality is developed as an individual learns to cope with basic anxieties stemming from parent-child relationships. She hypothesized three approaches to coping with anxiety: compliance, representing a strategy of moving toward people; aggressiveness, moving against people; and detachment, moving away from people. In one of the few studies relying on social theories of personality to explain purchase behavior, Cohen developed a **compliance-aggressiveness-detachment (CAD) scale**.[26] Cohen argued that trait theory was not adequate to explain purchasing behavior and that it would be more meaningful to organize traits into categories descriptive of a person's consistent means of relating to and coping with others.

Cohen measured CAD based on a thirty-five item inventory. The construction of this inventory differed from trait inventories in that Cohen began the study with the intention of measuring compliance, aggression, and detachment. Trait theorists "let the chips fall where they will" in terms of the ultimate construct of the scale based on factor analysis.

In applying the CAD scale, Cohen found that compliant types had a higher frequency of usage for mouthwash and toilet soaps and used more Bayer aspirin; aggressive types used more cologne and after-shave lotion and bought Old Spice deodorant and Van Heusen shirts; and, detached types drank more tea and less beer. These findings suggest advertising the use of mouthwash or toilet soap as a means of social approval; advertising colognes and after-shaves as a means of social conquest; and advertising tea in a nonsocial, more isolate context.

Measures such as Cohen's CAD scale are important because they were constructed for marketing applications and have a theoretical base in personality theory. In such cases, the researcher begins a study with defined hypotheses as to what to measure.

Another set of personality measures is based on **self-concept theory.** This theory holds that an individual has a concept of *self* measured on such criteria as happy, careful, dependable, confident, social, etc. and on a concept of the *ideal self*. The self-concept measures who consumers think they are; the ideal concept measures who consumers think they would like to be. Table 10–7 presents an example of a forty-item, self-concept inventory. The question asks respondents to describe how they see themselves on these items. An additional question could ask respondents to rate themselves on how they would like to be on the same forty items.

TABLE 10–7   Self-Image Inventory

Instructions to Respondents

Different words are used to describe different people. We would now like to find out what words you would use to describe yourself. Each of these cards contains one descriptive word. (Place 4 envelopes in front of respondent.) Please place each card on one of these envelopes depending on how much you think the word describes *you*. If you feel the word is *very descriptive* you would place the card here (point). If you feel the word is *somewhat descriptive, not too descriptive,* or *not at all descriptive* you would place the cards on one of these envelopes depending on how descriptive you feel the word is. Now, please sort these cards according to how descriptive you feel the word is of you. (At end of sort, place cards in envelopes and record after you have left the residence.)

	Very Descriptive	*Somewhat Descriptive*	*Not Too Descriptive*	*Not at All Descriptive*
Thrifty				
Hard working				
Healthy				
Happy				
Careful				
Friendly				
Dependable				
Modern				
Appealing				
Neat				
Efficient				
Humorous				
Enthusiastic				
Active				
Practical				
Energetic				
Serious				
Lovable				
Attractive				
Imaginative				

TABLE 10–7 Self-Image Inventory (cont.)

Psychographic Characteristics	Very Descriptive	Somewhat Descriptive	Not Too Descriptive	Not at All Descriptive
Flexible				
Religious				
Self-controlled				
Warm				
Social				
Cosmopolitan				
Sophisticated				
Successful				
Imaginative				
Intelligent				
Relaxed				
Sensitive				
Confident				
Useful				
Involved				
Creative				
Conscientious				
Aggressive				
Warm				
Open-minded				

Self-concept theory has taken two directions in marketing. One direction holds that the discrepancy between the self and the ideal self is a measure of personal dissatisfaction. Such dissatisfaction could be related to product usage, particularly for products that deal with self-enhancement. Thus, a woman who would like to be more efficient, modern, and imaginative may buy a different type of perfume or deodorant or tend to shop at different stores compared to a woman who would like to be more warm and attractive.

A second line of research holds that consumers buy on the basis of their self-image (either actual or ideal) and that there is congruence between brand image and self-image.

A study by White illustrates research based on the discrepancy between actual and ideal self-image. White defined three segments based on this discrepancy.[27] High discrepants are those who are dissatisfied with their self-image and wish for great and unrealizable changes; middle discrepants are those who are somewhat dissatisfied and want to improve themselves in a realistic way; and low discrepants are those who have accurate and often severe notions of themselves and tend to have little tolerance for fantasy. White related these categories to ownership of compact cars and found that a significantly greater proportion of the middle discrepants owned compact cars. Moreover, they had their current car two years longer, on average, than the other two groups. Thus, compact car ownership seems to be greater among a more realistic, somewhat better adjusted group, a group that could be effectively appealed to with a moderate amount of fantasy interspersed with a good dose of reality concerning appeals to durability and economy.

A study by Dolich illustrates self-concept research based on the relationship between self-image and brand image. Dolich studied this relationship for beer, cigarettes, bar soap, and toothpaste.[28] He found that respondents tend to prefer brands they rate as similar to themselves on both the actual and ideal dimensions. Several studies have shown the same relationship for automobiles.[29] An owner's perception of his or her car is consistent with self-perceptions. Further, the consumer's self-image is similar to his or her image of others with the same automobile.

Using Personality Characteristics in Marketing Strategy

Personality characteristics can influence marketing strategies, particularly in segmenting markets, positioning products, establishing media guidelines, and introducing new products. Although strategic applications of personality variables have not been as frequent as life-style and demographics, a number of such applications are worth mentioning.

Market Segmentation

In a study for Anheuser-Busch, two University of Pennsylvania professors developed personality profiles of beer drinkers which enabled them to determine which market segments the company's three major brands — Budweiser, Michelob, and Busch — were reaching.[30] Four drinking types were identified based on corresponding personality types: social drinkers, reparative drinkers, indulgent drinkers, and oceanic drinkers (see Table 10–8 for descriptions).

This typology led to a test to confirm the association between personality and beer drinking. A sample of 250 beer drinkers was first given a questionnaire to determine in which of the four personality groups each beer drinker belonged. Next, the sample was shown four TV commercials for four fictitious brands of beer. Each commercial showed each of the four personality types drinking one of the four brands. Each of the four beers was then tried. Consumers tended to choose the brand corresponding to their personality type, even though the four brands were identical. Furthermore, "all the subjects believed that the brands were different and that they could tell the differences between them. Most felt that at least one of the four brands was not fit for human consumption."[31]

This test led to a larger scale survey of 1200 beer drinkers in six cities. Respondents were asked to characterize those who drink each major beer brand in their area.

The researchers found that Michelob, Budweiser, and Busch appealed to different personality segments. This enabled the company to specify target segments to be reached by each of the three brands based on the personality types. The test also enabled the company to specify the kind of advertising

TABLE 10–8 Drinker Personality Types

Type of Drinker	Demographics	Personality Type	Drinking Patterns
Reparative Drinker	Middle-Aged	Sensitive and responsive to needs of others; adapts to these needs by sacrificing own aspirations; well adjusted to this situation.	Drinks at end of day, usually with a few close friends; controlled drinker, seldom drunk; drinking is self-reward for sacrifices made to others.
Social Drinker	Younger Adult	Driven by own ambitions; attempts to manipulate others to get what he/she wants; not yet attained level of aspirations, but expects to.	Drinks heaviest on weekends; in larger groups in social settings; drinks as means of acceptance of and by others; controlled drinker.
Indulgent Drinker		Considers self a failure; blames environment and others.	Heavy drinker; drinks in isolation as a form of escape.
Oceanic Drinker		Considers self a failure but blames own shortcomings.	Also heavy drinker and drinks to escape recognition of shortcomings; does not drink alone.

Source: Russell L. Ackoff and James R. Emshoff, "Advertising Research at Anheuser-Busch (1968–1974)," *Sloan Management Review* 16 (Spring 1975): 1–15.

messages that would be most effective in influencing these segments. Media implications also emerged. For example, the reparative drinker will watch much more TV; the oceanic drinker more likely reads *Playboy*. These personality descriptors permitted the company "to combine messages and media in such a way as to direct advertising messages at particular market segments in a more effective way."[32]

Advertising and Product Positioning

Personality characteristics provide a richness in describing consumer segments that may assist copywriters and may guide advertising content. One writer states:

> Suppose for example that you have a scale that measures impulsivity versus caution. Telling a copywriter that the people who are high in social status are heavy users of a particular product or that the people who are low in social status are the light users will help some, but not much. However, if you can tell a copywriter that the people who are important users of a product keep saying over and over again in different ways that they are impulsive, then I think the scale is of some value.

The personality typology reported by Young provides a good example of input into the creative process (see Table 10–6). As noted earlier, the profiles were used as an effective vehicle to segment the cosmetic market. For example, a product directed to a deference segment might use testimonials from authority figures. Cosmetics targeted to a narcissism segment may use advertising depicting meticulous grooming. Appealing to a dominant segment may warrant a campaign based on superiority, self-worth, and upward mobility.

Media Guidelines

Wells and Beard effectively make the case for the use of personality characteristics to select media:

> Personality traits might prove a useful adjunct to demographic data in the media-selection process. Perhaps the best prospect for a cleaning product is not just a middle-aged, middle-class housewife, but a middle-aged, middle-class housewife with a compulsive need for cleanliness. Perhaps the best prospect for an expensive set of books is not just a well-educated male, but a well-educated male who is substantially above average on achievement motivation. If media, for whatever reasons, draw disproportionate numbers of compulsive housewives or achievement-oriented males, personality characteristics might improve the product-media match.[33]

But few studies have used personality to improve the product-media match.

In one such study, consumers were grouped by similarity in TV-viewing behavior.[34] Five audience segments were identified by similarity in type of show most frequently watched: light viewers; heavy viewers; nonviolent viewers (situation comedies and light entertainment); action-oriented viewers (action and drama programs); and change-oriented viewers (a variety of programs). The personality, life-style, and demographic characteristics of each audience segment were identified. Although the association between personality traits and TV viewing was not strong, some traits proved revealing. Heavy viewers were discontent with their life, tended to be more isolate, were more conventional, and had a greater desire for security. These characteristics suggest heavy TV viewers are less likely to buy new products and may be more brand loyal. Nonviolent viewers were less confident in personal and social interactions and less likely to be independent. Action-oriented viewers tended to be more self-satisfied.

Such profiles are useful in identifying the media needed to reach target segments. For example, consumers identified as falling into a social inhibition segment may more likely be in the nonviolent viewer group, suggesting advertising should be scheduled for the situation comedy and light entertainment shows.

New Product Users

Several studies have attempted to identify the consumers most likely to buy new products (the innovators) by studying their personality characteristics. Studies cited earlier found that less dogmatic individuals are more likely to buy new products. The important implication here is that the less dogmatic individual is more receptive to factual advertising that focuses on product characteristics rather than to symbolic or emotional advertising that emphasizes ego and social needs.

Support for this finding comes from other studies that describe the new product purchaser as *inner*- rather than *other*-directed; that is, a consumer that relies on internal values and standards to guide behavior rather than peer values. One study identified purchasers of Ford's Maverick when it was first introduced in 1969 (innovators) and purchasers of the car in three succeeding years (followers). Innovators were significantly more inner-directed than followers.[35] A second study found that purchasers of five new grocery products were also significantly more inner-directed than those who were not purchasers.[36] Further, inner-directed consumers seem to prefer ads containing more factual content that enable them to use their own standards in evaluating products.[37]

The clear implication is that marketers of new products should advertise on a more factual basis in the early stages. Once the innovators have been reached, then advertising can gradually shift toward the social and ego-oriented appeals.

There is some danger in assuming such results may be relevant for all new products, however. Current evidence indicates that the innovator for one product category may not be an innovator for another. Therefore, it is not at all certain that the inner-directed or less dogmatic consumer is going to be favorably disposed to any new product. One study found that personality characteristics related to the personal grooming innovator were very different from those related to the apparel innovator.[38] Therefore, marketers should study personality predispositions toward new products on a product by product basis.

SUMMARY

Two consumer characteristics of importance to marketers are life-style and personality. Life-style is represented by a consumer's activities, interests, and opinions. Personality characteristics are more enduring and deep-seated and reflect consistent patterns of response developed since childhood. Life-style and personality characteristics make up a richer set of descriptors than demographics because they represent the psychological makeup of the consumer.

Life-style inventories have been constructed in marketing studies to measure consumers' activities and interests. These inventories have enabled marketers to measure many life-style characteristics. Like demographics, life-style characteristics have been used to identify current and prospective brand users, but they also have provided more specific guidelines for advertising and product positioning since a consumer's life-style is more descriptive of the individual.

Personality characteristics can also be used to describe consumer segments, guide advertising, help position products, and select media. However, personality variables are more difficult to use in marketing because they are not as closely related to brand usage as are life-style and demographics. One difficulty that arises is due to the fact that many of the personality inventories used in marketing were developed in psychology. There is a need for tailor-made psychological inventories for marketing purposes. Given the continued use of personality variables by marketers, several personality theories are reviewed in this chapter:

- **Trait theory** seeks to measure personality traits by the development of personality inventories. Trait theory is the most widely applied of the personality theories in marketing since specific personality variables can be measured and related to consumer usage.

- **Psychoanalytic theory** stresses the unconscious nature of personality as determined by childhood conflicts. Marketers have applied psychoanalytic theory by utilizing unstructured interviews to try to assess consumer motives.

- **Social theory** emphasizes environmental variables in personality development.

- **Self-concept theory** suggests that an individual's self-image or image of the ideal self determines behavior. Marketers have applied this theory in the belief that there may be a congruence between an individual's self-image and the image of the brand.

The chapter concludes by considering various uses for personality variables in guiding marketing strategies.

QUESTIONS

1. What are the marketing implications of a change in values from family to self for (a) product line strategies, (b) pricing, and (c) advertising strategies?

2. What are the marketing implications of a change in values from an emphasis on work to an emphasis on leisure for (a) product line strategies and (b) advertising strategies?

3. What are the marketing implications in using any of the life-style categories cited in Table 10–1 for describing users (or prospective users) of:
   - a new detergent that advertises that it makes washing easier?
   - personal care appliances such as curling irons or facial care appliances?
   - a new magazine designed to provide up-to-date marketing and financial information to the working woman?
   - a new breakfast cereal for the diet conscious and active adult?

4. A heavy-duty floor cleaner was positioned to emphasize its ability to remove dirt. Life-style research showed the target segment was more concerned with cleanliness from the standpoint of health rather than utilitarian homekeeping benefits.
   - Should the product be repositioned? How?

5. A life-style study of hair care appliances found two product groups most likely to own these products. One is more sociable and style conscious; the other is less concerned with style and with other people's opinions. Women in this group tend to be self-actualizers and are more upwardly mobile than the first group. Both groups are more likely to own hair care appliances, but the first group uses them more frequently.
   - What are the implications of positioning hair care appliances to each group?

- Should the same products be positioned to each group, or should separate product lines be developed?

6. Do you see any limitations in the use of consumer life-style characteristics to select media?

7. What would be the differences in advertising the following brands to low dogmatics versus high dogmatics: (a) Mercedes-Benz automobiles, (b) Brut after-shave, and (c) *Sports Illustrated?*

8. Psychoanalytic theory has been criticized as having little relevance to marketing because it deals with deep-seated needs and motives derived from childhood conflicts.
   - Do you agree?
   - For what types of product categories may psychoanalytic theory provide insights into consumer purchasing motives?

9. Under what circumstances or for what types of products might it be more appropriate to appeal to a consumer's (a) ideal self-image; (b) actual self-image; and (c) the difference between the two?

RESEARCH ASSIGNMENTS

1. You would like to distinguish users of natural food products (granola, wheat germ, etc.) from nonusers based on life-style criteria. You plan to utilize life-styles to position a new line of natural food products and develop guidelines for advertising.
   - Conduct a number of depth interviews with users of natural foods. On this basis, develop a life-style inventory designed to identify natural food users.
   - Submit the inventory to a sample equally divided between users and nonusers of natural foods. Does the life-style inventory discriminate between the two groups? If so, what are the distinctive life-style characteristics of natural food users?
   - What are the implications of these life-style characteristics for (a) advertising and (b) new product development?

2. Self-concept theory suggests that the disparity between a consumer's actual and ideal self-image could predict the purchase of brands or products related to the consumer's identity.
   - Select ten or fifteen items from Table 10–7. Submit these items to a sample of consumers and ask respondents to rate themselves on both actual and ideal self. Also ask consumers to identify brands that are regularly purchased for items such as perfume, clothing, magazines, automobiles, or any other items that may be related to self-image.
   - Determine the disparity between actual and ideal self-image by summing across the differences for each item in the scale. Are these differences related to brand or product ownership?

1. Joseph T. Plummer, "The Concept and Application of Life Style Segmentation," *Journal of Marketing* 38 (January 1974): 33–37.
2. "Focus Selling Efforts on Life Styles, Retailers Told," *Advertising Age,* Jan. 26, 1976, p. 10.
3. William D. Wells and Douglas J. Tigert, "Activities, Interests and Opinions," *Journal of Advertising Research* 11 (August 1971): 27–35.
4. Plummer, "The Concept and Application of Life Style Segmentation."
5. Joseph T. Plummer, "Life Style and Advertising: Case Studies," in Fred C. Allvine, *Combined Proceedings, 1971 Spring and Fall Conference* (Chicago: American Marketing Association, 1972), pp. 290–295.
6. Plummer, "Life Style and Advertising," p. 292.
7. Shirley Young, "Psychographic Research and Marketing Relevancy," in Charles A. King and Douglas J. Tigert, eds., *Attitude Research Reaches New Heights* (Chicago: American Marketing Association, 1971), pp. 220–222.
8. Ibid.
9. Douglas J. Tigert, "Are Television Audiences Really Different?" in Fred C. Allvine, ed., *Combined Proceedings, 1971 Spring and Fall Conference* (Chicago: American Marketing Association, 1972), p. 246.
10. Lewis Alpert and Ronald Gatty, "Product Positioning by Behavioral Life-Styles," *Journal of Marketing* 33 (April 1969): 65–69.
11. William D. Wells, "Backward Segmentation," in Johan Arndt, ed., *Insights into Consumer Behavior* (Boston: Allyn and Bacon, 1968), pp. 85–100.
12. Franklin B. Evans, "Psychological and Objective Factors in the Prediction of Brand Choice: Ford vs. Chevrolet," *Journal of Business* 32 (October 1959): 340–369.
13. Ralph Westfall, "Psychological Factors in Predicting Product Choice," *Journal of Marketing* 26 (April 1962): 34–40.
14. Arthur Koponen, "Personality Characteristics of Purchasers," *Journal of Advertising Research* 1 (September 1960): 6–12.
15. Robert P. Brody and Scott M. Cunningham, "Personality Variables and the Consumer Decision Process," *Journal of Marketing Research* 5 (February 1968): 50–57.
16. Robert A. Peterson, "Moderating the Personality-Product Usage Relationship," in Ronald C. Curhan, ed., *1974 Combined Proceedings,* (Chicago: American Marketing Association, 1975), pp. 109–112.
17. Jacob Jacoby, "Personality and Innovation Proneness," *Journal of Marketing Research* 8 (May 1971): 244–247.
18. Kenneth A. Coney, "Dogmatism and Innovation: A Replication," *Journal of Marketing Research* 9 (November 1972): 453–455.
19. Jacoby, "Personality and Innovation Proneness," p. 246.
20. Harold H. Kassarjian, "Personality and Consumer Behavior: A Review," *Journal of Marketing Research* 8 (November 1971): 409–419.
21. Morris J. Gottleib, "Segmentation by Personality Types," in Lynn H. Stockman, ed., *Advancing Marketing Efficiency,* Proceedings of the 1959 Conference (Chicago: American Marketing Association, 1960), pp. 148–158.
22. Shirley Young, "The Dynamics of Measuring Unchange," in Russell I. Haley, ed., *Attitude Research in Transition* (Chicago: American Marketing Association, 1972), pp. 49–82.
23. Mason Haire, "Projective Techniques in Marketing Research," *Journal of Marketing* 14 (April 1950): 649–656.
24. William D. Wells and Arthur D. Beard, "Personality Theories," in Scott Ward and Thomas S. Robertson, eds., *Consumer Behavior: Theoretical Sources* (Englewood Cliffs, N.J.: Prentice-Hall 1973), pp. 142–199.
25. Wells and Tigert, "Activities, Interests and Opinions," p. 27.
26. Joel B. Cohen, "An Interpersonal Orientation to the Study of Consumer Behavior," *Journal of Marketing Research* 4 (August 1967): 270–278.
27. Irving S. White, "The Perception of Value in Products," in Joseph W. Newman, ed., *On Knowing the Consumer* (New York: John Wiley, 1967), pp. 90–106.
28. Ira J. Dolich, "Congruence Relationships Between Self Images and Product Brands," *Journal of Marketing Research* 6 (February 1969): 80–85.
29. Al E. Birdwell, "Influence of Image Congruence on Consumer Choice," *Proceedings, Winter Conference, 1964* (Chicago: American Marketing Association, 1965), pp. 290–303; and Edward L. Grubb and Gregg Hupp, "Perception of Self Generalized Stereotypes and Brand Selection," *Journal of Marketing Research* 5 (February 1968): 58–63.
30. "Researchers Categorize Beer Drinkers to Aid Anheuser-Busch Brand Efforts," *Advertising Age,* June 23, 1975, pp. 17 and 22; and Russell L. Ackoff and James R. Emshoff, "Advertising Research at Anheuser-Busch, Inc." (1968–1974), *Sloan Management Review* 16 (Spring 1975): 1–15.
31. Ackoff and Emshoff, "Advertising Research at Anheuser-Busch, Inc.," p. 12.
32. Ibid., p. 14.
33. Wells and Beard, "Personality Theories," p. 177.
34. Kathryn E. Villani, "Personality/Life Style and Television Viewing Behavior," *Journal of Marketing Research* 12 (November 1975): 432–439.

260 35. James H. Donnelly, Jr. and John M. Ivancevich, "A Methodology for Identifying Innovator Characteristics of New Brand Purchasers," *Journal of Marketing Research* 11 (August 1974): 331–334.

36. James H. Donnelly, Jr., "Social Character and Acceptance of New Products," *Journal of Marketing Research* 7 (February 1970): 111–113.

37. Harold H. Kassarjian, "Social Character and Differential Preference for Mass Communication," *Journal of Marketing Research* 2 (May 1965): 146–153.

38. William R. Darden and Fred D. Reynolds, "Backward Profiling of Male Innovators," *Journal of Marketing Research* 11 (February 1974): 79–85.

PART THREE

Environmental Influences on Consumer Behavior

In Part Three the focus shifts from the individual consumer to the consumer's environment, the components of which can be viewed as an inverted pyramid. The broadest-based environmental influences — the consumer's culture and social class — will be considered first. Then, the influence of face-to-face groups on purchase behavior will be discussed, with particular emphasis on the family. Finally, the purchase and usage situation will be identified as an environmental condition that directly influences purchase behavior.

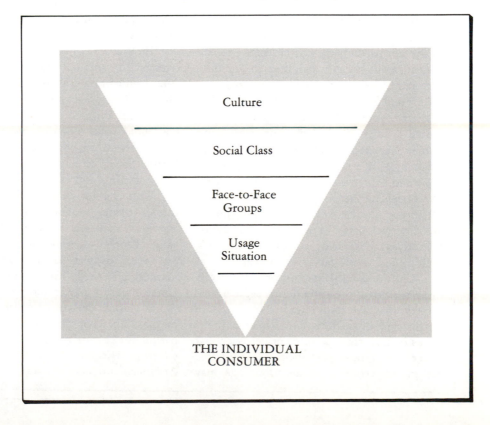

Culture

Social Class

Face-to-Face Groups

Usage Situation

THE INDIVIDUAL CONSUMER

ELEVEN

Cultural Influences

Focus of Chapter

The broadest environmental factor affecting consumer behavior is culture. **Culture** refers to the norms, beliefs, and customs that are learned from society and lead to common patterns of behavior. One cultural norm in the United States is the value placed on slimness and youth. John F. Kennedy represented a cultural ideal of youth and vigor to many Americans. That he would not wear a hat or coat encouraged others to do the same and led the hat and coat manufacturers to request that he carry these items in hand. Other manifestations of these cultural norms are diet products, weight-reducing salons, hair dyes, cosmetics to make one look young, and sports facilities to keep fit.

Culture is a diverse concept. Marketers often seek to specifically define segments of society that are tied together by common norms and characteristics. These **subcultures** demonstrate patterns of behavior that differ in certain respects from other groups. Religious, ethnic, or age groupings may constitute subcultures because of differences in norms, beliefs, and behavior.

International marketers may also be interested in cross-cultural comparisons. An American company introducing a detergent into the Puerto Rican market must be aware of cultural differences in attitudes toward household tasks and the role of the homemaker. Strategies that are successful in the United States cannot always be exported to other cultures and be expected to work.

This chapter will first focus on the nature of culture by describing cultural values and how they are measured. The cultural values central to American society will be considered as well as their application to marketing strategy. Subcultures within the United States, particularly the black consumer market, will be compared to the total market. The chapter will conclude by comparing our culture to other cultures and will consider the implications of marketing American products abroad.

THE NATURE OF CULTURE

One of the first writers to recognize the importance of culture in consumer behavior was an economist, James Duesenberry. He said, "In every case the kinds of activities in which people engage are culturally determined; nearly all purchases of goods are made . . . either to provide physical comfort or to implement the activities which make up the life of our culture."[1] Society instills in consumers basic norms and values that are likely to broadly influence consumers' behavior. For example, a high value placed on achievement may lead a consumer to demonstrate success by symbols of luxury and prestige, or a culturally derived desire to appear young and active may lead a consumer to buy cosmetics that advertise a "younger look" and enroll in an exercise program. In either case, the marketer must define the consumer's value orientation and determine what symbols appeal to these values.

The determination of commonly held values is central in applying culture to marketing strategies. For example, it would be logical for a furniture manufacturer to segment the market according to the value consumers place on beauty, social recognition, and comfort. Different product lines and marketing strategies would have to be developed for each segment. The beauty segment would desire highly styled and pleasurable furniture. Advertising symbols for this segment would appeal to the individual's integrity with the environment and to the individual's pleasure. The social recognition segment would desire furniture that demonstrates status. The furniture might be richer in design, and advertising would use symbols oriented to acceptance in a social environment. The comfort segment might desire furniture that is more practical and utilitarian. Advertising symbols for this segment would attempt to convey reality by demonstrating product features in an informative campaign. Cultural values are not held to the same degree by everyone. Values of comfort and social recognition are widely held in American society, but individual differences provide marketers with a basis for developing strategies.

In order to consider the implications of cultural values for marketing strategy, it is necessary to first understand (a) the nature of cultural values; (b) the characteristics of cultural values; (c) the widely held cultural values in American society; and (d) the measurement of cultural values.

Cultural Values

Rokeach defines **cultural values** as beliefs that some general state of existence is personally and socially worth striving for.[2] The vague state of success or achievement is an example of a value. An individual may have been instilled with this value by family and society from birth, and, as a result, much of day-to-day behavior may be directed to personal success. Similarly, beauty, youthfulness, comfort, leisure, social recognition, security, individuality, love, and happiness may all be regarded as cultural values directed toward desired end states. Rokeach developed an inventory of cultural or, as he termed them, terminal (end state) values. These values are listed in the first column in Table 11–1.

TABLE 11–1 Cultural and Consumption-Specific Values in American Society

Inventory of Cultural Values	Inventory of Consumption-Specific Values
a comfortable life	prompt service
an exciting life	reliable advertising claims
a world at peace	responsiveness to consumer needs
equality	accurate information
freedom	elimination of pollution
happiness	free repair of defective products
national security	convenient store locations
pleasure	no deceptive advertising
salvation	courteous and helpful sales people
social recognition	low prices
true friendship	solutions to urban decay and
a world of beauty	unemployment
family security	legislation to protect the consumer
mature love	no product misrepresentation
accomplishment	
inner harmony	

Source: Cultural values from Milton J. Rokeach, "The Role of Values in Public Opinion Research," *Public Opinion Quarterly* 32 (Winter 1968):554; Consumption-specific values from Donald E. Vinson, Jerome E. Scott, and Lawrence M. Lamont, "The Role of Personal Values in Marketing and Consumer Behavior," *Journal of Marketing* 41 (April 1977): 47.

Reprinted with permission from the *Journal of Marketing*.

Vinson, Scott, and Lamont distinguish between cultural values, consumption-specific values (see second column of Table 11–1), and product-specific values.[3] Examples of each are listed below:

Values:	Cultural Values →	Consumption–Specific → Values	Product–Specific Values
Definition:	Enduring beliefs concerning desired modes of behavior	Beliefs relevant to specific social, personal, and other activities	Evaluative beliefs about product attributes
Examples:	Security Happiness Freedom Social recognition	Prompt service Accurate information Convenient stores Nonpollution	Quiet Easy to use Durable Inexpensive

Product-specific values parallel the value component in the multiattribute attitude models described in Chapter 7.

Few marketing studies have utilized cultural values as descriptors of consumer behavior. Yet, cultural values should be regarded like other factors that influence consumer behavior such as life-style, personality, and social class. In each case, an inventory of factors has been established and used to describe behavior. Rokeach's inventory of values has been used on occasion to describe the automobile market, but its use has been limited.

Another cultural value inventory was developed by Kluckhohn and Strodtbeck.[4] It is composed of the following four variables:

Cultural Value	Alternative States
Individual's relation to nature	• Subjugated by
	• In harmony with
	• Mastery over
Time	• Past
	• Present
	• Future
Personal activity	• Being
	• Becoming
	• Doing
Individual's relation to others	• Traditional
	• Democratic
	• Individualistic

Only one study utilized this value inventory; again, it dealt with automobile purchases.

Given the importance of culture as an influence on consumer behavior, marketers should consider wider use of inventories like Rokeach's or Kluckhohn's. One reason for their limited use is that most marketing studies operate on a brand-by-brand basis. Cultural values are more likely to influence broad purchasing patterns, but it can be argued that a better understanding of the motivation behind brand purchases can be gained by understanding culturally derived purchasing values.

Characteristics of Cultural Values

A number of characteristics are common to all cultural values, as the following list describes.

1. *Cultural values are learned.* Children are instilled with cultural values at an early age. The process of learning the values of one's own culture from childhood is known as **socialization.** Learning the values of another culture is known as **acculturation.** Cultural learning can occur by imitative behavior (a foreigner copying local customs), by formal learning (a child taught by family members how to behave), and by technical learning (a child taught in a school environment). The process of acculturation is particularly important for business persons in foreign markets since an understanding of the local culture is necessary before product and advertising plans can be developed.

Hair and Anderson studied the process of acculturation among immigrants to America.[5] They found that respondents from developed countries were more quickly acculturated than respondents from developing countries. One explanation is that the heritages and life-styles of developed countries and the United States are more closely related. Hair and Anderson also found that acculturation takes place faster for consumer behavior than for other forms of behavior. The reason is that material objects are integrated more easily into one's behavior than more abstract, nonmaterial characteristics.[6]

2. *Cultural values are guides to behavior.*   Cultural values guide and direct an individual's behavior. Standards are established regarding proper social relations, means of insuring safety, eating habits, etc. If behavior deviates from the cultural norm, sanctions or restrictions may be placed on behavior.

3. *Cultural values are both permanent and dynamic.*   Cultural values are passed on from parents to children. Schools and religious groups are also important in maintaining the permanence of cultural values. The emphasis on values like freedom, self-respect, and individuality has not changed substantially over time. Yet, culture is also dynamic. Values must change as society changes. Basic changes in values have taken place in the American culture in the last forty years. The Depression, wars, and the development of a counterculture have drastically changed traditional values like the work ethic, the need to save, the desire to follow in parents' footsteps, and the respect accorded authority figures. Kotler has summarized some of the basic changes in cultural values as follows:[7]

From	*To*
self-reliance	government reliance
hard work	the easy life
husband-dominated household	wife-dominated household
parent-centered household	child-centered household
postponed gratification	immediate gratification
saving	spending
sexual chastity	sexual freedom
parental values	peer group values
independence	security

The increasingly rapid changes in cultural values require that marketers track these changes. A shift from the work ethic to the easy life means an increasing emphasis on leisure goods and services. A shift from saving to spending means the increased use of credit cards and a greater willingness to travel. A shift from sexual chastity to sexual freedom means more unisex styles in clothing and cosmetics. One marketing research firm has developed a "monitor" service to track such changes and provides its findings to clients on a syndicated basis. The service interviews 2,500 consumers annually to determine "how social values are impacting on consumer behavior."[8] Other services such as the Gallup and Harris polls provide similar information.

A good example of the marketing impact of cultural change is the current acceptance of instant food products. The Haire study in 1959, cited in the previous chapter, showed a resistance to the purchase of instant coffee because of the traditional cultural values that required the homemaker's care in meal preparation. An update of the study about ten years later showed the following changes in the image of the instant coffee purchaser:[9]

Percent who considered the purchaser of instant coffee:	*1950*	*1968*
lazy	48%	18%
poor planner	48%	27%
thrifty	4%	36%

It is apparent that there is much less resistance to the purchase of instant coffee than there was in 1950 because of the changing role of the homemaker. Time-saving devices in the kitchen are now accepted as necessary because of the increasing number of working women. With trends toward informality and leisure, formal meal preparations are no longer required. The breakdown of the extended family has also resulted in a greater informality at family meals.

4. *Cultural values are socially shared.* Cultural values are commonly accepted and widely held. The sharing of values is facilitated by a common language. In multilingual countries such as Canada, India, and the Soviet Union, the lack of a single cultural bond through language has led to divisiveness. In the United States, the mass media have facilitated the sharing of cultural norms. When two out of three households with TV sets view a particular program at the same time, they must share values. As a result, "advertising now compares with such long-standing institutions as the schools and the church in the magnitude of its social influence."[10]

Key Cultural Values in the United States

Each culture has certain key values that differentiate it from other cultures. Listed below are a number of widely held values in the United States that are important to marketing.

1. *Progress.* Americans place a high value on progress. They look toward the future rather than the past. Advances in the standard of living and in technology are taken for granted. One manifestation of the value placed on progress is the bias toward innovations and new products. The "disposable" society is willing to discard old products for new. This orientation toward progress may change as greater restrictions are placed on energy consumption. Adjustments may have to be made to lower the standard of living and stabilize rather than increase the rate of technological change.

2. *Personal achievement.* The value placed on achievement is closely tied to the work ethic and is reflected in product and home ownership. Justifications for vacations, leisure pursuits, and discretionary purchases are often made because the consumer "worked to enjoy it." One study of personal care appliances found that a frequently cited reason for purchase is "I like to spend money on myself because I think I deserve it."

3. *Materialism.* Americans place a great amount of importance on product ownership and consumption. The United States is the only country where ownership of television sets, telephones, and automobiles is close to universal. The acquisition of certain products and brands continues to be regarded as a mark of status and prestige. The more-is-better mentality is widespread. The feeling that material comfort is an American's right may have to change. Shortages in gas, coffee, and sugar in the 1970s have prompted the realization that the consumption of certain goods cannot be taken for granted. As a result, one writer has suggested the need for **demarketing**; that is, using promotional tools to *discourage* consumption.[11]

4. *Activity.* An outgrowth of the work ethic is activity. To many foreign visitors, Americans seem to be going at a frantic pace. The emphasis on activity is reflected in both work and play. Shorter work weeks, smaller families, and greater discretionary income have resulted in a boom for products related to hobbies, sports, cultural activities, and travel.

5. *Informality.* Informality has always been a trademark of the American culture, possibly as a reaction to the more traditional, formal values of European cultures. The emphasis on informality has been particularly evident since World War II. Since then, clothing styles have become more casual and meal patterns more informal. The reasons for the greater informality may be the more frequent interaction between social

groups and the changing structure of the American family. The increase in working women and a greater reliance on peer group norms mean less structured and less formal family roles.

6. *Individualism.*   Americans value independence and self-respect. They will tolerate a great deal more deviation from cultural norms than many other cultures. The emphasis on individuality is seen in advertising appeals aimed at self-enhancement and a desire to stand apart from the crowd. There is a counterbalancing force to maintain conformity to group norms, but the American value system calls for individuality, not conformity.

7. *Youthfulness.*   In America "young" and "new" are valued more than "old" and "traditional." Americans want to look young, thus advertising appeals to this desire. Ads for skin creams show youthful-looking grandmothers, ads for soaps compare the hands of mothers and daughters, ads for hair colorings say, "You're not getting older, you're getting better." The emphasis placed on a young and slender figure has led Americans to consume diet products in large quantities. The number of weight watchers is constantly increasing.

The Counterculture: A Reaction to American Values?

Not all Americans embrace the values described above. Events such as the Vietnam War and Watergate turned off many young people to traditional values. Achievement, progress, material possessions, and the work ethic are rejected by many. These Americans are turning to a new value system in which they seek "new family patterns, new sexual mores, new kinds of livelihood, new esthetic forms, new personal identities [divorced from] power politics, the bourgeois home, and the consumer society."[12] Marketers will have to use different appeals to attract this segment. The symbols of status, prestige, and social acceptance may not be relevant. Appeals to economy, conservation, product utility, and knowledge are likely to be more effective. On the other hand, there are indications of a declining countercultural influence. The Reagan landslide of 1980 suggests a turning back to more pragmatic emphasis on material possesions and the work ethic, and to a more traditional emphasis on family and religious values.

Measurement of Cultural Values

Four methods have been used to determine cultural values: development of cultural inventories, direct questioning, content analysis, and field studies. Despite the use of these techniques in other social sciences, they have rarely been used in studies of consumer behavior.

Cultural Value Inventories

Cultural value inventories are developed by studying a particular culture, identifying the shared values of that culture, and then determining whether these values are in fact widely held. The best known inventory is the **Rokeach Value Survey** described in Table 11–1.

Direct Questioning

Surveys have occasionally been conducted to determine cultural values. In such surveys, the interviewer refers to a particular value and asks the respondent if he or she would accept or reject it. An example of direct questioning is a survey of the values of college and noncollege youths. College youths place more value on money, sexual freedom, and minority protests. Noncollege youths place more value on law and order.

Content Analysis

Another technique for determining cultural values involves reviewing the content of the literature and mass communications of a particular culture. On this basis the values can be inferred. In a famous study McClelland identified the degree to which cultures were motivated by achievement by conducting a content analysis of the themes in children's stories.[13] Content analyses have also been performed to determine how blacks and females are portrayed in advertising as a reflection of their role in society.

Field Studies

Anthropologists have determined cultural values by direct observation of the customs and behavior of a particular culture. At times they have participated in the society to better understand its culture. Such field studies have not been used in marketing, but in some cases they may be relevant. For example, an Indian official investigating the possibility of introducing birth control devices in rural villages may wish to live in these villages for a period of time to determine people's values and their resistance to birth control. Or, an American business person interested in selling computer software packages in Japan may wish to live there for a period of time to determine the nature of customs and business.

APPLICATIONS OF CULTURAL VALUES TO MARKETING STRATEGY

The identification of cultural values can have implications for every aspect of marketing strategy. The lack of marketing studies in this area suggests that marketers should give more consideration to the measurement of cultural values. One recent study demonstrates the potential usefulness of doing so. Vinson, Scott, and Lamont selected two groups of students for study: one from a liberal, eastern university and another from a more conservative, southern university.[14] They asked students the importance of cultural values (using the items in column 1 of Table 11–1), consumption-specific values (using the items in column 2 of Table 11–1), and twenty automobile attributes. In addition to these values, the researchers collected information on the appeal of ten consumer products and services and on the importance of fifteen social issues.

The results are presented in Table 11–2. Students from the more liberal university placed greater value on equality, self-respect, intellect, logic, and an exciting life. Students from the more conservative university placed greater value on national security, salvation, manners, and social recognition. In regard to consumption-specific values, the liberal students placed more importance on durability, environmental controls, health, and ease of repair. In terms of automobile attributes, these concerns were translated into an emphasis on unleaded gas, performance criteria, and low pollution emissions. Conservative students emphasized prompt service on complaints and wanted a car that was large, luxurious, smooth riding, and prestigious. Differences on social issues reflected the liberal students' concern with pollution and racial equality and the conservative students' concern with law and order. Whereas the liberal students preferred a compact car, the conservative students preferred a standard size car.

Studies such as this one can have direct implications for market segmentation, product positioning, and promotional strategy.

Market Segmentation

A consumer's value orientation can provide an important basis for segmenting markets. The Vinson study identifies two distinct segments: those emphasizing self-enhancement and those emphasizing social recognition. Value orientation is closely associated with consumer needs. The self-enhancement segment wants

TABLE 11–2   Market Segmentation by Cultural Values

Cultural Values	Consumption-Specific Values	Automobile Attributes	Consumer Products	Social Issues
SEGMENT 1: The Self-Enhancement Group				
Exciting life	Durable products	Use of unleaded gas	Compact cars	Air pollution
Equality	Nonpolluting products	High speed capabilities	Outdoor recreation	Freedom of the press
Self-respect	Health-promoting products	Handling		Control of housing dis-crimination
Forgiveness	Easily repaired products	Quality workman-ship		
Intellect	Quiet products	Advanced engineering		
Logic	Products that help eliminate environmental pollution	Low level pollution emission		
SEGMENT 2: The Social Recognition Group				
National security	Prompt service on complaints	Smooth riding	Standard size cars	Crime control
Salvation		Luxurious	Stylish, attractive clothing	The drug problem
Politeness		Prestigious		
Social recognition		Large sized	Television	
		Spacious		

Source: Adapted from Donald E. Vinson, Jerome E. Scott, and Lawrence M. Lamont, "The Role of Personal Values in Marketing and Consumer Behavior," *Journal of Marketing* 41 (April 1977): 48. Reprinted with permission from the *Journal of Marketing.*

product performance; the social recognition segment wants prestige and style. An earlier study using the Rokeach Value Survey found similar results.[15] Two segments were identified: (1) a style segment oriented to pleasure and comfort, and (2) an antipollution segment concerned with social issues. One segment's values are related to self-gratification, the other to self-denial.

A third study used Kluckhohn's measure of values to determine differences between luxury, intermediate, and compact car owners.[16] Luxury car owners had patriarchal relations with others (i.e., clear lines of authority) and felt more subjugated by world events. These owners tended to be older, in the higher income group, but in the lower social class (e.g., independent businessmen with lower levels of education). Owners of intermediate size cars were more democratic in their relations with others and were in the lower income group. Appeals to the luxury car owners should be based on dominance (symbols of power and prestige) and control over the environment (getting what you want because you own a luxury car). Appeals to the intermediate group should use more democratic symbols (e.g., being a good person and sharing one's car in a car pool). For this group, symbols of power and prestige would not be as relevant.

Product Positioning

The Vinson study (see Table 11–2) demonstrates the importance of cultural values in product positioning. A car positioned to the self-respect segment must emphasize performance and quality; a car positioned to the social recognition segment must emphasize style and size. A study of owners of personal care appliances identified one important segment as those emphasizing self-respect and self-enhancement. A second segment was more style conscious. Appliances directed to the self-enhancement segment should emphasize pragmatic appeals such as convenience and additional features. Appliances directed to the style conscious group should emphasize grooming benefits.

Promotional Strategy

The studies cited above clearly suggest that advertising aimed at the self-respect segment should emphasize the utilitarian aspects of the product. The advertising should demonstrate a recognition that the consumer is capable of making product judgments and is in control. The informational content of advertising should dominate. Advertising for the social recognition segment should appeal to prestige, luxury, and social acceptance. The symbolic rather than the informational content of advertising should dominate.

Limitations of Influencing Cultural Values Through Advertising

Applications of cultural values to marketing strategy suggest that advertising should appeal to existing cultural values. If advertising attempts to change cultural values, it is doomed to fail. Cultural values are too deep-seated to be influenced by the mass media. Trends toward informality after World War II led to a decline in two product categories — men's hats and sterling silverware.

In both cases, manufacturers contributed to a cooperative advertising campaign in an attempt to counter declining demand. In both cases, the campaigns were a total failure.

If cultural values result in an upward demand trend, then advertising can contribute to this trend by creating product awareness. The introduction of diet sodas conformed to the value placed on slimness and youth. In this case, advertising was reinforcing a cultural trend rather than attempting to check it.

SUBCULTURAL INFLUENCES ON CONSUMER BEHAVIOR

In a society, individuals do not always have homogeneous cultural values. Certain segments of the society may be represented as subcultures because they have values and customs that distinguish them from others in the community. Given the diverse nature of American society, it is important that marketers identify the subcultures and determine whether specific strategies should be directed toward them. One writer feels that "Subcultures are the relevant units of analysis for market research. They represent definable target groups for specific products and logical units for segmenting of larger markets."[17] As shall be seen, subcultures in the United States can be identified by age, geography, national identity, and race.

Age

It can be debated whether age groups have values sufficiently different to constitute a subculture. Marketers have tended to identify two groups as subcultures: the youth market (primarily teenagers) and the elderly (those over age 65).

The Youth Market

The youth market is more consumption-oriented than most other groups. Teenagers have grown up in a prosperous and permissive age which has encouraged immediate gratification. Constant exposure to the mass media has made this group more aware of product and service alternatives. Many in this group were part of the counterculture's de-emphasis on achievement and the work ethic. However, recent evidence suggests a shift back to the more traditional values toward a career and hard work.[18] The youth market is more likely to buy discretionary products like records, cameras, stereo equipment, high style clothes, and personal care products.[19] They are also more likely to travel and to go to the movies.[20] Their media behavior is different. Young consumers are much more likely to listen to the radio, and to read magazines and newspapers.[21] They are less likely to watch television and are more skeptical of advertising.

The Elderly Consumer

Elderly consumers generally have been ignored by marketers, despite their different needs, values, and behavior. The neglect is probably due to the degree of orientation toward youth and to the belief that the elderly represent limited potential. It is true that incomes of the elderly are about half the average income level. However, the elderly are a fast growing segment whose income is rising because of better pension plans. The elderly consumer market will soon be close to $100 billion, but few studies have examined the purchasing, shopping, and media behavior of the elderly.

The elderly are more likely to spend their time reading, going to movies, gardening, and fishing.[22] They spend more on health care, public transportation, household maintenance, and food consumed at home.[23] They are less willing to shop at discount stores and more willing to travel to downtown shopping districts, even if it means paying higher prices. They are also heavier TV watchers, possibly because, as one writer notes, TV provides an escape from loneliness and is a substitute for social interaction.[24]

Some marketers have designed products for this segment. Campbell's recognized reduced appetites and the need for smaller portions in introducing Campbell's Soup-For-One. Bulova recognized the need for larger numbers on watches by introducing easy-to-read dials. Pfizer has introduced New Season, a shampoo conditioner for "people over 50."[25] Marketers should also be aware of the need for easier to open jars and packages because older people may suffer from a loss of dexterity. In general, though, marketers have not viewed the elderly as deserving of separate attention.

Geography

Geographic groups could also be identified as subcultures based on differences in tastes and behavior. Eastern, western and southern consumers differ in consumption habits. For example, consider the following differences:

- Westerners like coffee much weaker than easterners.
- Southerners drink more tea than the rest of the country and are more likely to use tea bags or loose tea to make iced tea.
- Southerners and midwesterners like soft bread. Consumers in the East and West consume a greater variety of breads — rye, whole wheat, French, etc. — and like their bread firmer.[26]
- Southern men are more likely to use mouthwash or deodorants than eastern men.[27]

Some marketers have also adjusted product offerings based on regional tastes. Several soft drink manufacturers use different formulations in different parts of the country to appeal to varying desires for sweetness, thickness, and carbonation.

National Identity

Numerous subcultures exist in the United States based on national identity. One could easily identify consumers by national origin — Poles, Italians, French, Irish, etc. In many cases, food and other types of products are purchased that reflect national customs and tastes. For example, stores frequently stock products of Chinese, Japanese, or Spanish origin.

One of the most important groups in the United States is the Spanish-speaking market. This is not a homogeneous group since it is composed of consumers of different national identities. But, as a group, it represents the nation's second largest minority with over fifteen million people.[28] (Blacks are the largest.) The three most important groups within this submarket are Mexican-Americans, Puerto Ricans, and Cubans. The Hispanic market tends to live in urban areas, is younger than average, and has a significantly lower than average income and educational level. It spends more on food due to larger family size, is highly brand loyal, and tends to be conservative in shopping. The brands this subgroup purchases are substantially different as the following brand share data illustrate:[29]

	Anglo	Hispanic
Soaps		
Tide	30.2%	15.3%
Cheer	15.0%	42.3%
Indigestion Remedies		
Alka Seltzer	31.6%	7.7%
Pepto Bismol	31.3%	65.4%
Cigarettes		
Winston	31.3%	7.0%
Marlboro	7.3%	21.6%

The Hispanic market may also be inhibited by language barriers. Hispanics tend to be reluctant to ask questions in stores and express confusion about multiple pricing and cents-off labels.[30]

Some marketers such as Pepsi-Cola, Coca-Cola, and Procter and Gamble advertise directly to the Hispanic market. Such advertising is facilitated by thirteen Spanish language television stations and over eighty Spanish language radio stations.[31]

Ethnic Subcultures: The Black Consumer Market

Subcultures can also be identified ethnically. The most important ethnic subculture is the black consumer market. The black consumer market is diverse. There are upper-, middle- and lower-class blacks; blacks who emphasize nutrition versus taste; and blacks who value self-enhancement versus social recognition. In other words, most of the same demographic, life-style, and value criteria used to segment the white market can also be used to segment the black market. Yet, marketers rarely segment the black consumer market into separate groups. Rather, they tend to treat the black consumer market as one homogeneous market.

Despite its diversity, there is some justification in viewing the black consumer market as a subculture. Blacks do differ from whites in their purchasing, shopping, and media behavior. This section will first review these differences and then consider the bases on which the black consumer market is segmented to account for its diversity.

Differences in Characteristics and Behavior

Characteristics. Blacks represent close to 12 percent of the total population in the United States. The average income of blacks is about one-third less than that of whites. Although the education level of blacks is improving, approximately half as many blacks go to college as whites. The average black consumer is six years younger than the average white consumer. Since a higher proportion of blacks will be growing into the prime consumer age range (18–35) in the next twenty years, the black consumer market is potentially very profitable. Blacks are also twice as likely as whites to live in central city areas, making them more accessible to mass media and retail distribution.[32]

Product Purchases. Differences exist in the purchasing patterns between blacks and whites. Such differences are most apparent when comparing the purchasing patterns of lower income blacks and whites.

Blacks spend proportionately more than whites for clothing, personal care, and home furnishings. Whites spend more on medical care, food, and transportation.[33] These differences suggest that blacks spend more on socially visible items compared to whites of the same income group. The substantial differences in products purchased are illustrated by the following data which have been taken from a comparison of purchases of black and white families in Chicago:[34]

Product Category	Percent of Black Families Purchasing	Percent of White Families Purchasing
Purchased more by blacks		
Cornmeal	81%	14%
Canned luncheon meats	20%	9%
Self-rising flour	34%	16%
Purchased more by whites		
Hair spray	21%	76%
Diet soft drinks	25%	49%
Cars	54%	84%
Regular Coffee	66%	92%

Blacks are also more likely to be innovators for socially visible products, particularly clothing.[35] A study in the 1960s found that black women were at least as fashion conscious as white women.[36] A more recent study of grooming products identified a segment of style conscious black consumers. These consumers were more likely to agree with statements such as, "I consider myself up to date regarding latest styles," "I am very concerned with my appearance," and "An important part of my life is dressing well." This segment was also much more price conscious and more concerned with brand names. Sexton believes that fashion items may "provide a visible way for blacks to achieve the middle-class style of life."[37]

Another difference between blacks and whites occurs in the nature of food preparation. One writer suggests that blacks view food as sustenance while whites view it as a pleasurable experience.[38] This appears to be true only for higher income consumers. High income whites were found to be more innovative in food purchases than high income blacks. But low income blacks were found to be more innovative than low income whites.[39]

Brand Purchases. Blacks are more likely to buy popular brands, possibly as a way of reducing risk.[40] Given a high level of social consciousness, purchasing a popular brand may be a means of social visibility and acceptance in a white-dominated society. The study comparing the purchases of black and white families showed blacks are also more likely to be brand loyal.[41] The same study also found significant differences between blacks and whites in brand preferences.[42] Blacks preferred Colgate to Crest by a ten-to-one margin whereas whites were evenly split. Blacks were also less likely to buy brands like Uncle Ben or Aunt Jemima because of negative associations. Although the study is dated, the following figures show the substantial differences in brand preferences:[43]

Product Category	Percent of Black Families Purchasing	Percent of White Families Purchasing
Corn Meal		
Quaker	94%	62%
Aunt Jemima	3%	23%
Rice		
Riceland	77%	35%
Uncle Ben	13%	23%
Cigarettes		
Kool	54%	36%
Salem	28%	45%
Hairspray		
VO–5	52%	17%
Aquanet	3%	20%
Cold Remedy		
Contac	19%	37%
Vicks	42%	18%

Shopping Behavior.   A study of shopping behavior found that blacks make fewer shopping trips than whites. Since price is of more concern to blacks, they are more likely to shop at discount houses and less likely to shop by mail or phone.[44]

There are also significant differences in shopping attitudes. Blacks are unhappier with supermarket facilities, tending to complain more about higher prices, overcrowding, and unfriendly employees.[45] Some of the same shopping inhibitions found among lower-class white consumers exist among blacks. Blacks tend to feel more alienated and defensive when shopping.[46] They are more likely to emphasize a friendly atmosphere, convenience, and service than do whites.[47] These shopping attitudes result in their reluctance to go shopping in downtown stores and, thus, result in a greater reliance on neighborhood outlets.

Pricing Behavior.   The question has frequently been raised whether inner-city blacks are subject to price discrimination by unscrupulous retailers, and, therefore, pay higher prices as a result. Sexton found that blacks do pay more, but not because of price discrimination.[48] Operating costs in inner-city stores tend to be higher because of the amount of pilferage and food spoilage. Once operating costs are considered, there is little difference in the prices charged in white and black areas.

Also contributing to higher priced merchandise is the fact that inner-city blacks are more likely to shop in independent stores which charge higher prices in general. In addition, blacks are more likely to buy higher priced, smaller sizes. The net result is that inner-city blacks pay about 1 percent more than whites for merchandise in chain stores and about 9 percent more for merchandise in independent stores.[49]

Media Behavior.   The major medium for blacks is radio. Blacks are more likely to listen to a radio than whites are and listen most frequently to black radio stations.[50] Magazines are also directed to blacks, particularly middle-class blacks. *Ebony* is a general audience black magazine; *Encore* is a black news monthly. *Essence* is directed to the fashion conscious black woman and covers beauty, health, fashion, food, book reviews, and music. Television continues to be a white-dominated medium. Some network shows feature blacks, but there is relatively little black television programming.

The dominant issue in selling to blacks is whether general or specialized media are more effective. The evidence is not clear-cut. Blacks can identify more closely with products if ads appear in black magazines or on black radio. Yet, for nationally advertised products, mass media will reach both blacks and whites. The best strategy for products with a broad appeal is to use specialized media vehicles to reach blacks and more general media to reach the mass audience. Sears allocated about 3 percent of its advertising budget to black media in 1975 in the expectation that the other 97 percent would reach some blacks.[51] For products directed primarily to blacks, black-oriented media should obviously be used. Television would be an inefficient medium for black-oriented products, whereas radio, magazines, newspapers, and outdoor advertising could be directed to specific segments of black consumers.

The foregoing section treated the black consumer market as a single subculture with values and marketing behavior similar to the white consumer market. In actuality, the black consumer market is almost as diverse as the white consumer market. As a result, specific segmentation, product development, advertising strategies, and distribution strategies are required when selling to the black consumer market.

Market Segmentation.   Some researchers have bemoaned the lack of segmentation and product positioning strategies directed toward black consumers. One writer says,

> Most of the major cosmetics houses — Revlon, Avon, L'Oreal for example — now have products specifically designed for black women. Having such products, they assume they are positioned in the black market.

> It would be a marketing howler, of course, if a company introduced a product for whites and then assumed it had positioned that product in the general market. To announce, "I have a product for whites," is hardly positioning.[52]

The writer went on to describe Johnson products — one of the largest black-managed and owned companies in the United States — as one of the few cosmetics companies "recognizing the black market is as segmented, demographically and psychographically, as the general market."[53] In 1965 Johnson introduced Ultra Sheen, the first product to "remedy the black woman's problem of relaxing curly hair."[54] In 1975 Johnson entered the men's fragrance market with Black Tie Cologne and Splash-On.

Johnson Products recognizes two broad segments of black consumers, those who strive for white middle-class values (the strivers) and those who feel financially blocked from such goals or rebel against them (nonstrivers).[55] Strivers feel they can achieve a middle-class life-style and are willing to put off immediate gratification to obtain these goals. The nonstrivers do not seek the material goods associated with being middle-class and instead seek to establish a separate identity. Two ads for hair coloring, one directed to strivers and the other to nonstrivers, are depicted in Figure 11–1. The ad for Radiance suggests middle-class values; the ad for Dark & Lovely suggests a denial of such values and a greater focus on black identity.

Johnson Products has positioned products to both segments. Some of its advertisements are more ethnically oriented; others attempt to portray middle-class values. An important consideration for Johnson is whether blacks will become more acculturated and accept the dominant middle-class values of American society or whether they will seek to maintain a separate identity and subculture.

Product Development.   Certain product categories must be geared to the specific needs of black market segments. Product development is particularly

FIGURE 11–1   Ads Directed to Strivers Versus Nonstrivers Based on Middle-Class Values

Source: Kelvin A. Wall, "Trying to Reach Blacks? Beware of Marketing Myopia," *Advertising Age,* May 21, 1979, p. 59.

important for grooming and cosmetic products. Susan Taylor, fashion editor of *Essence,* says, "Marketers of cosmetics should be doing much more basic R&D to create products that meet the black woman's needs."[56] She cites the following areas requiring product development:

1.   A penetrating time-stop-action protein conditioner "is needed for the new black hairstyles which have gone from Afro, to straight, to a mildly relaxed, more natural effect. The relaxing process takes out body and nutrients and there is a need for a wider range of products that address that need."

2.   In makeup, "there is still little range of shades. Companies think they are doing the job when they give us four shades." Products do not recognize black skin differences.

3.   Few eye shadows are made correctly for black women. "Colors are not intense enough to go over brown."

4.   "There is not one facial mask or acne clearing preparation product advertised to black women. . . . A sizeable number of black women need products with fewer allergens."

5.   More personal care appliance manufacturers should be developing products for black women since they are willing to trade dollars for convenience.[57]

Product development is also required to meet the needs of black males. As noted, Johnson Products introduced a line of fragrances for black men. Remington recently introduced a shaver designed for black males that helps prevent ingrown hairs and razor bumps (see Figure 11–2). A shaver for blacks is necessary according to Remington's marketing vice-president: "Shaving is a problem for many black men because their facial hairs tend to be very curly rather than straight, [and these] curly whiskers can become ingrown."[58] Regular electric shavers do not do a good job cutting curly hairs. As a result, Remington introduced its Black Man's Shaver.

Advertising.   Advertising to blacks must use relevant symbols and imagery. It must also meet the need for black identification. The ad for Canadian Club in Figure 11–3 is a good illustration of an ad with black identification. The ad has utilized research that showed that in brand selection for liquor products the black male has remained much more dominant than his white counterpart.[59] The two ads in Figure 11–3 for Cutty Sark and Johnnie Walker Red also appear in black magazines, but are not specifically oriented to blacks.

Cigarettes are also a good illustration of the need to direct ads specifically to blacks. Wall believes that brand imagery influences blacks more than whites.[60] Brands are often rejected based on imagery alone. Few blacks buy Marlboro because the cowboy is not a relevant symbol. Blacks are more likely to buy menthol cigarettes yet have not bought mentholated Merit because it relies on a scientific approach in describing tar and nicotine content. "With a product like cigarettes, blacks seek personal expression. . . . Blacks are more likely to respond to people and color in ads."[61] Kool and Salem, the leading brands among blacks, are people-oriented; Merit is not.

Some insight into the relevance of black-oriented themes is provided by Clarence Smith, president of *Essence* magazine. He says that marketers generally overlook the black woman's psyche:

FIGURE 11–2 Remington's "Black Man's Shaver"
Source: "Remington Shaver for Black Males Ends Test Market," *Product Marketing,* March 1978,
p. 65. By permission of Remington Products, Inc.

"Since childhood [black women] have been inundated with media images
of beauty as the white woman. They want to be attractive as possible
and show the black man that her beauty is fine. Marketers should see
that she is overcompensating in buying products to dispel negative stereotypes."[62]

Distribution.   Marketers must also gear distribution policies to black's purchasing behavior. Pepsi-Cola has intensified its merchandising program in supermarkets in its battle with Coca-Cola. Yet, its share among blacks is eroding.

WHEN IT'S TIME TO QUIET DOWN
AT THE END OF THE DAY, EVEN A FIRE
TURNS TO RED.

JOHNNIE WALKER RED
THE RIGHT SCOTCH WHEN ALL IS SAID AND DONE

AFTER 280 YEARS OF DEALING WITH ROYALTY, WE'VE LEARNED A LITTLE SOMETHING ABOUT TASTE.

The shop of Berry Brothers & Rudd, Ltd., wine merchants, has been a British landmark for nearly three centuries. For years, kings, queens, dukes and nobles from all over the world have sought advice on the best wines to serve with their sumptuous meals.

The Tasting Room at Berry Bros. & Rudd, Ltd.

On many occasions, Berry Brothers & Rudd, Ltd. were asked to suggest a Scotch Whisky of equal merit. Unable to recommend one with wholehearted enthusiasm, they created Cutty Sark Scots Whisky. The first Scotch ever made by wine experts to please the most demanding of palates.

The result is a Scotch with a delicate bouquet and a quality of smoothness which is quite singular.

Of course, you don't have to be of noble birth to appreciate Cutty Sark Scots Whisky. All that is required is noble taste.

CUTTY SARK

FIGURE 11–3   Ads Appearing in Black Magazines With and Without Black Identity

Source: Kelvin A. Wall, "Trying to Reach Blacks? Beware of Marketing Myopia," *Advertising Age,* May 21, 1979, p. 60. Ad for Canadian Club by permission of McCaffrey & McCall, Inc. Ad for Cutty Sark by permission of the Buckingham Corporation and Scali, McCabe & Sloves, Inc. Ad for Johnny Walker Red by permission of Somerset Importers, Ltd.

The **CC** man is back.
He's young. He's confident.
He's looking good. Drinking good.
Canadian Club Whisky.
Look who's drinking Canadian Club now.

From 65 percent to 70 percent of sales of soft drinks to blacks are made outside the supermarket.[63] Pepsi's efforts may be successful among whites, but are missing the mark among blacks. In another example of mismarketing to blacks, liquor companies began emphasizing on-premise consumption by blacks just when middle-class blacks were beginning to entertain more at home.

CROSS-CULTURAL DIFFERENCES BETWEEN CONSUMERS

The examination of subcultures demonstrates the diversity of norms, attitudes, and behavior within a single culture. An even greater diversity exists between cultures. The examination of cross-cultural differences is most important to international marketing firms. The scope of international operations is increasing and firms are placing more importance on cross-cultural research. Some American firms, such as Coca-Cola and IBM, do over half their business abroad; foreign firms, such as Unilever and Nestlé, have substantial operations in the United States.

Cross-cultural effects influence marketers in two ways. First, cultural norms and values in foreign countries must influence the manner in which business is conducted abroad. An American business person abroad cannot assume that his or her business customs apply elsewhere. Second, the customs of consumers in other countries must influence marketing strategy. Although there have been attempts to standardize marketing strategies abroad, such standardization is unlikely to be effective unless some consideration is given to local customs and values.

Cultural Influences of Doing Business Abroad

International businesses have come to recognize the importance of local customs when doing business abroad. Larger companies are sending American employees about to go abroad to courses specially designed to educate business people about local customs. Executive programs and business school courses dealing with such cross-cultural considerations are more commonplace.

The following examples illustrate the importance of recognizing local customs when doing business with executives from other countries:[64]

- The Japanese executive sucks in air through his teeth and exclaims "That will be very difficult." What he really means is just plain "no." But the Japanese consider an absolute "no" to be offensive and usually seek a euphemistic term. That's why in Japan the "difficult" really may be impossible. The American on the other side of the negotiating table knows none of this and presses ahead to resolve the "difficulty." The Japanese finds this inexplicable persistence to be abnormally pushy. The atmosphere deteriorates and, sure enough, the big deal falls through.

- A senior American executive was irked when an Asian businessman suggested changing the date of the American's visit ten days before the event. The American thought he was receiving shabby treatment. In fact, the Asian executive considered the meeting so important that he had consulted with a religious adviser who urged a more auspicious date for the talks. Anyone familiar with the local scene would have grasped the significance of the change, which the Asian meant as a compliment.

• American executives negotiating a contract in the Middle East found that there wasn't time to have their revised negotiating proposal typed, submitted a handwritten version, and thought nothing of it. But the Arabs across the bargaining table considered the gesture so bizarre that they began to analyze it intensely, seeking messages. Some concluded the Americans were trying to imply that they considered the whole contract unimportant.

• A common frustration many Americans feel overseas involves dealing with strikingly different concepts of time. In many Third World countries especially, anywhere from 50 percent to 80 percent of the time spent talking with businessmen will be spent discussing anything but business. But while the American often views this personal chitchat as a waste of time, it can be crucial to business.

Differing customs affect business relations not only in Asia, but in Europe as well. European business customs are more formal than those in the United States, and status and titles are much more important. "Not to give the German, Spaniard or Italian prospect his due is not only discourteous but poor business practice."[65] The reverse is also true. Americans should provide their title and qualifications in order to give European prospects information on their position and status. Greater formality also means that initial contacts in Europe should be in writing. Once written contact is established, oral communications are acceptable.[66]

Differing Consumer Customs and Attitudes

Different customs and attitudes in foreign countries will affect product usage. One study compared a broad range of consumer attitudes in the United States, Europe, and British Commonwealth countries.[67] Figure 11–4 compares consumer attitudes in these countries toward housecleaning, children, and deodorants. Italian women rate housecleaning much more important than women in other countries. Women in the United States rate it least important. Such differences suggest that an American producer of household products cannot merely export its strategy to Europe. Appeals to American women based on the functional benefits of the product may not be as relevant in Italy. Italian women probably view their roles in a more traditional manner and may find intrinsic benefits in housecleaning. Advertising a floor polish in Italy would require a basic shift in strategy from a pragmatic campaign to one based on symbolism and imagery. Appeals may be better directed toward praise from the husband for a shiny floor rather than toward a quick job that enables the woman to pursue other activities.

"A house should be dusted and polished three times a week."	"My children are the most important thing in my life."	"Everyone should use a deodorant."
100% Agreement	100% Agreement	100% Agreement
86% Italy	86% Germany	89% U.S.A.
59% U.K.	84% Italy/ French Canada	81% French Canada
55% France	74% Denmark	77% English Canada
53% Spain	73% France	71% U.K.
45% Germany	71% U.S.A.	69% Italy
33% Australia	67% Spain	59% France
25% U.S.A.	57% U.K.	53% Australia
	56% English Canada	
	53% South Africa	
	48% Australia	

FIGURE 11–4 Cross-Cultural Attitudes Toward Housecleaning, Children, and Deodorants

Source: Joseph T. Plummer, "Consumer Focus in Cross-National Research," *Journal of Advertising* 6 (Spring 1977): 10–11.

Reprinted with permission from the *Journal of Advertising*.

Attitudes toward children also differ by country. Women in Europe, the United States, and French Canada are more likely to consider children "the most important thing in my life" compared to women in the British Commonwealth countries. Such differences may have implications for advertising toys, children's clothes, and candy. For example, advertisements for children's clothing in Europe and the United States may more effectively appeal to parental love and concern. Advertisements in the British Commonwealth countries may do better to appeal to the utilitarian benefits such as price and durability.

Attitudes toward deodorants show that consumers in the United States and Canada are more likely to view usage as a social necessity than consumers in France or Australia. Appeals in the United States based on the risk of social ostracism due to not using a deodorant would be lost on many French and Australian consumers.

Differing customs are also likely to affect product usage. The Singer Company found that its predominant form of promotion — demonstration classes for women — had to be altered in Moslem countries.[68] Women were just not allowed to leave the home to attend sewing lessons at Singer centers. One Singer representative in the Sudan was jailed for attempting to encourage women to attend classes. Once men began to attend classes, they were convinced sewing lessons would be of value to their wives, and the women were then ordered to take lessons.

Women in the Cook Islands and in many Latin American countries are accustomed to stooping over their low stoves.[69] Attempts at introducing modern stoves failed because the women found it uncomfortable to have to stand upright and cook.

Stridsberg reports on several other examples of differences in product usage due to local customs, such as the following:

- Corn on the cob is an hors d'oeuvre in Britain.
- Oatmeal is a dessert in Northern Holland, North Germany, and Scandinavia.
- Vicks Vapo-Rub is used as a mosquito repellent in tropical areas.[70]

Even physiological differences between consumers in various countries will affect product usage. Powdered milk given to people in Peru and Bolivia by the United States is used to whitewash houses because the natives of these countries do not retain an enzyme enabling them to digest milk.[71]

Standardized Versus Localized Marketing Strategies

International marketers must seriously consider whether *one* promotional campaign can be directed to all their foreign markets or whether separate campaigns have to be developed to take into account local differences. During the 1960s the predominant view was that a standardized approach was possible. Such an approach offered greater simplicity and economies of scale. The belief was that consumers are motivated by similar appeals regardless of country. This view was stated by an American advertising executive:

> Different peoples are basically the same. . . . an international advertising campaign with a truly universal appeal can be effective in any market. . . . The desire to be beautiful is universal. Such appeals as "mother and child," "freedom from pain," "glow of health," know no

boundaries. In a sense, the young women in Tokyo and the young women in Berlin are sisters not only "under the skin," but on their skin and on their lips and fingernails, and even their hairstyles."[72]

Companies like Pepsi-Cola, Coca-Cola, Singer, Ford, and Goodyear followed this approach. A Pepsi-Cola executive said that Pepsi's aim was to establish "one Pepsi-Cola image that is the same throughout the world. . . . Management does not believe that each country requires an individual advertising and product approach."[73]

By the early 1970s many marketers "moved away from the earlier optimism about painless transfer of marketing strategy."[74] The predominant view was that promotional approaches had to be tailored to specific markets. Several studies illustrated major differences between consumers in different countries. One showed that Mexican consumers generally perceive less risk in product purchases because of a fatalism that characterizes Mexican society.[75] Mexicans feel they have less control over their destiny than do consumers in the United States. Advertising emphasizing risk-reducing benefits such as buying a well-known brand or one with a better warranty may not be as effective in Mexico. Another study found major differences between American and French consumers.[76] American consumers were more willing to experiment with new products and services because they were less bound by tradition. They relied more on sources of information outside the retail store. French consumers' greater traditionalism was reflected in more store loyalty and reliance on the local retailer for information and, indirectly, for social support. The study concluded that marketing strategy could not be exported from the United States to France without major revisions.

Dunn studied international companies and found a decrease in standardized advertising approaches.[77] Two-thirds of the executives interviewed thought that promotional emphasis on national traits would increase in the future. One said that there were really no multinational campaigns — only different degrees of similarity. Contributing to the emphasis on localization was "resentment at the sameness of the Coca-Cola campaigns, the sameness of the McDonald's stores, the sameness of the Holiday Inns and Howard Johnsons."[78] Some degree of standardization in international advertising is inevitable, but the trend is clearly toward accounting for local differences in customs and attitudes.

Marketing (and Mismarketing) Abroad

Various examples of marketing successes and failures illustrate the importance of adjusting marketing strategies to local markets. Such an adjustment is particularly relevant in two areas: product development and advertising.

Product Development

European companies have occasionally adjusted marketing strategies when introducing products in the United States. Nestlé first introduced freeze-dried coffee in Europe under the name Nescafé Lyophilisé, using a highly technical word — lyophilization — to describe the freeze-drying process.[79] Nestlé waited until General Foods introduced its freeze-dried brand — Maxim — in the United States before considering its entry. Rather than introduce the European brand, Nestlé did some research which suggested that the new brand should be separated from the traditional Nescafé name. It also decided on an entirely different appearance than the European brand (more granular) and chose the name Taster's Choice to designate quality while flattering the consumer. In each case, the strategy was changed to suit American tastes. Nestlé also recognized it was entering the market as the second brand and did not have to replicate the pioneering steps of the European strategy.

In a less successful example, Pepperidge Farm imported the Delacre line of luxury biscuits and realized that the recipes were too rich for American tastes. The line is being shifted to a more folksy positioning of traditional American cookies.[80] In another example, two dehydrated soups that were successful in Europe were launched in the United States. Both failed because they had to be constantly stirred to avoid boiling over. While European consumers may have been used to stirring prepared soups, Americans were not.[81]

Attempts at introducing American products abroad can also be cited as examples of mis-marketing. A leading American producer of condensed soups attempted to introduce its line in Britain. English consumers were used to ready-to-eat soups and were unaware of the condensed soup concept.[82] The cans were at a disadvantage in the store since they appeared small to English consumers. Initially, the company did not adequately explain the necessity of adding water. In addition, the variety of flavors was not tailored to English tastes. It took several years of low sales to make the company aware of the difficulties and the required adjustments.

Attempts to introduce American cake mixes in Britain have also encountered difficulties. English researchers felt that the American strategy of having the housewife add an egg to make her feel she was participating would be successful. The problem was that the cake mix was the wrong kind. British consumers did not want fancy cakes. They wanted "a tough rather spongy item which was traditional for tea."[83] The American company also made the mistake of assuming that professional-looking cakes would be important to British consumers and that exotic names such as angel or devil's food cake would be appealing. They failed to take into account British traditionalism. The market preferred simpler products such as tea cakes and fruit cakes.[84]

Sometimes, American companies lose sight of the obvious in introducing products abroad. One company attempted to introduce a filtered cigarette to an Asian country thinking that concern with cancer would cause Asian consumers to switch to the new brand. Company executives failed to realize that in a country with a life expectancy of twenty-nine years, fear of death is not going to be a motivating factor in cigarette use.

Advertising

Advertising campaigns must also be geared to local conditions. For example, the Ajax white tornado was not viewed as a symbol of power abroad. Ultra-Brite's sexy girl throwing kisses aroused a negative reaction among Belgian consumers, and the theme "Give Your Mouth Sex Appeal" had to be dropped.[85]

Two elephants are a symbol of bad luck in Africa and this forced Carlsberg to add a third elephant to its label for Elephant Beer.[86]

American companies must also be careful of direct translations into foreign languages. For example, "Body by Fisher" translates in French into "Corpse by Fisher." Meeting someone "at their convenience" would not translate well in England or Australia since a convenience in these countries is a toilet.[87] Product names also cause problems. Pledge, the Johnson wax product, was successfully launched in Germany as Pronto and in France as Pliz, but in Holland and Belgium the translation was an offensive word.[88]

Companies must also be sensitive to the use of color and symbolism in advertising. White is the color of mourning in Japan; purple is disapproved of in many Latin American countries because it is associated with death; brown and gray are disapproved of in Nicaragua. Feet are regarded as despicable in Thailand. Showing pairs of anything on the Gold Coast of Africa is a negative taboo.[89] Marketers have to be aware of different tastes and customs in developing advertising for foreign countries.

SUMMARY

This chapter introduces the environmental influences that affect consumer behavior by considering the broadest of the influences — culture. Cultural influence is transmitted through societal norms and values. These values are learned from childhood through a process of socialization and form permanent guides to understanding behavior. But cultural values are also subject to change, as exhibited by the de-emphasis in recent years of the work ethic in favor of the easy life, of saving in favor of spending, and of independence in favor of security. But, despite changes, certain values — such as achievement, materialism, individualism, and youthfulness — have remained fairly stable in the American culture.

Cultural values have rarely been used in the development of marketing strategy, but cultural inventories can be developed much like life-style and personality inventories and can be applied to segmenting markets, positioning products, and developing promotional strategies.

Subcultures can also be defined within societies by age, region, national identity, and race. The largest subculture in American society is the black consumer. Although the similarities with whites outweigh the differences, blacks do differ sufficiently in products purchased, shopping behavior, media behavior, and reactions to advertising messages to warrant separate attention. Some marketers have developed products directed toward the needs of black consumers, created advertising with a black identity, and have advertised in black media. One problem is that marketers tend to treat black consumers as a homogeneous market when, in fact, sufficient differences in needs and purchasing behavior warrant strategies for market segmentation.

The final section of the chapter deals with differences in customs and behavior between cultures. Cross-cultural differences influence marketers in two ways. First, cultural norms and values in foreign countries influence the manner in which business is conducted abroad. Second, different customs in foreign countries result in different patterns of purchasing behavior. Some marketers believe that a fairly standardized approach can be used in marketing to different countries, but the prevailing view is that marketing strategies must be adjusted to reflect local norms and values.

The next chapter will deal with another component of the consumer's environment — social class.

QUESTIONS

1. How would a furniture manufacturer use Kluckhohn's cultural inventory (one's relation to nature, to time, to personal activities, to others) to (a) segment the furniture market, and (b) develop separate product lines accordingly?

2. The U.S. Department of Transportation would like to encourage greater use of mass transit. It believes that attitudes toward transportation are deep-seated and tied to cultural values. It decides to use Rokeach's cultural inventory to identify cultural, consumption-specific, and product-specific values.

   • Identify relevant cultural, consumption-specific, and product-specific values for mass transit.

   • What are their implications for an advertising campaign designed to induce greater use of mass transit?

3. Consider the changes in cultural values Kotler describes. What are the implications of these changes for a company introducing a new line of (a) men's fragrances, (b) instant baking products, and (c) personal care appliances?

4. An automobile manufacturer recognizes the importance of cultural values in car ownership. Specifically, the manufacturer recognizes the importance of achievement, materialism, activity, informality, individualism, and youthfulness.

   • What are the implications of these values in developing and advertising new model cars?

5. Is there a counterculture in American society today? What are the marketing implications if such a counterculture exists?

6. Table 11–2 describes two segments based on cultural values: a self-enhancement group and a social recognition group. These two groups may be a reasonable basis for segmenting consumers in various product categories.

   • For what product categories may it be reasonable to segment the market based on self-enhancement versus social recognition? Why?

   • What would be the implications of such segmentation for (a) product development, (b) product positioning, and (c) advertising?

7. Can you cite any companies that have directed marketing strategy toward the black consumer market by

   • developing product lines directed to the needs of black consumers?

   • developing advertising campaigns depicting black consumers?

   • using media directed to black consumers?

8. An American company is considering the introduction of a line of housecleaning products into the Italian market. The company's domestic advertising campaign

is based on the time-saving conveniences and efficiency of its products for the busy woman.

- What changes would you suggest in advertising to appeal to the mass market in Italy (see Figure 11–4)? Specifically, what types of situations would you portray? What types of symbols and imagery would you use?

9. Are companies more likely to be successful in taking a standardized approach in their cross-national marketing strategies for certain types of products? For example, is a standardized campaign more likely to be effective for Pepsi-Cola or Tide detergent?

RESEARCH ASSIGNMENTS

1. The study by Vinson, Scott, and Lamont identified two segments based on cultural values — a self-enhancement segment and a social recognition segment. The two segments had very different need criteria for automobiles, different purchasing patterns, and different emphases on social issues. Use the five attitudes toward the following items to identify these two segments: (1) law and order, (2) national security, (3) religion, (4) individual freedom, and (5) logic. (The self-enhancement segment would place less emphasis on the first three items and more emphasis on the last two; the social recognition segment would do the reverse). Select a sample of respondents and place them into one of these two segments based on their responses. (You may wish to form a third segment composed of those who do not clearly fit into one of the two segments.) Then ask these respondents the criteria they emphasize in purchasing a particular durable good (e.g., criteria in buying a car, a stereo set, furniture, etc). Also determine particular brands or models owned.

- What are the differences in (1) need criteria emphasized, and (2) brand ownership between the self-enhancement and social recognition segment?
- Do your findings conform to the study by Vinson, Scott, and Lamont?

2. A large cultural institution was considering doing a study to determine needs and attitudes of black patrons toward theater productions in particular and artistic events in general. The study was to answer the following questions:

   1. Do blacks use different sources of information than whites regarding theater productions?
   2. Do they express different needs in attending theater productions?
   3. Do they have different attitudes toward the theater in general?
   4. Do they attend primarily black-oriented productions?

   Conduct three focused group interviews with blacks and three focused group interviews with whites to answer these questions. Act as a moderator and try to steer the discussion to theater in general and the specific questions listed above.

- In what ways do the needs, attitudes, sources of information, and behavior of blacks differ from whites?
- What are the marketing implications for theater producers in terms of (a) trying to attract a larger proportion of black audiences, and (b) performance and promotional strategies for doing so?

1. James S. Duesenberry, *Income, Saving and the Theory of Consumer Behavior* (Cambridge, Mass.: Harvard University Press, 1949), p. 19.

2. Milton J. Rokeach, "The Role of Values in Public Opinion Research," *Public Opinion Quarterly* 32 (Winter 1968): 547–549; and Milton J. Rokeach, "A Theory of Organization and Change Within Value-Attitude Systems," *Journal of Social Issues* (January 1968): 13–33.

3. Donald E. Vinson, Jerome E. Scott, and Lawrence M. Lamont, "The Role of Personal Values in Marketing and Consumer Behavior," *Journal of Marketing* 41 (April 1977): 44–50.

4. Florence Kluckhohn and Fred Strodtbeck, *Variations in Value Orientations* (Evanston, Ill.: Row, Peterson, 1961).

5. Joseph F. Hair , Jr. and Rolph E. Anderson, "Culture, Acculturation and Consumer Behavior: An Empirical Study," in Boris W. Becker and Helmut Becker, eds., *Combined Proceedings of the American Marketing Association,* Series No. 34 (1972), pp. 423–428.

6. Bernard Berelson and Gary A. Steiner, *Human Behavior: An Inventory of Scientific Findings* (New York: Harcourt Brace & World, 1964), p. 652.

7. Philip Kotler, *Marketing Management: Analysis, Planning and Control* 3rd ed. (Englewood Cliffs, N.J.: Prentice-Hall Inc., 1976), p. 43.

8. Daniel Yankelovich, *The Yankelovich Monitor* (New York: Daniel Yankelovich, Inc., 1974).

9. Frederick E. Webster, Jr. and Frederick Von Pechmann, "A Replication of the 'Shopping List' Study," *Journal of Marketing* 34 (April 1970): 61–63.

10. David M. Potter, *People of Plenty* (Chicago: University of Chicago Press, 1954).

11. Philip Kotler and Sidney J. Levy, "Demarketing, Yes Demarketing," *Harvard Business Review* 50 (November-December 1971): 74–80.

12. Theodore Roszak, *The Making of A Counter Culture: Reflections on the Technocratic Society and its Youthful Opposition* (Garden City, N.Y.: Doubleday, 1969), p. 66.

13. David C. McClelland, *The Achieving Society* (Princeton, N.J.: Van Nostrand, 1961).

14. Vinson, Scott, and Lamont, "The Role of Personal Values."

15. Jerome E. Scott and Lawrence M. Lamont, "Relating Consumer Values to Consumer Behavior: A Model and Method for Investigation," in Thomas V. Greer, ed., *Combined Proceedings of the American Marketing Association,* Series No. 35 (1973), pp. 283–288.

16. Water A. Henry, "Cultural Values Do Correlate with Consumer Behavior," *Journal of Marketing Research* 13 (May 1976): 121–127.

17. Gerald Zaltman, *Marketing: Contributions from the Behavioral Sciences* (New York: Harcourt, Brace & World, 1965), p.8.

18. Daniel Yankelovich, *The New Morality: A Profile of American Youth in the 70's* (New York: McGraw-Hill, 1974).

19. Melvin Helitzer and Carl Heyel, *The Youth Market* (New York: Media Books, 1970), p. 58.

20. "44 Million Adults - A New Wave of Buyers," *U.S. News and World Report,* January 17, 1972, pp. 16–19.

21. Edward Papazian, "Teenagers . . . and Broadcast Media," *Media/Scope* 11 (December 1967): 111–115.

22. Kenneth L. Bernhardt and Thomas C. Kinnear, "Profiling the Senior Citizen Market," in Beverlee B. Anderson, ed., *Advances in Consumer Research,* vol. 3 (Atlanta: Association for Consumer Research, 1976), pp. 449–452.

23. Herbert Zeltner, "You Can Sell to the Older Set if You Watch These Trends," *Advertising Age,* August 22, 1977, pp. 33 and 42.

24. Lawrence Wenner, "Functional Analysis of TV Viewing for Older Adults," *Journal of Broadcasting* 20 (Winter 1976): 77–88.

25. Zeltner, "You Can Sell."

26. Subhash C. Jain, "Life Cycle Revisited: Applications in Consumer Research," in Mary Jane Schlinger, ed., *Advances in Consumer Research,* vol. 2 (Ann Arbor, Mich.: Association for Consumer Research, 1975), p. 42.

27. Phillip H. Dougherty, "Matching Products to Lifestyle," *New York Times,* April 21, 1976, p. 58.

28. Phillip H. Dougherty, "Hispanic Population Pinpointed," *New York Times,* September 11, 1980, p. D14.

29. Richard P. Jones, "Spanish Ethnic Market Second Largest in U.S.," *Marketing Insights,* November 27, 1967.

30. David L. Loudon and Albert J. Della Bitta, *Consumer Behavior: Concepts and Applications* (New York: McGraw-Hill, 1979), p. 159.

31. Dougherty, "Hispanic Population Pinpointed," p. D14.

32. Johnson Products Company, *Annual Report,* 1975, p. 4.

33. Raymond A. Bauer and Scott Cunningham, "The Negro Market," *Journal of Advertising Research* 10 (April 1970): 3–13.

34. Carl M. Larson, "Racial Brand Usage and Media Exposure Differentials," in Keith Cox and Ben Enis, eds., *June Conference Proceedings of the American Marketing Association,* Series No. 27 (1968), pp. 208–215.

35. Thomas S. Robertson, Douglas J. Dalrymple, and Michael Y. Yoshino, "Cultural Compatability in New Product Adoption," In Philip R. McDonald, ed., *Proceedings of the American Marketing Association Educators Conference,* Series 30 (1969), p. 72.

36. Raymond A. Bauer, Scott M. Cunningham and Lawrence H. Wortzel, "The Marketing Dilemma of Negroes," *Journal of Marketing* 29 (July 1965): 3.

37. Donald E. Sexton, Jr., "Black Buyer Behavior," *Journal of Marketing* 36 (October 1972): 38.

38. Henry A. Bullock, "Consumer Motivation in

Black and White," *Harvard Business Review* 39 (May-June 1961): 98.

39. Robertson, Dalrymple, and Yoshino, "Cultural Compatability," p. 73.

40. Raymond A. Bauer, "Negro Consumer Behavior," in Joseph W. Newman, ed., *On Knowing the Consumer* (New York: John Wiley & Sons, 1966), pp. 161–165.

41. Carl M. Larson and Hugh G. Wales, "Brand Preferences of Chicago Blacks," *Journal of Advertising Research* 13 (August 1973): 15–21.

42. Larson, "Racial Brand Usage."

43. Ibid., pp. 214–215.

44. Laurence P. Feldman and Alvin D. Star, "Racial Factors in Shopping Behavior," in Keith Cox and Ben M. Enis, eds., *June Conference Proceedings of the American Marketing Association,* Series No. 27 (1968), pp. 216–226.

45. John V. Petrof, "Attitudes of the Urban Poor Toward Their Neighborhood Supermarkets," *Journal of Retailing* 47 (Spring 1971): 3–17.

46. Bullock, "Consumer Motivations," p. 99.

47. Dennis H. Gensch and Richard Staelin, "The Appeal of Buying Black," *Journal of Marketing Research* 9 (May 1972): 141–148.

48. Donald E. Sexton, Jr., "Comparing the Cost of Food to Blacks and to Whites — A Survey," *Journal of Marketing* 35 (July 1971): 40–46.

49. Donald E. Sexton, Jr., "Do Blacks Pay More," *Journal of Marketing Research* 8 (November 1971): 423.

50. Leon Morse, "Black Radio Market Study," *Television/Radio Age,* February 28, 1977, pp. A-1 –A-31.

51. Ibid., p. A-20.

52. Kelvin A. Wall, "Trying to Reach Blacks? Beware of Marketing Myopia," *Advertising Age,* May 21, 1979, p. 59.

53. Ibid.

54. Dennis F. Healy, "Johnson Products Company," in M. Wayne DeLozier, *Consumer Behavior Dynamics: A Casebook* (Columbus, Ohio: Charles E. Merrill Publishing Co., 1977), p. 116.

55. Bauer, Cunningham, and Wortzel, "The Marketing Dilemma of Negroes."

56. *"Essence* Urges Heavier Marketing to Blacks," *Product Marketing,* September 1977, p. 1.

57. Ibid., p. 30.

58. "Remington Shaver for Black Males Ends Test Market," *Product Marketing,* March 1978, p. 65.

59. Wall, "Trying to Reach Blacks," p. 60.

60. Ibid.

61. Ibid.

62. *"Essence* Urges Heavier Marketing," p. 31.

63. Wall, "Trying to Reach Blacks," p. 60.

64. Roger Ricklefs, "For a Businessman Headed Abroad Some Basic Lessons," *Wall Street Journal,* January 16, 1978, p. 2.

65. J. Douglas McConnell, "The Economics of Behavioral Factors on the Multi-National Corporation," in Fred C. Allvine, ed., *Combined Proceedings of the American Marketing Association,* Series No. 33, (1971), p. 264.

66. Ibid.

67. Joseph T. Plummer, "Consumer Focus in Cross-National Research," *Journal of Advertising* 6 (Spring 1977): 5–15.

68. McConnell, "The Economics of Behavioral Factors," p. 265.

69. Ibid., p. 266.

70. Albert Stridsberg, "Watch That Foreign Market — Everything Changes," *Advertising Age,* April 29, 1974.

71. Albert Stridsberg, "U.S. Advertisers Win Some, Lose Some in Foreign Market," *Advertising Age,* May 6, 1974.

72. Arthur C. Fatt, "The Danger of 'Local' International Advertising," *Journal of Marketing* 31 (January 1967): 60–62.

73. Norman Heller, "How Pepsi-Cola Does It In 110 Countries," in John S. Wright and Jac L. Goldstucker, *New Ideas for Successful Marketing* (Chicago: American Marketing Association, 1966), pp. 694–700.

74. S. Watson Dunn, "Effect of National Identity on Multinational Promotional Strategy In Europe," *Journal of Marketing* 40 (October 1976): 51.

75. Robert J. Hoover, Robert T. Green, and Joel Saegert, "A Cross-National Study of Perceived Risk," *Journal of Marketing* 42 (July 1978): 102–108.

76. Robert T. Green and Eric Langeard, "A Cross-National Comparison of Consumer Habits and Innovator Characteristics," *Journal of Marketing,* 39 (July 1975): 34–41.

77. Dunn, "Effect of National Identity."

78. Ibid., p. 56.

79. Stridsberg, "U.S. Advertisers."

80. Ibid.

81. Ibid.

82. Brian Toyne, "Home Products, Inc.," in M. Wayne DeLozier, *Consumer Behavior Dynamics: A Casebook* (Columbus, Ohio: Charles E. Merrill Publishing Co., 1977), p. 227.

83. Stridsberg, "U.S. Advertisers."

84. Montrose Sommers and Jerome Kernan, "Why Products Flourish Here, Fizzle There," *Columbia Journal of World Business* (March-April 1967): 93.

85. Dunn, "Effect of National Identity," pp. 54–55.

86. McConnell, "The Economics of Behavioral Factors," p. 264.

87. Ibid.

88. Stridsberg, "U.S. Advertisers."

89. Charles Winick, "Anthropology's Contribution to Marketing," *Journal of Marketing* 25 (July 1961): 59.

TWELVE

Social Class Influences

Focus of Chapter

A young college professor making $20,000 a year likes to drink bourbon, reads the *New Yorker,* and plays tennis. A forty-year-old factory foreman making $30,000 a year likes to drink beer, subscribes to *Reader's Digest,* and bowls with a team of fellow workers once a week. The college professor's wife works as an editorial assistant in a publishing firm. They make joint decisions for major purchases and frequently shop together. They are childless and have no immediate plans to raise children. They are willing to take the risk of buying new products because of a belief in their upward occupational mobility.

The factory foreman's wife does not have an outside job because they both share traditional norms that the wife should be the homemaker. He tends to make the major budgeting decisions. They have three children, 8, 14, and 16 years old. They are reluctant to change their life-style or to buy new products because of economic uncertainty caused by inflation and the possibility

of layoffs in a prolonged recession. Whereas the college professor is oriented to the future, the factory foreman is oriented to the present.

These two profiles illustrate the concept of social class. The college professor is in the *upper middle class;* the factory foreman is in the *upper lower class.*

Social class is another environmental component that is important to the marketer. It refers to the position of an individual or family on a social scale based on criteria valuable to society. In American society, an individual's occupation, education, and income may define the prestige or power of the individual, and, therefore, his or her position as upper, middle, or lower class. Social classes represent broad groups of people with similar occupations, incomes, and educations. Members of the same social class may never meet or communicate, but they are likely to share certain values, attitudes, and behavior because of their similar socioeconomic characteristics.

This chapter focuses on the concept of social class and its importance to marketers. The attributes of a social class and profiles of upper-, middle- and lower-class members are described. Each social class has different purchasing, shopping, media, and communications behavior. Differences in the attitudes and behavior of these groups and the effects of social class on purchasing behavior will be explored. The chapter also shows the weaknesses in using social class to describe market segments.

SOCIAL STRATIFICATION

The classifications of upper, middle, and lower class imply that certain members of society rank higher than others in prestige and power. Although contrary to the American creed that all people are created equal, **social stratification** suggests that some people are more equal than others. Berelson and Steiner define social stratification as "the ranking of people in society by other members of the society into higher and lower positions so as to produce a hierarchy of respect or prestige."[1]

A key question is: What are the indicators society uses as marks of respect and prestige? In American society income is not always the only criterion. In the example above, the college professor makes less money than the factory foreman. Therefore, as a measure of social class, income must be combined with occupation and education. One study used occupation as the primary criterion for measuring social class and found that physicians, scientists, government officials, college professors, and lawyers rated highest on the social scale.[2] These ratings are dependent on the ideals and values of American society. In Europe, college professors and lawyers would probably be rated lower than artists and writers.

THE IMPORTANCE OF SOCIAL CLASS
TO MARKETING STRATEGY

Social class groupings are important to the marketer since consumers in the same class exhibit broadly similar patterns in what they buy, where they live, how they shop, and what they read. Social class characteristics can be related to every aspect of marketing strategy.

Market Segmentation

Marketers seeking to define a target for their brand frequently describe a segment of the consumer market in socioeconomic terms. One study segmented the use of bank credit cards according to social class and life-style characteristics.[3] Credit card users were in the upper middle and upper classes (higher income, better educated, professional occupations). The study found that these individuals are more aware of their appearance, are achievement-oriented, are contemporary rather than traditional in outlook, and are willing to take risks. These findings are supported by earlier studies that found that consumers in the middle and upper classes are more likely to use credit cards for convenience, whereas consumers in the lower class tend to use them as a means of installment purchasing. The conclusion is that "different social classes reflect different values, and these differences are manifested in consumer buying behavior."[4]

In another study, AT&T sought to segment the residential, long-distance market by social class and demographic characteristics.[5] The measure of social class was an index of socioeconomic status (SES) representing occupation, family income, and education. The results showed that higher income consumers will spend more on long-distance calls regardless of their occupation and education, but among those in the middle- to lower-income range the higher the occupation and education, the greater the expenditure on long-distance calls. Thus, a middle-income college professor may spend a greater than average amount on long-distance calls compared to other middle-income consumers because a professor has a higher SES score.

Advertising

Social class characteristics can give direction to advertising. The language and symbols used in advertising must be understood by the social class to which the advertising is directed. Martineau found that middle-class mothers associated the words "darling" and "sweet" with baby, while lower-class mothers used words such as "more work" and "a darling but a bother."[6] Based on this, advertisements for infant clothing directed to the middle- and upper-class markets may attempt associations with care and love while advertisements directed to lower-class mothers may emphasize ease of cleaning and durability.

Figures 12–1 and 12–2 present advertisements for two products directed toward different social classes. The ad for After Six is directed toward the upper class. The appeal is clearly to prestige. The ad has appeared in media most likely to be read by upper-middle- and upper-class consumers. The ad for Amway reflects a greater emphasis on the part of lower middle- and lower-class consumers for financial security by citing a source of extra income. The ad has appeared in media most frequently read by those in lower socioeconomic groups.

The beer market is a good example of a market whose advertising has been influenced by social class characteristics. Frequent beer drinkers are more likely to be in a lower social class than those that drink less frequently. One study found that frequent beer drinkers are in the middle-income group and in blue-collar occupations. A member of this group is seen as:

> more pleasure-seeking toward life than the non-drinker. He seemed to have less regard toward responsibilities of family and job. More than the non-drinker, he tended to have a preference for a physical/male-oriented existence and an inclination to fantasize. Finally [he has] a great enjoyment of drinking, especially beer which he saw as a real man's drink.[7]

To appeal to this group, Schlitz developed the "Gusto man" campaign. In contrast to this, Lowenbrau appeals to a different social class with the theme "Here's to good friends." The appeal here is to sociability, not to masculinity. Rather than being oriented to males, the Lowenbrau ads frequently picture couples in a social gathering. The tone and orientation of both promotional

FIGURE 12–1 An Appeal to the Upper-Class Values of Prestige and Distinction
By permission of Chalk, Nissen, Hanft, Inc./After Six, Inc.

strategies are heavily dependent on the social class definitions of their target markets.

Distribution

Social classes frequently differ in store patronage. Lower-class consumers are more likely to shop in discount stores, in local stores, and by mail order.[8] Upper-class consumers are more likely to shop in regular department stores for products they consider risky and in discount stores for products with little risk.[9] One study classified department stores as being high fashion, price appeal, or broad appeal stores. Upper-class consumers were fifteen times more likely to shop in high fashion stores than were lower-class consumers. Lower-class

"I NEVER THOUGHT WE'D FEEL REALLY INDEPENDENT!"

"It takes *money* to feel really independent – and I never thought we'd have enough to give us at least a little sense of security. Then we discovered Amway."

Craig & Laurie Shreeve
Amway distributors

"Now we're earning extra income as independent Amway distributors. We started part-time, just like more than 500,000 other independent Amway distributors. Most of them are husband-and-wife teams like us.

"We serve our friends and neighbors with more than 150 Amway® home-care, personal-care, nutrition and diet, and housewares products. And we help people start their own Amway businesses – some of them are in these photos with us.

"We're building our Amway business *our* way. *We* run it. *We're* the boss. And that freedom makes us feel so good!"

When someone wants to tell you about Amway — listen! But don't wait for your Amway distributor to call. Talk to him or her today. If you need help in finding a distributor, dial toll-free (except in Hawaii and Alaska, write from there) 1-800-253-4463. (Michigan residents dial 1-800-632-8723). Do it now. Amway Corporation, Ada, MI 49355; Amway of Canada, Ltd., London, Ontario, N6A 4S5.

Get the <u>whole</u> story.

Amway
SHOP WITHOUT
GOING SHOPPING

FIGURE 12–2   An Appeal to the Lower-Class Value of Financial Security

consumers were four times more likely to shop in price appeal stores than were upper-class shoppers. Middle-class consumers were the most likely to shop in broad appeal stores.[10]

These findings suggest that social class characteristics can provide guidelines for distribution strategies. If the target market is more likely to be in the lower socioeconomic group, then neighborhood stores should be used rather than downtown shopping centers. Middle- and upper-class target groups suggest the use of regular department stores in downtown locations. Moreover, discount store managers would be wise not to trade up in quality of goods in an attempt to attract upper-class customers. Such customers are likely to continue to purchase at regular department stores, and attempts at trading up may alienate the regular discount store customers.[11]

Product Development

Social classes may also react differently to product characteristics and styles. A study by AT&T examined the style and color preferences for telephones among various social groups.[12] Lower-class consumers were not interested in a decorative or modern phone. They just wanted one that worked. The lower middle class placed the greatest emphasis on phones of different designs and colors. These findings demonstrate that the lower socioeconomic group would be a poor target for decorative phones. Surprisingly, a good prospect is the lower middle class. Had AT&T assumed that higher socioeconomic groups were most likely to prefer high style phones, it might have missed an important target group.

THE NATURE OF SOCIAL CLASS

Realizing how important social class is to consumer behavior requires an understanding of the following factors:

- the general attributes of social classes;
- social class groupings and the characteristics of each group;
- measures of social class to permit classification of individuals into higher or lower groups;
- the nature of social classes in the United States; and
- the limitations in using social class characteristics to describe consumer behavior.

The following discussion will include a review of these factors in order to better understand the nature of social class.

Social Class Attributes

Social classes have several characteristics that distinguish them from reference groups, culture, or other environmental factors.

Social classes have status. Status means the relative ranking of each social class according to criteria important to the society. Berelson and Steiner list the following factors that are important in determining status:

- authority over others
- power (political, economic, military)
- ownership of property
- income

- consumption patterns and life-style
- occupation
- education
- public service
- ancestry
- association ties and connections[13]

Social classes are hierarchical.   Social class exists as a position on a social scale. An individual is positioned on the social scale based on the status criteria described above. The individual may not agree with the norms and behavior of his or her social class, but is still a member of that class by virtue of socioeconomic characteristics. Thus, the teenager living in the comfort of upper-middle-class surroundings may reject values of materialism and upward, occupational mobility and be content to live in a commune someday. But that individual is still positioned on the higher end of the social scale.

Social classes serve as a frame of reference for individual norms, attitudes, and behavior.   The above example suggests that membership in a social class imparts specific norms, attitudes, and behavior. Individuals on the lower end of the social scale are more oriented toward traditional values. They are less likely to plan for future financial security, regardless of income, and are more likely to buy on impulse. The values of individuals at the higher end of the social scale are more contemporary. Husbands and wives are more likely to make purchases jointly on a budgeted basis. Purchasing behavior will also differ between classes. Several studies found that upper-class consumers are more likely to spend their leisure time playing cards, going to concerts, or playing tennis while lower-class consumers are more likely to spend their time bowling or in craftsmanlike activities such as model building and woodworking.[14]

Social classes are dynamic.   It is possible for an individual to move up or down the social scale. An important issue is whether the trend in American society is toward the middle of the social scale. A current belief is that American society has a leveling effect and that social class criteria are becoming blurred with the predominance of a large middle class. A contrary belief is that social class lines are still firm and inhibit association between members of different social classes.

Another issue is whether criteria for placement on the social scale are changing. Income does not appear to be as important a criterion as it used to be for placement on the social scale. At the turn of the century, income was closely correlated with occupation. Today, blue-collar workers may be making the same income as certain professionals and managers.

Social classes discourage contact with members of other class groups.   People tend to maintain social contact with others who have the same values and patterns of behavior. Such an association can be comfortable and reinforcing. As a result, members of the same social class are more likely to associate with each other and are less likely to associate with members of other social classes. Writers who believe that social class lines in the United States are becoming blurred point to the greater social mobility and contact between social groups. They would say that social class differences are no longer a barrier to communication and personal association. Others accept the traditional boundaries between class lines and agree that social classes still discourage contact.

Social Class Categories and Measurement

The definition of social class categories is multidimensional. The placement of an individual on the social scale is based on several socioeconomic measures that are combined into an index of social class. Two of the most widely used indices are Warner's **Index of Status Characteristics** (ISC)[15] and the U.S. Bureau of the Census Socioeconomic Status score (SES).[16] Warner developed his index in a study of social class lines in a New England city.[17] The ISC is based on the following socioeconomic indicators:

- occupation (weighted by a factor of 4)
- source of income (weighted by 3)
- house type (weighted by 3)
- dwelling area (weighted by 2)

An individual is classified into one of the categories listed in Table 12–1. The classification is then multiplied by the weight and summed across the four indicators to obtain the ISC score. On this basis, Warner developed a six-part classification of social class as follows:

- upper upper class (1.4 percent of respondents)
- lower upper class (1.6 percent of respondents)
- upper middle (10.2 percent)
- lower middle (28.1 percent)
- upper lower (32.6 percent)
- lower lower (25.2 percent)

The U.S. Bureau of the Census combines occupation, family income, and education into a Socioeconomic Status index. AT&T used this approach to measure the social class of a panel of residential telephone subscribers.[18] The income, occupation, and education classifications and the associated scores are presented in Table 12–2. These three scores were averaged for each individual to produce an overall SES score. AT&T then used these scores to identify four social class groups (see bottom of Table 12–2). Thus, anyone with an SES index of 0–44 would be classified in the lower class, anyone with an SES score of 45–69 in the lower middle class, etc.

There are other methods for developing indices of social class.[19] Methods have also been used to identify a consumer's social class based on perceived social position rather than an objective index. For example, consumers could be asked what social class they belong to; upper, middle or lower.[20] Or individuals could be asked to evaluate the social status of others in the community.[21] These more subjective methods have rarely been used in marketing studies. Marketing researchers favor a more empirical measure such as a social class index.

TABLE 12–1 Categories Used in Computing Warner's Index of Status Characteristics

Occupation (weight of 4)	Source of Income (weight of 3)	House Type (weight of 3)	Dwelling Area (weight of 2)
1. Professionals and priorietors of large businesses	1. Inherited wealth	1. Excellent houses	1. Very high: Gold Coast North Shore, etc.
2. Semiprofessionals and officials of large businesses	2. Earned wealth	2. Very good houses	2. High: the better suburbs and apartment house areas; houses with spacious yards, etc.
3. Clerks and kindred workers	3. Profits and fees	3. Good houses	3. Above average: areas all residential, larger than average space around houses; apartment areas in good condition, etc.
4. Skilled workers	4. Salary	4. Average houses	4. Average: residential neighborhoods, no deterioration in the area
5. Proprietors of small businesses	5. Wages	5. Fair houses	5. Below average: area not quite holding its own and beginning to deteriorate, business entering, etc.
6. Semiskilled workers	6. Private relief	6. Poor houses	6. Low: considerably deteriorated, run-down and semislum
7. Unskilled workers	7. Public relief and nonrespectable income	7. Very poor houses	7. Very low: slum

Source: W. Loyd Warner, Marchia Meeker, and Kenneth Eells, *Social Class in America: A Manual of Procedure for the Measurement of Social Status* (New York: Harper & Row, 1960), p. 123. Reprinted with permission from Harper & Row.

The diversity of measures of social class is illustrated by the fact that there are no standardized social class categories. Warner's six-part categorization is the most widely used. Others have proposed using five categories (upper class, upper middle, lower middle, working class, lower class). The AT&T study (Table 12–2) used four categories. A study by Martineau used a simple two-part comparison of lower class and middle class.[22]

Profiles of the Social Classes

The various social classes described in Warner's six-part classification have distinct norms, values, and life-styles. Research into the attitudes and behavior of these groups makes it possible to describe a general profile of each.[23]

TABLE 12–2 Categories Used by AT&T in Developing Socioeconomic Status Score

Income Category	SES Income Score	Education Category	SES Education Score	Occupation Category	SES Occupation Score
Under $3,000	15	Some Grade School	10	Laborers	20
$3,000–4,999	31	Grade School Graduate	23	Retired	33
$5,000–7,499	62	Some High School	42	Student	33
$7,500–9,999	84	High School Graduate	67	Housewife	33
$10,000–14,999	94	Some College	86	Unemployed	33
$15,000–19,999	97	College Graduate	93	Service Workers	34
$20,000–29,999	99	Graduate School	98	Operators	45
$30,000 & over	100			Craftsmen	58
				Clerical & Sales	71
				Managers	81
				Professionals	90

Socio-Economic Status Category
(Computed by averaging above three scores for each individual)

Social Class Category	SES Score
Lower	0–44
Lower Middle	45–69
Upper Middle	70–89
Upper	90–99

Source: Adapted from Richard B. Ellis, "Composite Population Descriptors: The Socio-Economic/Life Cycle Grid," in Mary Jane Schlinger, ed., *Advances in Consumer Research,* vol. 2 (Ann Arbor, Mich.: Association for Consumer Research, 1975), pp. 485–486. Reprinted with permission from Association for Consumer Research.

The Upper Upper Class (1.4 percent of the population)

This group is the social elite, the country club set. Most have inherited their wealth. They are likely to be in top management positions or they own long-established companies, are active in community and cultural activities, and emphasize breeding and community responsibility. They dress conservatively and well and avoid ostentatious purchases. According to one writer, this group tends to adopt the tastes and values of the British aristocracy.[24]

The Lower Upper Class (1.6 percent of the population)

This group is represented by successful professional and business people who have acquired their social status by wealth rather than inheritance. They represent the "new money." They are more likely to demonstrate wealth and status through ownership of large homes, luxury cars, and expensive clothes. Both the upper upper class and the lower upper class are unlikely to be specific targets for mass marketers since they represent less than 3 percent of the market.

They would make excellent targets for specialty items such as expensive clothing, jewelry, furniture, or boats.

The Upper Middle Class (10.2 percent of the population)

This group is also comprised of successful professional and business people, but they do not have the wealth or status of the upper class. They are career oriented and achievement motivated. The upper middle class emphasizes education. Many of these individuals have advanced degrees and demand high educational performance from their children. Given their level of education, this group is more likely to critically appraise product alternatives. They emphasize quality and value.

To the upper middle class, the home is a symbol of achievement. They are fashion oriented and also emphasize leisure activities as a means of balancing the career orientation. Women in this group are more likely to be aware, active, and self-expressive as compared to other groups.[25]

The Lower Middle Class (28.1 percent of the population)

This group is represented by white-collar workers, small businessmen, and highly paid blue-collar workers. They emphasize respectability and tend to conform closely to prevailing societal norms. The home is an important focus for this group. They want their homes to be neat, presentable, and located in a good neighborhood.

Lower-middle-class women are more home and family oriented than women in the higher classes. They pride themselves in their role of mother and homemaker. Whereas appeals to time-saving benefits in food preparation and appliances are likely to appeal to upper-middle-class families, they are unlikely to appeal to the lower-middle-class family. Rather, the orientation is more toward traditional, conservative benefits such as pride in meal preparation and satisfaction in upbringing of their children.

The Upper Lower Class (32.6 percent of the population)

The upper lower class consists primarily of blue-collar workers and is sometimes referred to as the working class. Uncreative jobs requiring manual activity frequently result in a routine and dull view of life. The upper lower class sees work as a means to an end — after-hour leisure and enjoyment. Work is not an end in itself. The security of union wages provides some discretionary income for this group. The narrow dimensions of their jobs and lack of self-expression lead to a pattern of impulse purchasing to escape from the dull routine. As a result, in-store displays may be particularly effective. This group would rather buy for today than plan for tomorrow; therefore, advertising appeals to fantasy and escape are more likely to be successful.

The Lower Lower Class (25.2 percent of the population)

This group represents the unskilled, poorly educated, and socially disadvantaged. The lower-lower-class family is frequently frustrated and angry about their economic status. Due to prolonged deprivation and the feeling of being boxed in by society, they may also tend to feel indifferent about their plight. This group is poorly informed about alternative prices, products, and stores. They often pay higher prices for goods compared to other groups because they lack price and product awareness. The lack of any prospect for upward occupational mobility has led to what one writer calls "compensatory consumption,"[26] that is, an attempt to compensate for a bleak future by trying to buy the symbols of the American way of life. As a result, high priced automobiles and color television sets are not uncommon in this group.

The Limitations of Social Class As a Determinant of Consumer Behavior

Several considerations may give marketers second thoughts about using social class as an important basis for segmenting markets or positioning products. These limitations of social class may be summarized by the following questions:

- What is the advantage of using a composite social class index over a simpler one-dimensional classification such as occupation or income?

- What happens if an individual is high in one component of the social class index and low in the other (e.g., high occupation, low education).

- Are there significant differences in socioeconomic status within a social class? Two scientists may both be in the upper-middle class based on social class indices, but one may be a Nobel laureate and the other a lab technician.

- Are social classes merging into one giant middle class? If so, what is the point of emphasizing social class if it is unlikely to discriminate consumer behavior?

Each of these questions will be considered below.

Composite Versus Single Measures of Social Class

Several studies have compared using a single measure of social class, such as occupation or income, versus using a composite measure such as Warner's ISC or the SES index. These studies have uniformly found that a single measure of social class is more closely related to consumer purchasing behavior than a composite index. Myers et al. compared income versus a social class index as predictors of ownership of ninety-three consumer packaged goods.[27] In seventy-nine cases, income was a better predictor of product ownership than social class. In a follow-up study Myers and Mount studied thirty-six appliance, clothing, and travel items. Income was a better predictor of ownership in thirty-two cases.[28] In a study of Israeli households, Wind found that occupation was a better predictor of ownership of packaged goods and appliances than was a social class index.[29]

These findings suggest that a researcher is better off using just occupation or income as a determinant of choice rather than social class; but such a conclusion is misleading. Hisrich and Peters looked at social class and income as predictors of both ownership and frequency of use.[30] They studied fourteen entertainment-type products and also found that income was a better predictor of ownership; but a social class index was a better predictor of frequency of use of these items. Thus, income level may be a good predictor of whether one travels abroad or not, but social class is a better predictor of how often one travels abroad. To marketers of packaged goods frequency of use is probably more important than ownership in measuring purchase performance. Just owning a jar of Sanka does not mean too much since it may not have been used for weeks. Frequency of use is the determining criterion. Social class indices must therefore be regarded as important if they are more closely linked to frequency of use.

Social Class Incongruence

Social class incongruence occurs if an individual is high on one measure in the social class index and low in the other. The problem with frequent social class incongruence is that it can distort an index of social class. The poorly paid intern (high on occupation, low on income) would achieve the same rating as the middle-income, white-collar worker (middle on occupation and income). Yet, they are not in the same social class. Few studies have examined the degree of social class incongruence.[31] If social class incongruence within a target group is frequent, it is better to use a single measure of social class (preferably occupation) rather than a composite index.

Differences in Status Within Social Classes

Another problem with social class groupings is that they may mask substantial variation in status within each class. The better paid production-line worker may be in the same social class as the poorly paid production-line worker, but their purchasing behavior may be very different. Coleman suggested using occupation as the measure of social class and identifying consumers in each social class grouping who are above or below the group's average income.[32] He referred to those with above average income as the **overprivileged** and those with below average income as the **underprivileged.** Thus, the highly paid blue-collar worker and wealthy lawyer would both be in the overprivileged group. Peters found that the underprivileged group was more likely to buy compact cars and the overprivileged group luxury cars, regardless of social class. Thus, "the buying behavior of relatively well-off blue-collar workers is more like that of affluent white-collar and professional workers than that of less well-off blue-collar workers."[33] If this finding is true (and several studies have supported it),[34] then it suggests that social class by itself is not as good a determinant of consumer behavior as relative income within social class.

Is America Becoming a Classless Society?

Another question that may inhibit the use of social class in consumer behavior studies is whether social class lines are becoming more blurred. The universal ownership of television sets means everyone is exposed to the same mass communications. The rise of mass merchandising and the standardization of consumer packaged goods means that most people buy similar brands. The universal ownership of automobiles means greater mobility. As a result of these trends, many believe that sharp distinctions between classes no longer exist. Differences between the working class and the middle class have become blurred.[35]

Recent evidence suggests that differences between social classes have not diminished. Occupational differences are still well-defined. Greater income equality between the working and middle classes is due to spouses joining the work force and to the strength of union demands. Differences in norms, attitudes, and values between groups still exist.[36] One writer describes an erosion of the egalitarian spirit and a reemergence of the class system in the "me decade" of the 1970s.[37] A wider gap between the educated and noneducated, between the haves and have nots, increases the opportunities to market products that bestow status. Moreover, there is no evidence that it is easier to move from one class to another. Chase found that men have little opportunity for upward social mobility through occupational changes since they are likely to inherit the status of their fathers.[38] Social class in America is still very much a reality and a component to be considered in explaining consumer behavior.

DIFFERENCES IN BEHAVIOR BETWEEN CLASSES

Despite some shortcomings in the use of social class indices, marketers have found social class measures important because of substantial differences in behavior between classes. Social classes differ in their purchasing behavior, shopping behavior, media behavior, communications behavior, and information search behavior.

Purchasing Behavior

Substantial differences exist between social classes in the purchases of clothing, furniture and appliances, leisure goods and services, financial services, and food products.

Clothing

Upper- and middle-class consumers are more style conscious and more interested in fashion. They are more likely to read fashion magazines, go to fashion shows, discuss fashions with others, and observe what others wear.[39] They are twice as likely to use cosmetics compared to lower-class consumers.[40] Lower-class consumers are more likely to dress for comfort than fashion.[41]

Furniture and Appliances

Furniture has a symbolic function for consumers who are higher on the social scale, whereas it has a utilitarian function for those lower on the social scale. Higher classes emphasize self-expression by buying either modern or traditional, highly styled furniture pieces, art, and sculpture. Lower classes are more likely to emphasize sturdiness, comfort, and maintenance.[42] The same preferences carry over to appliances. Upper classes are more likely to buy modern appliances and colored appliances. Lower class consumers are more likely to emphasize appliances that work.[43]

Leisure Goods and Services

Consumers higher on the social scale are more likely to engage in sports such as tennis, swimming, ice skating, and skiing. Lower-class consumers are more likely to spend their leisure time hunting, fishing, or bowling. Some researchers have felt that the upper-class activities may be a compensation for a more sedentary existence since they involve active movement.[44] Individuals in the lower classes do not require the same level of activity since they are more likely to be in physically active occupations. Upper- and middle-class families are also more likely to engage in leisure activities together. In lower-class families, leisure activities such as hunting and fishing tend to be male-dominated.

Financial Services

Upper- and middle-class consumers are more likely to use credit cards for luxury products such as entertainment, restaurants, antiques, and gasoline. Lower-class consumers are more likely to use credit cards for necessities such as furniture, clothing, and medical expenses.[45] Differences also exist in the sources of credit. Upper- and middle-class consumers are more likely to cite banks and insurance policies as credit sources, while lower-class consumers cite personal loan companies, credit unions, and friends.[46]

Food Products

Food is used in a more symbolic fashion at the higher end of the social scale, while it is used more pragmatically at the lower end.[47] This suggests that upper-class families may buy particular foods as an expression of their self-image while lower-class families are more likely to buy standard, well-known brands. Upper-class consumers are also more likely to be self-indulgent in their eating and drinking habits compared to lower-class consumers.[48]

Shopping Behavior

Upper- and middle-class women shop more frequently than lower-class women. They are more likely to shop with their husbands for appliances, whereas lower-class women are more likely to shop with their husbands for groceries.[49] Upper- and middle-class women are also more likely to discuss shopping with friends, whereas lower-class women discuss shopping with family members.[50]

Attitudes toward shopping also differ. One study of women in the Chicago area found that upper-middle-class women organize the shopping task efficiently, lower-middle-class women work more at their shopping and show more anxiety about it, and lower-class women shop more impulsively.[51] Comments by women in each social class illustrate the difference:

Upper-Middle-Class Woman

"I shop in Wanamakers, Lord and Taylor, Bonwit's and Snellenberg, depending on what I want at the time I'm shopping. I go shopping with a specific thing in mind. I usually group my shopping for the coming season's needs for clothing for myself and the children. I shop for food regularly once a week at Penn Fruit."

Lower-Middle-Class Woman

"I'm always buying clothing for the family. I look around and buy the best I can for as a little as I can. With supermarkets, I watch for ads on Thursdays. For example, I just bought a blanket and I went to three stores to look. As it happened, we bought at Lits; they had the nicest blanket for the best price."

Lower-Class Woman

"My shopping is very broad and vague. I don't go anywhere in particular but for food and that I get at Best Market. For clothing, I usually go to one of the department stores or when they have an advertisement to show what is on sale and what is different than the usual run of things. I just shop wherever I find what I want."[52]

Lower-class women are also more likely to shop in neighborhood stores where they feel more comfortable and are likely to get a friendlier reception. One study found that lower-class women who shopped in higher status department stores felt that clerks punished them in various ways. One woman waiting to be helped was finally told, "We thought you were a clerk."[53]

Media Behavior

Middle- and upper-class consumers are more likely to subscribe to newspapers and magazines.[54] They are more likely to read magazines such as *New Yorker, Ladies Home Journal* or *Playboy;* whereas lower-class consumers are more likely to read *True Story* or *Hustler.* Middle- and upper-class consumers are likely to watch less television and are more concerned about the viewing habits of their children. They are more likely to watch current events and drama, while lower-class consumers are more likely to be interested in soap operas, quiz shows, and situational comedies.[55]

Communications Behavior

Consumers in different social groups tend to have different speech patterns and expressions. One study found that speakers with "upper-class" voices and speech patterns were viewed as more credible than "low-status" sounding persons.[56] Different norms and values between groups also means that certain advertising symbols may be relevant to one group but totally meaningless to another. A marketer of lower priced watches used symbols such as a top hat and champagne glasses to try to convey quality. The target market did not relate to the symbols used.

Levy has found that lower-class consumers are more receptive to "advertising that is strongly visual in character, that shows activity, ongoing work and life, impressions of energy, and solutions to practical problems in daily requirements. . . ."[57] In contrast, upper-class consumers are more open to subtle symbolism, to approaches that are more "individual in tone, . . . that offer the kinds of objects and symbols that are significant of their status and self-expressive aims."[58]

Pricing Behavior

In general, lower-class consumers are more poorly informed about price and product alternatives.[59] They are not more likely to buy products on sale or products priced lower.[60] Because they have more limited product information, lower-class consumers are more likely to use price as a cue for quality. Higher class consumers feel better able to judge products on their own merits rather than rely on price as an indication of quality.[61]

Information Search Behavior

Middle- and upper-class consumers are more likely to search for information prior to purchase. Foxall found that these consumers are more likely to read brochures, newspapers, and test reports before buying appliances. Lower-class consumers are much more likely to use in-store sources such as displays and salespeople.[62] These consumers buy with less prepurchase deliberation. Therefore, evaluation of the product in the store is more important.

SUMMARY

The consumer's social class influences purchasing behavior and represents another component of the environment. Social class refers to a consumer's position on a social scale based on occupation, education, and income criteria. Social class groupings are important to marketers since consumers in the same social class exhibit broad patterns of similarity in what they buy, how they shop, and the media they select. Thus, social class criteria are used to identify market segments, to suggest the language and symbols in advertising, to develop in-store strategies, and to indicate appropriate product characteristics and styles.

In order to develop strategic implications for marketing, consumers must be classified on the social class hierarchy. The most frequently used categorization is the six-part classification developed by Warner ranging from a very small, elite upper class to a sizeable middle and lower class. Warner's classification weights occupation most heavily in determining social class position, with source of income, house type, and dwelling area used as additional criteria.

Each group has distinctive norms, values, family roles, and patterns of purchasing behavior. For example, the upper middle class is motivated by achievement and places a great deal of emphasis on education. Quality, value, and convenience are the most important purchasing criteria, and the home is a symbol of achievement. The lower middle class places greater emphasis on societal norms. The family is more traditionally oriented with the wife taking pride in child-rearing and meal preparation. The upper lower class emphasizes security and seeks escape from the routine of its work environment. Buying is often impulsive and used as an escape.

As a result of these differences, social classes demonstrate marked variations in the purchase of such items as clothing, furniture, leisure goods, and even food items. Attitudes toward shopping also vary, with the upper-middle-class shopper planning ahead, the lower-middle-class shopper being more concerned with price, and the lower-class shopper buying impulsively.

Despite the potential importance of social class in influencing behavior, some doubts have been expressed about the use of social class indices such as Warner's. Studies have shown a closer link to behavior when one variable such as occupation is used, rather than when a composite index is used. Many people may not fit neatly into a social class, such as a highly paid executive with a high school education. There are also marked differences in behavior within social classes. And, given the greater mobility and blurring of class lines, some feel social class may not be a powerful consumer descriptor. But there is sufficient evidence to suggest that social class lines do exist, providing barriers to communication between groups, and that social classes do serve as a frame of reference for the values and purchasing patterns of individual consumers. As a result, social class criteria are likely to provide marketers with relevant insights into consumer behavior.

QUESTIONS

1. Two companies produce different lines of furniture. One company directs its line toward upper-middle-class consumers, the other to lower-middle-class consumers.
   - What are likely to be the differences in (a) product styles and features; (b) print media used; and (c) distribution and in-store environment?

2. A leading domestic beer manufacturer is considering buying the rights to produce an imported beer in the United States. The objective is to compete with Lowenbrau, now owned by Miller.
   - How could the manufacturer use social class to (a) define the target market for the new beer, and (b) provide guidelines for advertising?

3. Two positions were stated in the chapter regarding the current status of social class in the United States: one, that social class differences are becoming less important, and that there are fewer barriers in communication and mobility between groups; two, that social class characteristics are still sharp and social barriers between groups are firm.
   - What is your position?
   - What trends do you project in relation to future social class distinctions?

4. A magazine publisher decides there are sufficient differences in the orientation, role, and purchasing behavior of working women in different social classes to segment the magazine market by introducing three different magazines: one directed to the working woman in the upper middle class, another to the working woman in the lower middle class, and a third to the working woman in the upper lower class.
   - Do you agree with the publisher's premise?
   - Specifically, how may each magazine differ in (a) editorial content, and (b) advertising?

5. A company is introducing a new line of instant baking products designed to facilitate the preparation of more complicated recipes for breads, cakes, and pies.
   - Should the company segment its line so that one set of products is directed to higher social classes and another to lower social classes?
   - How would the advertising campaigns to each group differ?
6. The chapter implies that leisure activities serve a different purpose for the middle class versus the lower class.
   - In what way?
   - What does this imply for a large producer of sporting equipment such as AMF?
7. The chapter also suggests that different social groups have very different orientations to their children. What might these differences suggest regarding the following:
   - The likelihood of mothers in different social groups acceding to the child's purchase request?
   - The differences in the impact of television on children in different social classes?
8. Differences in parents' orientation to children in different social classes are likely to affect the marketing strategies of manufacturers of children's clothing.
   - What different approaches might a manufacturer of a more expensive line of children's clothing take compared to a manufacturer of a less expensive line regarding (a) references to children in the ads; (b) references to the mother's purchase role in the ads; and (c) the specific benefits of the line of clothing emphasized in the ads?
9. Differences in shopping orientation between social classes are likely to affect retail store policies. Compare three retail stores located in upper-middle-, lower-middle-, and lower-class neighborhoods.
   - How are differences in shopping orientations likely to affect these stores' (a) advertising, (b) store layout, and (c) in-store displays?

RESEARCH ASSIGNMENTS

Using the SES score (Table 12–2), classify a sample of consumers by social class. Develop three categories: (1) lower — SES score of 69 or under; (2) middle — SES score of 70–89, and (3) upper — SES score of 90 or over. Try to interview twenty consumers in each category. Ask consumers about the following:

1. life-styles (based on questions such as those in Chapter 10, Table 10–1);
2. product and brand ownership for selected durables (car, stereo, kitchen appliances) and leisure goods (sporting equipment);
3. price paid for these items;
4. magazines read most frequently;
5. demographics (to be used as basis for determination of social class).

- What are the most significant differences between the upper, middle, and lower classes in relation to the above?
- Are these differences due primarily to income level or to different norms and values between social classes?
- What are the marketing implications of these differences?

1. Bernard Berelson and Gary A. Steiner, *Human Behavior: An Inventory of Scientific Findings* (New York: Harcourt, Brace & World, 1964), p. 453.

2. Robert W. Hodges, Paul M. Siegel, and Peter H. Rossi, "Occupational Prestige in the United States, 1925–1963," *American Journal of Sociology* 70 (November 1964): 290–292.

3. Joseph T. Plummer, "Life Style Patterns and Commercial Bank Credit Card Usage," *Journal of Marketing* 35 (April 1971): 35–41.

4. H. Lee Mathews and John W. Slocum, Jr., "Social Class and Commercial Credit Card Usage," *Journal of Marketing* 33 (January 1969): 73–74.

5. A. Marvin Roscoe, Jr. and Jagdish N. Sheth, "Demographic Segmentation of Long Distance Behavior: Data Analysis and Inductive Model Building" in M. Venkatesan, ed., *Proceedings of the 3rd Annual Conference, Association for Consumer Research* (1972), p. 268.

6. Pierre Martineau, *Motivation in Advertising* (New York: McGraw-Hill, 1957), p. 166.

7. Joseph T. Plummer, "Life Style and Advertising: Case Studies," in Fred C. Allvine, ed., *Combined Proceedings of the American Marketing Association,* Series #33 (1971), p. 292.

8. Stuart U. Rich and Subhash C. Jain, "Social Class and Life Cycle as Predictors of Shopping Behavior," *Journal of Marketing Research* 5 (February 1968): 41–49.

9. V. Kanti Prasad, "Socioeconomic Product Risk and Patronage Preferences of Retail Shoppers," *Journal of Marketing* 39 (July 1975): 42–47.

10. Rich and Jain, "Social Class and Life Cycle."

11. Leon G. Schiffman and Leslie L. Kanuk, *Consumer Behavior* (Englewood Cliffs, N.J.: Prentice-Hall, Inc., 1978), p. 323.

12. A. Marvin Roscoe, Jr., Arthur LeClaire, Jr., and Leon G. Schiffman, "Theory and Management Applications of Demographics in Buyer Behavior," in Arch G. Woodside, Jagdish N. Sheth, and Peter D. Bennett, eds., *Consumer and Industrial Buying Behavior* (New York: North-Holland, 1977), p. 74.

13. Berelson and Steiner, *Human Behavior,* p. 454.

14. William R. Cotton, Jr. "Leisure and Social Stratification," in Gerald W. Thielbar and Saul D. Feldman, eds., *Issues in Social Inequality* (Boston: Little, Brown, 1972), pp. 520–538; Alfred C. Clarke, "Leisure and Occupational Prestige," *American Sociological Review* 21 (June 1956): 305–306; Bert N. Adams and James E. Butler, "Occupational Status and Husband-Wife Social Participation, *Social Forces* 45 (June 1967): 501–507.

15. W. Loyd Warner, Marchia Meeker, and Kenneth Eells, *Social Class in America: Manual of Procedure for the Measurement of Social Status* (New York: Harper & Brothers, 1960.)

16. Methodology and Scores of Socioeconomic Status, Working Paper No. 15 (Washington D.C.: U.S. Bureau of the Census, 1963.)

17. W. Loyd Warner and Paul S. Lunt, *The Social Life of a Modern Community, Yankee City Series,* vol. 1 (New Haven: Yale University Press, 1941.)

18. Richard B. Ellis "Composite Population Descriptors: The Socio-Economic/Life Cycle Grid," in Mary Jane Schlinger, ed., *Advances in Consumer Research,* vol. 2 (Ann Arbor, Mich.: Association for Consumer Reasearch, 1975), pp. 481–493.

19. For example, see August B. Hollingshead, *Elmtown's Youth: The Impact of Social Class on Adolescents* (New York: Wiley, 1949); James M. Carman, *The Application of Social Class in Market Segmentation* (Berkeley, Calif.: Institute of Business and Economic Research, University of California Graduate School of Business Administration, 1965).

20. Richard Centers, *The Psychology of Social Class* (New York: Russell and Russell, 1961), p. 233.

21. Warner, Meeker and Eells, *Social Class in America* pp. 56–57.

22. Pierre Martineau, "Social Classes and Spending Behavior," *Journal of Marketing* 23 (October 1958): 121–129.

23. For a description of the profiles of Warner's six social class groups see: Richard P. Coleman, "The Significance of Social Stratification in Selling," in Martin L. Bell, ed., *Marketing: A Maturing Discipline* (Chicago: American Marketing Association, 1960), pp. 171–184; Warner, Meeker, and Eells, *Social Class in America,* pp. 11–21; Sidney J. Levy, "Social Class and Consumer Behavior," in Joseph W. Newman, ed., *On Knowing the Consumer* (New York: John Wiley & Sons, 1966), pp. 146–160.

24. M. C. Pirie, "Marketing and Social Classes: An Anthropologist's View," *Management Review* 49 (September 1960): 45–48.

25. Levy, *Social Class and Consumer Behavior.*

26. Kim B. Rotzoll, "The Effect of Social Stratification on Market Behavior," *Journal of Advertising Research* 7 (March 1967): 22–27.

27. James H. Myers, Roger R. Stanton, and Arne F. Haug, "Correlates of Buying Behavior: Social Class vs. Income," *Journal of Marketing* 35 (October 1971): 8–15.

28. James H. Myers and John F. Mount, "More on Social Class vs. Income as Correlates of Buying Behavior," *Journal of Marketing* 37 (April 1973): 71–73.

29. Yoram Wind, "Incongruency of Socioeconomic Variables and Buying Behavior," in Philip R. McDonald, ed., *American Marketing Association Fall Conference Proceedings,* Series No. 30 (1969), pp. 362–367.

30. Robert D. Hisrich and Michael P. Peters, "Selecting the Superior Segmentation Correlate," *Journal of Marketing* 38 (July 1974): 60–63.

31. Gerhard E. Lenski, "Status Crystallization: A Non-Vertical Dimension of Social Status," *American Sociological Review* 21 (August 1956): 458–464; Wind, "Incongruency."

32. Coleman, "The Significance of Social Stratification."

314 33. William H. Peters, "Relative Occupational Class Income: A Significant Variable in the Marketing of Automobiles," *Journal of Marketing* 34 (April 1970): 77.

34. Ibid.; R. Eugene Klipper and John F. Monoky, "A Potential Segmentation Variable for Marketers: Relative Occupational Class Income," *Journal of the Academy of Marketing Science* 2 (Spring 1974): 351–354.

35. R. A. Nisbet, "The Decline and Fall of Social Class," in R. A. Nisbet, ed., *Traditional Revolt* (New York: Random House, 1968).

36. Norval D. Glenn, "Massification versus Differentiation: Some Trend Data from National Surveys," *Social Forces* 46 (December 1967).

37. Florence Skelly, "Prognosis 2000," Speech before New York Chapter of the American Marketing Association, Dec. 15, 1977.

38. Ivan D. Chase, "A Comparison of Men's and Women's Intergenerational Mobility in the United States," *American Sociological Review* 40 (August 1975): 483–505.

39. Rich and Jain, "Social Class and Life Cycle."

40. William D. Wells, "Seven Questions About Lifestyle and Psychographics," in Boris W. Becker and Helmut Becker, eds., *Combined Proceedings of the American Marketing Association,* Series No. 34 (1972), p. 464.

41. Roscoe, LeClaire, and Schiffman, "Theory and Management Applications," p.75.

42. Levy, *Social Class and Consumer Behavior,* p. 158.

43. Roscoe, LeClaire, and Schiffman, "Theory and Management Applications," pp. 74–75.

44. Doyle W. Bishop and Masaru Ikeda, "Status and Role Factors in the Leisure Behavior of Different Occupations," *Sociology and Social Research* 54 (January 1970): 190–208.

45. Mathews and Slocum, Jr., "Social Class."

46. Pierre D. Martineau, "Social Class and its Very Close Relationship to the Individual's Buying Behavior," in Martin L. Bell, ed., *Marketing: A Maturing Discipline* (Chicago: American Marketing Association, 1960), p. 191.

47. Levy, *Social Class and Consumer Behavior,* p. 158.

48. Ibid.

49. Gordon R. Foxall, "Social Factors in Consumer Choice," *Journal of Consumer Research* 2 (June 1975): 60–64.

50. Rich and Jain, "Social Class and Life Cycle," p. 45.

51. Levy, *Social Class and Consumer Behavior,* pp. 153–154.

52. Ibid., p. 154.

53. Martineau, "Social Classes and Spending Behavior," p. 121.

54. Levy, *"Social Class and Consumer Behavior,"* p. 155.

55. Ibid., p. 155.

56. L. S. Harms, "Listener Judgments of Status Cues in Speech," *Quarterly Journal of Speech* 47 (April 1961): 164–168.

57. Levy, *Social Class and Consumer Behavior,* p. 156.

58. Ibid., p. 156.

59. Andre Gabor and S. W. J. Granger, "Price Sensitivity of the Consumer," *Journal of Advertising Research* 4 (December 1964): 40 –44; and David Caplovitz, *The Poor Pay More* (New York: The Free Press, 1963.

60. Frederick E. Webster, Jr., "The Deal-Prone Consumer," *Journal of Marketing Research* 1 (August 1964): 32–35.

61. Joseph N. Fry and Frederick H. Siller, "A Comparison of Housewife Decision Making in Two Social Classes," *Journal of Marketing Research* 8 (August 1970): 333–337.

62. Foxall, "Social Factors in Consumer Choice," p. 62.

THIRTEEN

Reference Group Influences

Focus of Chapter

One of the most important environmental influences on consumer behavior is the face-to-face group. In Chapters 13 through 16, group influence and communications will be examined in detail.

The framework for considering the influence of groups is based on the **reference group;** that is, a group that serves as a reference point for the individual in the formation of his or her beliefs, attitudes, and behavior. Reference groups are important to the marketer for they are sources of information and influence. Marketers frequently advertise their products in a group setting — the family eating breakfast cereals, the neighbor admiring a sparkling floor, etc.

Marketers utilize experts or well-known personalities in commercials as well, assuming consumers will more readily believe spokespersons than direct appeals from advertisers. Consumers are likely to identify with the norms and values expressed by the spokesperson.

In this chapter various types of reference groups will be described, the roles they play will be considered, and the ways they influence the individual consumer will be explored. In introducing the topic of group influence, this chapter sets the stage for a later consideration of family decision making and group communications in Chapters 14–16.

TYPES OF REFERENCE GROUPS

Reference groups provide points of comparison on which to evaluate attitudes and behavior. The consumer can either be a member of a reference group, like the family, or aspire to associate himself or herself with a group of which he or she is not a member, (e.g., a tennis buff's association with tennis pros). In the first case, the individual is part of a **membership group;** in the second, the individual is part of an associative or **aspiration group** (see Figure 13–1).

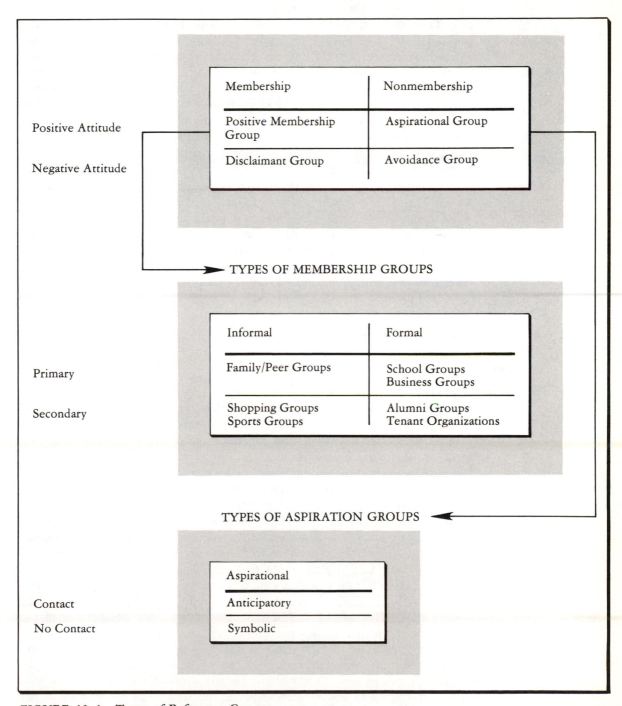

FIGURE 13–1 Types of Reference Groups

Reference groups can also be negatively viewed. For example, an individual may either belong to or join a group and then reject the group's values. This type of group would be a **disclaimant group** for the individual.[1] Moreover, an individual may regard membership in a particular group as something to be avoided; thus, there may be an **avoidance group** as well.

These classifications define the four types of reference groups shown at the top of Figure 13–1. From a marketing standpoint, the positive reference group is more important than the negative one because consumers are generally motivated to buy things based on positive beliefs and attitudes, not negative ones. On occasion, consumers will buy some visible product to stand apart from a membership group they have no desire to belong to or to stand apart from other social groups. In fact, Thorstein Veblen's theory of conspicuous consumption, which states that consumption is largely motivated by a desire to stand apart from other social groups, is based on the distinction between positive and negative reference groups.[2]

However, Veblen lived at the turn of the century when social class divisions in the United States were sharper. Today, purchasing based on dissociation from groups is not common. Advertisers rarely appeal to the negative desire to avoid or disclaim groups. Rather, they appeal to the positive desire to be part of a group. Even appeals to nonconformity are made on the positive note of being different from everyone else, not on the negative note of dissociating oneself from certain groups. Marketers, therefore, will tend to focus on positive reference groups.

Types of Membership Groups

Given the importance of positive reference groups, Figure 13–1 further breaks down membership and aspiration groups into specific types. In the middle of Figure 13–1, positive membership groups are classified by whether they are primary or secondary groups and whether they are informal or formal groups. If a person is in regular contact with certain individuals, such as family, friends, and business associates, then those individuals are a primary group. Shopping groups, political clubs, and fellow skiers or joggers constitute secondary groups. Primary groups are more important to the consumer in developing product beliefs, tastes, and preferences and are of more direct influence on purchasing behavior. As a result, they are more interesting to the marketer.

Groups can also be divided by whether they have a formal structure (a president, secretary, and treasurer) with specific roles (fund raising, teaching, transmitting information) or an informal structure. Informal groups have structures and roles, but they are implicit.

This classification produces four types of membership groups as defined in Figure 13–1. Primary informal groups are represented by the family and by peer groups. They are by far the most important groupings because of the frequency of contact and the closeness between the individual and group members. As a result, advertisers frequently portray product consumption among friends (e.g., the commercial for Lowenbrau — ''Here's to good friends, tonight is kind of special. . . .'') or within a family context (Mrs. Olsen comes with a cup of Folgers to rescue the wife whose husband turns his nose up at her regular coffee).

Primary formal groups are groups that the consumer frequently comes into contact with and that have a more formal structure than family or friends, such as, for example, school class groups assigned to a project or business groups working together on a daily basis. Advertisers may wish to portray membership in such groups as a means of winning product approval. For example, one TV commercial for a car depicted six business associates in a daily car pool squashed together in a compact car. One of them then purchased a roomier compact car and immediately won the gratitude of the group. The direct message was that compact cars can be roomy, but the indirect message was group acceptance.

Secondary informal groups are groups without a formal structure that meet infrequently. Examples are shopping groups that get together once a week or every two weeks and sports groups that get together on a seasonal basis. Such groups may directly influence purchases. One of the difficulties Prince Manufacturing had in introducing the oversized Prince tennis racket was overcoming the fear among some players that they would be subject to ridicule or accused of playing with an unfair advantage by their tennis peers.[3] As one tennis player wrote, "When the racquet came in, I was real eager to try it. Took some courage to walk out on the court, though. I mean people would say 'Hey Benton, where'd you get that mongoloid racquet?' Carrying it is an admission to people that you've got a problem with your game."[4] Besides being an example of the influence of secondary informal groups, Benton's experiences reflect the desire to conform to group norms out of fear of ridicule and group censure. (See Figure 13–2.)

Another example of the influence of secondary informal groups is a study of shopping groups by Granbois.[5] He found that when an individual shops in a group of three or more persons, there is twice as much chance the original purchase plans will not be fulfilled when compared to when the consumer shops alone. More purchases than originally planned will be made when shopping with others. The influence of "relevant others" influences the shopper to stray from his or her original plans.

Secondary formal groups are the least important to the consumer, and therefore to the marketer, since they meet infrequently, are structured, and are not closely knit. Examples include alumni groups, business clubs, and tenant organizations. Marketers of particular products may have some interest in these groups (travel agents, developers of executive programs) but marketers generally do not appeal to these groups.

Types of Aspiration Groups

At the bottom of Figure 13–1 aspiration groups are classified by whether contact with these groups is direct or indirect. Two types of aspiration groups, anticipatory and symbolic, are defined. **Anticipatory aspiration groups** are groups the individual anticipates joining at some future time and, in most cases, has direct contact with. The best example of this is a higher group in the organizational hierarchy that an individual wishes to join. This desire is based on the rewards that have been generally accepted to be most important in Western culture — power, status, prestige, and money. Marketers will appeal to the desire to enhance one's position by climbing to a higher aspiration group. Clothing and cosmetics are frequently advertised within the context of business

Berry's World

© 1976 by NEA Inc

"I know there's nothing illegal about that new racket of yours but don't you feel a wee bit guilty using it?"

FIGURE 13–2   Pressure to Conform from Secondary Groups
Reprinted by permission. © 1976 NEA, Inc.

success and prestige. Manufacturers of men's clothing and fragrances have traditionally used such themes. Women's products rely on appeals to organizational aspirations because of the increasing number of women in the work force. A good example of a direct appeal to aspiration group norms within the organization is the ad for Johnnie Walker Black Label featured in Figure 13–3. The appeal in this ad is toward the anticipation of eventually arriving at the top. The purchase of the product, therefore, represents an acceptance of aspirational group norms.

Symbolic aspiration groups are groups in which an individual is not likely to receive membership, despite the acceptance of the group's beliefs and

On the way up, the work may not get easier
but the rewards get better.

Johnnie Walker
Black Label Scotch
YEARS 12 OLD

12 YEAR OLD BLENDED SCOTCH WHISKY, 86.8 PROOF. BOTTLED IN SCOTLAND. IMPORTED BY SOMERSET IMPORTERS, LTD., N.Y.

FIGURE 13–3   An Appeal to Aspiration Group Norms
By permission of Somerset Importers, Ltd.

attitudes. Marketers appeal to symbolic aspirations by using experts to advertise certain products. Arthur Ashe's endorsement of the Head tennis racquet is an example. If the tennis buff identifies with certain players, these experts may be used to endorse products outside their field. Vitas Gerulaitis's endorsement of Brut (see Figure 13–4) is an example of an expert in one field who has become a spokesman for a product in another field.

FIGURE 13–4   Use of a Spokesperson to Represent a Symbolic Aspiration Group
Courtesy of Vitas Gerulaitis and by permission of Faberge, Inc.

THE NATURE OF REFERENCE GROUPS

Reference groups have certain characteristics that affect the nature of their influence on the consumer. Reference groups establish norms, roles, status, socialization, and power. Each of these characteristics is described below.

Norms

Norms are the rules and standards of conduct (generally undefined) established by the group. Group members are expected to conform to these norms, which may be established in relation to the appropriateness of clothes, eating habits, makes of cars, or brands of cosmetics. A few years back, for example, Rossignol skis became the norm among a number of ski clubs, and there was general conformity in ownership of this brand.

Roles

Roles are functions that the individual assumes or that are assigned to the individual by the group in the attainment of group objectives. In group purchasing behavior, specific roles can be identified in an attempt to select the best available brand or product category. The following roles have been identified in organizational buying behavior[6] and are equally relevant to family decision making: the influencer; the gatekeeper (the individual who has most control over the flow of information into the group); the decision maker; and the consumer. In organizational buyer behavior, these roles are formally specified; in family decision making, they are implicit.

Status

Status refers to the position the individual occupies within the group. High status implies greater power and influence. A chairman of the board has the highest status within an organization but may be the weakest member of a weekly bridge club. Symbols of dress or ownership are frequently associated with both high and low status. For example, the chairman's oak-paneled office symbolizes status, but so does the maintenance man's uniform.

Products are sometimes purchased to demonstrate status in a broader societal sense so that the message is one of wealth and implied superiority. The elegant dress and the expensive car may be status symbols, but in some groups symbolism operates in exact reversal to one's wealth and position. Jeans and small cars may be the norm among wealthy suburbanites. Large cars and more expensive clothes may be status symbols among lower socioeconomic groups.

Status can also operate on a product-specific basis. The expert skier may have status within the ski club and may be constantly asked advice on the purchase of equipment. This individual would be regarded as an opinion leader within the group, but in other contexts (tennis, travel, financial holdings) the individual may have little expertise and influence and therefore less status.

Socialization

The process by which the individual learns the norms and role expectations of the group is referred to as socialization. The individual moving from one job to another must learn the formal rules and expectations of the organization, but must also learn the informal rules and expectations from primary work groups.

Consumer socialization is the process by which consumers acquire the knowledge and skills necessary to operate in the marketplace. The two most important types of consumer socialization are the socialization of children and the socialization of new residents in a community.

Children learn the norms and values of the family and develop product preferences accordingly. The process of socialization is sometimes used as a basis for advertising appeals, especially in cases where product preferences can be maintained between generations. Johnson and Johnson used a theme depicting a bride getting ready for the ceremony and using Johnson and Johnson's baby powder to freshen up. The mother breaks into tears and says she used it on her as a baby.

Children's socialization is also receiving more attention because of television's impact. To some degree, television has replaced the family as a means of socialization, and children's commercials have received increasingly closer scrutiny as a result.[7]

Consumers must also go through a process of socialization when they move to a new community. The availability of unfamiliar brands and store outlets must be learned as well as the brand preferences of the neighborhood peer group. A study by Sheth of foreign students found a process of socialization to be taking place since many of the students were buying the same brands as their friends who had been in this country for a longer period.[8]

Power

The degree of influence that a group has on an individual is closely related to the power of the group. Various sources of group influence have been identified,[9] but three are particularly relevant for marketing strategy: expert power, referent power, and reward power.

Expert Power

Expert power relies on the expertise of the individual or group based on experience and knowledge. A friend's purchase recommendation may be accepted if the friend is regarded as more knowledgeable or experienced with the product. A sales representative may also be regarded as an expert source as long as the salesperson has established credibility with the consumer.

Figure 13–5 shows an example of one advertiser's use of expert power. Rafer Johnson, an Olympic decathlon champion, is endorsing sports equipment made by AMF by extolling the virtues of exercise. His expertise is accepted in his answers to questions about exercise. These are questions that any consumer considering a strenuous sport may ask.

Advertisers also create their own experts. General Motors has established Mr. Goodwrench as an expert in car maintenance. Betty Crocker was created by General Mills in 1921 and has become "a sort of 'First Lady of Food,' the most highly esteemed home service authority in the nation."[10] Folgers is trying to establish the same level of expertise with Mrs. Olsen as the Betty Crocker of coffee.

"Each time you exercise, you come back stronger. Before long, you flat-out get tough. Both mentally and physically."

Rafer Johnson

(Today, 1960 Decathlon Olympic Gold Medal winner Rafer Johnson is still on the run. As V.P. of Community Relations for Continental Telephone, he travels 42 states. As a concerned citizen, he is deeply involved with the President's Council on Physical Fitness in a nationwide track and field program for youngsters, as well as with the Special Olympics for the Retarded.)

Q. The old sound mind in a sound body idea?

A. It's true. You really can work better with your head when your body is in better shape. Physical and mental pressures are a part of life. But if you stay fit, you can deal with them better. You'll have the stamina you need to stand the strain.

Q. What if I'm too tired to exercise?

A. You're not that tired. Often, that's just your mind talking. You wouldn't cancel an important meeting just because you felt a bit tired. So don't cancel that hour or so of recreation. Just don't do as much as on the days you feel fresh. But do something. You'll be surprised how less tired you feel.

Q. You're into the racket sports. Any special reason?

A. They're basically running sports. And with my background I feel a running program is best for me. So I sprint, and play racquetball and tennis. When you move on those courts, it's amazing how much running you get. Quick starts, direction changes, jumping— you're using all your running muscles.

Q. What fitness program is best?

A. It depends. An ex-athlete should go at it differently than a businessman or woman. I'd say start out easy. Test yourself. Find your own level. Pick a game or sport you really like, then do it regularly. That's the secret— regularity.

Q. What about age?

A. Whether you're five or twenty-five or seventy-five, it doesn't matter. The idea is to be where you want to be. Not where someone else is or says you should be. Just try to be in the best shape you can on any given day. It's that simple— whether you're going for the Gold Medal or just trying to live a healthy life.

Another message brought to you by AMF. We make **American Athletic** Gymnastics Equipment; **Whitely** Physical Fitness Products; **Voit** Sporting Goods; **Harley-Davidson** Motorcycles and Golf Cars; **Roadmaster** Bicycles and Mopeds; **Crestliner** and **Slickcraft** Boats; **Hatteras** Yachts; **Alcort** Sunfish Sailboats; **Mares** Swim Products; **AMF** Bowling Products; **Ben Hogan** Golf Equipment; **Tyrolia** Ski Bindings; **Head** Skis, Tennis Rackets and **Head** Sports Wear.

AMF
We make weekends

FIGURE 13–5   An Example of Expert Power

By permission of Benton & Bowles, Inc.

Referent Power

The basis for **referent power** is the identification of the individual with members of the group. The greater the similarity of the individual's beliefs and attitudes with those of group members, the greater the referent power of the group. The individual desires to be associated with the group because of common interests.

Advertisers frequently rely on referent power by using a "typical consumer" approach in their advertising. Such an appeal demonstrates to the consumer that other customers have similar needs and offers a solution to these needs. The advertisement in Figure 13–6 is an example of this. The individual pictured is a typical consumer in a typical situation, experiencing the anxiety of meeting a deadline. She serves as a spokesperson for Extra Strength Tylenol by stating that it gives her relief from headaches. An individual in a similar situation could easily identify with the ad and the solution.

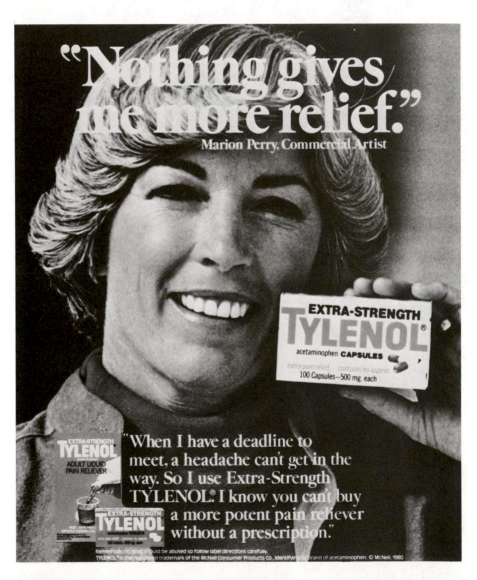

FIGURE 13–6 An Example of Referent Power: The "Typical Consumer" Approach

By permission of McNeil Consumer Products Company.

Another basis for using referent power is to encourage the consumer to identify with an individual that he or she would like to be similar to. The advertisement using Vitas Gerulaitis for Brut (Figure 13–4) is an example of an aspiration referent, whereas the typical consumer in Figure 13–6 is an example of a membership referent. In the first case, the individual would like to be similar to the referent; in the second case, the consumer actually considers himself or herself similar.

Reward Power

Reward power is based on the ability of the group to reward the individual. The business organization can reward the individual with money and status. The family can reward the child with praise and approval. Social groups can also provide rewards in purchasing behavior. Compliments on one's clothes or looks provided by a relevant other reinforces the consumer's choice.

Marketers have used reward power by depicting social approval in advertising. Praise for a good cup of coffee, a shiny floor, glorious hair, good sherry, and a quiet and comfortable ride are all examples of advertising's simulation of social approval. In each case, an individual that is important to the consumer (husband, wife, neighbor, friend, business associate) has expressed approval of the consumer's choice. The Johnny Walker ad in Figure 13–3 also shows reward power by associating the product with societal rewards for achievement.

Groups that have reward power also may have **coercive power** over the individual. The group "giveth and taketh away." The greater the importance of the group, the greater its power to express disapproval and even censure. Marketers have depicted such coercive power through the use of fear appeals. For example, the fear of social disapproval due to loose dentures is brought out by Poligrip; the fear of group ostracism due to body odor is demonstrated by Dial. In each case, however, use of the product changes disapproval to approval demonstrating the fact that coercive power and reward power are linked.

REFERENCE GROUP INFLUENCES ON THE CONSUMER

The discussion about power and influence suggests that groups influence consumer choice in three ways.[11] First, groups supply the consumer with information. The testimonial of an expert or the experiences of a friend are informative communications. In addition, the visible consumption of certain products (cars, appliances, clothes, etc.) provide consumers with information as to what brands and products are most popular in the group.

Second, reference groups are a **comparative influence** in permitting a comparison of the individual's beliefs, attitudes, and behavior to that of the group. As referents, groups provide the consumer with the basis for evaluating one's self-image. In fact, one way to define self-image is by how we think others see us.

Third, reference groups are a **normative influence** in that they directly influence attitudes and behavior based on group norms and thus encourage compliance with these norms.

TABLE 13–1   Types of Influence Exerted by Reference Groups

Nature of Influence	Objectives	Perceived Characteristics of Source	Type of Power	Behavior
Informational	Knowledge	Credibility	Expert	Acceptance
Comparative	Self-Maintenance and Enrichment	Similarity	Referent	Identification
Normative	Reward	Power	Reward or Coercion	Conformity

Source: Adapted from Robert E. Burnkrant and Alain Cousineau, "Informational and Normative Social Influence in Buyer Behavior," *Journal of Consumer Research* 2 (December, 1975): 207.

Reprinted with permission from the *Journal of Consumer Research.*

These three functions closely parallel the expert (informative), referent (comparative), and reward (normative) powers of groups. Table 13–1 shows each type of influence within the context of consumer behavior by citing the type of influence exerted on the consumer, the benefits to the consumer, and the effects on behavior.[12]

Informational Influence

A consumer will accept information from a source if the consumer believes the information will enhance knowledge about product choices.[13] A consumer may visit an automobile showroom to test drive a car and obtain information about features and specifications from the salesperson. The consumer will accept the salesperson's information if the salesperson is regarded as a credible source. Credibility also implies that the salesperson is regarded as an expert. The result is that the consumer accepts the source of influence.

Table 13–1 illustrates this process by citing the nature of influence as informational, the consumer's objective as obtaining knowledge, the condition for accepting information as credibility, the source of power as expertise, and the final behavior as acceptance of influence. Table 13–2 lists various types of statements that illustrate informational, comparative, and normative influences. The statements were used in a study by Park and Lessig to determine the relative importance of these three influences in the selection of twenty products.[14] Statements 1–5 all reflect an objective of seeking information from expert sources or friends and neighbors with reliable information. In addition, observation (statement 5) is regarded as an important source of information.

Most of the evidence in marketing studies suggests that informational influences come primarily from personal rather than commercial sources. Consumers tend to rely on friends, neighbors, and family members more than on advertisers or salespersons in obtaining product information. Personal sources seem to be more credible than commercial sources. A study by Robertson found that personal sources of information were much more important than commercial sources in purchasing small appliances and were somewhat more important in purchasing food items.[15] This study suggests that expert power may be based

Informational Influence

1. The individual seeks information about various brands of the product from an association of professionals or independent group of experts.

2. The individual seeks information from those who work with the product as a profession.

3. The individual seeks brand-related knowledge and experience (such as how Brand A's performance compares to Brand B's) from those friends, neighbors, relatives, or work associates who have reliable information about the brands.

4. The brand which the individual selects is influenced by observing a seal of approval of an independent testing agency (such as *Good Housekeeping*'s).

5. The individual's observation of what experts do influences his or her choice of a brand (such as observing the type of car which police drive or the brand of TV which repair people buy).

Comparative Influence

6. The individual feels that the purchase or use of a particular brand will enhance the image which others have of him or her.

7. The individual feels that the purchase of a particular brand helps show others what he or she is, or would like to be (such as an athlete, successful business person, etc.)

8. The individual feels that those who purchase or use a particular brand possess the characteristics which he or she would like to have.

9. The individual sometimes feels that it would be nice to be like the type of person which advertisements show using a particular brand.

Normative Influence

10. The individual's decision to purchase a particular brand is influenced by the preferences of people with whom he or she has social interaction.

11. The individual's decision to purchase a particular brand is influenced by the preferences of family members.

12. The desire to satisfy the expectations which others have of him or her has an impact on the individual's brand choice.

Source: Adapted from C. Whan Park and V. Parker Lessig, "Students and Housewives: Differences in Susceptibility to Reference Group Influence," *Journal of Consumer Research* 4 (September, 1977): 105.
Reprinted with permission from the *Journal of Consumer Research.*

---

on usage and experience by friends and neighbors as well as on professional expertise.

Personal sources of information also play an important part in organizational buyer behavior. Two separate studies found that personal contacts with peers were a primary source of information and influence in new product adoptions.[16]

Comparative Influence

Consumers constantly compare their attitudes with those of members of important groups. In so doing, consumers seek to support their own attitudes and behavior by associating themselves with groups with which they agree and by dissociating themselves from groups with which they disagree. As a result, the basis for comparative influence is in the process of comparing oneself to other members of the group and of judging whether the group would be supportive.

For example, assume a family moves into a new home and meets various neighbors. The parents compare neighbors' attitudes toward political issues, education, and child rearing with their own. They also identify brands and products purchased by the neighbors. A new resident will naturally be attracted to individuals similar to themselves because they tend to enhance his or her self-concept. But a new resident may also seek to join neighborhood groupings whose attitudes and behavior differ if the individual admires these groups. In both cases a process of comparison and identification with group attitudes and behavior is taking place.

Table 13–1 cites the nature of this process as comparative influence. The individual's objective is to enhance the self-concept by associating with groups that will provide reinforcement and ego gratification. The source of power is referent power, and the individual's behavior toward the group is one of identification. Table 13–2 shows that the types of conditions relating to comparative influence deal with the enhancement of one's self-image (statements 6 and 7) or identification with other people that are liked and admired (statements 8 and 9). Thus, the ad for AMF using Rafer Johnson is an example of informational influence because of the demonstrated expertise, but the ad for Brut using Vitas Gerulaitis is an example of comparative influence because the ad will be effective with those consumers who admire and identify with Gerulaitis.

Comparative influence implies that those being influenced should have characteristics similar to those doing the influencing. This notion has been investigated in customer-salesperson interactions. Several studies have found that when a customer sees the salesperson as similar in terms of tastes, attitudes, and even religion, the salesperson is likely to be more effective.[17]

Few studies have compared the characteristics of influencers and influencees when they are friends and neighbors. One of the exceptions is a study by Moschis of female users of cosmetics.[18] He found that consumers are more likely to seek information from friends whom they view as similar to themselves and to regard such sources as credible. Thus, credibility can be the result of perceived expertise of the source of information or the result of perceived similarity to the source. Moschis concludes that advertising should not just rely on experts but should try to use spokespersons that consumers perceive as being similar to themselves (i.e., use a "typical consumer" approach).

A number of other studies have shown that influencers and influencees tend to live close to each other.[19] One study of elderly residents found that 81 percent of the exchange of information and advice about a new product occurred between persons who live on the same floor.[20] Given this proximity, it is a safe assumption that patterns of influence are comparative since residents are likely to live near those who provide support and self-enhancement.

Normative Influence

Normative influence refers to the influence exerted by a group to conform to their norms and expectations. According to Park and Lessig, a consumer is motivated to conform to the norms and behavior of the group if (1) the group provides significant rewards for compliance and punishment for lack of compliance; and (2) the individual's behavior in conforming is visible to members of the group.[21]

Visibility is essential in exerting normative influence. If the action is not visible to group members, then the group cannot exert normative influence. A group can exert normative influence in the purchase of clothes, furniture, and appliances because these items are visible. Normative influence may also occur for items like mouthwash and denture adhesive, even though the items themselves are not visible, because of fear that lack of use may be visible (bad breath, loose dentures). Normative influence is unlikely to occur for products like paper towels or canned vegetables because of lack of visibility, but informational group influence could occur for these items. Visibility is not as important in exerting informational and evaluative influence because, in these cases, the objective is not conformity but knowledge and self-enhancement. The consumer could obtain information from the group and gain satisfaction in identifying with the group without any overt action.

The importance of visibility was demonstrated in a study of air conditioners in a Philadelphia suburb when they first began to be purchased on a widespread basis in the late 1940s.[22] The pattern of ownership could easily be traced because of visibility of air conditioners. Research indicated the direct influence of friends and neighbors in purchasing the product, but the most apparent influence was *seeing* an air conditioner in a neighbor's window.

Table 13–1 cites normative influence as being based on the desire to receive the rewards of the group and to avoid group censure. The basis for power is reward or coercive power; the resulting behavior toward the group is conformity and compliance. Table 13–2 indicates that conditions reflecting normative influence deal with a desire to conform to group preferences (statements 10 and 11), and to satisfy the expectations of group members (statement 12).

Conformity in Consumer Behavior

Conformity to group norms means that consumers will imitate the behavior of the group and buy the brands and product categories of the group leader. Marketers are interested in such imitative behavior because it implies a snowball effect once products are accepted by the most influential members of a group. The idea of "keeping up with the Joneses" reflects imitative behavior.

Various studies have confirmed that individuals do imitate group behavior. These studies have been largely experimental in nature and have been inspired by social psychology studies demonstrating an individual conforming to group norms. One of the most famous of these experiments brought groups of seven to nine college students together to judge the length of lines drawn on a card.[23] All but one group member were instructed to give the same incorrect response. The subject who was not aware of the experiment was confronted with the obviously incorrect choice of a unanimous group. Yet in 37 percent of the cases, the unaware subject went along with the group, even though the choice appeared to be going against his or her senses.

In another experiment, three identical men's suits labeled "A," "B," and "C" were described to respondents as being of different quality and manufacture.[24] Three of four students in each group were told to pick suit B. In the majority of cases the fourth student then picked suit B. But when pressure was put on the individual to go along with the other three, the chances of conforming went down. Students were reacting negatively to such pressure. This situation, known as **reactance,** suggests that consumers will only conform to group pressures up to a certain point. When group pressures become too intense, the consumer will reject group norms and demonstrate independent behavior.

Hansen questioned these studies as a demonstration of the importance of conformity in influencing consumers on the grounds that they were experimental.[25] He sought to determine whether consumers do imitate the group in a realistic setting. He determined friendship links between first-year secretarial students and identified nineteen groups in this way. He also identified the leaders in each group. Preferences and frequency of use were determined for ten products and fourteen brands in a first interview and then eight months later. Since these were newly formed groups, conformity would be demonstrated if brand preferences became more similar over time. No such effect was found. Contrary to previous experiments, consumers were not imitating the behavior of others in the group.

Hansen concluded that conformity may be overrated as an influence on consumer behavior. He did not rule out the importance of personal influence on consumers. Rather, he felt that informational influence may outweigh normative influence in affecting behavior.

Conformity by Product and Brand

Even though there are limits to the degree of pressure a group can exert on an individual consumer, it is likely that such pressure may be greater for certain types of products than for others. Bourne examined a number of studies of reference group influence and found that pressures to conform to group norms were more likely for visible brands and products.[26] Pressures to conform could influence the purchase of a product, the purchase of a brand, or both. As a result, Bourne developed the typology of reference group influences on product and/or brand in Figure 13–7. The upper right quadrant means that groups influence the purchase of the product and the selection of a brand within the product category. The upper left represents group influence on brand only, the lower right represents group influence on product only, and the lower left represents no group influence on either product or brand selection.

1. *Influences on product and brand.* Bourne found that cars, cigarettes, beer, and drugs were subject to group pressures for both the product and brand decision. The frequency of purchase of a new car, as well as the type of car purchased, is subject to the norms of the community. Certain groups are more likely to condone smoking than others. Moreover, if smoking is the norm, the group is likely to express a preference for a certain brand. In the case of beer, the purchase of premium or regular, as well as the brand, will be subject to group norms.

2. *Influence on brand only.* Reference groups are also likely to influence the purchase of brands but not the purchase of the product itself. It is obvious that items like clothing, furniture, magazines, refrigerators, and toilet soap are not subject to group influence since they are used by almost everyone. But brands within these categories may be representative of group norms. In particular, clothing, magazines,

REFERENCE
GROUP
INFLUENCES
BY BRAND

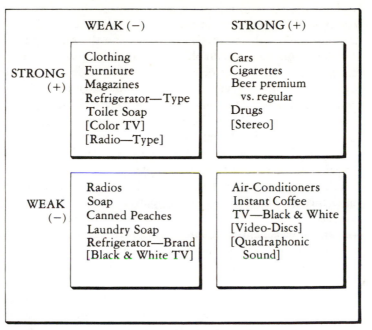

FIGURE 13-7   Reference Group Influences by Product and Brand

Source: Adapted from Francis S. Bourne, "Group Influence in Marketing and Public Relations," in Rensis Likert and Samuel P. Hayes Jr., eds., *Some Applications of Behavioral Research* (Paris: UNESCO, 1957). © Unesco 1957. Reproduced by permission of Unesco.

Note: Products in brackets were included by the author to show more current positionings. For example, Bourne writing in 1957 put black and white TV in the product (+) brand (−) quadrant. Today, it might more appropriately belong in the product (−) brand (−) quadrant.

and furniture represent highly visible product categories subject to group preferences. One group may emphasize designer clothes, another leisure wear; one group may establish reading of high brow magazines as the norm, another reading of gossip sheets.

3. *Influence on product only.*   Certain product categories may be so distinctive that ownership in itself may be representative of group norms. Bourne placed air conditioners, black and white TV, and instant coffee in this category because he was reporting on studies done in the late forties. Today, these three categories have achieved widespread acceptance, and their use or ownership is no longer subject to group pressures.

4. *No group influence.*   The last category in Bourne's typology represents products that are not subject to group influence. Bourne cites products such as kitchen soap, canned peaches, and radios since neither the product nor brand are socially visible. In such cases, consumers decide based on the product's attributes rather than on group influence. The strength, sudsiness, or bleaching power of a laundry detergent is more likely to influence choice than the comments of a neighbor.

The Social Multiplier Effect

Today, Bourne's typology of products is outdated. The products in brackets in Figure 13-7 represent Bourne's typology updated. Black and white TV sets now may be more appropriately placed in a category of no group influence.

Color TVs can be placed in a category of brand influence since ownership is widespread, but a group could also influence the purchase of a brand. Stereo equipment can be placed in the category of product and brand influence since a group could influence both ownership and the brand purchased.

Video discs and quadraphonic sound can be placed in the product influence category because they are new and distinctive, and ownership may be influenced by group norms. As video disc is introduced into the American market, a demonstration principle may begin to operate. First formulated by an economist, James Duesenberry,[27] the **demonstration principle** states that with the increased mobility and purchasing power of the American consumer, consumers will come into increasing contact with new products and will have the purchasing power to buy them. Once one family buys a video disc, friends and neighbors will come into contact with the product. Since they are likely to have the same level of purchasing power, they will buy. In turn, other individuals will come into contact with the recently acquired product and the pattern of ownership will spread within the group and to other groups. This demonstration effect is referred to as a **social multiplier effect** because ownership increases in multiples as a function of group influence and product visibility.

The social multiplier effect illustrates the volatility of group influence in the American economy. Certain brands or product categories may be highly visible today and representative of group norms; but, five or ten years from now such influence may become minimal.

Information, Comparison, or Conformity?

Is group influence on consumer purchasing behavior due primarily to the information supplied by groups, the identification with groups, or the pressure that groups bring to bear on individuals? The obvious answer is that all three components influence the consumer. But the type of influence that is most important may be a function of the type of product being evaluated.

Influence by Product Type

Park and Lessig measured the relative effects of informational, comparative, and normative influence in the purchase of twenty products.[28] A sample of college students was asked to rate the twenty products by the statements listed in Table 13–2. The results showed that the following products were most subject to the three types of influences:

Informational	*Comparative*	*Normative*
1. Color TV	1. Automobiles	1. Automobiles
2. Automobiles	2. Clothing	2. Clothing
3. Physician services	3. Furniture	3. Beer
4. Insurance	4. Color TV	4. Physician services
5. Beer		5. Color TV
6. Air conditioners		6. Coffee
7. Headache remedies		7. Furniture

It appears that the types of products most likely to be subject to informational influences are products that are technologically complex (autos, color TVs, air conditioners) or products requiring objective informational criteria for selection (insurance, physicians, headache remedies). The fact that beer is subject to informational influence seems to be a function of the importance of the product to a sample of college students.

The three products most subject to comparative influence — autos, clothing, and furniture — are a means of self-expression. Therefore, it is logical that they would be regarded as means for group identification and support.

Automobiles and clothing are also subject to normative influences. This suggests that college students view these products as a basis for conforming to group norms. Beer as a means of normative compliance again appears to be a function of a college sample.

The study also found that ratings of informational influence were higher than ratings of the other influences for ten of the twenty products studied. Ratings of the comparative function were lowest across product categories. This implies that the informational component of group influences outweighs the need to rely on groups for identification and reward.

Is Information the Most Important Component?

The answer to this question is probably yes, although the evidence is conflicting. Consumers may well use groups more for the information supplied than as a means of identification and reward.

Hansen felt that many of the studies purporting to find conformity to group norms may actually represent the processing of information supplied by groups.[29] If a consumer tends to buy the products and brands purchased by the group, this can be interpreted in two ways: One, the consumer is conforming to the norms of the group; or two, given the uniformity of purchasing behavior within the group, the consumer assumes the popular brand is in fact highest in quality and buys it. The latter case does not represent conformity; it represents action based on credible information.

Burnkrant and Cousineau support the notion that groups are more important in supplying information than in influencing compliance to group norms.[30] They asked individuals to rate a new brand of instant coffee under two sets of conditions: (1) group consensus regarding the brand evaluation versus no consensus, and (2) evaluations that were visible to group members versus private evaluations. They found that a group's consensus was more important than visibility in influencing coffee evaluations. It was not the pressure to conformity but the belief in the credibility of information provided by peers that most influenced ratings of the coffee brand. The importance of groups as sources of information rather than of conformity is also supported in the study by Moschis.[31] He found that consumers seek information from individuals similar to themselves not because of compliance but because of identification and knowledge.

These findings suggest that marketers should place more emphasis on the group as a source of information than as a source of compliance. Ads should picture typical consumers citing their experiences and providing information on relevant product attributes. Rather than picturing a woman marveling at a sparkling floor (compliance to group norms of cleanliness), it may be more relevant to have the woman transmit information on a new and improved version of the same product. Such an approach shifts the emphasis from conformity to information. Moreover, ads utilizing the typical consumer may be more effective than ads utilizing the expert. It may be easier for the consumer to identify with other consumers and accept their judgments, even if the ad is sponsored by the manufacturer. The increasing use of typical consumers who are presumably unaware they are being filmed is an example.

Group Influence Versus Product Evaluation

Given the importance of group influence as a source of information, does group influence supplant objective product evaluation? That is, do many consumers say, "Since most of my friends use it, I may as well use it because it must be good," and as a result forego a process of brand evaluation? In may cases, yes — reference group influence is a substitute for brand evaluation. This may be especially true in cases where there is a low level of involvement with the product category; it may not be worth the time and energy to evaluate alternative brands. If this is so, then it would contradict traditional group theories that say groups are most likely to influence the purchase of meaningful products. The use of groups as a means to short-circuit the necessity for brand evaluation means that groups may be more influential in the purchase of relatively unimportant products.

There is some support for the idea that in supplying information, groups eliminate the need for brand evaluation. Moschis concluded that reliance on peers for information results in "consumers often choos[ing] products without evaluating them on the basis of objective attributes."[32] In addition, Bourne studied the relative influence of groups versus objective product evaluations and consistently found that group influence outweighs the consumer's evaluation of a product's attributes.[33]

SUMMARY

This chapter focuses on reference group influences on consumer behavior. Reference groups can be classified into membership groups and aspiration groups. Membership groups can further be classified into formal and informal groups, and primary and secondary groups. By far the most influential groups are informal primary groups, represented by family and peer groups. Aspiration groups can also be divided into groups that the consumer anticipates membership in (anticipatory groups) and groups that the consumer admires at a distance (symbolic groups).

These group designations are important since advertisers frequently portray group influences directly (e.g., one friend influencing the other) or employ spokespersons to influence consumer aspirations.

Reference groups serve a number of important functions. They provide norms of conduct, assign roles within the group to individuals, designate status positions within the group, and are a vehicle for consumer socialization. The influence of the group on the individual can be measured in terms of the power of the group. Three types of power are most relevant for marketers: expert power (as demonstrated by the use of expert spokespersons in ads); referent power (as demonstrated by a typical consumer approach); and reward power (as demonstrated by social approval or rejection based on product usage in ads).

Reference groups can also be viewed as influencing consumers by the nature of these three types of influences. Groups exert informational (expert) influence, comparative (referent) influence, and normative (reward) influence. Informational influence depends on the credibility of the source of information, comparative influence on the degree of similarity between the consumer and influencer, and normative influence on the levels of reward or punishment meted out by the group.

Normative influence has been emphasized most by marketers since it results in conformity to group norms. Conformity is most likely when products are visible and related to group norms. Such conformity may produce a social multiplier effect — one consumer buys a product; others come into contact with the consumer and are influenced to buy resulting in a spread of ownership throughout the group and, eventually, to other groups.

The chapter suggests that marketers may be placing too much emphasis on normative influence at the expense of emphasis on informational influence. Frequently, groups are used as sources of information rather than influence. Reliance on the experiences of the group is a good way to reduce purchase risk.

The next chapter will consider the most important face-to-face group, the family.

QUESTIONS

1. When would it be more relevant to use an aspiration referent in advertising versus a membership referent?

2. What types of products are more likely to be influenced by anticipatory versus symbolic aspiration groups?

3. The Tylenol ad (Figure 13–6) used referent power. Why?

4. For what types of products are personal sources of information likely to be more important than commercial sources?

5. Given the fact that shopping in groups tends to increase the number of purchases what strategies may a retailer use to encourage group shopping?

6. Both the ads for AMF and Brut use spokespersons. The ad for AMF portraying Rafer Johnson is based on informational influence. The ad for Brut using Vitas Gerulaitis is based on comparative (evaluative) influence.
   - Why did both advertisers for these two different products use spokespersons?
   - Why is one based on informational influence and the other on comparative influence?

7. Over time, product categories may move from one box to another in Bourne's classification of group influence (see Figure 13–7).
   - Can you trace such movement for several product categories?

8. Was the social multiplier effect more prevalent in American society at the turn of the century or today? Why?
   What is the distinction between the social multiplier effect and the theory of conspicuous consumption?

9. This chapter suggests that there may be too much emphasis on normative group influences in advertising.

   • Under what conditions may advertisers be better advised to portray informational rather than normative group influence?

RESEARCH ASSIGNMENTS

Ask a group of students to evaluate four identical unlabeled cans of soda. Four students should do the evaluation at the same time. Three students acting as "ringers" will be asked to state a preference for the same can of soda. The fourth student will be an actual respondent. Conduct about twenty such tests so there are twenty actual respondents. In one-half of the cases the ringers should express a preference in a low-keyed manner. In the other half of the cases, they should be adamant about their preference (e.g., "Wow, this soda is much better"). One should expect that on a random basis, the fourth student would agree with the other three 25 percent of the time.

• Is the proportion who conform significantly greater than the 25 percent chance expectation?

• Is there a difference in acceptance between those who were subjected to a low-keyed preference versus those who were subjected to a more definite preference?

• Once the taste test is completed, ask the actual respondents to rate themselves on (1) self-confidence, and (2) predisposition to take risk (see new brand tryers in Table 10–1). Do those who conformed differ from those who did not on these two characteristics?

NOTES

1. Leon G. Schiffman and Leslie L. Kanuk, *Consumer Behavior* (Englewood Cliffs, N.J.: Prentice-Hall, Inc., 1978), p. 214.
2. Thorstein Veblen, *The Theory of the Leisure Class* (New York: Macmillan, 1899).
3. M. Wayne DeLozier, *Consumer Behavior Dynamics. A Casebook* (Columbus, Ohio: Charles E. Merrill Publishing Co., 1977), Prince Tennis Racquet Case, pp. 146–161.
4. Ibid., pp. 150–151.
5. Donald H. Granbois, "Improving the Study of Customer In-Store Behavior," *Journal of Marketing* 32 (October 1968): 28–33.
6. Frederick E. Webster, Jr. and Yoram Wind, *Organizational Buying Behavior* (Englewood Cliffs, N.J.: Prentice-Hall, Inc., 1972), pp. 78–80.
7. For example see: *FTC Staff Report on Television Advertising to Children* (Washington, D.C.: Federal Trade Commission, 1978); M. Goldberg and G. Gorn, "Some Unintended Consequences of TV Advertising to Children," *Journal of Consumer Research* 5 (June 1978): 22–29; National Science Foundation, *Research on the Effects of Television Advertising on Children* (Washington, D.C.: U.S. Government Printing Office, 1977).
8. Jagdish N. Sheth, "How Adults Learn Brand

Preference," *Journal of Advertising Research* 8 (September 1968): 25–36.

9. John R. French and Bertram Raven, "The Bases of Social Power," in D. Cartwright, ed., *Studies in Social Power* (Ann Arbor, Mich.: Institute for Social Research, 1959), pp. 150–167.

10. Julian L. Watkins, *The 100 Greatest Advertisements* (New York: Dover Publications, Inc., 1959), p. 205.

11. H.C. Kelman, "Processes of Opinion Change," *Public Opinion Quarterly* 25 (Spring 1961): 57–78.

12. Robert E. Burnkrant and Alain Cousineau, "Informational and Normative Social Influence in Buyer Behavior," *Journal of Consumer Research,* 2 (December 1975): 206–215.

13. Ibid., p. 207.

14. C. Whan Park and V. Parker Lessig, "Students and Housewives: Differences in Susceptibility to Reference Group Influence," *Journal of Consumer Research* 4 (September 1977):102–110.

15. Thomas S. Robertson, *Innovative Behavior and Communications* (New York: Holt, Rinehart and Winston, Inc., 1971).

16. Frederick E. Webster, Jr., "Informal Communication in Industrial Markets," *Journal of Marketing Research* 7 (May 1970):186–189; and John A. Martilla, "Word-of-Mouth Communication in the Industrial Adoption Process," *Journal of Marketing Research* 8 (May 1971):173–178.

17. F.B. Evans, "Selling as a Dyadic Relationship - A New Approach," *American Behavioral Scientist* 6 (May 1963):76–79; and Timothy C. Brock, "Communicator-Recipient Similarity and Decision Change," *Journal of Personality and Social Psychology* 1 (June 1965):650–654.

18. George P. Moschis, "Social Comparisons and Informal Group Influence," *Journal of Marketing Research* 13 (August 1976):237–244.

19. See William H. Whyte, "The Web of Word of Mouth," *Fortune* (November 1954): 140–143;

and Sidney P. Feldman, "Some Dyadic Relationships Associated with Consumer Choice," in Raymond M. Haas, ed., *Proceedings of the American Marketing Association,* Series No. 24 (1966), pp. 758–775.

20. Leon G. Schiffman, "Social Interaction Patterns of the Elderly Consumer," in Boris W. Becker and Helmut Becker, eds., *Combined Proceedings of the American Marketing Association,* Series No. 34 (1972), p. 451.

21. Park and Lessig, "Students and Housewives."

22. Whyte, "The Web of Word of Mouth."

23. S.E. Asch, "Effects of Group Pressure Upon the Modification and Distortion of Judgments," in Harold Geutzkow, ed., *Groups, Leadership and Men* (Pittsburgh, Pa.: Carnegie Press, 1951).

24. M. Venkatesan, "Experimental Study of Consumer Behavior Conformity and Independence," *Journal of Marketing Research* 3 (November 1966):384–387.

25. Flemming Hansen, "Primary Group Influence and Consumer Conformity," in Philip R. McDonald, ed., *Proceedings of the American Marketing Association's Educators Conference,* Series No. 30 (1969), pp. 300–305.

26. Francis S. Bourne, "Group Influence in Marketing and Public Relations," in Rensis Likert and Samuel P. Hayes, Jr., eds., *Some Applications of Behavioral Research* (Paris: UNESCO, 1957).

27. James Duesenberry, *Income, Savings and the Theory of Consumer Behavior* (Cambridge, Mass.: Harvard University Press, 1949).

28. Park and Lessig, "Students and Housewives."

29. Hansen, "Primary Group Influence and Consumer Conformity."

30. Burnkrant and Cousineau, "Informational and Normative Social Influence."

31. Moschis, "Social Comparisons."

32. Ibid., p. 240.

33. Bourne, "Group Influence."

FOURTEEN

Family Decision Making

Focus of Chapter

Reference groups may not only influence consumers, they may also be the decision-making unit. Many purchasing decisions involve more than one person. In particular, the family is frequently involved in joint decision making. Parts One and Two of this book have been devoted almost exclusively to the individual consumer. But the realization that many purchasing decisions are made jointly by several members of a family suggests that it may be equally relevant to refer to a family decision unit as well as to the individual consumer.

This chapter will focus on joint decision making within the family. Though consumers may be involved in other decision-making units, by far, the most important and most frequent joint decisions made by consumers occur within the family setting. In the first part of this chapter a model of family decision making will be described. The relative influence of the husband and wife will be considered next. Last but not least, the child's influence on the parents and the parent-child interaction in the purchasing process will be looked at.

THE NATURE OF FAMILY DECISION MAKING

Since family decision making involves more than one person, several factors that were not considered when the focus was on the individual consumer become important. One factor involves the different roles family members play in the decision-making process. Another concerns the conditions in which a decision is likely to be made individually or by several family members. The necessity to resolve conflicts when family members have different goals and brand evaluations is a third consideration. Each of these factors is considered below.

Roles in Family Decision Making

Family members play a variety of roles in decision making. There are five roles that could be played by one or more members of the family:

1. *The information gatherer:* The individual who has the greatest expertise in the particular decision area and is most knowledgeable regarding the decision criteria. The information gatherer will be more aware of appropriate sources for additional information search.

2. *The influencer:* The person most likely to influence the manner in which alternative brands are evaluated. This means that the influencer will establish the decision criteria by which brands are compared and will be instrumental in deciding which brands most closely conform to the decision criteria. The influencer may be the same as the information gatherer, but not necessarily.

3. *The decision-maker:* The individual who makes the final decision. Again, this could be the same person as the information gatherer and influencer, but not necessarily.

4. *The purchasing agent:* The family member who actually purchases the product. The purchasing agent may or may not have discretion regarding the brand to buy. This decision may have already been made. The purchasing agent may only have discretion regarding the store. When an in-store decision is made, the purchasing agent and decision maker are the same.

5. *The consumer:* The user of the product. This could mean the whole family or an individual member.

From the marketer's standpoint one of the most important distinctions is that between the purchaser and consumer. Many strategic decisions are made without recognizing this important distinction. In many cases, the purchasing agent may be relatively inconsequential since the consumer is making the postpurchase evaluation and will decide on future brand purchases. In other cases, the purchaser may decide the brand for others in the family. Coulson believes that the "purchasing agent has the strategic role in the brand decision."[1] He cites a study by McCall's magazine that found almost one-third of beer consumers delegated the brand decision to the purchasing agent (in most cases the wife), and that the purchasing agent was aware of the consumer's beer preferences 90 percent of the time. These findings suggest that beer advertising should be partially directed to the wife.

A more recent study by Haley and Overholzer found that wives were twice as likely as husbands to be both decision maker and purchasing agent for a wide variety of food and toiletry items.[2] Wives were more influential not only in determining when to buy, but what brands to buy. Wives were also more influential in purchasing small appliances and carpeting, and were the prime information gatherers for these products. The only exceptions to the more dominant role of the wife in family decision making involved liquor and automobile purchases where the pattern was reversed.

Family Roles by Stage in Decision Making

In Figure 14–1 family roles are compared to decision making stages described in Chapter 2. The information gatherer (sometimes referred to as the "gate-

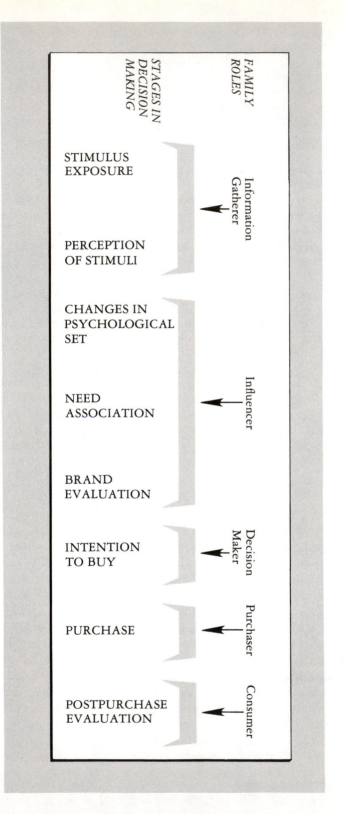

FIGURE 14–1 Roles by Stage in Decision Making

keeper") influences the level and type of stimuli the family is exposed to and the way the stimuli are interpreted. The individual who is most influential in determining brand choice will establish the most important evaluative criteria (cost, durability, etc.) and will influence the other family members' evaluation of the alternatives. In so doing, the influencer will determine those brands that most closely adhere to the family's needs. The decision maker will decide on the make or brand to be purchased, probably because he or she has budgetary power and therefore final approval. The purchasing agent will fulfill the decision. The consumer will use the product and evaluate it, resulting in some feedback to other family members regarding the degree of satisfaction with the chosen brand and the desirability of purchasing the same brand again. In most cases, several of these roles will be performed by the same individual.

Family Roles by Purchase Influence

Family roles can also be specified by the nature of the purchase influence. The most important classification by purchase influence defines instrumental versus expressive roles in family purchasing.[3] **Instrumental roles** are related to task-oriented functions meant to provide direction to the group. Decisions on budgets, timing, and product specifications would be task oriented. **Expressive roles** are related to the group's needs for social and emotional support through self-expression. Decisions regarding color, style, and design would be examples of expressive roles since they deal with means of self-expression.

Historically, the husband has been associated with the instrumental role and the wife with the expressive role.[4] A study by Davis supports this view since he found that husbands were more influential on decisions when to buy and how much to spend, whereas wives were more influential on decisions regarding style and color.[5] But the instrumental and expressive roles are more likely to become intermingled between husband and wife as more women enter the work force. One study found that working wives are less likely to play an expressive role.[6] A study by Ferber and Lee suggests that the wife may be just as likely to fulfill certain instrumental roles as the husband.[7] They identified the financial officer in the family; that is, the individual that pays the bills, keeps track of expenditures, and determines the use of leftover money. Clearly this is an instrumental rather than an expressive role since it is budgetary. Ferber and Lee found that in the first year of marriage, the husband and wife were equally likely to assume this role. In one-fourth of the families the husband was the financial officer, in one-fourth the wife, and in one-half both assumed this responsibility. But in the second year of marriage, the wife was more likely to be the financial officer, with 36 percent of the families saying the wife assumed these duties compared to only 27 percent for husbands.

Joint Versus Individual Decisions

Under what conditions are purchasing decisions likely to be made jointly by the family and under what conditions are they likely to be made by an individual family member? Sheth defines several situations in which joint decision making is more likely.[8]

Joint decisions are more likely when the level of perceived risk in buying is high. Since a wrong decision will affect the whole family, a joint decision is likely to occur to reduce risk and uncertainty. A decision regarding the purchase of a new home is invariably a joint decision because of the financial risks, the social risks involved in neighborhood interaction, and the psychological risks. There is some evidence that joint decision making may encourage the group to make riskier decisions because in this way, the failure of a wrong decision can be shared by all members of the group. This so-called **"risky shift" phenomenon** would mean that a decision made by the husband and wife may result in the purchase of a more expensive house than if the decision was made by the husband or wife alone.

Woodside studied whether a risky-shift occurs in consumer decisions and found that housewives were more willing to make riskier decisions for a variety of products after group discussion.[9] Yet another study found that such a shift is likely to occur only if the risks are not too great.[10] Thus, if the decision is whether to buy a more expensive color TV, the family may opt for the riskier choice. But in the case of a house, a joint decision may actually lead to a more conservative choice since the risk is great. Family members will be more concerned with the negative consequences of a wrong decision and will exert a moderating influence on each other, producing a negative risky shift.

Joint decisions are more likely when the purchasing decision is important to the family. Importance is closely related to risk. Yet in some cases, the decision may be important and the risk low, as in, for example, deciding whether to go back to the same vacation resort the family has gone to for the last five years. Decisions to buy major appliances and automobiles are generally joint decisions because of their importance. Low involvement products are more likely to involve individual decisions.

Joint decisions are more likely when there are few time pressures. Time pressures will encourage one member of the family to make the purchase decision. It may not be worth the time and effort to engage in family decision making for many products. The greater incidence of working wives has created greater time pressures within the family, encouraging individual decision making for many products that might ordinarily be purchased on a joint basis.

Joint decision making is more likely for certain demographic groups. There are several demographic factors that are also likely to encourage joint decision making:

1.   Joint decision making is less likely among upper and lower socioeconomic groups. The downscale groups (the lower income households) are more wife dominant, the upscale groups (the higher income households) are more husband dominant. The middle income groups are most likely to engage in joint decision making.[11]

2.   Younger families (those under 24) show a higher frequency of joint decision making.[12] The study by Ferber and Lee found the greatest amount of shared decisions in the first year of marriage.[13] As the family gets older, joint decisions tend to decrease because family members learn to make decisions that are acceptable to each other. Therefore, there is no need for shared decisions.[14]

3.   Joint decision making is more likely if only one of the parents is working since time pressures will be less. A working wife is more likely to make many decisions

on an individual basis without consulting her husband because there is no time to do so.

4. Kenkel suggests that as children are added to the family, roles become more clearly defined, and husband and wife are more willing to delegate authority for individual decisions.[15]

Conflict in Family Decision Making

Any time two or more people are involved in decision making, there is likely to be some degree of conflict in purchasing objectives, attitudes toward alternatives, and the selection of the most desirable alternative. The family is no exception. Sprey states that the normal state for the family is not one of agreement and stability.[16] Close interdependence of family members means that joint decisions will lead to conflict. Blood states that since families are small in size and are involuntary groups, conflict is the norm.[17] But these writers were referring to family decisions in general, not purchasing decisions.

Are purchasing decisions likely to create conflict in the family? Davis believes so. He states that "families quite often bargain, compromise and coerce rather than problem-solve in arriving at decisions."[18] He cites studies of husband-wife decision making for housing,[19] automobiles,[20] and family planning[21] that show substantial differences in choice criteria, perceptions, and attitudes. In family planning for example, husbands emphasized the positive effects of low fertility on living costs and children's education, while wives viewed low fertility as an advantage in giving them more time. Davis studied a number of product categories and found conflict regarding the roles to be played in the decision. There were three types of conflict: (1) who should make various purchase decisions; (2) how should the decision be made (degree of information search, reliance on advertising, etc.); and (3) who should implement the decision.

Therefore, it is clear that family decision making is not just a simple process of arriving at a joint decision through consensus. It frequently requires the resolution of the conflicting goals and attitudes of family members. Conflict between members of the decision-making unit is therefore an important consideration that does not arise in individual decision making. The marketer must be aware of such conflicts and adjust marketing strategies accordingly. Differing emphasis on style, economy, and luxury by the husband and wife means that different benefits should be directed to different members of the family. The wife may be more interested in the functional aspects of carpeting, its wear and durability. The husband may be more concerned with the style and luxuriousness. Advertising in women's magazines may emphasize the functional aspects; advertising in more general media may emphasize style and luxury.

Similarly, salespersons should be aware of any potential conflict in family decisions. Families frequently visit automobile showrooms together and talk to dealers jointly. The husband may emphasize roominess and style to impress business associates, whereas the wife may be concerned with gas economy and service costs. Or, conversely, the husband may emphasize cost and the wife style. In any case, differences are likely to occur, and the sales representative must appeal to both parties.

The existence of conflict in family decisions raises the important question of how such conflicts are resolved. Families use various strategies to arrive at a joint decision, and in the process resolve any conflicts to the satisfaction of all family members.

Davis classifies different family strategies by whether family members agree about goals (consensus) or disagree (accommodation).[22] In the latter case, conflict requiring some resolution is likely to arise. Cited in Table 14–1 are various strategies to arrive at a decision in cases of consensus and accommodation. Consensus does not always mean the family will come together and mutually arrive at a decision. An alternative to problem solving is to delegate the responsibility for a decision to one member of the family, the *specialist*. Taking this approach means that the family has opted for individual rather than joint decision making.

Another alternative to problem solving is to use the budget as a guide to most decisions. The *controller* in the family (the family financial officer) determines the size and allocation of the budget. There is still room for decision making within the budget. A family may have allocated a certain amount for a vacation, and will jointly decide where to go, but the amount of expenditures is predetermined.

Problem solving involves various modes of decision making that are likely to lead to a decision that is satisfactory to all family members. *Experts* can be

TABLE 14–1   Alternative Strategies in Family Decision Making

Goals	*Strategy*	*Ways of Implementing*
	Role structure	The Specialist
Consensus (Family members agree about goals)	Budgets	The Controller
	Problem solving	The Expert The Better Solution The Multiple Purchase
Accommodation (Family members disagree about goals)	Persuasion	The Irresponsible Critic Feminine Intuition Shopping Together Coercion Coalitions
	Bargaining	The Next Purchase The Impulse Purchase The Procrastinator

Source: Harry L. Davis, "Decision Making Within the Household," *Journal of Consumer Research* 2 (March 1976): 255.
Reprinted with permission from the *Journal of Consumer Research*.

relied on to determine the best alternative. Family discussion may lead to a *better solution* than that proposed by any one member of the family. Also, *multiple purchases* may be a way of avoiding conflict.

Davis cites two strategies used when family members disagree about goals: persuasion and bargaining. Persuasion is a means of influencing someone to agree to a decision he or she would not otherwise make. Bargaining leads to some "give-and-take" since both parties are likely to gain. Various methods of persuasion are listed in Table 14–1. The *irresponsible critic* criticizes the decision of the family by disassociating himself or herself from the decision. If the decision is right, there is nothing to lose; if it is wrong the irresponsible critic can always say, "I told you so." *Feminine intuition* could be grouped together with masculine intuition as a means for one spouse to take advantage of the weaknesses or empathy of another. The husband may realize the wife is susceptible to guilt and in trying to win her over to his favorite vacation spot may say, "I work myself to the bone and now I can't even go where I want."

Shopping together is a form of conflict resolution by getting the agreement of a member of the family through direct involvement. *Coercion* involves direct threat; for example, the threat by the parent to reduce a child's allowance if most of it is used to purchase candy. One spouse can also threaten another (since you bought that suit, I have a right to buy the winter coat I saw). *Coalitions* may also be formed within the family. Children may support one parent or the other in a conflict. Coalitions may be formed to bring dissenters into line. Everyone in the family wants to buy a stereo console except the teenage son who wants to buy components. The weight of family opinion forces the teenage son to comply.

Sheth regards coercion and coalitions as a form of "politicking" and says this is the least desirable form of conflict resolution.[23] Such politicking is most likely to occur when family members disagree not only about buying goals, but about life-styles and fundamental attitudes. The family with a child that is alienated by the political and economic values of his or her parents is more likely to resort to coercion or coalitions. The family in which parents are constantly arguing may encourage children to take sides and form coalitions. On the other hand, when conflict in the family is not so fundamental, other forms of persuasion, such as shopping together or various forms of bargaining, are more likely. Under these conditions, the argument is not over basic values but over purchasing criteria. It is a lot easier to resolve conflict when the disagreement is over the relative emphasis to be placed on economy or style than when the disagreement is over whether a second car is an expression of unjustified capitalistic values.

Bargaining is the second basic method of resolving purchasing conflicts within the family. Table 14–1 lists three bargaining strategies. One is to allow one member of the family to buy the desired item on this purchase if the other will be able to have his or her way on the *next purchase*. The husband might buy the car as long as it is agreed the wife will plan the vacation. Another strategy is to buy on *impulse* and bargain later. A third is to *procrastinate;* that is, delaying the purchase even after the decision is made in the hope that new information will become known or the situation will be changed. As examples,

"By the time I got to the store they were out" or "I found a new brand we didn't consider" are familiar statements. In each case, however, bargaining requires some give and take since family members are trading off their rights to decision making and influence.

When Is Conflict Less Likely?

There are three situations when family conflicts are less likely to occur. The first occurs when one person is recognized as the legitimate authority. If decision making is delegated to this individual, conflict is unlikely. The Davis study showed that the husband is generally delegated authority on how much to spend for a car, the wife on the style of furniture. The second occurs when one family member is more involved in the decision than the others. It may be agreed that the highly involved individual will make the decision. And the third situation is when one member of the family may be much more empathetic to the needs of another.

Burns and Granbois studied the influence a husband and wife had in automobile decisions to determine if these three factors reduce conflict.[24] Each factor facilitated conflict resolution. Conflict was less likely if the husband and wife agreed that the decision should be made jointly or by one of them alone. Even if the couple failed to agree on authority, conflict was less likely if one of them was much more involved in the purchase. Finally, conflict was also less likely if one of the spouse's was more empathetic. For autos, the husband was more involved and less empathetic to the needs of the wife. Therefore, the wife was more likely to cede decision authority to the husband.

Cox also studied family conflict in purchasing automobiles, but focussed on the relationship of demographic characteristics to conflict.[25] He found that spouses who have been married longer and who are in the later stages of the life cycle are more likely to agree with each other's decisions. This is not surprising since the very fact that a husband and wife have stayed together suggests a capacity for avoiding or resolving conflicts. In addition, the presence of children in the family tends to bring about an agreement in goals.

A MODEL OF FAMILY DECISION MAKING

Figure 14–2 attempts to summarize many of the above considerations by presenting a model of family decision making. A brief glance at the model suggests that family decision making may be a more complex process than individual decision making because of the need to delegate decision roles to two or more people and because of the need to resolve conflicts.

Assume a four-member family is considering its vacation plans for the year. The needs, attitudes, and past vacation experiences of each family member (the psychological set) will influence attitudes toward vacation alternatives. For the last five years, the family has been going to the same resort area about two hundred miles from their home. This year, the two children approach their parents and ask if there is any possibility they may take a trip instead. The parents consult about budget and alternative expenditures and decide to explore

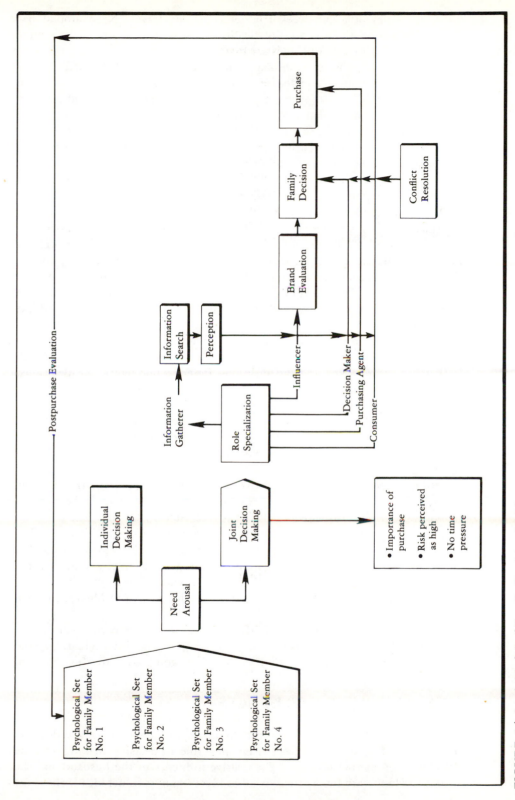

FIGURE 14–2 A Model of Family Decision Making

the possibilities of a two-week trip requiring air travel. Need arousal has occurred based on the attitudes of the family members who tended to agree that a change in vacation plans is warranted.

At this point, the decision may be made to delegate all authority to one of the parents because of expertise or a high level of involvement with the decision. But given the importance of the decision to the family, joint decision making is much more likely. Moreover, the perceived risks of making a poor decision (the expense, the fact the family will be close together, and the desire to have a good time) are fairly high. Finally, there is no time pressure since it is March and the family is planning for an August vacation.

Given the need for a joint decision, specification of roles will occur. Such specification may be made explicit or it may be assumed. Before the children made the suggestion on the change in vacation plans, they began to collect information about alternative areas. One collected information on Mexico, the other on several Caribbean islands. Although they initiated the process of information search, the whole family may be regarded as information gatherers since the husband and wife also begin to be aware of travel information. The prime influencers in the decision are the children since they initiated the decision process. They have also specified two primary alternatives—Mexico and the Caribbean.

The decision maker will be the family financial officer. This family is an example of the most common type specified by Ferber and Lee in which both husband and wife make budgetary decisions. Based on budgetary considerations, the parents decide to consider Mexico and the Caribbean. A third alternative is a car trip through Eastern Canada. This third alternative may be necessary if the parents decide they cannot afford the additional expense of four air fares by summer time. The purchasing agent will be the wife since she is a part-time travel agent and can easily make the arrangements. The consumers will of course be the whole family.

In the process of collecting information and evaluating alternative vacation spots, a conflict arises between the two children. The son would like to go to one of the Caribbean islands because he is interested in surfing. The daughter would like to go to Mexico because she is interested in Aztec architecture. The parents would prefer Mexico to the Caribbean and decide to resolve the conflict by using the "next purchase" and "multiple purchase" strategies. They tell the son that if they also go away next year, his choice would prevail over his sister's. But in any case, they will spend a few days in a beach area in Mexico to allow for surfing.

By summertime the family finds it can afford the trip to Mexico. The purchase is made, they all enjoy the vacation (postpurchase evaluation), and agree that if they can afford it they will consider going back to Mexico again.

HUSBAND-WIFE INFLUENCES

The husband and wife are clearly the dominant influences in family decision making. Most studies have focused on their role in decision making and the dominance of one or the other. The relative influence of the husband and the wife is likely to vary by (1) the type of product being considered, (2) the stage in decision making, (3) the type of decision being made, and (4) the characteristics of the family.

Husband-Wife Influences by Type of Product

Various studies have identified husband dominance, wife dominance, and shared influence by product category. Husbands dominate decisions regarding automobiles[26] and liquor.[27] Wives tend to dominate decisions for food, toiletries, and small appliances.[28] Joint decision making is likely for decisions regarding housing,[29] vacations, and furniture.[30]

Davis and Rigaux undertook one of the most detailed studies of husband-wife influences by product category.[31] They studied family decision making in Belgian households for twenty-five products and classified these products into four categories:

1. products where the husband tends to be the dominant influence;
2. products where the wife tends to be the dominant influence;
3. products where decisions are made by either the husband or the wife and either one is equally likely to be dominant (referred to as **autonomic decisions**);
4. products where decisions are made jointly by husband and wife (referred to as **syncratic decisions**).

Results of their study are outlined in Figure 14–3. The higher up the product on the vertical axis, the more likely it is the wife will be the dominant influence. The further to the right on the horizontal axis, the more likely it is the decision will be a joint one. Therefore, products in the upper left are wife dominant, products in the middle left are based on individual decisions by either husband or wife (autonomic), and products in the lower left are husband dominant. Products to the right are joint decisions (syncratic) and must involve both husband and wife as equal influences. Products to the left are individual decisions.

With some exceptions, the product classifications in Figure 14–3 tend to confirm previous studies. Husbands dominate decisions for insurance and to a lesser extent cars and savings. Wives dominate decisions for food, clothing, household products, and toiletries. Either the husband or the wife will make decisions for liquor and for the husband's clothing on an individual basis. Joint decisions will most likely be made for furniture, housing, vacations, and schools.

The classifications in Figure 14–3 have important implications for marketers. If a product is in the husband or wife dominant category, messages have to be tailored to one spouse or the other. Media have to be selected that are male or female dominant. If the product is in the syncratic category, the message has to be tailored for the couple, and media have to be purchased that are likely to reach both spouses. If the product is in the autonomic category, marketing strategy is more difficult. The decision could be made by either spouse, although in some cases the husband is dominant, in others the wife is dominant. Therefore, there are two audiences and two campaigns may be necessary. Advertising alcoholic beverages may require one campaign stressing husband-oriented appeals and another wife-oriented appeals. Trying to develop one campaign to appeal to both spouses may be ineffective.

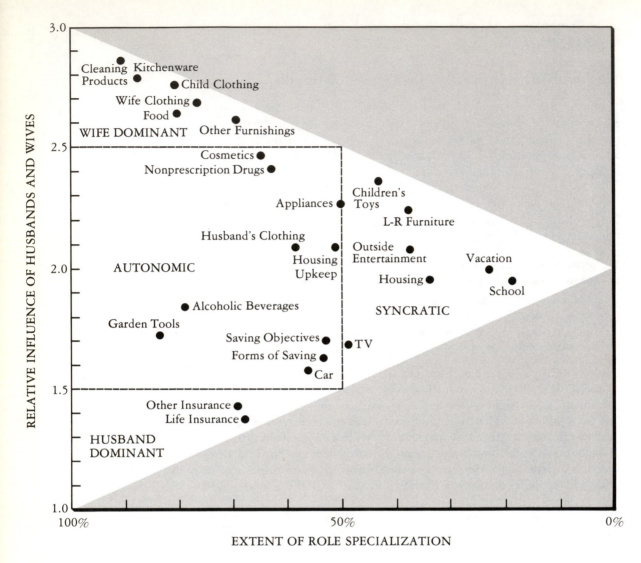

FIGURE 14–3 Husband-Wife Roles in Family Decisions by Product Category
Source: Harry L. Davis and Benny P. Rigaux, "Perception of Marital Roles in Decision Processes,"
Journal of Consumer Research 1 (June 1974): 54.
   Reprinted with permission from the *Journal of Consumer Research.*

Husband-Wife Influences by Stage in Decision Making

The influence of the husband or wife may also vary according to the stage in decision making. One spouse may initiate a decision, another may dominate in gathering information, and both may make the final decision. In the family planning area, both husband and wife are likely to initiate decision making, but the wife is more involved than the husband in searching for information.[32] One study of the adoption of IUDs in India found that in 44 percent of the cases, the husband made the final decision.[33]

In the Davis and Rigaux study, husband-wife influences were studied in

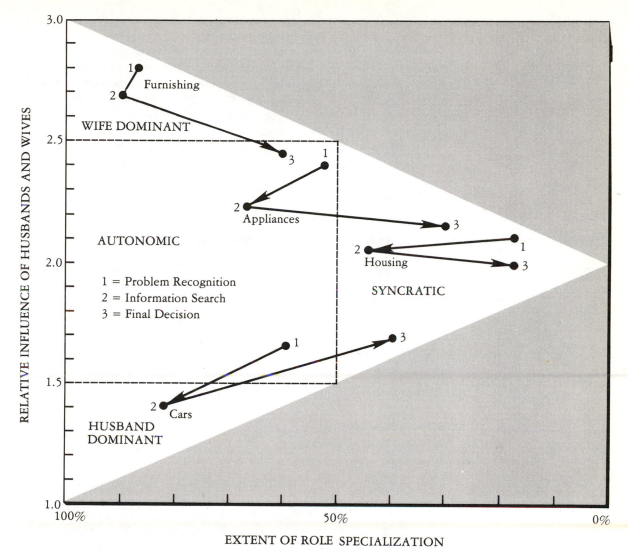

FIGURE 14–4 Changes in Husband-Wife Roles from Problem Recognition to Information Search

Source: Adapted from Harry L. Davis and Benny P. Rigaux, "Perception of Marital Roles in Decision Processes," *Journal of Consumer Research* 1 (June 1974): 56, 57.

Reprinted with permission from the *Journal of Consumer Research*.

three phases of the decision process: (1) problem recognition, (2) information search and (3) the final decision.[34] Davis and Rigaux traced the pattern of influence for the twenty-five products cited in Figure 14–3 across these three decision phases. They found that in going from problem recognition to information search, the husband became more of a dominant influence for most products. On the other hand, when moving from information search to the final decision, the pattern of influence became more equal. Information search was likely to be an individual process, whereas the final decision was more likely to be made jointly.

The findings for four of the products are presented in Figure 14–4. Using automobiles as an example, when going from problem recognition (represented as #1 in Figure 14–4) to information search (#2 in Figure 14–4) the husband becomes more of a dominant influence (downward sloping arrow from #1 to #2). Moreover, since the arrow swings to the left, this means information search for a car is more likely to be an individual process. When moving from information search to the final decision (#2 to #3), the arrow for the car now swings up and to the right, meaning that the wife's influence increases and the final decision is more likely to be joint.

These findings clearly show that the husband's and wife's influences are likely to vary depending on the stage of the decision. The husband's influence does appear to increase when information is being gathered, illustrating the husband's traditional instrumental role in the family. The final decision is likely to be made on a more equal basis between husband and wife.

Husband-Wife Influences by Type of Decision

The husband's and wife's influences can also vary by the type of decision being made within a product category. For example, husbands may be more influential in determining how much to spend for certain products while wives may be more influential in determining what make or brand to buy. Davis studied husband and wife influences by type of decision for furniture and automobiles.[35] He defined six types of decisions for each product:

1. When to buy
2. Where to buy
3. How much to spend
4. What make or type to buy
5. What model or style to buy
6. What color to select

In studying one hundred families in four Chicago suburbs, he found what one would expect: husbands dominated purchase influence for automobiles; wives dominated purchase influence for furniture. But, there were wide variations in the degree of purchase influence by the six factors cited above. The husband dominated the decision on when to buy a car and how much to spend. But, the wife was almost as influential as the husband on where to buy the car and the color. The wife dominated the decision on what style and color of furniture to buy. But, the husband was almost as influential as the wife on when to buy furniture and how much to spend.

The pattern of influence is consistent between cars and furniture. The husband is most influential regarding the amount of money to spend and the timing of the decision. The wife is most influential regarding style and color. These findings reflect the instrumental role of the husband and the expressive role of the wife in family purchasing decisions.

Husband-Wife Influences by Family Characteristics

Even though husbands tend to dominate decisions for certain product categories and wives for others, there is likely to be variation in the degree of dominance within each family. In certain families, the husband may be more dominant regardless of the product being considered (patriarchal families); in others the wife may be more dominant (matriarchal families).

Studies have associated the characteristics of the family to the degree of husband or wife dominance. These results can be summarized as follows: The husband will be more influential in the purchase decision than the wife when

1. his level of education is higher than that of the wife;
2. his income and occupational status are higher than that of the wife;
3. the wife is not employed;
4. the couple is at an earlier stage in the family life cycle (young parents);
5. the couple has a greater than average number of children.[36]

The opposite would hold for a wife-dominant family: Wife is employed, has a higher level of education than the husband, etc.

The profile of the husband-dominant family suggests a family with traditional values and attitudes toward marital roles. The husband's higher income provides him with financial power within the family. A nonworking wife with a lower level of education suggests more traditional values.

The traditional orientation of the husband-dominant family is supported in a study by Green and Cunningham.[37] They surveyed 257 married women and classified them as conservative, moderate, or liberal with regard to female roles. Women who had more contemporary views of their role were much more likely to make purchase decisions than were conservative women. They were also more than twice as likely to make decisions regarding family savings, vacation plans, and major appliances when compared to conservative women. Therefore, it appears the one most important factor in defining the relative influence of a husband versus a wife is attitudes toward marital roles. Traditional views encourage greater male influence, contemporary views encourage greater female influence.

Changing Patterns of Husband-Wife Influences

The rapid increase in the number of working wives in the last twenty years has probably resulted in some substantial changes in purchasing roles within the family. Holter argues that an employed wife results in a more equal distribution of family power between husband and wife and will therefore lead to more joint decisions.[38] Cunningham and Green also cite labor-saving devices in the home and more effective family planning as providing the married woman with increased time to participate in activities outside the home.[39]

In order to determine whether family purchasing roles have changed, Cunningham and Green replicated a study of purchasing influence conducted in 1955.[40] Results of the two studies are presented in Table 14–2. For three of the products studied — autos, vacations, and housing — the likelihood of a joint decision increased substantially from 1955 to 1973. In two cases — food and financial decisions — the chances of the wife's making the decision by herself increased. In one case — life insurance—the husband's influence increased between 1955 and 1973.

The tendency toward more joint decision making in the selection of hous-

TABLE 14–2   Changes in Husband-Wife Purchase Roles: 1955 Versus 1973

Decision Area	1955 (%)	1973 (%)
Food and Groceries		
Husband usually decides	13	10
Both husband and wife	33	15
Wife usually	54	75
Number of cases	(727)	(248)
Life Insurance		
Husband usually	43	66
Both husband and wife	42	30
Wife usually	15	4
Number of cases	(727)	(247)
Automobile		
Husband usually	70	52
Both husband and wife	25	45
Wife usually	5	3
Number of cases	(727)	(248)
Vacation		
Husband usually	18	7
Both husband and wife	70	84
Wife usually	12	9
Number of cases	(727)	(244)
House or Apartment		
Husband usually	18	12
Both husband and wife	58	77
Wife usually	24	11
Number of cases	(727)	(245)
Money and Bills		
Husband usually	26	27
Both husband and wife	34	24
Wife usually	40	49
Number of cases	(727)	(248)

Source: Isabella C.M. Cunningham and Robert T. Green, "Purchasing Roles in the U.S. Family, 1955 and 1973," *Journal of Marketing* 38 (October 1974): 63.

Reprinted with permission from the *Journal of Marketing.*

ing, vacation spots, and autos may be the result of a trend toward greater equality between spouses. The greater involvement of the wife in food decisions may also suggest more female influence since working wives may just not have the time to consult husbands on many grocery items.

The implications for marketing are direct. The findings show that in most cases, marketers were not selling to the same group in 1973 that they sold to in 1955. The most marked change was for automobiles. Automobile purchase decisions once dominated by the husband are being made more jointly. Automobile marketers should direct promotional themes toward both the husband and the wife and should not rely only on male-dominant media.

PARENT-CHILD INFLUENCES

Children play an important part in family decision making for a wide range of products, and in many cases may themselves be the sole decision makers. Younger children may decide on expenditures for candy, snack items, and movies. As the child grows older and his or her purchasing power increases, the child may be the primary decision maker for toys, record albums, and reading material. Moreover, children are likely to influence decisions for products consumed by the whole family such as food items, vacation plans, entertainment and restaurant decisions, and even decisions for small appliances.

Given the potential influence of children, it is surprising that almost all studies of family purchase decisions have focused on husband and wife influences and have excluded children. In noting this lack of research on children's influence, one copywriter asked, "How can researchers ask questions about family decision making for cookies, ice cream, peanut butter, pudding, cereals, chewing gum, family vacations, children's clothes, and hamburgers from fast food restaurants without finding out if children are involved?"[41]

Since 1972, more attention has been devoted to the effects of advertising on children because of government reports from the Federal Trade Commission suggesting unwarranted influence of advertising on younger children.[42] But even these studies do not consider the interaction between the parent and the child in family decision making.

The few studies done on parent-child influences in purchasing have been divided between research on younger children (12 or under) and research on adolescents (teenagers). Research on younger children has focused on the role of the mother and the mother-child interaction in purchasing. Research on adolescents has been directed toward the relative influence of parents and peer groups in teenage purchasing decisions. This focus is due to the general belief that children rely more on parents for norms and values when they are younger, and more on their peer groups as they grow older. The section below will first consider the mother-child interaction and then the peer group-adolescent interaction.

Mother's Response to Child's Purchase Request

Several studies have considered the mother's response to a child's request to purchase various products. These studies recognize that younger children can not obtain most products directly and must ask the mother. The mother serves as the final decision maker and the purchasing agent, but mother and child interact as sources of influence.

Berey and Pollay studied the mother's acceptance of the child's favorite brand of ready-to-eat cereals.[43] They thought children would be more likely to get their way if (1) they are more assertive, and (2) the mother is more child centered. They interviewed elementary school students, their mothers, and their teachers to assess the child's assertiveness. The more assertive children were not more likely to get their way. Also, contrary to the researcher's expectations, the more child-centered the mother, the *less* likely she was to buy the child's favorite brand. Berey and Pollay conclude that if a mother is child-centered, she will buy what she thinks is right for the child, not what the child wants. It is the less child-centered mother that may give in to a child's request for a tastier and less nutritious cereal as the easiest way out because she just can not be bothered.

Ward and Wackman did a more extensive study of twenty-two categories by age of the child (5–7, 8–10, 11–12).[44] They found that the older the child, the more likely the mother would yield to his or her request. Yet the older the child, the less frequently did they make purchase requests to the mother. As children become older, they may be able to make decisions independently because they may get more money from the parents, or possibly because they begin to look to the peer group and disregard parents as sources of information. Mothers are more likely to go along with the child's request because they may regard the older child as being more competent in making purchasing judgments.

Mother-Child Negotiations

The two studies cited only considered whether the mother will yield to the child's request or not. Popper suggested three other possibilities: (1) positive negotiation, (2) avoidance, and (3) negative negotiation.[45] Positive negotiation would require an "I will buy it if . . ." response from the mother; for example, if the child pays for part of it or if the child provides a rational explanation for the purchase. Negative negotiation would require an "I won't buy it, but . . ." response from the mother; for example, the mother is willing to buy a substitute or explains why she will not buy it. Avoidance is essentially a procrastination strategy such as "Ask your father" or "We'll talk about it later." These three strategies all reflect bargaining with the child rather than persuasion since they deal with some give and take; either further communication, another alternative, or a delayed response.

Popper tested these three strategies plus the yield or not yield alternative on mothers by giving them two scenarios: in one the child requests a candy bar, in the other a game. The mothers are then asked to respond to the child's request. The distribution of responses is in Table 14–3. The results show that just yielding or not yielding is an oversimplified representation of mother-child interactions in the purchasing process. Some form of negotiations took place in over half the cases. Moreover, there was some variation in the strategy used by product. The candy bar resulted in more negative negotiation. This could be because mothers are more likely to resist a product like a candy bar.

Mother's Role in the Purchasing Process

Mothers can serve as information gatherers, influencers, and decision makers in interactions with the child. Wackman identified these roles in a mother-child context.[46] He broke out the informational role into two parts: one, educating the child (mother serves as consumer educator), and two, conveying relevant information about products to the child (mother serves as information mediator).

	Response to Scenario #1 (candy bar)	Response to Scenario #2 (game)
Yield[a]	24.3%	26.5%
Positive negotiation[b]	24.3%	22.7%
Avoid[c]	10.3%	13.4%
Negative negotiation[d]	28.0%	21.8%
Not yield[e]	6.9%	8.7%
Other	6.2%	6.9%

Example of response in each category:
[a] "I would buy the product."
[b] "I'll buy it if the child pays part . . ."
[c] "Ask your father."
[d] "I won't buy this product but would buy a substitute."
[e] "I would not buy this product."

Source: Edward T. Popper, "Mothers' Mediation of Children's Purchase Requests," in Niel Beckwith et al., eds., *Proceedings of the American Marketing Association Educators' Conference.* Series #44 (1979), p. 646.

Reprinted with permission from the American Marketing Association.

In addition, the mother may serve as the prime consumption motivator by asking the child what he or she wants as a gift, by providing the child with money to make a purchase, or by yielding to the child's request and thus encouraging future requests. Finally, the mother can serve as a block to the child's desire by denying a purchase request. Wackman refers to this role as establishing a *countervailing* force to the child.

A number of studies by Wackman and his colleagues show that the mother does not frequently serve an informational role as either a consumer educator or a supplier of information. In most cases, it is the child that initiates discussions about product purchases and consumption. The primary role of the mother is to facilitate the final decision by either letting the child buy what is wanted or blocking the purchase. Therefore, the mother's role as final decision maker seems to be more important than her role as influencer or information gatherer.

Child's Role in the Purchasing Process

The extent of children's influence varies sharply by product category. In their extensive study of mothers of five- to twelve-year-olds, Ward and Wackman found that 87 percent of the mothers interviewed yielded to the child's request for breakfast cereals.[47] (Results of the study are in Table 14–4.) Other product categories resulting in a high proportion of yielding are snack foods, games and toys, soft drinks, candy, toothpaste, and clothing. It is logical that children will exert influence on parents for all of these product categories except clothing. But Table 14–4 shows that influence for clothes increases with age. Only 21 percent of the mothers yielded to clothing requests from 5–7-year-old children,

TABLE 14–4 Percent of Mothers Who Usually Yield to Children's Requests (by Product Category)

Product	Percentage of yieldings			
	5–7 years old	8–10 years old	11–12 years old	Total
Foods				
Breakfast cereal	88	91	83	87
Snack foods	52	62	77	63
Candy	40	28	57	42
Soft drinks	38	47	31	46
Jell-O	40	41	26	36
Durables for child's use				
Game, toy	57	59	46	54
Clothing	21	34	57	37
Bicycle	7	9	9	8
Hot wheels	29	19	17	22
Record album	12	16	46	24
Camera	2	3	0	2
Notions, toiletries				
Toothpaste	36	44	40	39
Bath soap	9	9	9	9
Shampoo	17	6	23	16
Aspirin	5	6	0	4
Other products				
Automobile	2	0	0	12
Gasoline brand	2	0	3	2
Laundry soap	2	0	3	2
Household cleaner	2	3	0	2

Source: Adapted from Scott Ward and Daniel B. Wackman, "Children's Purchase Influence Attempts and Parental Yielding," *Journal of Marketing Research* 9 (August 1972): 317.

Reprinted with permission from the *Journal of Marketing Research.*

but 57 percent yielded to requests from 11–12-year-old children. Record albums is another category where the child's influence increases markedly with age.

Children have the greatest influence over categories one would expect — snack foods, candy, and toys — and almost no influence over products normally associated with adults such as autos and household items. Overall, the extent of children's influence is high. What Wackman refers to as "child power" may be growing with the greater independence of children. Greater affluence and increased divorce rates may be resulting in a greater likelihood that children will get their way.

Effects of Advertising on Mother-Child Interaction

The effects of television advertising on children have definite ethical and public policy implications. The focus here is on advertising's effect on decision making. The results on this score are mixed. One study found that if the child requested a product because it was seen on TV, the parent was more likely to buy it.[48]

The reason is that the request was coupled with some persuasive argument obtained from the commercial such as ease of use or economy. Two studies found the opposite: Exposure to television commercials resulted in mothers being somewhat more likely to refuse the child's request.[49] If this is so, it may be risky to advertise to both mother and child because of the possibility of outright rejection by the mother. But it can also be argued that if mother and child see the commercial together, the mother has an opportunity to moderate the claim. If the claim is acceptable, the mother is more likely to yield to the child's request when the commercial is seen jointly. Otherwise, an ad seen by the child alone may result in a denial of his or her request. Therefore, advertisers should consider not only the traditional Saturday morning timing for children's commercials, but evening prime time as well.

Parent Versus Peer Group Influences Among Adolescents

The traditional view maintains that parents' purchasing influence decreases as children enter adolescence, due to the shifting of allegiances to the peer group as the primary reference group. Recent studies suggest that children continue to rely on parents for information and influence into adolescence. One study found that high school students were just as concerned with parents' approval as elementary school students.[50] Another found that 16–19 year olds were more likely to be influenced by parents than friends in the purchase of sports equipment and small appliances.[51] When products are expensive and complex, teenagers tend to rely more on parental rather than peer influence.[52]

These findings are supported by a comprehensive study of parent and peer group purchasing influences among adolescents. Moschis and Moore conducted a study of purchase influences for eight product categories among 734 adolescents.[53] They found that adolescents preferred parents to friends as a source of information by almost two to one. Parents were also preferred as a source of influence. The fact the parent liked the product was a much more important criterion than the fact that a friend liked the product. Also, adolescents were almost three times as likely to buy these products with a member of the family along rather than with a friend. Parents' influences were particularly important for more expensive products such as wristwatches, dress shoes, and pocket calculators. Friends were more important than parents as sources of information and influence for only one product, sunglasses!

The importance of parents in purchasing decisions does not exclude the peer group as an important source of influence. In fact, the more the family talks about purchase alternatives, the more likely it is that the adolescent will also communicate these alternatives to his or her friends.[54]

FAMILY DECISION MAKING AND MARKETING STRATEGIES

Research on family decision making influences every phase of marketing strategy — the advertising message, the media selected, product development, pricing, and distribution.

Content of Advertising Messages

The nature of family decision making will influence the content of advertising messages. If the wife or husband is dominant in making the decision, the advertising message must be directed to the needs of the dominant party. The finding by Green and Cunningham that automobile decisions are increasingly joint decisions means that the evaluative criteria used by both husband and wife must be taken into account in developing advertising themes. A finding in a recent study that the child directly influences the choice of fast food restaurants means that these establishments must advertise by combining adult and child orientations.[55] Both McDonald's and Burger King consistently portray the whole family. They also directly appeal to children by such characters as Ronald McDonald and the Magic Burger King.

Advertising Media

The selection of advertising media will be based on who is involved in the decision. Husband- or wife-dominant decisions require the selection of magazines and TV programs that are male or female oriented. If the decision is autonomic — that is, the decision is made by husband or wife and either one is equally likely to make it — the marketer is faced with a difficult choice. Should the advertising budget be split equally between male- and female-dominated media, or should the marketer follow a segmentation strategy and appeal to one or the other?

Men's clothing is a good example. The marketer could advertise men's clothing in women's magazines, in men's magazines, or in both. If both are used, two separate campaigns would be required; one aimed toward men, the other toward women. The danger of this approach is the media budget may be too diffused with little impact. The marketer may choose to direct advertising toward those families in which the wife is more likely to be the dominant influence in men's clothing. This would involve a single campaign and a more simplified media strategy. But the danger is that a substantial part of the market could be lost.

A syncratic decision does not pose the problem of choosing between male- or female-dominated media since the decision is made jointly by both parties. But then the question is how to split the budget between general and specialized media. Should the marketer attempt to reach both husband and wife together, or should there be an attempt to reach each separately with essentially the same theme?

The nature of parent-child influences also provides implications for media strategy. The fact that the mother yields to the child's preferred breakfast cereal in almost 90 percent of the cases means that advertising cereals directly to the child is a rational approach. When the mother is less likely to yield to the child's wishes (snack foods, candy, toys) children's requests initiated by advertising may reduce the chances the mother will go along. In these cases, the marketer may wish to re-evaluate advertising primarily to children. Advertising to both mother and child may be effective to erase doubts regarding product claims.

Product Development

Products designed for one member of the family provide the marketer with less of a problem than products designed for two or more members. Life insurance is usually designed to the specifications of the husband, childrens' clothing is designed primarily to the specifications of the wife.

Garden tools could be designed to the specifications of either the husband or the wife since either one may make the decision. In designing a trowel or hoe, the marketer could introduce a lighter weight material or an easier grip to facilitate use by the wife. Or heavier duty material and a thicker handle could be introduced to appeal to the husband. The strategy could be to (1) segment the market by introducing one product to a certain member of the family, (2) expand the product line to appeal to all members of the family, or (3) introduce an all-purpose product so the family could buy one item to be used by everyone.

Pricing

Pricing strategies may also be influenced by the identity of the decision maker. One study identified the price-oriented consumer for toothpaste as the husband.[56] The marketer cannot assume that the coupon redeemer and price sensitive consumer is necessarily the wife.

The fact that husbands generally determine how much to spend for automobiles and wives for furniture, means that price levels must be established based on the price sensitivity of these individuals.

Children will also exert pricing influences. One study found that mothers were more willing to yield to children's requests when the explanation was that the brand was economical or was being sold at a premium.[57] Parents were willing to accept arguments when economy was the rationale.

Distribution

The nature of family decision making may also influence distribution strategies. If decisions are made jointly, stores may be required to stay open longer to accommodate both the husband and the wife. The orientation of a product to one member of the family means separate merchandising displays.

In-store promotional displays must reflect purchase influence as well. Wackman found that children are more likely to get their preferred brand when they make a request in the store rather than in the home.[58] This implies that in-store promotions for cereals, snacks, candy, or toothpaste should be directed toward the child as well as the adult.

THE MEASUREMENT OF FAMILY INFLUENCE

Studies of family decision making rely on measures of family influence that are assumed to be valid. Two questions arise: Who should be interviewed to determine relative influence, and how should influence be measured?

Who to Interview

Three approaches have been used in determining husband-wife influences: (1) interview both together, (2) interview each separately, (3) interview the wife to determine her influence and the husband's.

Most studies that have interviewed husbands and wives separately have found a close level of agreement between them as to their respective influence. Davis and Rigaux found little difference between spouses in positioning products into husband- versus wife-dominant categories.[59] They found that 68 percent of husbands and wives agree about their roles across the twenty-five product categories studied. Where disagreement over influence exists, it tends to deal with who makes the decision.

Davis concludes that if the purpose of the study is to determine relative influence of husbands or wives in general, then interviewing the wife is sufficient. If the purpose is to study the nature of family decision making, interviewing only one spouse may provide a distorted picture.[60] In such cases, data should be obtained from both spouses separately or in joint interviews.

The question also arises, who should be interviewed, in parent-child studies. In most cases, the mother is interviewed to estimate the child's influence. But the validity of the mother's response as a true reflection of the child's influence has not been tested. A comparison of the mother's and child's perception of relative influence would be difficult because of the complexities of interviewing children. But comparisons could certainly be made between parental and adolescent responses regarding family influence to determine whether they agree.

How to Measure Influence

Most studies have measured the relative influence of the husband and wife on some scale from husband dominant to wife dominant. The simplest scale is a three-point scale: husband decides, equal influence, and wife decides. Other studies have divided the equal influence category into syncratic (both decide) and autonomic (sometimes one spouse decides, sometimes the other). Influence has also been measured by asking each spouse to divide up ten points to show the relative "share" of husband and wife influences.

Once again, these measures are adequate to measure relative influence, but are not adequate to measure the nature of the influence. If the wife decided about a piece of furniture, was it because the husband was not interested, because a decision was made to delegate authority to the wife for the purchase, or was it the result of a process of negotiation in which the wife gave something in return?[61] Determination of the nature of influence requires more complex measures and in-depth interviews involving both husband and wife.

SUMMARY

This chapter focuses on the most important group — the family. The family was defined as a decision-making unit with prescribed roles and purchase influence. Family members can perform the role of information gatherer, influencer, decision maker, purchasing agent, and consumer. Reference is made to expressive versus instrumental roles in the process of family decision making. Expressive roles are related to decisions regarding styles, colors, and models. Instrumental roles are related to decisions regarding budgets, timing, and product specifications. Traditionally, the wife performs the expressive roles and the husband the instrumental roles, although in families with working wives these roles have begun to merge.

Decisions within the family can be made on a joint or individual basis. Joint decisions are more likely when perceived risk is high, the purchase decision is important to the family, and there are fewer time pressures. Joint decisions invariably produce some conflict in purchase objectives. As a result, families develop strategies to resolve purchase conflicts. Conflicts can be resolved by strategies of persuasion or by strategies of bargaining.

The fact that joint decision making requires multiple roles and strategies of conflict resolution means that the process of brand evaluation will be more complex than in the case of individual decision making. The model of family decision making (Figure 14–2) incorporates role specialization and conflict resolution in the process of brand evaluation.

The second portion of this chapter deals with husband-wife influences in the purchase process. Four types of decision processes are defined: husband-dominant, wife-dominant, autonomic (either husband or wife is equally likely to make an individual decision), and syncratic (joint) decision making. Traditionally, husbands tend to dominate decisions for cars and insurance, wives for food and toiletries, and joint decisions are made for vacations, housing, and education. But recent evidence suggests a greater trend toward joint decision making.

Parent-child influences are also considered. Studies suggest that the mother does not always either give in to or resist children's purchase requests. Frequently, there is a more complex process of negotiation between mother and child. In addition, the mother rarely performs the function of a "marketing educator." The role of television in this regard has brought it under close scrutiny by governmental agencies.

The chapter concludes by considering strategic implications of family decision making. The nature of family decision making will influence all facets of marketing strategy, especially since the family decision-making process defines the nature of information seeking, purchase influence, and brand evaluation.

The next two chapters focus on communications within and between groups.

QUESTIONS

1. Instrumental roles have traditionally been associated with the husband and expressive roles with the wife.

- What changes have taken place in American society that have caused a blurring of these traditional roles?

2. Using the categories in Table 14–1, cite two or three strategies for resolution of family conflicts that could be used in the following cases:
   - The wife wants a smaller house than the husband because it is easier to maintain. The husband wants a larger house to impress friends and business associates.
   - The daughter wants a TV set in her room to have freedom of choice in program selection. The parents resist the idea for fear less attention will be given to homework.
   - The teenage son wants a car. The teenage daughter wants to go on a summer vacation with friends. Parents cannot afford both.

3. ·Why is conflict likely to arise in each of the cases cited in question 2?

4. Advertising campaigns for products where decisions are made on an autonomic basis are more difficult to formulate because an individual decision could be made by either husband or wife. The advertiser could try to develop (a) separate campaigns for each spouse, (b) a joint campaign for both, and (c) a campaign aimed at one or the other.
   - Under what conditions will each of the above strategies be most effective?

5. Why do you suppose the decisions for garden tools and alcohol are autonomic (Figure 14–3), whereas the decisions for vacations, schooling, and entertainment are syncratic?

6. Interpret the shifts in roles by stages in the decision process in Figure 14–4 for (a) housing, (b) appliances, and (c) furnishings.

7. What may be the effect of a contemporary versus a traditional view of the woman's role in the family on (a) the purchase of convenience foods, (b) family shopping behavior, and (c) the criteria used in selecting food products?

8. There has been a greater shift toward joint decision making for many product categories that have been within the traditional domain of the husband (autos, financial planning) and wife (appliances, furniture).
   - What are the implications of this shift for (a) new product development, (b) product line strategies, and (c) advertising?

9. Mothers are more likely to yield to a child's request when it is made in the store rather than in the home.
   - Why do you suppose this is true? What are the strategic implications of this finding for (a) advertising and (b) in-store promotional policy?

RESEARCH ASSIGNMENTS

1. Trace a family decision for a higher and a lower socioeconomic family. Make sure the product or service involves joint decisions by parents and children (e.g., a family vacation, selection of a college, purchase of an automobile). Identify each family member's (a) specific roles; (b) perceptions and attitudes of the alternatives being considered; (c) conflicts in decision making; (d) modes of conflict resolution; and (e) postpurchase evaluation.

- Does the decision process conform to the model in Figure 14–2?
- What are the differences in the decision processes between the higher and the lower socioeconomic family?
- What are the implications of decision making for (a) advertising, (b) product-line development, (c) product positioning, and (d) pricing?

2. Conduct separate interviews with third or fourth grade children and their mothers to determine perceptions of each child's influence. A good vehicle for doing this is to make contact with an elementary school class. Interviews would be conducted in class with the cooperation of the teacher. Mothers could then be interviewed at home.

- Ask mothers about the influence of the child and ask children about their influence relative to their mothers for products such as cereal, toothpaste, candy, or fast food restaurants. Use a simple scale that children can understand such as "I make the decision," "My mother makes the decision," "We both make the decision." Ask both mothers and children what brand they last purchased and to rate the brand from excellent to poor.
- Is there agreement between mother and child on (a) degree of influence; (b) brand purchased, and (c) brand ratings?

3. Replicate assignment no. 2 for 12–13-year-old girls buying clothes. In this case, ask children and mothers to divide up ten points based on purchase influence. Determine degree of agreement on (a) purchase influence, (b) evaluation of store in which purchased, and (c) evaluation of clothing purchased.

4. Present a sample of twenty to thirty mothers with a scenario in which a child requests a specific cereal (scenario no. 1) and suggests a fast food restaurant (scenario no. 2). Determine the mother's reaction to the child's purchase request based on the categories developed by Popper (see Table 14–3). Do your findings conform to Popper's?

NOTES

1. John S. Coulson, "Buying Decisions Within the Family and the Consumer-Brand Relationship," in Joseph W. Newman, ed., *On Knowing the Consumer* (New York: John Wiley & Sons Inc., 1967), p. 60.
2. Haley, Overholser and Associates, Inc. *Purchase Influence: Measures of Husband/Wife Influence on Buying Decisions* (New Canaan, Conn.: Haley, Overholser Inc., 1975.)
3. Bernard Berelson and Gary A. Steiner, *Human Behavior: An Inventory of Scientific Findings* (New York: Harcourt, Brace & World Inc., 1964), p. 314.
4. William F. Kenkel, "Husband-Wife Interaction in Decision-Making and Decision Choices," *Journal of Social Psychology* 54 (1961): 260.
5. Harry L. Davis, "Dimensions of Marital Roles in Consumer Decision Making," *Journal of Marketing Research* 7 (May 1970): 168–177.
6. William F. Kenkel, "Family Interaction in Decision-Making on Spending," in Nelson Foote, ed., *Household Decision-Making* (New York: New York University Press, 1961), p. 152.
7. Robert Ferber and Lucy Chao Lee, "Husband-Wife Influence in Family Purchasing Behavior," *Journal of Consumer Research* 1 (June 1974): 43–50.
8. Jagdish N. Sheth, "A Theory of Family Buying Decisions," in Jagdish N. Sheth, ed., *Models of Buyer Behavior* (New York: Harper & Row, 1974), pp. 17–33.
9. Arch G. Woodside, "Informal Group Influence on Risk Taking," *Journal of Marketing Research* 9 (May 1972): 223–225.
10. Peter H. Reingen, "Comment on Woodside," *Journal of Marketing Research* 11 (May 1974): 223–224.
11. Mira Komarovsky, "Class Differences in Family Decision-Making on Expenditures," in Nelson Foote, ed., *Household Decision-Making* (New York: New York University Press, 1961), pp. 255–265.

12. Elizabeth H. Wolgast, "Do Husbands or Wives Make the Purchasing Decisions?," *Journal of Marketing* 22 (October 1958): 151–158.
13. Ferber and Lee, "Husband-Wife Influence."
14. Donald H. Granbois, "The Role of Communication in the Family Decision-Making Process," in Stephen A. Greyser, ed., *Proceedings of the American Marketing Association Educators' Conference* (1963), pp. 44–57.
15. Kenkel, "Family Interaction."
16. J. Sprey, "The Family as a System in Conflict," *Journal of Marriage and the Family* 31 (November 1969): 699–706.
17. R.O. Blood, Jr., "Resolving Family Conflicts," *The Journal of Conflict Resolution* 4 (June 1960): 209–219.
18. Harry L. Davis, "Decision Making Within the Household," *Journal of Consumer Research* 2 (March 1976): 252.
19. Raymond Loewy/William Snaith, Inc., *Project Home: The Motivations Towards Homes and Housing.* Report prepared for the Project Home Committee, 1967.
20. P. Doyle and P. Hutchinson, "Individual Differences in Family Decision Making," *Journal of the Market Research Society* 15 (October 1973): 193–206.
21. T. Poffenberger, *Husband-Wife Communication and Motivational Aspects of Population Control in an Indian Village* (Green Park, New Delhi: Central Family Planning Institute, 1969).
22. Davis, "Decision Making Within the Household."
23. Sheth, "A Theory of Family Buying Decisions," p. 33.
24. Alvin C. Burns and Donald H. Granbois, "Factors Moderating the Resolution of Preference Conflict in Family Automobile Purchasing," *Journal of Marketing Research* 14 (February 1977): 77–86.
25. Eli P. Cox III, "Family Purchase Decision Making and the Process of Adjustment," *Journal of Marketing Research* 12 (May 1975): 189–195.
26. Davis, "Dimensions of Marital Roles"; and Haley, Overholser, *Purchase Influence.*
27. Haley, Overholser, *Purchase Influence.*
28. Ibid.
29. G. M. Munsinger, J.E. Weber, and R. W. Hansen, "Joint Home Purchasing Decisions by Husbands and Wives," *Journal of Consumer Research* 1 (March 1975): 60–66.
30. H.L. Davis and Benny P. Rigaux, "Perception of Marital Roles in Decision Processes," *Journal of Consumer Research* 1 (June 1974): 51–62.
31. Ibid.
32. J. Palmore, "The Chicago Snowball: A Study of the Flow and Diffusion of Family Planning Information," in D.J. Bogue, ed., *Sociological Contributions to Family Planning Research* (Chicago: Community and Family Planning Center, University of Chicago, 1967), pp. 272–363.
33. D.C. Dubey and H.M. Choldin, "Communication and Diffusion of the IUCD: A Case Study in Urban India," *Demography* 4 (1967): 601–614.
34. Davis and Rigaux, "Perception of Marital Roles."
35. Davis, "Dimensions of Marital Roles."
36. Benny Rigaux-Bricmont, "Explaining the Marital Influences in the Family Economic Decision-Making," in Subhash C. Jain, ed., *Proceedings of the American Marketing Association Educators' Conference,* Series #43 (1978), pp. 126–129.
37. Robert T. Green and Isabella C.M. Cunningham, "Feminine Role Perception and Family Purchasing Decisions," *Journal of Marketing Research* 12 (August 1975): 325–332.
38. Harriet Holter, "Sex Roles and Social Change," *Acta Sociologica* 14 (Winter 1971): 2–12.
39. Isabella C.M. Cunningham and Robert T. Green, "Purchasing Roles in the U.S. Family, 1955 and 1973," *Journal of Marketing* 38 (October 1974): 61–64.
40. Ibid.
41. George J. Szybillo, Arlene K. Sosanie, and Aaron Tenenbein, "Should Children Be Seen But Not Heard?" *Journal of Advertising Research* 17 (December 1977): 8.
42. *FTC Staff Report on Television Advertising to Children* (Washington, D.C.: Federal Trade Commission, 1978).
43. Lewis A. Berey and Richard W. Pollay, "The Influencing Role of the Child in Family Decision Making," *Journal of Marketing Research* 5 (February 1968): 70–72.
44. Scott Ward and Daniel B. Wackman, "Children's Purchase Influence Attempts and Parental Yielding," *Journal of Marketing Research* 9 (August 1972): 316–319.
45. Edward T. Popper, "Mothers' Mediation of Children's Purchase Requests," in Neil Beckwith et al., eds., *Proceedings of the American Marketing Association Educators' Conference.* Series #44 (1979), pp. 645–648.
46. Daniel B. Wackman, "Family Processes in Children's Consumption," in Neil Beckwith et al., eds., *Proceedings of the American Marketing Association Educators' Conference.* Series #44 (1979), pp. 649–652.
47. Ward and Wackman, "Children's Purchase Influence."
48. Pat L. Burr and Richard M. Burr, "Parental Responses to Child Marketing," *Journal of Advertising Research* 17 (December 1977): 17–20.
49. Popper, "Mothers' Mediation"; and Wackman, "Family Processes."
50. David C. Epperson, "Reassessment of Indices of Parental Influence in the American Society," *American Sociological Review* 29 (February 1964).
51. Paul Gilkison, "What Influences the Buying Decisions of Teenagers?" *Journal of Retailing* 41 (Fall 1965): 36–41.
52. Russell L. Langworthy, "Community Status and Influence in a High School," *American Sociological Review* 24 (August 1959): 537–539.
53. George P. Moschis and Roy L. Moore, "Decision Making Among the Young: A Socialization Perspective," *Journal of Consumer Research* 6 (September 1979): 101–112.
54. Gilbert A. Churchill, Jr. and George P. Moschis, "Television and Interpersonal Influences on Adolescent Consumer Learning," *Journal of Consumer Research* 6 (June 1979): 23–25.

55. Szybillo, Sosanie, and Tenenbein, "Should Children Be Seen?"
56. Russell I. Haley, "Benefit Segmentation: A Decision-Oriented Research Tool," *Journal of Marketing* 32 (July 1968): 30–35.
57. Burr and Burr, "Parental Responses to Child Marketing."
58. Wackman, "Family Processes."
59. Davis and Rigaux, "Perception of Marital Roles."
60. Davis, "Decision Making Within the Household."
61. Harry L. Davis, "Measurement of Husband-Wife Influence in Consumer Purchase Decisions," *Journal of Marketing Research* 8 (August 1971): 305–312.

FIFTEEN

Word-of-Mouth Communication and Opinion Leadership

Focus of Chapter

This chapter considers direct communication between individuals within a group. A central concept in direct communication between individuals in a group is *opinion leadership*. An **opinion leader** is the individual who influences the purchasing behavior of another consumer through face-to-face communication. The consumer being influenced is the **follower**.

Research on opinion leadership has centered on the flow of word-of-mouth communications between consumers and the reasons why consumers offer and receive product opinions. In the first section of the chapter the process of word-of-mouth communications is considered. Key issues regarding opinion leadership will then be explored, such as: Does opinion leadership cut across product categories? Can the characteristics of an opinion leader be described? Is the word-of-mouth process best described as one of opinion leadership or opinion transmission? The next section then shows how marketers use the concept of opinion leadership. Finally, the measurement of opinion leadership will be considered.

OPINION LEADERSHIP VERSUS SOCIAL COMMUNICATION

Although the designations opinion leader and follower have commonly been used for almost thirty years to identify influencer and influencee, these terms are very misleading. The opinion leader is not a leader in the true sense of the word. He or she may influence another consumer for a particular product in a particular situation, but probably does not exert general leadership influence. There is no reason to believe that an opinion leader for fashion should also be an opinion leader for financial services. Opinion leadership is not a personality trait, it is specific to the product category or categories.

Furthermore, a number of studies have consistently found that the individual who transmits information to others is also more likely to receive information from others. That is, a consumer who frequently expresses opinions about sports equipment will also be more likely to listen to others' opinions about such equipment. One study found that doctors who influenced others in adopting a new drug were also influenced by others in their social group.[1] A study of the adopters of stainless steel blades when they were first introduced found that 75 percent of "opinion leaders" were also influenced by others.[2] A study of women's influence in four product categories found that 80 percent of the influencers also received information from others.[3]

These findings suggest that the key element in face-to-face influence is not opinion leadership but *social communications*. Those who are more likely to do the influencing are also more likely to be influenced. Word-of-mouth communication is, therefore, the key in transmitting influence within groups.

Despite the shortcomings of the opinion leadership versus follower dichotomy (opinion giver versus receiver would be more appropriate), the traditional terminology will be used in this chapter to identify influencer and influencee.

WORD-OF-MOUTH COMMUNICATION AND PERSONAL INFLUENCE

The Importance of Word-of-Mouth Communication

The adage "a satisfied customer is your best salesperson" illustrates the importance of word-of-mouth communication to the marketer. Positive opinions about a product from friends and relatives are more likely to influence choice than any other source of information. Personal influence is most powerful because consumers generally regard such sources as more credible and trustworthy than commercial sources. Moreover, information from reference and family groups is a means of reducing the risk in a purchase decision. A consumer considering the purchase of an expensive item such as a car, or socially visible items such as clothing or furniture, is likely to obtain the opinion of "relevant others." Such opinions not only provide information to reduce financial and performance risk, but also are a means of group sanction to reduce social risk.

One of the first studies establishing the importance of word-of-mouth communications was conducted by Katz and Lazarsfeld in a small Midwestern community shortly after World War II. They found word-of-mouth communication was the most important form of influence in the purchase of food products and household goods. It was twice as effective as radio advertising in influencing consumers to switch brands, four times as effective as personal selling, and seven times as effective as newspapers and magazines.[4] Similarly, Whyte's study of the transmission of influence in the purchase of air conditioners in a Philadelphia suburb also concluded that word-of-mouth communication was the determining factor.[5] He found that ownership clustered in certain locations, tended to group on one side of the street, but did not cross the street. He concluded that the pattern of ownership reflected the pattern of social communication.

Though both studies were conducted before television became a major medium, more recent studies have also confirmed the dominance of personal influence in choice decisions. Arndt found that respondents who received positive word-of-mouth communications about a new food product were three times as likely to purchase it compared to those who received negative communications.[6] Feldman and Spencer found that two-thirds of new residents in a community relied on word-of-mouth communications to select a doctor, and that over 40 percent requested additional advice from the same individuals on other products and services.[7] In a study of four product categories, Summers and King found that over two-thirds of the respondents discussed new products in these categories with friends and relatives in the last six months.[8] Robertson concluded that personal sources generally outweighed commercial sources in influencing the consumer for a wide range of product categories.[9]

Word-of-mouth communication will not be the dominant factor for every product category. It will be most important, however, when reference groups are more likely to be sources of information and influence. This will occur when

- the product is visible and therefore behavior is apparent;
- the product is distinctive and can more easily be identified with style, taste, and other personal norms;
- the product has just been introduced;
- the product is important to the norms and belief system of the reference group (e.g., teenagers' reactions to a new rock album; older consumers' reaction to a new salt-free breakfast product);
- the purchase of the product is likely to be seen as risky, encouraging a search for additional information; and
- the consumer is involved in the purchase decision.

The Two-Step Flow of Communication

Katz and Lazarsfeld were among the first to identify the process of word-of-mouth communication. They described the process as a two-step flow from the mass media to opinion leaders, and from opinion leaders to followers (see top of Figure 15–1.)[10] They believed that opinion leaders are more exposed to the mass media than are those whom they influence.[11] As a result, the opinion leader is viewed as an intermediary between the mass media and other consumers. The majority of consumers—the followers—are viewed as passive recipients of information.

The principal contribution of the two-step flow theory is that it rejected the long-standing notion that the mass media were the principal means of

THE MULTISTEP FLOW MODEL

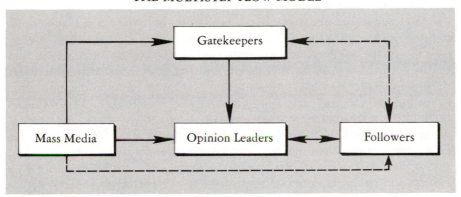

FIGURE 15–1   Two Models of Word-of-Mouth Communication

influencing consumers and the principal source of information. Although evident today, the importance of personal influence relative to commercial influence was not that clear after World War II. Advertising was considered the dominant force. It was only in the 1950s and, paradoxically, with the advent of television, that advertising began to be viewed as a weaker force that was unlikely to change group-influenced purchasing choices. Advertising would reinforce existing product preferences but could not change negative opinions, particularly when they are strongly held.[12] The two-step flow theory encouraged the view that personal influence was the principal means of communication and influence, not advertising.

Personal Influence and the Two-Step Flow for Low-Involvement Products

It was of course recognized by sociologists that this view of the importance of personal influence is only relevant when reference group influence is operative; that is, for distinctive and involving products. For less important products, a low involvement perspective would be more relevant; one which would view personal influence as unimportant relative to advertising. Under such conditions, advertising may be the dominant force just from the power of repetition.[13] The product may not be important enough to seek information from friends and relatives.

A Multistep Flow of Communication

Although the two-step flow was important in understanding the process of personal influence, it was not an accurate representation of the flow of information and influence for several reasons. First, the follower is not passive. He or she may initiate requests for information as well as listen to the unsolicited opinions of others. Summers found that in most cases the traditional view held — opinion leaders offered unsolicited opinions. But in one-third of the cases, opinion leaders were asked for their opinions about new products. [14]

Second, those who transmit information are also more likely to receive it. Opinion leaders are also influenced by followers. Conversely, those who seek out information are also more likely to give it. Word-of-mouth influence is frequently a two-directional flow between transmitter and receiver.

Third, the opinion leader is not the only one to receive information from the mass media. Followers will also be influenced by advertising. Moreover, the opinion leader may not control the flow of information from the mass media to the group. Katz and Lazarsfeld recognized that there may be a "gatekeeper" or "information gatherer" who serves this function. [15] The **gatekeeper** may be distinct from the opinion leader since the gatekeeper may introduce ideas and information to the group but may not disseminate them. For example, a consumer may be an avid reader of fashion magazines, may introduce certain information on the latest styles, but may not influence the adoption of these styles within the group.

Katz and Lazarsfeld did not introduce the concept of the gatekeeper in a marketing context. Yet it is recognized that certain consumers may be able to introduce information without exerting influence. In family decision making, the child may serve as a gatekeeper for candy by informing the mother of the various alternatives, but the mother may make the final decision. In organizational buying behavior, the purchasing agent may be the gatekeeper for information on alternative vendors, but the engineer and production manager may be the opinion leaders within the buying group.

Given these limitations in the concept of a two-step flow, a more realisitic model of word-of-mouth communication would be a multistep flow, as represented in the bottom of Figure 15–1. This model recognizes that the mass media can directly reach either gatekeeper, opinion leader, or follower, but are less likely to reach the follower (as represented by the dotted line). The gatekeeper is represented as a source of information to both opinion leaders and followers, but is more likely to disseminate information to opinion leaders. Furthermore, word-of-mouth communication between opinion leaders and followers is represented as a two-directional flow since opinion leaders may seek information from followers, and followers may solicit information from opinion leaders.

Categorization of Consumers in the Multistep Flow

The recognition in the multistep model that opinion leaders and followers may both transmit and receive information leads to four possibilities (see Figure 15–2). The **socially integrated consumer** is one who is high on both opinion

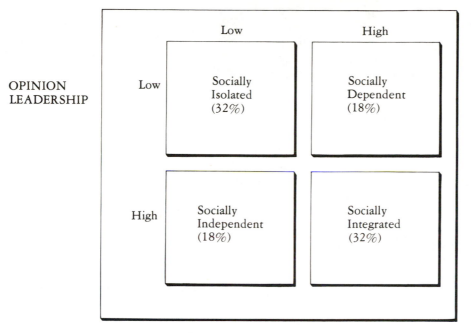

FIGURE 15–2   A Categorization of Consumers by Opinion Leadership and Information Seeking

Source: Adapted from Fred D. Reynolds and William R. Darden, "Mutually Adaptive Effects of Interpersonal Communication," *Journal of Marketing Research* 8 (November 1971): p. 451
Reprinted with permission from the *Journal of Marketing Research.*

leadership and information seeking. This consumer is the most socially active in encouraging word-of-mouth communications. The **socially independent consumer** scores high on opinion leadership but low on information seeking. This consumer represents the traditional view of opinion leadership in the two-step model; a consumer who transmits information and influence but does not solicit it. The **socially dependent consumer** is low on opinion leadership but high on information seeking. This consumer represents the traditional view of a follower — an individual who is socially active in soliciting word-of-mouth communication, but is not an influencer. The **socially isolated consumer** scores low on opinion leadership and information seeking. This consumer is a passive individual who receives information but does not seek it. This group is not socially active and may avoid personal influence.

Reynolds and Darden classified women into one of these four groups based on their transfer of information and influence about women's clothing fashions.[16] One third of the women were categorized as socially integrated, one-third as socially isolated, and the remainder were split equally between the socially independent and socially dependent consumer. Therefore, only one-third of the sample conformed to the traditional definitions of opinion leader and follower.

Reynolds and Darden then determined the fashion interest and media behavior of each group. The socially integrated consumer was twice as likely to express a high level of interest in fashion as the socially independent consumer. A high level of interest will therefore encourage both the giving and receiving of information and influence. This means that the opinion leadership concept is not sufficient to explain word-of-mouth communication. Word-of-mouth communication is most likely to be the result of interest in the subject rather than leadership within the group.

Why Consumers Engage in Word-of-Mouth Communication

Why do consumers engage in word-of-mouth communication? The question applies to motives for transmitting and motives for seeking information and influence.

Motives for Transmitting Word-of-Mouth Communications

There are a number of motives for talking about brands or products. First, product involvement is likely to encourage a consumer to transmit information and influence. The study by Reynolds and Darden showed that this factor is important in encouraging consumers to transmit and to receive word-of-mouth communication. Katz and Lazarsfeld found that those most likely to transmit information are not those with experience but those who are experiencing product decisions.[17] The opinion leader for children's vitamins is not likely to be the mother with six grown children and past purchasing experience, but the mother with younger children who has direct interest in the product category. Summers found that 86 percent of all transmitters of word-of-mouth communications owned the product before discussing it.[18] Therefore, product involvement is an essential ingredient in personal communications.

Another motive for transmitting information is to erase any doubts about product choice. A consumer may attempt to reduce dissonance by describing the positive qualities of a recently purchased car to friends and relatives. If a friend buys the same make, this will be seen as confirmation of the consumer's original judgment.

A third reason for word-of-mouth communication is involvement with the group. The greater the importance of the group, the greater the likelihood the consumer will seek to transmit information to it. A new resident in a leisure community may want to become more involved with his or her neighbors and will transmit information on new products of interest to elderly consumers. Dichter suggests that such communication is a means of ensuring involvement with the group by various strategies such as gaining attention, suggesting expertise, or showing inside information.[19]

Transmission of word-of-mouth communication may be encouraged by other types of involvement besides product and group involvement. Dichter suggests that consumers who are involved with advertising messages (the gatekeepers) are also likely to transmit this information through word-of-mouth communications. Certain people enjoy talking about commercials or product experiences as a means of social interaction.

Motives for Seeking Word-of-Mouth Communications

Several motives may also be cited for seeking word-of-mouth communication. One motive is that friends and relatives are a good source of product information. A second motive for seeking information from personal sources is that it facilitates the purchase task. A consumer might find out from a relative that a store does not have the desired item, that it is priced too high, or that it is not made of the desired material. Shopping time has thereby been reduced. A saving has been made in time, effort, or money as a result of personal communications. A third motive for seeking word-of-mouth communications is that it reduces purchase risk. Consumers who see risk in the purchase are more likely to initiate product-related conversations and to request information from friends and relatives. The flow of word-of-mouth communications is therefore from those who see less risk in purchasing to those who see more risk.[20]

Woodside and DeLozier describe a number of possible outcomes when a consumer seeks information from a group to reduce risk (see Figure 15–3).[21] Assume a consumer is considering purchasing a Beta-Max video recorder, an expensive item that is not widely owned. The consumer decides to ask a group of friends for their advice. First it is possible the group does not know very much about the product. If so, it is likely the consumer will explain the nature of the product and its benefits to the group and will then seek their advice (right-hand branch in Figure 15–3).

If group members are familiar with the video recorder (left-hand branch), then the question is whether communication with the group has reduced the consumer's uncertainty about buying. If so, it is likely the product will be purchased. If not, then the question is whether the group believes the benefits gained by purchasing are greater than the risk. If so, the consumer will probably purchase. Assume the feeling among group members is that the cost and the uncertainty about performance outweigh product benefits. This opinion may be sufficient to dissuade the consumer from buying a video recorder. But if the purchase is of great importance, the consumer may look for other sources to support the purchase. Product information may be obtained from *Consumer Reports* or from other groups such as business associates or relatives.

WORD-OF-MOUTH COMMUNICATION AND OPINION LEADERSHIP

The influence of word-of-mouth communication in consumer behavior is closely tied to the concept of opinion leadership since a study of group communication requires an understanding of the transmitter (opinion leader) and receiver (follower).

The Nature of Opinion Leadership

The point was made earlier that opinion leadership is not a general trait, but is particular to the product category of interest to the consumer and to the

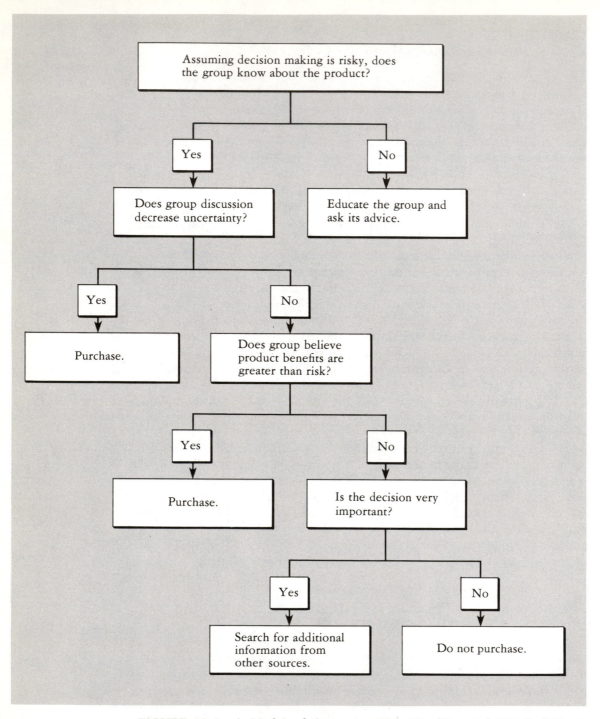

FIGURE 15–3 A Model of Consumer Risk Handling and Word-of-Mouth Communication

Source: Adapted from Arch G. Woodside and M. Wayne DeLozier, "Effects of Word-of-Mouth Advertising on Consumer Risk-Taking," *Journal of Advertising* 5 (Fall 1976): 17 Reprinted with permission from the *Journal of Advertising*.

situation. Several questions must therefore be answered before the marketer can consider directing appeals to opinion leaders or attempt to stimulate positive word-of-mouth communications: 1. To what degree is opinion leadership product-specific? 2. Is opinion leadership dependent on the purchase situation? 3. Is opinion leadership dependent on the social setting for communication? 4. Is opinion leadership really leadership?

Is Opinion Leadership Product-Specific?

There is general agreement that opinion leadership does not extend across unrelated product categories. The classic study by Katz and Lazarsfeld found that there was no overlap in opinion leadership in marketing, fashion, and public affairs. An opinion leader in one of these three areas was not necessarily an opinion leader in the other.[22] But marketing can cover anything from autos to toothpaste. So the question still remains, what is the degree of opinion leadership across product categories.

Several more recent studies show that there is some overlap in opinion leadership. An opinion leader in one category is likely to be an opinion leader in a closely related product category. For example, King and Summers found that opinion leaders for small appliances were also likely to be opinion leaders for large appliances. Influence was also closely related for women's clothing, fashion, and cosmetics. And, those who were influential for packaged foods were also likely to be influential for household cleansers and detergents.[23] Similar findings were obtained by Myers and Robertson: Opinion leaders for household furnishings were likely to be opinion leaders for household appliances.[24]

Therefore, opinion leadership and word-of-mouth communications are not general, but rather are related to the product category. However, sufficient overlap exists to safely conclude that an opinion leader in one category is likely to be an opinion leader in a related category.

Is Opinion Leadership Situational?

Consumers do not generally meet and launch into a discussion of product experiences. Product-related conversations occur in a more casual setting that generally involves some relevant situational cue to stimulate a product discussion, such as the use of the product.

Belk did one of the few studies that examined the situation in which word-of-mouth communication is likely to take place.[25] He interviewed women in the Minneapolis-St. Paul area when Maxim coffee was first introduced. Respondents were asked, "How was it that the subject of Maxim happened to come up?" Replies are found in Table 15–1. First, it is apparent that word-of-mouth communication takes place within a context relevant to the product. Almost 80 percent of all word-of-mouth communication about Maxim — both received and sent — took place in a situation relevant to food. In over one-third of the situations, discussion was prompted by use of the product category.

Belk also concluded that a leader-follower role in word-of-mouth communication does not seem to occur. Word-of-mouth communication is more dependent on the situation than on the parties involved. Therefore, product discussion is more likely to be generated by the fact that two people are drinking

TABLE 15–1 Situations in Which Word-of-Mouth Communications Occurred

Situation	Percent Received	Percent Sent	Total Percent
Food-Related Context			
Drinking coffee	25	38	30
Drinking Maxim	9	0	6
Conversing about food	35	29	33
Shopping for food	5	8	6
Eating	5	0	3
Totals	79	75	78
Non-Food Context			
Spontaneously given	7	17	11
Spontaneously received	0	4	1
Viewing/hearing Maxim ad	5	4	4
Unclear	9	0	6
Totals	21	25	22

Source: Adapted from Russell W. Belk, "Occurrence of Word-of-Mouth Buyer Behavior a Function of Situation and Advertising Stimuli," in Fred C. Allvine, ed., *Combined Proceedings of the American Marketing Association,* Series No. 33 (1971), p. 420.
Reprinted with permission from the American Marketing Association.

coffee together, than by the fact that one of them can be regarded as a group leader.

This finding again brings into question the concept of leadership. It suggests that the marketer should be more concerned with identifying relevant situations that may stimulate product discussion rather than spending time and money trying to identify a group of opinion leaders. The implication seems to be that advertising should try to present a situation that simulates product discussion. The alternative — developing an advertisement that emphasizes the influence of one individual over another — would be less relevant according to Belk's findings.

Is Opinion Leadership Related to Social Setting?

Opinion leadership is also related to the setting for communications. Summers examined the setting for word-of-mouth communication regarding four new products.[26] He asked consumers whether product-related conversations involved the family, just the transmitter and receiver (the dyad), or other people as well (the group), and whether conversations took place in the home or in other locations.

The importance of the family is evident since about half of all conversations involved the family (see Table 15–2). Family-related word-of-mouth communication was least likely for nylon hose and most likely for the electric toothbrush. Word-of-mouth communication was also heavily weighted toward two-person conversations. Two thirds of all communications were between transmitter and receiver only. Summers concludes that the dominance of two-person

TABLE 15–2   The Social Setting for Word-of-Mouth Communication

Social Setting	Percent of Time Word-of-Mouth Communications Occurs Four Product Categories				
	Durable Press Clothing	New Type of Nylon Hose	New Snack Food	Electric Toothbrush	Total
Family vs. Non-family					
Family	45	35	44	51	45
Nonfamily	55	65	56	49	55
Group vs. Dyad					
Dyad	72	77	54	63	66
Group	28	23	46	37	34
Physical Location					
Private Home	65	50	74	77	69
Other	35	50	26	23	31

Source: Adapted from John O. Summers, "New Product Interpersonal Communications," in Fred C. Allvine, ed., *Combined Proceedings of the American Marketing Association,* Series # 33 (1971), pp. 431–432.

Reprinted with permission from the American Marketing Association.

conversations "suggests a casual passing on of product information rather than 'lecturing' by transmitters."[27] Summers therefore agrees with Belk that word-of-mouth communication is likely to be determined by passing circumstance rather than by any strong desire to communicate feelings and opinions about products.

Table 15–2 also shows that most word-of-mouth communication takes place in the home. Only for nylon hose were discussions equally likely to occur outside the home. It appears that the fashion character of the product makes it more relevant outside the casual atmosphere of the home.

Since family and home are closely related to personal influence, Summers' findings suggest the importance of physical proximity in encouraging word-of-mouth communication. This finding was supported by a study of physician selection which showed that among those transmitting and receiving opinions about physicians, 67 percent had visited the other person's home.[28]

Is Opinion Leadership Really Leadership?

If opinion leadership implies that the transmitter of information is likely to be the group leader, the answer is "no." The individual who transmits information and influence regarding a product does not have to be a group leader. The transmitter is most likely to be involved with the product and to have knowledge about the product. This provides the individual with credibility and legitimacy in communicating product information. Moreover, opinion leadership does not occur in the sense of one individual dominating another or communicating in a one-sided way. The studies cited above consistently show that communication occurs both ways between transmitter and receiver. Further, word-of-mouth communication about products is fairly casual and does not generally involve pressures to conform to the opinions of a group leader. Opinion leadership is really the transmission of opinion through social communication in a matter-of-fact setting.

Characteristics of the Opinion Leader

Marketers are interested in identifying opinion leaders since these consumers may exert a high level of influence within the product category. Opinion leaders are more aware of product information and are more likely to discuss products with others. Identification of the demographic characteristics that distinguish opinion leaders from other purchasers in a product category would permit marketers to select media most likely to reach this influential group. Identification of the attitudes or life-styles of opinion leaders would permit marketers to develop promotional themes to appeal to this group.

The effectiveness of such a strategy is doubtful because of the fact that opinion leaders tend to communicate with consumers similar to themselves. Personal influence tends to occur when source and receiver have similar attitudes, beliefs, and characteristics.[29] This view was confirmed by Myers and Robertson in a study of twelve product categories.[30] They found little difference between the demographic and life-style characteristics of opinion leaders and followers.

Another reason why developing a profile of the opinion leader is difficult is that such a profile has to be product-specific. The characteristics of the fashion opinion leader may be totally different from those of the food opinion leader. Few generalizations can be made across product categories.

Despite the difficulties of identifying an opinion leader, some useful generalizations have emerged.

Product-Related Characteristics

Opinion leaders have generally been found to display certain product-related characteristics. They usually are:

- more knowledgeable about the product category;
- more interested in the product category;
- more active in receiving communications about the product from personal sources;
- more likely to read magazines and other print media relevant to their area of product interest.

In addition, opinion leaders have consistently expressed greater interest in new products in the particular product category. Thus, fashion opinion leaders will be more interested in the latest styles, appliance opinion leaders more interested in new appliances, etc. A study of intention to buy personal care appliances such as hair dryers and curlers also found that opinion leaders express a greater willingness to buy new products.[31]

Demographic Characteristics

Few generalizations can be made about the demographic characteristics of opinion leaders. Katz and Lazarsfeld found that women with more children were more likely to be opinion leaders for household products, possibly because they are more likely to buy a wider range of products and, therefore, have more purchasing experience. Katz and Lazarsfeld also found that younger women in the higher socioeconomic bracket were somewhat more likely to be opinion leaders. They speculated that higher income may provide for more time in obtaining product information and more status in associating with other consumers.[32] A study of clothing also found that fashion opinion leaders were more likely to be younger and upscale.[33] But most marketing studies have found few demographic differences between opinion leaders and followers in a product category. This means that selecting media to reach opinion leaders based on demographic differences is not a viable strategy.

Personality Characteristics

Two generalizations can be made about the personality characteristics of opinion leaders across product categories: Opinion leaders are more likely to be *self-confident* in their appraisal of the product category,[34] and are more likely to be *socially active*.[35] Self-confidence is probably a function of greater knowledge of product characteristics and interest in the product. Social activity is probably a function of a greater willingness to communicate with others in a group setting. In other respects, personality variables have not discriminated between opinion leaders and followers. Robertson and Myers related a large number of personality variables to opinion leadership for three product categories and concluded that "a marketer trying to reach innovative or influential individuals will find little help by identifying these people in terms of basic personality variables."[36]

Life-Style Characteristics

Few studies have identified the life-style characteristics of opinion leaders. A Canadian study by Tigert and Arnold of opinion leadership across many product categories found that opinion leaders were more involved with clubs and community affairs, more independent, more price conscious and more style conscious.[37] If these findings are replicated, they may suggest that life-style is a more likely basis for identifying opinion leaders than either personality or demographics.

Media Habits

Few marketing studies have been able to confirm Katz and Lazarsfeld's original conclusion that opinion leaders are more exposed to the mass media. Rather, the general finding is that opinion leaders will read publications relevant to their product category. Studies of automotive[38] and fashion[39] opinion leaders found that they are more likely to read magazines in their area of interest.

In summary, there is little evidence, overall, to suggest that a generalized opinion leader can be described. Further, marketers are unlikely to identify any distinctive demographic or personality traits of opinion leaders even on a product-specific basis. This means that a strategy of trying to pinpoint opinion leaders and reaching them through specific media is likely to fail. If this is true, it does not mean that the study of word-of-mouth communication provides the marketer with few strategic applications. What these findings suggest is that strategic applications are best directed to stimulating word-of-mouth communications. They should not be directed toward trying to reach word-of-mouth transmitters.

STRATEGIC APPLICATIONS OF OPINION LEADERSHIP

Given the difficulty of directing advertising to opinion leaders through the mass media, several alternative strategies can effectively use word-of-mouth communication to increase sales. These strategies may seek to (1) identify opinion leaders directly, (2) create opinion leaders, (3) simulate word-of-mouth communication in advertising, and (4) stimulate word-of-mouth communications through advertising. It is also possible that if substantial negative word-of-mouth communication occurs, the marketer may have to (5) undertake a defensive strategy to counter negative information. This section will consider each of these strategies.

Identifying Opinion Leaders Directly

Opinion leaders can be identified directly through company purchase records. Given the close relationship between opinion leadership and new product adoption, it is possible to identify consumers who are among the first to adopt a new appliance or other product with a purchase record. Another means of identifying opinion leaders is through consumer contests or ads offering additional information. Individuals who respond to contests and offers of information are likely to have a high interest in the product and to be opinion leaders.

Once opinion leaders are identified, direct mail can be used to promote the company's products and provide additional information. Such contacts would stimulate the social multiplier effect referred to in Chapter 13, since these individuals would disseminate information and exert a disproportionate amount of influence on friends and relatives. Opinion leaders could also be given free samples, or in the case of expensive durables, products on loan to stimulate usage. Lincoln Continental dealers in one city recruited a group of opinion leaders to drive the car during the introduction of the model.[40] Attitudes and usage of opinion leaders could also be tracked so that the level of adoption of new products could be projected.

Creating Opinion Leaders

It may also be possible to create opinion leaders for a particular product among a group of socially active consumers. In one well-known application of this strategy, an attempt was made to transform an unknown pop record into a hit in several cities.[41] Opinion leaders in high school were identified — class presidents, class secretaries, sports captains, cheerleaders. These individuals were invited to join a panel to evaluate rock records. Panel members were told they would receive free records in appreciation for their participation and were encouraged to discuss their choice with friends. Several of the records provided to the group reached the top ten in the trial cities without making the top ten in other cities.

Ford also attempted to create opinion leaders when they introduced the Mustang. College newspaper editors, disc jockeys, and airline stewardesses were loaned Mustangs on the assumption that these individuals were more likely to discuss the automobile with others.[42]

Simulating Word-of-Mouth Communication

Advertising can simulate word-of-mouth communication by portraying conversations between typical consumers. In portraying personal influence, these ads seek to replace the need for direct contact by the consumer with friends and relatives. The assumption is that the typical person in the ad is sufficiently credible so that the consumer will believe the information provided by this individual. (See the ad in Figure 13–6 as an example.)

The most frequent approach used in advertising is one consumer telling another about the virtues of the product. Another approach is the hidden camera showing people in TV commercials making unsolicited recommendations for the product. A current campaign for toilet tissue uses an unsolicited recommendation for the product by the husband. The wife is then shown the videotape and is amazed the husband is aware of brand differences. Such ads assume that the consumer believes the testimonial is spontaneous and unsolicited and that the typical consumer has some believable relation to the product.

Stimulating Word-of-Mouth Communication

Advertising can also try to encourage consumers to talk about the product. One strategy is to generate curiosity through planned secrecy. Ford kept the Mustang under wraps before it was introduced, yet generated curiosity by a well-planned publicity campaign. The result was "the most talked about —and least seen — auto of this year."[43]

Another approach is to encourage consumers to "tell your friends" or to "ask your friends." Such a strategy assumes that the product is in a strong position and that word-of-mouth communication will be positive. Obviously, using such a strategy first requires confirmation that the word-of-mouth communications are uniformly positive.

A third strategy is to use original and entertaining themes that are likely to be repeated. Certain themes become part of the everyday jargon during an advertising campaign and even for a period of time after the slogan is no longer used. A number of years ago Tareyton used the slogan "I'd rather fight than switch." Although irritating to many people, it did generate communication and increase product awareness. Another example was Alka Seltzer's theme, "Try it, you'll like it" which also generated considerable word-of-mouth communication.

"Setting the Record Straight" Through Word-of-Mouth Communication

Sometimes, advertisers attempt to encourage word-of-mouth communication to set the record straight. Consumers may have misconceptions about a product which warrants corporate advertising to combat negative information. A good

(the rumor)

Esther Coley

"So many rumors travel through the grapevine you can't always tell what's true and what's not. There's one rumor going around that I'd like to set straight right now. You may have heard that Hunt-Wesson Foods is owned by a man from Texas, named Hunt. It's not so. Hunt-Wesson Foods is located in California. Always has been. We're part of Norton Simon, Incorporated. We have nothing, not a thing to do with any other Hunt. That's the truth. Won't you tell your neighbor and help set the record straight? We'd be grateful."

Esther Coley
Esther Coley
Home Economist
Hunt-Wesson Foods

FIGURE 15–4   Using Word-of-Mouth Communication to Set the Record Straight

By permission of Hunt-Wesson Foods, Inc.

example is the ad in Figure 15–4. The misperception existed among consumers that Hunt-Wesson was owned by a rich Texas magnate called Hunt. The ad dispels the false rumor by identifying the true owner, the Norton Simon company, and the true company location, California. The ad is also a good example of a direct attempt to simulate word-of-mouth communication to counter consumer misperceptions.

Advertisers may also wish to directly discourage rumors that are proving harmful. An example of this was rumors among children that a new chewing gum — Bubble Yum — caused cancer and had spider eggs in it. The rumors were so rampant that they became nationwide. The company placed full page ads in thirty newspapers that stated, "Someone Is Telling Your Kids Very Bad Lies About a Very Good Gum."[44] The rumors eventually disappeared.

MEASURING OPINION LEADERSHIP

Three methods have been used to measure opinion leadership: the sociometric technique, the key informant method, and the self-designating technique.

Sociometric Technique

In the **sociometric technique** group members are asked to reveal whom they would go to for advice and information about a product or idea. Specific individuals are identified and can in turn be interviewed to trace the network of communication. A study by Coleman traced word-of-mouth communications between doctors.[45] Figure 15–5 shows the pattern of communication between nine doctors in a community. This network is known as a *sociogram*. Obviously doctor 5 is an opinion leader since the eight other doctors seek his advice. Doctor 5 also adopted a new drug sooner than the other eight doctors.

Several marketing studies have used the sociometric technique. Arndt asked 332 women in an apartment complex about adoption of a new brand.[46] Women were asked three names of others they go to for advice or others who offer advice about new products. Responses were then cross-checked by comparing names given by both parties.

In a study of organizational buying influence, Martilla studied word-of-mouth communication among representatives of thirty-three paper converting plants.[47] Once again, specific sources of information were identified.

In all three studies cited, members of a particular social system (doctors in a community, members of an apartment complex, associates in an industry) could be identified and the patterns of communication traced. Therefore, the sociometric technique can be used only when such a closed grouping is being studied. But most brand and product studies involve influence extending beyond a single social system. Therefore, other techniques must be used.

The Key Informant Method

Key informants in a social system are asked to identify opinion leaders. For example, key informants could be used to rate the prestige or leadership of members of their group. The method is limited in that it seeks to study only

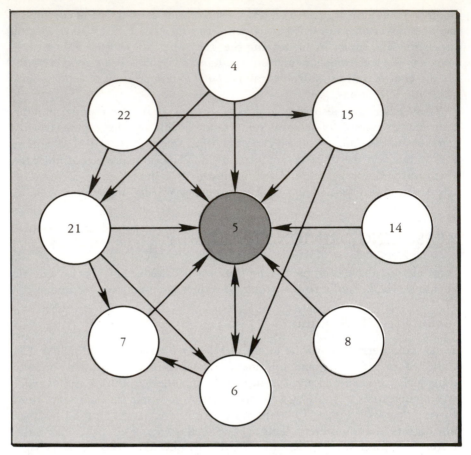

FIGURE 15–5   A Sociogram of Word-of-Mouth Communications Between Doctors

Source: James Coleman, "Social Processes in Physicians' Adoption of a New Drug," *Journal of Chronic Diseases* 9 (1959): 1–19
        Reprinted with permission from James Coleman.

opinion leaders. It is also restricted to a particular social system and cannot be used for the large number of marketing studies that require a sample from a population of consumers that includes many diverse groups.

The Self-Designating Technique

The **self-designating technique** asks a consumer a series of questions to determine the degree to which the consumer perceives himself or herself as an opinion leader. The most frequently used battery of questions is presented in Figure 15–6.[48] On the basis of answers to these questions, the researcher will develop a single score to permit categorization of the individual as an opinion leader, a follower, or some middle category. Most studies utilize this multiple questioning procedure because it provides greater reliability in identifying opinion leaders. But some studies have used one or two questions to identify

OPINION LEADERSHIP SCALE

1. In general do you like to talk about _____ with your friends?
   Yes _____1   No _____2
2. Would you say you give *very little information, an average amount of information,* or *a great deal of information* about _____ to your friends?
   You give very little information .... _____1
   You give an average amount of information .... _____2
   You give a great deal of information .... _____3
3. During the *past six months,* have *you told anyone about* some _____?
   Yes _____1   No _____2
4. compared with *your circle of friends,* are *you less likely, about as likely,* or *more likely* to be asked for advice about _____?
   Less likely to be asked .... _____1
   About as likely to be asked .... _____2
   More likely to be asked .... _____3
5. If you and your friends were to discuss _____, what part would *you* be most likely to play? Would you *mainly listen* to your friends' ideas or would *you try to convince them* of your ideas?
   You mainly listen to your friends' ideas .... _____1
   You try to convince them of your ideas .... _____2
6. Which of these happens more often? Do *you tell your friends* about some _____, or do *they tell you* about some _____?
   You tell them about some _____ _____1
   They tell you about some _____ _____2
7. Do you have the feeling that you are generally regarded by your friends and neighbors as a good source of advice about _____?
   Yes _____1   No _____2

Source: Everett M. Rogers and F. Floyd Shoemaker, *Communication in Innovations* (New York: The Free Press, 1971). Copyright © 1971 by the Free Press, a division of Macmillan Publishing Co., Inc.

opinion leaders, For example: "Let's consider how much you feel you influence friends and relatives on each of the following topics (check one):
"I influence people —— Quite a bit —— To some extent —— Very little."[49]

Most of the marketing studies cited in this chapter have used the self-designating technique. These studies are surveys of brand and product influence that extend beyond a single social system. Therefore, a self-designating method is necessary.

SUMMARY

Word-of-mouth communication between consumers is the most important source of information and influence in consumer behavior. The individual who influences the purchasing behavior of another consumer is the opinion leader; the consumer being influenced is the follower. But these designations may be misleading for two reasons. First, an individual is an opinion leader only for a particular product category or categories. There is little evidence of a general opinion leader. Second, the opinion leader is as likely to receive information as to give it. Therefore, certain consumers are more likely to engage in word-of-mouth communication independent of group leadership.

Several studies have documented the greater importance of word-of-mouth communication compared to commercial information sources. Word-of-mouth influence is more likely to be important when the product is visible, distinctive, and important to the belief system of the group. The process of word-of-mouth communication can best be described as a transmission of information from mass media to both opinion leaders and followers, with gatekeepers (those most sensitive to product information) serving as intermediaries in the information flow.

The nature of word-of-mouth communication was considered by examining several issues. Word-of-mouth communication appears to be product-specific. Social communication tends to be initiated by interest in a product category rather than by any specific leadership role. As a result, word-of-mouth communication is likely to be situational. Discussions are most likely initiated when the product is seen or is in use. Moreover, product-related conversations are most likely to take place in a family setting. These findings again support the conclusion that word-of-mouth communication is more a function of the product environment than of opinion leadership.

Since opinion leadership is product-specific, few characteristics have been associated with an opinion leader across product categories. Opinion leaders do tend to be more knowledgeable about the product of interest and more likely to read magazines about the product. They are also more interested in new brands in the product category. They are more likely to be currently involved in decision making for the product. They are also more self-confident in their product decisions. But few specific demographic, life-style, and personality characteristics can be associated with opinion leadership.

Strategically, the concept of opinion leadership offers marketers several options. Marketers can attempt to identify and reach opinion leaders directly in an effort to initiate a social multiplier effect. They can attempt to create opinion leaders. They can simulate word-of-mouth communications by picturing social influence in advertising. Or, they can stimulate word-of-mouth communications by using original themes and story-lines that are likely to be repeated in a social setting.

The next chapter will consider the diffusion of communications across groups.

1. This chapter suggests that an alternative categorization to an opinion leader is a social communicator since individuals most likely to transmit information on a product are also more likely to receive such information. What is the distinction between the concept of an opinion leader and a social communicator in terms of (a) the nature of influence, (b) the role of the influencer, and (c) possible characteristics of the influencer?

2. Two of the major studies documenting the importance of word-of-mouth communication — Whyte's study of air conditioner ownership and Katz and Lazarsfeld's study of influence in a Midwestern town — were conducted before the advent of TV. Some have argued that TV provides a basis for simulating word-of-mouth communication and thereby reduces the importance of word-of-mouth influence.

   - Do you agree?
   - Is it possible that TV is a more important force than word-of-mouth influence for certain groups (e.g., children, the undereducated, etc.)?

3. In most cases, opinion leaders provide their opinions of brands and products unsolicited. But in some cases, others in the group institute word-of-mouth communication by asking about particular brands and products.

   - Under what conditions will the views of the opinion leader be solicited by others?

4. Assume that you are studying group influence in the purchase of men's cosmetics and fragrances. You hypothesize that they are likely to be socially independent, dependent, integrated, or isolate consumers depending on their degree of opinion leadership and communication (see Figure 15–2).

   - What questions would you ask consumers to test your hypothesis?
   - Assume that these four groups could be identified. What would be the strategic implications for the marketing of men's cosmetics and fragrances?

5. Studies by Belk and Summer suggest that the situation is more important in generating word-of-mouth communication than is the role of the opinion leader.

   - If this is true, what would be the implications for using advertising to attempt to generate word-of-mouth communication?

6. Marketing studies have not identified any distinctive characteristics of opinion leaders.

   - Given the difficulty in identifying opinion leaders, can the concept of opinion leadership be used for purposes of market segmentation?

7. A record company feels that word-of-mouth communication is a key element in the creation of hit records and would like to document this fact by studying the nature of word-of-mouth communication among groups.

   - Develop a study design to trace word-of-mouth influence in the purchase of records.
   - What measurement technique would you use and why?

8. Is it feasible to attempt to "create" opinion leaders? If so, for what types of product categories?

9. Would you recommend a sociometric technique to measure opinion leadership in evaluating patterns of influence in the:

   - adoption of a new product in a retirement community?
   - purchase of a new line of high-styled jeans?
   - role of the purchasing agent in the purchase of a new industrial product?

1. Use a sociometric technique to trace conversations between a group of eight or nine teenagers or college students regarding opinions of rock/pop albums. Make sure the persons you interview know each other. Try to develop a network to show who talks to whom. Then ask these individuals to rate themselves on opinion leadership. (You can use questions 2 and 4 in Figure 15–6 to measure opinion leadership.)

   • Do the sociometric and self-designating techniques agree regarding the identity of opinion leaders?

   • Ask the sample to rate themselves on their (a) interest in records, (b) self-confidence in buying and evaluating records, and (c) level of social activity compared to friends and acquaintances.

   • Opinion leaders would be expected to score high on these three criteria. Do your findings confirm this hypothesis?

2. Select about five or six diverse product categories such as jeans, casual wear, record albums, stereo equipment, books for leisure reading, camera equipment, etc. Make sure some of these products are interrelated (e.g., record albums and stereo equipment; jeans and casual wear). Ask a sample of twenty to thirty respondents to rate themselves on opinion leadership for each category (using questions 2 and 4 in Figure 15–6). In addition, ask them to rate themselves on a life-style inventory (select items from Table 10–1) and to determine their demographic characteristics.

   • Is there a generalized opinion leader that rates high on opinion leadership on most categories? If so, does the generalized opinion leader differ from others in demographic and life-style characteristics?

   • Do consumers who rate high on one product also rate high on a related product category? (E.g., do those who rate high on jeans also rate high on casual wear?) What are the demographic and life-style characteristics of the product-specific opinion leaders?

   • What are the marketing implications of defining the demographic and life-style characteristics of the generalized opinion leader (if there is one)? Of the product-specific opinion leader?

NOTES

1. James Coleman, Elihu Katz, and Herbert Menzel, "The Diffusion of an Innovation Among Physicians, *Sociometry* 20 (December 1957): 253–270.
2. Jagdish N. Sheth, "Word-of-Mouth In Low-Risk Innovations," *Journal of Advertising Research* 11 (June 1971): 15–18.
3. John O. Summers and Charles W. King, "Interpersonal Communication and New Product Attitudes," in Philip R. McDonald, ed., *Proceedings of the American Marketing Association's Educators' Conference,* Series #30 (1969), pp. 292–299.
4. Elihu Katz and Paul F. Lazarsfeld, *Personal Influence* (Glencoe, Ill.: The Free Press, 1955).
5. William H. Whyte, Jr., "The Web of Word of Mouth," *Fortune* 50 (November 1954): 140–143.
6. Johan Arndt, "Role of Product-Related Conversations in the Diffusion of a New Product," *Journal of Marketing Research* 4 (August 1967): 291–295.
7. Sidney P. Feldman and Merlin C. Spencer, "The Effect of Personal Influence in the Selection of Consumer Services," in Peter D. Bennett, ed., *Proceedings of the Fall Conference of the American Marketing Association* (1965), pp. 440–452.
8. Summers and King, "Interpersonal Communication," p. 295.
9. Thomas S. Robertson, *Innovative Behavior and*

Communications, (New York: Holt, Rinehart and Winston, Inc., 1971.)

10. Katz and Lazarsfeld, *Personal Influence.*
11. Ibid., pp. 309–312.
12. R.A. Bauer, "The Obstinate Audience," *American Psychologist* 19 (May 1964): 319–328.
13. Herbert E. Krugman, "The Impact of Television Advertising: Learning Without Involvement," *Public Opinion Quarterly* 29 (Fall 1965): 349–356.
14. John O. Summers, "New Product Interpersonal Communications," in Fred C. Allvine, ed., *Combined Proceedings of the American Marketing Association,* Series #33 (1971), pp. 428–433.
15. Katz and Lazarsfeld, *Personal Influence,* pp. 118–119.
16. Fred D. Reynolds and William R. Darden, "Mutually Adaptive Effects of Interpersonal Communication," *Journal of Marketing Research* 8 (November 1971): 449–454.
17. Katz and Lazarsfeld, *Personal Influence,* Chapter 10.
18. Summers, "New Product Interpersonal Communication," p. 430.
19. Ernest Dichter, "How Word-of-Mouth Advertising Works," *Harvard Business Review* 44 (November–December 1966).
20. Scott M. Cunningham, "Perceived Risk as a Factor in the Diffusion of New Product Information," in Raymond M. Haas, ed., *Proceedings of the American Marketing Association Fall Conference,* (1966), pp. 698–721.
21. Arch G. Woodside and M. Wayne DeLozier, "Effects of Word-of-Mouth Advertising on Consumer Risk Taking," *Journal of Advertising* 5 (Fall 1976): 12–19.
22. Katz and Lazarsfeld, *Personal Influence,* pp. 332–334.
23. Charles W. King and John O. Summers, "Overlap of Opinion Leadership Across Consumer Product Categories," *Journal of Marketing Research,* 7 (February 1970): 43–50.
24. James H. Myers and Thomas S. Robertson, "Dimensions of Opinion Leadership," *Journal of Marketing Research* 9 (February 1972): 41–46.
25. Russell W. Belk, "Occurrence of Word-of-Mouth Buyer Behavior as a Function of Situation and Advertising Stimuli," in Fred C. Allvine, ed., *Combined Proceedings of the American Marketing Association,* Series #33 (1971), pp. 419–422.
26. Summers, "New Product Interpersonal Communication.
27. Ibid., p. 433.
28. Feldman and Spencer, "The Effect of Personal Influence," p. 450.
29. Katz and Lazarsfeld, *Personal Influence.*
30. Myers and Robertson, "Dimensions of Opinion Leadership."
31. Proprietary study by a large appliance manufacturer.
32. Katz and Lazarsfeld, *Personal Influence,* Chapter 10.
33. John O. Summers, "The Identity of Women's Clothing Fashion Opinion Leaders," *Journal of Marketing Research* 7 (May 1970): 178–185.
34. Reynolds and Darden, "Mutually Adaptive Effects;" Summers, "The Identity of Women's Clothing."
35. Ibid.
36. Thomas S. Robertson and James H. Myers, "Personality Correlates of Opinion Leadership and Innovative Buying Behavior," *Journal of Marketing Research* 6 (May 1969): 168.
37. Douglas J. Tigert and Stephen J. Arnold, *Profiling Self-Designated Opinion Leaders and Self-Designated Innovators through Life Style Research,* (Toronto: School of Business, University of Toronto, June 1971).
38. James F. Engel, Robert J. Kegerreis, and Roger D. Blackwell, "Word-of-Mouth Communication by the Innovator," *Journal of Marketing* 33 (July 1969): 15–19.
39. Summers, "The Identity of Women's Clothing."
40. James H. Myers and William H. Reynolds, *Consumer Behavior and Marketing Management,* (Boston: Houghton Mifflin Co., 1967), p. 309.
41. Joseph R. Mancuso, "Why not Create Opinion Leaders for New Product Introductions?" *Journal of Marketing* 33 (July 1969): 20–25.
42. David L. Loudon and Albert J. Della Bitta, *Consumer Behavior,* (New York: McGraw-Hill Book Co., 1979), p. 282.
43. *Time,* March 13, 1964, p. 91.
44. John E. Cooney, "Bubble Gum Maker Wants to Know How the Rumors Started," *The Wall Street Journal,* March 24, 1977, p. 1.
45. James Coleman, "Social Processes in Physicians' Adoption of a New Drug," *Journal of Chronic Diseases* 9 (1959): 1–19.
46. Arndt, "Role of Product-Related Conversations."
47. John A. Martilla, "Word-of-Mouth Communication in the Industrial Adoption Process," *Journal of Marketing Research* 8 (May 1971): 173–178.
48. Everett M. Rogers and F. Floyd Shoemaker, *Communication in Innovations,* (New York: The Free Press, 1971).
49. Myers and Robertson, "Dimensions of Opinion Leadership," p. 42.

SIXTEEN

Communications Across Groups: The Diffusion Process

Focus of Chapter

Two streams of research have focused on personal influence and communications. The first, communications within groups, was considered in the last chapter. The second, communications across groups — that is, the diffusion of information and influence — will be considered in this chapter.

Research on opinion leadership views communications on a *micro* level since communications are between individual consumers. Diffusion research views communication on a *macro* level since communications and product ownership are traced across a large number of individuals over time.

This chapter focuses on **diffusion,** the process by which ideas and products are spread across consumers through communications. The categorization of consumers

by time of adoption (innovators, early adopters, the early majority, the late majority, and laggards) and the characteristics of adopter groups will be described. In addition, some of the same questions raised concerning opinion leaders can also be raised concerning innovators. Is the propensity to buy new products specific to the product or general? Is it situational? Are innovators *really* innovators?

From the marketer's standpoint, the most relevant area of study is the diffusion of new products, particularly new products that can be classed as innovations. But diffusion is also relevant in other marketing areas, such as in the diffusion of information about existing products, in the diffusion of information about public positions of companies, or in the diffusion of misinformation.

THE IMPORTANCE OF NEW PRODUCTS

Most research on diffusion has been concerned with the spread of new products across markets, primarily because new product development is an important area that affects profitability. Profit margins for mature products may peak even before sales begin to decline, therefore, a company must systematically introduce new products to ensure that profits are maintained. Otherwise, the firm's profit position will be overly sensitive to the life cycle of one or several products.

Diffusion research traces the spread of product acceptance. In identifying early adopters, the firm is identifying its primary target market at the time the product is introduced. Media strategy, promotional themes, and pricing policy can be geared to the needs of the early adopters. As the product gains wider acceptance, the firm can decrease its price, widen its promotional appeal, and use more general media vehicles to appeal to later adopters. Therefore diffusion research has a direct relevance to the marketer in (1) tracing the rate of acceptance of a new product in a particular market, and (2) identifying those who are adopting it.

DIFFUSION AND WORD-OF-MOUTH COMMUNICATION

There is a close link between diffusion research and the research on word-of-mouth communication. Ideas are disseminated by word-of-mouth communication, and new product ideas are no exception. Moreover the innovators — those who adopt first and are instrumental in disseminating information — are also likely to be opinion leaders. Innovators demonstrate a higher degree of interest in the product category and a greater level of knowledge. These characteristics are shared by opinion leaders. Several studies have shown that there is better than a 50 percent chance that an opinion leader is also likely to be an innovator.[1] It is not surprising then, that many of the findings that apply to opinion leadership also apply to diffusion research.

The reason there is no one-to-one correspondence between an innovator and an opinion leader is that some innovators are much more socially independent and rely on their own norms and values rather than the group's. These individuals tend to be the very first to buy new products and do not exert influence on others. Conversely, some opinion leaders may not be innovators. They may communicate information and exert influence on others, but may not be among the first to buy new products. Therefore, despite the similarity, opinion leadership and diffusion are two separate communications processes that have differing implications for marketing strategy. The implications from opinion leadership tend to be applied to promotional strategies, the implications from diffusion tend to be applied to market segmentation and new product development.

WHAT IS AN INNOVATION?

Given this focus on the adoption of innovations, it would be relevant to ask: What is an innovation? Is it synonymous with a new product?

Actually, most marketing diffusion studies have not dealt with true innovations such as an electric car, but with more limited advances such as freeze-dried coffee, electric toothbrushes, or new car models. Robertson defines three types of categories:

1. **A continuous innovation** involves an extension of existing products. Examples are fluoridated toothpaste, low-tar cigarettes, and cook-in-the-bag vegetables.

2. **A dynamically continuous innovation** is a new product but not a major technological advance. It does not change existing consumer behavior patterns. Examples are electric toothbrushes, color TVs, or Touch-Tone telephones.

3. **A discontinuous innovation** is a major technological advance involving the establishment of a new product and new behavior patterns. Examples are solar energy, electric cars, or the video-disc.[2]

Not surprisingly, most marketing studies involve continuous innovations. Patterns of diffusion for continuous innovations are not as striking and well-defined as are those for discontinuous innovations. Electric toothbrushes were not as widely talked about as air conditioners or color TVs. Nor was the pattern of personal influence as marked. In fact, when marketers study more mundane products, they find it hard to describe a general innovator for the same reason they find it hard to describe a general opinion leader — the individual who is among the first to buy a new type of deodorant is not necessarily the same as the individual who is among the first to buy a new type of coffee. When discontinuous innovations are studied, however, a profile of a general innovator emerges — a higher income, self-confident individual who is not as reliant on group norms and not as concerned with product risk. The reason for this more precise profile is due to the fact that the individual who is most likely to be among the first to buy a video-disc will also be among the first to consider buying an electric car or adopting solar energy. The General Motors study of owners of Olds diesels, previously cited in Chapter 9, supports this contention. Owners of Olds diesels were also likely to own a microwave oven and a digital watch.[3]

THE DIFFUSION PROCESS

Diffusion is the process by which the *adoption* of an innovation is spread by *communication* to members of a *target market* over a period of *time*. An understanding of the diffusion process in marketing, therefore, requires a description of (1) adoption, (2) communications, (3) the target market, and (4) the element of time.

The Adoption of an Innovation

The adoption of an innovation requires that an individual or a group of consumers makes a decision regarding a new product. The model of complex decision making described in Chapter 2 can be used in new product decision making since the consumer must recognize a need for the product, search for information, evaluate alternatives, and make a decision. But two elements in the new product decision make it distinct from other decisions. First, awareness of the product becomes more critical because it is new, and second, product risk is likely to be higher. As a result, the product may go through a trial period before it is adopted.

In Figure 16–1 a series of steps in the adoption of an innovation are shown. For example, a consumer considering the purchase of a battery-powered car would go through these six steps. First the consumer must be *aware* of the existence of a battery-powered car. The potential adopter may have very little information and no specific attitudes toward the innovation. The consumer will search for additional information to gain some *knowledge* of the capabilities of a battery-powered car. Based on this information, the consumer will *evaluate* the innovation. The decision may be that further information is necessary. Or, a favorable attitude may be formed toward the product leading to a decision that the purchase of a battery-powered car should be given serious consideration *(legitimation)*.[4] The consumer will also consider alternative versions of battery-powered cars produced by various manufacturers.

At this point, outright adoption may be too risky. Therefore, *trial* will take place. Trial of an innovation is difficult since the manufacturer cannot give out free samples. But, the consumer can test drive the car, rent one for a few weeks, lease one, or try a model owned by a friend. In each case, the innovation is used for a short period to evaluate performance. If product performance is satisfactory during the trial period, the consumer may then decide to *adopt* the innovation by purchasing a battery-powered car.

These stages in decision making are important to the marketer because they indicate the acceptance of the product and the effect of the promotional campaign. To what degree is the public aware of the new innovation? Is the public's information accurate? What are the consumer's attitudes toward the innovation? What is the likelihood of trial and subsequent adoption?

One essential element that is missing in the six-step description of the adoption process is the *time of adoption*. Was the consumer one of the first to adopt the battery-powered car? Did adoption occur after a number of friends had adopted? Or, looking ahead to the next century, was the consumer one of the last to adopt once battery-powered cars began replacing conventional cars? This question is important to the marketer because it permits identification of the early and late adopters. Identification of the early adopters allows the marketer to target price, promotional, and media strategies to this group. Identification of the later adopters permits adjustments in the marketing plan to account for diffusion of the product to a larger group.

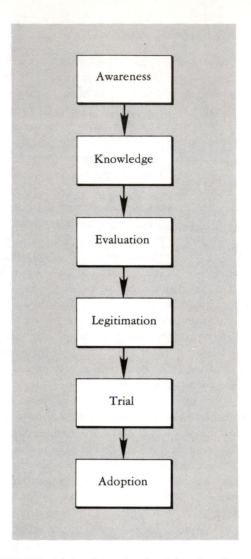

FIGURE 16–1   Steps in the Adoption Process

Categories of Adopters

A classification of adopters by time of adoption was developed by Rogers. Rogers examined over 500 studies of diffusion and concluded that there are five categories of adopters: innovators, early adopters, the early majority, the late majority, and laggards.[5] Based on past research, Rogers decided that these categories follow a normal distribution (see Figure 16–2), and described each category as follows:

- *Innovators* represent the first 2½ percent of all those who adopt. They are eager to try new ideas and products almost as an obsession. They have higher incomes, are better educated, are more cosmopolitan, and are more active outside of their community. They are less reliant on group norms and are more self-confident. They are more likely to obtain their information from scientific sources and experts.

- *Early adopters* represent the next 13½ percent to adopt the product. They are not the very first, but they adopt early in the product's life cycle. This group is distinct from innovators since they are much more reliant on group norms and values. They are also more oriented to the local community in contrast to the innovator's cosmopolitan outlook. Early adopters are most likely to be opinion leaders because of their closer affiliation to groups.

- *The early majority* (the next 34 percent to adopt) are very deliberate before adopting a new product. They are likely to collect more information and evaluate more brands; therefore, the process of adoption will take longer. They rely on the group for information but are not likely to be opinion leaders. They are likely to be the friends and neighbors of opinion leaders. The early majority is an important link in the process of diffusing new ideas since they are positioned between earlier and later adopters.

- *The late majority* (next 34 percent to adopt) are described by Rogers as skeptical. They adopt because most of their friends have already done so. Since they also rely

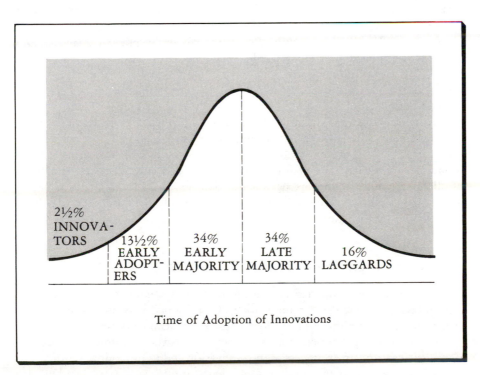

FIGURE 16–2 Distribution of Adopter Categories

Source: Everett M. Rogers, *Diffusion of Innovations* (New York: The Free Press, 1962), p. 162. Copyright © 1962 by The Free Press of Glencoe, a Division of Macmillan Publishing Co., Inc.

on group norms, adoption is the result of pressure to conform. This group tends to be older and below average in income and education. They rely primarily on word-of-mouth communication rather than the mass media.

- *Laggards* (the final 16 percent to adopt) are similar to innovators in not relying on the norms of the group. They are independent because they are tradition-bound. Decisions are made in terms of the past. By the time laggards adopt an innovation, it has probably been superseded by something else — for example, the purchase of the first television set when color television is already widely owned. Laggards have the longest time of adoption and the lowest socioeconomic status. They tend to be suspicious of new products and alienated from a rapidly advancing society.[6]

Adopters Versus Nonadopters

Rogers' classification assumes that everyone will eventually adopt a new product or an innovation. His classification does not make room for a nonadopter category. This assumption is, of course, unrealistic. All families do not own stereos, electric toothbrushes, food processors, or even color televisions. A simpler three-part classification of innovators, later adopters, and nonadopters may be more realistic. The innovator group would combine Rogers' innovators and early adopters. In most studies of the diffusion of new products, such a classification is used because it simply is not feasible for management to direct marketing resources to the $2\frac{1}{2}$ percent of all adopters represented by the true innovator. The late adopters would combine the early and late majority and laggards. The nonadopter group would provide for the possibility that a sizeable part of the market may simply decide not to buy the new product. (Since most diffusion studies include early adopters when referring to innovators, this broader definition of innovators will be used in this chapter.)

A hypothetical projection of the adoption of video-discs makes use of the more common three part categorization (see Figure 16–3). Assuming that by the year 2000 60 percent of all American households will own a video-disc, innovators represent 10 percent of all households and later adopters 50 percent of all households. Innovators have adopted prior to 1986 and later adopters after. Nonadopters are the remaining 40 percent of all households who have not adopted by the year 2000.

Communication in the Diffusion Process

The second requirement in the diffusion process is the communication of the new product idea across a total market. Communications are required from marketer to consumer; word-of-mouth communications are required between consumers. Communication from the marketer to the consumer is most important in creating an awareness of the innovation and in providing information. A study of early users of a new automobile diagnostic center in a Midwestern city found that early adopters of the service relied primarily on magazines and radio for information.[7] A study of early adopters of stainless steel blades found that their principal source of information was from the mass media.[8] But both studies concluded that the greatest influence on consumers in evaluating the

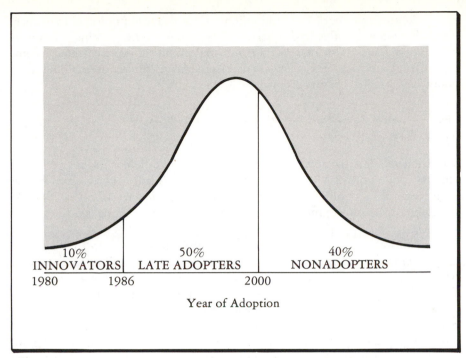

FIGURE 16–3 Hypothetical Projection of Diffusion of Video-Discs

innovation and deciding on whether to adopt or reject it came from friends and relatives. These findings suggest that advertisers should emphasize an informational campaign to attract those who are not familiar with the new product, and should try to stimulate favorable word-of-mouth communications to try to encourage adoption.

The studies cited above also show the importance of word-of-mouth communication in the diffusion process. If the adoption of a new product is to be diffused across a large number of people, word-of-mouth communication is required within and between groups.

Word-of-Mouth Communication Within Groups

The last chapter showed that opinion leaders are more likely to communicate and receive product information. Given the link between opinion leadership and innovativeness, it is not surprising that innovators are also more likely to communicate about new products. The study of the new automotive diagnostic centers found that innovators (early users of the center) were three times as likely to be asked about new products compared to noninnovators, and twice as likely to communicate their experiences without being asked.[9]

Lambert studied the adoption of seven new products ranging from cook-in-the-bag vegetables to water spray devices for cleaning teeth.[10] He found that innovators were more likely to tell friends and acquaintances about the products purchased. Baumgarten characterized the innovator who is most likely to engage in word-of-mouth communication as the **innovative communicator.** He found that close to 50 percent of all fashion innovators also communicated frequently about fashion and influenced others.[11] The various studies linking innovators to opinion leaders also demonstrate the importance of word-of-mouth communication within groups as a means of disseminating information and influence about new products across groups.[12]

Word-of-Mouth Between Groups: Trickle Down Versus Trickle Across

Diffusion requires the spread of information across different groups.[13] One of the basic questions is whether information and influence travels from higher socioeconomic groupings to lower ones (**a trickle down effect**) or whether diffusion occurs across groups regardless of socioeconomic status (**trickle across effect**).

Traditionally, the view has been that diffusion occurs from the higher to the lower social classes. This view was stated by two famous sociologists, Veblen[14] and Simmel.[15] Both believed that the upper classes bought primarily for status and ostentation (conspicuous consumption), and that lower quality duplicates of these products were made for the lower classes. Communication and influence moved from one class down to the next in the social hierarchy.

There is some support for the notion of a trickle down effect in fashion. The high fashion lines generally originate in Paris and are aimed at the upper income groups. Those lines that are accepted by the fashion innovators will be duplicated by lower cost manufacturers and directed to a broader base of adopters. A trickle down effect can also occur through word-of-mouth communications. Liu and Duff cite the adoption of IUD devices in the Philippines as being speeded by the fact that information often traveled from a higher status to a somewhat lower status housewife.[16] Information spread most easily among housewives of similar social status, but some flow of information to housewives of differing social status was necessary to cause widespread diffusion of the innovation.

King tends to discount the trickle down effect in today's American society.[17] The Depression and the post-World-War-II period produced a leveling effect in socioeconomic status which eliminated the sharper distinctions between upper and lower classes that were true at the turn of the century. Moreover, the mass media rapidly diffuse information on innovations to all classes. Writing about fashion adoption, King states:

> "The traditional upper class fashion leader directing the lower levels is largely short-circuited in the communication process. Within hours after the exclusive Paris and American designers' showings, the season's styles have been passed to the mass audiences via newspaper and television."[18]

In a study of fashion adoption in the Boston area, King found that early buyers of new fashions were *not* the upper crust elite. Almost two-thirds were middle class or lower. Moreover, there was no evidence that communications went from individuals of a higher social class to those of a lower class. Four-fifths of respondents were influenced by members of their own social class. Early buyers were more likely to be influenced by those in a higher social class. The trickle down theory would hold that later buyers should have received influence from higher socioeconomic groups.

King's study tends to confirm a trickle across rather than a trickle down effect in the diffusion of fashion styles. King's ideas closely conform to the social multiplier effect suggested by Duesenberry that individuals are more likely to come into contact with new products and ideas because of the leveling of social status in American society, and that as a result, influence will travel in a lateral fashion across markets.[19] It is not surprising that social influence went from upper- to lower-class housewives in the Philippines. Social class distinctions are much more marked in that country than in the United States. In a society with a broad middle class, a trickle of information and influence across groups is more likely to result in the diffusion of new products.

The Target Market

The third component in the diffusion process is a market to which the innovation is targeted. In a study of the diffusion of color television, the target market would ultimately be identified as all households in the United States. But the definition of the target market will differ over the diffusion process. When color televisions were first introduced, they were targeted to a higher income group who was more willing to take the risk of adoption (i.e., the definition of the general innovator). As adoption increased and the price was lowered, the definition of the target market broadened.

Diffusion studies have sometimes focused on very specific target markets. For example, one of the first diffusion studies involved the adoption of hybrid seed among farmers in two Iowa communities.[20] Other studies have involved the adoption of a new drug among doctors in several cities;[21] community antenna television among residents of a Wisconsin town;[22] and a new diet product among residents of a geriatric community.[23]

The norms and values of the target market will influence the rate of diffusion. Rogers and Shoemaker have defined markets that are modern versus traditional.[24] Members of a target market who tend to be "modern" in orientation are more likely to accept change, have a greater respect for education and science, and are more cosmopolitan. Such a group is more likely to adopt new products. The opposite characteristics describe a traditional orientation resulting in less chance of new product adoption.

The marketer must determine attitudes toward change and product risk among members of the target market. A conservative and traditional orientation would suggest difficulty in introducing a new product, particularly a discontinuous innovation.

Time

By definition, time is an essential component of the diffusion process. The categorization by Rogers describes consumers by time of adoption. Moreover, the communication process resulting in diffusion of information and influence occurs over time.

The element of time creates a problem in diffusion research. Most diffusion studies occur at a given point in time rather than over time. Say, for example, a study was performed in 1986 on the adoption of video-discs. At that point, anyone who adopted most recently would be considered a late adopter, and anyone who had not yet adopted would be classified as a nonadopter. But such a categorization may be misleading since the later adopters in 1986 may actually be innovators (e.g., they may still be among the first 10 percent to adopt) and nonadopters may shortly become adopters. Diffusion research requires time-series data to trace the proportion of consumers adopting at various time intervals and the rate of diffusion. Only then can adequate definitions be established of true innovators. Yet time series data are expensive to gather and may lead to sensitization of the market if repeated interviews take place.[25]

Rate of Diffusion

The rate of diffusion is the most important time-oriented measurement. It reflects the cumulative level of adoption of a new product over time. An example of a diffusion curve for television is shown in Figure 16–4. The adoption of black and white television increased on a straight line basis from 1950 to 1962. By 1962, it had been adopted by most households in the United States. Color television showed a very slow rate of adoption from its introduction in 1955

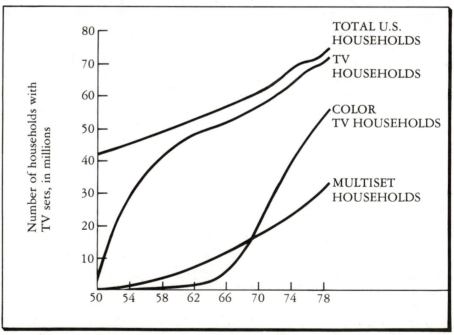

FIGURE 16–4   Diffusion Curve for Black and White and Color Television: 1950–1978

Source: Figures for 1950–1974 from *Advertising Age,* April 19, 1976, p. 112. Figures for 1975–1978 from A.C. Nielsen.

Reprinted with permission from the April 19, 1976 issue of *Advertising Age.* Copyright 1976 by Crain Communications, Inc. and with permission from the A. C. Nielsen Company.

to 1964, possibly because of a high price, a lack of widespread programming in color, and a high level of perceived risk.[26] After 1964, prices decreased, programming increased and more households began to adopt. The result is a rapid diffusion curve paralleling that of black and white. Adoption is now also close to the point of saturation.

Product Characteristics That Encourage Rapid Adoption and Diffusion

Some products can be diffused faster than others. The rate of diffusion depends on the product characteristics the consumer perceives. It helps if the marketer can anticipate a product's diffusion rate because strategies can be adjusted accordingly. For example, projecting a slow rate of diffusion may suggest the need for higher initial prices to sustain product entry.

Rogers and Shoemaker[27] identified these five characteristics that increase the rate of acceptance and diffusion of a new product:

- *Relative advantage* is the degree to which consumers perceive a new product as superior to existing substitutes; for example, the relative advantage of a microwave oven in cooking time, or of a food processor in versatility.

- *Compatibility* is the degree to which the product is consistent with the consumer's needs, attitudes, and past experiences. In one study by a large appliance manufacturer, consumers concerned with their appearance were more likely to buy personal care appliances. In another study, consumers who looked for time-saving products were more likely to buy new kitchen appliances such as food processors.

- *Observability* is the ease with which the product can be observed and/or communicated to potential consumers. Products that are highly visible are more easily diffused. Fashion items and cars are good examples. Whyte's study of air conditioners suggests that an important element of diffusion is the high visibility of the product.

- *Simplicity* is the ease in understanding and using a new product. Products such as electric toothbrushes, instant food products, and cook-in-the-bag vegetables are easy to understand and use. More complex innovations such as food processors require an instruction booklet. Such complexity may inhibit diffusion.

- *Trialability* is the degree to which a product can be tried before adoption. Discontinuous innovations such as a video-disc or battery-powered car have little trialability. Limited trial is possible by demonstrations in show rooms or test runs. One element that is related to trialability is *divisibility*. If a product can be purchased in small quantities, then trial is relatively easy. A study of five packaged goods[28] found that almost two-thirds of consumers made trial purchases of new brands in smaller quantities than they usually purchased.

Several studies have demonstrated the importance of these five factors in influencing the rate of diffusion. Feldman and Armstrong compared adopters of the Mazda rotary engine when it was first introduced (innovators) to later adopters (those buying eighteen months later) and to those who purchased a conventional compact (nonadopters).[29] Early buyers of the rotary engine rated the Mazda's five product characteristics described above as significantly higher than nonadopters.

In another study, Ostlund asked consumers to test six new packaged foods on the same five product characteristics.[30] Once again, adopters rated the products higher than nonadopters on each of the product characteristics. The one factor that was most important in encouraging adoption and diffusion was *relative advantage*. Ostlund categorized relative advantage into savings in time, effort, and money. Adopters were much more likely to rate the new product high on savings in time and effort. Ostlund also found that consumers' perceptions of the product's characteristics were much more important than the consumer's demographic and personality characteristics in predicting adoption. This finding suggests that an individual is more likely to be an innovator because of advantages that he or she perceives in the product, not because of any innate personal characteristics.

THE INNOVATOR IN THE DIFFUSION PROCESS

The innovator is central to the diffusion of new product information and ownership across groups, just as the opinion leader is the main stimulus in the communication of product information within a group. This section will ask some key questions about the nature of innovativeness and will describe the characteristics of the innovator.

The Nature of Innovativeness

The same types of questions asked about the opinion leader can be asked about the innovator. The first question is whether innovativeness is general or product-specific. An answer to this question will help the marketer determine if marketing strategy can be directed to a general group of innovators, or whether specific target segments of early buyers have to be defined on a product-by-product basis. The second question is whether there is a negative as well as a positive innovator. That is, can one trace a negative diffusion process leading to rejection of an innovation? And, third, is innovativeness dependent on the situation?

Is Innovativeness Product-Specific?

It is likely that a general innovator exists for true (discontinuous) innovations. Various studies have shown that across product categories, innovators tend to be:

- more likely to accept risk;
- more inner-directed and independent of group norms;
- less dogmatic about new ideas and change;
- more cosmopolitan; and
- better educated and in the higher income group.

This profile of the generalized innovator may be most relevant for more expensive innovations such as videotape recorders, rotary engines, or battery-powered cars for several reasons. First, higher income groups can better afford such products and are therefore less subject to financial risk. Second, a general willingness to act independently of group norms and to be more tolerant of change and risk is more likely to lead to new product acceptance. Third, a cosmopolitan life-style subjects a consumer to newer and more varied products, also leading to a greater likelihood of new product acceptance.

Despite the likelihood of the existence of a generalized innovator for discontinuous innovations, most findings suggest that for less innovative products, a generalized innovator does not exist. That is, the individual who is most likely to accept the newest style in clothes will not necessarily be one of the first to have tried cook-in-the-bag vegetables or freeze-dried coffee. The same finding applies as for opinion leadership: Innovativeness is likely to extend across *related* product categories, but an innovator in one category is not likely to be an innovator in an unrelated category.

There is support for the conclusion that innovativeness is product-specific. Summers studied six product categories and found some overlap in innovativeness across them.[31] The closest overlap was between packaged food products and household cleaners, both home-related product categories. The innovator for small appliances was also likely to be an innovator for large appliances. But there was little overlap in unrelated lines such as appliances and cosmetics.

Robertson and Myers studied innovativeness for new appliances, clothing, and food items.[32] They found some overlap in innovativeness across these three categories, but not to a significant degree. They concluded that the marketer cannot rely on identifying a general innovator group and target new products to this group. These findings suggest that for most new products, the marketer must define the target market on a product-by-product basis.

Are There Positive and Negative Innovators?

So far, the discussion has assumed that the innovator group for a particular product category is going to react positively to the product, leading to an increase in the rate of adoption and diffusion. But what if a sizeable group of innovators dislikes the product? Midgley proposes three categories of adopters:

1. *Active adopters* are those who have tried the product and will give favorable information on it.
2. *Active rejectors* are those who have tried the product, found it deficient, and will give unfavorable information about it.
3. *Passives* are those who have tried the product but do not give information or exert influence. They are innovators, but not opinion leaders.[33]

Several studies have distinguished the innovator who is less likely to communicate (the passive) from the innovator more likely to communicate (the active adopter).[34] For example, one study of fashion innovation among males found that the passive innovator was more likely to be in the higher income group, was older, and was more involved in social organizations.[35] But no marketing study has distinguished between Midgley's categorization of the active adopter versus the active rejector. This means that there has been *no documentation of a negative diffusion process,* one leading to rejection of a new product because of negative word-of-mouth advertising. Possibly, marketers are reluctant to provide evidence of failures, but studies of negative diffusion may be important in providing insights to marketers on how to avoid future market failures.

Is Innovativeness Situational?

It is likely that the usage situation will directly influence adoption of a new product. A battery-powered car may be feasible for local family use, but may not be feasible for the salesperson who has to travel frequently. Likewise, a consumer may feel that premixed liquors are fine for home consumption, but not for guests.

Despite the logic of tying the usage situation to new product adoption, few if any marketing studies have examined this area. The marketer of a new product should determine consumer reactions to a new product in a situational context. Thus, a new snack food should be presented to the consumer as an "energy-providing breakfast food," an "in-between-meal pick-me-up," or a "late-night snack." In each case, the usage situation is linked to the benefits provided by the new product.

Characteristics of the Innovator

There is a close link between innovativeness and market segmentation. The marketer seeks to identify the segment of the market that is most likely to adopt the new product when it is first introduced. The *personality* and *life-style* characteristics of the innovator will suggest the nature and tone of advertising. An innovator group that is self-confident and independent of group norms would probably find a straight informational campaign more appealing. An innovator segment that is younger and more socially active may be more attracted by group-related themes simulating social communication. *Perceptions of risk* may identify those consumers most willing to try a new product and suggest an acceptable price level for the target segment. *Demographic* characteristics of the innovator segment would have implications for media selection. These innovator characteristics will be considered in turn.

Personality Characteristics

A number of personality characteristics have been related to innovativeness. Innovators have been found to be more *inner-directed*. The inner-directed person relies on his or her internal standards and values to guide behavior; the other-directed person relies on the values of friends and associates.[36] Donnelly studied five new consumer packaged goods and found that in each case, the individuals who had tried the product were significantly more likely to be inner-directed.[37] In a later study, Donnelly found that those who purchased the Maverick in the first three months after it was introduced were much more likely to be inner-directed than those who purchased later.[38] These findings suggest that the innovator is more likely to be independent of group norms and pressures to conform.

Innovators have also been found to be less *dogmatic*. Dogmatism is related to perceived threat and anxiety resulting in a closed mind toward change. Low dogmatics are more likely to accept change in a variety of situations.[39] Jacoby related consumers' scores on dogmatism to their likelihood to select fifteen new products and confirmed that low dogmatics are likely to be more innovative.[40] Since consumers who are low in dogmatism tend to "act on relevant information from the outside on its own intrinsic merits, unencumbered by irrelevant factors,"[41] Jacoby concluded that the most effective appeal to innovators is a straight, informational campaign focusing on product attributes rather than an emphasis on ego or social factors such as the approval of friends and neighbors.

Baumgarten studied the male fashion innovator among college students and found him to be more impulsive, self-loving, exhibitionistic, and less intellectually oriented than the noninnovator.[42] This profile suggests that advertising should emphasize the appearance-enhancing value of clothes and that the retailer should anticipate a fair amount of impulse purchasing by the fashion innovator. These findings are contradictory to Jacoby's conclusion that advertising to innovators should be devoid of ego and social factors. Clearly, the fashion innovator should be appealed to by ego and socially oriented themes. These contradictions strongly suggest that innovators must be studied on a product-by-product basis.

Life-Style Characteristics

A study by a manufacturer of personal care products demonstrates the use of life-style characteristics in identifying the innovator. A sample of women were asked to rate themselves on the life-style characteristics listed in Table 16–1. A factor analysis produced the eleven items listed in the table. For example, respondents who were classified as style and appearance conscious tended to agree with statements such as "I consider myself up to date regarding the latest styles," and "I am very concerned with my appearance." Women who are classified as isolate/conservative tended to agree that "I would rather spend a quiet evening at home than go to a party," and "I prefer to cook a good meal at home rather than go out to eat."

Women were then classified by their willingness to buy new products when they first come on the market. About 14 percent of the women were classified as innovators and the other 86 percent as noninnovators. The eleven life-style factors were then related to innovativeness (see Table 16–2). Personal care innovators were more likely to:

- be style and appearance conscious;
- be socially oriented and self-confident;
- communicate to friends in general and communicate about new products in particular;
- look for products that save time;
- change hairstyles and be careful about products used on their hair; and
- rely on the brand name.

Understandably, this group was found to be less isolate/conservative.

TABLE 16–1   Life-Style Characteristics Used to Identify Adopters of New Personal Care Products

Factor 1:   **Style and Appearance Conscious/Self-Indulgent**

I consider myself up to date regarding the latest styles.
I am very concerned with my appearance.
It is worth it to me to spend a lot of time on my hair.
I like to spend money on myself because I think I deserve it.

Factor 2:   **Isolate/Conservative**

I would rather spend a quiet evening at home than go to a party.
I prefer to cook a good meal at home rather than go out to eat.
I like to dress conservatively.

Factor 3:   **Social/Self-Confident**

I entertain frequently.
When I set my mind to doing something, I can usually do it.
I am more independent than most people.
I am frequently invited to social gatherings.

Factor 4:   **Bargain Seekers**

I tend to shop around for the best bargains.
When I consider buying a new product, the first thing I consider is price.

Factor 5:   **Outdoor Types**

I love the outdoors.
I love to participate in active sports.

Factor 6:   **New Product/Social Communicators**

I often ask the advice of friends regarding new products.
I enjoy discussing new products.
I feel I am regarded by friends and neighbors as a good source of information about new products.

Factor 7:   I look for products that help save time.

Factor 8:   I tend to rely on the name of the manufacturer when I buy new products.

TABLE 16–2   Life-Style Characteristics of Innovators of Personal Care Products

Life-Style Characteristics	Innovators (14% of Sample)	Noninnovators (86% of Sample)
Style and Appearance Conscious/Self-Indulgent	39%	28%
Isolate/Conservative	25%	32%
Social/Self Confident	44%	27%
Bargain Seekers	28%	30%
Outdoor Types	31%	32%
New Product/Social Communicators	39%	26%
Look for Time-Saving Products	39%	25%
Rely on Manufacturer's Name	26%	20%

These findings portray an innovator who is a self-confident individual concerned with her appearance and who is probably an opinion leader. The study also found that the innovator is more likely to be upscale and employed, resulting in an emphasis on time-saving products. Assume that the manufacturer is considering the introduction of a new hair conditioner and cream-rinse combined. Appeals to the most innovative consumer would require portraying a self-confident and socially aware woman who is concerned with her appearance and busy enough to emphasize the time-saving qualities of a two-in-one hair care product.

A study of men's personal care products produced a similar life-style profile of the innovator. Men who were most likely to buy products such as hair spray, hand lotion, and hair stylers were higher in self-confidence and self-esteem and had a more positive attitude toward change.[43] They were also more likely to be fashion-conscious.

Social Activity

Social activity is closely related to life-style characteristics. The innovator is more socially active. Adopters of push-button telephones were found to be better accepted by friends and to be more socially involved than nonadopters.[44] Adopters of a new coffee product were more likely to be cited as close friends by nonadopters.[45] Innovators are also more likely to communicate with friends and associates about new products. Innovators of eight new consumer products were more likely to seek out information and to tell friends about new products compared to noninnovators.[46] Laggards will communicate about new products, but tend to seek advice from the immediate family rather than go outside the family.[47]

Innovators are also more likely to belong to social and civic groups. College fashion innovators were more active in student groups[48] and adopters of community antenna television were found to be more involved in social and civic clubs.[49]

Perceived Risk and Innovativeness

Perceived risk has been closely identified with innovativeness. Innovators tend to perceive less risk in product adoption than noninnovators. For example, adopters of a new salt substitute were less likely to see a taste or health risk in using the product than nonadopters.[50] Lambert found that innovators of eight fairly diverse products were less likely to see uncertainty in buying the product.[51] They were also less likely to be concerned with negative consequences such as disapproval of the purchase by friends and relatives, and a possible waste of money. Uhl, Andrus, and Poulsen studied laggards rather than innovators for sixteen new grocery products and found that laggards avoid the risk of trying new products by remaining loyal to established brands.[52] One strategy to induce laggards to try new brands is to extend their brand loyalty to the firm's entire line. For example, if a laggard is loyal to Nestlé's Tasters Choice, then it may be easier to get him or her to try a new line of packaged soups that are being introduced by the company. In this way, risk is reduced by remaining loyal to the company name.

Demographic Characteristics

The innovator tends to be younger and have a higher income, education level, and occupational status. The innovator is also more likely to be mobile. This profile has been found to be true for innovators of a new automotive diagnostic service,[53] community antenna television,[54] new grocery products,[55] and new personal care products. Yet the demographic profile of the innovator is not always consistent. For instance, Darden and Reynolds found that the fashion and grooming innovator is less educated and in a lower income group.[56] This inconsistency again points to the need for marketers to develop specific profiles for their product categories.

Media

Marketers attempt to select mass media that are most likely to reach adopters of their products. Evidence suggests that innovators are more likely to read newspapers and magazines than noninnovators. A study of female fashion innovators found that early adopters had a higher readership of general interest magazines.[57] A study of the adoption of eight consumer goods found that innovators were more likely to read magazines.[58]

But marketers can not select any magazine indiscriminately. Summers studied six broad product categories and found that innovators were selective in their exposure to the mass media.[59] Innovators tended to read magazines with editorial content relevant to the product category. For example, female fashion innovators are more likely to read *Glamour, Vogue,* and *Harper's Bazaar;*[60] male fashion innovators are more likely to read *Playboy, Esquire,* and the *New Yorker.*[61] Appliance innovators are more likely to read *Consumer Reports.*[62] These findings suggest that it would be more efficient for the marketer to select media on a product-specific basis by utilizing specialty magazines.

Findings for print media do not seem to apply to radio and television. Innovators are not more likely to be exposed to these media.[63] Television's mass outreach does not make it a particularly effective medium for reaching specific and well-defined segments of consumer innovators.

A summary of the personality, life-style, demographic and media characteristics of the innovator are presented in Table 16–3. The table presents a cohesive profile of the consumer innovator as distilled from the studies cited above.

STRATEGIC APPLICATIONS OF DIFFUSION THEORY

Diffusion theory can provide marketers with guidelines for adjusting strategies depending on the projected rate of diffusion. The marketer has two strategic options in influencing the rate of diffusion. As defined in Table 16–4, these are a skimming policy and a penetration policy. In a **skimming policy,** the marketer projects a slow rate of diffusion. As a result, prices have to be set higher initially to sustain the costs of introduction. The policy aims at "skim-

TABLE 16–3   A Profile of the Innovator Versus the Noninnovator   413

Characteristic	Innovator	Noninnovator (or later adopter)
Product Interest	More	Less
Opinion Leadership	More	Less
Personality:		
Dogmatism	Open-minded	Closed-minded
Social character	Inner-directed	Other-directed
Venturesomeness	More	Less
Perceived Risk	Less	More
Purchase and Consumption Traits		
Brand loyalty	Less	More
Usage	More	Less
Media Habits		
Total magazine exposure	More	Less
Special interest magazines	More	Less
Television	Less	More
Social Characteristics		
Social integration	More	Less
Social striving (e.g., social, physical, and occupational mobility)	More	Less
Group memberships	More	Less
Demographic Characteristics		
Age	Younger	Older
Income	More	Less
Education	More	Less
Occupational status	More	Less

Source: Leon G. Schiffman and Leslie Lazar Kanuk, *Consumer Behavior,* © 1978, p. 425. Reprinted by permission of Prentice-Hall, Inc., Englewood Cliffs, New Jersey.

ming the cream off the market" by aiming at the small, price inelastic segment.

Such a segment is likely to be well defined by demographic and life-style characteristics. Advertising will probably be informationally oriented to create awareness and supply necessary technical information. Distribution of the product will be selective. A skimming policy is most likely for discontinuous innovations. There are few close competitors to create price competition. There may be greater barriers to widespread acceptance because the product is not likely to be simple and may not be compatible with existing products or systems. Therefore, it is logical to establish a smaller and more specific target for adoption. The video-disc would be a good example of a product that qualifies for an initial skimming strategy based on lack of competition (only a few companies are entering the market) and newness. It is likely that RCA and MCA will define a small target segment initially, will use an informational advertising campaign and will distribute the product selectively.

The alternative to a skimming policy is a **penetration strategy.** In this case, the marketer encourages rapid and widespread diffusion by introducing

TABLE 16–4   Strategic Alternatives Based on the Diffusion Curve

Strategic Alternatives	Skimming	Penetration
Rate of Diffusion	Slow	Fast
Initial Price	High	Low
Market Segmentation	Target market is • small, • well specified by demographics and life-style.	Target market is • larger, • harder to specify by demographics and life-style.
Advertising	Informational approach	Use of symbols and imagery
Distribution	Selective	Intensive
Product Characteristics	Discontinuous innovation	Continuous innovation

the product at a low price. The intention is to try to sell to a general market through a more intensive campaign that uses imagery and symbolism. Distribution is widespread. Since the market is so general, it may be more difficult to identify the characteristics of early adopters. A penetration policy is more likely for continuous innovations such as diet soda or freeze-dried coffee since closely competitive products exist and there is no inhibition to try the product due to lack of compatibility or simplicity. Both diet soda and freeze-dried coffee were introduced at competitive prices on a widespread basis with intensive advertising campaigns utilizing symbolism and imagery.

Once an initial strategy is established, diffusion theory can also provide the marketer with guidelines as to changes in marketing strategy depending on where the product is on the diffusion curve. A product introduced based on a skimming strategy will eventually move more toward a penetration strategy (move right on the continuum from skimming to penetration in Table 16–4). For example, as video-discs gain awareness and acceptance, prices will be reduced, distribution will be more widespread, and more competitors will enter the market. Eventually, advertising will shift toward a greater use of imagery when product features become standardized across competitors. Knowledge of the diffusion curve can help marketers define the proper time for such shifts to begin to take place.

Similarly, marketers introducing a penetration strategy may find that a slow increase in prices is warranted given widespread acceptance of the product. Advertising and distribution will remain intensive, but the proper time for a change in pricing policy may be defined by the diffusion curve.

MEASURING INNOVATIVENESS

Innovativeness is distinct from opinion leadership in that it is a behavioral variable. It is defined as the actual adoption of a new product. In contrast, opinion leadership is measured by the consumer's perception regarding his or her interpersonal communications with others.

Innovativeness has been measured by two criteria. First, and most frequently, it has simply been measured by adoption at a given point in time. A survey is taken and those who have adopted the new product are classified as innovators. This measure is not very reliable because it does not take account of adoption over time. Several studies have attempted to measure adoption over time. For example, one study identified early adopters of the Maverick as those who purchased the car in the first three months after it was introduced, middle adopters as those who purchased in the second and third model year, and later adopters as those who purchased thereafter.[64] Such a measure of innovativeness accounts for the rate of diffusion of the product.

A second criterion used to identify innovators is the number of new products adopted. Summers categorized consumers by those who adopted from zero to six new products.[65] Such a criterion is useful in distinguishing between the product-specific and the generalized innovator. Any consumer who adopts innovations in all six product areas under study is likely to be a general innovator.

In some cases, innovativeness is measured by self-designating methods similar to those used to measure opinion leadership. Such measures are used when the researcher wants to determine the orientation of the consumer to new products rather than measuring specific adoption. Innovativeness could be determined by a two-question sequence as follows:

1. How do you see yourself with regard to buying new products?
    ————As one of the first to buy
    ————Purchasing after a few others have tried the product
    ————Purchasing after many people have bought the product
    ————Will not purchase

2. If you intend to buy the product, how soon after its appearance are you likely to buy?
    ————Immediately
    ————Within a week
    ————Within a month
    ————Within a year
    ————Longer[66]

SUMMARY

This chapter focuses on communication across groups in contrast to the previous chapter's focus on communication within groups. A process of diffusion is described, which leads to the dissemination of ideas and products across consumers. Diffusion research provides marketers with insights into the process of new product acceptance. Such insights are particularly important given the close link between the success of new product introductions and the profit position of the firm.

The diffusion process involves the adoption of an innovation and communication to other groups over time. Adoption of a new product requires awareness, knowledge, evaluation, legitimation, and trial. Communication between groups is likely to take place based on a trickling down of information from higher to lower socioeconomic groups, or a trickle across similar groups regardless of economic status. Given the greater mobility and lack of sharp socioeconomic distinctions in the United States, diffusion is more likely based on a trickle across effect. Time is a critical part of the diffusion process. It determines the rate of diffusion. New products will be diffused across markets faster if they are visible, simple to understand, compatible with consumers' needs and past experiences, and easily tried. Time is also important in defining adoption. Adopter categories are defined based on time of adoption such as innovators, early adopters, the majority, and laggards.

Research has identified specific characteristics of each adopter group with greatest attention given to the innovator. This group tends to be better educated, more self-confident, more willing to take risks and accept change, and more socially active. Innovators are also more likely to be opinion leaders.

But some doubt is cast on these general designations because in most cases, the characteristics of innovators are product-specific rather than general. An innovator for one product may not be an innovator for another. The exception is discontinuous innovations — that is, innovations that represent a marked change in product specifications and consumer behavior. In this case, the same individual is likely to be predisposed to adopt true innovations.

Despite the fact that most findings are product-specific, diffusion research does provide important strategic implications. It helps marketers define those who are first to adopt. Further, it provides some basis for predicting the diffusion process and suggests guidelines for changes in strategy as the marketer proceeds on the diffusion curve.

QUESTIONS

1. What marketing implications can diffusion research provide RCA or MCA when they first introduce the video-disc? Specifically, what are the implications of diffusion research for:
   - definition of a target segment?
   - pricing the product when it is first introduced?
   - advertising the product to the innovators?
   - distribution?

2. Diffusion research not only provides marketers with implications regarding the introductory phase in marketing a new product, it also provides implications for changes in strategy along the diffusion curve. What are the implications for changes in marketing strategy after the video-disc begins to be accepted; particularly for changes in:
   - definition of new target groups?
   - pricing?

- advertising strategy?
- product specifications?
- distribution?

3. Assume RCA introduces a new type of remote control switch for color television which permits more finely tuned color. What are the differences in the marketing implications of diffusion research for this product compared to the video-disc?

4. The diffusion curve in Figure 16–2 has the same shape as the product life cycle curve. Is the diffusion curve in fact the same as the product life cycle curve? What are the marketing implications of your answer?

5. The chapter cites two theories of communication between groups: a trickle down versus a trickle across effect.

- In what types of societies is a trickle down flow of communication more likely?
- Are there any groups or regions in the United States where a trickle down flow is more likely to occur?
- Is a trickle up flow also possible? Cite examples.

6. Based on the five characteristics specified by Rogers and Shoemaker, what prediction would you have made regarding the speed of adoption of: (a) fluoride toothpaste, (b) the automobile, (c) pocket calculators?

7. Ostlund's study of adoption of six consumer packaged goods found that there is no generalized innovator. Consumers' perceptions of the product were more important than any personal characteristics, such as demographics or personality, in identifying the innovator.

- Why was it unlikely that Ostlund would have found the same consumers buying new products across the six categories he studied?

8. The chapter cites an important gap in diffusion research — the lack of any research on a negative diffusion process. Marketing managers never like to advertise failures; thus the lack of research on negative diffusion. But such studies might provide insights on how to avoid product failures.

- Cite an example of negative diffusion for a product.

9. Assume a company is introducing a new facial care appliance. How could the company best appeal to the target market based on the profile of the personal care innovator in Table 16–2?

10. What insights might the marketing manager have gained from studying negative diffusion to better understand (a) word-of-mouth communication, and (b) product positioning?

RESEARCH ASSIGNMENTS

1. Use the following type of questions to identify the innovator for men's cosmetics. "How do you see yourself with regard to buying a new facial care preparation for men? As one of the first to buy? As purchasing after a few others have tried it? As purchasing after many people have bought it? Not purchasing?" Identify the innovator as the individual who says he would be one of the first to buy. In addition to the innovativeness question, ask the sample of males: (a) life-style

questions based on those listed in Table 16–1; (b) an opinion leadership question based on questions 2 and 4 in Figure 15–6; (c) self-confidence questions in selecting cosmetics and toiletry items; and, (d) questions about their demographic characteristics.

- What are the differences between the innovators and noninnovators on each of the above items? (If your sample is large enough, split it into three groups: innovators, those tending to be innovators, and noninnovators and determine differences between these groups.)

- What are the implications of these differences for a marketing strategy for men's cosmetics in regard to (a) market segmentation, (b) advertising and product positioning, (c) pricing, (d) product development, and (e) distribution?

2. One of the hypotheses in the chapter is that there may be a generalized innovator for discontinuous innovations. Determine ownership of discontinuous innovations by asking a sample of forty to fifty consumers about ownership of items such as microwave ovens, digital watches, CB radios, diesel cars, rotary engines, videotapes, etc. Also determine (a) life-styles, (b) opinion leadership, and (c) demographics.

- Do consumers who own one discontinuous innovation tend to own others?

- Split the sample between those who do and do not own two or more discontinuous innovations. What are the differences in characteristics between the two groups?

NOTES

1. Thomas S. Robertson, "Determinants of Innovative Behavior," in Reed Moyer, ed., *Winter Conference of the American Marketing Assocation.* Series #26 (1967), pp. 328–332; and James F. Engel, Robert J. Kegerreis, and Roger D. Blackwell, "Word-of-Mouth Communication by the Innovator," *Journal of Marketing* 33 (July 1969): 15–19.

2. Thomas S. Robertson, "The Process of Innovation and the Diffusion of Innovation," *Journal of Marketing* 31 (January 1967): 14–19.

3. "Who Buys a G.M. Diesel Car?", *The New York Times*, November 9, 1978, p. D7.

4. Thomas S. Robertson, *Innovative Behavior and Communication* (New York: Holt, Rinehart & Winston, Inc. 1971), pp. 75–77.

5. Everett M. Rogers, *Diffusion of Innovations* (New York: The Free Press, 1962).

6. Ibid., pp. 168–171.

7. Engel, Kegerreis, and Blackwell, "Word-of-Mouth Communication."

8. Jagdish N. Sheth, "Word-of-Mouth in Low-Risk Innovations," *Journal of Advertising Research* 11 (June 1971): 15–18.

9. Engel, Kegerreis, and Blackwell, "Word-of-Mouth Communication."

10. Zarrel V. Lambert, "Perceptual Patterns, Information Handling, and Innovativeness," *Journal of Marketing Research* 9 (November 1972): 427–431.

11. Steven A. Baumgarten, "The Innovative Communicator in the Diffusion Process," *Journal of Marketing Research* 12 (February 1975): 12–18.

12. See Johan Arndt, "Role of Product-Related Conversations in the Diffusion of a New Product," *Journal of Marketing Research* 4 (August 1967): 291–295; and John O. Summers and Charles W. King, "Interpersonal Communication and New Product Attitudes," in Philip R. McDonald, ed., *Proceedings of the American Marketing Association Educators' Conference*, Series #30 (1969), pp. 292–299.

13. Everett M. Rogers, "New Product Adoption and Diffusion," *Journal of Consumer Research* 2 (March 1976): 290–301.

14. Thorstein Veblen, *The Theory of the Leisure Class* (New York: MacMillan, 1912).

15. George Simmel, "Fashion," *International Quarterly* 10 (October 1904): 130–155.

16. W.T. Liu and R.W. Duff, "The Strength in Weak Ties," *Public Opinion Quarterly* 36 (Fall 1972): 361–366.

17. Charles W. King, "Fashion Adoption: A Rebuttal to the 'Trickle Down' Theory," in James U. McNeal, ed., *Dimensions of Consumer Behavior* (New York: Appleton-Century-Crofts, 1969), pp. 169–184.

18. Ibid., p. 172.

19. James Duesenberry, *Income, Savings and the Theory*

of Consumer Behavior (Cambridge, Mass.: Harvard University Press, 1949).

20. B. Ryan and N.C. Gross, "The Diffusion of Hybrid Seed Corn in Two Iowa Communities," *Rural Sociology* 8 (March 1943): 15–24.

21. James Coleman, Elihu Katz, and Herbert Menzel, "The Diffusion of an Innovation Among Physicians," *Sociometry* 20 (December 1957): 253–270.

22. Ronald B. Marks and R. Eugene Hughes, "The Consumer Innovator: Identifying the Profile of the Earliest Adopters of Community Antenna Television," in Kenneth L. Bernhardt, ed., *Proceedings of the American Marketing Association Educators' Conference,* Series #39 (1976), pp. 568–571.

23. Leon G. Schiffman, "Perceived Risk in New Product Trial by Elderly Consumers," *Journal of Marketing Research* 9 (February 1972): 106–108.

24. Everett M. Rogers and F. Floyd Shoemaker, *Communication of Innovations,* 2nd ed (New York: The Free Press, 1971).

25. Rogers, "New Product Adoption," p. 294.

26. Leon G. Schiffman and Leslie L. Kanuk, *Consumer Behavior* (Englewood Cliffs, N.J.: Prentice-Hall Inc., 1978), pp. 412–413.

27. Rogers and Shoemaker, *Communication of Innovations.*

28. Robert W. Shoemaker, and F. Robert Shoaf, "Behavioral Changes in the Trial of New Products," *Journal of Consumer Research* 2 (September 1975): 104–109.

29. Laurence P. Feldman and Gary M. Armstrong, "Identifying Buyers of a Major Automotive Innovation," *Journal of Marketing* 39 (January 1975): 47–53.

30. Lyman Ostlund, "Perceived Innovation Attributes as Predictors of Innovativeness," *Journal of Consumer Research* 1 (September 1974): 23–29.

31. John O. Summers, "Generalized Change Agents and Innovativeness," *Journal of Marketing Research* 8 (August 1971): 313–316.

32. Thomas S. Robertson and James H. Myers, "Personality Correlates of Opinion Leadership and Innovative Buying Behavior," *Journal of Marketing Research* 6 (May 1969): 164–168.

33. David F. Midgley, "A Simple Mathematical Theory of Innovative Behavior," *Journal of Consumer Research* 3 (June 1976): 31–41.

34. Elizabeth C. Hirschman and William O. Adcock, "An Examination of Innovative Communicators, Opinion Leaders and Innovators for Men's Fashion Apparel," in H. Keith Hunt, ed., *Advances in Consumer Research,* vol. 5 (Ann Arbor: Association for Consumer Research, 1978), pp. 308–314.

35. Baumgarten, "The Innovative Communicator."

36. David Riesman, N. Glazer, and R. Denney, *The Lonely Crowd* (New Haven, Conn.: Yale University Press, 1950).

37. James H. Donnelly, Jr., "Social Character and Acceptance of New Products," *Journal of Marketing Research* 7 (February 1970): 111.

38. James H. Donnelly, Jr. and John M Ivancevich,

"A Methodology for Identifying Innovator Characteristics of New Brand Purchasers," *Journal of Marketing Research* 11 (August 1974): 331–334.

39. Howard J. Ehrlich and Dorothy Lee, "Dogmatism, Learning and Resistance to Change: A Review and a New Paradigm," *Psychological Bulletin* 71 (April 1969): 249–260.

40. Jacob Jacoby, "Personality and Innovation Proneness," *Journal of Marketing Research* 8 (May 1971): 244–247.

41. Milton Rokeach, *The Open and Closed Mind* (New York: Basic Books, 1960), p. 57.

42. Baumgarten, "The Innovative Communicator," pp. 17–18.

43. William R. Darden and Fred D. Reynolds, "Backward Profiling of Male Innovators," *Journal of Marketing Research* 11 (February 1974): 79–85.

44. Thomas S. Robertson, "Determinants of Innovative Behavior," in Reed Moyer, ed., *Proceedings of the Winter Conference of the American Marketing Association,* Series #26 (1967), pp. 328–332.

45. Arndt, "Role of Product-Related Conversations."

46. Lambert, "Perceptual Patterns."

47. Kenneth Uhl, Roman Andrus, and Lance Poulsen, "How Are Laggards Different? An Empirical Inquiry," *Journal of Marketing Research* 7 (February 1970): 51–54.

48. Baumgarten, "The Innovative Communicator."

49. Marks and Hughes, "The Consumer Innovator."

50. Schiffman, "Perceived Risk."

51. Lambert, "Perceptual Patterns."

52. Uhl, Andrus, and Poulsen, "How Are Laggards Different?"

53. Engel, Kegerreis, and Blackwell, "Word-of-Mouth Communication."

54. Marks and Hughes, "The Consumer Innovator."

55. Uhl, Andrus, and Poulsen, "How Are Laggards Different?"

56. Darden and Reynolds, "Backward Profiling of Male Innovators."

57. Charles W. King, "Communicating with the Innovator in the Fashion Adoption Process," in Peter D. Bennett, ed., *Proceedings of the Fall Conference of the American Marketing Assocation* (1965), p. 430.

58. Lambert, "Perceptual Patterns."

59. John O. Summers, "Media Exposure Patterns of Consumer Innovators," *Journal of Marketing* 36 (January 1972): 43–49.

60. Ibid., p. 46.

61. Baumgarten, "The Innovative Communicator," p. 16.

62. Summers, "Media Exposure," p. 46.

63. Ibid.; and King, "Communicating with the Innovator," p. 430.

64. Donnelly and Ivancevich, "A Methodology," p. 332.

65. Summers, "Generalized Change Agents," p. 314.

66. Philip Kotler and Gerald Zaltman, "Targeting Prospects for a New Product," *Journal of Advertising Research* 16 (February 1976): 7–18.

SEVENTEEN

Situational Determinants of Consumer Behavior

Focus of Chapter

One essential environmental factor that has not yet been explored is the usage situation. In asking a consumer to rate preferences for brands of paper towels or makes of automobiles, it would be perfectly reasonable for the consumer to say, "The brand I select depends on how, when, where, and why I'm going to use it." A consumer may prefer one brand of paper towels for heavy duty cleaning and another for wiping; one brand of coffee to have alone and another to serve guests; and one make of automobile for long business trips and another for local shopping trips.

Therefore, the usage situation will directly affect consumers' perceptions of brands, preferences for brands, and purchasing behavior.

This chapter will focus on situational variables as determinants of consumer behavior. The importance of the usage situation in developing marketing strategies will first be considered. Second, the nature of situational variables will be discussed, particularly the need for an inventory of situations relevant to consumption. Third, a model of consumer behavior centered on situational effects will be described. Fourth, recent studies will be presented that take account of the usage situation to better explain and predict consumer attitudes and behavior.

IMPORTANCE OF THE USAGE SITUATION IN MARKETING STRATEGY

The usage situation directly influences marketing strategy because it affects the manner in which markets are *segmented*, products are *positioned*, and brands are *advertised*. These factors will be considered below.

Market Segmentation

Market segmentation often depends on the consumer's use situation. In a snack food study, situational determinants were important in defining the segments. Nutritional snackers were light users. When snack foods were eaten, they tended to be eaten at meals in combination with other foods. Guilty snackers tended to eat snack foods between meals. Party snackers obviously ate and served snacks primarily at social occasions. The only segment for which situational factors were not important was the indiscriminate snacker who tended to eat snacks on most usage occasions.

Product Positioning

A study of paper towel usage found that consumers divided usage occasions into heavy duty uses (cleaning ovens, washing windows, cleaning cars), light duty usage (wiping hands, wiping kitchen counters, wiping dishes), and decorative uses (as a napkin, placemat). Positioning a paper towel requires the recognition of the usage situation. A positioning toward heavy duty usage will dictate the product's characteristics (multiple ply), the target segment to which the product should be positioned (the heavy-duty user), the promotional appeals (strength and durability), and possibly the media to be used (based on the demographic characteristics of the heavy-duty segment).

Promotional Direction

The usage situation will also dictate the promotional appeals to be used. If a soft drink is purchased primarily for social occasions, it should be advertised in the context of a social occasion. If a food processor is purchased by a certain segment primarily for cooking for guests, it should be advertised in the context of meal preparations for guests rather than family. The paper towel study concluded that advertising to the lighter duty segment required appeals based on absorbency rather than strength. A positioning to the decorative segment required appeals to color and design. The snack food study concluded that advertising to the nutritional segment required appeals to nutrition in a situational context emphasizing snacks in combination with other foods. Appeals to the guilty snackers required an attempt to alleviate the anxiety of eating snacks in the situation in which they are most likely to be eaten, between meals.

Limited Use of Situational Variables

Given the importance of the usage situation in affecting brand choice, it is surprising that most marketing studies do not account for the situation. Consumers are asked to rate a brand (on nutrition, taste, convenience, etc.) without reference to the usage situation. Most of the attitudinal studies described in Chapter 7 failed to take account of the usage situation. The assumption is that attitudes toward a brand are the same, regardless of the usage situation. Fennell comments on the weakness of this assumption as follows:

A moment's thought makes it clear that words such as power, ease of handling, complexion care, cleansing, etc., while referring to product benefits that may satisfy wants, do not in themselves tell us anything about the situations in which consumers find themselves — the situations that make power, complexion care, and the like desirable to them. . . . The marketing concept implies that the meaning of such product use situations differs in important ways across consumers. . . .[1]

It is clear that if marketing strategy is to be geared to consumer needs and preferences, then these needs and preferences must be measured for a particular usage situation. A marketing practitioner, commenting on the general lack of use of situational variables, said:

When my colleagues talk about my ideal cigarette, I am tempted to ask them whether they mean ideal for work or ideal for play, ideal for the beginning of the month when I'm rich or ideal for the end when I am poor. When they talk about shampoos. . . . I want to know whether the ideal they are asking me about is my ideal when I am on holiday sea-bathing, my ideal when the shopping has to be done as quickly as possible. The markets may be [situationally] homogeneous — it seems I am not.[2]

THE NATURE OF SITUATIONAL VARIABLES

If the usage situation is to be considered in the development of marketing strategy, it is important to understand the nature of situational variables. The first consideration is the types of situations managers must consider. Given an understanding of the types of situations, the next consideration is how to develop a situational inventory so that consumer behavior in different situations can be measured.

Types of Situations

There are three types of situations relevant to the marketer — the consumption situation, the purchase situation, and the communications situation.[3]

The Consumption Situation

The consumption situation refers to the anticipated usage situation for the brand. For example, Belk asked consumers what types of snack foods they would buy for the following usage situations:

- a snack the family can eat while watching TV in the evening
- a snack to have around for a few close friends at a party
- a snack for a long automobile trip
- a between meal snack
- a snack to have around in case friends drop by
- a snack to have with lunch[4]

The Purchase Situation

Practically all the studies cited in this chapter will involve the consumption situation, but it is important to recognize that the purchase situation may also affect marketing strategy. For example, assume that the manufacturer of a leading line of cereals wants to assess the impact of the in-store environment on consumer choice. Situational factors such as out-of-stock, change in price, competitive deals, and ease of shopping become relevant in the consumer's choice and may affect the manufacturer's distribution and pricing policies. As a result, the manufacturer asks a sample of consumers how the following purchase-related situations may affect brand choice:

- You are in the store and find your favorite brand of cereal is not in stock. (Do you go to another store, buy a substitute, or delay the purchase?)
- Your favorite brand of cereal is five cents more than it was last time.
- A brand of cereal that you have used occasionally has a price deal.
- You need cereal yet there is a long line at the check-out counter as you come into the store.
- You have some difficulty finding your favorite brand of cereal. (Do you ask a clerk or buy a competitive brand?)

The importance of the purchase situation is documented in many studies that have demonstrated the effects of price changes, displays, and salesperson influences on consumer behavior as a result of the in-store environment.[5]

Another purchase-related situation is buying a product either as a gift or for oneself. The purchase of an appliance for someone else may result in the use of different evaluative criteria and selection of a different brand than if the purchase was for oneself.

The Communications Situation

The communications situation is also of interest to the marketer. Did a consumer hear a radio commercial while riding in the car or while sitting in the living room? Was a magazine read inside or outside the home? Was the magazine read as a pass-on issue? Was a TV commercial seen alone or with a group of people? Was it in the middle of an involving program? All of these situations are likely to affect the probability of exposure, attention, comprehension, and retention of the ad. The communications situation differs from the purchase and usage situation in that the consumer is not asked to anticipate what would be done in a given situation. It would not make sense to ask a consumer to anticipate how his or her reaction to a commercial would differ if people were in the room or not. In these cases, it would make more sense to directly test the effect of different situations on recall, comprehension, and retention.

Single Versus Multiple Use Situations

Given the importance of the consumption situation, Belk further classified usage into *single use consumption situations* (a good is purchased for use in a single, frequently anticipated consumption situation) and *multiple use consumption situ-*

ations (a good is purchased that best satisfies the various demands of several anticipated consumption situations).[6]

Products purchased for single use consumption situations are most likely to be consumer packaged goods. Studies of soft drinks,[7] snack foods,[8] beer,[9] meat products,[10] and breath fresheners[11] have all shown that the consumption situation directly affects behavior. Products purchased for multiple uses are more likely to be durable goods. It is unlikely that consumers will own different television sets for different viewing occasions, or different stereo sets for different listening occasions. But even here, situational effects may be important. For example, many two-car families use one car primarily for work purposes and another for local shopping or evening entertainment. Some camera buffs may have several cameras for different types of situations, etc. Belk concludes that even though situational effects are less likely to be important for durable goods, "there are few if any product and service purchases which are devoid of potential consumption situation influences."[12]

The Situation Versus the Product

Belk is right in emphasizing the importance of the situation, but may be overstating the case. In some cases, consumers will buy a certain brand regardless of the situation. This can be true even for consumer packaged goods. For example, a consumer may be very loyal to Michelob beer. The consumer makes no distinction between drinking Michelob when alone, with guests, while watching TV, with meals, in-between meals, or any other time. This consumer happens to like Michelob and the consumption situation will not influence purchasing behavior. The product is paramount in determining behavior, not the situation.

It can generally be stated that *the greater the degree of brand loyalty, the less important are situational influences.* The brand loyal consumer is likely to use the favorite brand of beer, coffee, or snack food regardless of the situation. Conversely, where loyalties are not strong, the consumption situation may be the determining factor in brand choice. A consumer may prefer a certain brand of beer because it is adequate and less expensive than most beers. On occasion, an intermediate priced brand may be purchased for home consumption when the consumer is willing to spend more. For social occasions, a higher priced beer will be purchased. The price sensitivity of this consumer causes him or her to consider the consumption situation in buying different brands.

Another principle is that *the higher the level of product involvement, the less likely it is that situational factors will determine behavior.* In cases of high product involvement, the benefits provided by alternative products will influence behavior. In cases of low involvement, the consumer is not committed to any particular brand. Therefore, the consumption situation rather than the brand's characteristics may determine behavior. Clarke and Belk studied involvement in the situation and involvement in the product for four product categories.[13] They found that when involvement in the product is low, the situation tends to determine behavior. When product involvement is high, the situation is not as important.

Characteristics of Consumption Situations

Not only is it necessary to identify specific types of consumption situations, it is also necessary to consider the more general characteristics of such situations. Belk identifies five characteristics of situations :

1. *The Physical Surroundings.*   For example, a store's decor and shelf layout; being indoors or outside; being in a noisy room.
2. *Social Surroundings.*   Whether guests are present, the social occasion, the importance of friends and neighbors that are present.
3. *Time.*   Breakfast, lunchtime, between meals; seasonal factors such as winter versus summer relative to clothing; the time that has passed since the product was last consumed.
4. *Task Definition.*   Shopping for oneself or for the family, shopping for a gift; cooking for oneself, for the family or for guests.
5. *Antecedent States.*   Momentary conditions such as shopping when tired or anxious, buying a product on impulse because of an excess of cash on hand, using a product when in an excited state. [14]

Situations are likely to be made up of several of these characteristics. For example, the situation "shopping for a snack that the family can eat while watching television in the evening,"[15] is made up of the physical surroundings (TV set present), the social surroundings (family), time (evening), and task definition (consumer is doing the shopping and family will do the eating).

Development of Situational Inventories

An important step in accounting for the effects of consumption situations on behavior is development of an inventory of situations closely related to behavior. The procedures for developing a situational inventory are similar to those for developing a life-style inventory. A group of consumers are brought together for an open-ended discussion of the nature of usage of a certain product category. From these discussions, a large number of consumption situations are identified. The number of situations are then reduced by eliminating any redundancy between situations (e.g., a between meal snack and an afternoon snack frequently represent the same situation) and also selecting those situations that seem to be most closely related to brand choice.

Once the situational inventory is developed, consumers can then be asked one or more of the following questions:

• What is the frequency with which the situation arises?
• What is the likelihood of buying a particular product in that situation?
• What is the likelihood of buying a particular brand in that situation?

Table 17–1 presents two situational inventories, one from a snack food study,[16] the other from a study of beer drinkers.[17] In each case, ten situations

TABLE 17–1 Examples of Situational Inventories for Snack Foods and for Beer

SNACK FOODS INVENTORY

1. You are shopping for a snack that you or your family can eat while watching television in the evenings.

2. You are planning a party for a few close friends and are wondering what to have around to snack on.

3. Snacks at your house have become a little dull lately and you are wondering what you might pick up that would be better.

4. You are going on a long automobile trip and are thinking that you should bring along some snacks to eat on the way.

5. You suddenly realize that you have invited a couple of friends over for the evening and you have nothing for them to snack on.

6. You are at the grocery store when you get an urge for a between meal snack.

7. You are at the supermarket and notice the many available snack products; you wonder if you should pick something up in case friends drop by.

8. You are thinking about what type of snack to buy to keep around the house this weekend.

9. You are at the store to pick up some things for a picnic you are planning with friends and are trying to decide what kind of snack to buy.

10. You are thinking about a snack to have with lunch at noon.

Source: Russell W. Belk, "An Exploratory Assessment of Situational Effects in Buyer Behavior," *Journal of Marketing Research* 11 (May 1974): 160
Reprinted with permission from *Journal of Marketing Research.*

BEER INVENTORY

1. Entertaining close friends at home.

2. Giving a party at home where the guests include people you know at work and friends you come in contact with only once or twice a week.

3. Going to a tavern after work.

4. Going to a restaurant or lounge on Friday or Saturday night.

5. Watching a sports event or some favorite TV show.

6. Attending some social event for which you are asked to supply your own refreshments.

7. Engaging in some sports activity or hobby such as golf, bowling, softball, fishing, etc.

8. Taking a weekend or vacation camping trip, beach trip, or extended picnic.

9. Working at home on the yard, house, or car.

10. Simply relaxing at home.

Source: William O. Bearden and Arch G. Woodside, "Consumption Occasion Influence on Consumer Brand Choice," *Decision Sciences* 9 (April 1978): 275.
Reprinted with permission from *Decision Sciences.*

were identified. In each case, these situations were selected based on preliminary in-depth interviews with consumers.

In the snack food study, the ten situations were factor analyzed to reduce them to a smaller number of situational dimensions. Four situational dimensions were identified:

427

The Nature of Situational Variables

- informal serving situations (represented by items 5, 7, and 8 in Table 17–1)
- nutritive situations (items 4, 9, and 10)
- impulsive consumption situation (items 3 and 6)
- planned purchasing situations (items 1 and 2)

These situations were then related to the purchase of three types of snack foods: substantial snacks (sandwiches, cheese, crackers), light/salty snacks, and sweet snacks. Consumers were not homogeneous in the types of snack foods they purchased for the four situations. One segment tended to purchase substantial snacks for all occasions except unplanned purchases. For unplanned purchases they tended to buy light/salty snacks. A second segment bought light/salty snacks primarily for informal serving situations. A third segment bought sweet snacks primarily for impulsive situations.[18]

The study has important implications for marketing strategy. Marketers of light/salty snacks such as potato chips and pretzels would do best to portray these products in informal situations. Appeals to nutritive situations are likely to fall short because of lack of association of these products with nutritional benefits. Marketers of sweet snacks such as cookies could emphasize the impulsive nature of consumption — the urge to buy and to liven up a snacking occasion. Such a situation could be linked to the pleasure of eating sweets.

The snack food study demonstrates the use of situational inventories in behavioral research, but it assumes that situational inventories should be product-specific. This assumption has been questioned.

General Versus Product-Specific Situational Inventories

There are two approaches to developing a situational inventory. In one, the researcher may attempt to classify all possible situations affecting consumer behavior in general; in the other, the researcher could classify all relevant situations affecting behavior toward the product. An example of an attempt to develop a general situational inventory is found in the work of Mehrabian and Russell.[19] They developed a classification of three situational characteristics: pleasure, arousal, and dominance. All situations could be classified into one of these three categories. The types of general situations defined by Mehrabian and Russell are situations such as "plunging into a cool pool on a hot day," "sitting alone late at night in a roadside rest stop," "being a champion racer at the Indianapolis 500 in a tight competitive race," etc. Thus, plunging into a cool pool is associated with arousal, sitting in a quiet room with pleasure, and being a champion racer with dominance.

Although this type of general situational inventory may have some relevance in studies of behavioral predispositions, it has little application to marketing. The situational inventory must be related to consumer behavior. Situations that affect the choice of a snack food are totally different from those which affect the choice of a cosmetic. Therefore, situational inventories must be product-specific.[20] The inventories in Table 17–1 are good examples of product-specific inventories with potentially important implications for marketing strategy.

A MODEL OF SITUATIONAL DETERMINANTS

The simple model of consumer behavior in Chapter 1 described three possible influences on purchasing behavior: (1) the consumer, (2) environmental influences, and (3) marketing strategy. A model of situational determinants on consumer behavior would describe behavior as a function of the same three basic forces, except that the consumer's environment would be represented by the consumption situation and marketing strategy would be represented by the product being consumed.

This model of situational determinants is presented in Figure 17–1.[21] The model is derived both from a stimulus-response and a cognitive framework. From a stimulus-response view, the two outside forces acting on the consumer are the product and the consumption situation (the stimuli). The consumer (the organism) reacts to the product and the situation and decides on the brand to be purchased (response). From a cognitive standpoint, it is recognized that the interaction between the consumer, situation, and product will result in a process of choice leading to behavior. Further, the situation and product can be viewed within the cognitive principles of context since the product is the

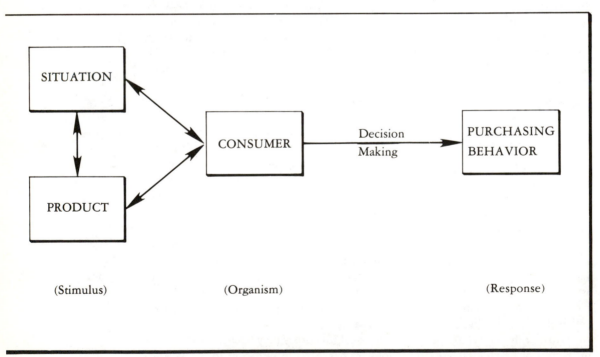

FIGURE 17–1   A Model of Situational Determinants of Consumer Behavior

Source: Adapted from Russell W. Belk, "Situational Variables and Consumer Behavior," *Journal of Consumer Research* 2 (December 1975): 158.
    Reprinted with permission from the *Journal of Consumer Research*.

figure and the situation is the ground. This distinction is clear in viewing almost any print advertisement. The product generally appears in the foreground and the situation in the background. (See the ads in Chapter 5, Figure 5–5, as an example.)

Although the situational model may seem simple compared to the descriptions of decision making in Chapters 2 and 3, it is not as simple as it appears. Several issues require attention. First, it must be determined what the relationship between the product, the situation, and the consumer is. Is behavior primarily due to loyalty to the product regardless of the situation? Is it due to the situation regardless of the product? Is it due to some interaction between product, situation and consumer? (The possibility of such interactions is recognized in the model by the double arrows between situation, product, and consumer.)

A second and related issue is whether the consumer attributes behavior to the situation, to the product, or to both. Attributing behavior to the product implies that behavior will be consistent across situations and that a degree of brand loyalty exists. Attributing behavior to the situation implies variation in behavior across brands since different brands will be purchased for different situations. Attribution theory sheds light on the role of consumption situations and product characteristics in influencing behavior.

A third issue is the contiguity of the situation to behavior. If the situation is close to behavior, then it is more likely to be the determining factor in influencing behavior (e.g., buying soft drinks at the last minute for a party, regardless of price or brand). If the consumption situation is not closely linked to the purchase, it is less likely to be an influence. Each of these three issues will be explored.

The Interaction of Situation, Product, and Consumer on Behavior

A number of studies have considered the influence of the situation, the product, and the consumer on purchasing behavior. Belk has summarized seven of these studies in Table 17–2 for product categories ranging from beverages to motion pictures.[22] The percentage of variance accounted for by the three components in the model — the consumer, the product, and the situation — is represented as well as the interaction between these components. These percentages represent the level of importance of each factor in influencing consumer behavior.

The table shows that the situation alone (second row) is relatively unimportant in influencing behavior. The major influence is the situation in combination with the product (fourth row). A situation like a party will not influence the purchase of beverages regardless of the type of beverage purchased (e.g., it is unlikely someone will say, "I buy more of all kinds of beverages when there is a party"). A party will determine the type of beverage purchased (e.g., "I buy more soft drinks, or more colas, or more beer when I have a party").

The second most important influence on behavior is the product in interaction with the consumer (sixth row in Table 17–2). This means that certain types of products will be purchased by certain consumers regardless of the

TABLE 17–2   Effects of Situation, Product and Consumer on Behavior for Six
Product Categories

Source	Response Category (%)					
	Beverage Products	Meat Products	Snack Products	Fast Foods	Leisure Activities	Motion Pictures
Consumers (C)	0.5	4.6	6.7	8.1	4.5	0.9
Situations (S)	2.7	5.2	0.4	2.2	2.0	0.5
Products (P)	14.6	15.0	6.7	13.4	8.8	16.6
P × S	39.8	26.2	18.7	15.3	13.4	7.0
S × C	2.7	2.9	6.1	2.2	4.0	1.9
P × C	11.8	9.7	22.4	20.1	21.2	33.7
Residual[a]	27.8	36.4	39.0	38.7	46.1	39.4
Total	100.0	100.0	100.0	100.0	100.0	100.0

[a] The residual represents the variance left over once the effects of the consumer, situation, and product, and the interaction between them are accounted for. The above residual also includes the three-way, product-by-situation-by-consumer interaction.

Source: Adapted from Russell W. Belk, "Situational Variables and Consumer Behavior," Journal of Consumer Research, 2 (December 1975): 160.
Reprinted with permission from the Journal of Consumer Research.

situation. For example, teenage suburbanites in the middle income group (the consumer type) buy more colas (the product) regardless of the situation. This consumer-by-product interaction demonstrates the importance of brand or product loyalty since certain consumer segments buy a particular product across most situations. The table thus shows that (1) situational influences frequently determine the product or brand purchased, and (2) where this does not occur, brand or product loyalty tends to be operating.

The same studies cited by Belk in Table 17–2 are also instructive in showing differences between product categories. For example, the situation-by-product interaction was important for every category except motion pictures. It was especially important for beverage and meat products, meaning that these products are particularly prone to situational influences: Certain types of beverages and meats are likely to be served for certain occasions. The consumer-by-product interaction was important for all product categories, but especially for motion pictures and less so for snack and beverage products. This means that certain types of people are "loyal" to certain types of motion pictures regardless of the situation. Some people may see every Woody Allen or Al Pacino picture that comes out. Motion pictures may be less subject to situational influences because they may be more involving. For beverage and meat products, loyalty to a certain product regardless of the situation is much less likely.

The studies cited by Belk strongly support the situational model in Figure 17–1. Products tended to be purchased for specific consumption situations.

Consumer Attribution of Situational Factors

One important consideration in the situational model is whether consumers attribute their behavior to the product's characteristics or to the situation. Attribution theory suggests that people examine their prior behavior and attribute a cause to the behavior after-the-fact.[23] If a consumer attributes behavior to the product rather than to the situation, attitudes toward the product will be more positive, increasing the likelihood the product will be purchased again.[24] Thus, if a consumer attributes the purchase of a cereal to its nutritional content (a product attribute) rather than to the fact that it was on sale (a situational determinant), attitudes toward the cereal are likely to be positive and the cereal is likely to be repurchased. On the other hand, if attribution is to the situation (e.g., "I purchased because it was on sale"), attitudes toward the brand are not likely to be more positive and the consumer will probably revert to the regular brand when the sale is over.

Attribution theory seems to support the notion that brand loyalty and situation-specific behavior are opposites. Brand loyalty suggests that behavior was due to the product independent of the situation. Situation-specific behavior suggests that the purchase was due to environmental circumstance, and that if the situation changes, brand choice will also change.

Contiguity Between Situation and Behavior

Another issue relevant to the situational model in Figure 17–1 is the degree of contiguity between the situation and behavior. If the purchase and the situation are close in time, then the situation is likely to influence brand choice. A consumer who is shopping for food for a big dinner party that evening may buy items not ordinarily purchased. A consumer who sees a sharp reduction in price for a particular brand (a purchase situation), may buy it even though it is not among those brands regularly purchased. In both cases, behavior is situation-specific.

Sternthal and Zaltman refer to these types of situations as *facilitators*.[25] The situational facilitators are less likely to lead to consistent behavior over time. Thus, the consumer who buys items for a dinner party is not likely to purchase them on a day-to-day basis. The consumer who buys a less preferred brand because of a sharp price reduction is not likely to continue to do so when the price returns to normal. Situations that are not contiguous to behavior are situational *inhibitors*. The consumer buying food items for normal usage may just be "stocking up" for the future. Situational requirements are not apparent, and the preferred brands will be purchased. Under such conditions, behavior is due to preferences for the product rather than to the urgency of any situation.

SITUATIONAL INFLUENCES ON CONSUMER DECISIONS

Research on situational influences has tended to focus on three areas: (1) situational influences on product choice; (2) situational influences on product perceptions and attitudes; and (3) situational influences on decision making.

The research by Belk and others cited in the previous section has sufficiently substantiated the fact that products are frequently purchased for particular situations. Research has also shown that perceptions of products will vary by situation (Shake 'n Bake chicken may be rated as convenient to prepare for dinner, but not for lunch); and that the decision process will vary by situation (a greater number of product attributes are considered when selecting a hair dryer as a gift than when selecting it for oneself).

Influence of Situations on Product Attitudes and Perceptions

A number of studies have shown that consumers' attitudes toward products vary depending on the situation.[26] These studies have tended to take a multiattribute approach by having consumers rate product attributes for various situations. The basic multiattribute model described in Chapter 7 is used on a situation-specific basis so that

$$A_o = \sum_{i=1}^{n} b_{ois} \, a_{is}$$

where:

A_o = the attitude towards the brand (o).

b_{ois} = the belief about the brand o on attribute i (e.g., convenience) in situation s (e.g., between meals).

a_{is} = the importance of attribute i (convenience) in situation s (between meals).

The inclusion of the situation in the basic multiattribute model allows the researcher to determine whether consumers regard certain attributes more important than others (the a term in the model) in certain situations. Thus, "convenience" and "easy to prepare" may be more important for lunch or snack occasions than for a dinner occasion. Conversely, "good for the family" may be more important for dinner occasions than for lunch or snacks. The model also can determine if consumers vary their beliefs about brands (the b component in the model) depending on the situation. For example, a consumer may rate Schlitz "refreshing" for "when I'm thirsty" but not for "at mealtime." The consumer may also rate Schlitz high on taste for "when I am drinking beer alone" but not for "when I serve beer to guests."

Differences in importance ratings and brand beliefs by situation have important implications for marketing strategy. If many consumers regard the benefits of "convenience" and "easy to prepare" as more appropriate for lunchtime, then it is obvious that these benefits should be advertised in a lunchtime situation. Differences in brand perceptions by situations might also indicate strengths and weaknesses of brands. If a certain snack food is rated particularly low on taste for parties and social occasions, the marketer would want to further explore this potential weakness. Is it a problem with the product formulation or with the brand's image? Further, if a brand is stronger in a particular situation, then this strength should be exploited. If Schlitz is regarded as a good beer to have on isolate rather than social occasions, then perhaps taste benefits should be emphasized for situations when the beer drinker is alone.

One of the most comprehensive studies of the situational determinants of product attitudes was undertaken by Miller and Ginter.[27] They asked consumers to rate eight fast food restaurants (Burger Chef, Burger King, McDonald's, etc.) on attributes such as speed of service, variety, cleanliness, convenience, and so on, for four situations:

- lunch on a weekday
- snack during a shopping trip
- evening meal when rushed for time
- evening meal with the family when not rushed for time

Consumers were asked to rate the importance of each of the attributes for each situation (the a_{is} term in the multiattribute model). They were then asked to rate each of the fast food restaurants on convenience for the four situations. Results are in Table 17–3. The first part of the table shows the importance ratings when no situation was mentioned (the first column) and the importance ratings for each of the four situations. Convenience and speed of service were considered most important for lunch on a weekday and for evening meals when rushed. Variety of menu and popularity with children were most important for evening meals with the family when not rushed for time. Thus, consumers do differentiate product benefits by situation.

The second part of Table 17–3 shows the ratings of the eight fast food restaurants on convenience for the four situations. There were substantial differences in ratings by situation. Arby's and Burger King received higher ratings on convenience for snack occasions during a shopping trip than for the other three occasions. Borden Burger, Burger Chef, and McDonald's were seen as more convenient for both evening meal occasions compared to the other two occasions. Hungry Herman's was the only restaurant that received higher ratings for convenience on lunch on a weekday compared to the other three situations. These findings may suggest how to gain a competitive advantage based on convenience. For example, Hungry Herman's is generally rated low compared to the other restaurants, but it is rated higher on lunchtime situations than on other occasions. Therefore, the restaurant may increase its popularity by advertising convenient and quick service at lunch.

The final element in Miller and Ginter's analysis was to evaluate the ability of the multiattribute model to predict consumer behavior without taking account of the situation versus with taking account of the situation. The results are in the last part of Table 17–3 on p. 436. In each case, the situational model (model S) correctly predicted a greater proportion of consumer's restaurant choices than the nonsituational model (model G). For example, the situational model predicted the right choice for lunchtime occasions 41.3 percent of the time compared to 30.5 percent of the time for the nonsituational model. This result shows the importance of the situation in explaining consumer behavior. The basic model of consumer behavior can not be as effective without the situational component in Figure 17–1.

TABLE 17–3 Situational Determinants of Consumer Attitudes

RELATIONSHIP OF SITUATIONS TO CONSUMER IMPORTANCE RATINGS

Attribute	Nonsituational	Lunch on a weekday (Sit. A)	Evening meal when rushed for time (Sit. B)	Evening meal with family when not rushed for time (Sit. C)	Snack during a shopping trip (Sit. D)
1 Taste of food	4.76[a]	4.64	4.60	4.72	4.48
2 Cleanliness	4.54	4.32	4.31	4.41	4.35
3 Convenience	3.47	4.32	4.32	3.40	4.23
4 Price	3.64	3.92	3.84	3.83	3.89
5 Speed of service	3.65	4.45	4.45	3.05	3.98
6 Variety of menu	2.83	2.70	2.62	3.43	2.79
7 Popularity with children					
(n = 62)	2.28	1.95	2.69	3.21	2.58

[a] Importances were measured on a scale from 1 = very unimportant to 6 = very important.

TABLE 17–3 (cont.)

RELATIONSHIP OF SITUATIONS TO PERCEPTIONS OF CONVENIENCE

Brand	Nonsituational	Lunch on a weekday (Sit. A)	Evening meal when rushed for time (Sit. B)	Evening meal with family when not rushed for time (Sit. C)	Snack during a shopping trip (Sit. D)
1 Arby's	2.50[a]	1.56	2.09	2.26	2.49
2 Borden Burger	3.64	3.00	3.64	3.67	3.43
3 Burger Chef	2.81	2.04	2.71	2.87	2.53
4 Burger King	2.99	2.89	3.34	3.49	3.64
5 Hungry Herman's	.88	1.24	.69	.74	.87
6 McDonald's	3.75	3.29	3.82	3.82	3.72
7 Wendy's	2.80	2.63	2.74	2.94	2.83
8 White Castle	2.65	2.27	2.18	2.35	2.18

[a] Perceptions of convenience were measured on a scale from 1 = out of the way to 6 = close to where I am.

TABLE 17-3 cont.

PREDICTION OF BEHAVIOR USING A NONSITUATIONAL MODEL (G) VERSUS A SITUATIONAL MODEL (S)

Situation	n^a	Mean proportion correct	
		Model G	Model S
Lunch on a weekday	210	.305	.413
Evening meal when rushed for time	159	.386	.440
Evening meal with family when not rushed for time	128	.459	.495
Snack during a shopping trip	94	.316	.347

[a] Sample size is number of respondents who purchased on each occasion during the course of the study.

Source: Kenneth E. Miller and James L. Ginter, "An Investigation of Situational Variation in Brand Choice Behavior and Attitudes," *Journal of Marketing Research* 16 (February 1979): 117, 119, and 121. Reprinted with permission from the *Journal of Marketing Research*.

Situational Determinants of Decision Making

Few studies have focused on the effects of different situations on decision making. Yet it is likely that the number of brands considered, the amount of search, the type of information sought, and the sources of information are likely to vary by the consumption and purchase situation.

There is some evidence to support this belief. Ryans compared gift purchasing situations to purchases for oneself in the selection of electrical appliances.[28] Information search was more extensive in gift purchasing situations. In-store sources of information were more likely to be used compared to out-of-store sources. Moreover, a price limit was more likely to be set beforehand in the gift purchasing situation.

Clarke and Belk identified a gift-purchasing situation as more involving than a personal use situation. They felt that "giving the product as a gift increases the overall level of arousal and causes more effort to be expended."[29] They found that the gift-purchasing situation did increase the amount of time and effort devoted to shopping for low involvement products but not for high involvement products. They reasoned that for high involvement products the purchase situation was not likely to increase involvement any further. For low involvement products, the situation could increase the level of involvement. This finding supports a suggested strategy for increasing involvement in less important products by linking the product to an involving situation.[30] Thus, linking bubble bath (one of the low involvement products studied by Clarke and Belk) to a gift-giving situation is likely to increase involvement in the product.

In another study of the purchasing situation, Granbois identified purchasing situations where the shopper is alone and is with others.[31] When the shopper is with others more store locations are visited and more unplanned purchases are made.

The three studies cited above all evaluated differences in decision making for various purchasing situations. Ptacek and Shanteau focused on differences in decision making for various consumption situations. They defined four situations in the purchase of paper towels:

- heavy-duty jobs
- lighter jobs
- as napkins and for cleaning up at a barbecue
- just to have on hand.[32]

They identified consumers based on three types of decision strategies: those who made a decision based on one criterion for all brands; those who made decisions based on two criteria for all brands; and those who varied the criteria used across brands (an interactive strategy). When the consumption situation was for light duty work and for the barbecue, purchasing strategies were likely to be more complex and interactive. When towels were purchased for heavy duty jobs, simpler one- or two-dimensional strategies were used. This is probably due to the fact that the selection of a towel for heavy duty use rests on a simpler evaluation based on strength and durability. For light duty work, more attributes were probably needed to evaluate the towels, thus requiring a more complex decision strategy. The study by Ptacek and Shanteau is one of the few that examined decision making by situation. The findings suggest that consumers are likely to vary their method of selecting brands depending on the situation.

USE OF SITUATIONAL VARIABLES IN MARKETING STRATEGY

Situational variables have been used most frequently for purposes of positioning products and segmenting markets. Several studies will be cited to illustrate the use of situational factors for these strategic applications.

Product Positioning

A large food manufacturer undertook a study to determine the association of a broad range of food products for four types of occasions:

- special meal occasions
- family meals
- regular day-to-day meals
- snacks and quick meals

A sample of consumers was asked to associate sixteen products to these occasions. Results of the analysis are presented in Figure 17–2. Each quadrant in the figure represents one of the four mealtime occasions. For example, cold cuts, grilled cheese, and English muffins are associated with quick meals and snacks. Hamburgers and hot sandwiches are associated with regular meal occasions.

The study has several implications for marketing strategy. First, it provides a rational basis for grouping products in a situational context. Although not previously apparent, a logical product grouping could be cold cuts and cheeses, or packaged potatoes and vegetables. Second, the study provides guidelines for advertising in a situational context. Whereas one may have assumed that hamburgers are associated with quick meals, the study showed it would be more logical to advertise hamburgers and accessory products in a regular meal occasion.

Market Segmentation

A study of soft drink usage sought to segment consumers by situation.[33] Three segments were identified: (1) light users who bought soft drinks primarily for social occasions; (2) heavier users who bought soft drinks for many occasions; and (3) heavier users who bought soft drinks for a number of occasions but used

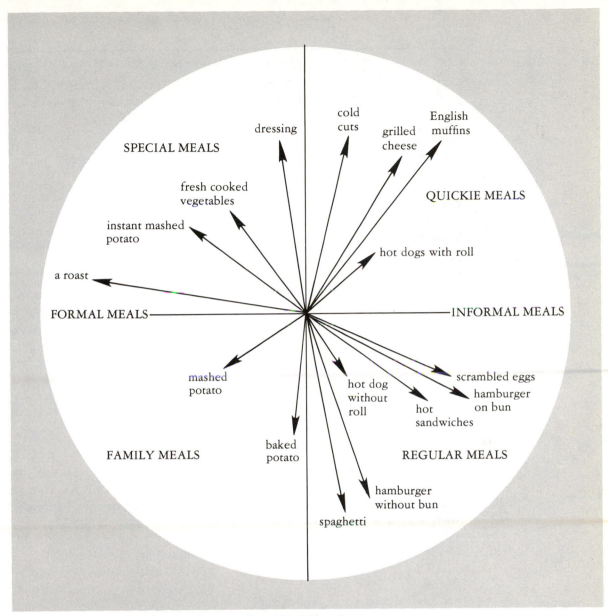

FIGURE 17–2   Positioning Products by Four Meal Situations

soft drinks particularly as a mixer with liquor.

Once these three segments were situationally defined, their needs, brand preferences, and demographic characteristics were identified. Table 17–4 presents these results. The lighter users who purchased for social occasions preferred

TABLE 17–4 Defining Market Segments by Situational Variables for Soft Drinks

	Distinguishing Characteristics of Each Situational Segment		
	Segment 1	*Segment 2*	*Segment 3*
	Light users/buy for social occasions	Heavier users/buy for most occasions	Heavier users/buy for mixed drinks
Product Attribute Preferences	lighter weaker noncola flavor fruit flavor	sweet want bottle	stronger thicker want cans
General Association	old-fashioned	modern	modern
Brand Preferences	Seven-Up Hires Root Beer	Coca-Cola Pepsi	Coca-Cola Pepsi
Demographic Characteristics	older	females	male younger

Source: Adapted from Louis K. Sharpe and Kent L. Granzin, "Market Segmentation by Consumer Usage Context: An Exploratory Analysis," *Journal of Economics and Business* 26 (1974): 227–228. Reprinted with permission from the *Journal of Economics and Business.*

lighter and weaker soft drinks. They liked noncola and fruit flavors. They also tended to associate soft drinks with old-fashioned values. This group was much more likely to drink Seven Up and Hires Root Beer. Demographically, they tended to be older.

The heavier users who drank soft drinks regardless of the situation preferred a sweet drink and liked bottles rather than cans. They tended to think of soft drinks as being more modern. They were more likely to drink Coke and Pepsi compared to the lighter users and were more likely to be females. The heavier users who used soft drinks as mixers preferred a stronger drink. They also thought of soft drinks as being more modern and were more likely to drink Coke and Pepsi. This group was younger and more likely to be male.

This study is a good illustration of segmentation by situational factors. The needs of the segments provide a basis for positioning and promoting products to each group. For example, a logical new product to be positioned to the lighter users would be a noncola, light, fruit-flavored drink. Advertising should emphasize traditional values to an older group.

SUMMARY

The usage situation is an important environmental factor that directly influences the consumer's brand choice, yet it has been largely overlooked by marketers. The usage situation should influence marketing strategy by affecting the manner in which markets are segmented, products are positioned, and brands are advertised.

Although the chapter emphasized the usage situation, two other situations also have important implications for marketing: the purchase situation and the communications situation. The purchase situation refers to the conditions under which a decision is made (e.g., whether purchasing as a gift or for oneself) and the in-store conditions at the time of the purchase. The communications situation refers to the conditions in which advertising exposure occurred (e.g., a radio commercial heard in a car or at home; TV watched alone or with friends, etc.).

An important facet of utilizing situational variables in explaining consumer behavior is the development of a situational inventory. Situational inventories such as those in Table 17–1 require the identification of relevant usage, consumption, or communication situations. The importance of the situation is determined and brands are rated for each relevant situation. Frequently, a multiattribute approach will be taken in evaluating the situation so that marketers can determine variations in importance of product benefits and variations in brand attitudes on a situation-by-situation basis. Most of these inventories define situations specific to the product category. Attempts to develop general situations that can be used across many products have not been productive.

The chapter describes a simple model of the decision process incorporating situational factors. The model recognizes that a consumer's decision can be a function of the brand, the situation, the consumer's own predispositions, or as is more likely, some combination of these factors. Various studies are cited demonstrating that for many products, the most important factor in explaining behavior is the interaction between situation and product. That is, choice of brands is likely to vary by situation regardless of consumer characteristics. But the situation will not be important in all cases. Where a high level of brand loyalty exists and/or a high level of product involvement, the consumer may buy a particular brand regardless of the situation. Therefore, the second most important influence on consumer choice is the interaction between the product and the consumer's characteristics (e.g., consumers with certain characteristics favor a particular brand regardless of the situation).

The chapter concludes by citing two studies that utilized situational variables to provide implications for product-line determination, product positioning, and definition of target segments.

QUESTIONS

1. A manufacturer of instant coffee is considering the introduction of a new line of continental flavors to be advertised for special occasions. The objective is to gear marketing strategy to the situations that warrant distinctive coffee that can be conveniently prepared.
   - For what types of situations should the coffee be positioned?
   - What are the implications for (a) defining a target segment, and (b) developing an advertising strategy?

2. A product manager for a leading brand of paper towels notices substantial variation in sales performance for the brand between stores in the same trading area. The manager hypothesizes that there may be marked differences in the in-store purchase situation causing variation in sales.

   - Specify the differences in in-store purchase situations that may be causing differences in sales.

3. A manufacturer of hair dryers identifies two types of purchase situations that lead to differences in brand evaluation: (a) purchase for self, and (b) purchase as a gift.

   - What are the marketing implications for positioning a product to appeal to each of these purchasing situations?
   - What may be the differences in brand evaluation in each condition?

4. Develop a list of communications situations that may affect a consumer's awareness and comprehension of (a) print advertising, and (b) television advertising.

5. A company marketing a leading brand of yogurt has always focused on yogurt's nutritional benefits without considering the possibility of varying its appeal to depend on the usage situation.

   - Could the product benefits consumers see in yogurt vary by the usage situation? Specify.
   - What are the marketing implications of variations in perceived benefits by usage situation?

6. Market segments can be defined by usage situation; for example, between meal snackers and party snackers.

   - What market segments could be identified by usage situation for: (a) deodorants, and (b) paper towels?

7. Provide examples of the interaction of (1) situation and product, and (2) situation and consumer in influencing the purchase of: (a) soda, (b) records, and (c) men's suits.

8. What are the strategic implications of Table 17–3 for a new chain of fast food restaurants in competition with those listed in Table 17–3. Specifically, what may be the implications for:

   - situations and benefits to be emphasized in advertising?
   - store hours and service policy?

9. What marketing implications other than those stated in the text are provided by Figure 17–2?

RESEARCH ASSIGNMENTS

1. Select a product category that you feel is likely to be affected by the usage situation (e.g., soft drinks, paper towels, coffee, snacks, etc.). Conduct several depth interviews with consumers to define:

   a. the most frequent usage situations for the category, and

   b. a vocabulary of evaluative product attributes.

   Then develop a questionnaire in which consumers are asked to rate:

   a. the importance of each of the attributes by the four most important situations you defined in the depth interviews (e.g., How important is a soft drink that is refreshing when drinking it alone? When drinking it at a party?).

b.   the three leading brands by the vocabulary of product attributes for the four most important situations (e.g., rate Pepsi on "refreshing" when drinking it alone, drinking it at a party, etc.).

- What is the variation in importance ratings by situation?
- What is the variation in brand ratings by situation?
- What are the implications of variations in importance ratings and brand image by situation for (a) positioning a new product, (b) repositioning an existing product, (c) advertising strategy, and (d) definition of a target group?

2.   Do a series of depth interviews with consumers to develop a comprehensive situational inventory for snacking products. Make sure the inventory contains the five elements defined by Belk: physical surroundings, social surroundings, time, task definition, and antecedent states. Submit the inventory to a small sample of consumers (ten to twenty) and determine the frequency with which various snack foods (potato chips, pretzels, cheese, crackers, fruit, cookies) are considered for each usage occasion. What are the implications of your findings for (a) product line strategy, (b) new product development, and (c) advertising?

NOTES

1. Geraldine Fennell, "Consumers' Perceptions of the Product-Use Situation," *Journal of Marketing* 42 (April 1978):39.
2. J. A. Burdus, "Attitude Models — The Dream and the Reality," in Philip Levine, ed., *Attitude Research Bridges the Atlantic* (Chicago: American Marketing Association, 1975), p. 161.
3. Flemming Hansen, *Consumer Choice Behavior* (New York: The Free Press, 1972.)
4. Russell W. Belk, "An Exploratory Assessment of Situational Effects in Buyer Behavior," *Journal of Marketing Research* 11 (May 1974): 160.
5. See Chapter 21 in this text.
6. Russell W. Belk, "A Free Response Approach to Developing Product-Specific Consumption Situation Taxonomies," in Allan D. Shocker, ed., *Analytic Approaches to Product and Market Planning* (Cambridge, Mass.: Marketing Science Institute, 1979), p. 178.
7. William O. Bearden and Arch G. Woodside, "Interactions of Consumption Situations and Brand Attitudes," *Journal of Applied Psychology* 61 (1976): 764–769.
8. Belk, "An Exploratory Assessment"; Louis K. Sharpe and Kent L. Granzin, "Market Segmentation by Consumer Usage Context: An Exploratory Analysis," *Journal of Economics and Business* 26 (1974): 225-228.
9. William O. Bearden and Arch G. Woodside, "Consumption Occasion Influence on Consumer Brand Choice," *Decision Sciences* 9 (April 1978): 273–284.
10. Belk, "An Exploratory Assessment."

11. Rajendra K. Srivastava, Allan D. Shocker, and George S. Day, "An Exploratory Study of the Influences of Usage Situation on Perceptions of Product Markets," in H. Keith Hunt, ed., *Advances in Consumer Research,* vol. 5 (Ann Arbor, Mich.: Association for Consumer Research, 1978), pp. 32–38.
12. Belk, "A Free Response," p. 178.
13. Keith Clarke and Russell W. Belk, "The Effects of Product Involvement and Task Definition on Anticipated Consumer Effort," in William L. Wilkie, ed., *Advances in Consumer Research,* vol. 6 (Ann Arbor, Mich.: Association for Consumer Research, 1979), pp. 313–318.
14. Russell W. Belk, "Situational Variables and Consumer Behavior," *Journal of Consumer Research* 2 (December 1975): 159.
15. Belk, "An Exploratory Assessment," p. 160.
16. Ibid.
17. Bearden and Woodside, "Consumption Occasion," p. 275.
18. Belk, "An Exploratory Assessment."
19. Albert Mehrabian and James A. Russell, *An Approach to Environmental Psychology* (Cambridge, Mass.: M.I.T. Press, 1974.)
20. Belk, "A Free Response," p. 179.
21. Belk, "Situational Variables," p. 158.
22. Ibid.
23. D. Bem, "Self Perception Theory," in L. Berkowitz, ed., *Advances in Experimental Social Psychology* (New York: Academic Press, 1972), pp. 1–62.
24. Brian Sternthal and Gerald Zaltman, "The

444   Broadened Concept: Toward a Taxonomy of Consumption Situations," in Gerald Zaltman and Brian Sternthal, eds., *Broadening the Concept of Consumer Behavior* (Ann Arbor, Mich.: Association for Consumer Research, 1975), p. 144.

25. Ibid., p. 146.

26. See Eric N. Berkowitz, James L. Ginter, and W. Wayne Talarzyk, "An Investigation of the Effects of Specific Usage Situations on the Prediction of Consumer Choice Behavior," in Barnett A. Greenberg and Danny N. Bellenger, eds., *Proceedings of the American Marketing Association Educators' Conference,* Series #41 (1977), pp. 90–94; and William O. Bearden and Arch G. Woodside, "Situational Influence on Consumer Purchase Intentions," in Arch G. Woodside, Jagdish N. Sheth, and Peter D. Bennett, *Consumer and Industrial Buying Behavior* (New York: North-Holland, 1977), pp. 167–177.

27. Kenneth E. Miller and James L. Ginter, "An Investigation of Situational Variation in Brand Choice Behavior and Attitude," *Journal of Marketing Research* 16 (February 1979): 111–123.

28. Adrian B. Ryans, "Consumer Gift Buying Behavior: An Exploratory Analysis," in Barnett A. Greenberg and Danny N. Bellenger, eds., *Proceedings of the American Marketing Association Educators' Conference,* Series #41 (1977), pp. 99–104.

29. Clarke and Belk, "The Effects of Product Involvement," p. 314.

30. Tyzoon T. Tyebjee, "Refinement of the Involvement Concept: An Advertising Planning Point of View," in John C. Maloney and Bernard Silverman, *Attitude Research Plays for High Stakes* (Chicago: American Marketing Association, 1979), p. 100.

31. Donald H. Granbois, "Improving the Study of Customer In-Store Behavior," *Journal of Marketing* 32 (October 1968): 28–33.

32. Charles H. Ptacek and James Shanteau, "Situation Determinants of Consumer Decision Making," working paper, 1980.

33. Sharpe and Granzin, "Market Segmentation by Consumer Usage Context," pp. 225–228.

PART FOUR

Applications

Part IV represents the key component of this book since it deals with each element of the marketing plan — product, promotion, distribution, and price — from the perspective of consumer behavior principles and findings. Chapter 18 will focus on product positioning. Market segmentation is closely tied to this since products have to be positioned to defined target markets. In Chapter 19 advertising is considered within a communications framework. Chapter 20 is concerned with distribution as seen from the standpoint of the consumer's shopping behavior and store choice. Chapter 21 focuses on the remaining elements of the marketing plan — price and personal selling. In Chapter 22 the focus is shifted from consumer behavior to organizational buyer behavior.

EIGHTEEN

Market Segmentation and Product Positioning

FOCUS OF CHAPTER

Market segmentation is a strategy designed to allocate marketing resources to defined segments. Product positioning is a strategy designed to communicate product benefits to meet consumer needs. Although each strategy serves a different purpose, they are closely linked to each other. Products must be positioned to defined target segments. Therefore, the identification of the needs and characteristics of target groups is a prerequisite to product positioning. Further, the success of positioning strategies depends on how the target segments react to the marketing strategies directed to them. Given the link between market segmentation and product positioning, both of these topics are treated together in this chapter.

The chapter is organized around the distinction between marketing strategy and analysis as follows:

- Market segmentation strategy seeks to differentially allocate resources to defined segments

- Market segmentation analysis defines the characteristics of target segments to permit such allocation

- Product positioning strategy communicates product benefits to achieve a distinctive position in the market

- Product positioning analysis determines whether consumers perceive the brand in the manner intended by the marketer

The first two sections of the chapter deal with market segmentation strategies and analysis. The remaining two sections will consider product positioning strategies and positioning analysis.

Market segmentation strategy is not uniform. Various approaches can be taken to define target segments, depending on the marketer's objectives. If a marketer wishes to identify opportunities for new product introductions, the first step should be the identification of consumer needs. Consumers would be segmented by differences in needs. For example, the snack food market could be segmented into those who are nutritionally oriented, taste oriented, socially oriented, and weight watchers. New products are then developed to meet these needs. This type of segmentation is called **benefit segmentation.**

Assume a natural snack food product has been introduced to appeal to the nutritional segment. Now the questions are: Who are the purchasers of the product? What are their demographic and psychographic characteristics? What is their attitude toward the new brand? In this case, the basic distinction is a *behavioral* one; that is, marketers are trying to identify the characteristics of users and nonusers. This segmentation approach will be referred to as **behavioral segmentation.** Logically, it is used to describe differences in behavior for existing products. Demographic differences betweeen users and nonusers may guide media strategy. Differences in brand attitudes between users and nonusers may guide advertising strategy.

A third type of segmentation is **response elasticity.** Marketers may wish to identify consumers by their responsiveness to marketing strategy. For example, they may wish to determine which consumers are most likely to switch brands when price changes (i.e., the price elastic segment) or which consumers tend to buy most frequently by deal or coupons (the deal prone segment). They may also wish to know if a segment can be influenced by advertising or sales promotion (the advertising elastic segment).

This information is essential for evaluating marketing strategies. The characteristics of the price elastic segment define those customers most likely to switch out of a marketer's brand given a price increase. The characteristics of the deal or coupon prone consumer provide guidelines for directing price promotions to certain segments. Coupons could be sent by direct mail to those geographic regions that best match the demographic profile of the heavy coupon redeemer. Knowledge of the characteristics of segments most responsive to advertising permits marketers to direct advertising dollars to these groups.

There are other bases for segmenting markets; for example, segmentation by store purchasing behavior (store loyalty, frequency of purchasing in certain stores, comparison shopping behavior). But the most important strategic bases for segmentation are by benefit, behavior, and responses.

To summarize, benefit segmentation defines new product opportunities, behavioral segmentation provides guidelines to develop marketing strategies for existing products, and segmenting by response elasticity helps direct marketing strategies to those consumers most likely to respond.

Benefit Segmentation

A consumer oriented approach to marketing requires developing product strategies based on known consumer needs. It is obvious that marketers cannot allocate resources based on the needs of single individuals. Therefore, some criterion for aggregating consumers is required and the most logical criterion is similarity in needs. Strategies are developed to appeal to the relatively homogeneous needs of target segments.

As an example, three important needs expressed by consumers in the instant coffee market are "freshly brewed flavor," "lets me sleep," and "economy." Consumers who place emphasis on one of these needs would be in a particular benefit segment. A producer of instant coffee could satisfy the "freshly brewed flavor" segment by introducing freeze-dried coffee and advertising it as similar to ground roast. It could satisfy the "let's me sleep" segment by introducing a decaffeinated coffee, perhaps even a freeze-dried decaffeinated to capture consumers that emphasize both "freshly brewed flavor" and "let's me sleep." And, it could satisfy the "economy" segment by introducing a lower priced regular instant coffee or by promoting an instant coffee priced at parity but with frequent price-off promotions and couponing.

Consider the data presented below for the three coffee benefit segments. The data are in disguised form, but are based on an actual study:

Primary Benefit Desired	Percent of All Buyers of Instant	Percent of All Buyers of Decaffeinated	Average Age	Average Income	Percent of Purchasers of Brand A Decaffeinated
"Lets me sleep"	15	26	46	$13,000	17
"Economy"	38	49	32	$22,000	9
"Brewed flavor"	39	20	31	$16,000	4

A producer of decaffeinated coffee would certainly aim at the "let's me sleep" segment but could not ignore the "economy" segment since it represents almost twice as many consumers as the "lets me sleep" segment. Moreover, appeals to the two segments require different media allocations since the "lets me sleep" segment is older and downscale while the "economy" segment is younger and upscale. The company's brand (last column above) has a much higher market share among the "lets me sleep" segment suggesting a need to increase effort to the "economy" segment. This can be accomplished by increasing deals and coupons for its existing brand, or by introducing a new brand of decaffeinated that will be heavily dealed.

Most companies will have a decaffeinated, an instant, and a freeze-dried coffee in their product line to appeal to all three benefit segments. The appeal to several segments gives the marketer an opportunity to differentially allocate resources to better maximize profits. Theoretically, the marketer could "operate at the margin" for each segment by continuing to allocate resources to one segment or the other until the ratio of marginal revenue to marginal cost is equal for each segment. If the ratio is greater for one segment than another, additional marketing expenditures should be allocated to that segment to maximize profits.[1] Granted it is difficult to estimate revenues and costs at the margin for each segment, but the principle of differential allocations at the margin could be followed assuming adequate consumer information to identify benefit segments.

There is a danger in appealing to several benefit segments simultaneously. Appeals to one segment could alienate another. If a coffee producer introduced both a freeze-dried and a lower priced brand, would the lower priced brand tarnish the image of the freeze-dried product? Possibly, given strong corporate identification with both brands. Therefore, marketers must consider the effects of strategies directed to one segment on all segments so as to maximize corporate profits.

Other examples of benefit segmentation may be found in studies by Calantone and Sawyer[2]; Anderson, Cox, and Fulcher[3]; and Young, Ott, and Feigin.[4]

Behavioral Segmentation

In behavioral segmentation, segments are defined by consumer characteristics that distinguish:

- brand users versus nonusers,
- brand loyalists versus occasional buyers,
- product users versus nonusers, and
- heavy versus light users

By Brand Usage

The most frequently used form of behavioral segmentation is to distinguish those who purchase the company's brand versus those who purchase competitive brands.

Once brand users are defined, two approaches prevail. The first approach directs resources to those segments with the highest probability of purchasing the brand. For example, assume 20 percent of higher income suburbanites buy a brand compared to 10 percent of all other consumers. Product and advertising appeals are directed to this segment on the assumption that it will be easier to get higher income suburbanites who are not buying the brand (that is, the other 80 percent) to buy. Underlying this approach is the presupposition that nonpurchasers who have the same characteristics as brand purchasers are more likely to buy the brand.

The second approach is to appeal to segments that are unlikely to buy the brand by directing new product offerings to this group. If current offerings are unlikely to be purchased by lower income consumers, then perhaps the company should develop a product to appeal to this group and, thus, expand its customer base. But the company must insure that such offerings do not alienate its current users. Both approaches are compatible. Both require a segmentation of the market into brand users versus nonusers by demographic or attitudinal characteristics.

The segmentation of the hand lotion market cited in Chapter 9 is a good example of behavioral segmentation based on brand usage. Users of the company's brand were distinguished from nonusers by demographic characteristics (see Figure 9–6). The best target segment for the product was females in the north-central states with incomes under $12,500. This group represented 5 percent of the sample but 20 percent of the regular users of the brand. The company directed marketing resources to this group to capture those downscale females in the north-central states who were not using the brand.

By Brand Loyalty

Segments have also been defined based on brand loyalty.[5] This behavioral criterion is more specific than brand usage since a subgroup of users is identified — those who consistently buy the brand — and is compared to nonloyalists. In defining the characteristics of nonloyalists, the purpose may be to get occasional buyers of the brand to become loyal, or loyalists of competitive brands to try the company's brand.

By Product Usage

Product usage (as distinct from brand usage) is a common basis for behavioral segmentation. Marketers may wish to identify those consumers who buy a product category rather than a brand. Purchasers of decaffeinated coffee may tend to be older consumers in the middle to lower income brackets, regardless of whether they buy Sanka or Taster's Choice decaffeinated. Their demographic characteristics are a reflection of the need for the product. In such cases, marketers are more likely to use product rather than brand purchase as a guide in selecting media or determining advertising appeals. The key in marketing Bayer, Anacin, or Bufferin may be more closely related to the characteristics of the analgesics user rather than specific differences between users of the three brands. On the other hand, developing a strategy for a brand of dry cereals may depend more on brand differences because of the general appeal of dry cereals across demographic and psychographic lines.

There have been numerous attempts to identify product usage segments. For example, Peters defined segments of compact, medium-sized, large-sized, and foreign car owners.[6] Hisrich and Peters identified users of a wide range of entertainment services.[7]

By Degree of Usage

A common practice among marketers is to segment markets by degree of product usage into heavy versus light user segments. For most consumer packaged goods, a few consumers account for a disproportionate share of purchases. The principle most commonly stated is that 50 percent of the consumers account for 80 percent of product volume. This group is known as the "heavy half." The key question is: What are the demographic, attitudinal, or need characteristics that identify the heavy half?

A good example of segmentation by degree of usage is provided in a study conducted by a manufacturer of iced tea. The objective was to identify heavy versus light users by the benefits they associate with iced tea. Five segments were identified:

Primary Benefits Associated with Iced Tea	No. of Glasses Consumed in Last Month	Percent of All Consumers[a]	Percent of Iced Tea Volume
1. Restores energy *and* is year round drink	47.5	17.0	34.7
2. Restores energy only	21.1	14.7	13.3
3. Low in calories	24.0	29.1	30.0
4. Good taste	15.4	21.6	14.3
5. None	4.3	8.7	1.6

[a] 9 percent of sample not represented by above segments

The analysis shows that segment no. 1 is the key. This group sees iced tea as providing both energy and versatility (year around drink). They drink at least twice as much as the other segments. They represent 17 percent of all consumers but account for 35 percent of iced tea volume. The second segment emphasizes energy only. Therefore it would not represent a separate segment in terms of marketing appeal. Marketing effort can be directed to both segments simultaneously. Segment 3 represents the other major target group — consumers who associate iced tea with less calories. This group represents almost one-third of iced tea volume. Clearly, a separate campaign could be directed to this segment. Alternatively, two iced tea products could be introduced, one directed to the fitness seekers concerned with energy, the other directed to the weight watchers concerned with calories. The next logical step would be to determine if there are demographic or psychographic differences between these two groups to further guide media and promotional appeals.

Other studies that have used level of product usage as a basis for behavioral segmentation have been by Bass, Tigert, and Lonsdale for ten food products and toiletries,[8] and by Assael in identifying frequent users of long distance for the residential[9] and business[10] markets.

Segmenting by Response Elasticity

The third basis for segmenting markets is by consumer sensitivity to marketers' strategies, known as **response elasticity.** Some customers will be more sensitive to a price increase, a change in advertising expenditures, or an increase in deal effort than others. Response elasticity measures a consumer's sensitivity to a particular marketing stimulus by associating a percentage change in the stimulus with a percentage change in quantity purchased. The most common example is price elasticity.

Consumers can be segmented by elasticity criteria. For example, assume a company is considering a price increase and tests a number of alternative prices in a simulated shopping environment. It derives a measure of price elasticity based on consumer responses and segments consumers on this basis using demographics as descriptors. It finds that white collar, middle income families with children are the most price elastic. But these are also the heavy buyers of the product category. Since this segment is the most likely to switch out of the brand given a price increase, this could mean that sales will decrease more than expected if the company raises its prices.

Consumers can be segmented by their responses to other marketing stimuli as well. For example, deal, coupon, advertising, and even package size elasticity. The value of segmenting by response elasticities is that it provides management with a basis to:

1. direct price or advertising appeals to the most sensitive groups;
2. estimate the groups most likely to reduce purchases with a price increase (an important consideration in an inflationary period);
3. direct deals and coupons to the most responsive consumers;
4. identify groups most likely to respond positively to increases in advertising expenditures.

Underlying segmentation by response elasticities is the basic principle that marketers should increase or decrease allocations to a segment based on the response of that segment. If all segments respond in the same manner to marketing effort, then there would be no basis for differentially allocating resources. Few studies have used response elasticity to segment markets. Massy and Frank[11] and McCann[12] analyzed consumer purchases over time to estimate advertising and price elasticities. Cunningham and Peterson asked consumers to estimate changes in gas usage based on various projected price increases.[13] Inelastic and elastic segments were identified. Not surprisingly, inelastic consumers had higher incomes; elastic consumers had lower incomes and were more likely to be nonwhite. The most interesting differences between segments were attitudinal. Customers that were elastic were more likely to feel that the petroleum companies were responsible for the energy problem and that there is no basis for charging higher prices. They were also more likely to agree that the energy problem placed a substantial strain on their budgets. The inelastic segment was less likely to hold these attitudes.

MARKET SEGMENTATION ANALYSIS

In order to segment by benefits, behavior, or response elasticities, marketers must be able to describe these segments. What are the demographic, psychographic or attitudinal characteristics of the nutritional segment in the snack food market (benefit segmentation), of the heavy snackers (behavioral segmentation), or of the price sensitive snackers (segmenting by price elasticity).

The aim of **market segmentation analysis** is to develop a cohesive profile of each segment. For example, the benefit segmentation analysis cited in Chapter 10 (Table 10–2) identified a nutritional snacker segment demographically as having younger children and being better educated, and psychographically as being more controlled and self-assured. This profile was developed in two steps by a computer program known as cluster analysis. The first step grouped together respondents with similar needs so that there would be greatest similarity between respondents in a given segment and greatest differences between segments. In this way, the respondents in the nutritional segment were identified. The second step then determined each segment's demographic, psychographic, and need characteristics.

The behavioral segmentation of users of a brand of hand lotion (in Figure 9–6) is also a good example of market segmentation analysis. Those consumers who were most likely to use the brand were identified based on demographic characteristics, permitting identification of a group who had a 62 percent chance of using the brand. Once again, a computer program was used to develop a multivariate profile (i.e., inclusion of many variables in the analysis) to identify the most profitable segment.

It is beyond the scope of this book to describe the quantitative techniques used in market segmentation analysis.[14] Suffice it to say that the basic purpose is to develop guidelines for positioning new brands, repositioning existing brands, and developing advertising, media, and pricing strategies. The remainder of this chapter will focus first on product positioning strategies and then on product positioning analysis.

PRODUCT POSITIONING STRATEGIES

Marketers have followed two general approaches in product positioning strategies. One is to focus on the consumer, the other on competition. In both cases, the end result should be to associate the product with consumer needs. **Consumer positioning** associates the product directly with needs, or appeals to needs indirectly through product imagery. Crest communicates a benefit of decay prevention directly, whereas Ultra-Brite uses more indirect social and sexual themes to communicate the benefits of pleasant breath and white teeth.

Competitive positioning communicates product benefits by establishing a distinctive position for the product compared to competition. A classic example is 7-Up's positioning as the Un-Cola.

> "By linking the product 7-Up to what is already in the mind of their prospect, 7-Up has established itself as an alternative to Coke and Pepsi. No product features, no customer benefits, no company image. Only the mental leverage factor of one word. The 'un-cola.' Today, 7-Up is the third largest company in the soft-drink industry."[15]

Consumer Positioning

Products can be positioned to consumers by two criteria: specific versus general positioning, and direct versus indirect positioning.

Specific Versus General Positioning Strategies

Products can be positioned to appeal to the needs of a specific market segment, or positioning can be broader and more ambiguous to appeal to several segments. There are trade-offs in both strategies. Specific positioning has the advantage of a direct product-to-benefit link and more explicit guidelines for resource allocation, but it also runs the risk of restricting the market by a narrow focus or by alienating segments that may buy the product. Ultra-Brite's positioning is primarily toward the teenage and young adult market. Such a positioning may be overly restrictive in excluding family-oriented purchasers more likely to emphasize decay prevention. Yet introduction of a fluoridated version of Ultra-Brite with appeal to decay prevention may alienate the primary market because of a shift away from socially oriented benefits.

A more general and ambiguous positioning strategy has the advantage of allowing the consumer to "read in" the desired benefits. Effective advertising may be vague enough to be many things to many people, yet sufficiently specific to create a product-to-benefit link. The danger is that the ambiguity may overwhelm the association of product to benefit. In attempting to appeal to many segments, the product may appeal to none.

Positioning strategies fall on a continuum from specific to general. The proper positioning on this continuum could be determined by consumers' purchase motives. Five purchase motives are listed below from specific to general:

1. The solution of a particular problem (toilet soap for dry skin)
2. Prevention of a problem (mouthwash to prevent bad breath)
3. Buying when out of stock (primarily for low involvement goods such as canned vegetables)
4. Exploration and novelty seeking (the focus is on information and new products such as buying a new magazine)
5. Sensory reaction (enjoyment of taste, color, hearing or smell sensation such as wines, perfumes, records, etc.).[16]

This classification clearly views positioning as requiring a definition of consumer needs. The approach would require a very specific positioning if a snack food is directed to weight watching (the solution of a problem), and a more ambiguous positioning if its focus is on good taste (sensory reaction). The problem with some segments is that needs may be directed to both problem solution and sensory enjoyment. For example, appeals to guilty snackers should be based both on the solution of the weight problem and the desired sensory enjoyment of the snack. This dual requirement complicates a positioning strategy to the guilty snacking group.

Positioning by Claims Versus Imagery

Another distinction in consumer positioning is establishing a direct product-to-benefit link by citing claims versus a more indirect approach of establishing a mood through imagery and symbolism. Direct claims tend to be more specific and imagery more general, but not always. The use of symbolism and imagery can be used to target specific segments. For example, personal care appliances can be directed to the upwardly mobile, self-actualizing woman by linking the product to an image of competence and success.

Cigarette advertising uses both direct claims and imagery. Cigarettes such as True or Merit appeal directly to health-oriented benefits by citing figures on tar and nicotine content. Virginia Slims and Marlboro rely on imagery to establish positive brand associations, in one case utilizing appeals to feminine self-awareness and in the other to masculinity and fantasy.

Competitive Positioning

A second approach to positioning is to achieve a product-to-benefit link by focusing on competition. The advantage of this approach is that the marketer can "link the product to what is already in the mind of the prospect."[17] Competitive positioning provides a clear frame of reference for the consumer by relating claims to other brands. But a brand's positioning cannot be on a "me too" basis. Successful competitive positioning requires the establishment of a distinctive positioning associated with consumer needs.

The success of competitive positioning is demonstrated by 7-Up relative to Coke and Pepsi, and by Avis relative to Hertz. In both cases, these companies were able to utilize awareness of the market leaders to their advantage, yet maintain a distinctive position. Competitive positioning can be as consumer oriented as consumer positioning, since both require direct or indirect association with consumer needs.

The danger in utilizing competitive positioning is that a distinctive position may not be established. B.F. Goodrich was forced to use a competitive positioning approach because, as stated in one of its ads, "It's one of fate's cruel accidents that our biggest competitor's name turns out to be almost identical to our founder's. Goodyear. Goodrich. Awfully confusing. Especially since Goodyear has advertised more than we have." Goodrich introduced steel-belted radials. Yet when consumers were asked who makes steel-belted radials, 56 percent cited Goodyear first, although at the time Goodyear did not make them.[18]

Another problem with competitive positioning is that consumers may confuse the brand's position with that of competitors. Comparative advertising — naming competitors in the ad — has become an important means of competitive positioning. Increased use of comparative advertising caused Ogilvy-Mather, a large advertising agency, to evaluate its effectiveness. A study of eight comparative commercials led the agency to conclude that comparative advertising was more likely to lead consumers to confuse the company's brand with competitors than noncomparative advertising.[19]

Despite these shortcomings, competitive positioning remains a viable strategy to establish a distinctive product-to-benefit link in the consumer's mind, using competition as a reference point.

PRODUCT POSITIONING ANALYSIS

Product positioning analysis identifies consumer perceptions of brands or products. The purpose is to evaluate where a product should be positioned (normative analysis) or where it is currently positioned (descriptive analysis). Normative analysis evaluates alternative positionings for new products; descriptive analysis evaluates the current position of existing products. In each case, a new product concept or an existing brand is positioned relative to competitive brands based on consumer perceptions.

Perceptual Mapping

The position of several product concepts and/or brands requires introducing the notion of a perceptual map. As noted in Chapter 2, consumers evaluate brands by desired benefits and product characteristics. Consumers might evaluate beer on criteria such as light, full bodied, and thirst quenching. Assume a sample of 1,000 consumers rate Miller, Michelob, Budweiser, and Schlitz on lightness. The average ratings for the four brands are as follows:

	Mil-ler	Bud	Shl-itz	Miche-lob	
LIGHT	X	X	X	X	HEAVY
	1 2	3 4	5	6 7	

These ratings represent the perceived positioning of the brands from light to heavy for the sample of consumers. It is apparent that Miller is seen as a lighter beer and Michelob as a heavier beer.

In most cases, positioning is based on more than one attribute. Introducing a second attribute — mild to bitter — requires positioning products in two-dimensional perceptual space as in Figure 18–1. Each dimension represents an attribute, and products are positioned on each attribute based on consumer perceptions. The result is a **perceptual map** of the beer market.

Figure 18–1 shows that Miller is seen as the mildest and lightest beer. Budweiser is similar to Miller in this respect. Schlitz is in a distinctive position as the most bitter beer, and Michelob is distinctive as the heaviest beer. Such a map is valuable in demonstrating the effectiveness of advertising in positioning a brand by specific consumer benefits. The map also summarizes the relative strengths and weaknesses of each brand.

Multidimensional Positioning

The above is a simple example of positioning brands by one or two product dimensions. A more realistic application would position products on a fuller range of evaluative dimensions as in Figure 18–2.[20] A new food concept is being tested against six brands by eight product benefits. Consumers were given a description of the concept (a complete, nutritional breakfast food) and were asked to rate the similarity of the brands and the concept. (E.g., which are most similar to the test concept, brands A, B, C, etc.; which are most similar to each other, brands A, B, C, etc.). This data was fed into a computer program known as **multidimensional scaling**.[21] The program determines the relative position of brands and concepts in a perceptual map based on the consumers' similarity ratings. The positions of the test concept and Brands A–F in Figure 18–2 were derived by this program. It is apparent that consumers see the test concept as similar to Brands A and B, suggesting a danger of a positioning as a "me too" brand.

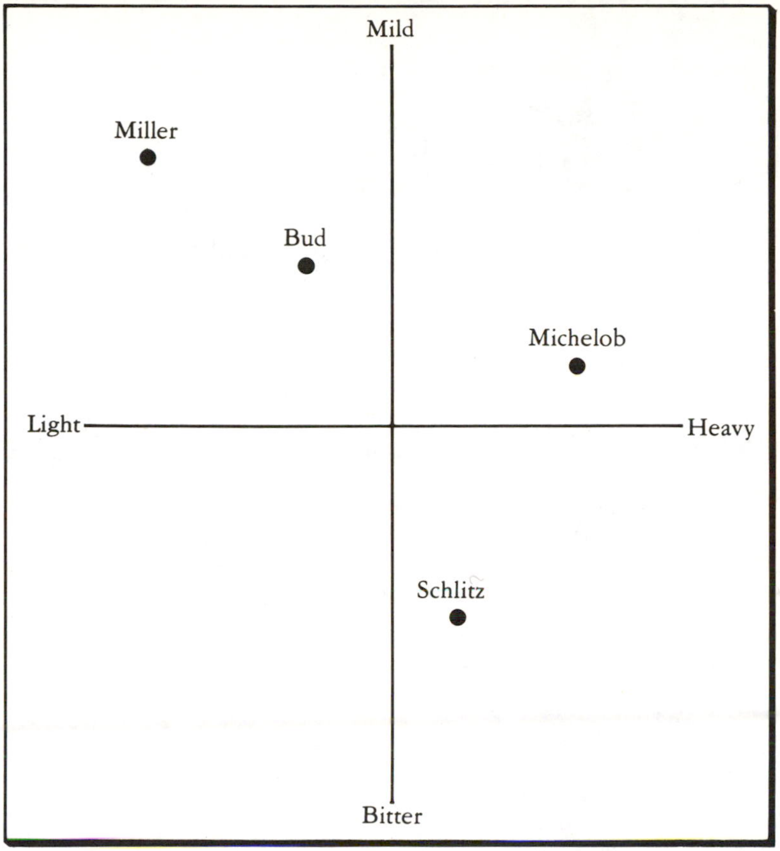

FIGURE 18–1   Perceptual Map of Four Brands of Beer by Two
Evaluative Dimensions

Consumers were also asked to rate each brand by eight product benefits. Another computer program known as **PROFIT (property fitting)** was used to determine the association of the benefits with the brands.[22] The program identifies the positon of each attribute by determining a vector that provides the best fit between the attributes and the brands in the perceptual map. This analysis produced the eight lines representing the attributes in Figure 18–2. It is apparent the concept and Brands A and B were most closely associated with nutritious and good for the family, and were not associated with economy. Brands C and D were associated with good for snacks and little preplanning, Brand E with economical, and Brand F with good tasting.

Finally, consumers were asked to rank order their preference for each brand and the concept (e.g., which brand/concept do you prefer most, second, third, etc.). Each consumer was positioned on the perceptual map so that he or she would be closest to the brand preferred most and furthest from the brand preferred least. The asterisk in Figure 18–2 represents a single consumer positioned in Segment 1. This consumer preferred Brand A most, the test concept second, Brand B third, and Brands E and F least. Groups of consumers preferring similar brands are represented by circles. These circles were defined by a third computer program, **cluster analysis.**[23] The program grouped consumers to-

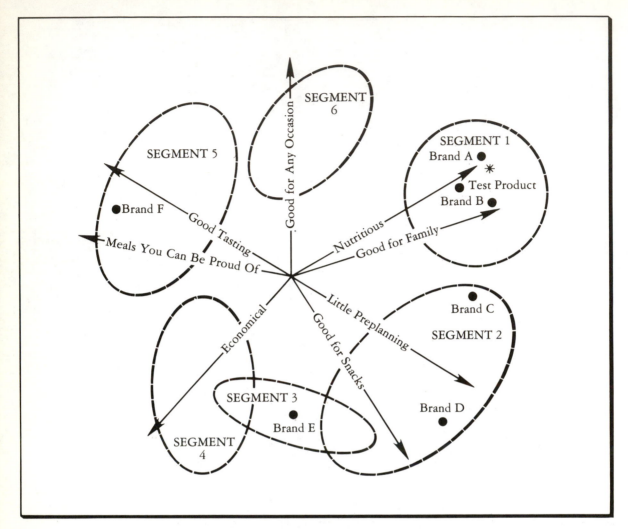

FIGURE 18–2 Perceptual Mapping to Position a New Food Product Relative to Existing Brands

Source: Adapted from Henry Assael, "Evaluating New Product Concepts and Developing Early Predictions of Trial," *Marketing Review* (May 1975): 13.
Reprinted with permission from *Marketing Review.*

gether with similar preferences. The cluster program identified six segments (the six circles in Figure 18–2), each segment representing consumers who prefer the same brand(s). The size of the circle represents the number of consumers in each segment. Thus, the largest segment (segment 1) preferred the test concept and Brands A and B. The second largest segment preferred Brands C and D. Generally, consumers preferring the brand also tended to emphasize the benefits associated with the brand, segment 1 emphasizing nutrition, segment 2 little preplanning, segments 3 and 4 economy, and so on.

What does Figure 18–2 tell us? Quite a lot. First it provides management with a picture of the market for the concept and competitive brands. It suggests there is a danger of competing head-on with Brands A and B. On the other hand, there may be room for the concept since all three brands are positioned to the largest segment. Secondly, Figure 18–2 shows the concept is closely positioned to appeal to nutritional benefits, a positioning intended by management. Third, the analysis provides implications for new product possibilities by defining "gaps" in the perceptual space. The most obvious is the failure of any product to be perceived as "good for any occasion," (breakfast, main meal, in-between meals). A product positioned so it can be eaten at any occasion may best appeal to segment 6. In addition, the map suggests a need for an economical snack since consumers in segment 3 are buying two different brands to fulfill snacking and economy benefits.

Three criteria are used to evaluate the positioning of the new concept. First, is it in a distinctive position relative to competition? In this case, no. Second, is the positioning in line with managerial objectives? Yes, because the concept is perceived as having nutritional benefits. Third, does it appeal to a sufficiently large segment to warrant further testing? Yes, since Segment 1 is the largest segment.

Further testing is required before a positioning strategy is selected and a decision made to introduce the product. Even though the concept and Brands A and B appeal to a nutritional segment, can the concept be distinguished from brands A & B on key nutritional benefits? What are the needs and characteristics of consumers in Segment 1 who would definitely buy the concept? If the concept is tested in use, will the same positioning be maintained, or will consumers change their perceptions?

Limitations of Perceptual Mapping

Perceptual mapping is a useful device for representing consumer perceptions of relative brand positions, but it has several limitations. Most perceptual maps are based on similarity ratings. In positioning products by similarity it is assumed that consumers will react similarly to brands perceived as being similar. If the test concept is perceived as similar to Brands A and B, then consumers preferring the concept also tend to prefer these brands. Similarity ratings are thus assumed to reflect cross-elasticity between brands.

Researchers have criticized this assumption on the following counts. First, brands that are seen as similar may not be preferred. A consumer may rate Coke and Pepsi as similar for generic reasons (they are both colas). But if the preferred cola brand is not available, the consumer may next prefer 7-Up or even mineral water. Therefore, similarity and preference may not be equivalent. Second, two brands may be seen as similar on one set of attributes and different on another. A representation in perceptual space would cancel out these similarities and dissimilarities, resulting in a misleading representation of the brand's relative position. Third, brands may be seen as similar for certain occasions and different for other occasions. Fourth, certain segments may see certain brands as similar and other segments may see the same brands as dissimilar. Adults may view Pepsi and Coke as similar. Teenagers may be more aware of cola beverage attributes and may rate the two brands as dissimilar.

Because of these limitations, several refinements have been made in perceptual mapping applications. For one, researchers sometimes develop separate maps for preference and similarity ratings. The similarity map provides the cognitive structure (how brands are seen by evaluative attributes). The preference maps provide the affective structure (degree of substitutability between brands). Thus, the two maps may provide different dimensions of attitude. Second, maps can be developed separately by occasion. Figures 18–6 and 18–7 below provide an example of positioning foods and beverages by lunchtime and snacking occasions. Third, separate maps may have to be developed by segment where there is reason to believe different segments may see the market differently. For example, it would be logical to develop separate brand positionings for those segments that emphasize performance, cost, and styling in the automobile market.

Another limitation of perceptual mapping is in the nature of the techniques used. The relative positioning of brands by consumer ratings is at best an imperfect representation of the structure of the market. Multidimensional scaling techniques are designed to convert rank order data (e.g., I prefer Brand A more than Brand B) into precise metric configurations of brands. The exactitude of these representations is deceiving since there is sometimes a large degree of error in converting these ratings into maps. For example, a consumer may prefer Brand A first, Brand F second, and Brand C third. In such a case, the consumer's preferences could not be represented by the solution provided in Figure 18–2.

These limitations require care in the selection of consumer rating procedures and recognition of the assumptions of statistical programs used if perceptual mapping is to be an effective tool in portraying brand positions.

Developmental Analysis

In Figure 18–2 it is assumed that a product concept has been developed and is ready to be tested. The concept itself represents a bundle of attributes designed to position the brand. The concept in Figure 18–2 was described to consumers as a high protein natural and complete breakfast food product. Therefore, the positioning was clearly established toward nutritious and good for the family.

But suppose the company does not have a concept and is investigating the appropriate combinations of benefits to offer the consumer. In this case, perceptual mapping would not be suitable since there is no product or concept to map.

Defining the Evaluative Attributes

The company starting from scratch would first want to determine the relevant attributes consumers use to evaluate products. The most frequently used approach to derive a vocabulary of attributes is the depth and focused group interview (see bottom of pp. 46 and 47).

Another approach is to ask consumers why they see certain brands as similar, and identify the attributes used most frequently to describe brand similarities. Assume Great Snacks Inc. is investigating the possibility of developing a concept for a low calorie chiplike snack. It has not identified the consumer vocabulary used in evaluating chiplike snacks and, as a result, has not formalized a concept statement. The company conducts a small test on one hundred consumers. It asks them to rate existing brands for similarity. Three brands are selected — Wise, Pringles, and Lay potato chips. Consumers are asked which two are most similar, why, and how they differ from the third brand. The attributes used to define similarities and differences are recorded. Another set of three brands is then introduced and the process is repeated. This technique, known as the **Kelly Repertory Grid**[24], defines five key attributes: crispiness (keeps fresh), easy open package, low price, not oily, and no artificial ingredients.

Trade-Off Analysis

Given the introduction of a sixth benefit, low calorie, the question becomes what combination of benefits to introduce. Obviously, the ideal would be to introduce all six benefits, but this may be too costly or technologically impossible. Therefore, it is necessary to test concepts representing alternative combinations of characteristics. One possibility would be to test all possible combinations of the six benefits. If each attribute has two levels (either the product has it or not) then there would be sixty-four possible concepts (two to the sixth power), obviously too many concepts to test.

An alternative to testing every possible concept formulation would be to present consumers with a limited number of concepts, say ten. Figure 18–3 defines ten concepts by listing the attributes in each concept (Y for Yes; N for No). Thus, concept 1 is crispy, easy to open, and low in calories. Consumers would be presented with these alternatives and asked to rank order their preferences for each concept from 1 for the most preferred to 10 for the least preferred.

A single respondent's ratings are presented in the last column of Figure 18–3. This respondent places the highest value on the combination of low calorie and not oily (the fifth concept which is the consumer's first choice). This consumer's second and third choices also reflect the desire for low calorie and not oily (concepts 6 and 10). When forced to give up one or the other, the consumer chooses low calorie combined with low price (concept 2 which is the fourth choice). But when faced with choosing either low calorie, or the combination of low price and not oily (concept 1 versus 4), the consumer is ready to give up the former for the latter (fifth choice is concept 4).

This technique, known as **trade-off analysis,**[25] provides a basis for determining the consumer's optimal combination of characteristics. Through a statistical technique known as **conjoint analysis,** an estimate can be made of the evaluation of all sixty-four possible concepts, even though only ten were tested. The program develops utilities for each attribute tested based on rank order preference ratings of all consumers. Sample utilities derived from a conjoint analysis are presented on the bottom of Figure 18–3. The first attribute that should be introduced to maximize consumer preferences is low calorie; the second is crispiness in combination with low calorie; the third is no artificial ingredients in combination with crispiness and low calorie. The ideal concept is therefore a low-calorie, crispy snack with no artificial ingredients.

On this basis, the company may decide that an easy-open package is not necessary, but that a package ensuring crispiness is. Further, it appears that the ideal concept can be sold at a moderate to high price compared to other chip type snacks. It is important to note that the ideal concept — low calorie,

Concept	Crispy	Easy-Open Package	Low Price	Not Oily	No Artificial Ingredients	Low Calorie	Sample Respondent's Rank Order of Preference
1	Y	Y	N	N	N	Y	6
2	Y	N	Y	N	N	Y	4
3	Y	Y	N	N	Y	N	7
4	Y	N	Y	Y	Y	N	5
5	Y	Y	N	Y	N	Y	1
6	Y	N	Y	Y	N	Y	2
7	N	Y	N	N	Y	N	10
8	N	N	Y	N	Y	N	9
9	N	Y	N	N	N	Y	8
10	N	N	Y	Y	N	Y	3
Relative Utilities for All Consumers	.23	.06	.12	.10	.19	.30	

FIGURE 18–3   Example of Trade-Off Analysis: Evaluation of Ten Concepts to Identify Ideal Concept Formulation

(Y = Yes;   N = No)

crispy, no artificial ingredients — was not tested, but could be identified based on conjoint analysis because consumers place the highest value on these three benefits.

The company is now ready for a concept test. The result will be a perceptual map as in Figure 18–2 depicting the positioning of the concept relative to other brands. The sequence of steps in the positioning process was:

1. Generate a vocabulary of evaluative attributes through application of the **Kelly repertory grid.**
2. Test a large number of alternative concepts by **trade-off analysis** and select one or two best concept positionings.
3. Conduct a **product concept test** asking consumers to rate the concept(s) and competitive brands by similarity and preference.
4. Utilize multivariate statistical techniques to develop a **perceptual map** positioning the concept relative to existing brands.

Use of Quantitative Techniques for Positioning

Product positioning analysis is an excellent example of the link between consumer behavior and quantitative applications for marketing. The positioning analysis described in the previous section demonstrated utilization of multivariate statistical techniques (techniques capable of analyzing a large number of variables simultaneously) for the evaluation of consumer data. Conjoint analysis can be used to screen a large number of concepts and identify several candidates for further testing. Multidimensional scaling can analyze results of a concept test based on consumer similarity or preference ratings. In addition to multidimensional scaling, other multivariate techniques such as discriminant analysis[26] and factor analysis[27] can be used for positioning. The PROFIT program can be used to associate brand positions with evaluative attributes, and cluster analysis will identify consumer segments. These techniques are used sequentially in a planned approach to positioning analysis.

As noted, it is not within the scope of this book to discuss these techniques. Yet, it is important for the student of consumer behavior to recognize the indispensable role of statistical analysis in evaluating brand positionings and in defining market segments.

EVALUATING NEW PRODUCTS BY PERCEPTUAL MAPPING

The remainder of this chapter will describe applications of perceptual mapping analyses in two key areas: the normative evaluation of new products to determine where they should be positioned, and the descriptive evaluation of existing products to determine where they are positioned. A third area to be described, longitudinal analysis of consumer perceptions, is designed to track changes in a product's position over time as a means of evaluating repositioning strategies.

Perceptual mapping has been used in new product development for:

1. screening and evaluating new product concepts, and
2. evaluating shifts in the product's position once the product has been used.

Screening and Evaluating New Product Concepts

In 1972 a large auto manufacturer conducted a survey of 1,000 car owners in one of their foreign markets. The objectives of the study were to determine the position of possible new models relative to competitive makes and to define the characteristics of the best target segment for each prospective entry.

The automobile market presents particular problems for positioning analysis since it is difficult to evaluate cars in use tests. Furthermore, the investment of going into pilot plant production for a test model is substantial. As a result, reliance must be placed on concept tests to evaluate positioning strategies against competing models.

Three new economy car concepts were presented to consumers (concepts S, T, and U in Figure 18–4), as well as four existing makes. Concept S was designed to compete primarily with the Renault R-12 and secondarily with the VW Brazilia. Concept U was to compete with the R-12, and Concept T with the Datsun 1600. All cars were stationwagons. The VW Beetle was also included in the analysis as a leading economy car at the time. Respondents were given a complete set of specifications for the concepts and for existing cars, as well as positioning statements outlining the advantages of each make.

Respondents were then asked to rank order their preferences for each of the seven cars.

Preference data were analyzed by multidimensional scaling and a map was produced. Figure 18–4 shows that the U-car is closely positioned with the Renault R-12 since those that prefer one tend to pick the other as their second choice. The S-car is positioned close to the Brazilia. The T-car is not in its intended position since it is not preferred by those who like the Datsun 1600.

The next step was to position consumers on the perceptual map to identify target groups for each new car concept. Consumers were positioned closest to the cars they preferred most and furthest from those they liked least. Thus, consumers in segment 4 represent 22 percent of the sample and like the S-car the most, and the U-car and R-12 the least.

Based on this analysis, the T-car was eliminated from further consideration. Ordinarily, a distinctive position is desirable, but in this case the T-car had few prospective consumers. It was the least preferred concept.

Although the U-car was positioned as intended, it did not appeal to a

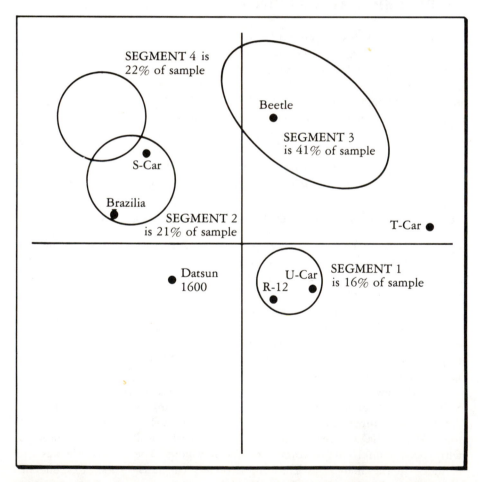

FIGURE 18–4   Position of Seven Popular Car Concepts Based on Customer Preferences

sufficiently large segment for further consideration and was eliminated. The limited size of the prospective market for the Renault R-12 was surprising since in previous years it was in a stronger position.

The S-car was in a viable positon for market entry on two counts. First, it was positioned well against one of the market leaders, the Brazilia. Second, it straddled two segments representing 43 percent of all economy car prospects. Segment 2 differed from segment 4 in being younger and more interested in technical specifications. Consumers in this segment preferred both the S-car and the Brazilia. Segment 4 preferred the S-car with no strong secondary preference. Consumers in this group were older, more upscale and more interested in comfort and roominess.

Given two distinct segments, the implication is to develop two positioning strategies directed to each; one describing the technical specifications of the S-car, possibly compared to the Brazilia. This campaign would use media most likely to be read by younger prospects. Another positioning would emphasize styling and comfort utilizing imagery more suited to older more established prospects.

Based on this positioning analysis, the company achieved its objectives to:

1. identify the best potential entry into the market;
2. evaluate positioning strategies relative to existing makes;
3. determine the size and characteristics of the target segment(s) for the prospective entry; and
4. assess whether the target market's perceptions of the car's features are in line with managerial objectives.

Other examples of concept positioning analysis may be found in approaches described by Wind[28] and by Stefflre.[29]

Evaluating Shifts in Positioning After Usage

Chapter 9 described a new concept tested by a leading food manufacturer — a low-calorie, artificial bacon product. Respondents were asked to evaluate the concept and three nationally distributed brands on attributes such as looks lean, crisp, convenient, versatile, good for the family, appetizing, etc. The concepts and the three brands were then positioned on these attributes.

In this case, factor analysis was used to position the concept and brands. The program grouped together "good for the family," "gives you energy," and "provides nutritional benefits" because respondents who rated a brand high on one of these attributes tended to rate the brand high on the other two. These three attributes were called the nutritional factor. The concept and the brands were grouped on this and other factors defined by the factor analysis.

The new product was then given to those consumers who had eaten bacon within the past year and said they would definitely or probably buy the concept. This group was asked to use the concept and their regular brand. The same ratings were obtained as in the concept test. A perceptual map was developed based on the use test and compared to results from the concept test. Figure 18–5 shows the shift in perception from concept to use for the test concept and

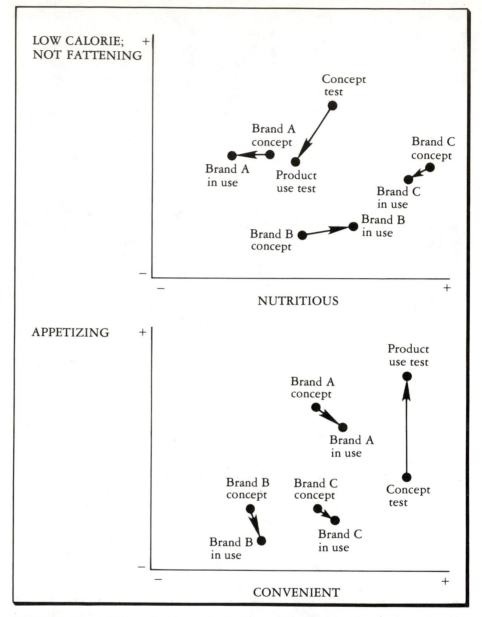

FIGURE 18–5 **Determination of the Concept Product Fit by Perceptual Mapping**

the three brands on four factors: low calorie/not fattening, nutritious, appetizing, and convenient.

The top of Figure 18–5 shows little change in the positioning of the three brands from the concept to use test (changes are shown by arrows), but the perception of the concept deteriorates when it is used in the home. It is rated more negatively on both low calorie and nutrition. Consumers expected more from the new product on these key benefits based on the concept statement than they received. The bottom of Figure 18–5 shows that there was no change in perceptions of the convenience of the new product, but consumers saw the new product as more appetizing in use than they were led to believe by the concept statement.

Apparently, the concept and the picture of the product conveyed the impression of a nutritious but not particularly appetizing product. When consumers used it, they found more fat than expected, yet a better taste. The net result was to dilute one of the key benefits — low calorie/non fattening — and position the concept closer to Brand A. Although the product could have been positioned as "a tasty bacon that has fewer calories than your present brand," the danger of being perceived as just another bacon product with no distinctive benefits was too great. The in-home use test strongly suggested further product modifications to ensure that the product in use met the expectations aroused by the concept's positioning. Once the product was modified, further tests suggested two positioning strategies: one directed to older consumers emphasizing health benefits such as easier to digest and low in cholesterol; another directed to middle-aged consumers emphasizing dietary and nutritional benefits.

EVALUATING EXISTING PRODUCTS
BY PERCEPTUAL MAPPING

It is important for management to evaluate not only where they should be but where they are. Descriptive positioning studies have been conducted to evaluate the relative positon of:

1. *types of products* such as liquor, small appliances, or even more broadly, foods
2. *competitive brands* within a specific product category.

Positioning Products

Positioning by product type is sometimes referred to as **market structure analysis** because it provides a broad view of a market based on consumer perceptions. Such analyses are conducted to evaluate the positioning of alternative product categories by consumer needs (e.g., the relative position of freeze dried, instant, decaffeinated, and ground roast coffees by key consumer benefits). Market structure analysis will also assess the potential for entry into a particular product category (the potential for a freeze-dried decaffeinated).

At one time, Campbell's Soup was interested in determining the position of its Chunky and regular condensed soups relative to related food and beverage products. It would be logical for Campbell's to conduct a study by product type rather than brand, since it represents the lion's share of canned soups. A proposed study was to position Chunky and condensed soups relative to related products. Consumers were to rate the degree of similarity between the soup, beverages, and food products. It was also hypothesized that canned soups were perceived differently by serving occasion. Therefore, similarity ratings were obtained separately for lunch time and snacking occasions.

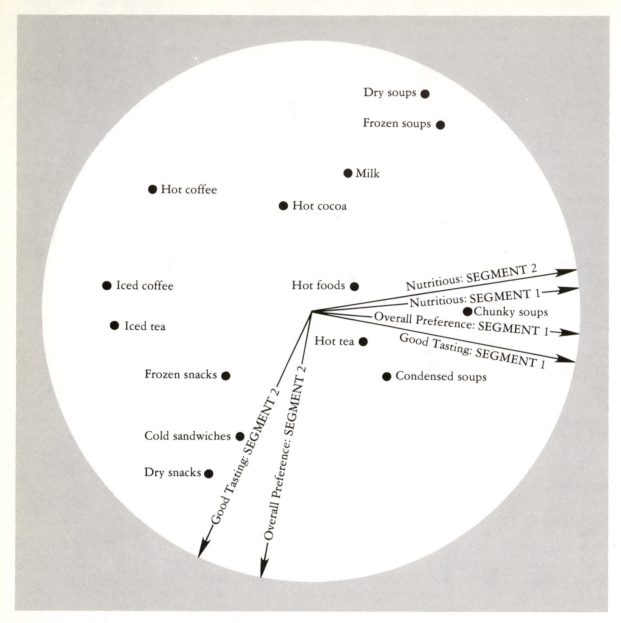

FIGURE 18–6 Market Structure Analysis:
Positioning Soups, Foods, and Beverages by Lunch-Time Occasions

Hypothetical results are presented in Figures 18–6 for lunch and 18–7 for snacking occasions. Multidimensional scaling was used to position the products and the PROFIT program to relate evaluative attributes to products. Figure 18–6 shows that canned soups are positioned closest to hot tea and hot foods for lunch. Cold sandwiches and snack products form a separate cluster. A third cluster is composed of iced coffee and iced tea. Consumers appear to be grouping soups and hot foods together as complementary, and view hot tea as a substitute

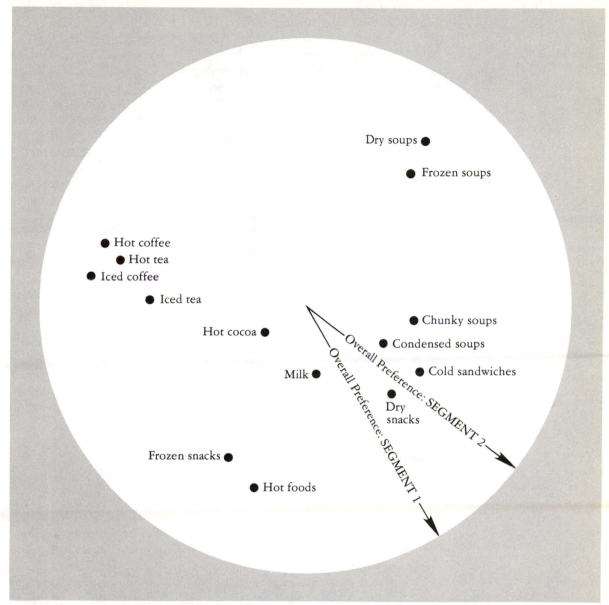

FIGURE 18–7 Market Structure Analysis:
Positioning Soups, Foods and Beverages by Snacking Occasions

for soup at lunch. If this is true, a positioning of soup and sandwiches for lunch does not appear to be suitable.

As part of the proposed positioning study, consumers were first segmented by benefits desired. Two segments were identified: Segment 1 emphasized nutritional benefits and was more likely to be composed of middle-aged respondents with children; Segment 2 emphasized taste and was more likely to be composed of teenagers and young adults. The lines in the figure show the evaluations of these two segments. Product-to-benefit associations show marked differences between the two segments. The nutritional segment (Segment 1) prefers the hot foods cluster for lunch. (This is represented by the line showing overall preference for Segment 1 in Figure 18–6.) Segment 1 associates hot foods with good taste. The taste segment (Segment 2) prefers snacks and cold foods or cold beverages, and associates them with good taste. Both segments agree that hot foods are more nutritious.

The best positioning for "soup for lunch" would be as a hot meal in itself or as a supplement to a hot meal rather than as a quick "pick-me-up." The target would be segment 1 — families concerned with providing nutrition at lunch.

The picture changes significantly when products are rated by snacking occasions (Figure 18–7). Now, hot tea and hot foods are no longer grouped with soups. Soups group with cold sandwiches and dry snacks. Coffee, tea, and hot foods are not viewed as suitable for snacking. Furthermore, there is little difference between the nutrition and taste segment in their preferences for snacking products. Preferences are clearly for the soup, sandwich, and dry/cold snack cluster.[30]

This analysis demonstrates the significance of analyzing consumer perceptions by occasion. Consumers position brands and products differently by usage occasion. Perceptual mapping analyses generally fail to identify usage occasions and tend to position brands across situations. Positioning strategies frequently must be varied by usage occasion. It is clear that if Campbell's is to position its soups relative to other food products, it will have to develop separate positioning strategies by lunch and snacking occasion. The analysis also demonstrates the importance of positioning by segments. A different positioning was required for soup at lunch for the nutrition and taste segments.

Positioning by Brands

Positioning analyses are conducted most frequently by brand. Yet few such studies are reported due to their proprietary nature. Exceptions to this are brand positioning studies reported by Johnson in the beer market[31] and by Wilkes in the automobile market.[32] Consumers' perceptions of brands provide a basis for evaluating advertising strategies and determining whether brand repositioning is necessary

Figure 18–8 illustrates a hypothetical brand positioning analysis for paper towels. Consumers rated five brands and their ideal paper towel on fifteen attributes. Factor analysis was used to position brands and market segments. Two of the factors produced in the analysis were strength and decorativeness. The strength factor represents attributes such as strong when wet, firm bodied and strong when dry. The decorative factor represents attributes such as cheerful and impulsive. The five brands and the ideal were then positioned on these two factors based on consumer brand ratings. The analysis shows that Northern and Bounty are seen as similar — strong towels that are not decorative. Gala and Scott are seen as weaker and more decorative towels.

The most important component of this analysis is differences in brand perceptions by segments. Two types of segments are portrayed: frequent versus infrequent purchasers of paper towels, and brand users versus nonusers. Frequent

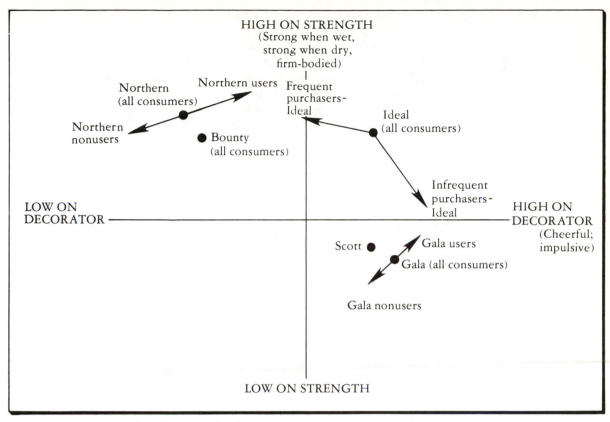

FIGURE 18–8 Brand Positioning Analysis:
Positioning Paper Towel Brands by Two Evaluative Dimensions

purchasers view an ideal brand as much stronger and less decorative than infrequent purchasers. (Differences in perception of the ideal by frequent and infrequent users are shown by the two lines extending from the ideal.) Northern users and nonusers view the brand as strong, but Northern users view it as more decorative than nonusers. Based on brand positioning by segments, the following conclusions can be drawn:

1. Appeals to frequent purchasers should be made based on strength, to infrequent purchasers based on decorativeness.
2. Northern is well positioned to meet the needs of the frequent purchaser. Frequent purchasers want a strong, moderately decorative brand and this is Northern's positioning among users.
3. Gala is well positioned to appeal to infrequent purchasers since Gala users emphasize decorativeness.

REPOSITIONING ANALYSIS

A corollary of any positioning analysis is that communication can influence consumers to change their perceptions of a brand in the desired direction. The success of brand repositioning strategies can only be evaluated by tracking consumer perceptions over time. Changes in a brand's position would be a measure of the effectiveness of the advertising campaign.

Repositioning strategies were discussed in Chapter 8 under the heading of strategies of attitude change. The basic premise in that chapter is that adaptive (positioning) strategies are easier to implement than change (repositioning) strategies, although the latter are viable under certain conditions.

The problem with attempting to reposition established brands is that beliefs and perceptions become entrenched and harder to change. Repositioning becomes a long-term communications strategy, and the company must assess the costs and utility of attempting to change beliefs. For example, Mead Johnson, producers of Metrecal, sought to reposition the brand by changing the image from an established product with medical acceptance sold in drugstores to a flavorful diet food sold in supermarkets.[33] It changed both its product and advertising strategy. New products were introduced in addition to the basic diet drink such as canned meals and flavored milkshakes. Its advertising emphasized themes such as taste, variety, and flavor while maintaining the em-

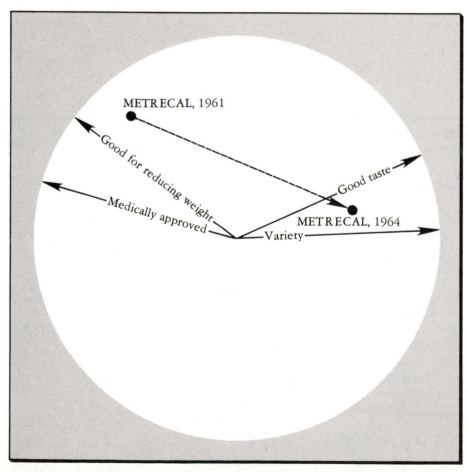

FIGURE 18–9   Attitude Change Strategy of Metrecal in 1961

phasis on low calories. The motivation for these changes was a loss of market share to other brands such as Pet Food's Sego and Carnation's Slender, both of which were advertised as diet foods distributed in supermarkets.

The objectives of respositioning are illustrated in Figure 18–9. Metrecal's position in 1961 is shown as a medically approved diet drink used primarily by people who are overweight. The purpose of the new campaign was to expand the market to those who used diet products to remain slim by emphasizing Metrecal as a food product that was tasty and came in many varieties.

Recently, multidimensional scaling techniques have been used to evaluate repositioning strategies. Studies by Perry et al.,[34] Moinpour et al.,[35] and Narayana[36] are representative. These studies report shifts in consumer perceptions by portraying differences in perceptual maps before and after an advertising campaign or other promotional stimulus.

An interesting extension of repositioning strategy is a case of forced repositioning by federal regulation requiring corrective advertising. The Federal Trade Commission's ruling requiring Listerine to cease further advertising of the brand as a cold remedy requires future corrective advertising. Listerine must change consumer perceptions, and in so doing, reposition the brand.

Whether repositioning is willful or forced, communications strategies designed for change must measure change, and perceptual mapping is an effective mode of analysis for doing so.

SUMMARY

This chapter describes market segmentation and product positioning from the standpoint of marketing strategy and behavioral analysis. Market segmentation and product positioning are closely linked since products are generally positioned to meet the needs of defined market segments.

The first part of the chapter considered market segmentation strategies and analysis. Segmentation strategies require allocating marketing resources to defined segments. Three approaches were identified. In *benefit segmentation,* consumers are defined by similarity in needs (e.g., consumers emphasizing cavity prevention versus whitens teeth versus economy in the toothpaste market). New products are developed and existing products are repositioned to meet these needs. In *behavioral segmentation,* marketers identify users of their brand, users of the product category, or distinguish between heavy and light users. Segments are described by demographics, psychographics or brand attitudes to provide guidelines for developing advertising and media strategies. Markets can also be segmented by consumer *response elasticities;* that is, consumer sensitivity to changes in price, advertising, or other marketing stimuli. The purpose is to identify the characteristics of consumers who may be induced to buy by a deal, or who may be influenced by an increase in advertising expenditures.

Market segmentation analysis seeks to identify and describe the benefit, behavioral, or response segments. For example, statistical analyses may identify snack food purchasers by similarity in needs (e.g., nutritional snackers, weight watchers, etc.), and then determine the demographic, psychographic, and attitudinal characteristics of these segments.

Product positioning also has its strategic and analytical components. Product positioning strategies can be based on positioning to consumers or positioning to competitors. Positioning to consumers requires identification of consumer needs and positioning products accordingly. Such positioning can be based on specific benefits directed to specific segments, or on more ambiguous appeals to broader segments. Competitive positioning requires using a competitive brand as a frame of reference and developing a product claim accordingly — for instance, 7-Up as the un-cola.

Product positioning analysis requires developing and testing new product concepts, or evaluating repositioning strategies for existing products. If the marketer feels an opportunity exists and wishes to determine the appropriate combinations of characteristics for a new product, then trade-off analysis can be used to identify an "ideal" product concept. Once a concept is defined, perceptual mapping techniques can be used to assess its position based on how the concept is perceived by consumers relative to other brands. A key question is whether the concept will fulfill its promise in a product-use test.

The chapter concludes by considering uses of perceptual mapping to (1) evaluate new products, (2) define the position of existing products, and (3) track changes in consumer perceptions of the product's position.

The next chapter will consider another component of marketing strategy, advertising, within the framework of marketing communications.

QUESTIONS

1. What benefit segments may be identified for the following markets: (a) soft drinks, (b) household cleaners, (c) personal care appliances, and (d) credit cards?
   - What are the implications of identifying these segments for (a) positioning new products, or (b) repositioning existing products?

2. Under what circumstances would a marketer wish to segment by the following behavioral criteria: (a) brand users versus nonusers; (b) product users versus nonusers; (c) brand loyalists versus occasional users; and (d) heavy versus light users of the product category?

3. Table 10–2 in Chapter 10 cited a nutritional, weight-watching, and guilty segment in the snack food market. What would be the usefulness of identifying each of these segments by (a) demographics, (b) psychographics, (c) brand attitudes, and (d) brands regularly purchased?

4. What are the strategic implications of segmenting the coffee market according to (a) deal or coupon sensitivity, and (b) sensitivity to changes in package size?
   - How would marketers identify the deal and package sensitive segments?

5. What are the advantages of positioning a brand by specific versus general criteria?
   - How would you position the following on the continuum from specific to general based on the five purchase motives specified on page 454? (Specify a possible positioning strategy for each product): (a) a new skin conditioner for men; (b) a decaffeinated coffee with chicory added to improve taste; and (c) a

new fruit-flavored soft drink with the fruit derivative imported from Brazil?

6. What are the advantages and disadvantages of positioning a brand relative to competition?

- Given 7-Up's successful positioning against colas and Avis's against Hertz, under what circumstances should competitive positioning be used?

7. Assume that a company wants to develop a new snack food to appeal to those consumers who would like a snack that is nutritious and can be eaten at any time (morning, afternoon, after dinner, before bedtime).

- How can the company use (a) the Kelly Repertory Grid and (b) trade-off analysis to develop an appropriate concept?

8. How could the US Postal Service utilize market structure analysis in positioning a new electronic message delivery service relative to other forms of communications?

9. How can the Federal Trade Commission utilize perceptual mapping techniques to determine if required corrective advertising (e.g., Listerine) has the desired effects on consumer perceptions of the brand in question?

RESEARCH ASSIGNMENTS

1. Select a product category and identify three or four key benefits. Select a sample of product users and ask them to identify the most important benefit desired. On this basis, form three or four benefit segments (e.g., consumers who emphasize "lets me sleep," "freshly brewed coffee," or "economy" for coffee). Try to ensure there are at least ten consumers in each benefit segment. Ask the sample for information on the following: (a) demographic characteristics (b) brand regularly used (c) frequency of use, and (d) a select number of life-style characteristics, based on Table 10–1.

- What are the differences between benefit segments based on the above information?

- What are the implications for: (a) new product positioning, (b) repositioning existing products, (c) advertising, (d) media selection, and (e) pricing strategies?

2. Select a product category that might warrant a new product entry (e.g., a new after-shave product, a faster acting and safer analgesic, a three-in-one shampoo, cream rinse, and conditioner, etc.). Use the Kelly Repertory Grid technique on a small sample of consumers to identify relevant attributes that might be introduced into a new product concept. Then use trade-off analysis to test various combinations of attributes that might be included in a new product (see Figure 18-3). Ask a sample of about 20 to 30 consumers to rank their preferences for the combinations of attributes (concept formulations) you have developed.

- Based on an examination of the data, what appears to be the best prospective product formulation?

- Can you identify one group of consumers that tends to prefer one concept and another group that prefers another? What are the differences in the demographic or brand usage characteristics of the two groups?

- What are the implications of your findings for (a) the way the product should be positioned, and (b) the target group it should be positioned to?

NOTES

1. Ronald E. Frank, William F. Massy and Yoram Wind, *Market Segmentation,* (Englewood Cliffs, N.J.: Prentice-Hall, 1972), pp. 175–176.
2. Roger J. Calantone and Alan G. Sawyer, "The Stability of Benefit Segments," *Journal of Marketing Research* 15 (August 1978): 395–404.
3. W. Thomas Anderson, Jr., Eli P. Cox III, and David G. Fulcher, "Bank Decisions and Market Segmentation," *Journal of Marketing* 40 (January 1976): 40–45.
4. Shirley Young, Leland Ott, and Barbara Feigin, "Some Practical Considerations in Market Segmentation," *Journal of Marketing Research* 15 (August 1978): 405–412.
5. See William Massy, Ronald E. Frank, and Thomas M. Lodahl, *Purchasing Behavior and Personal Attributes,* (Philadelphia, Pa.: University of Pennsylvania Press, 1968); Ronald E. Frank, Susan P. Douglas, and R.E. Polli, "Household Correlates of Brand Loyalty for Grocery Products," *Journal of Business* 41 (April 1968): 237–245; Ronald E. Frank, "Brand Loyalty as a Basis for Market Segmentation," *Journal of Advertising Research* 7 (June 1967): 27–33; George S. Day, "A Two-Dimensional Concept of Brand Loyalty," *Journal of Advertising Research* 9 (September 1969): 29–36.
6. William H. Peters, "Using MCA to Segment New Car Markets," *Journal of Marketing Research* 7 (August 1970): 360–363.
7. Robert D. Hisrich and Michael P. Peters, "Selecting the Superior Segmentation Correlate," *Journal of Marketing* 38 (July 1974): 60–63.
8. Frank M. Bass, Douglas J. Tigert, and Ronald T. Lonsdale, "Market Segmentation: Group vs. Individual Behavior," *Journal of Marketing Research* 5 (August 1968): 264–270.
9. Henry Assael, and A. Marvin Roscoe, Jr., "Approaches to Market Segmentation Analysis," *Journal of Marketing* 40 (October 1976): 67–76.
10. Henry Assael, "A Research Design to Predict Telephone Usage Among Bell System Customers," *European Research* 1 (January 1973): 38–44, and (March 1973): 59–61.
11. William F. Massy and Ronald E. Frank, "Short Term Price and Dealing Effects in Selected Market Segments," *Journal of Marketing Research* 2 (May 1965): 171–185.
12. John M. McCann, "Market Segment Response to the Marketing Decision Variables," *Journal of Marketing Research* 11 (November 1974): 399–412.
13. William H. Cunningham and Robert A. Peterson, "Market Segmentation by Gasoline Consumption Intentions," in Barnett A. Greenberg and Danny N. Bellinger, eds., *Proceedings of the American Marketing Association Educators' Conference,* Series 41 (1977), pp. 105–109.
14. For descriptions of quantitative techniques used in segmentation analysis, see: Paul E. Green and Donald S. Tull, *Research for Marketing Decisions,* 3rd ed. (Englewood Cliffs, N.J.: Prentice-Hall, 1975), Part IV; and Henry Assael, "Segmenting Market Segmentation Strategies and Techniques," *European Research* 1 (September 1973): 190–194; and *European Research* 1 (November 1973): 256–258.
15. Jack Trout, "Marketing in the '70's: Product Positioning," *The Conference Board Record* (January 1976): 42.
16. Adapted from Geraldine Fennell, "Consumers' Perceptions of the Product Use Situation," *Journal of Marketing* 42 (April 1978): 38–47.
17. Trout, "Marketing in the '70's." p. 42.
18. Ibid.
19. Philip Levine, "Commercials That Name Competing Brands," *Journal of Advertising Research* 16 (December 1976): 7–16.
20. Henry Assael, "Evaluating New Product Concepts and Developing Early Predictions of Trial," *Marketing Review* (May 1975): 12–13.
21. For a full description of multidimensional scaling applications in marketing, see: Paul E. Green and Frank J. Carmone, *Multidimensional Scaling and Related Techniques in Marketing Analysis* (Boston: Allyn and Bacon, 1970).
22. For a description of property-fitting techniques, see Green and Carmone, *Multidimensional Scaling,* pp. 58–59.
23. For a description of clustering techniques, see Paul E. Green and Donald S. Tull, *Research for Marketing Decisions,* 3rd ed. (Englewood Cliffs, N.J.: Prentice-Hall, 1975), Chapter 15.
24. W. A.K. Foost and R.L. Braine, "The Application of the Repertory Grid Technique to Problems in Market Research," *Commentary* 9 (July 1967): 161–175.
25. For examples of two different approaches to trade-off analysis, see: Richard M. Johnson, "Trade-Off Analysis of Consumer Values," *Journal of Marketing Research* 11 (May 1974): 121–127; and Paul E. Green and Yoram Wind, "New Ways to Measure Consumers' Judgements," *Harvard Business Review* 53 (July-August 1975): 107–117.
26. For an example of the use of discriminant analysis to position brands, see: Richard M. Johnson, "Market Segmentation: A Strategic Management Tool," *Journal of Marketing Research* 8 (February 1971): 13–19.
27. For an example of the use of factor analysis to position products see: Henry Assael, "Perceptual

Mapping to Reposition Brands," *Journal of Advertising Research* 11 (February 1971): 39–42.

28. Yoram Wind, "A New Procedure for Concept Evaluation," *Journal of Marketing* 37 (October 1973): 2–11.

29. Volney Stefflre, "Market Structure Studies," in F.M. Bass, C.W. King, and E.A. Pessemier, eds., *Applications of the Sciences in Marketing Management* (New York: John Wiley & Sons, 1968), pp. 251–268.

30. For an example of a market structure study positioning types of iced tea, see Assael, "Perceptual Mapping."

31. Johnson, "Market Segmentation: A Strategic Management Tool."

32. Robert E. Wilkes, "Product Positioning by Multidimensional Scaling," *Journal of Advertising Research* 17 (August 1977): 15–22.

33. Roger D. Blackwell, James F. Engel, and David T. Kollat, *Cases in Consumer Behavior* (New York: Holt, Rinehart and Winston, 1969), Mead Johnson and Co. (A), pp. 3–8 and Mead Johnson and Co. (B), pp. 113–120.

34. Michael Perry, Dov Izraeli, and Arnon Perry, "Image Change as a Result of Advertising," *Journal of Advertising Research* 16 (February 1976): 45–50.

35. Reza Moinpour, James M. McCullough, and Douglas MacLachlan, "Time Changes in Perception: A Longitudinal Application of Multidimensional Scaling," *Journal of Marketing Research* 13 (August 1976): 245–253.

36. Chem L. Narayana, "The Stability of Perceptions," *Journal of Advertising Research* 16 (April 1976): 45–49.

NINETEEN

Marketing Communications and Consumer Information Processing

Focus of Chapter

In order to position products to meet consumer needs product benefits must be communicated to the consumer. Through marketing communications consumers learn about new products, the prices and availability of existing products, and the characteristics of alternative brands. Marketing communications are central to any marketing plan. Marketers communicate by mass media advertising, package information, in-store displays, and personal selling.

The *communication* of information by the marketer and the *processing* of marketing information by the consumer are key elements in the study of consumer behavior. Without information, the consumer cannot act. Without communication, the marketer cannot sell.

Chapter 8 presented a basic model of communication in relation to the individual consumer. The focus was on strategies of attitude change. In Chapter 15, communication in a group context was considered in discussions of group influence and word-of-mouth communications. In this chapter the process of marketing communication, and more particularly, the process of communication through advertising, will be described in detail. The focus of the chapter will be on consumer information processing.

The following two chapters will consider the effects of marketing communications other than advertising; namely, in-store stimuli and salesperson-consumer communications.

A MODEL OF ADVERTISING COMMUNICATIONS

The most important form of marketing communications is advertising. A detailed model of the advertising communications process is presented in Figure 19–1. The model incorporates the basic communications process described in Chapter 8 — development of an idea to be communicated, encoding the idea into a marketing message, transmitting the idea to a defined target group of consumers, the decoding of the message by the consumer, acting on the message, and the process of feeding back consumer reactions to the marketer. The model in Figure 19–1 goes beyond the description of the basic communications process in Chapter 8 by considering the barriers to advertising communications, and by accounting for the possible results of marketing communications on consumer behavior.

Barriers to Communication

Barriers to communication can occur at each step in the communications process: at the source, with the sender, in the transmission, or with the receiver.

In the first step in the communications process, the idea to be defined by the source is generally a product concept. The advertiser must ensure the message conforms to the basic product concept. The barrier to communication at the *source* is an inadequate definition of the concept, or the marketer's failure to communicate the concept to the advertising agency. Such a failure is most likely to lead to an advertising message that is unrelated to consumer needs.

For example, a large pharmaceutical company once developed an aspirin that could be taken without water in the belief that it would offer quick relief when water was not available. Initial tests of the product were encouraging and an advertising campaign was developed based on the key concept of instant relief anywhere at any time. The product was a failure because the concept did not reflect consumer needs: Consumers wanted the soothing effects of water when taking aspirin. As a result, the campaign was doomed to failure, illustrating the fact that a good advertising campaign cannot sell a poor product.

Failures in marketing communications can also be attributable to the *sender.* At times, copywriters and artists may be more interested in developing creative, original advertising than in conveying product benefits. The result may be a message that is eye-catching, but not able to communicate to the consumer. Another barrier to communication at the sender level is deceptive advertising. Deception occurs when consumers acquire false beliefs because of exposure to advertising. One study exposed a group of consumers to deceptive advertisements while another group received nondeceptive ads.[1] The results showed that 64 percent of the group exposed to deceptive ads formed strong and false beliefs about the product. This figure suggests that deception can be accepted by a large number of consumers, increasing its potential seriousness as a barrier to effective communication.

Barriers to communication can also occur in the process of *transmission.* An

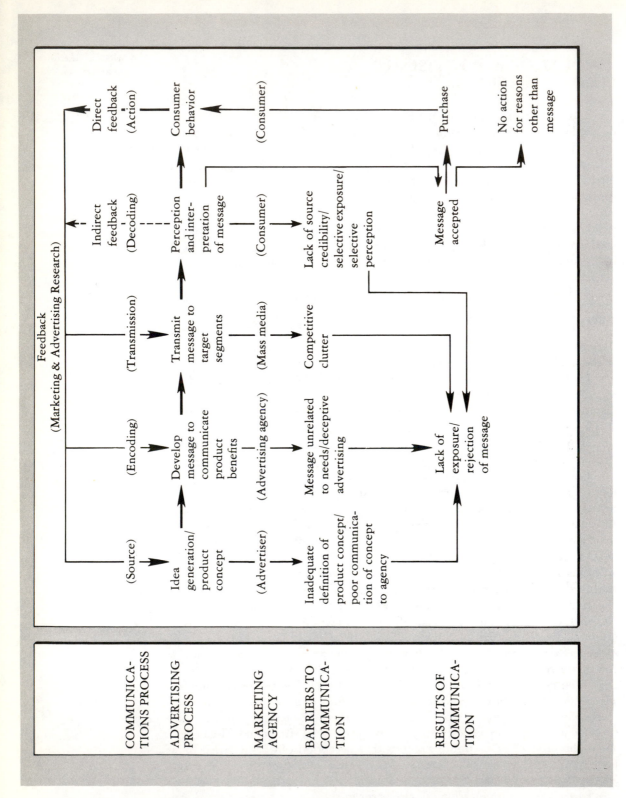

FIGURE 19–1   A Detailed Model of the Advertising Communication Process

example of this is a garbled television message due to some mechanical failure. Perhaps the most wearisome barrier in transmission is competitive clutter. The number of commercials and print advertisements has been increasing. With greater leisure time, the opportunity to be exposed to these ads has also been increasing. This is demonstrated by the fact that the average TV set is on for six hours and eighteen minutes a day.[2] Competitive clutter has produced negative attitudes on the part of consumers. The most uniform attitude toward television among consumers is that there are too many commercials on the air. These negative attitudes lead to overestimates as to the amount of time taken up by commercials on TV. A study by Webb found that viewers overestimate commercial time on TV by from 33 to 100 percent.[3]

A failure to develop a product concept or to create an advertising message related to consumer needs is likely to lead to barriers to communication in the *decoding process*. Consumers will selectively ignore messages of no interest to them. Further, if consumers find that the source of the message is not credible, the message will be rejected. An advertisement from a large oil company explaining the nature of gas shortages and justifying higher profits to ensure further exploration may be rejected by consumers for lack of credibility. A similar message from the Department of Energy is more likely to be accepted.

Rejection of an advertising message by the consumer may be independent of the source or message content. Such rejection may be a result of the consumer's attitudes, past experiences, and beliefs. A consumer who has had consistently poor performance from a certain automobile make is unlikely to accept the validity of a claim that the car is well engineered, durable, and provides maximum performance on the road.

Results of the Communication Process

Figure 19–1 recognizes that the consumer may decide not to purchase for reasons other than the information in the communication. Price and availability are obvious restrictions to purchase. Another may be a lack of an immediate need. A consumer may find a car very attractive based on the advertising, but will not be in the market for a car for two years.

The most desirable result of the communications process from the advertiser's standpoint is a *purchase*. Marketers would like to assess the effect of the marketing communication on the purchase. Evaluation of the communication by marketing and advertising research provides the marketer feedback. *Direct feedback* is provided when a marketing communication can be linked to sales results. Retail advertising announcing a sale on a given day can be judged by the number of shoppers. The effects of in-store displays can be evaluated by comparing them to sales with no display. Coupon returns can be related back to the advertising source. But the sales effectiveness of an advertising message in the mass media is harder to judge. *Indirect feedback* is produced when the marketing communication is evaluated based on the consumer's thought process. Indirect criteria of effectiveness relate to the ability of the advertisement to produce exposure, awareness, comprehension, and retention of the advertising message.

Key Questions in Evaluating the Effects of Advertising

The model in Figure 19–1 raises some important questions regarding the effects of advertising on consumer behavior. These questions can be illustrated by considering the relationship between the components of the model.

The first question concerns the relationship between idea generation and encoding. *Can the benefits in the product be easily encoded?* The benefit of gas economy can be easily conveyed to the consumer, but there may be more difficulty in conveying a safety benefit for two reasons: First, there may be difficulty in linking specific product characteristics to safety benefits. (Is a bigger, heavier car safer or more dangerous?) Second, unfortunately safety is not one of the consumer's top priorities in purchasing. Generally, product benefits will be more difficult to encode when they are related to secondary needs, and when they cannot be linked to product features.

The second question concerns the link between encoding and decoding. *Does the consumer decode the message in the manner intended by the sender?* Selective perception may cause the consumer to misinterpret the message. Or, the message may be rejected because it does not conform to the consumer's beliefs about the product. As cited in Chapter 6 a number of conditions exist when messages are more likely to be misperceived or rejected, namely when the message:

- conflicts with strongly held beliefs;
- conflicts with past experience;
- is too anxiety producing;
- is too ambiguous; and
- does not attract sufficient attention.

A third question involves the link between transmission and the receiver. *Are the selected media efficient in reaching the target segments defined by the advertiser?* An effective communications campaign is useless unless it reaches the intended receivers.

Fourth, it must be determined what the relation is between decoding and action. *Does exposure to and acceptance of the message lead to a purchase?* Advertising tests frequently link interpretation of messages to changes in attitudes or intention to buy the brand. This requires determining attitudes and purchase intent before exposure to the message, and subsequent changes in attitudes and purchase intent after exposure. Such tests must be under controlled conditions to ensure that changes in attitudes and purchase intent can be attributable to the advertising message.

Fifth, it is necessary to know what the relation is between action and future idea generation and encoding. *Does the advertiser learn from the current campaign how to better develop and communicate product concepts?* Adequacy of feedback will ensure that the advertiser can learn from current mistakes and can improve the process of generating and communicating product benefits.

Consumer Information Processing

The communications model focused on one source for the advertising message. In actuality, consumers are exposed to multiple sources of information, both from the mass media in the form of advertising and from personal sources in the form of word-of-mouth communications. Figure 19–2 reflects the consumer's need to process information from multiple sources. Consumer information processing requires evaluating the source of the message and the message itself. Figure 19–2 also recognizes that the consumer may choose to initiate a search for additional information when the level of information is considered inadequate to make a choice. Such search behavior may take the form of asking the advice of friends or relatives, shopping in various stores, buying specialty magazines, considering evaluations from impartial sources such as *Consumer Reports,* or taking notice of advertisements for new or unknown products.

The remainder of this chapter will consider the marketing communications process within the framework of consumer information processing. The primary components of the advertising communications model in Figure 19–1 will be considered: the *source,* the *message* (encoding), the *media* (transmission), the *consumer* (decoding), and *feedback.*

SOURCE EFFECTS ON INFORMATION PROCESSING

The source of information (advertisers, salespersons, friends, relatives) directly influences a consumer's acceptance and interpretation of the message. It is important to consider the nature and credibility of the source to understand the impact of the source on consumer information processing.

Types of Sources

There are three types of information sources: commercial (advertising, sales representatives, sales promotions); personal (friends, relatives); and neutral (news articles, *Consumer Reports* magazine, government sources). Most researchers agree that the commercial and neutral sources are most important in providing information about products, but the personal sources are most likely to influence the consumer's actions.

These results are reflected in a study of information sources for three categories, small appliances, clothing, and food.[4] Consumers were asked how they first heard of the product, how else they heard about the product before they purchased, and which source of information was most important in the purchase decision (Table 19–1). The commercial sources were clearly relied on as the initial source of information about the product for all three product categories. Personal sources of information dominated as the most important influence on the purchase decision. A study by Newman and Staelin of sources of information for automobiles and major appliances found even less reliance

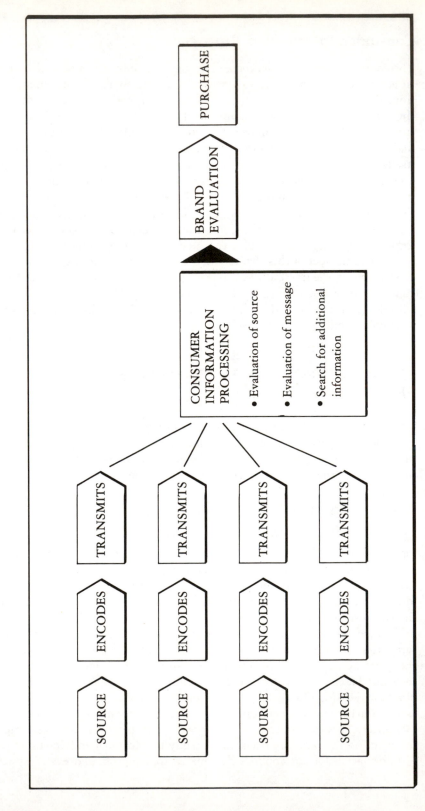

FIGURE 19–2 Consumer Processing of Multiple Messages

TABLE 19–1 Sources of Information in the Purchase Decision

Source	Small appliances			Clothing			Food		
	First	Else	Most important	First	Else	Most important	First	Else	Most important
Commercial Sources:									
Advertising	48	23	8	35	27	16	45	25	19
Salesmen	1	1	1	4	1	6	0	0	0
Sales promotion.[a]	9	7	9	19	14	32	26	16	27
Interpersonal Sources:									
Friends, neighbors, relatives[b]	23	41	53	27	29	33	16	19	29
Immediate family	8	7	11	2	4	0	12	12	21
Professional advice	6	8	13	0	0	0	1	0	0
Editorial and News Sources[c]	1	0	1	6	6	6	0	0	1
No Mentions	4	13	4	7	19	7	0	28	3
Total (N = 99)	100%	100%	100%	100%	100%	100%	100%	100%	100%

[a] includes sampling, displays, in-store promotions, packaging

[b] includes actual discussion as well as noticing the item or trying the item (e.g., in the home of a friend)

[c] includes *Consumer Reports*

Source: From *Innovative Behavior and Communications* by Thomas S. Robertson. Copyright © 1971 by Holt, Rinehart and Winston, Inc. Reprinted by permission of Holt, Rinehart and Winston.

on advertising.[5] When consumers sought information, they were more likely to go to the automobile showroom or retail store than to advertising sources, and, the sources of information consumers had most confidence in were retail outlets, friends, and neighbors.

Advertising is a more important source of information for packaged goods compared to autos and major appliances, possibly because packaged goods have a greater number of alternative brands. The alternatives for autos and major appliances are fewer and the financial risks are greater. As a result, a friend or a salesperson in a retail outlet is more likely to be an important source of information.

The findings in both these studies conform to the conclusion in Chapter 15 that advertising is a relatively weak source of influence compared to word-of-mouth communications. Yet advertising has an essential role in informing the public of the existence of new products and the attributes of alternative brands.

Source Credibility

One of the reasons that advertising does not exert as much influence on the consumer as personal sources is due to the fact that consumers are more likely to believe messages from friends and neighbors. Advertising is viewed as less credible because of the obvious desire of the advertiser to sell the brand. Credibility is associated with believability, objectivity, and expertise. Neutral sources are also more likely to be regarded as credible because they make no attempt to change attitudes or to influence behavior. Newscasters are generally viewed as credible for this reason. Walter Cronkite has been repeatedly cited as the most credible American figure because of a perceived objectivity in reporting.

Studies have concluded that the greater the perceived credibility of the source, the greater is the likelihood the receiver will accept the message.[6] For example, Craig and McCann studied the effects of messages from Con Edison and from the New York State Public Service Commission asking consumers to save money by reducing the consumption of electricity used for air conditioning.[7] The message was enclosed in the monthly utility bill. A control group did not receive the message. Results of the study are in Figure 19–3. The findings show the two groups that received the message consumed less electricity in August than the group that received no message. But the group receiving the message from the Public Service Commission — a more credible source — consumed substantially less electricity compared to the group receiving the message from Con Edison. By September, the weather cooled and the message was no longer relevant. The authors conclude that "the effectiveness of a communication advocating energy conservation can be enhanced by using a source of greater credibility."[8]

Source credibility in itself does not ensure message acceptance. Other studies have found:

1.   Source credibility increases the acceptance of the message only for low involvement products.[9] When involvement is great and the consumer does not agree with the message, it will be rejected even if it is from a credible source.

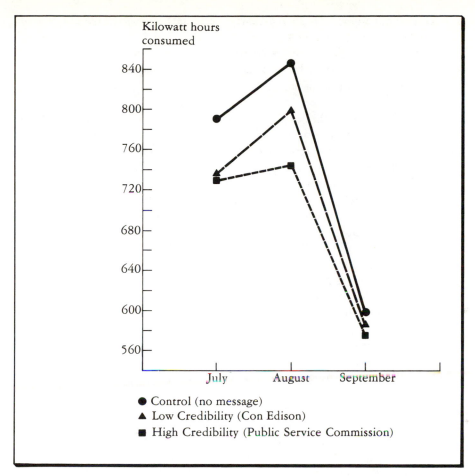

FIGURE 19–3 Effects of Source Credibility on Changes in Electrical Consumption

Source: C. Samuel Craig and John M. McCann, "Assessing Communication Effects on Energy Conservation," *Journal of Consumer Research* 5 (September 1978): 87.
    Reprinted with permission from the *Journal of Consumer Research*.

2.   Source credibility increases the acceptance of the message if there is little experience with the product.[10] If consumers can rely on their own experience, the credibility of the source is not as important in influencing message acceptance.

3.   Source credibility increases the likelihood of message acceptance if the message does not conflict with the consumer's best interests. If such conflict occurs, credibility will not improve the chances of message acceptance.[11]

4.   Source credibility increases message acceptance if the message is not threatening.[12] Fear appeals from a credible source are likely to be rejected if they arouse too much anxiety.

Increasing Source Credibility

Given that a lack of credibility is a major limitation in the acceptance of advertising messages, advertisers may reasonably consider how they can increase their credibility. Behavioral research has suggested four factors that increase credibility:

1. Don't say the product is good for everything. State its benefits but also indicate what the product cannot do.
2. Emphasize the familiarity of the source.
3. Emphasize the similarity between the source and the receiver.
4. Stress the expertise of the source.

Research suggests that *two-sided messages* increase source credibility. Settle and Golden used attribution theory to prove this point.[13] Attribution theory states that a receiver will attribute certain motives to a communication source. When all the ads seen by a consumer are making uniformly positive claims (gets your teeth whiter, your clothes cleaner, your meat more tender, etc.), the consumer begins to doubt the motives of the advertiser. Uniformly positive claims lead the consumer to attribute the message to the advertisers' desire to sell the product. But if a message provides some variation in the claim, (e.g., analgesic A is stronger and provides quick relief, but it is also more likely to produce side effects), then the consumer is more likely to accept the source as credible. The claim is more likely to be attributed to the actual characteristics of the product than to the desire of the advertiser to sell.

Settle and Golden tested two sets of ads. In one set, the messages claimed superiority on all product attributes. In the other set, the messages claimed superiority on three of five product features and disclaimed superiority on the other two. Consumers had more confidence in the claims that cited the pros and cons of a brand. The conclusion is that advertisers may be better off if they disclaimed at least one product feature so as to increase believability in the message and credibility in the source. The advertiser that argues its brand is always best under every circumstance may encourage the consumer to reject the source and the message. Advertisers that admit their brands may not be best under certain circumstances are likely to win credibility and possibly acceptance of the brand.

A second factor that may increase source credibility is *familiarity.* Consumers frequently accept information provided by nationally known companies as more reliable compared to information produced by local and lesser known companies.

Third, *similarity between the source and the consumer* is likely to increase source credibility. Research has shown that when consumers see salespersons as similar to themselves, consumers are more likely to accept and be influenced by their messages.[14] The salesperson is seen as a legitimate source of information and influences the consumer in much the same way as a friend or peer.

Fourth, source credibility is likely to increase if *the source is seen as having expertise.* Research has shown that salespeople who are viewed as experts *and* are seen as similar to the consumer are likely to be more credible in a sales situation.[15] Similarly, advertising that employs spokespersons who stress their similarity to the consumer and their expertise is likely to increase credibility. The problem is that, more often than not, similarity and expertise may conflict. Jimmy Connors might be an excellent individual to provide a testimonial for a tennis racket, but there is very little similarity between Jimmy Connors and most tennis players. Although he may be regarded as a credible source, his effectiveness may be limited by too much distance from the typical tennis player.

The advertising message is meant to inform and persuade. Informational objectives may be directed toward announcing new products or changes in existing products, informing the consumer of product characteristics, or providing information on price and availability. Persuasive objectives may be directed toward convincing the consumer of product benefits, trying to induce trial, or reducing uncertainty after the purchase is made. The methods of developing and presenting advertising messages are beyond the scope of this book, but certain aspects of message content bear directly on the likelihood that the consumer will accept and act on the message. The following questions have been considered by consumer researchers:

1. Should the message be one-sided (supportive) or two-sided (refutational)?
2. Is comparative advertising (naming a competitor in the ad) an effective means of communicating product benefits using a two-sided approach?
3. What are the advantages of using fear appeals?
4. What is the appropriate role of humor in advertising?

One-Sided Versus Two-Sided Appeals

The study by Settle and Golden suggested that two-sided appeals are more effective because they increase source credibility. Another reason for favoring two-sided appeals is they may provide the consumer with a means of refuting arguments against the chosen brand. For example, an ad may convey the benefits of the purchase of an economy car — better gas mileage, economical maintenance, good performance — and frankly refer to a potential loss of prestige or status for former owners of luxury cars. But the ad may also present the counter-argument to this concern by pointing out that the car is sufficiently roomy and has the luggage space of a luxury car. Thus, the loss is in status, not comfort. Such an ad would provide ammunition to the purchaser of an economy car who may be contradicting the norms of his or her peer group requiring the purchase of a more expensive car. A negative remark from a friend may prompt the consumer to cite the arguments made in the ad — "give me economy and comfort any day and I'd be glad to sacrifice status."

Support for a two-sided approach to provide the consumer with counter-arguments comes from two studies. Szybillo and Heslin found that refutational appeals were more effective than supportive appeals in countering opposing views.[16] They presented messages supporting the use of air bags (one-sided) and messages both supporting the use of air bags and considering some of the arguments against them (two-sided). The two-sided ads were more effective in countering arguments against air bags and convincing consumers of their merits.

Sawyer also found that two-sided messages were more effective in refuting competitive claims as long as there was sufficient repetition of the two-sided statement.[17] He concluded that refutational ads would be effective in introducing a new product which must overcome some consumer objections. Anti-pollution devices on cars or nondisposable containers may be examples. Refutational ads would also be effective for brands with lower market shares that want to refute a large competitor's claims of superiority. Avis's campaign against

Hertz is an example. A refutational campaign could have been used by Heinz several years ago when they introduced Great American soups to compete against Campbell's. Eventually Heinz's brand went off the market because of the dominance of Campbell's. But a campaign similar to Avis's might have been effective (We're number two but our quality is just as good and we try harder).

Refutational ads are not always more effective than supportive ads. Evidence suggests that one-sided ads are more effective when the consumer possesses little information, when there is agreement with the advertiser's position, and when the consumer is loyal to the advertiser's brand.[18] But in today's competitive environment these conditions are less likely to occur. This means that more sophisticated advertisers will increase their use of refutational advertisements in an attempt to provide consumers with a more realistic presentation of product benefits.

Comparative Advertising

The best example of refutational messages is **comparative advertising.** Advertisers sometimes name a competitor, cite the claimed benefits of the competitor's product, and then refute these benefits by citing the strength of their brand. The argument for the use of comparative advertising is that (1) users of competing brands are more likely to notice the ad and are therefore more subject to the claims of the advertiser; (2) users of competing brands will be more likely to consider the advertiser's brand, and (3) claims made in comparative ads are more likely to be considered objective.[19]

The evidence on the effectiveness of comparative advertising is mixed. A study by Ogilvy & Mather found that consumers frequently confused the sponsor for the competitor in many comparative ads. Further, there was no difference in awareness of persuasiveness between comparative and noncomparative advertising.[20] In contrast, Prasad found that recall was higher for comparative ads,[21] and Sawyer found that consumers did not generally confuse the competitor and the sponsor in comparative advertising.[22]

One study attempted to resolve these different findings by examining the use of comparative advertising for different product categories. The research findings questioned the use of comparative advertising for consumer packaged (convenience) goods because these products do not require advertising to explain differences in quality, style, price, or other features between brands. For shopping goods such as major appliances and automobiles, a comparative ad was found to represent a potentially powerful alternative because such advertising could present consumers with key differences in product attributes. Interestingly, the Ogilvy & Mather study was of packaged goods, whereas the Prasad and Sawyer studies included shopping goods. Therefore, it is not surprising that the Ogilvy & Mather study found comparative advertising less effective than the research by Prasad or Sawyer.

Comparative advertising will most likely increase given greater sensitivity on the part of consumers to brand alternatives. It should have a more limited role for consumer packaged goods compared to "big ticket" items. Thus, one may question its use by Pepsi relative to Coke, but it is a reasonable approach for Avis relative to Hertz.

Fear Appeals

Fear appeals were considered in Chapter 6 as an example of messages that consumers frequently seek to avoid. Various campaigns were cited (e.g., American Cancer Society) using fear appeals that dealt with such stark consequences (death, job loss) that the appeal was rejected. As noted, fear appeals are more likely to be effective when the level of anxiety is moderate rather than high, and when the consumer can take some action based on the appeal.[23] Research has also shown that moderate appeals to fear are more likely to be persuasive when the credibility of the source is high,[24] and when the individual is self-confident and less subject to anxieties.[25] A fifth factor involves product usage. One study found that fear appeals are more effective among nonusers than users.[26] Thus, fear appeals would be more effective in getting nondeodorant users to use the product than they would be in getting deodorant users to switch brands.

Humor in Advertising

Humorous messages are used as a means of attracting attention and because advertisers believe that humor can sometimes be persuasive. But, humor may be a poor vehicle for communicating information and ensuring retention of the message. One of the better known commercials based on humor was the use of "Bert and Harry Piels" to advertise Piels beer. The results of the campaign were mixed. Although recall was very high, there were indications that consumers were focused more on the characters than on the product benefits. The advertising was attention getting, but it was not really communicating.

Sternthal and Craig conclude there are pros and cons for the use of humor in advertising.[27] On the positive side, humor is likely to increase attention and enhance the credibility of the advertiser. Humor may create a positive mood toward the advertiser, increasing the persuasiveness of the message. It may also distract users of competitive products from developing counter-arguments against using the advertiser's brand, and may lead them to accept the message. But distraction may have a negative effect on message comprehension because of the dominance of humor. Product benefits may not be communicated. If this is the case, then humor cannot be said to be effective, regardless of greater attention and source credibility. Message effectiveness requires comprehension of the benefits communicated in the ad.

MEDIA EFFECTS

The third component in the communication model is message transmission. Advertisers must ensure the message reaches the intended target. Therefore the characteristics of the target segment must be identified by demographic and life-style criteria, and media must be selected that can best reach these segments. The selection of media by consumer characteristics was described in Chapter 9. In this section, the communications effects of media selection will be considered.

The Medium and the Message

Marshall McLuhan's statement "The medium is the message" implies that the medium communicates an image independent of any single message it contains.[28] Magazines like *New Yorker, Reader's Digest,* and *Playboy* have different images based on different editorial content, reputation, and subscribers. The interpretation of an advertising message is therefore a function of the medium by which it is transmitted as well as the content of the message.

The role of the medium in communications is illustrated by the fact that the same advertisement will result in different communications effects when run in different media. In a study by Aaker and Brown, identical ads were included in two magazines, *New Yorker* and *Tennis World*.[29] The two magazines were chosen as contrasts, *New Yorker* representing a prestige magazine and *Tennis World* a specialty magazine. Aaker and Brown found that *New Yorker* was more effective in persuading nonusers to consider a product when the ad stressed product quality. *Tennis World* was more effective when the ad stressed reasons for usage. These findings suggest that the medium's environment conveys a message: Specialty media were more effective as vehicles for conveying information; prestige media were more effective as vehicles for conveying image.

Media Environments

The previous section suggested that magazines will convey different images based on differing editorial content. Given differences between media environments within a particular category (e.g., magazines), can any generalizations be made about different environments between categories (e.g., magazines versus TV)?

High Versus Low Involvement Media

The most important distinction is between broadcast (TV and radio) and print (newspapers and magazines). Krugman describes the broadcast media as "cool" or low-involvement media and the print as "hot" or high involvement media.[30] Television, in particular, produces low personal involvement because the rate of viewing and understanding is out of the viewer's control. There is little opportunity to dwell on a point in television advertising. In contrast, the print media and magazines in particular allow the reader to set the pace.[31] There is more opportunity for making connections and dwelling on points of interest in advertising. The result is that the print media allow for a more traditional learning environment in which information can be absorbed and integrated. The print message is more likely to lead to a change in attitude and in behavior. Radio falls between TV and magazines since some involvement is required to visualize the advertising message, but not to the degree required by print.

Krugman equates the environment for television as the equivalent of **random or "unanchored" learning**. Advertising messages are retained without a process of perception and comprehension. On this basis, television may be a more effective medium for quick messages designed to maintain familiarity with the brand and reinforce positive experiences. Magazines may be more effective in providing information on product attributes and persuading consumers when brand alternatives must be carefully compared.

Other Environmental Characteristics

There are other environmental factors that distinguish media categories. Television is a good medium for products that require a physical demonstration or action (automobiles, children's toys). Radio is an effective medium for products requiring sound — records, theater productions, political candidates. Magazines are important as sources of information on product attributes because of the ability to present messages in print. Newspapers are a particularly effective source of information on sales and local merchandise. Newspapers permit consumers to preshop and can be carried around as sources of shopping information. Product samples are another type of medium that marketers can use to communicate. In this case, the message is direct product experience rather than the symbolism and imagery provided in advertising. Product samples are particularly useful in the introduction of a new product since they provide immediate experience in an attempt to encourage further trial.

CONSUMER INFORMATION SEARCH

The most important component of the communications model in Figure 19–1 is the consumer. Of central concern to advertisers is how consumers *process* information, that is, perceive, interpret, and act on the multiple messages received from friends and the mass media. But consumers are not passive receivers of information. More often than not, they actively seek information on brand alternatives. Therefore there are two components to keep in mind considering the consumer's role in communications: first, *the active search for information,* and second, *the processing of information.*

These two components are summarized in Figure 19–4. The amount of search for information for a given product is contingent on the nature of the product (high risk or high price will generate more search), the situation (an involving situation will generate more search), the consumer's past experience and characteristics (less experience will generate more search), brand attitudes (weakly held attitudes will generate more search), and group influences (products important to the group will result in more search). The search process will provide information from several sources which is then decoded. In the process of perceiving and interpreting various messages, consumers will employ different processing strategies; for example, processing by brand (compare individual brands across various attributes), or processing by attributes (examine an individual attribute such as gas mileage across brands). One of the key questions in processing multiple messages is the degree of information load, that is the amount of information that consumers can reasonably handle. Given a process of decoding multiple messages, consumers are then in a position to evaluate brand alternatives and make a purchase decision.

This section will consider the process of information search. The next section will review consumer information processing.

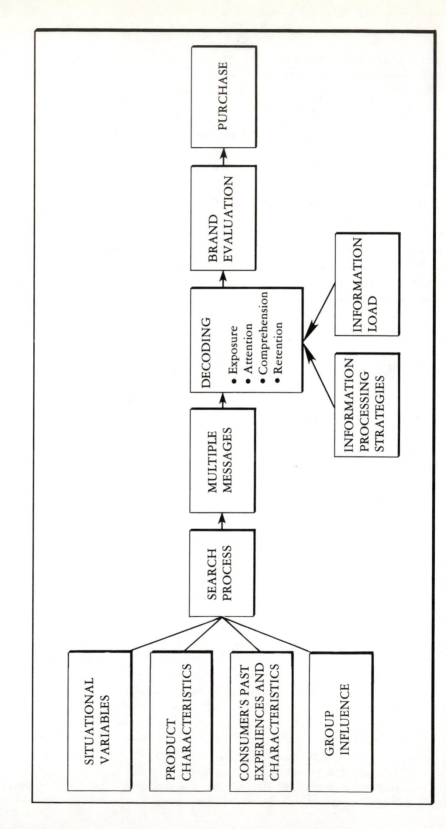

FIGURE 19–4 Consumer Search and Information Processing

Amount of Information

Consumers do not engage in extensive information search unless they think it is necessary. A principle of parsimony seems to exist in information search. Consumers weigh the time and cost of searching for information against the benefits gained by additional information. They thus pick and choose information sources.

The limited nature of consumer search is illustrated by an experiment by Jacoby and his colleagues.[32] They presented consumers with information in a matrix of sixteen brands by thirty-five product characteristics (560 pieces of information in all). On average, consumers selected eleven pieces of information or less than 2 percent of the information available prior to making a decision. Furthermore, information acquisition was centered on only six of the thirty-five informational dimensions.

Other studies have focused on different aspects of information search. Table 19–2 summarizes the results of five studies by the number of retail stores visited.[33] Most purchasers of toys and small appliances visit only one store. Purchasers of refrigerators and furniture are more likely to visit three or more stores. Interestingly, half the purchasers of cars and major appliances visited only one showroom. The amount of shopping for these products is not as great as one might expect based on the risks involved.

Studies have also considered the number of alternative brands. One study[34] found that the proportion of consumers considering more than one brand was

- 59 percent for refrigerators
- 53 percent for cars and household appliances[35]
- 39 percent for washing machines
- 35 percent for electric irons
- 29 percent for vacuum cleaners

TABLE 19–2   Number of Stores Visited for Five Product Categories

Product	Percentage of Purchases by Number of Stores Visited		
	One Store	Two Stores	Three or More Stores
Toys	87.4	6.1	6.5
Small electrical appliances	60.0	16.0	22.0
Refrigerators	42.0	16.0	42.0
Living room furniture	22.0	13.4	62.1
New cars and major appliances	49.0	26.0	23.0

Source: Compiled from five studies by David L. Loudon and Albert J. Della Bitta, *Consumer Behavior* (New York: McGraw-Hill, Inc., 1979), p. 463.
Reprinted with permission from McGraw-Hill, Inc.

These figures suggest that the number of brands considered is typically small. Although the evidence points to limited information search, this does not mean the buyer is ill informed. A prospective consumer may be going into the decision-making process with a large amount of past experience and purchase information. Therefore, the necessity for extensive information search may be low.

Determinants of Information Search

What factors determine the extent of information search? Studies have found the following factors to be related to the extent of the search:

1. *Price.* The higher the price, the greater the amount of information search. This was found to be true for women's apparel,[36] appliances, and cars.[37]

2. *Perceived Differences in Alternatives.* Claxton et al. found that furniture and appliance buyers who saw significant differences between brands visited more stores.[38]

3. *Product Importance.* Jacoby et al. found that the more important the product to the consumer, the greater the amount of information acquired.[39]

4. *Perceived Risk.* The higher the perceived risk in purchasing, the greater the amount of information search. Locander and Herman found that when risk was high, information search from neutral sources such as *Consumer Reports* and from personal sources such as friends and neighbors was greater. The lower the risk, the greater the likelihood the consumer would buy with a minimum of information search.[40]

5. *Past Experience.* Several studies suggest that as consumers learn from past experience, information search decreases. Bennett and Mandell found that past experience with a product reduces the need for information only as long as the consumer is satisfied with the product.[41] Negative experiences with products may increase the need for information search. This means that brand loyalty based on past reinforcement will reduce information search.

6. *Situational Factors.* Certain situational factors may influence the amount of search. For example, Newman and Staelin found that an immediate need reduces information seeking.[42] Lack of product availability may force an extension of information search.

Since durable goods tend to be higher price, higher risk items, they are likely to require more information search. The advertiser that can assist this search by providing catalogues, brochures, and informational advertising may gain a competitive advantage. For example, manufacturers of furniture may be well advised to provide consumers with more information on product characteristics, possibly within the context of two-sided messages stating a competitor's claim and demonstrating the advantages of the advertiser's product.

Advertisers of consumer packaged goods do not have the same need to provide information because of lower product importance and risk. Therefore, much of the advertising for cosmetics, toiletries, and food products relies on imagery rather than hard information. Yet, if a consumer packaged goods advertiser can demonstrate a difference in attributes to consumers, such a difference may encourage information search. A producer of toiletries introducing a dry-spray deodorant has communicated a new feature. Consumers may begin to compare products on the criterion of dry to wet. This process of comparison will require greater information search.

Costs of Information Search

There are monetary and nonmonetary costs associated with the process of information search. Information search frequently involves traveling to various retail stores. The higher cost of gasoline increases the monetary cost of search and may inhibit the acquisition of additional information.

Another cost of search is the time involved in traveling, shopping in alternative retail outlets, reading advertisements, asking the advice of friends, etc. Search time must be weighed against alternatives such as leisure or making money. One study concluded that "today's shopper must weigh the opportunity cost involved in expending time for prolonged search against the probable benefits to be derived from it."[43]

A third cost is psychological. The search process may not be desirable to the individual whose time is valuable. Information may not be available or the source of information may not be apparent. Further, the process of information search may be complex, as when a buyer is comparing stereo components without knowing what criteria to use to evaluate quality. Consumers who see the purchase as risky and who are not confident in the criteria for choice are particularly likely to see psychological costs in the search process.

The consumer will weigh the costs of search against the benefits of additional information. When the consumer finds the monetary, psychological, or time costs too great compared to the information to be gained, then search will be restricted.

The Information Seeker

Do certain consumers ordinarily seek more information than others? The evidence suggests that an *information seeker* can be identified based on demographic and life-style criteria. Thorelli et al. equated information seeking with readership of *Consumer Reports*.[44] They found that the subscriber to *Consumer Reports* is richer, better educated, a more careful planner, and more likely to be an opinion leader. Subscribers are more active in seeking information from print sources but watch less TV. The conclusion is that the information seeker is a person with money, the communications skills and the motivation to use objective product information. McEwen found essentially the same profile of consumers who use toll-free telephone services to obtain information on products and product performance.[45]

Most of these studies, however, have sought the existence of a generalized information seeker without examining the question of whether information seeking is product specific. Studies that have examined information seeking by product category have found results similar to the Thorelli and McEwen studies: Upscale consumers are more likely to search for information. Claxton et al. studied information search for appliances and furniture.[46] They classified consumers into thorough and nonthorough searchers. The nonthorough searchers tended to be in the lower income, less educated group.

The profile of the information seeker indicates that information-seeking behavior may be a function of knowing what to look for and where to look for it. As the Thorelli study indicates, the information seeker has the money and is communications oriented. Those with a higher income and better education probably know of a wider range of alternatives and are more confident of the criteria to use in evaluating brand alternatives for high-priced items. If this is the case, then a government-sponsored informational program may be required to educate and inform lower income, disadvantaged consumers about (1) product and price alternatives, (2) criteria in comparing brands, and (3) product availability in specific store locations.

CONSUMER INFORMATION PROCESSING

Figure 19–4 depicted information processing as a process of decoding representing a sequence of steps from exposure to attention to comprehension and retention. But this sequence only describes the processing of a single message. Central to the concept of information processing is a strategy for processing multiple messages, integrating this information, and using it in evaluating brands.

Information Processing Strategies

The nature by which consumers process information depends on (1) the amount of information search, (2) the sequence by which multiple information is processed, and (3) the decision rule the consumer uses for processing the information and evaluating brands. The amount of information search was considered in the previous section. Attention here will focus on the sequence of processing information and decision rules used.

Sequence of Information Processing

In a study of information acquisition for cold cereals, Jacoby et al. identified four strategies of information acquisition: (1) rely on the brand name only (no sequence of information); (2) process by brand (consider all the characteristics of one brand, then move to the next brand, etc.); (3) process by attribute (compare all brands on one attribute, then compare all brands on another attribute, etc.); and (4) a combination of the above.[47] About the same number of consumers used a brand sequence and an attribute sequence processing strategy. Reliance on brand name alone was rare. Jacoby and his colleagues found that those who did not engage in extensive information search used an attribute processing strategy, whereas those who were heavier information users utilized a brand processing approach.

Other studies have found that consumers tend to process by attribute rather than by brand.[48] Furthermore, in processing by attribute, subjects had difficulty in considering more than two attributes at a time. That is, both the gas mileage and price may be evaluated simultaneously for the Dasher, Toyota, etc. But if the consumer adds front-wheel drive or cost of parts, then the trade-offs between the characteristics of the cars become difficult to evaluate.

If consumers find it easier to process information by attribute rather than brand, this will have important implications for comparative advertising and in-store displays. The prevalent approach is to cite one competitive brand and then cite the various advantages of the advertiser's brand. But a potentially more effective approach would be to cite one or two attributes, and then compare the advertiser's brand to others on these attributes.

The effectiveness of processing by attribute rather than brand also has implications for in-store displays. Bettman argues that retailers should present information on brands one attribute at a time in an in-store display board, particularly for nutritional information.[49] Such a display board would provide information on the vitamin content of various breakfast cereals, the price, the calories, etc. Breakfast cereals would then be compared one attribute at a time. Similarly, other products could be compared on such display boards. Bettman's argument for such an approach is that processing all brands one attribute at a time facilitates comparisons by providing relative information. The amount of information to be processed is thereby reduced.

Given the fact that retailers are unlikely to provide such display boards because of a lack of any profit incentive, Bettman argues for a role by the Federal Trade Commission in supplying nutritional information by such in-store displays on an attribute-by-attribute basis.

Decision Rules for Information Processing

The decision rule consumers use determines how information is treated in evaluating alternative brands. This question was reviewed in Chapter 7 under the heading of multiattribute models. Various decision rules were considered. In the compensatory model, information processing is by brand across attributes. In the noncompensatory models (disjunctive, conjunctive, lexicographic), information processing is by attribute across brands. The noncompensatory models therefore recognize that the decision rules used to process information will evaluate brands on an attribute-by-attribute basis.

Information Load

An important consideration in consumer information processing is whether more information is better. The assumption among some consumer advocates and government agencies is that consumers should be supplied with as much information as possible to permit a comparison of brand alternatives. The same assumption underlies economic theory: Optimal choice requires access to information on all alternatives.

However, consumers do not seek to make optimal choices. They are not information processing machines. They carefully weigh the amount of information and rarely utilize all the available information. The cost of search and the complexity of processing are just too great to attempt to consider all brand alternatives. Therefore, more information is not necessarily better. In fact, too much information may create **information overload,** that is, confusion in the decision task resulting in a less effective decision.

Jacoby et al. found that information overload exists.[50] He and his colleagues provided consumers with from eight to seventy-two items of information on alternative laundry detergents. They then related the amount of information to the effectiveness of brand choice. Effectiveness of choice was determined by the degree to which consumers chose brands that were similar to their ideal laundry detergent. The results are summarized in Figure 19–5. Up to twenty-four pieces of information, the "more is better" notion seems to hold. But more than twenty-four pieces of information seem to cause consumers to choose brands that were not similar to their ideal. Too much information complicated the decision task and resulted in a less effective choice.

Other researchers have challenged the reliability of the methodology used in the study,[51] but the idea that at some point too much information may have negative consequences on decision tasks is not challenged. The implication is

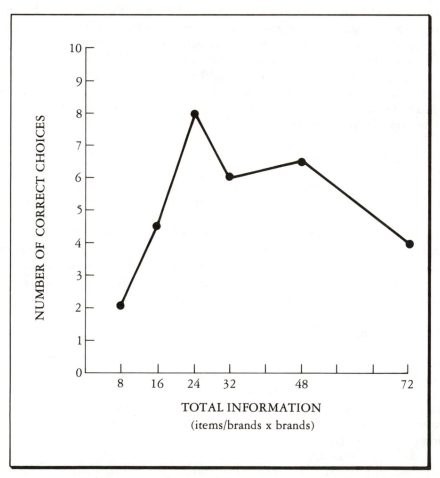

FIGURE 19–5 Relation of Information Load to Effectiveness of Decision Making

Source: Jacob Jacoby, Donald E. Speller, and Carol A. Kohn, "Brand Choice Behavior as a Function of Information Load," *Journal of Marketing Research* 11 (February 1974):66.
Reprinted with permission from the *Journal of Marketing Research*.

that both advertisers and public agencies must be careful not to overload the consumer with information. Aggravating this problem is the sheer magnitude of commercials on the air. (It is estimated that the average consumer is exposed to from 250 to 2,000 print and broadcast advertisements a day.) Therefore, it is not surprising that researchers like Bettman have made proposals to facilitate information processing by offering consumers simpler brand comparisons on an attribute-by-attribute basis.

COMMUNICATIONS FEEDBACK

The final step in the communication process is action and subsequent feedback to the advertiser to evaluate the effectiveness of the marketing communication. As indicated in Figure 19–1, the advertiser can try to establish a direct link between message effectiveness and purchase behavior, or an indirect link by evaluating the impact of the message on information processing. Most of the work in advertising research has been based on indirect feedback; that is, evaluating the effect of the message on exposure, attention, comprehension, and retention. McGuire summarizes the types of feedback provided in each step of the decoding process in Figure 19–6.[52] In addition to the basic steps in decoding, McGuire adds **yielding** to the correctly comprehended message, or what is referred to in the advertising communications model as message acceptance.

Presentation or exposure can be measured by a magazine's circulation or a television program's ratings. Circulation and program reach may measure exposure to the medium, but they do not necessarily measure exposure to a message. An individual may be watching a TV program and step out of the room during a commercial. An individual may read some sections of a magazine and miss the advertisement. Therefore, other techniques may be required to determine exposure to the marketing communication. For example, the Starch service, the oldest measure of print ad exposure, asks consumers whether they noted an advertisement in a magazine. The noted score measures exposure. Subsequent measures attempt to determine attention and comprehension.

Attention can best be measured by recognition of an advertisement. The Starch service also computes a "seen-associated" measure in which consumers are asked to associate the ad with a brand or manufacturer. Such an association provides some assurance that the consumer was attentive to the ad at the time of exposure.

Comprehension is measured primarily by tests of recall of copy points. The Gallup and Robinson readership service asks respondents to recall and describe sales messages of specific ads. In this manner, comprehension of the ad's theme can be evaluated. Checklists can also be used to determine whether respondents remember seeing particular components of an ad. Such checklists would represent aided recall since they provide consumers with a cue as to what was in the ad.

Yielding or message acceptance is best measured by its impact on brand attitudes or purchase intent. For example, attitudes toward the brand can be measured prior to and after message exposure. Comparisons of matched groups

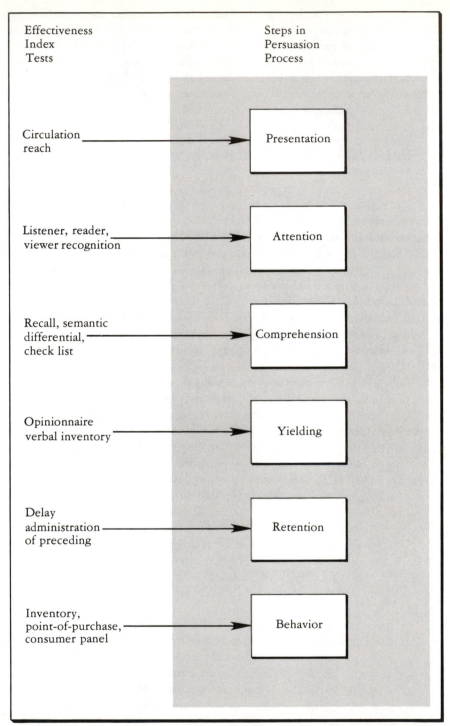

FIGURE 19–6   Methods of Obtaining Feedback in the Decoding Process

Source: Adapted from William J. McGuire, "An Information-Processing Model of Advertising Effectiveness," in H.L. David and A.J. Silk, eds., *Behavioral and Management Sciences in Marketing* (New York: Ronald/Wiley, 1978), p. 161.

Reprinted with permission from J. Wiley & Sons, and William J. McGuire.

of consumers exposed to the message and those not exposed can show the effect of the message on attitude change. Wind and Denny describe such a procedure for testing television commercials on a "before and after" exposure basis.[53] Two matched groups are selected and asked questions about brand attitudes and purchase intent. The test group is asked to watch a particular TV program. The test group is then asked the same brand attitude questions after exposure as well as questions regarding the message. The effectiveness of the commercial is measured based on the degree of positive attitude change and favorable shifts in intention to buy.

Retention is measured by the same type of instruments as comprehension and yielding, but after a period of time. Since marketing communications are likely to "wear-out" over time, the degree of retention is an important determinant of message effectiveness.

The final step, *purchase behavior,* can be measured by pantry checks to determine if a brand is on hand, observation of purchases at the point of sale, or the use of consumer panels that report on purchases on a periodic basis. The problem with these measures is that they cannot be directly linked to message effectiveness. The question remains, to what degree does the marketing communication influence the purchase decision?

The issue of linking the message to purchasing behavior raises the question of direct feedback from sales results. It is extremely difficult to link a particular message with purchasing behavior at the individual consumer level. Advertising effects are cumulative. Further, a wide range of variables impact on consumer behavior. Yet the ultimate criterion of the effectiveness of an advertising campaign must be sales results. The problem remains much as John Wanamaker stated it over a century ago: "I know half my advertising is effective, but I don't know which half."

Mathematical models have been developed to assess the effects of advertising campaigns on sales results at the aggregate sales level rather than the individual purchase level. Such approaches have occasionally used sophisticated designs to vary ad expenditure levels and arrive at an optimal advertising budget based on expected sales results. But the evaluation of marketing communications is largely tied to consumer processing of the message as illustrated in Figure 19–6.

SUMMARY

A detailed communications model is first presented, stipulating the basic communications process (development of an idea to be communicated, encoding of the idea, transmission, decoding, action, and feedback). The model also identifies the marketing agencies carrying out each step in the communications process and potential barriers to effective communication at each stage. The key questions in evaluating the effectiveness of advertising and other marketing communications are:

1. Has the communications idea (generally a product concept) been formulated to reflect consumer needs?
2. Has the product concept been adequately encoded by the advertising agency?

3. Has the message been transmitted to the target segment by utilizing the right media?

4. Was the message decoded by the consumer in the manner intended by the advertiser?

5. Does exposure to and acceptance of the message lead to a purchase?

The remainder of the chapter deals with the primary components of the communications model: the source, the message, media, the receiver (consumer), and feedback. These factors are considered within the framework of consumer information processing and marketing communications.

Source effects focus on the credibility of the source of the message. The greater the credibility of the source, the greater the likelihood the message will be accepted. Reference groups, family, and impartial sources such as *Consumer Reports* and government agencies are regarded as more credible than commercial sources of information. Methods are considered by which marketers could increase their credibility.

The main issue in the effect of the message is whether the communication should be one-sided or two-sided. Research supports the greater effectiveness of two-sided appeals, comparative advertising being an example of such an approach. But one-sided appeals can be effective if the consumer agrees with the advertiser's position and is loyal to the advertiser's brand.

Studies of *media* effects demonstrate the importance of the media environment in affecting a consumer's perception of an ad.

The most important component of the communications model is the *consumer*. Two components are considered in the consumer's evaluation of marketing communications: (1) the search for information, and (2) the processing of the information. Consumers generally limit the extent of information search so as to collect information required for a satisfactory rather than an optimal decision. Otherwise, the costs of information search may be too high. An information seeker — i.e., one who is more likely to seek out product information — is described as an upscale and better educated consumer more aware of price and brand alternatives.

Consumer information processing is described as a sequence of steps from exposure to attention, comprehension, and retention. An important question is consumer strategies for information processing; that is, whether consumers process information by brand across product attributes, or by attribute across brands. Evidence suggests it is easier for consumers to process by attribute rather than by brand.

The chapter concludes by considering certain key issues in *feedback,* namely, the measurement of indirect feedback through consumer thought variables, and the desirability yet difficulty of evaluating advertising based on direct consumer purchase response.

The next chapter will consider another key component of the marketing plan influencing consumer behavior — the store.

1. Assume that state and local agencies in California wish to undertake an educational campaign to alert the public to the dangers of earthquakes. They use several ads to show the devastation that earthquakes can produce to try to convince the public of the importance of the educational campaign.
   - What factors are likely to encourage and discourage the acceptance of the message?

2. Assume that Exxon initiates a campaign to convince the public that rising gas prices are justified as a means of encouraging increases in domestic exploration for oil, and that, as a result, the windfall profits tax on oil is unjustified.
   - What principles could Exxon use to increase its credibility based on the principles stated in the text?

3. Would a comparative advertising campaign be likely to be effective for:
   - MCA relative to RCA in introducing its new video-disc system?
   - Anacin relative to Tylenol in advertising pain-killing benefits and relief for arthritis sufferers?
   - *Newsweek* relative to *Time* magazine?

4. Consider the following situations:
   a. A husband and wife have tentatively decided to buy a certain type of carpeting from a local carpet retailer. They consider visiting several department stores to compare prices and quality.

   b. A high school student considers the desirability of adding a fourth and fifth school to the list of colleges to be applied to.

   c. An individual considers investigating the credentials of various specialists to obtain a second opinion on a health problem.
   - What factors would influence the consumer's assessment of the cost of information search, particularly the psychological costs and the costs in time and effort, in each of the above cases?
   - At what point is further search for information likely to cease in each of the above cases?

5. Is there a general information seeker or is information seeking product-specific?
   - Is the information seeker the same as the (a) gatekeeper, (b) opinion leader, and (c) innovator?

6. Is there a more cognitively complex consumer? That is, is there a consumer who (1) tends to use more attributes in evaluating brands; (2) is more tolerant of complex and contradictory information; and (3) generally uses more complex decision rules in information processing?
   - If so, develop some hypotheses as to the characteristics of such a consumer.
   - What are the marketing implications of the existence of a cognitively complex consumer?

7. What are the implications for in-store promotional displays and advertising if consumers tend to process information (a) by brand across attributes and (b) by

attributes across brands?

8. Develop a proposal for the FTC to facilitate in-store processing by encouraging the presentation of brand information by attribute.

9. Given the difficulties in evaluating the effects of an advertising message on a consumer's purchase decision, advertisers have used consumer attitudes, perceptions, and intentions as criteria of effectiveness.

- What are some of the limitations of using attitudes, perceptions, and purchase intent as criteria of advertising effectiveness?

- Under what conditions is it possible to provide advertisers with more direct feedback of advertising effectiveness to establish the link between the advertising message and consumer behavior?

RESEARCH ASSIGNMENTS

1. Select two product categories, a high and a low involvement category. Evaluate the processing of information for a particular brand in each category by interviewing in depth four or five users or owners of the product. Use Figures 19–1, 19–4, and 19–6 as aids in determining the nature of information processing. In so doing, be sure to determine the following:

1. sources of the message (including friends and relatives)
2. evaluation of the source's credibility
3. awareness and comprehension of the message
4. attitudes toward the brand or product
5. possible consumer action

- Does the processing of information you have identified conform to the models in Figures 19–1 and 19–4?

- Are there differences in information processing between the high and low involvement category (i.e., differences in source, message, brand evaluation, etc.)?

- Are there differences in source, message, or brand evaluation between different types of consumers?

- What are the implications of your findings for evaluating (a) the source, (b) message effects on brand image, and (c) message effects on consumer action?

2. Develop an information board for automobiles and another information board for cereals. Such an information board will require listing a number of brands or models across the top and their attributes down the side. Include at least four brands across the top and eight attributes down the side. Show the boards to about ten consumers for each brand. Ask consumers to describe out loud their process of evaluating the brands on each board. At the end of the process of evaluation, ask consumers to fill out a short questionnaire to determine (a) demographics, (b) selected life-style items, (c) brand or model used, and (d) frequency of usage or number of miles driven in a year.

- What are the differences in evaluation between the cereals and the autos? The material in Chapters 7 and 19 suggests that consumers are more likely to evaluate cars by brand and cereals by attribute. Is this true?

- Are there differences in evaluation between consumers? That is, are certain consumers more likely to evaluate by brand and others by attribute? If so, are there differences in the characteristics of brand evaluators versus attribute evaluators?

NOTES

1. Jerry C. Olson and Philip A. Dover, "Cognitive Effects of Deceptive Advertising," *Journal of Marketing Research* 15 (February 1978): 29–38.
2. *Broadcasting Yearbook,* 1971.
3. Peter H. Webb, "Perceptual Discrepancies in the Time Duration and Number of Television Commercials," in William L. Wilkie, ed., *Advances in Consumer Research,* vol. 6, (Ann Arbor, Mich.: Association for Consumer Research, 1978), pp. 85–89.
4. Thomas S. Robertson, *Innovative Behavior and Communications,* (New York: Holt, Rinehart and Winston, Inc., 1971).
5. Joseph W. Newman and Richard Staelin, "Information Sources of Durable Goods," *Journal of Advertising Research* 13 (April 1973): 19–29.
6. See W. Watts and William McGuire, "Persistence of Induced Opinion Change and Retention of the Inducing Message Contents," *Journal of Abnormal and Social Psychology* 68 (1964): 233–241; and G. Miller and J. Basehart, "Source Trustworthiness, Opinionated Statements and Response to Persuasive Communication," *Speech Monographs* 36 (1969): 1–7.
7. C. Samuel Craig and John M. McCann, "Assessing Communication Effects on Energy Conservation," *Journal of Consumer Research* 5 (September 1978): 82–88.
8. Ibid., p. 87.
9. Richard W. Mizerski, James M. Hunt, and Charles H. Patti, "The Effects of Advertising Credibility on Consumer Reactions to an Advertisement," in Subhash C. Jain, ed., *Proceedings of the American Marketing Association Educators' Conference,* Series #43 (1978), pp. 164–168.
10. Ruby Roy Dholakia and Brian Sternthal, "Highly Credible Sources: Persuasive Facilitators or Persuasive Liabilities?" *Journal of Consumer Research* 3 (March 1977): 223–232.
11. A. Eagly and S. Chaiken, "An Attribution Analysis of the Effect of Communicator Characteristics on Opinion Change: the Case of Communicator Attractiveness," *Journal of Personality and Social Psychology* 32 (1975): 136–144.
12. H. Sigall and R. Helmreich, "Opinion Change as a Function of Stress and Communicator Credibility," *Journal of Experimental Social Psychology* 5 (1969): 70–78.
13. Robert B. Settle and Linda L. Golden, "Attribution Theory and Advertiser Credibility," *Journal of Marketing Research* 11 (May 1974): 181–185.
14. Timothy C. Brock, "Communicator-Recipient Similarity and Decision Change," *Journal of Personality and Social Psychology* 1 (June 1965): 650–654; and Arch G. Woodside and J. William Davenport, Jr. "The Effect of Salesman Similarity and Expertise on Consumer Purchasing Behavior," *Journal of Marketing Research* 11 (May 1974): 198–202.
15. Woodside and Davenport, "The Effect of Salesman Similarity;" and Paul Busch and David T. Wilson, "An Experimental Analysis of a Salesman's Expert and Referent Bases of Social Power in the Buyer-Seller Dyad," *Journal of Marketing Research* 13 (February 1976): 3–11.
16. George J. Szybillo and Richard Heslin, "Resistance to Persuasion: Inoculation Theory in a Marketing Context," *Journal of Marketing Research* 10 (November 1973): 396–403.
17. Alan G. Sawyer, "The Effects of Repetition of Refutational and Supportive Advertising Appeals," *Journal of Marketing Research* 10 (February 1973): 23–33.
18. Carl I. Hovland, Arthur A. Lumsdaine, and Fred D. Sheffield, *Experiments on Mass Communication* (New York: John Wiley, 1949), pp. 182–200; and W.E.J. Faison, "Effectiveness of One-Sided and Two-Sided Mass Communications in Advertising," *Public Opinion Quarterly* 25 (1961): 468–469.
19. William L. Wilkie and Paul W. Farris, "Comparison Advertising: Problems and Potential," *Journal of Marketing* 39 (October 1975): 7–15.
20. "The Effects of Comparative Television Advertising That Names Competing Brands," Ogilvy & Mather Research, New York (Private Report.)
21. V. Kanti Prasad, "Communications-Effectiveness of Comparative Advertising: A Laboratory Analysis," *Journal of Marketing Research* 13 (May 1976): 128–137.
22. Sawyer, "The Effects of Repetition."
23. John R. Stuteville, "Psychic Defenses Against High Fear Appeals: A Key Marketing Variable," *Journal of Marketing* 34 (April 1970): pp. 39–45.
24. Gerald R. Miller and M.A. Hewgill, "Some Recent Research on Fear Arousing Message Appeals," *Speech Monographs* 33 (1966): 377–391.
25. Michael Ray and William L. Wilkie, "Fear: The Potential of an Appeal Neglected by Marketing," *Journal of Marketing* 34 (January 1970): 54–62.
26. John J. Wheatley, "Marketing and the Use of Fear-Anxiety Appeals," *Journal of Marketing* 35

508

(April 1971): 62–64.

27. Brian Sternthal and C. Samuel Craig, "Humor in Advertising," *Journal of Marketing* 37 (October 1973): 12–18.

28. Marshall McLuhan, *The Medium Is the Message,* (New York: Random House, 1967).

29. David A. Aaker and Phillip K. Brown, "Evaluating Vehicle Source Effects," *Journal of Advertising Research* 12 (August 1972): 11–16.

30. Herbert E. Krugman, "The Impact of Television Advertising: Learning Without Involvement," *Public Opinion Quarterly* 29 (Autumn 1969): 349–356.

31. Herbert E. Krugman, "The Measurement of Advertising Involvement," *Public Opinion Quarterly* 30 (Winter 1966-67): 583–596.

32. Jacob Jacoby, Robert W. Chestnut, Karl C. Weigl and William Fisher, "Pre-Purchase Information Acquisition," in Beverlee B. Anderson, ed., *Advances in Consumer Research,* vol. 3 (Atlanta: Association for Consumer Research, 1975), pp. 306–314.

33. Compiled from five studies by David L. Loudon and Albert J. Della Bitta, *Consumer Behavior* (New York, McGraw-Hill Inc. 1979), p. 463.

34. W.P. Dommermuth, "The Shopping Matrix and Marketing Strategy," *Journal of Marketing Research* 2 (May 1965): 128–132.

35. Joseph W. Newman and Richard Staelin, "Prepurchase Information Seeking for New Cars and Major Household Appliances," *Journal of Marketing Research,* 9 (August 1972): 249–257.

36. W.P. Dommermuth and E.W. Cundiff, "Shopping Goods, Shopping Centers and Selling Strategies," *Journal of Marketing,* 31 (October 1967): 32–36.

37. Newman and Staelin, "Prepurchase Information Seeking."

38. John D. Claxton, Joseph N. Fry, and Bernard Portis, "A Taxonomy of Prepurchase Information Gathering Patterns," *Journal of Consumer Research* 1 (December 1974): 35–42.

39. Jacob Jacoby, Robert W. Chestnut, and William A. Fisher, "A Behavioral Process Approach to Information Acquisition in Nondurable Purchasing," *Journal of Marketing Research* 15 (November 1978): 532–544.

40. William B. Locander and Peter W. Hermann,

"The Effect of Self-Confidence and Anxiety on Information Seeking in Consumer Risk Reduction," *Journal of Marketing Research* 16 (May 1979): 268–274.

41. Peter D. Bennett and Robert M. Mandel, "Prepurchase Information Seeking Behavior of New Car Purchasers — The Learning Hypothesis," *Journal of Marketing Research* 6 (November 1969): 430–433.

42. Newman and Staelin, "Prepurchase Information Seeking."

43. Dommermuth and Cundiff, "Shopping Goods," p. 32.

44. Hans B. Thorelli, Helmut Becker, and Jack Engledow, *The Information Seekers* (Cambridge, Mass.: Ballinger Publishing Co., 1975).

45. William J. McEwen, "Bridging the Information Gap," *Journal of Consumer Research* 4 (March 1978): 247–251.

46. Claxton, Fry, and Portis, "A Taxonomy."

47. Jacoby, Chestnut, and Fisher, "A Behavioral Process Approach."

48. J. Edward Russo and Barbara A. Dosher, "Dimensional Evaluation: A Heuristic for Binary Choice," working paper, University of California, San Diego (1975).

49. James R. Bettman, "Issues in Designing Consumer Information Environments," *Journal of Consumer Research* 2 (December 1975): 169–177.

50. Jacob Jacoby, Donald E. Speller, and Carol A. Kohn, "Brand Choice Behavior as a Function of Information Load," *Journal of Marketing Research* 11 (February 1974): 63–69.

51. William L. Wilkie, "Analysis of Effects of Information Load," *Journal of Marketing Research* 11 (November 1974): 462–466; and John O. Summers, "Less Information is Better?" *Journal of Marketing Research* 11 (November 1974): 467–468.

52. William J. McGuire, "An Information-Processing Model of Advertising Effectiveness," in H.L. David and A.J. Silk, eds., *Behavioral and Management Sciences in Marketing* (New York: Ronald/Wiley, 1978), pp. 156–180.

53. Yoram Wind and Joseph Denny, "Multivariate Analysis of Variance in Research on the Effectiveness of TV Commercials," *Journal of Marketing Research* 11 (May 1974): 136–142.

TWENTY

Store Choice and Shopping Behavior

Focus of Chapter

Up to this point, the focus of the book has been on brand choice and product choice. Consumer behavior also involves *store choice.* In fact, the choice of a store may be more important to the consumer than the choice of a brand, and may involve a more complex set of decision criteria.

The distinction between brand and store choice also requires that there be a distinction between buying behavior and shopping behavior. Consumers frequently shop from store to store for a variety of products, and the motives for shopping may be quite distinct from the motives for buying a particular product. Consumers may shop because of a desire to search for bargains or seek social interaction with sales personnel. Neither of these reasons would be directly related to brand or product choice.

The emphasis on store influences on consumer behavior also requires a shift from a focus on out-of-store marketing commu-

nications (advertising) to in-store marketing communications (package, display, coupons, price, salespersons). The manager's relative emphasis on out-of-store and in-store stimuli determines the approach to the consumer. Heavier emphasis on advertising is an attempt to create demand prior to entering the store. Advertising is especially important if the consumer plans the purchase beforehand. Emphasis on displays, price promotions, and personal selling influences demand within the store environment.

The differing focus of this chapter therefore requires an orientation toward shopping behavior rather than purchasing behavior, in-store stimuli rather than advertising, and store choice rather than brand choice. On this basis, the chapter is organized to discuss (1) shopping behavior, (2) in-store purchasing behavior, and (3) store choice behavior.

SHOPPING BEHAVIOR

Although related to the process of store choice, shopping behavior is a distinctive form of consumer behavior. Two consumers may shop at the same set of stores for reasons of convenience, courteous sales help, or good decor, but one consumer's orientation to shopping can be totally different from the other's. The first consumer may find shopping a burden, something to be done quickly with a minimum of effort. The second may enjoy shopping, particularly the satisfaction of buying a desired item at a bargain price. This consumer does not mind spending time searching for alternatives.

Importance of Shopping Behavior

The frequency of search in alternative stores is demonstrated by a study that found 51 percent of large appliance purchasers visited more than one store.[1] Moreover, for those consumers who tended to seek more information on an appliance outside the store, 70 percent visited more than one store. In addition to visiting several stores, consumers frequently make more than one shopping trip to the same store, further increasing the incidence of shopping behavior.[2]

Shopping frequency is likely to increase with inflation and reductions in discretionary income. The greater emphasis on consumer protection and greater awareness of differences in quality between products will also increase the frequency of comparison shopping.

Why Do People Shop?

The previous section suggested the existence of an "apathetic" shopper and an "economy" shopper. Such different orientations to shopping led Tauber to make the distinction between "Why do people shop where they do" (store selection) and "Why do people shop" (shopper behavior).[3] Tauber studied different motives for shopping through a series of individual depth interviews. Based on this exploratory research, he found a number of shopping motives such as the following:

- *Diversion* from the routine of daily life
- *Self gratification* based on the expected utility of the buying process itself
- *Learning about new trends* when visiting the store
- *Physical activity* since an urban environment provides little opportunity to exercise
- *Sensory stimulation* such as handling merchandise, trying it on or trying it out
- *Social experiences outside the home* such as encounters with friends or salespersons
- *Pleasure of bargaining* as a means to make a wise purchase

Shopper Profiles

Classifications such as Tauber's have led some researchers to profile consumers by their orientation to shopping, and then determine the characteristics of these shopper types. One of the earliest and most widely used typologies was developed by Stone based on interviews with 150 women in Chicago.[4] Stone identified four types of shoppers:

- *The economic consumer* (33 percent of the women) regards shopping as buying and is oriented to shopping efficiency. The store is judged by objective standards such as price, quality, and the assortment of merchandise, rather than by store personalization or convenience. The economic shopper is likely to be socially mobile with a high aspiration level.
- *The personalizing consumer* (28 percent) lacks the opportunity for social contact and forms strong personal attachments with store employees as a substitute. Stores that are more intimate are preferred.
- *The ethical consumer* (18 percent) is motivated by normative criteria of what should be done to help out local store merchants, particularly the "little guy."
- *The apathetic consumer* (17 percent) does not like to shop and finds little satisfaction in establishing personal relations with store personnel. Convenience is paramount to minimize the time and trouble of shopping.

Stone found that the higher socioeconomic groups are more likely to be in the ethical segment, the lower socioeconomic groups in the apathetic segment. New residents who are more socially isolated are more likely to be personalizing consumers.

Darden and Reynolds tested Stone's typology in a small Southeastern community.[5] Consumption patterns conformed to Stone's typology. For example, the economic shoppers demonstrate their emphasis on social mobility by buying products with high social visibility (face makeup, hand cream, etc.). The personalizing shoppers demonstrate their social isolation by being less likely to buy socially visible products. A later study by Darden and Ashton expanded Stone's typology to seven groups so as to focus on shopping in supermarkets. Groups such as stamp preferers, stamp haters, and convenient location shoppers were described.[6]

Shopper profiles like Stone's are useful in helping retail managers position their store and appeal to different segments of the market. A price appeal to the economy shopper should be coupled with emphasis on quality and product assortment. A retail store can emphasize friendly sales personnel to the personalizing consumer, with less concern for price and assortment. Appeals to convenience and shopping speed can be directed toward the apathetic shopper. Groups of local small businessmen can effectively appeal to the ethical shopper.

Moschis provides another strategic dimension to shopper profiles by relating shopping orientation to effectiveness of marketing communications.[7] He defines six types of shoppers based on the purchase of cosmetic products:

- special sales shoppers;
- brand loyal;
- store loyal;
- problem solving (find it hard to decide on cosmetic products);
- socializing (buy cosmetics that friends use); and
- name conscious (judge cosmetics by store that sells them).

Advertising is used as a source of information about cosmetics mainly by the brand loyal and name conscious shopper. Socializing shoppers rely on friends or neighbors for information. Problem solvers spend the most time watching TV. Special sales shoppers rely on free samples more than others, and have more of a need for objective price and product information.

A communications profile of shopper types provides retail management with guidelines for determining the types of information demanded by these segments and for reaching them. The special sales consumer should be given price and other information on alternative products, and can best be reached by home-oriented magazines. The name conscious consumer can best be reached by fashion magazines and should be told the brand alternatives that are carried by various stores.

Planned Versus Unplanned Shopping Behavior

The fact that shopping behavior satisfies certain needs independent of purchasing behavior also suggests that certain shopping trips may be unplanned —a spur of the moment decision to enter a record store or an apparel shop and browse around. Tauber believes the likelihood of shopping on impulse has increased because of less time spent at home, more leisure time, greater mobility, and increases in discretionary income.[8]

However, Tauber was writing in 1972, before consumers became conscious of energy shortages. If, as is likely, energy conservation will be necessary through the rest of this century, more shopping trips will probably be planned. The number of shopping trips is also likely to decrease to conserve fuel, leading to a greater use of in-home shopping by telephone or catalogue.

Impulse shopping is likely to decrease, but not necessarily impulse buying. That is to say, a shopping trip may be planned, but certain items bought on the trip may be unplanned. Therefore, it is necessary to distinguish planned and unplanned *shopping behavior* from planned and unplanned *purchasing behavior*.

IN-STORE PURCHASING BEHAVIOR

Many purchase decisions are not preplanned, but are made within the store. As a result, the influence of in-store stimuli such as displays, shelf position, packaging, and price become more important in the purchase decision. If the decision is unplanned, in-store stimuli become more important. This does not mean that advertising and in-store stimuli are separate. Advertising can reinforce in-store stimuli by reminding consumers of product benefits once they see the product on the shelf. Conversely, displays and good shelf position are a necessity if advertising is to be effective. However, relative emphasis on each is important. It determines whether the marketer is emphasizing a *pull* or a *push* strategy. Advertising "pulls" the products from the store by creating demand beforehand; in-store stimuli "push" the product through the store by influencing the consumer at the point of sale.

The model of complex decision making in Chapter 2 assumed that a preplanning process tended to place more emphasis on the pull or advertising aspects of marketing strategy. But preplanning does not occur for many purchase decisions, particularly for food items. Therefore, in certain cases, the push or in-store stimuli require greater emphasis.

Unplanned purchasing behavior conforms more closely to the model of low involvement purchasing behavior than the model of complex decision making. Utilizing the low involvement framework, there would be two basic reasons for an unplanned purchase. One, the time and effort involved in searching alternatives outside the store is not worth it, resulting in the consumer buying largely on a reminder basis. Or two, the consumer seeks variety or novelty and buys on impulse.

The Nature of Unplanned Purchasing

Unplanned purchasing is not necessarily impulse buying, the latter denoting a tendency to buy on whim, with little thought given to it. For example, a parent may be reminded that there is no breakfast cereal in the house by seeing the product on the supermarket shelf. The decision to buy is made in the store. The parent decides to examine nutritional information on various packages and carefully selects a cereal judged to be most nutritious. This is an unplanned purchase, not an impulse purchase. The package, not the advertising, becomes the primary means of communicating the product's benefits. In-store stimuli outweigh the influence of out-of-store communications in this decision.

Stern suggests four different types of unplanned purchases:

- *Pure impulse* for variety or novelty. This type of behavior represents a departure from the normal set of products or brands purchased.
- *Reminder effect* because the item is needed, but was not included in shopping intentions prior to entering the store. The trigger is seeing the product on the shelf or on display.
- *Suggestion effect* for a new product based on in-store stimuli. For example, the consumer is not previously aware of a nondetergent laundry product. Seeing it on the shelf or in a counter display generates a purchase because the product is related to the consumer's needs.
- *Planned impulse* refers to a consumer's intention to buy on the basis of price specials or coupons for an unanticipated item once in the store. Buying on special sale or by coupon is planned, but the purchase of the item itself is not.[9]

The Importance and Scope of Unplanned Purchases

The importance of unplanned purchases is documented by several studies. DuPont conducted a study of consumer purchasing of toiletries, health-care, and pharmaceutical products in supermarkets.[10] Decisions made before entering the store (specifically planned) were identified in addition to three types of in-store decisions: generally planned, substitute (consumer substitutes another brand for the intended brand in the store), and unplanned purchases. Of all health care and beauty aid items, 72 percent are in-store decisions and 61 percent are unplanned. Among pharmaceuticals and vitamins, 57 percent are in-store decisions and 51 percent are unplanned decisions. Kollat and Willett found that over one-half of the food items purchased in supermarkets are unplanned.[11]

Even purchases outside of supermarkets are frequently unplanned. Prasad found that 39 percent of department store shoppers and 62 percent of discount store shoppers purchased at least one item on an unplanned basis.[12]

Kollat and Willett attempted to relate consumer demographic and purchasing characteristics to the likelihood of buying on an unplanned basis.[13] In each case, they offered two explanations for unplanned purchases: one, the shopper is exposed to in-store stimuli (the reminder or suggestion effect), and two, the shopper is unwilling to spend the time and effort to itemize purchase plans (lack of customer commitment).

The study found that unplanned purchases increase the longer one is married. This could be because as children grow, the quality and variety of food increases making preplanning more time consuming. Unplanned purchases also increase with the number of different products purchased. This could be due to the fact that the greater the number of products purchased, the greater the exposure to in-store stimuli. The alternative explanation is that the more products purchased, the more difficult and time consuming it is to itemize purchases. Unplanned purchases were also found to be more likely on major shopping trips rather than "fill-in" trips. On major trips, shoppers' needs are not as well-defined as they are on fill-in trips. As a result, the shopper is more receptive to in-store stimuli. Also, major trips involve more time and effort. Therefore, there may be less willingness to itemize and preplan. In each of the above cases, unplanned purchases could be explained either by exposure to in-store stimuli or by lack of consumer commitment to a brand.

In-Store Stimuli

The consistent finding in studies of unplanned purchases is that in-store exposure to marketing stimuli are the most influential factors in the purchase decision. The in-store stimuli include:

- displays
- shelf position (eye level is best)
- shelf space (manufacturers vie for the greatest amount of room on the shelf)
- information on the package (size, content, price)
- the nature and attractiveness of the package
- in-store pricing promotions

The frequency of unplanned purchases means that in-store stimuli deserve as much attention as advertising, especially for consumer packaged goods distributed in supermarkets. Store layout, shelf allocations to products, and positioning of displays are all within the control of the retailer and directly influence the in-store environment. Price level is also influenced by the retailer. The main influence of the manufacturer on in-store stimuli is through package development, general price level, and allocation of funds to in-store displays and promotions.

STORE CHOICE BEHAVIOR

The decision processes described in Chapters 2–4 apply to stores as well as brands. In some cases, consumers go through a process of complex decision making in selecting stores based on extensive search (shopping). In other cases, store loyalty may develop based on past experience, and store selection may become routinized. The principles of low involvement decision making apply equally well to stores. Consumers may select a certain store because it simply is not worth the time or effort to shop around. In such a case, images and attitudes toward the store may be the result of an emphasis on convenience and location. In contrast to this, complex shopping behavior involves the formation of attitudes that lead to store selections based on consumer expectations. The strategic implications of these differing store decision processes also parallel those for brands: Use frequent advertising for reminder effects for low involvement store selection; use image oriented advertising for high involvement store selection.

Market segmentation and product positioning applications are also equally relevant to store selection. Numerous studies have sought to segment customers by store patronage based on demographics, store attitudes, and consumer lifestyles. Researchers are also beginning to use perceptual mapping techniques to position competitive stores based on key store selection criteria. In both cases, the purpose is to better understand the store's customers so that product lines can be developed and promotional resources directed toward customer needs.

This section will parallel the considerations of brand choice by describing the process of store selection, the formation of store images, and the development of store loyalty.

A Model of Store Choice

A model of store choice developed by Monroe and Guiltinan is presented in Figure 20–1.[14] The consumer's demographic, life-style, and personality characteristics (Box 1) lead to the development of certain shopping and purchasing needs (Box 2). These needs establish certain priorities in evaluating store alternatives. These priorities are based on store attributes such as convenience, store personnel, breadth of selection, attractive decor, etc. (Box 3).

An image of a particular store (Box 4) is developed based on the consumer's characteristics, the consumer's needs, and retailer's strategies (retail advertising and in-store stimuli are in Box 5). The closer the store's image is to consumer's needs (the closer Box 4 to Boxes 2 and 3), the more positive the attitude toward the store (Box 6) and the greater the likelihood the consumer will shop in the store (Box 7). If the consumer is satisfied with the store environment based on in-store information processing (Box 8) and the selection of products and brands within the store (Box 9), then a positive image of the store is reinforced (feedback to Box 2), leading to the likelihood the store will be revisited. A continual process of such reinforcement is likely to result in store loyalty.

As an example of the operation of the model, consider a young woman

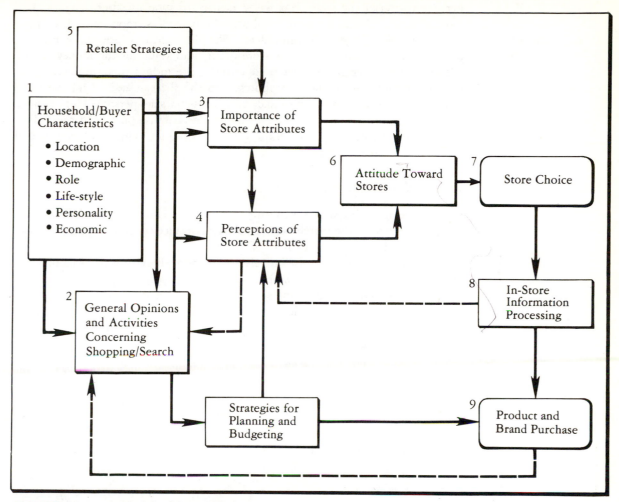

FIGURE 20–1   A Model of Store Choice

Source: Kent B. Monroe and Joseph B. Guiltinan, "A Path-Analytic Exploration of Retail Patronage Influences," *Journal of Consumer Research* 2 (June 1975): 21.
Reprinted with permission from the *Journal of Consumer Research*.

lawyer who just moved to New York City after graduating from law school. She is very clothes and style conscious. Initially, she does her shopping in four stores—B. Altman, Lord & Taylor, Bergdorf-Goodman and Bloomingdale's, primarily because her friends shop in these stores.

She can best be described by Stone's typology as an "economic consumer" because she judges stores primarily based on the objective criteria of quality of merchandise, breadth of assortment, and value. After shopping in these stores she tends to do more and more of her shopping in Bloomingdale's for several reasons: Her personal characteristics (Box 1) tend to conform with her image of the Bloomingdale's shopper since she is upwardly mobile and views herself as a self-actualizer. Bloomingdale's advertising (Box 5) pictures the same type of person. Secondly, her shopping and purchasing needs (Box 2) conform to her perception of the store (Box 4)—a facility to shop for alternatives and to acquire value. Third, the store attributes she considers important (Box 3) are in line with her image of Bloomingdale's. She places greatest priority on breadth of assortment, quality, attractive store decor, and value for the money spent. Although the other stores meet these criteria, she judges Bloomingdale's best on the combination of these attributes. Fourth, she can easily find the merchandise she requires in Bloomingdale's and finds the sales personnel informative (Box 8). And fifth, she is satisfied with the merchandise purchased there (Box 9). As a result, positive attitudes toward the store are reinforced (box 6) and store loyalty develops (box 7).

Criteria of Store Selection

One of the most important determinants of store choice in the Monroe and Guiltinan model is the match between the importance consumers place on store attributes and the image they have of the store. This raises the question: What are the criteria consumers use in selecting stores? Based on a series of forty depth interviews focusing on store patronage motives, Kelly and Stephenson developed thirty-five criteria for store selection.[15] They suggested using a semantic differential scale to determine a store's image based on these criteria (see Table 20–1). A factor analysis of these criteria[16] suggested that there are eight basic dimensions in store choice:

- general store characteristics
- physical characteristics of the store
- convenience of reaching the store from the consumer's location
- products offered
- prices charged by the store
- store personnel
- advertising by the store
- friends' perception of the store

The thirty-five criteria are broken out by these store dimensions in Table 20–1.

Kelly and Stephenson have developed a fairly comprehensive basis for evaluating store choice, but retailers have been researching consumer motives in store selection for close to fifty years. Most of these earlier studies have concentrated almost exclusively on the third factor listed above — store location. In the 1920s, William Reilly studied consumer shopping behavior in Texas and developed what became known as Reilly's **law of retail gravitation** — two cities will attract customers to their respective shopping facilities in direct proportion to their population and in inverse proportion to the distance of a prospective consumer to each town.[17] More recent studies have found Reilly's law simplistic and have modified the estimate of the locational impact of stores,[18] but the important point is that store patronage motives are likely to incorporate many more criteria than just location. Kelly and Stephenson's list of store attributes present a more realistic basis for evaluating store image and store choice.

TABLE 20–1 Evaluative Criteria for Store Selection

GENERAL CHARACTERISTICS OF THE COMPANY

well known generally	: : : : : : :	unknown generally
small number of stores	: : : : : : :	large number of stores
operated by company	: : : : : : :	operated by company
long time in community	: : : : : : :	short time in community

PHYSICAL CHARACTERISTICS OF THE STORE

dirty	: : : : : : :	clean
unattractive decor	: : : : : : :	attractive decor
easy to find items you want	: : : : : : :	difficult to find items you want
easy to move through store	: : : : : : :	difficult to move through store
fast checkout	: : : : : : :	slow checkout

CONVENIENCE OF REACHING THE STORE FROM YOUR LOCATION

near by	: : : : : : :	distant
short time required to reach store	: : : : : : :	long time required to reach store
difficult drive	: : : : : : :	easy drive
difficult to find parking place	: : : : : : :	easy to find parking place
convenient to other stores I shop	: : : : : : :	inconvenient to other stores I shop

Store Choice and
Shopping Behavior

TABLE 20–1 Evaluative Criteria for Store Selection (cont.)

PRODUCTS OFFERED

wide selection of different kinds of products	:	:	:	:	:	:	limited selection of different kinds of products
fully stocked	:	:	:	:	:	:	understocked
undependable products	:	:	:	:	:	:	dependable products
high quality	:	:	:	:	:	:	low quality
numerous brands	:	:	:	:	:	:	few brands
unknown brands	:	:	:	:	:	:	well known brands

PRICES CHARGED BY THE STORE

low compared to other stores	:	:	:	:	:	:	high compared to other stores
low values for money spent	:	:	:	:	:	:	high values for money spent
large number of items specially priced	:	:	:	:	:	:	small number of items specially priced

STORE PERSONNEL

courteous	:	:	:	:	:	:	discourteous
cold	:	:	:	:	:	:	friendly
unhelpful	:	:	:	:	:	:	helpful
adequate number	:	:	:	:	:	:	inadequate number

TABLE 20–1 Evaluative Criteria for Store Selection (cont.)

ADVERTISING BY THE STORE

uninformative	___	___	___	___	___	___	informative
unhelpful in planning purchases	___	___	___	___	___	___	helpful in planning purchases
appealing	___	___	___	___	___	___	unappealing
believable	___	___	___	___	___	___	misleading
frequently seen by you	___	___	___	___	___	___	infrequently seen by you

YOUR FRIENDS AND THE STORE

unknown to your friends	___	___	___	___	___	___	well known to your friends
well liked by your friends	___	___	___	___	___	___	disliked by your friends
poorly recommended by your friends	___	___	___	___	___	___	well recommended by your friends
numerous friends shop there	___	___	___	___	___	___	few friends shop there

Source: Robert F. Kelly and Ronald Stephenson, "The Semantic Differential: An Information Source for Designing Retail Patronage Appeals," *Journal of Marketing* 31 (October 1967): 45.
Reprinted with permission from the *Journal of Marketing*.

Store Image

The model of store choice in Figure 20–1 centers on the development of a store image. Therefore, it is important for retailers to determine consumer perceptions. Measurement of store image assists retailers in determining their competitive strengths and weaknesses. Several studies have evaluated consumer images of competitive stores utilizing the semantic differential scale, and more recently, perceptual mapping as an analytic tool. These studies have used the multiattribute approach proposed by Kelly and Stephenson.

In one study, store images were determined based on the six evaluative criteria listed in Figure 20–2.[19] Consumers were asked how important each of the attributes was in store selection. They then rated each of these stores on the same six criteria. The rating of the store was weighted by the importance

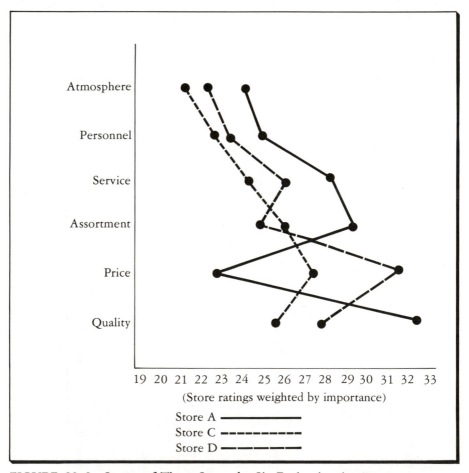

FIGURE 20–2   Image of Three Stores by Six Evaluative Attributes

Source: Don L. James, Richard M. Durand, and Robert A. Dreves, "The Use of a Multi-Attribute Attitude Model in a Store Image Study," *Journal of Retailing* 52 (Summer 1976): 23–32.
Reprinted with permission from the *Journal of Retailing,* Vol. 52, No. 2 (Summer 1976).

of an attribute. Two consumers may rate a store equally positive on the breadth of assortment, but the store will receive a higher image rating only if the consumer considers assortment important. This attitude measurement approach is an offshoot of the multiattribute models described in Chapter 7. Most multiattribute attitudinal models have been applied to brand selection, but they are equally applicable to store selection.

Results for three of the stores are shown in Figure 20–2. The values on the horizontal axis are the ratings on a seven-point semantic differential scale weighted by importance. Store A is perceived to be a high price/high quality store with a broader assortment and better service. Consumers recognize that in store A they have to pay for quality and service. Store D is perceived as having the lowest price. It is in between stores A and C on quality, service, personnel, and atmosphere. Given the lowest price and intermediate value, it may in fact be perceived as providing the best value for the money. Store C seems to be in a relatively weak position — intermediate price yet lowest quality with no distinctive strength in any of the other attributes.

Retailers can determine if these perceptions are in line with their strategies or if repositioning of the store is required. Store A does in fact stress high quality, carrying primarily name brands. Store D is a checkout, mass merchandiser. It does emphasize low price, limited assortment, and medium quality. Store C would clearly be a candidate for repositioning given the low quality perception despite intermediate prices.

Store image has also been studied through the development of perceptual maps. Singson asked consumers to rate the similarity of nine department stores to each other.[20] The department stores were then positioned based on these similarity ratings by a multidimensional scaling computer program. The assumption, as stated in Chapter 18, is that consumers who view objects as being similar will behave similarly to these objects. Results of the analysis are in Figure 20–3. Singson identified the horizontal axis as a price/quality dimension and the vertical axis as an assortment dimension. House of Values, Valu-Mart, and White Front are seen as similar in being lowest on price and quality with an average level of assortment. Sears and Penney's are also similar in providing the greatest breadth of product assortment at an intermediate price/quality level. The remaining stores are more dispersed, but are seen as providing higher prices and quality at a lower assortment level than Sears or Penney's.

Singson analyzed his findings by differences between socioeconomic groups. He found that subjects in the lower socioeconomic groups placed greater emphasis on the breadth of product assortment and were more likely to shop in Sears and Penney's. Shoppers in the higher socioeconomic groups put more emphasis on the depth of assortment — that is, a better stock of fewer items. As a result, they were more likely to shop in specialty stores such as Nordstrom Best.

Store Loyalty

The model of store choice suggests that if the image of a store conforms to consumer priorities, store loyalty could develop. The consumer emphasizing convenience above all else is likely to be loyal to the closest supermarket. The

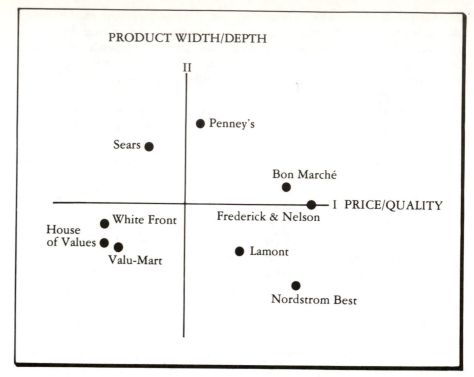

FIGURE 20–3   Relative Position of Nine Stores on Two Evaluative Dimensions

Source: Ricardo L. Singson, "Multidimensional Scaling Analysis of Store Image and Shopping Behavior," *Journal of Retailing* 51 (Summer 1975): 38–52.
    Reprinted with permission from the *Journal of Retailing,* Vol. 51, No. 2 (Summer 1975).

shopper who enjoys personalized relationships is most likely to become loyal to the store in which he or she feels at home with the sales personnel.

Inflationary pressures are likely to increase price consciousness and reduce store loyalty. A study by *Progressive Grocer* magazine found that in 1954, 41 percent of housewives shopped in one supermarket exclusively. In 1975, only 10 percent shopped in one supermarket.[21] Although this decrease in loyalty may be due in part to an increase in the number of supermarkets, it is also likely that shoppers became more selective and price conscious over a twenty year period.

Despite the apparent decrease in store loyalty, it is still profitable for retailers to attract store-loyal customers. In a study of store loyalty, Enis and Paul found that stores with a larger share of store loyal customers tend to be more profitable since they attract a larger share of consumer expenditures.[22] Further, loyal customers are no more expensive to serve than nonloyal customers.

The profitability of attracting the store loyal consumer has led to several attempts to identify the personal characteristics of consumers that do most of their shopping in the same stores. Reynolds et al. related life-style characteristics to store loyalty.[23] They identified store loyalty by the willingness of a sample of women to shop in the same stores and to avoid the risk of shopping in new stores. They found that the store loyal woman is less likely to be venturesome, gregarious, an opinion leader, and urban oriented. The socioeconomic profile suggests that the store-loyal homemaker tends to be older and more downscale.

These findings are supported in a study by Goldman.[24] He found that store loyal consumers engaged in less comparative prepurchase search, knew about the existence of fewer stores, and were less likely to shop even in stores known to them. Further, these consumers tended to be in the lower income group. Goldman concludes that store loyal behavior appears to be "part of a low search, a low knowledge and low utilization level shopping style," and that this shopping style is more likely to exist among low income consumers because they are constrained by their inability to shop much.[25] The clear implication is that store loyalty is an inefficient mode of shopping and is more likely to exist among low income consumers because of limited information and less discretionary income.

The two studies cited above also indicate that perceived risk in purchasing is an important determinant of store selection. Several studies have documented the importance of perceived risk in store choice,[26] leading to the conclusion that stores are "susceptible to the same kind of risk-handling analysis typically accorded only products."[27] The lower income and educational level of the store loyal consumer may heighten the sense of risk in shopping behavior. The careful and conservative nature of these customers suggests that store loyalty may be a means of reducing the risk of shopping in unknown stores. One obvious strategy in reducing risk in store choice is to shop in one or a select number of stores.

Segmentation by Store Choice

Given the importance of store choice to retailers, it is logical that consumers should be segmented based on store choice. The three basic approaches to market segmentation described in Chapter 18 can be applied to store choice — behavioral segmentation, benefit segmentation, and segmenting by response elasticities.

Behavioral segmentation determines the demographic, life-style, or shopping characteristics of consumers who frequent certain stores in comparison to consumers who frequent competitive stores. Based on this information, retailers can develop advertising to appeal to their frequent shoppers and can select those media most likely to be read or seen by their patronage group.

Benefit segmentation divides consumers into groups by shopping needs and priorities. Shoppers can be identified based on the store attributes they tend to emphasize. Thus, certain consumers may be oriented to convenience, others to quality or price. Retailers can attempt to position their stores by appealing to a particular benefit segment. The key question is whether the store image conforms to the needs of the target group. Consumers can also be segmented by shopping orientation. The identification of the economic consumer or the personalizing consumer provides a retailer with a more complete profile of shopping needs and shopper characteristics. Positioning a store's image to appeal to those who emphasize intimacy and personal contact, or to those who emphasize shopping efficiency would be a viable strategy.

Segmentation by response elasticity emphasizes differences in consumer responses to in-store variables. Reaction to price is the most logical basis for categorizing consumers. Further, since price stimuli are largely in-store stimuli, segmenting by price elasticity is of direct interest to the retailer. Shoppers can be categorized by the likelihood of buying items on sale, buying by price deals, or using coupons. If retailers can identify the demographic, life-style, and shopping characteristics of the price sensitive shopper, then price deals, coupons, and private brand advertising can be more effectively directed to this group.

Response elasticity can also be based on other in-store variables. For example, consumers can be classified by sensitivity to changes in package size, to changes in display, or to changes in shelf position. In each case, retailers can more effectively develop in-store stimuli to maximize sales if they know the characteristics of those consumers most sensitive to a particular stimulus.

Unfortunately, few if any attempts to segment by benefits or response elasticity have been reported in retailing. Segmentation has been restricted to the behavioral variety — namely segmenting by store choice behavior. Most of the studies in this area have identified the characteristics of consumers frequenting certain types of stores (discount, department, specialty, etc.) rather than identifying those loyal to a particular store (Sears, Penney's, etc.).

Segmentation by Store Type

Identification of the characteristics of consumers most likely to frequent certain types of stores is useful to retailers in developing an advertising approach and in selecting media. Bearden et al. surveyed the characteristics of patrons of convenience food stores, department stores, discount stores, and fast food outlets.[28] Compared to nonpatrons, convenience food store shoppers are younger, upscale, less traditional, less outgoing, and less socially oriented. Fast food patrons are also younger and more upscale than nonpatrons, but they are more outgoing and socially oriented. The implication is to advertise fast food outlets in media more likely to be seen or read by better educated, higher income consumers and to use advertising themes portraying outgoing customers in a social setting.

Hirschman examined differences in the characteristics of frequent patrons of traditional department stores, chain stores, and discount stores.[29] She found that traditional department store customers are drawn from the higher social classes and are better educated; they place more emphasis on store atmosphere and less importance on price. Discount store customers are more likely to have children, to be in the lower social classes, and to be less educated. The sharp distinction in the profile of traditional department store versus discount store customers suggests sharply different positionings on basic store selection criteria and the likelihood that these types of store are not closely competitive.

SUMMARY

The change in focus from brand to store considerations requires an orientation toward shopping rather than purchasing behavior, in-store stimuli rather than advertising, and store choice rather than brand choice. The chapter is organized around these three considerations.

Shopping behavior is important to retailers since consumers are likely to be motivated by different needs in shopping. Consumers may view shopping as a diversion, a means of self-gratification, a source of sensory stimulation, a means of socialization, or a basis for bargaining. These different motivations have led researchers to define various shopper profiles such as an economic shopper, a personalizing shopper, or an apathetic shopper. Such profiles assist retailers in defining shopper segments by benefits sought.

In-store stimuli are important to retailers because many decisions are made within the store, particularly unplanned decisions. Unplanned purchases may be made on impulse because of the reminder of the product on the shelf, or because of the stimulus of a price special or coupon offer. Various studies have shown that unplanned purchases tend to be the rule for food items, toiletries, and pharmaceuticals. This suggests that the "push" of in-store stimuli may be more important than the "pull" of advertising for these product categories.

Store choice is important in enabling retailers to understand why consumers prefer certain stores over others. A model of store choice suggested that the store decision is a function of the consumer's characteristics, shopping needs, image of the store, and of course the retailer's strategies. Retailers can take a multiattribute approach in determining the competitive position of their store relative to other stores. The attributes consumers use in selecting a store can be identified (see Table 20–1) and the image of the store can be determined on this basis (e.g., Figure 20–2). Identification of the store's image will demonstrate the store's strengths and weaknesses relative to competition and assist retailers in developing positioning and repositioning strategies. Retailers can also use segmentation strategies by identifying (1) either the demographic or life-style characteristics of their regular customers versus customers of competitive stores, (2) the benefits sought by various segments of consumers (e.g., a convenience segment versus a quality segment), and (3) consumer sensitivity to prices or in-store displays.

The next chapter will deal with the behavioral implications of two other components of marketing strategy — price and personal selling.

QUESTIONS

1. How could the following retailers position their store to one or more of Stone's shopper types? Specify the advertising appeals and retail store policies relevant for positioning to one or more of Stone's shopper types.
   - a high fashion men's clothing store in a suburban location
   - an independent chain of bakery shops specializing in home-baked products
   - a large department store merchandiser considering opening a new store in a suburban mall
   - a group of independent gas station dealers
2. Assume that a large department store chain would like to follow a policy of store segmentation. It uses the differing shopping motives specified by Tauber on page 511 as a basis for a segmentation policy.

- What differences might be formulated in (a) local advertising, and (b) store policies to appeal to the differing shopping motives specified by Tauber?

3. How can a retailer of cosmetics and toiletries adjust its price, advertising, or in-store policies to the needs of the six segments specified by Moschis on page 512?

4. On the one hand, gas shortages are likely to inhibit unplanned shopping trips. Yet, on the other hand, increases in discretionary income are likely to encourage unplanned shopping trips.
   - What do you think is the future trend?
   - Should retailers attempt to encourage unplanned shopping trips? What types of retailers? How?

5. What strategies can a retailer use to encourage the four types of unplanned purchases specified by Stern, namely:
   - pure impulse purchases,
   - reminder effect purchases,
   - suggestion effect purchases,
   - planned impulse purchases?

6. A large retailer of sports equipment in an urban area finds sales slipping. As a result, the retailer wishes to conduct a study to determine (a) how consumers decide on a store for sports equipment, and (b) the image of the store relative to competition.
   - Specify how the model of store choice (Figure 20–1) and the criteria specified in Table 20–1 may be of help in determining the required information.

7. The chapter cites segmenting consumers by the individual store they frequent most as well as by the type of store in which they shop. Some researchers have also suggested segmenting consumers by locational criteria; namely, distinguishing between those who shop within their trading area versus those who shop outside their trading area (outshoppers).
   - What are the likely demographic and life-style characteristics of the outshopper?
   - Should retailers attempt to attract outshoppers? If so, what types of retailers? How?

8. Another distinction made by researchers is between store and in-home shoppers. The distinction is becoming particularly important with the growth of in-home shopping.
   - What factors have caused an increase in in-home shopping?
   - What are the likely demographic and life-style characteristics of the in-home shopper?
   - Should retailers encourage in-home shopping? If so, what types of retailers? How?

9. What would be the strategic implications to retailers of segmenting by
   - store choice behavior?
   - benefits?
   - response elasticity?

1. Select a particular product category in which the choice of a store is particularly important (clothing, furniture, rugs and carpets, etc.). Then identify consumers who have bought the item within the last six months. Conduct seven or eight depth interviews with such consumers to identify the process of store choice.

   • Describe the decision process.

   • Does the process of store choice conform to the model described in Figure 20-1?

   • What are the implications of the decision process for the retailer regarding

      (a) positioning of the store,

      (b) selection of merchandise,

      (c) pricing,

      (d) in-store promotions,

      (e) customer-salesperson interaction, and

      (f) market segmentation?

2. Select three or four competitive stores in your local area (they can be department stores, food or specialty stores, discount retailers, etc.). Develop a rating scale (use the semantic differential scale) to determine consumer images of the stores. Use the items in Table 20-1 as a guide to the types of store attributes that should be included. Develop a questionnaire including (1) the rating scale, (2) the stores the consumer frequents most often, (3) local media read or watched most frequently, and (4) demographics.

   • Portray the image of each store using the format shown in Figure 20-2. This will require determining the average rating for each store on each attribute.

   • Does the image of a particular store differ by (a) those who go there regularly versus those who do not, and (b) demographic characteristics of consumers?

   • What are the implications of your findings for

      (a) possible repositioning strategies,

      (b) in-store promotional policies,

      (c) customer-salesperson interactions,

      (d) pricing,

      (e) advertising, and

      (f) media selection?

NOTES

1. Joseph W. Newman and Richard Staelin, "Prepurchase Information Seeking for New Cars and Major Household Appliances," *Journal of Marketing Research* 9 (August 1972): 249–257.

2. Jon G. Udell, "Prepurchase Behavior of Buyers of Small Electrical Appliances," *Journal of Marketing* 30 (October 1966): 50–52.

3. Edward M. Tauber, "Why Do People Shop," *Journal of Marketing* 36 (October 1972): 46–49.

4. Gregory P. Stone, "City Shoppers and Urban Identification: Observations on the Social Psychology of City Life," *American Journal of Sociology* 60 (1954): 36–45.

5. William R. Darden and Fred D. Reynolds, "Shopping Orientations and Product Usage Rates," *Journal of Marketing Research* 7 (November 1971): 505–508.

6. William R. Darden and Dub Ashton, "Psycho-

530   graphic Profiles of Patronage Preference Groups," *Journal of Retailing* 50 (Winter 1974–75): 99–111.

7. George P. Moschis, "Shopping Orientations and Consumer Uses of Information," *Journal of Retailing* 52 (Summer 1976): 61–70.

8. Tauber, "Why Do People Shop," p. 49.

9. Hawkins Stern, "The Significance of Impulse Buying Today," *Journal of Marketing* 26 (April 1962): 59–62.

10. "Marketing Emphasis," *Product Marketing*, February 1978, pp. 61–64.

11. David T. Kollat and Ronald P. Willett, "Customer Impulse Purchasing Behavior," *Journal of Marketing Research* 4 (February 1967): 21–31.

12. V. Kanti Prasad, "Unplanned Buying In Two Retail Settings," *Journal of Retailing* 51 (Fall 1975): 3–12.

13. Kollat and Willett, "Customer Impulse Purchasing Behavior."

14. Kent B. Monroe and Joseph B. Guiltinan, "A Path-Analytic Exploration Of Retail Patronage Influences," *Journal of Consumer Research* 2 (June 1975): 19–28.

15. Robert F. Kelly and Ronald Stephenson, "The Semantic Differential: An Information Source for Designing Retail Patronage Appeals," *Journal of Marketing* 31 (October 1967): 43–47.

16. Ronald Stephenson, "Identifying Determinants of Retail Patronage," *Journal of Marketing* 33 (July 1969): 57–61.

17. William J. Reilly, *Methods for the Study of Retail Relationships* (Austin, Tex.: Bureau of Business Research, University of Texas Press, 1929).

18. John R. Thompson, "Characteristics and Behavior of Out-Shopping Consumers," *Journal of Retailing* 47 (Spring 1971): 70–80.

19. Don L. James, Richard M. Durand, and Robert A. Dreves, "The Use of a Multi-Attribute Attitude Model in a Store Image Study," *Journal of Retailing* 52 (Summer 1976): 23–32.

20. Ricardo L. Singson, "Multidimensional Scaling Analysis of Store Image and Shopping Behavior," *Journal of Retailing* 51 (Summer 1975): 38–52.

21. Robert F. Dietrich, "Know Thy Consumer: A Quiz That Shows How Well You Do," *Progressive Grocer*, March 1975, p. 55.

22. Ben M. Enis and Gordon W. Paul, "Store Loyalty as a Basis for Market Segmentation," *Journal of Retailing* 46 (Fall 1970): 42–56.

23. Fred D. Reynolds, William R. Darden, and Warren S. Martin, "Developing an Image of the Store-Loyal Customer," *Journal of Retailing* 50 (Winter 1974–75): 73–84.

24. Arieh Goldman, "The Shopping Style Explanation for Store Loyalty," *Journal of Retailing* 53 (Winter 1977–78): 33–46.

25. Ibid., p. 46.

26. Robert D. Hisrich, Ronald J. Dornoff, and Jerome B. Kernan, "Perceived Risk in Store Selection," *Journal of Marketing Research* 9 (November 1972): 435–439; and Joseph F. Dash, Leon G. Schiffman, and Conrad Berenson, "Risk and Personality Related Dimensions of Store Choice," *Journal of Marketing* 40 (January 1976): 32–39.

27. Hisrich, Dornoff, and Kernan, "Perceived Risk," p. 439.

28. William O. Bearden, Jesse E. Teel, and Richard M. Durand, "Media Usage, Psychographic and Demographic Dimensions of Retail Shoppers," *Journal of Retailing* 54 (Spring 1978): 65–73.

29. Elizabeth C. Hirschman, "Intratype Competition Among Department Stores," (working paper, New York University, 1979).

TWENTY-ONE

Price and Salesperson Influences on Consumer Behavior

Focus of Chapter

Store-related stimuli are an important influence on consumer behavior. Two other influences, the price and the salesperson, logically follow any consideration of store influences since they are frequently represented within the store environment.

A consideration of consumer pricing behavior will include (1) consumer awareness of prices, (2) the link between price and quality, and (3) the degree of consumer sensitivity displayed toward pricing policies and changes in price.

The second influence to be considered in this chapter, the interaction between the salesperson and the consumer, has increasingly become the province of consumer research rather than of sales research. The focus of sales evaluation has shifted from what characteristics make a good salesperson to "how can the salesperson best meet the consumer's needs." Customer-salesperson considerations include (1) the nature of the interaction process, (2) the salesperson as a source of social reinforcement and/or expertise, and (3) salesperson strategies to influence consumers within a behavioral framework.

PRICING INFLUENCES

Price is an important influence on both brand and store choice. Price not only represents the monetary cost of an item, but also indicates to the consumer the quality of a brand or product and the satisfaction to be expected. Consumers also link a store's image to price based on price expectations and the quality of merchandise within the store.

Economic theory has logically played an important role in the study of price effects. Two traditional views based on Alfred Marshall's theory of demand are (1) in order to maximize satisfaction, consumers must have a complete knowledge of prices and brand alternatives, and (2) the higher the price, the less the quantity demanded. As the price increases — if the percentage decrease in quantity is more than the percentage increase in price — demand is elastic. If the percentage decrease in quantity is less than the percentage increase in price, demand is inelastic.

These traditional views of the effect of price on demand do not take into account the realities of consumer behavior. Consumers' knowledge of prices is very limited. Furthermore, consumers do not always buy less at higher prices. Studies have shown a close link between price and quality perceptions. Even the traditional behavioral view of pricing (higher prices connote better quality) may be oversimplified. As multiattribute models show, many factors other than price influence quality perceptions and brand preference.

The lack of simple explanations about the influence of price on consumer behavior means that the consumer's *price awareness, price perceptions,* and *price sensitivity* must be studied on a product-by-product basis and linked to consumer characteristics.

Price Awareness

Consumer awareness of retail prices is low. A 1974 study by *Progressive Grocer* magazine of forty-four supermarket items found that consumers were able to identify the correct price only one-fourth of the time.[1] A correct price was considered a price within 5 percent of the actual price. The exact price to the cent was estimated only 8 percent of the time. A comparison to a similar study by *Progressive Grocer* ten years earlier showed a marked decrease in price awareness.[2] In 1963 customers were able to estimate a correct price 32 percent of the time and were able to estimate the exact price 20 percent of the time.

No reason was given for the decrease in awareness of the actual price, but this may not mean a decrease in price consciousness. Actually, the study found that national brands had poorer recognition in 1974 than in 1963, but price recognition of private label brands was higher. Therefore, price awareness for lower priced products was increasing while awareness for higher priced products was decreasing.

A study by Gabor and Granger found that the incidence of misperception of prices was higher for lower income and less educated respondents.[3] The exception was the very poor; they were more aware of prices. This finding suggests that lower income consumers have more limited price information than do higher income respondents and may not be as efficient in comparative shopping. However, if income is low enough, comparative shopping is sufficiently worthwhile. Brown also found that higher income consumers tended to perceive price more accurately, as did respondents who were single and/or employed full time.[4] The fact that fully employed shoppers are more accurate in price perceptions than those not employed means that more shopping time may not increase the accuracy of price information. Brown confirmed this fact — more frequent shopping *does not* improve the accuracy of price perceptions.

Greater price awareness among more advantaged consumers may be related to their having access to more accurate price information and to their greater willingness to process such information.

In-Store Information Programs

The quality of in-store price information has improved with the introduction of unit pricing. **Unit pricing** is the posting of the price for an item in a common unit like an ounce, even though the actual size of the item may be more than an ounce. Unit pricing permits comparisons of various brands in common units.

Some stores have combined unit pricing with other information to assist the consumer to shop and compare. Jewel advertised a Compar-A-Buy program to provide shopper assistance.[5] Mott's Shop-Rite stores have introduced in-store consultants to assist shoppers. These consultants inform shoppers of price-reduced, antiinflation items, answer consumer complaints, and maintain store services.[6] In addition to unit pricing, other important components of an in-store information program are open code dating and nutritional labeling. The importance of these three sources of information to consumers is reflected in a 1976 study by *Progressive Grocer* that shows that 94 percent of the consumers interviewed frequently rely on open dating, 51 percent frequently use nutritional labeling information, and 70 percent frequently use unit price information.[7]

Given the importance of in-store price information, the question arises whether unit pricing merely confuses consumers or whether it leads to economies. Houston found that "the consumer is better able to determine the most economical item in a product class at stores with unit pricing than at stores that provide less information regarding unit price."[8] Consumers frequently use this information to buy a lower priced item, although not necessarily the lowest priced item.

Unit pricing therefore leads to consumer economies. But who is most likely to use unit price information? Once again, the consistent finding is that it is the better educated consumer with higher income that uses unit pricing and is therefore better informed regarding price alternatives. Isakson and Maurizi found that less educated respondents with low income do not employ unit price as much in their shopping, possibly as a "result of their inability to understand or use the labels."[9] Jewel stores studied use of their Compar-A-Buy program and found that stores in lower socioeconomic neighborhoods registered less awareness of the program.[10] The fact that better educated respondents tend to be more aware of price means that educating minority and low income consumers to in-store information such as how to use unit prices "is a difficult proposition, but perhaps the most rewarding when successful."[11] It is these consumers that most need the information.

Price Perceptions

Consumers frequently perceive price as an indicator of product or store image, independent of the objective information provided by price.

The most important cue provided by price is product quality. When a consumer does not have sufficient information about product quality, price serves as a good proxy for quality. This implies that as more information is made available regarding product quality, the role of price as an indicator of quality should be reduced.

Early studies tended to examine the relationship between price and quality when price was the only information supplied.[12] Logically, a strong relationship was found between price and quality, especially when price differences between alternatives were substantial and when the consumer believed that there were differences in the quality of brands. These single cue studies (price only) came to be regarded as unrealistic because the importance of price may be reduced when other information is made available. As a result, a number of multicue experiments were conducted. Jacoby et al. manipulated price, product composition, and brand image in a beer taste test. They found that brand image had a significant effect on quality perceptions. Price level did not influence quality perceptions except when it was considered alone.[13] Monroe found that when housewives had prior experience with the brand, that experience overcame price as the dominant factor in brand choice.[14] Wheatley and Chiu found that in the purchase of carpeting, the store image and color combined with price to create a quality image.[15]

The multicue studies tend to support the multiattribute nature of consumer decisions. Generally, consumers do not make decisions based on price alone, and product perceptions are not a function of price alone.

Psychological Pricing

Another element in price perception is the sensitivity to certain price points. For example, consumers appear to be more sensitive to prices ending with an odd number of just under a round number (odd-even pricing). Or they may find products priced in multiples such as four for $.79 (multiple pricing) preferable to single item prices. These pricing policies are referred to as psychological pricing because they rely on consumers' perceptual sensitivity to certain price points.

Odd-even pricing is used by retailers in the belief that an item priced at $2.99 is seen by the consumer as substantially less expensive than an item priced at $3.00. It is felt the consumer would associate a $2.99 price to a $2.00, rather than a $3.00 frame of reference. Lambert found some justification for this conclusion.[16] In presenting groups of products to consumers at odd and even prices, but at the same price level, he found that in the majority of cases consumers perceived the odd prices as being substantially lower than the even prices. Lambert's study is one of the few carefully controlled studies of odd-even pricing.

Multiple pricing also conveys an image of economy to the consumer. Obtaining a product at four for $.79 implies a small saving over a single unit purchase at $.20. A study of multiple pricing shows that consumers are likely to buy in multiples as long as it is a frequently purchased product and the consumer recognizes a clear saving,[17] but if multiple pricing becomes too complicated, consumers are likely to reject multiple purchases.

Price Sensitivity

Another factor that directly influences retailer and manufacturer pricing strategies is the degree of consumer sensitivity to price changes. As noted, the measure of price sensitivity used most often is a consumer's price elasticity or response to changes in price.

Price Elasticity

Chapter 18 noted that an important approach in segmenting markets is to classify consumers by the degree of price elasticity. If the more price-sensitive consumers have particular demographic or regional characteristics, then deals, coupons, or sales strategies can be directed to these consumers. Some attempt has been made to define consumers more responsive to deals and coupons by zip code and to use direct mail to send coupons to these consumers. Price promotions could also be directed to zip code areas demonstrating greater price sensitivity.

In Chapter 18 it was noted that there have been few studies attempting to segment markets by price elasticity. Most studies have been on the total market level rather than the individual consumer level. The energy crisis has prompted a number of studies of the price elasticity of individual consumers for gasoline. Willenborg and Pitts studied purchase intentions for autos and gasoline among a panel of South Carolina consumers from 1973 to 1975, a period when gas prices began to increase.[18] By the end of 1973, three and a half times as many consumers stated an intention to buy a compact car as a full-sized car. Yet when gas prices stabilized in 1975, intentions went back to a normal ratio — about even between compacts and full-sized cars. Furthermore, although registration of compacts increased in 1974, with stabilization of gas prices by 1975, registration of compacts began to decrease.

The majority of consumers indicated that they would begin driving less frequently when prices increased by eight to ten cents a gallon. But once prices stabilized, consumers expressed little willingness to drive less. Data on gas consumption supports the fact that there was little reduction in driving.

Overall, there seems to be a disparity between what people say and what they do regarding gasoline consumption. Consumers seemed to *express* greater price elasticity in the face of price increase, but, in actuality, there was little change in consumption, suggesting that consumers were much more inelastic in their demand for gasoline than their own perceptions would indicate.

Supporting the finding of price inelasticity for gasoline is a 1976 study that found drivers patronizing gasoline stations charging ten cents more a gallon compared to neighboring stations.[19] This apparent disregard for price occurred despite a 52 percent increase in gas prices over 1973 levels and a more price conscious public. The authors believe that drivers were patronizing higher priced stations so they could develop a reliable source of gasoline should serious shortages recur. Such patronage did not avoid waiting in line during shortages in mid-1979. But, even during this period, some motorists disregarded substantial price differences between stations. Apparently, the American consumer's need for mobility and the continued love affair with the automobile exempts gasoline from price sensitivity.

Elasticity of demand for gasoline was estimated in a period of increasing prices. Monroe makes the distinction between **upside elasticities** (sensitivity to price increases) and **downside elasticity** (sensitivity to price decreases).[20] In a study of three products, he found that consumers were more elastic on the downside than on the upside. That is, they were more likely to increase consumption with a decrease in price and less likely to decrease consumption with an increase in price. Monroe concludes that small price increases may increase profits since they are likely to produce insignificant changes in response.

Other studies of consumer price sensitivity have focused on factors that may increase such sensitivity. For example, one study found that the consumer's price elasticity decreases when the consumer is accompanied by a friend,[21] and another found less price sensitivity when the salesperson is viewed as an expert.[22] Consumers are more likely to be price elastic when they are shopping alone and when they are self-confident in their own appraisal of the product.

Price Expectations

An important determinant of a consumer's sensitivity to prices is his or her expectations regarding a normal price level and price range. Consumers develop a **standard price** for most items — what they regard as a fair price. The standard price serves as a basis for judging other prices. There is a range around the standard price that is not likely to produce a change in quantity consumed or a switch in brands. But, outside this range, significant changes may occur producing greater price elasticity. For example, a consumer may expect to pay $1.29 for a three-pound box of bleach. A variation of five cents either way would not be noticed. But, more than a five-cent increase in price may cause the consumer to look for another brand. More than a five-cent decrease may cause the consumer to purchase two boxes. A five-cent charge is therefore the point where some price sensitivity comes into play (i.e., the "just noticeable difference" referred to in Chapter 5).

Price expectations also refer to an **acceptable price range** across brands in a product category. The consumer buying bleach for $1.29 may be skeptical of a three-pound box selling for less than $.80, thinking something must be wrong with a brand priced that low. On the other hand, if the consumer is in a small grocery store on Sunday and needs bleach to do the wash, the upper price limit he or she sets is $1.49. Therefore, the acceptable price range for bleach based on this consumer's price expectations is between $.80 and $1.49. Gabor and Granger confirmed the existence of an acceptable range of prices. In a study of five product categories they found "an upper limit above which the article would be judged too expensive and a lower limit below which the quality of the item would be suspect."[23]

The Price-Sensitive Consumer

Inflationary pressures have increased consumer price sensitivity. Price consciousness has resulted in increased use of coupons and price specials, in shifts to private label brands, and in decreases in the number of shopping trips. After a 33 percent increase in the Consumer Price Index for food from 1973 to 1974, *Progressive Grocer* surveyed consumer reactions to increased prices as well as store

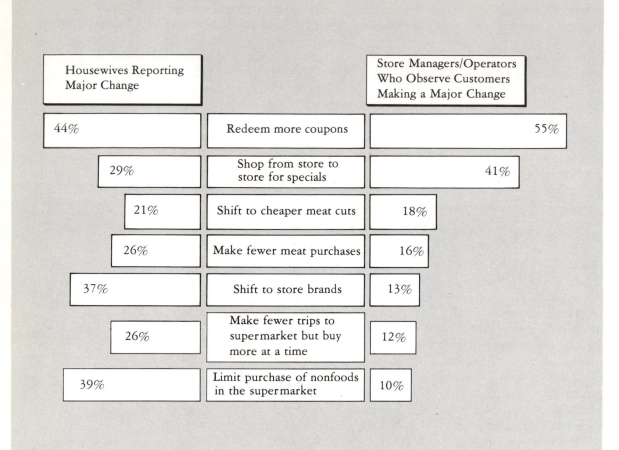

Housewives Reporting Major Change		Store Managers/Operators Who Observe Customers Making a Major Change
44%	Redeem more coupons	55%
29%	Shop from store to store for specials	41%
21%	Shift to cheaper meat cuts	18%
26%	Make fewer meat purchases	16%
37%	Shift to store brands	13%
26%	Make fewer trips to supermarket but buy more at a time	12%
39%	Limit purchase of nonfoods in the supermarket	10%

FIGURE 21–1   Housewives and Store Managers Reporting Changes in Shopping Behavior

Source: Robert F. Dietrich, "Shopping Smart," *Progressive Grocer,* April 1975, p. 50. Reprinted with permission from *Progressive Grocer,* April 1975.

manager perceptions of how consumers were reacting.[24] Results of the survey are presented in Figure 21–1. The most important changes were increases in the redemption of coupons, a decrease in the purchase of nonfood items in supermarkets, increased purchases of store (private label) brands, and a search for price specials from store to store. A second survey by the same magazine showed that consumers who tended to worry about prices spent more time and money on food shopping (see Table 21–1). These consumers were more information oriented. They were more likely to use unit pricing and open dating information and were more likely to utilize shopping aids such as shopping lists and mechanical counters. They were also more shopping-oriented. If they could not find a desired item, they were more likely to shop elsewhere to find it.[25]

	Worries a Lot	Worries a Little	Worries Not at All
% of all shoppers	57%	31%	12%
Minutes spent shopping	28.9	29.5	23.7
Amount spent	$28.52	$26.01	$21.88
Amount spent per minute	.99¢	.88¢	.92¢
Discarded items at checkstand	6%	4%	———
Shopping Aids:			
Used shopping list	44%	44%	29%
Used mechanical counter	8	2	1
Redeemed in-ad coupons	17	11	1
Redeemed manufacturer coupon	22	22	6
Unit Pricing:			
Apparent observed use (Intense and moderate)	38%	29%	30%
Claimed use (Frequently and occasionally)	73	70	61
Rated helpfulness by users (Very and somewhat)	79	79	70
Freshness Dates:			
Apparent observed use (Intense and moderate)	42%	34%	32%
Claimed use (Frequently and occasionally)	81	80	63
Rated helpfulness by users (Very and somewhat)	89	87	77
Missing/out-of-stock items:			
Encountered missing items	27%	22%	26%
Substituted for missing items*	28	10	33
Asked employee help*	22	20	32
Complained to store employee*	16	2	20
Intend to look elsewhere*	54	50	44
Store Rating:			
Called store their "regular" supermarket	85%	86%	88%
Called store their "favorite" supermarket	77%	79%	78%
Miles traveled to shop (median)	1.2	1.4	.9
Other supers shopped (Past four weeks)	2.05	2.16	1.89

* Based on those who could not find items

Source: "The Uptight Consumer, What Is She Up To?" *Progressive Grocer*, November 1975, p. 49. Reprinted with permission from *Progressive Grocer*, November 1975.

It is clear that more consumers are becoming sensitive to increased prices. But what types of consumers are most likely to be price-sensitive? Several studies have related consumer demographic characteristics to the likelihood of buying private label brands or buying on deal. No clear profile emerged of the more price-sensitive consumer. In a recent study, Blattberg et al. studied the characteristics of consumers more likely to buy on deal. They concluded that buying on deal is a function of demographic characteristics of the household, household costs (shopping, storage, and transportation costs), household resources (home and car ownership), and the household's usage rate for the product.[26] They found that the deal-prone consumer was most likely to have a higher income. Further, they found that among households owning a car and a home, one-third were deal prone. Among households owning neither, only 20 percent were deal prone.

These findings indicate that consumer price sensitivity is more a function of product and information search than of low income. Consumers who had the means to travel and to store items were better able to take advantage of price deals. Low income and disadvantaged consumers were not likely to buy on deal because of restricted resources (no car and limited storage space) and probably because of limited knowledge of deals.

SALESPERSON INFLUENCES

Purchasing behavior frequently requires direct contact with salespeople. In fact, personal selling may be the most important form of marketing communication. Kotler estimates that American firms spend 50 percent more on personal selling than on advertising.[27] A survey of executives in consumer durable and nondurable companies found that selling was 1.8 times more important than advertising in their company's marketing efforts for durable goods and 1.1 times more important for nondurable goods.[28]

Direct sales influence can be a potent force on the consumer. Most research on sales influence has dealt with the personal characteristics of an effective salesperson. Recently, such research has become more consumer oriented by studying the nature of the interaction process between buyer and seller.

Consumer-Salesperson Interaction

A salesperson's influence on the consumer comes from two sources. First, the salesperson may be seen as a means of personal identification, a source of friendship, attraction, or shared identity. Chapter 13 referred to this source of influence as **referent power**. The personalized shopper in need of socialization in the retail sphere may be most subject to this type of influence. In the context of referent power, a consumer's perception of the salesperson as having similar needs and characteristics is likely to exert a direct influence on the sale.

Second, the salesperson may be considered to be knowledgeable about the product category and a legitimate source of information. Chapter 13 referred to this source of influence as **expert power**. A third source of influence is the consumer's influence on the salesperson as represented by the consumer's **bargaining power**. Where negotiation with the salesperson is feasible, the consumer willing to bargain could exert direct influence by obtaining price, delivery, or other concessions. Such individuals may be more self-confident and independent. They may not need the social contact with the salesperson or see the salesperson as an expert. Rather, they view the buyer-seller interaction as a bargaining process.

Consumer-Salesperson Similarity (Referent Power)

Several studies have demonstrated the importance of referent power by showing that when customers see the salesperson as similar to themselves, a sale is more likely to occur. Evans found that if a life insurance prospect thought the sales representative preferred the same political party and had the same religion, a sale was much more likely to occur.[29] Brock studied the success of paint sellers who were characterized as similar to the consumer but inexperienced (referent but not expert power) and dissimilar to the consumer but experienced (expert but not referent power).[30] The results indicated that referent power was more important than expert power. Almost twice as many customers exposed to similar but inexperienced salespersons changed their decision in line with the salesperson's suggestion as compared to those who were exposed to dissimilar but experienced salespersons.

The Salesperson's Expertise (Expert Power)

These findings in no way reduce the potential influence of the salesperson as an expert. In an experiment studying the relative influence of referent and expert power on life insurance decisions, Busch and Wilson found that expert power is more important than referent power in gaining the customer's trust.[31] Woodside and Davenport came to the logical conclusion that the combination of both referent and expert power maximizes sales influence in the purchase of a specialty item.[32] They introduced four conditions — expert salespersons who are either similar or dissimilar to the customer and nonexperts who are similar or dissimilar. The results were as follows:

- customers exposed to expert salespersons seen as similar — 80 percent bought
- customers exposed to expert salespersons seen as dissimilar — 53 percent bought
- customers exposed to nonexpert salespersons seen as similar — 30 percent bought
- customers exposed to nonexpert salespersons seen as dissimilar — 13 percent bought

Consumer Bargaining Power

In situations where negotiation is possible, the willingness and ability of the consumer to bargain will directly influence the sales outcome. One study found that the major reason certain customers can obtain the same item for a lower price is the bargaining strength and knowledge of the consumer.

What type of individual is most likely to be successful at bargaining in a sales situation? The limited evidence seems to point to an efficient and dominant person, high in need achievement but less tolerant of others.[33] This may well be the type of individual least likely to view a salesperson as a source of expertise or as a source of socialization.

The three sources of influence imply three general approaches to customer-salesperson interactions. One, the salesperson can attempt to reinforce the ego and social needs of the customer by demonstrating similar needs, concerns, and predispositions (referent influence). Two, the salesperson can be an objective source of information (expert influence). Three, the salesperson can take a more detached view and engage the customer in bargaining. It is obvious that some combination of these three approaches may be best in most cases, but the burden falls on the salesperson to develop a proper impression of the customer and to formulate a sales strategy accordingly. These abilities require emphasis on the salesperson's perception of consumer characteristics and needs and the development of communications strategies to meet these needs. Such behavioral emphasis is required in any sound sales training program.

A Model of the Sales Process

A model of customer-salesperson interactions was developed by Weitz (Figure 21–2).[34] In the first step, the salesperson combines past sales experience with specific information gained from contact with the customer to form an impression of the customer. The salesperson then analyzes his or her impression of the customer and formulates a strategy. As the salesperson delivers the message, the effects on the customer are evaluated and adjustments are made. The salesperson can change his or her impressions of the consumer, change the strategic objectives, change the message, alter the style of communicating the message, or just repeat the original message if it seems to have been effective.

The model emphasizes two factors — (1) the salesperson's formation of an impression of the customer, and (2) the development of a strategy to influence the customer.

Impression of the Customer

If the salesperson is able to accurately estimate the needs and product perceptions of the customer, then the salesperson will be in a better position to formulate a communications strategy for the product in question. A sale is thus more likely to result. Weitz evaluated the accuracy of a salesperson's impression of customer needs for an industrial product. He compared the salesperson's estimation of a customer's needs and product perceptions with the customer's own estimation. The more accurate the salesperson was in estimating (1) customer emphasis on particular product attributes, and (2) customer product perceptions, the better the salesperson's performance was. This finding confirms a consumer-oriented approach to evaluating sales performance: Sales success can best be predicted by the process of customer-salesperson interaction rather than by any general characteristics of the salesperson such as personality attributes.

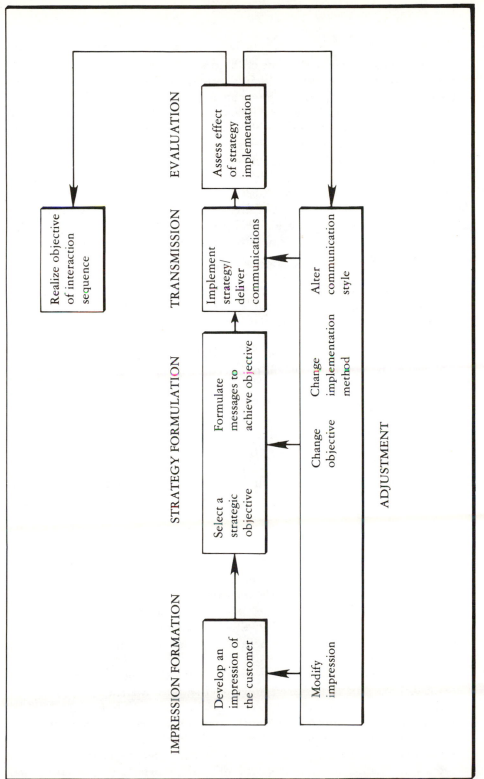

FIGURE 21–2   A Model of Customer-Salesperson Interaction

Source: Barton A Weitz, "The Relationship Between Salesperson Performance and Understanding of Customer Decision Making," *Journal of Marketing Research,* 15 (November, 1978):502. Reprinted with permission from the *Journal of Marketing Research.*

Strategy to Influence the Customer

The second important component of Weitz's model is the ability of the sales-person to develop an effective communications strategy once an impression of the customer is formulated. Assuming an understanding of consumer needs and product perceptions, the salesperson can develop four strategies to influence the customer. First, new product criteria could be communicated — for example, automatic color controls on a television set. Second, the salesperson could attempt to change the importance of existing criteria. If a consumer emphasizes portability, the salesperson may suggest that portability can only be obtained by sacrificing excellence in color and automatic lock-in color features. Third, the salesperson could attempt to change perceptions of an existing brand. The customer may have judged a particular brand as always being poor in color tone. The salesperson may demonstrate the set and convince the customer otherwise. Fourth, the salesperson may introduce an unknown brand or model to the customer.

The effectiveness of each of these strategies is dependent on the salesperson's accuracy in estimating the customer's decision process. Attempting to change brand perceptions of an attribute that is relatively unimportant to the customer would obviously be an ineffective strategy. In addition, as pointed out in Chapter 8, customer needs are harder to change than brand perceptions. If a salesperson attempts to change the priority of customer needs, then such change requires a fuller understanding of the customer.

Weitz found that the best salesperson was not just the individual who could assess a customer's needs, but the individual who could also develop the appropriate change strategy — whether it is a change in awareness of a product attribute, in customer priorities, or in brand perceptions. The logical conclusion of this type of research is that "salespeople might improve their performance if they attempted to improve their understanding of their customers' choice decisions."[35]

SUMMARY

This chapter considers two important sources of influence on the consumer — price and the salesperson. Price is important since it frequently influences a brand's image and a store's image. Studies have demonstrated strong price-quality associations for brands. Yet, when consumers have experience with the brand and are confident in their selections, price is not the dominant cue in indicating quality.

An important consideration in pricing is the consumer's awareness of and sensitivity to prices. Studies have suggested that price awareness of lower priced brands is increasing, while awareness of national brands is decreasing. Further, the low income consumer tends to be less aware of prices suggesting the need for in-store information programs to better inform these consumers.

Studies of consumer price sensitivity became more frequent in the 1970s because of inflation and the energy crisis. These studies suggested that, for gas at least, consumers are more price inelastic than they think. Behavior changed less than anticipated with gas price increases. Inflation has also resulted in greater coupon redemption for food products and in a shift to lower priced store brands. Attempts to identify the price-sensitive consumer have not been successful.

Consideration of salesperson influences emphasizes the interaction process between buyer and seller. Salespersons can influence consumers by identifying with the consumer's needs and values (referent power) or by demonstrating knowledge (expert power). Studies suggest that the combination of both referent and expert power is most likely to produce sales rather than one or the other. A model of customer-salesperson interactions is presented in which the salesperson's evaluation of consumer needs and development of a sales strategy in accordance with these needs is emphasized.

The next chapter will shift the focus from the final consumer to the organizational and industrial buyer.

QUESTIONS

1. Why do you think price awareness of national brands decreased between 1963 and 1974, whereas price awareness of private brands increased?
2. Studies have found that higher prices suggest higher quality. Under what circumstances might this association not hold?
3. How do you explain the disparity shown between consumer perceptions of what they would do if gas prices increased further and what they did when gas prices did actually increase?
4. How would you measure a consumer's price sensitivity to a product? Cite both a perceptual and a behavioral measure of price sensitivity.
   - What do the studies of consumer perceptions of responses to possible increases in gas prices suggest about the validity of perceptual measures?
5. Figure 21–1 reports on a survey of housewives' reported reactions to increased prices and store managers' observations of customers' reactions to increased prices. The findings show a disparity between how the housewife thinks she reacted and how the store manager thinks the housewife reacted.
   - Why is there a disparity in perceptions?
   - What are the likely effects of the disparity on store policies?
6. Compare the characteristics of the consumer who worries a lot, a little, and not at all about price increases based on the information in Table 21–1.
   - What are the implications of these findings for (a) in-store informational programs, and (b) pricing policies?
7. Under what conditions are a salesperson's (a) referent power, (b) expert power, and (c) bargaining power likely to be more important in influencing the consumer?
8. The study by Weitz suggests that salespersons can develop four strategies to influence customers. They can:

- introduce a new product attribute or attributes,
- attempt to change the priority of consumer needs,
- attempt to change brand perceptions, and
- introduce a new brand.

Under what circumstances are each of these strategies more likely to be effective?

RESEARCH ASSIGNMENTS

1. Ask a sample of consumers to estimate their reactions to a 10 percent, 20 percent, 50 percent, and 100 percent increase in gas prices. Also obtain the following information:

   (a) number of miles driven in the last year;
   (b) average miles per gallon obtained in driving;
   (c) future expectations regarding the economy; and
   (d) demographic characteristics.

   In addition to this information, ask consumers whether there is a price of gas below which they will not buy because of a concern that the gas may be defective, or a price above which they will not buy. This question is meant to obtain the current acceptable price range for gas for each consumer.

   - What are the average changes in estimated driving with each increase in price?
   - Is there an acceptable price range for gas? What is the average acceptable price range?
   - Divide the sample into those who are more and those who are less sensitive to price increases. Are there differences between these groups in terms of their:
     (a) demographic characteristics,
     (b) frequency of driving,
     (c) future economic expectations, and
     (c) acceptable range for gas prices?

2. Identify a salesperson who is willing to cooperate in an experiment. The salesperson could be a local merchant or a student in a sales position. Develop a scenario in which the salesperson attempts to influence customers by (1) expressing similar interests and opinions (referent appeals), (2) acting knowledgeable (expert appeals), and (3) a combination of both. Then determine influence on the customer based on sales results or likelihood of a purchase.

   - Which appeals were most successful? Why?
   - If possible, replicate the above experiment in another type of store.
     a) Were the same results obtained?
     b) If not, why were there differences between the two types of stores? To what extent did differences in the product categories influence the results of the experiment?

1. Walter H. Heller, "What Shoppers Know and Don't Know About Prices," *Progressive Grocer,* November 1974, pp. 39–41.

2. Colonial Study, *Progressive Grocer,* January 1964, pp. C-81–C-96.

3. Andre Gabor and C.W.J. Granger, "Price Sensitivity of the Consumer," *Journal of Advertising Research* 4 (December 1964): 40–44.

4. F.E. Brown, "Who Perceives Supermarket Prices Most Validly," *Journal of Marketing Research* 8 (February 1971): 110–113.

5. Joseph S. Coyle, "Dual Pricing Settles In" *Progressive Grocer,* February 1971, pp. 46–50.

6. "See Who's Talking to the Customers Now," *Progressive Grocer,* February 1975, pp. 34–38.

7. Robert F. Dietrich, "Some Signs of Our Times on the Road to Smarter Shopping," *Progressive Grocer,* November 1976, p. 43.

8. Michael J. Houston, "The Effect of Unit-Pricing on Choices of Brand and Size in Economic Shopping," *Journal of Marketing* 36 (July 1972): 51–54.

9. Hans R. Isakson and Alex R. Maurizi, "The Consumer Economics of Unit Pricing," *Journal of Marketing Research* 10 (August 1973): 277–285.

10. Coyle, "Dual Pricing Settles In," pp. 47–48.

11. Ibid., p. 48.

12. See for example, Douglas J. McConnell, "Effect of Pricing on Perception of Product Quality," *Journal of Applied Psychology* 52 (August 1968): 331–334; and Folke Olander, "The Influence of Price on the Consumer's Evaluation of Products and Purchases," in B. Taylor and G. Wills, eds., *Pricing Strategy* (Staples Press, 1969), pp. 50–69.

13. Jacob Jacoby, Jerry Olsen, and Rafael Haddock, "Price, Brand Name, and Product Composition Characteristics as Determinants of Perceived Quality," *Journal of Applied Psychology* 55 (December 1971): 470–479.

14. Kent B. Monroe, "The Influence of Price Differences and Brand Familiarity on Brand Preferences," *Journal of Consumer Research* 3 (June 1976): 42–49.

15. John J. Wheatley and John S.Y. Chiu, "The Effects of Price, Store Image and Product and Respondent Characteristics on Perceptions of Quality," *Journal of Marketing Research* 14 (May 1977): 181–186.

16. Zarrel V. Lambert, "Perceived Prices as Related to Odd and Even Price Endings," *Journal of Retailing* 51 (Fall 1975): 13–22.

17. "How Multiple-Unit Pricing Helps and Hurts," *Progressive Grocer,* June 1971, pp. 52–58.

18. John F. Willenborg and Robert E. Pitts, "Gasoline Prices: Their Effect on Consumer Behavior and Attitudes," *Journal of Marketing* 41 (January 1977): 24–30.

19. William S. Penn, Jr. and Harold W. Fox, "Puzzling Price Latitude at Service Stations," *Business Economics* (March 1977): 12–16.

20. Monroe, "The Influence of Price Differences," p. 47.

21. Arch G. Woodside and J. Taylor Sims, "Retail Sales Transactions and Customer 'Purchase Pal' Effects on Buying Behavior," *Journal of Retailing* 52 (Fall 1976): 57–64.

22. Arch G. Woodside and J. William Davenport, Jr., "Effects of Price and Salesman Expertise on Customer Purchasing Behavior," *Journal of Business* 49 (January 1976): 51–59.

23. Andre Gabor and C.W.J. Granger, "Price as an Indicator of Quality: Report on an Enquiry," *Economica* 46 (February 1966): 43–70.

24. Robert F. Dietrich, "Shopping Smart," *Progressive Grocer,* April 1975, pp. 48–52.

25. "The Uptight Consumer, What is She Up To?" *Progressive Grocer,* November 1975, pp. 41–57.

26. Robert Blattberg, Thomas Buesing, Peter Peacock, and Subrata Sen, "Who is the Deal Prone Consumer," in H. Keith Hunt, ed., *Advances in Consumer Research,* vol. 5 (Ann Arbor, Mich.: Association for Consumer Research, 1978): pp. 57–62.

27. Philip Kotler, *Marketing Management: Analysis, Planning and Control,* 3rd ed. (Englewood Cliffs, N.J.: Prentice-Hall Inc., 1976).

28. Jon G. Udell, *Successful Marketing Strategies in American Industry* (Madison, Wis.: Mimir Publishers, 1972).

29. F.B. Evans, "Selling as a Dyadic Relationship — A New Approach," *American Behavioral Scientist* 6 (May 1963): 76–79.

30. Timothy C. Brock, "Communicator-Recipient Similarity and Decision Change," *Journal of Personality and Social Psychology* 1 (June 1965): 650–654.

31. Paul Busch and David T. Wilson, "An Experimental Analysis of a Salesman's Expert and Referent Bases of Social Power in the Buyer-Seller Dyad," *Journal of Marketing Research* 13 (February 1976): 3–11.

32. Arch G. Woodside and J. William Davenport, Jr., "The Effect of Salesman Similarity and Expertise on Consumer Purchasing Behavior," *Journal of Marketing Research* 11 (May 1974): 198–202.

33. G. David Hughes, Joseph B. Juhasz, and Bruno Contini, "The Influence of Personality on the Bargaining Process," *Journal of Business* 46 (October 1973): 593–603.

34. Barton A. Weitz, "The Relationship Between Salesperson Performance and Understanding of Customer Decision Making," *Journal of Marketing Research* 15 (November 1978): 501–516.

35. Ibid., p. 514.

TWENTY-TWO

Organizational Buyer Behavior

Focus of Chapter

Consumer behavior refers to the behavior of a type of customer in the marketplace — the final consumer. An equally important category of customer is the organizational buyer as represented by the industrial purchaser (the purchaser who buys products for industrial purposes such as input into manufacturing processes) and by the institutional purchaser (the purchaser for institutions such as hospitals, government agencies, or schools). Organizational buying behavior represents a larger segment of the economy by sales volume than consumer behavior. Webster estimates that over half of all economic activity in America is represented by the industrial purchaser.[1] Furthermore, most of the personal selling activity referred to in the previous chapter is directed to organizational buyers.

Organizational buyer behavior has certain similarities to consumer buying behavior, but the needs, decision processes, and behavior of organizational buyers are sufficiently different from consumer buyers to warrant separate consideration. Recognition of these differences and the consequent differences in marketing strategies have resulted in the development of a body of literature in marketing, particularly since 1970, devoted to the study of organizational buyer behavior.

The first part of this chapter will consider the similarities and differences between consumer behavior and organizational buyer behavior. A model of organizational buyer behavior will be described. In the next two sections, the decision process in (1) selecting a supplier and (2) selecting a product to meet the needs of the organization will be examined. The chapter will conclude by describing organizational buyer behavior as a process of group decision making and by considering the role of the buying center in the organization.

THE NATURE OF ORGANIZATIONAL
BUYER BEHAVIOR

549

The Nature of
Organizational
Buyer Behavior

Similarities to Consumer Behavior

Frequent reference has been made to a belief that the organizational buyer operates primarily on the basis of rational criteria of cost and product quality. As far back as 1924, Paul Converse stated "The [industrial] buyers are generally experts and often buy on the basis of chemical analysis and physical tests. . . . Buying tends to become scientific. Quality, price and delivery are the controlling factors."[2] Over thirty years later, Shoaf studied 137 managers engaged in industrial buying and concluded: "The industrial buyer may be more human than we're inclined to realize."[3] Shoaf found that the greater the standardization in industrial products, the more likely emotional factors such as subjective attitudes, desire to avoid risky decisions, and longevity of supplier relations come into play.

Other studies have also found that the organizational buyer does not necessarily follow the model of rational, economic man. Wilson et al. identified two decision styles in a study of 132 Canadian industrial purchasers.[4] A normative (rational) decision style was one in which expected monetary value was maximized in the purchase. This style conforms to the traditional view of the industrial purchaser. A conservative decision style was one in which expected value was not maximized, primarily because of a greater level of risk associated with the purchase and a consequent need for more certainty. This suggests that a conservative decision style would be followed by someone who does not want to rock the organizational boat and who is more interested in protecting his or her position. Wilson and his colleagues found that only 30 percent of the managers conformed to the rational decision style.

The notion of an organizational buyer operating by personal rather than organizational motives, and by subjective attitudes and perceptions rather than economic utility, means that certain components of the model of consumer behavior may apply equally well to organizational buyer behavior. For example, the organizational buyer enters the purchasing situation with a psychological set. The organizational buyer develops attitudes toward vendors based on past experience, the vendor's marketing strategy, and the buyer's own predispositions. As a result, preferences develop that may favor certain vendors on other than economic grounds. The result may be the development of vendor loyalty, just as the consumer is likely to develop brand or store loyalty. Studies suggest that vendor loyalty may be an inefficient basis for vendor selection reflecting inadequate information search.[5] These findings parallel results reported in Chapter 20 that store loyalty may be the result of inertia and inadequate information on price and product quality.

Further evidence shows that interpersonal influences may operate in organizational buyer behavior as they do in consumer behavior. Martilla reports on the importance of word-of-mouth influence on industrial buyers.[6] Two studies have also identified opinion leaders as an important source of influence in organizational buying.[7] Clearly, organizational buying cannot be understood by economic analysis alone. Behavioral principles must be applied within a framework of buyer behavior research.

Differences with Consumer Behavior

Despite its similarities, organizational buyer behavior is substantially different from consumer behavior in several ways. The importance of these differences is the rationale for this chapter.

Most importantly, organizational buyer behavior is generally a *group decision process*. Several people playing different roles may be involved — the purchasing agent, the engineer, the production manager. These individuals represent a decision-making unit in the organization referred to as a **buying center.** In consumer behavior, concepts and applications have focused on the individual as the unit of analysis. In organizational buying behavior, the group is most frequently the unit of analysis. In this respect, there may be more parallels between studies of family decision making (Chapter 14) and organizational buyer behavior than between studies of individual consumers and organizational buyers.

A second difference is the *technical complexity* frequently involved in organizational buying. Webster states, "Even when the unit of analysis in consumer marketing is the household rather than the individual consumer, consumer buying behavior never reaches the complexity of industrial buying. . . "[8] Third, the *interdependence between buyer and seller* is likely to be greater in organizational buying. The buyer may have fewer alternatives for a given item, while the seller may be seriously affected by losing a large industrial account. Fourth, the *postpurchase process* is likely to be more important because of the necessity for installation, service calls, and warranty. Fifth, because of the greater need for interaction between buyer and seller, a *negotiation process* is more likely to take place. As a result, personal selling assumes more importance.

A sixth difference is that organizational buyers are much more likely to have individual needs requiring sellers to design products to meet *specifications*. As a result, organizational buyers are less likely to be presold based on advertising compared to consumers. The need to meet particular demands increases the length of the organizational buying process. Another outcome of producing to specification is that segmentation of industrial markets becomes less relevant. Some segments may be represented by one or two companies.

Characteristics of Organizational Buying Decisions

The differences between organizational and consumer buying require a fuller understanding of the process of organizational buying. Before presenting a model of organizational buying behavior, several characteristics must be understood that will differentiate one organizational buying decision from another.

Type of Decision

Organizational buying situations are likely to differ by degree of complexity. Organizational buying decisions are frequently classified into three types:

1. *The straight rebuy* is a recurring purchasing requirement and can be handled on a routine basis. Little information search is required and vendors are selected from a prespecified list. This type of decision parallels routinized purchases in consumer behavior described in Chapter 3.

2. *The modified rebuy* is also a recurring purchasing situation, but either the vendor alternatives or product specifications have changed requiring some information search. Vendors who are not on the buyer's supplier list will try to change a straight rebuy to a modified rebuy. This type of decision parallels the limited decision-making process in Chapter 3.

3. *The new task* is a buying decision that has not occurred before. Since there is little past experience, extensive information search is required to identify alternative suppliers and develop proper product specifications. New task decisions are important because they may set the pattern for future rebuy decisions. Particularly important in this respect is the adoption of new products and innovations by the organization. This type of decision parallels complex decision making in Chapter 2.

Vendor Versus Product Selection

Another distinction is the one between a decision regarding alternative suppliers and a decision regarding product adoption. Frequently the two are intertwined, but different criteria are used to select vendors (delivery, sales personnel, reliability) and products (price, quality, engineering specifications). The normative model of economic utility suggests that product specifications should determine vendor selection. But, frequently it is the other way around — loyalty to a certain vendor or criteria of supplier dependability and reliability determine product choice. This is particularly true in straight rebuy situations.

Individual Versus Group Decisions

Most decisions involving selection of new suppliers or products are made by buying centers. Some may be made by individual purchasing agents, although individual decisions are more likely in a straight or modified rebuy situation. Decision making by buying centers requires considering the different roles of members of the buying center, differing interpretations of objectives, interpersonal influences, relative power, and the need for some resolution of possible conflicts between members of the buying group. These factors are not as relevant in individual decisions.

Influences on the Buying Decision

The distinction between individual and group decisions is not always clear in organizational buying. The purchasing agent may have ultimate decision responsibility but may be influenced by superiors within the organization and by peers outside the organization. The buying center is still composed of individuals subject to their own attitudes, perceptions, and biases. Therefore, two components in any organizational buying decision are the influence of *the individual* and the influence of *the group*. A third component is the *organization* itself; a fourth is the *environment* in organizational buying. Webster and Wind summarize these four influences on the organizational buyer in Figure 22–1.[9]

I. THE ENVIRONMENT (Environmental determinants of buying behavior)

Physical	Economic	Legal
Technological	Political	Cultural

Suppliers	Customers	Govern-ment	Labor Unions	Trade Associations	Professional Groups	Other Business Firms	Other Social Institutions

Information about Suppliers (Marketing Communications)	Availability of Goods and Services	General Business Conditions	Values and Norms

II. THE ORGANIZATION (Organizational determinants of buying behavior)

THE ORGANIZATIONAL CLIMATE: PHYSICAL, TECHNOLOGICAL, ECONOMIC, CULTURAL

ORGANIZA-TIONAL TECHNOLOGY	ORGANIZA-TIONAL STRUCTURE	ORGANIZA-TIONAL GOALS AND TASKS	ORGANIZA-TIONAL ACTORS
TECHNOLOGY RELEVANT FOR PURCHASING	ORGANIZATION OF THE BUYING CENTER AND THE PURCHASING FUNCTION	BUYING TASKS	MEMBERS OF THE BUYING CENTER

Technological Constraints and Technology Available to the Group	Group Structure	Group Tasks	Member Characteristics and Goals, Leadership

III. THE BUYING CENTER (Interpersonal determinants of buying behavior)

TASK	NON TASK
Interactions, Activities, Sentiments	Interactions, Activities, Sentiments

GROUP PROCESSES

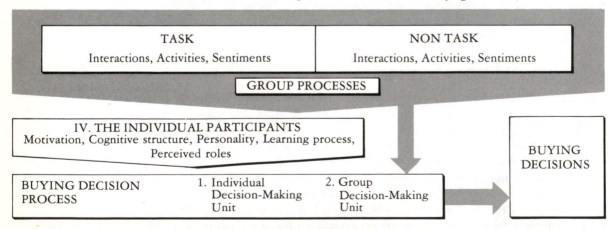

IV. THE INDIVIDUAL PARTICIPANTS
Motivation, Cognitive structure, Personality, Learning process, Perceived roles

BUYING DECISION PROCESS

1. Individual Decision-Making Unit
2. Group Decision-Making Unit

BUYING DECISIONS

FIGURE 22–1   Influences on Organizational Buying Behavior

Environmental influences (Part I of Figure 22–1) include the technological state of the arts in the buyer's industry, the state of the economy, government regulations, and legal and cultural factors. These factors influence the organizational climate. Organizational variables that impact on buyer decisions (Part II of Figure 22–1) are the technology available to the buyer, the organizational structure for decision making, the goals and responsibilities assigned to various members of a buying group, and the makeup of the buying center.

Group influences are summarized in the operation of the buying center (Part III of Figure 22–1). These represent the interpersonal relations within the buying center. Group influences are broken out into task-related interactions (interactions based on the work to be performed in the buying task) and nontask interactions (personal motives, the interplay of personalities, different views of the buying function by members of the buying center). The individual's motives, perceptions, personality and role within the organization (Part IV of Figure 22–1) influence his or her interactions within the buying center and the final decision process.

The four influences summarized in Figure 22–1 will influence the buying decision, whether it is an individual decision or whether it is made by a group decision-making unit.

A Model of Organizational Buyer Behavior

A model of organizational buyer behavior should take these distinctions into account. Such a model is presented in Figure 22–2 and is an adaptation of one developed by Sheth.[10] The key component of the model is the expectations of buyers (purchasing agent, engineer, production manager, etc.) about suppliers and brands (Number 1 in the model). The more positive the expectations about performance, the more likely the supplier or brand will be selected. Expectations can be measured by determining the buyer's assessment of the vendor or brand on key evaluative criteria. Using a multiattribute approach similar to that used in the evaluation of brands, the buyer would first identify the most important objectives (product quality, delivery time, reliability, after-sale service, price, etc.) and rate each vendor or each brand on these criteria. The supplier and brand most likely to meet the buyer's objectives based on the key evaluative criteria would be selected.

The buyer's expectations (evaluation of vendors or brands) are based on four factors. The first factor is the background of the decision maker (1a in Figure 22–2). The decision maker's demographic characteristics, life-style, and job expectations are likely to affect his or her assessment of suppliers and brands. Educational differences in particular may result in different expectations. For example, Haksansson and Wootz found that the most important influence on industrial purchasing behavior is the buyer's education.[11] Purchasers with a higher level of education spend more time on the purchase decision, contact a more diverse set of suppliers, and are more willing to make a risky decision.

Source for Figure 22–1: Adapted from Frederick E. Webster and Yoram Wind, "A General Model for Understanding Buying Behavior," *Journal of Marketing* 36 (April 1972): 15.
Reprinted with permission from the *Journal of Marketing*.

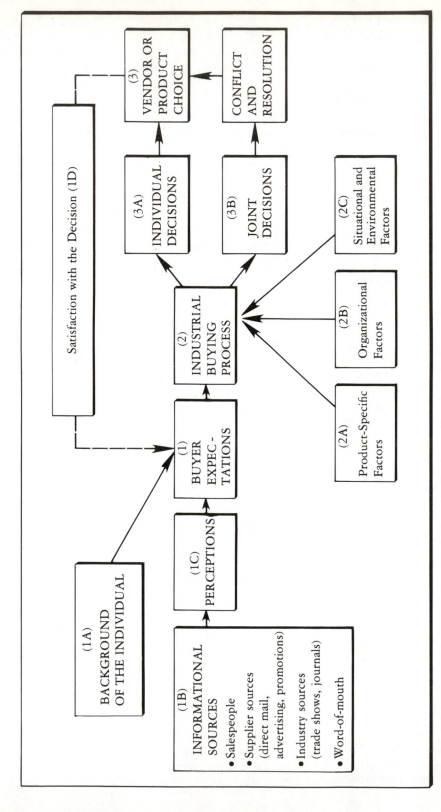

FIGURE 22–2   A Model of Organizational Buyer Behavior

Source: Adapted from Jagdish N. Sheth, "A Model of Industrial Buyer Behavior," *Journal of Marketing* 37 (October 1973): 51.   Reprinted with permission from the *Journal of Marketing.*

The second factor influencing buyer judgments is the nature and source of information (1b in the model). Informational sources are from personal selling, supplier promotion and advertising, industry sources, and word-of-mouth influences from other buyers. The purchasing agent is more likely to engage in active search and to obtain information from advertising and promotion. Engineers and production managers are more likely to obtain information from industry sources.[12]

The buyer's perceptions of the supplier and the brand (1c) will directly influence expectations. Previous chapters have suggested that information processing is likely to be selective. Since engineers, purchasing agents, and production managers operate based on different goals and values, they are likely to evaluate the same information differently. Selectivity in perception is illustrated in a study by Weigand which found that purchasing agents rated their own involvement in buying decisions higher than did other executives.[13] Similarly, a study by Grashof and Thomas found that participants in joint decisions consistently inflated their own roles in the organizational buying process.[14]

The final factor influencing buyer expectations is past experience with a supplier or brand (1d). Here also, different individuals in the organization may interpret the same experience differently. Sheth notes that the purchasing agent is rewarded for economy, the engineer for quality control, and the production manager for efficient scheduling.[15] Therefore, if a high quality product is purchased from a supplier with a quick delivery date but at substantially higher cost, it is likely to be evaluated more positively by engineering and production personnel and more negatively by purchasing agents.

The industrial buying process (2 in the model) and ultimately the final decision regarding a supplier or brand (3) will be influenced by several factors. First is the buyer's expectations (1). These expectations represent the sum of the individual influences on the buying decision. Second, the decision will be influenced by the nature of product choice (2a). Is the decision for a straight rebuy, a modified rebuy, or a new task? A related factor is the degree of risk associated with the decision. The level of risk is likely to be greater in selecting a new product. Another product-related consideration is the dollar amount budgeted for the item. Time pressures in the decision will also affect the outcome.

A third set of factors directly influencing the decision is organizational (2b). Company orientation will influence the decision process. A company that is technologically oriented is likely to assign more responsibility to engineers. A cost-conscious company is more likely to assign responsibility for buying to the purchasing agent. Other organizational factors are size and degree of centralization. Companies that are larger and more decentralized are more likely to develop joint responsibilities for purchasing in buying centers composed of purchasing, engineering, and production.

Situational and environmental factors also affect the decision process and outcome (2c). A recession will increase the level of risk in decisions and possibly increase the power of cost-conscious purchasing agents compared to quality-conscious engineers. Strikes or machine failures will affect the importance of delivery dates and the role of the production manager.

The model takes account of the fact that the decision may be an individual one (3a) or a joint decision by a buying center (3b). Whether the decision is individual or joint is dependent on the nature of the decision process, particularly the product and organizational factors. For example, if risk is high, the decision is more likely to be made by a buying center because more deliberation and a greater diversity of opinion are warranted. Higher cost decisions and decisions on new products are also more likely to be made by buying centers for the same reason. Given the greater deliberation of a joint versus an individual decision, time pressures cannot be as great. Regarding the organizational factors, joint decisions are more likely in technologically complex organizations because the engineer will probably join the purchasing agent in taking responsibility for buying. As noted, joint decisions are also more likely if the organization is large and decentralized.

Given the inputs of individual expectations, product and organizational characteristics, environmental influences, and individual versus joint decision making, a decision will be reached regarding a supplier and brand. The decision will be evaluated individually or jointly. Postpurchase evaluation will then affect future expectations of buyers regarding the chosen supplier and brand.

SUPPLIER CHOICE BEHAVIOR

The model of organizational buyer behavior is useful in outlining the factors that influence supplier and brand choice, but it does not adequately describe the process of decision making. The key elements in this process are the formulation of buying objectives and the development of criteria for evaluating alternatives. This section will consider *supplier choice;* the next section will focus on *product choice.*

The Process of Supplier Choice

The process of choosing a supplier involves a sequence of steps. Webster and Wind define five steps in the process:

1. *Identify needs:*   Some member of the organization perceives a problem that can be solved through the purchase of a product or service.

2. *Establish objectives and specifications:*   Specifications will grow out of need identification and may be submitted to alternative suppliers. Such specifications may describe technical requirements, delivery dates, price limits, and service.

3. *Identify vendors and obtain bids:*   The market is searched for alternative sources of supply. Bids are then obtained from qualified suppliers indicating price and conformity to other specifications.

4. *Evaluate alternative suppliers:*   Supplier bids are compared to the buyer's specifications. Since most decisions involve multiple criteria, a multiattribute approach would be logical in which various criteria are weighted by the importance to the buyer. Suppliers are then rated, and the supplier who most closely meets specifications on the most important criteria is selected.

5. *Select the supplier.*[16]

A sixth step should be added: postpurchase evaluation of the supplier. The degree to which the supplier met the promised specifications and fulfilled service obligations is evaluated and will directly influence the likelihood of repurchasing.

Webster and Wind's description of supplier selection is more typical of a new task and possibly a modified rebuy than a straight rebuy situation. In a straight rebuy, need identification may be a function of out-of-stock, specifications may be preset, vendors may already be identified from an approved list, and evaluation may be based on one or two criteria like price and delivery date.

Given the need for a decision process in supplier selection, some key issues are (1) the criteria used in evaluating alternative suppliers, (2) the sources used to obtain information on suppliers, and (3) the degree of risk involved in choosing a supplier.

Criteria in Supplier Choice

The criteria used in evaluating alternative suppliers are likely to differ from those used in evaluating specific product alternatives. In a study of purchasing agents in forty-five companies, Lehmann and O'Shaughnessy identified seventeen attributes used to evaluate suppliers (see Table 22–1).[17] These can be grouped into criteria related to price, ordering convenience, supplier reputation, service, supplier technical capabilities, and product-operating characteristics. Lehmann and O'Shaughnessy found that price and delivery were more important if the product is less likely to cause operating problems. Under these conditions, current suppliers are more likely to be selected. If a product is likely to cause operating problems, then technical service, supplier flexibility in adjusting to the company's needs, and product reliability become much more important.

Criteria used in evaluating suppliers are likely to differ by organization. In one study, five large manufacturing firms were contacted and were asked to review past purchasing decisions based on the seven criteria listed in Table 22–2.[18] The low bidder obtained the contract 89 percent of the time in Company 4 but only 40 percent of the time in Company 1. The buyer had prior experience with the vendor 100 percent of the time in Company 3 but only 11 percent of the time in Company 4. Compared to other companies, Company 4 emphasized low price and short delivery time and was not concerned with prior experience with the vendor. Company 3 also emphasized low price but would deal only with vendors on an approved list. Company 2 was more likely to emphasize the existence of spare parts, possibly in an attempt to ensure uninterrupted production.

This study demonstrates that buyers do not always rely on objective factors such as price, delivery date, service, and lack of duplication. The fact that Company 3 dealt only with past suppliers shows that prior relationships may be more important than the supplier's product capabilities. Cardozo and Cagley found the same results in a study of sixty-four industrial purchasers.[19] Supplier visibility and prior relationships were more important than price, product specifications, delivery, or the amount of information provided to the buyer. Having a well-known name was more important if the buyer had little other information about the supplier. This does not mean that the product plays little role in the purchase decision. Of the bids accepted, 84 percent met product specifications.[20] But, in most cases, product specifications were met by well-known companies or companies with a prior relationship with the buyer.

Information Sources

An important input into the process of choosing a supplier is the nature and source of information on product choice. Dempsey focused on sources of in-

TABLE 22–1 Attributes Used to Evaluate Suppliers

1. Overall reputation of the supplier
2. Financing terms
3. Supplier's flexibility in adjusting to your company's needs
4. Experience with the supplier in analogous situations
5. Technical service offered
6. Confidence in the salespeople
7. Convenience of placing the order
8. Data on reliability of the product
9. Price
10. Technical specifications
11. Ease of operation or use
12. Preferences of principal user of the product
13. Training offered by the supplier
14. Training time required
15. Reliability of delivery date promised
16. Ease of maintenance
17. Sales service expected after date of purchase

Source: Donald R. Lehmann and John O'Shaughnessy, "Difference in Attribute Importance for Different Industrial Products," *Journal of Marketing* 38 (April 1974): 38.
    Reprinted with permission from the *Journal of Marketing*.

TABLE 22–2   Percentage of Time Successful Bidder Possessed Following Characteristics

	Co. 1	Co. 2	Co. 3	Co. 4	Co. 5
Low bidder on price	40%	46%	76%	89%	64%
Bid met specifications	100%	100%	100%	100%	100%
Equal or shortest delivery time	48%	61%	56%	77%	64%
Buyer had prior experience with vendor	52%	50%	100%	11%	36%
Duplication of existing equipment	36%	57%	4%	22%	48%
Spare parts available in buyers inventory	8%	21%	0	0	4%
Future maintenance evaluated	12%	14%	0	0	0

Source: J. Patrick Kelly and James W. Coaker, "Can We Generalize about Choice Criteria for Industrial Purchasing Decision," in Kenneth L. Bernhardt, ed., *Proceedings of the American Marketing Association Educators' Conference,* Series #39 (1976), p. 332.
    Reprinted with permission from the American Marketing Association.

formation for vendors such as catalogs, purchasing records, direct mail, journal advertising, and financial reports.[21] He found that a supplier's quality of workmanship was evaluated using catalogs, purchasing records, and plant visits. Pricing information was obtained from advertising, internal company records, and purchasing managers in other firms. Dempsey concludes that industrial marketers can improve their quality-workmanship image by placing more emphasis on the distribution of their catalogs.

Perceived Risk in Supplier Selection

Perceived risk is another element in the process of supplier selection. One strategy to reduce risk is to buy from the same vendor. Such vendor loyalty protects the buyer's position within the firm. Since the decision is routinized, the buyer is in a sense abdicating responsibility for it. This strategy is followed by Company 3 in Table 22–2. Another strategy for risk reduction is to reduce the possible negative consequences of a decision by selecting the lowest bidder, as represented by Company 4 in Table 22–2.

Vendor Loyalty

Vendor loyalty is a natural outgrowth of satisfaction with a particular supplier and a desire to forego decision making for routine purchases. In this respect, vendor loyalty is similar to store or brand loyalty, but organizational buyers sometimes continue to buy from a particular supplier even when a search for alternative vendors may result in cost savings or better quality products. Vendor loyalty may be based on a number of individual and organizational factors that do not conform to the model of a rational buyer.

Bubb and van Rest cite a number of objective and subjective reasons for vendor loyalty based on a study of industrial buying behavior of a new metal product in Europe.[22] The most important factors encouraging vendor loyalty are administrative inertia (reluctance to change to new sources because of an inability to cope with any complications resulting from change) and familiarity (the desire to ensure that unexpected difficulties will not occur). Both motivations reflect a desire to reduce risk and may result in a slow adaptation to a changing environment. Other reasons cited for vendor loyalty are persistence (the advantages of building up a long-term relationship with the same supplier) and reciprocity.

Despite the potential inefficiencies of vendor loyalty, some limitation on a search for alternative vendors is necessary. Otherwise, the organizational buyer will be engaged in a decision process for every straight rebuy. A balance between vendor loyalty and decision making is therefore required, with vendor loyalty typically occurring for straight rebuys and with a search for alternative vendors occurring in the modified rebuy or new task situation.

Wind did an extensive study of the purchase history of an electronics firm and concluded that vendor loyalty was a function of a buyer's past experience with the supplier, organizational pressures for cost savings, and time pressures resulting in simplification of rules for buying.[23] These factors are enumerated in Figure 22–3. A fourth factor is the vendor's product or service offering. Price is most important in maintaining vendor loyalty because it is assumed the

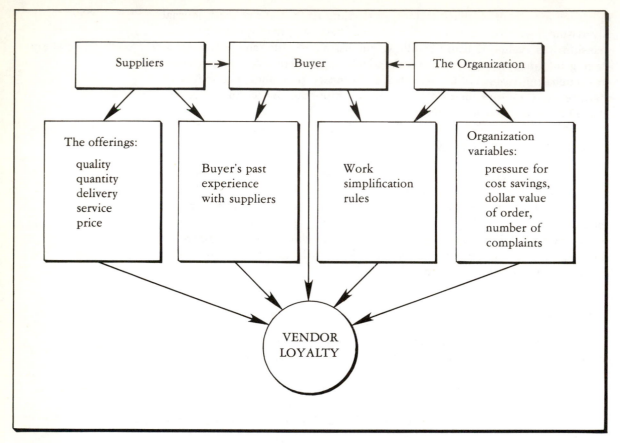

FIGURE 22–3   Factors Encouraging Vendor Loyalty

Source: Adapted from Yoram Wind, "Industrial Source Loyalty," *Journal of Marketing Research* 7 November 1970): 451.   Reprinted with permission from the *Journal of Marketing Research.*

favored vendor will maintain the price of the product. A price increase will lead to a greater probability of considering alternative vendors.

Based on his research, Wind concludes that vendor loyalty is more likely to occur under the following conditions:

1. *The dollar value of the order is small:*   No significant cost savings are expected by a switch in vendors. Therefore, the cost of search for alternative vendors is not worth it.

2. *Past cost savings by dealing with the favored vendor are high:*   There is little pressure for reducing costs, decreasing the motivation to search for alternative suppliers.

3. *The prices charged by the favored vendor are stable or decreasing:*   This means the buyer is achieving the desired cost savings without information search.

4. *A specific brand is recommended by the favored vendor:*   In most cases, the buyer will accept the brand recommendations of a favored vendor. This alleviates the organizational buyer from engaging in a decision process regarding brand selection.

Organizational buying behavior involves the selection of a product, as well as a vendor. The two decisions are closely related since one often determines the other. But certain areas in the organization may exert more influence on vendor selection, while others may exert more influence on product choice. For example, Cooley et al. found that engineers had the dominant power in selecting products, while the purchasing department had the dominant power in selecting suppliers.[24] Moreover, the criteria used in evaluating products are likely to differ from those used in evaluating suppliers. McMillan developed the following product and supplier selection criteria:

Product Variables	*Supplier Variables*
Total cost	Delivery on schedule
Performance	Service
Quality	Innovative nature
Quality consistency	Dependability
	Technical capability
	Emergency assistance
	Supplying future demand[25]

The process of product choice is likely to center on the question of adopting a new product or process. Technical specifications are likely to dominate. This is why engineers have the most power in selecting new products. Price is not as important as product specifications in the selection of a new product. Price becomes important once product specifications are met. In the study by Cardozo and Cagley, the low price bidder received the contract only 32 percent of the time.[26]

The importance of new products and innovations in industrial firms has extended adoption and diffusion theory (Chapter 16) to organizational buying behavior. Studies have focused on the nature of the new product adoption process in industrial buying, the characteristics of early adopters of innovations, and sources of information and influence in the adoption decision.

The Industrial Adoption Process

A description of the industrial adoption process is presented in Figure 22–4.[27] The process requires an *awareness* of the product by the prospect, sufficient *interest* based on organizational needs, an *evaluation* of the product by determining product specifications and by comparing them to company needs, a period of *trial* in which product performance is directly assessed, and, finally, a decision on *adoption*.

The inputs into the decision process are the organizational factors (age of firm, R&D commitment, size, environment, etc.) and the characteristics of the buying center (size, age, education of members, etc.). Informational sources regarding the new product are central to the process of adoption. Two types of sources are specified in Figure 22–4, impersonal (advertising, brochures, trade shows) and personal (salesperson contacts, contacts with buyers in other

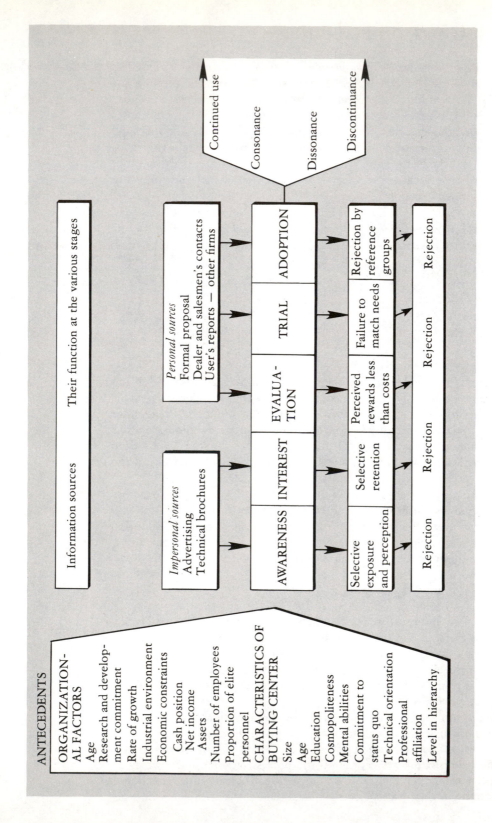

FIGURE 22–4   The Industrial Adoption Process

Source: Adapted from Urban B. Ozanne and Gilbert A. Churchill Jr., "Five Dimensions of the Industrial Adoption Process," *Journal of Marketing Research* 8 (August 1971): 323. Reprinted with permission from the *Journal of Marketing Research.*

firms). The model assumes that the impersonal sources will be most influential in the creation of new product awareness and interest, whereas the personal sources will be most important in product evaluation, trial, and the adoption decision. This means that industrial marketers must rely on brochures and advertising for initial awareness and must then shift to personal sources such as sales representatives and word-of-mouth to influence buyers in the evaluation and adoption stages.

The model allows for three outcomes. First, rejection of the product because of lack of awareness (selective exposure or perception), a failure to meet economic criteria or to match product specifications to needs in the evaluation and trial phase, or a rejection of the product after trial by the buying center for any of the above reasons. Second, given adoption, the product may be discontinued because of poor performance. Third, the product may achieve continued use within the firm.

Characteristics of Adopters

Interest has focused on the characteristics of firms more likely to adopt innovations, and more precisely the characteristics of early adopting firms. O'Neal et al. suggest that firms are more likely to adopt an innovation if they:

1. are *large* relative to the required investment;
2. are in industries with a high rate of *technical change*;
3. face intense *competition*;
4. have sufficient positive information about the innovation to *reduce uncertainty*;
5. view the innovation as presenting a *relative advantage* as measured by comparing the gross margin of the innovation to the least favorable product carried by the firm; and
6. view the innovation as *compatible* with products previously adopted.[28]

Webster adds a seventh criterion, the firm's *level of aspiration* as measured by market share and profitability objectives.[29] Firms with a higher level of aspiration are more likely to be adopters.

Not only the adoption process, but the time of adoption has been studied by researchers. Czepiel studied the continuing casting process in the steel industry[30] and found that younger firms and firms with a more open decision style were more likely to adopt early. A freer and more open decision process could encourage risk taking. Further, younger firms may be more likely to engage in such a decision style.

Information Sources

An essential element in the adoption process is the nature and source of information. Webster asked industrial buyers their preference for sources of information by stage in the adoption process.[31] The industrial salesperson is seen as the most valuable source in all phases of the adoption process. But buyers and engineers in other companies are almost as important in the process of evaluating alternative products. Interpersonal sources of influence therefore seem to be important in the product evaluation phase.

A study by Martilla of paper buying practices in 106 firms supports the importance of personal sources in the later stages of the adoption process.[32] He found that interpersonal contacts with persons in the buyer's firm and in other firms was much greater in the evaluation phase. Impersonal sources such as product literature, trade journals, and trade shows were more important in gaining product awareness. Martilla also found that personal contacts were important to the buyer *after* the purchase as a means of reducing postpurchase uncertainty. Confirming information was sought to justify the purchase.

Both the Webster and Martilla studies suggest that commercial sources of information are most important in creating awareness of new products, but that personal influence is most important in the decision to adopt new products.

Sources of information have also been studied by time of adoption. Traditional adoption and diffusion theory holds that early adopters rely more on external sources of information (technical journals, catalogues, etc.) whereas later adopters are more subject to personal sources. Several studies found the opposite to be true in industrial adoptions: Early adopters were less likely to rely on external sources of information.[33] It appears that the early *industrial* adopter relies more on interpersonal influence than does the early *consumer* adopter. One possible explanation is that industrial buyers consider an innovation as a risky decision for the firm and for themselves, especially if they are one of the first to adopt the product. Millions of dollars could be lost if the wrong decision is made. As a result, when it comes down to making the decision, industrial buyers might tend to rely on the most valid and legitimate source they know — other buyers in their firm and in other firms. Baker and Parkinson found that the early industrial adopter did see more risk in the decision than the later adopter, particularly regarding the likelihood that the product would match manufacturers' performance claims and that it would be easy to service.[34]

Industrial Segmentation by Product Choice

A segmentation of organizational buyers is a viable approach for industrial marketers. Yet as Wind and Cardozo note, "Industrial marketers by no means use market segmentation strategies as widely or effectively as they might. Segmentation appears to be largely an after-the-fact explanation of why a marketing program did or did not work, rather than a carefully thought-out foundation for marketing programs."[35]

One reason why segmentation may be less frequent in industrial than consumer markets is the unique nature of product demand. If a product must be developed to the specifications of one or two firms, then there is no basis for grouping customers together by similarities in need or product choice. Another factor is that industrial marketing research has lagged behind the consumer area in development of data bases and application of quantitative techniques required for segmentation analysis.

Despite these limitations, some segmentation studies have been reported in the industrial area. Most of these can be classified as behavioral segmentation, that is, identifying the characteristics of a firm's customers by product choice. Wind and Cardozo surveyed segmentation practices of twenty-five companies. In two-thirds of the cases the criteria were behavioral (sales, market share, profit performance of a particular product). In only 5 percent of the cases did the firms cite customers' needs as the criterion (i.e., benefit segmentation).[36]

An analysis by AT&T of its industrial purchasers is illustrative of behavioral segmentation in the industrial sphere.[37] The company sought to identify the organizational characteristics (total sales, number of employees, location, etc.) of heavier versus lighter users of the telephone. Results of this analysis are presented in Table 22–3. The average monthly telephone bill for the industrial customer in the sample is $910, but among companies with more than 500 employees, the average bill is $6,033. These companies are only 3 percent of AT&T's industrial customers, but they represent 20 percent of AT&T's revenues from industrial accounts. Despite its small size, Segment 1 is worth targeting for promotions and personal selling effort.

Another important segment is companies with less than 500 employees that utilize central switching (PBX) facilities and have at least fifty employees in other locations (Segment 2). These companies represent 8 percent of the industrial customers and another 21 percent of AT&T's industrial revenues. Thus, about 10 percent of AT&T's industrial customers account for 40 percent of the revenue, illustrating the extreme degree of concentration in the industrial telecommunications market.

Although these results are not surprising, the analysis was valuable in identifying the characteristics of the heaviest telephone users. The analysis also demonstrated the importance of further study of the small business segment with switching facilities (segment 3) since this group accounted for almost half of all companies and one-half of AT&T's revenues.

One of the few examples of *benefit segmentation* in industrial buying is found in a study by Wind, Grashof, and Goldhar. They attempted to define the components for a new Scientific and Technical Information (STI) service based on the needs of 274 scientists and information specialists.[38] Conjoint analysis was used to define the combination of components in an information system that would best meet the needs of these individuals. Five segments were identified based on differences in their emphasis on the twelve STI components listed below:

- speed of information
- purchase arrangement
- nature of output
- output format
- mode of search
- distribution

- mode of payment
- type of supplies
- language used
- topical coverage
- period coverage
- price

The distinctive characteristics of each segment are summarized below:

- *Segment 1* (48 percent of all respondents) is *systems rather than price oriented,* and emphasizes the system's language and extent of coverage. Firms in segment 1 are larger and the orientation is more toward *information* support rather than R&D.
- *Segment 2* (8 percent of all respondents) is also systems rather than price oriented, but this group is more concerned with *output format.* Firms in segment 2 are smaller with a smaller proportion of employees with advanced degrees. Job responsibility is more likely to be with an R&D manager rather than a scientist or general manager.

TABLE 22–3 Segmentation of the Industrial Telecommunications Market

Organizational Charac- teristics of Segment	Average Monthly Telephone Bill ($)	Segment Is This Percent of All In- dustrial Compa- nies	Segment Accounts for This Percent of Total Revenue
TOTAL SAMPLE	$ 910	100%	100%
Segment 1			
Companies with 500 or more employees	6,003	3%	20%
Segment 2			
Less than 500 employees, but has PBX facilities and 50 or more employees elsewhere	2.412	8%	21%
Segment 3			
Less than 500 employees, but has PBX facilities and less than 50 employees elsewhere	995	46%	50%
Segment 4			
Less than 500 employees and has key facilities	180	43%	8%

Source: Adapted from Henry Assael and Richard B. Ellis, "A Research Design to Predict Telephone Usage Among Bell System Business Customers," European Research 1 (1973): 38–42.

- **Segment 3** (20 percent of respondents) is both *price and systems oriented,* emphasizing output format and distribution. Segment 3 is more research oriented, with a higher proportion of employees with advanced degrees.

- **Segment 4** (11 percent) is the most *price-sensitive* segment and is more likely to emphasize nature of output. This group tends to assign job responsibility to general managers rather than the R&D function.

- **Segment 5** (13 percent) is a *speed-of-information* segment. This group is composed of small, research-oriented firms with particular emphasis on engineering research.

The results of the segmentation analysis demonstrated that there is no universally desirable STI system. The researchers suggest using a product-line approach and offering five STI systems to appeal to each of the five benefit segments. The alternative would be to offer a very flexible basic system with a large number of options that could appeal to all five segments. A third option would be to focus on segment 1 only since it represents almost one-half of all respondents.

The study illustrates the desirability of a benefit segmentation approach in industrial markets since it provides guidelines for product development. Systems options can be developed by segment. Once the systems are designed, a perceptual mapping approach could be applied to determine if the various systems options are in fact positioned toward the desired segment, and if new systems configurations are required to better meet the needs of defined segments.

Organizational buyer behavior is generally a process of group decision making, especially in new task situations. Therefore, an understanding of organizational buyer behavior requires an understanding of the buying center within the organization.

The Roles of Members of the Buying Center

Central to an understanding of decision making in a buying center is the different roles of members of the buying group. These roles closely parallel those that can be identified in family decision making; the user, the influencer, the buyer, the decision maker, and the gatekeeper. Webster and Wind summarize these roles by stages in the decision process (Figure 22–5).[39]

FIGURE 22–5   Roles of Members of the Buying Center by Decision Stage

	User	Influencer	Buyer	Decider	Gate-keeper
Identification of need	X	X			
Establishing specifications and scheduling the purchase	X	X	X	X	
Identifying buying alternatives	X	X	X		X
Evaluating alternative buying actions	X	X	X		
Selecting the suppliers	X	X	X	X	

Source: Frederick E. Webster, Jr. and Yoram Wind, *Organizational Buying Behavior,* © 1972, p. 80. Reprinted by permission from Prentice-Hall, Inc., Englewood Cliffs, New Jersey.

Users and influencers have a role in all aspects of the decision process. The *user* may be the worker within the plant. Requirements of labor may be represented by unions, or plant foremen may convey user reactions to management. Users may also be represented by doctors using hospital supplies or teachers using educational materials.

Influencers may be users or may manage the process of usage. Production managers are likely to influence purchasing when production scheduling is important, engineers will exert influence regarding technical specifications, and purchasing agents will exert influence regarding cost and delivery criteria.

Buyers have formal authority for selecting the supplier and arranging terms of purchase. The buyer is generally the purchasing agent. The buyer may have authority to negotiate terms and may be the decision maker. At times, buyers may have only authority for implementing a decision. For example, engineering may establish technical specifications that only one or two suppliers can fulfill, leaving the buyer responsibility for implementing the decision.

Decision Makers have final authority for vendor selection. Decision-making authority is based on the importance of the choice criteria. If cost considerations are predominant, it would be logical to give the purchasing agent responsibility for deciding. In some cases, purchasing agents cannot go beyond an upper cost limit. Decision responsibility for larger investments may be placed with top management.

Gatekeepers control the flow of information into the buying center. The purchasing agent may have authority for allowing salespersons to call on engineers or other members of the buying center. The purchasing agent is restricting the access of vendors to the buying center and is therefore assuming a gatekeeper role. Responsibility for developing an approved list of vendors would reflect such a role.

Joint Decision Making

Several other factors influence the joint decision process in addition to the roles of members of the buying center.[40] *Individual factors* such as the members' background, attitudes, and personality will influence the decision process. Common backgrounds and attitudes of members of the buying center are likely to encourage consensus and speed the process of decision making.

Group factors such as the structure of the group (open or bureaucratic), cohesiveness, and size will also influence the decision outcomes. Spekman and Stern found that higher uncertainty leads to a more open style of decision making within the group, resulting in more joint decisions.[41] Smaller and more cohesive groups are more likely to reach consensus quickly.

Organizational and environmental factors such as the responsibilities of group members and the organizational rewards also influence the group decision process. Particularly important is the degree of risk in purchasing perceived by the buying group. Spekman and Stern found that greater perceived risk encouraged more open communications between members of the buying group and a more flexible organizational style. The result "permitted buying group members to react more quickly and more easily to the increased contingencies of a more highly uncertain environment."[42]

Conflict in Group Buying Decisions

A logical outgrowth of joint purchasing responsibilities is conflict between members of the buying center. Such conflict can be constructive if it leads to a closer examination of the alternatives and eventual agreement on suppliers and product choice. Yet conflict can be destructive if members begin questioning each others' motives and roles. In such cases, some external arbitration may be necessary and if conflict persists, the buying group might be dissolved.

An example of conflict within the buying center is cited by Gorman in a study of seventy-six purchasing agents and production managers in the machinery manufacturing industry.[43]

The purchasing department, in its capacity as "watchdog" over the organizations' interests, determines that it has the right to purchase from a supplier other than the one specified by the production department if the firm can get "substantially the same product at lower cost." The production department, responsible for the manufacture of the firm's goods, insists that it has been delegated the authority to choose the source of supply and that purchasing is a service function only.

The result of these differing perceptions of role leads to destructive conflict as reflected by the following statements:

> The company doesn't realize that we (purchasing department) are an important contributor to profits and not merely a service-providing mechanism for other departments.

> Those people in purchasing are trying to build their own little empire without regard for our (production) needs. It's about time they were put in their place![44]

According to March and Simon, there are three reasons for such conflict.[45] First, close interdependence between purchasing, production, and at times engineering requires joint decision making, but the closer the interdependence, the greater the likelihood of conflict. Second, different roles within the organization will lead to different perceptions of what is required in the buying task. Selective perceptions of members of the buying group will lead to conflict. Third, different roles will lead to different formulations of goals within the buying group. As a result, members of the group may formulate buying objectives based on their own position (suboptimization) rather than on the broader objectives of the firm.

The key question is whether conflict in organizational buying objectives and procedures can be resolved constructively. Sheth cites three types of conflicts in the buying group.[46] First, disagreements may occur regarding capabilities of suppliers. Such conflict is likely to be resolved constructively when the buying center obtains more information. Second, conflict may occur when members disagree on the criteria for evaluation — purchasing may place more emphasis on cost, engineering on product specifications. Such conflict is likely to be resolved constructively by persuasion. Dissenting members are persuaded to take an overall corporate view rather than be swayed by their departmental objectives. Third, conflict can occur when there are differences in personality or in the style of decision making (centralized versus shared). Such conflict will result in politicking and is likely to lead to destructive consequences for the buying center.

In summary, it is important to regard organizational buyer behavior as a joint decision process that is in some ways more complicated to study and understand than individual decision making. Multiple attitudes and perceptions must be understood and reconciled in a process of conflict resolution. Furthermore, the outcome of the buying task is not simply a purchase. Other components must be evaluated such as the speed and effectiveness of the decision process, the likelihood the chosen supplier can be used on a repetitive basis in the future (postpurchase evaluation), and most important, the attainment of corporate goals.

SUMMARY

Organizational buyer behavior represents a larger sales volume than consumer behavior in the American economy. Therefore, the organizational buyer deserves separate consideration.

There are more similarities than differences between organizational and consumer buying, but substantial differences do exist, particularly the greater dependence on group decision making, the greater importance of personal selling, and the greater technical complexity of products in organizational buying.

A model of the organizational buying process suggests four influences on choice: the economic and industrial environment in which the firm operates, the organizational characteristics of the firm, the buying group, and the individual decision maker. These factors combine with the buyer's expectations to yield a decision regarding a supplier or a product.

The choice of a supplier depends on the evaluation by the buyer based on criteria such as reputation, service, technical capabilities, price, and convenience. Buyers frequently develop loyalties to specific vendors. These loyalties sometimes transcend rational economic criteria and are motivated by familiarity, administrative inertia, and reciprocity.

Product decisions may involve a recurring purchase (straight rebuy), a change in specifications for a recurring purchase (modified rebuy), or a new decision (new task). In the latter case, a decision must be made regarding the adoption of a new product. As in consumer adoption, industrial adoption requires awareness, interest, evaluation, and trial. Information sources are particularly important in this process, particularly impersonal sources of information in the early stages of adoption and personal sources in the later stages.

The selection of new vendors or the adoption of new products is frequently decided by a buying center. Members of the buying center have specific roles that parallel those in family decision making, namely, influencers, gatekeepers, decision makers, buyers, and users. Members of the buying center are likely to have varying degrees of influence over the nature of the decision. For instance, engineers have the dominant power over product choice, purchasing agents have the greatest say over price, and production managers have the most influence over delivery dates.

Given the varying organizational positions and perspectives of members of the buying group, some conflict is inevitable in the buying decision. Such conflict is likely to be resolved if it deals with differences over product or vendor selection, or differences regarding the criteria for evaluation. But when differences center on personalities or decision styles, conflict may not lead to the attainment of organizational objectives.

QUESTIONS

1. Select an example of an industrial buying decision.
    - To what extent is the industrial decision process you cited similar to a consumer decision process?
    - To what extent does it differ?

2. A pharmaceutical company is considering converting its plant to reduce industrial emissions so as to limit environmental pollution. It is considering proposals from various vendors to adapt its plants. What are likely to be the differences in criteria used to evaluate alternative vendor's proposals by the (a) purchasing agent, (b) engineering department, (c) sales manager, and (d) head of the legal department?

3. Develop a hypothetical profile of each company in Table 22–2, being sure to specify the (a) organizational environment, and (b) departments that seem to be dominant in the vendor selection process.

4. Based on the six criteria cited in the study by O'Neal on page 563, would the firms in the following situations likely be classified as innovators, early adopters, late adopters, or laggards? Why?
    - A large retailer adopting on-line terminals for managers in each department to identify out-of-stock conditions and to permit quick analyses of markups
    - A prestigious Wall Street law firm adopting Picturephones to facilitate communications between executives in branch offices
    - A large steel company adopting a continuous casting process
    - A brokerage house adopting an ongoing marketing research information system to track needs and attitudes of its customers toward financial packages

5. Several studies of the industrial adoption process have found that early adopters are more likely to rely on personal rather than impersonal sources for information about new products. This finding contradicts consumer studies that found early adopters were more likely to rely on mass media for information.
    - Does the reliance on group communication mean that there is more likely to be a "risky shift" phenomenon (i.e., greater risk taking in group compared to individual decisions) in industrial adoption decisions compared to consumer adoption decisions? That is, is the industrial buyer group more predisposed to take risks in considering new products compared to the family buying group?
    - Is a risky shift more likely for certain types of industrial companies than others?

6. What are the pros and cons of the three strategic alternatives in offering a Scientific and Technical Informational System, namely to (a) develop a separate system for each of the five benefit segments; (b) offer one flexible system to all five segments; and, (c) offer one system to meet the specific needs of the largest segment?

7. Assume a company decides to develop a new Scientific and Technical Information System to meet the needs for flexibility in language and extent of coverage required by Segment 1.
    - Develop a hypothetical perceptual map positioning the system relative to five

or six of the need criteria cited.

- Show the position of each of the five segments on the map.
- Interpret the meaning of the map you developed.

8. Can you draw any parallels between purchasing roles in industrial and family buying decisions?

- Cite an example of industrial and family decision making specifying the parallel roles in each case.

9. Under what circumstances is conflict likely to occur within the industrial buying group? When is such conflict likely to be helpful or harmful in achieving the objectives of the firm?

RESEARCH ASSIGNMENTS

1. Select an industrial product that has been introduced in the last five or ten years (e.g., Centrex telephone facilities, automatic check-cashing machines, electronic fund transfers, etc.). Sample a number of firms (thirty to forty) and determine the date of adoption of the innovation. In addition, determine the organizational characteristics of the firm (number of employees, type of business, annual sales, degree of centralization, etc.), and, if possible, the sources of information utilized in making the adoption decision.

- What was the pattern of diffusion for the new product?
- What organizational characteristics differentiate the early from the late adopters?
- Did the early adopters rely on different sources of information compared to the later adopters?

2. Select a particular company for study. Then contact four or five of its customers and interview purchasing agents, engineers, production managers, and any others involved in buying from the company. Ask these individuals to rate the company based on the criteria listed in Table 22–1.

- What are the differences in ratings between purchasing agents, engineers, and production managers?
- Are there greater differences in evaluation of the company between customers, or between purchasing agents, engineers, and production managers across customers?
- What are the implications of your findings for the company's policy regarding (a) services and warranties, (b) pricing, (c) personal selling, (d) customer training for product use, (e) product development, and (f) advertising?

1. Frederick E. Webster, "Management Science in Industrial Marketing," *Journal of Marketing* 42 (January 1978): 21–27.

2. Paul D. Converse, *Marketing Methods and Policies* (New York: Prentice-Hall Inc. 1924), p. 147.

3. F. Robert Shoaf, "Here's Proof — The Industrial Buyer *Is* Human," *Industrial Marketing* 44 (May 1959): 126.

4. David T. Wilson, "Industrial Buyers' Decision-Making Styles," *Journal of Marketing Research* 8 (November 1971): 433–436.

5. Peter Lawrence Bubb and David John van Rest, "Loyalty as a Component of the Industrial Buying Decision," *Industrial Marketing Management* 3 (1973): 25–32.

6. John A. Martilla, "Word-of-Mouth Communication in the Industrial Adoption Process," *Journal of Marketing Research* 8 (May 1971): 173–178.

7. Martilla, "Word-of-Mouth Communication"; and Leon G. Schiffman and Vincent Gaccione, "Opinion Leaders in Institutional Markets," *Journal of Marketing* 38 (April 1974): 49–53.

8. Webster, "Management Science," p. 23.

9. Frederick E. Webster and Yoram Wind, "A General Model for Understanding Buying Behavior," *Journal of Marketing* 36 (April 1972): 12–19.

10. Jagdish N. Sheth, "A Model of Industrial Buyer Behavior," *Journal of Marketing* 37 (October 1973): 50–56.

11. Hakan Haksansson and Bjorn Wootz, "Risk Reduction and the Industrial Purchaser," *European Journal of Marketing* 9 (1975): 35–51.

12. Sheth, "A Model of Industrial Buyers," p. 53.

13. Robert Weigand, "Identifying Industrial Buying Responsibility," *Journal of Marketing Research* 3 (February 1966): 81–84.

14. John F. Grashof and Gloria P. Thomas, "Industrial Buying Center Responsibilities," in Kenneth L. Bernhardt, ed., *Proceedings of the American Marketing Association Educators' Conference* Series #39 (1976): pp. 344–347.

15. Sheth, "A Model of Industrial Buyers," p. 53.

16. Frederick E. Webster and Yoram Wind, *Organizational Buyer Behavior* (Englewood Cliffs, N. J.: Prentice-Hall, Inc., 1972), pp. 31–33.

17. Donald R. Lehmann and John O'Shaughnessy, "Difference in Attribute Importance for Different Industrial Products," *Journal of Marketing* 38 (April 1974): 36–42.

18. J. Patrick Kelly and James W. Coaker, "Can We Generalize About Choice Criteria for Industrial Purchasing Decisions," in Kenneth L. Bernhardt, ed., *Proceedings of the American Marketing Association Educators' Conference,* Series #39 (1976), pp. 330–333.

19. Richard N. Cardozo and James W. Cagley, "Experimental Study of Industrial Buyer Behavior," *Journal of Marketing Research* 8 (August 1971): 329–334.

20. Ibid. p. 333.

21. William A. Dempsey, "A Canonical Analysis of Vendor Attributes and Industrial Buyer Information Sources," in Edward M. Mazze, ed., *Combined Proceedings of the American Marketing Association,* Series #37 (1975), pp. 267–271.

22. Bubb and Van Rest, "Loyalty as a Component."

23. Yoram Wind, "Industrial Source Loyalty," *Journal of Marketing Research* 7 (November 1970): 450–457.

24. James R. Cooley, Donald W. Jackson, and Lonnie L. Ostrom, "Analyzing the Relative Power of Participants in Industrial Buying Decisions," in Barnett A. Greenberg and Danny N. Bellinger, *Proceedings of the American Marketing Association Educators' Conference,* Series #41 (1977), p. 244.

25. James R. McMillan, "The Role of Perceived Risk in Industrial Marketing Decisions," in Boris W. Becker and Helmut Becker, eds., *Combined Proceedings of the American Marketing Association,* Series #34 (1972), pp. 412–417.

26. Cardozo and Cagley, "Experimental Study," p. 333.

27. Urban B. Ozanne and Gilbert A. Churchill, Jr. "Five Dimensions of the Industrial Adoption Process," *Journal of Marketing Research* 8 (August 1971): 322–328.

28. Charles R. O'Neal, Hans B. Thorelli and James M. Utterback, "Adoption of Innovation by Industrial Organizations," *Industrial Marketing Management* 2 (1973): 235–250.

29. Frederick E. Webster, Jr. "New Product Adoption in Industrial Markets: A Framework for Analysis," *Journal of Marketing* 33 (July 1969): 35–39.

30. John A. Czepiel, "Decision Group and Firm Characteristics in an Industrial Adoption Decision," in Kenneth L. Bernhardt, ed., *Proceedings of the American Marketing Association Educators' Conference,* Series #39 (1976), pp. 340–343.

31. Frederick E. Webster, Jr. "Informal Communication in Industrial Markets," *Journal of Marketing Research* 7 (May 1970): 186–189.

32. Martilla, "Word-of-Mouth Communication."

33. Michael J. Baker and Stephen T. Parkinson, "Information Source Preference in the Industrial Adoption Decision," in Barnett A. Greenberg and Danny N. Bellenger, eds., *Proceedings of the American Marketing Association Educators' Conference,* Series #41, (1977) pp. 258–261; and Czepiel, "Decision Group."

34. Baker and Parkinson, "Information Source Preference."

35. Yoram Wind and Richard Cardozo, "Industrial Market Segmentation," *Industrial Marketing Management* 3 (1974): 153–166.

36. Ibid. p. 163.

37. Henry Assael and Richard B. Ellis, "A Research Design to Predict Telephone Usage Among Bell System Business Customers," *European Research*

574   1 (1973): 38–42.

38. Yoram Wind, John F. Grashof, and Joel D. Goldhar, "Market-Based Guidelines for Design of Industrial Products," *Journal of Marketing* 42 (July 1978): 27–37.

39. Webster and Wind, *Organizational Buying Behavior,* p. 80.

40. Robert E. Krapfel, Jr., "A Decision Process Approach to Modelling Organizational Buyer Behavior," in Subhash C. Jain, ed., *Proceedings of the American Marketing Association Educators' Conference,* Series #43 (1978), pp. 116–120.

41. Robert E. Spekman and Louis W. Stern, "Environmental Uncertainty and Buying Group Structure: An Empirical Investigation," *Journal of Marketing* 43 (Spring 1979): 54–64.

42. Ibid. p. 58

43. Ronald H. Gorman, "Role Conception and Purchasing Behavior," *Journal of Purchasing* 7 (February 1971): 62.

44. Ibid. p. 57

45. James G. March and Herbert A. Simon, *Organizations* (New York: John Wiley & Sons Inc., 1958), pp. 121–129.

46. Sheth, "A Model of Industrial Buyers," p. 55.

Conclusion

TWENTY-THREE

Consumerism and Marketing's Responsibility to the Consumer

Focus of Chapter

A discussion of consumerism and marketing's responsibility to the consumer is a fitting conclusion to this book. In previous chapters, it has been assumed that the marketplace affords the consumer an adequate choice of goods and the likelihood of satisfaction with that choice. In fact, this is not always the case. At times, the consumer may not be adequately informed, may be purposefully misled, may be offered a restricted choice of alternatives, or may be offered unsafe products. The consumer has few channels to seek redress for these wrongs.

Fortunately, these inequities are the exception rather than the rule, but they have occurred with sufficient regularity to promote what has come to be known as the consumer movement.

This concluding chapter will first explore consumerism, its historical antecedents, and its rationale as a countervailing force to the powers of big business. The rights of consumers will be reviewed next, and in the last section, the marketer's responsibilities to the consumer will be considered.

CONSUMERISM

Consumerism is the set of activities of independent organizations, government, and business designed to protect the consumer.[1] The primary concern is with ensuring the consumer's rights in the process of exchange. These rights include the right to information, to be told the truth, to be given adequate alternatives, and to be assured of health and safety in the process of consumption.

These activities have come to be known as the consumer movement, but the term is misleading because it implies an integrated set of organizations that represent consumers much as the labor movement came to represent workers. Hermann states:

> Because of the lack of an overall philosophy and program of action, there is, in a sense, no real consumer movement. Consumerism is, instead, a conglomeration of separate groups each with its own particular concerns which sometimes form temporary alliances on particular issues. The constituent groups in these coalitions include labor organizations, consumer cooperatives, credit unions, consumer educators, the product-testing and consumer education organization (Consumers Union), state and local consumer organizations, plus other organizations with related interests. . . .[2]

The vehicle for consumer protection can be summarized as three types of organizations: consumer-oriented groups concerned primarily with increasing consumer consciousness and providing consumers information to improve their basis for choice; government through legislation and regulation; and business through competition and self-regulation. Sheth and Mammana summarize these forces in Figure 23–1.[3]

The most visible of the forces in the consumer movement have been three consumer activists that came to prominence in the 1960s: Ralph Nader, Esther Peterson, and Betty Furness. Nader established himself in the muckraking tradition of social activism by his exposés of the automobile industry's failures to maintain safety standards. Peterson and Furness moved from positions as presidential advisors on consumer affairs to national prominence as consumer activists in their own right. But these individuals represented disparate forces with no close integration of efforts. There is still no national consumer organization that seeks to represent consumers. The closest is Consumers Union, established in 1936 as a product testing and consumer education agency.

The consumer movement has therefore failed to establish the countervailing force to big business that the labor movement established for its workers. The reason for this failure is that consumers are difficult to organize and galvanize. The issue in the labor movement was salary and working conditions; the issues in consumerism are less central to the day-to-day well-being of the consumer. There have been occasions when consumers have grouped together to protest higher prices. Supermarket boycotts beginning in Denver in 1966 and meat boycotts in 1973 received national attention, but such group action is rare.

The rapid increase in prices in the late 1970s and the likelihood of continued inflation may cause the emergence of a national consumer movement. It is possible that "Nader's raiders" or Consumers Union may be the basis for such a movement. Both have broadened their activities beyond their original concerns. Nader's group has investigated such disparate areas as credit terms and funeral costs. Consumers Union, with a membership of two million, has undertaken broad consumer education programs regarding interest rates, life insurance, product safety, and doctor selection. It has also financed research into the problems of low income consumers and publishes *Consumer Reports*.

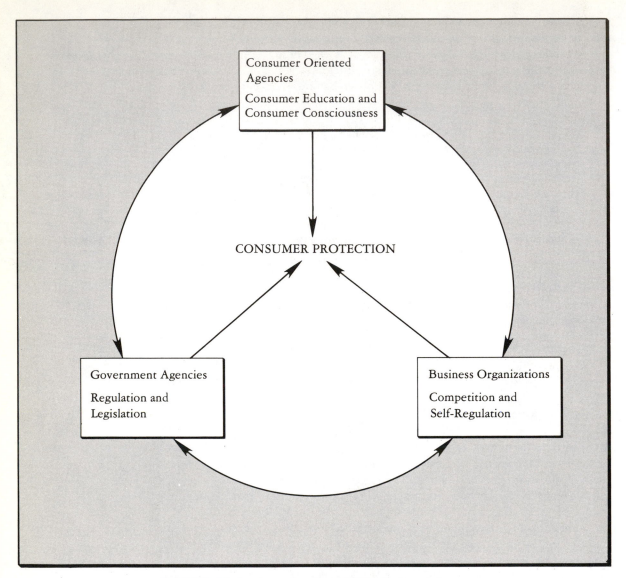

FIGURE 23–1   Agencies Involved in Consumerism

Source: Adapted from Jagdish N. Sheth and Nicholas Mammana, "Why Consumer Protection Efforts Are Likely to Fail," Faculty Working Paper, no. 104, College of Commerce and Business Administration, University of Illinois at Urbana-Champaign, April 11, 1973, p. 3.

Historical Antecedents of Consumerism

The consumer movement is not new. There have been three distinct periods in which consumer protection became a national issue. Each of these periods was marked by rising consumer prices and declines in real income.[4]

1900–1915

The emphasis on consumer protection at the turn of the century came during a period of increasing prices, resulting in resentment of the growing trusts.

One of the early manifestations of this resentment was the formation of the Consumers League in 1899 (no relation to the present Consumers Union). In 1906, Upton Sinclair's *The Jungle* exposed working conditions in Chicago's meat packinghouses. The book created such an outcry that Congress passed the Meat Inspection Act in 1906. In the same year the Food and Drug Act created the Food and Drug Administration.

A consumer movement could develop only at the turn of the century for several reasons. First, by the late 1800s the domination of big business and the trusts began to lead to consumer resentment. Second, national brands began to be prominent, permitting consumers to focus on the performance of these brands. Third, standardized packaging and branding reduced reliance on local merchants. Consumers felt a loss of control over merchandise and some degree of alienation resulted. One of the outcomes of this conflict with big business was the establishment in 1914 of the Federal Trade Commission to curb monopoly and unfair trade practices.

1935–1940

The consumer movement of the 1930s took place during the Great Depression, but it was primarily higher prices after 1935 that provided the impetus for consumer concerns. Consumer awareness was aroused in 1933 by a book by Kallet and Schlink, *100,000,000 Guinea Pigs.* The book exposed unsafe medicines, cosmetics, and foods. It led to a rash of other exposés of industry such as the following:

- *Our Master's Voice* (1934), an indictment of advertising as a symptom of deep social exploitation in a profit-motivated society.

- *The Popular Practice of Fraud* (1935), an examination of the excessive claims in advertising food and drugs, and a plea for launching programs of consumer education.

- *Eat, Drink and be Wary* (1935) by F.J. Schlink, then President of Consumers' Research Inc. which subsequently became Consumers Union. Schlink employed a group of chemists to test food, cosmetic and drug products and found unsanitary food processing, use of dangerous preservatives and chemicals in food, and false promises about health and safety.

- *American Chamber of Horrors: The Truth About Food and Drugs* (1936), pointed to the dangers of various food and drug products in an attempt to promote an updating and strengthening of the Food and Drug Act of 1906.

The result of these exposés was the formation of Consumers Union in 1936 and the enactment of the Wheeler-Lea amendment to the Federal Trade Commission Act in 1938. The amendment enlarged the powers of the Federal Trade Commission to prosecute unfair and deceptive trade practices, particularly advertising. The Commission did not fully use these powers until the 1960s when it began to examine children's advertising and also began to order advertisers to cease misleading claims and to take corrective action.

1965 to Present

World War II and post-war prosperity led to another dormant period for the consumer movement. President Kennedy's involvement with consumer issues and an inflationary period in the mid-1960s again aroused national concern with consumer rights. As in previous periods, it took several exposés of big business to galvanize the consumer movement. In 1962, it was shown that the drug thalidomide created birth defects when taken by pregnant women. A national tragedy was narrowly averted by a member of the Food and Drug Administration who used bureaucratic delaying tactics to prevent marketing the product in this country (it was marketed in Europe) until further testing. The thalidomide scare resulted in the passage of the Kefauver-Harris amendment to the Food and Drug act, a long-sought updating of that act.

In 1962, Rachel Carson's *Silent Spring* appeared, an investigation of the dangers of pesticides and other chemicals in foods and other products. The book did much to arouse consumers' ecological concerns. Then in 1965, Ralph Nader's *Unsafe at Any Speed* launched him in his career as a consumer advocate. The book exposed the automobile industry's disregard for even rudimentary safety precautions and documented instances of fatalities due to these defects. It was instrumental in the passage of the National Traffic and Motor Vehicle Safety Act to set safety standards for new and used automobiles. The 1960s also saw the passage of the following acts:

- *Cigarette Labeling Act* (1965), which requires cigarette manufacturers to label cigarettes as hazardous to health.
- *Fair Packaging and Labeling Act* (1966) which declares the deceptive packaging of certain consumer commodities illegal.
- *Child Protection Act* (1966) which allows the FDA to remove dangerous children's products from the market.
- *The Truth-in-Lending Act* (1968) which requires full disclosure of all finance charges in consumer credit agreements.[5]

The 1970s has seen greater emphasis on in-store information with requirements for unit pricing, open dating on perishables, and nutritional labeling. The emphasis on consumer protection initiated in the 1960s continued with passage of the Consumer Products Safety Act in 1972. This act created an independent agency empowered to set safety standards for products to protect consumers from the risk of injury. The decade also saw greater concern with environmental issues due to pollution and increasing gasoline prices. Environmental concerns became an issue in the consumer movement. The Federal Trade Commission also began to take a much more activist stance during this period, especially regarding the regulation of advertising.

Will continued inflation and environmental concerns prolong the period of consumer awareness and activism? An answer to this question requires considering the reasons behind the current period of consumerism and current consumer attitudes toward business and consumer organizations.

The Reasons Behind Consumerism

Each of the three consumerist periods described above was marked by increasing prices coupled by muckraking type exposés resulting in consumer protection legislation. The current causes of the consumer movement were investigated by Gaedeke in a study of the attitudes of businessmen, consumer spokesmen, and government officials.[6] Gaedeke found agreement for several underlying causes of the current focus on consumerism:

1. There has been a greater concern with the appeals made in advertising and greater awareness of the potential for misleading advertising.

2. There has been an increase in the awareness of social problems, particularly problems relating to the disadvantaged and to the environment. Both of these are concerns of consumer activists.

3. A feeling that the concern of business should go beyond the maximization of profits to encompass social concerns. Businessmen have begun to recognize the necessity of broadening their view of the business function to incorporate what Hensel refers to as consumerism management systems.[7] In fact one author notes that many businessmen have preempted criticism by putting more emphasis on consumer affairs.[8]

4. Changing consumer attitudes resulting in greater involvement with consumer issues.

Hendon cites several other causes for consumerism:

1. Imperfections in the state of information available to consumers
2. Improved technology and more complicated products
3. Better educated and informed consumers
4. Publicity given by advertising to consumer activists
5. The institutionalization of activists such as Nader, with sufficient resources to pursue specific causes and issues
6. The increased role of government, especially regulatory agencies
7. The rise of militancy in the United States, resulting in a greater willingness to protest rising prices[9]

If one adds inflationary pressures to the foregoing reasons, then it is likely that consumerism is going to be part of the marketing environment for a long-term period.

Consumer Attitudes Toward Business and the Consumer Movement

One of the issues regarding the consumer movement is whether consumer activists and consumer organizations reflect the needs and attitudes of the public. If consumers place a relatively low priority on safety in buying a car or an oven, should consumerist policies "force" consumers to do what is best for them? If there were no consumer movement, would there be a difference between what consumers do and what they are required to do by government regulation (e.g., buy seat belts for cars, wear helmets when riding motorcycles, buy cars with emission controls and air bags, etc.)?

There is sufficient evidence that attitudes of consumers differ from those of consumerists. In most cases, the consumerists are more "out in front" than consumers in attacking business policies and in proposing corrective action. Gazda and Gourley studied the attitudes of businesspersons, consumers, and consumerists toward five issues:

- product information
- product safety
- advertising
- government protection
- the environment[10]

The results are in Table 23–1. Attitudes of consumerists were stronger than those of consumers or businesspersons on each issue. Consumerists sought greater govenment involvement in regulation, were more doubtful of business's potential for self-regulation, and were generally more critical of business actions. Consumer attitudes were midway between those of consumerists and businesspersons. These findings demonstrate the disparity in attitudes between consumers and consumerists and suggest that most consumers are not as concerned with issues of information, safety, and the environment as the consumerists would hope.

TABLE 23–1 Attitudes of Businesspersons, Consumers, and Consumerists Toward Consumer-Related Issues

Statements	Attitudes of Businesspersons	Attitudes of Consumers	Attitudes of Consumerists
Attitudes Toward Advertising			
Companies should prove in advance any claims which they plan to use in their advertisements.	3.86	4.27	4.54
If a company uses false advertising, it should be forced to correct such statements in future advertising.	4.34	4.59	4.54
Advertising tries to persuade consumers to buy products they don't really need.	3.22	3.94	4.27
Attitudes Toward Government Protection			
The government should test competing brands of products and make the results of the tests available to consumers.	2.96	3.60	3.71
Industry, rather than government, should establish safety standards for consumer products.	2.57	2.51	1.59
Laws are necessary to protect the consumer in the marketplace.	4.34	4.59	4.54
Attitudes Toward the Environment			
Businesses should make products that do not pollute the environment.	3.78	4.11	4.22

TABLE 23–1   (cont.)   **583**

Manufacturers should be fined if they do not eliminate pollution.	3.38	3.79	4.09
Businesses not meeting pollution control standards should be closed.	2.91	3.45	3.53
Attitudes Toward Product Information			
Business should be required to supply more information to consumers.	3.40	4.14	4.47
Products should carry an information tag which would give information about performance, materials, care and characteristics.	4.07	4.31	4.51
Attitudes Toward Product Safety			
Manufacturers should be forced to prove that a product is safe before it can be sold to consumers.	3.76	4.30	4.28
Businesspersons are very concerned with designing and producing safe products.	2.67	2.02	1.65
The lack of product safety has been exaggerated.	2.37	1.97	1.20

Note: Data represent averages on a five-point scale with 1 = strongly disagree and 5 = strongly agree.

Source: Adapted from Gregory M. Gazda and David R. Gourley, "Attitudes of Businessmen, Consumers, and Consumerists Toward Consumerism," *Journal of Consumer Affairs,* 9 (Winter 1975): 178–183.

Reprinted with permission from the *Journal of Consumer Affairs.* © 1975 by the Regents of the University of Wisconsin.

The study also shows a significant disparity between views of consumers and businesspersons. It is clear that consumers would like to see more government involvement, more information, better products, and more accurate advertising than businesspersons feel is needed. The disparity between consumer and business opinions is demonstrated in a more recent poll by the Harris organization.[11] Key results are presented on page 584, top.

These findings show that consumers think things are getting worse. Manufacturers' claims are not as consistent with product performance as they used to be, products are no longer as durable, standards regarding products and services are lower, and products are more difficult to repair. With the exception of difficulty of product repair, businesspersons were much less likely to hold these attitudes.

	Percentage Who Agree		
	Consumers	*Consumerists*	*Businesspersons*
Differences between manufacturers' claims and actual product performance have increased	48	42	33
Products do not last as long as they used to	78	78	43
It is more difficult to get things repaired	64	76	69
Expectations about standards of products and services have gotten lower	44	50	24

The Harris study also identified the issues of greatest concern to consumers. The seven most important issues were:

1. High prices, especially for medical care
2. Poor product quality
3. Failure to live up to advertised claims
4. After-sale service and repairs
5. Lack of concern by manufacturers
6. Products breaking or going wrong soon after being brought home
7. Misleading packaging or labeling[12]

Harris also found consumers rejecting the view among some businesspersons that consumerists are "troublemakers piling unnecessary costs on business and the public."[13] Two-thirds of all consumers said things would be worse if government regulation stopped, but 60 percent of business managers said things would be the same or better. Concern with consumerist issues is likely to continue as long as this disparity of views between consumers and businesspersons prevails.

These findings seem to suggest a state of conflict between consumer interests and business actions. Apparently, widespread acceptance of the marketing concept has not eliminated defective products, misleading advertising, and occasional price gouging. Are things getting better? The Harris study suggests not, but the changes may be in consumer perceptions and awareness, not in the actions of businesses. It could be that businesses have improved marketing practices, but greater consumer awareness has created a perception of a worsening situation. In fact, consumers recognize improvements in marketing practices in certain areas. A study by Barksdale et al. found an improvement in consumer attitudes between 1971 and 1975 toward the variety of products in the marketplace and toward the amount of information provided by marketers.[14] Although abuses continue to exist, greater recognition of the legitimacy of consumer issues among businesspersons may be beginning to resolve some consumer grievances.

On March 15, 1962, President John F. Kennedy sent to Congress a *Special Message on Protecting the Consumer Interest*. This was the first message ever delivered by a president on this topic. Kennedy stated that legislative and administrative action was required for the Federal Government to meet its responsibilities to consumers in the exercise of their rights. He spelled out these rights to include:

1. *The right to safety* — to be protected against the marketing of goods which are hazardous to health or life.

2. *The right to be informed* — to be protected against fraudulent, deceitful, or grossly misleading information, advertising, labeling or other practices, and to be given the facts needed to make an informed choice.

3. *The right to choose* — to be assured access to a variety of products and services at competitive prices, and in those industries in which competition is not workable and government regulation is substituted, to be assured satisfactory quality and service at fair prices.

4. *The right to be heard* — to be assured that consumer interests will receive full and sympathetic consideration in the formulation of government policy.[15]

Two additional rights could be added:

5. *The right to a clean environment* — to be assured that industry will not squander precious resources or pollute the environment.

6. *The right to be in the minority without disadvantage* — to ensure that minority groups or low income consumers will not be at a disadvantage in relation to any of the above rights compared to other groups.

A Consumer Advisory Council was established by President Kennedy to provide advice on "governmental programs protecting consumer needs, and on needed improvements in the flow of consumer research material to the public."[16] This section will review these six consumer rights.

The Right to Safety

Day and Aaker describe the right to safety as the least controversial and oldest aspect of consumerism.[17] There is agreement between businesspersons and consumerists that abuses related to product safety must be eliminated. The greatest spur to eliminating these abuses was the establishment of the Consumer Product Safety Commission in 1972. The Commission can ban the sale of products, require manufacturers to perform safety tests, and require repair or recall of unsafe products. The Commission operates a hotline to report hazardous products and also runs a National Electronic Injury Surveillance System, a computer-based system that monitors 119 hospital emergency rooms across the country. On the basis of this system, the Commission computes a product Hazard Index. Among products with the highest hazard index are bicycles, stairs and ramps, cleaning agents, swings and slides, and liquid fuels.[18] The intent of the Commission is not to emphasize reports of post-sales injuries but to encourage preventive safety through better product design. To this end, it develops safety standards for products.[19]

One of the positive outcomes of the Commission's work is the greater emphasis on product safety. The Commission has influenced firms such as Westinghouse and Philco to formalize their product safety procedures. Philco has established a National Safety Alert program to speed up detection of potentially unsafe products.[20]

An important role of governmental agencies in ensuring the right to safety is the ability to recall products. The National Highway Traffic Safety Administration will recall cars whenever substantial numbers of safety-related defects appear, and the Environmental Protection Agency will recall cars for failure to meet emission standards. The Consumer Product Safety Commission has played a role in over 1,200 product recalls from 1973 to 1979. And, the Food and Drug Administration has the authority to ban or seize food and drug products it regards as a menace to the public's health.[21]

The Right to Be Informed

President Kennedy's statement regarding the right to be informed had two components: the right to be protected against deceptive and misleading information, and the right to be given information to make an informed choice.

Misleading and Deceptive Information

Over the years, the Federal Trade Commission has established a set of clearly defined guidelines for determining what is deceptive advertising under the Wheeler-Lea amendment. Advertising need only have the capacity to deceive to be deceptive. There is no need for the FTC to prove deception actually occurred. Further, the advertiser can be ignorant of any false claim and still be liable. The question that consumer researchers have tried to grapple with is where does puffery end and deception begin. Gardner identified three types of deceptive advertising.[22] The first is the straightforward lie. The second is a *claim-fact discrepancy*. In this case, the benefits claimed by the product will be fulfilled only under certain conditions which may not be clear in the advertising; that is, the product must be used in a certain manner or certain precautions are required in use. For example, a dandruff shampoo may work as claimed only for people with certain problems, but these may not be the most common problems in causing dandruff. A third type of deception is a *claim-belief interaction*. In this case, an advertisement interacts with certain consumer beliefs and results in a misleading claim. For example, a detergent manufacturer discovers that by putting red and blue crystals in some detergents, a certain number of housewives will attribute more cleaning power to the product.

The recent period of consumerism has seen heightened activity by the FTC in prosecuting deceptive advertising. The Commission has asked some companies to desist from making misleading claims. For example, it asked several major firms to cease making claims that enzymes in detergents eliminate stains,[23] but it has also developed a doctrine of full disclosure requiring some companies to undertake corrective advertising. For example, the Commission has insisted on company advertising to correct a misleading claim that Listerine kills germs. Another dimension of full disclosure is requiring companies to state the negative as well as the positive aspects of their products in advertising — for instance, requiring tobacco companies to state the tar and nicotine content in their brands.

The Provision of Adequate Information

Does the right to information go beyond the right not to be deceived and include adequate information to ensure a wise purchase? Day and Aaker feel that the requirement for disclosure of information is the most controversial and debated aspect of consumerism.[24] There are two polar positions on this issue. The view of business is that the buyer should be guided by his or her judgment of the brand's quality. The consumer activist feels that full information should be provided by business and by impartial sources and should reveal performance characteristics.

Regardless of the position one takes, it is evident the trend is toward more disclosure of information. An increasing number of states are requiring unit pricing of grocery products and open dating of perishables. In 1975, rules formulated by the Food and Drug Administration went into effect requiring more information on certain food labels.

The general increase in disclosure requirements is documented in Table 23–2.[25] The table categorizes type of disclosure by information on:

- prices
- performance
- ingredients
- perishability
- warnings on product usage
- forms of product usage

The disclosure requirements implemented by law between 1968 and 1975 are in the second column, and probable future disclosure requirements are in the last column.

The question of the efficacy of providing more information to consumers has not been resolved. Obviously minimal information requirements are necessary to make an informed choice. But research cited in Chapter 19 suggests that more information is not necessarily better because of possible information overload. Further, when information is provided it is not always used. Day cites research that found:

- only 9 percent of consumers used nutritional labels at least once.
- 30 to 50 percent of consumers used unit pricing in the buying decision.
- 10 percent of all credit buyers used information supplied by the Truth in Lending Bill in the last purchase of a durable.
- 39 percent used open dating information on one or more products during the last shopping trip.[26]

TABLE 23–2 Recent and Prospective Information Disclosure Requirements

Type of Disclosure	Implemented in Past Five Years	Probable in the Future
1. Comparative prices	Truth in lending	Prescription prices
	Unit pricing	Truth in life insurance
	Automobile list prices	Costs of operation of appliances and automobiles
		Truth in consumer leasing
2. Comparative performance and efficiency	Nutrition labeling of food products	Automobile gas mileage
	Lumen and life data for light bulbs	Appliance energy consumption and comparative efficiency
	Stereo amplifier power output	Appliance performance
	Octane labeling	Tire mileage, stopping ability, and high speed resistance to heat
	Automobile performance (vehicle stopping distance, acceleration and passing ability, and tire reserve load)	Carpet and upholstery wear characteristics
		Quality grade labels for food products
		Sun screen efficacy of suntan preparations
		Standards of drug efficacy
		Detergent efficacy
		Vocational school drop-out rate

TABLE 23–2 Recent and Prospective Information Disclosure Requirements (cont.)

3. Ingredients (including additives)	Cosmetics Food Liquor Phosphate content of detergents	Labeling of fat content in food Presence of pesticides Pigment content of paint Labeling to explain purpose of food ingredients and additives
4. Life/perishability	Open dating of foods	Appliance durability and life Expiration dates for drug potency Automobile damage susceptibility and repair costs
5. Warnings/clarifications	Cigarette health hazards Lack of efficacy of vitamins Flammability (children's sleepwear)	Flammability of cellular plastic insulation
6. Form and usage of product/terms of contract and warranties	Size standards (i.e., TV screens and refrigerators) Truth in warranties and service contracts Tire construction and load rating	Standards specifying amount of product to use (i.e., detergents) Care labeling for clothing Terms of land sales contracts Truth in imports (country of origin) Truth in savings (interest payments) Disclosure of manufacturer, packer, and distributor of food products Net and drained weights of canned and frozen food

Source: George S. Day, "Assessing the Effects of Information Disclosure Requirements," *Journal of Marketing* 40 (April 1976): 43.

Reprinted with permission from the American Marketing Association.

These figures certainly do not suggest the overwhelming use of information when supplied to consumers. Yet, there are compelling arguments for supplying more information to consumers. First, such information *is* used even if by a minority of consumers. Unfortunately, evidence suggests that the information is used by those who need it least — the better educated and higher income consumers.[27] Second, when used, the information does create more effective purchases. Several studies have found that consumers who use unit pricing information tend to shift their purchases toward lower unit priced goods.[28] Third, "mere availability of information increases buyer confidence."[29] Labels with nutritional information and dates regarding perishability increase the consumer's confidence in buying the product. Similarly, while only 10 percent of consumers used credit information in making a durable purchase, 54 percent said they felt better about knowing the rates and charges.[30]

The Right to Choose

The right to choose means that the consumer has a sufficient number of brand alternatives available to enable selection of a satisfactory brand. The ultimate goal is a satisfied consumer, and consumer satisfaction requires the ability to evaluate alternatives in the marketplace. Consumerists argue that there is a tendency on the part of large corporations to restrict choice by discouraging market entry. The marketer of a leading brand may advertise heavily, preempt shelf space within the store, and offer frequent price deals and coupons. Such actions tend to make competitive entry more difficult, thus restricting choice. Heinz's attempt to introduce Great American Soups was thwarted by Campbell's dominant position in canned soups. Scott Paper's attempt to enter the disposable diaper market failed because of the dominance of Pampers, produced by Procter and Gamble. In the case of disposable diapers, supermarkets will generally not stock more than two brands because of space restrictions, and Scott had difficulty gaining adequate coverage.

The potential for market dominance raises the question of monopoly powers. Such powers naturally restrict consumer choice. The Federal Government has played an active role in preventing the restraint of competition through the provisions of the Sherman Antitrust Act passed in 1890. The Clayton Act (1914) was aimed at more specific practices not covered by the Sherman Act such as price discrimination and tying contracts that limited distribution of certain goods. The Federal Trade Commission Act specified that the Commission was to be concerned with unfair methods of competition. The persistent restriction of monopoly powers by the Federal Government has been successful in guaranteeing a wide range of products to consumers.[31]

Consumerists have not made monopoly powers an important issue because of the success of governmental agencies in curbing such powers. Rather, some consumerists have taken the paradoxical position that consumers should *not* always have freedom of choice because sometimes they do not choose products that are in their own best interests. One writer, takes the position that some restraint is required on consumer choice because the consumer is "beguiled by style at the expense of safety and stamina, by gleam instead of guts, by features and gimmicks in place of performance and economy."[32] Such views reflect the statements of some of the better known critics of marketing that advertising encourages consumers to spend money on wasteful luxuries when they would be better off spending their money on social necessities such as education and health-care.[33]

Such opinions raise an even more difficult question: Who is to make the decision for the consumer? Government? Few consumer activists would propose such an extreme solution. In some cases, restraint on consumer choice is warranted where public safety is an issue — for example, consumers do not have the right to buy cars without seat belts or emission controls. Controls on expenditures for luxuries which could be better spent on food or education is an entirely different matter. Such a policy would constrain the consumer's right to establish his or her own priorities in a free society.

The Right to Be Heard

The consumer has the right to express dissatisfaction with a product and to have complaints resolved (redress). Most surveys agree that the overall level of product dissatisfaction among consumers is low. One study by a consumerist group found that 20 percent of recent purchases were considered unsatisfactory. A study by General Electric found 6 percent of appliance customers were dissatisfied.[34] And a survey of personal care products found dissatisfaction averaged less than 3 percent per product category.[35]

However, the level of dissatisfaction is increasing, particularly for all types of repair services, mail order products, toys, and automobiles.[36] Consumerists and businesspersons have differing explanations for the increase in consumer dissatisfaction. Consumerists argue that the quality of products is deteriorating. Business people feel that product quality and performance is improving, but consumer expectations are rising even faster. Therefore, there is a perception of decreasing quality. Further, in inflationary periods the perception of deteriorating quality is reinforced because the same amount of money will buy less. The central issue is (1) whether the consumer will seek redress if dissatisfied, and (2) if so, what channels of redress are available.

The most frequent response of dissatisfied customers is simply not to buy the product again. Few customers bring their complaints directly to the attention of the marketer. The study of personal care products found that among those consumers who were dissatisfied (a minority to begin with), only 8 percent returned the product to the store and 1 percent to the manufacturer. Another 12 percent complained to the store, the manufacturer, or the Better Business Bureau without returning the product. Therefore, only one-fifth of dissatisfied consumers took some overt action.[37] A study by A.C. Nielsen Co. of food products and health and beauty aids found that only 3 percent of all dissatisfied consumers brought their complaints to the attention of the manufacturer.[38] Both studies demonstrate that the manufacturer is almost totally cut off from direct consumer feedback regarding dissatisfaction with the product. As a result, the manufacturer may not be totally at fault for not adjusting products to consumer complaints.

Why do so few consumers bother to take some overt action in expressing their dissatisfaction? One study found that consumers said it was simply not worth the time and effort.[39] Given the low involvement nature of many product categories, it is not surprising that consumers do not express their dissatisfaction or return products. The two studies that found low levels of complaint behavior dealt with consumer packaged goods. When more expensive products are examined, complaint behavior increases. A study of a wide array of higher priced products found that one-third of all dissatisfied customers voiced complaints to manufacturers or retailers.[40]

Another possible explanation for the lack of consumer follow-up when dissatisfied is that there are no formal channels for redress. Letters of complaint are usually too much trouble to write and are more likely to be written by a minority of better educated consumers. Product returns are frequently discouraged by excessive red tape in retail stores. A study by the Center for Study of Responsive Law found that when consumers do report problems to businesses, they are not always satisfactorily resolved. In fact, only 56 percent of such problems are resolved by business to the consumer's satisfaction.[41] In some cases, the manufacturer has provided a direct form of redress to the consumer. One of the best known examples is the institution of a "Cool Line" by Whirlpool to provide a 24-hour-a-day facility for consumers to make complaints and inquiries directly to company headquarters. Whirlpool's sales increased following the introduction and promotion of this service.[42]

The Right to a Clean Environment

On April 22, 1980, thousands of environmentally conscious consumers gathered across the country to celebrate the tenth anniversary of Earth Day. Earth Day 1970 was acknowledged as the start of the movement toward a cleaner environment. The drive to reduce pollution and conserve scarce resources has been linked to consumerism because these issues impact directly on the consumption of detergents, canned goods, gasoline, fertilizers, and other products that affect the environment.

Earth Day 1970 touched off what William K. Reilly, President of the Conservation Foundation, called an "astonishing record of legislation" to protect the environment and the consumer.[43] Consider the following environmental legislation passed in the 1970s:

- The Clean Air Act
- The National Environmental Quality Act
- The Water Quality Improvement Act
- The Occupational Safety and Health Act
- The Toxic Substances Control Act
- The Resource Conservation and Recovery Act
- The Safe Drinking Water Act

Furthermore, during the 1970s the Federal Government created the following regulatory bodies to oversee environmental protection:

- The Environmental Protection Agency
- The Council on Environmental Quality

- The Occupational Safety and Health Administration
- The Oceanic and Atmospheric Administration[44]

Most important was the creation of a cabinet-level post to deal with energy conservation and the environment.

Paralleling this governmental activity is the greater willingness on the part of the consumer to purchase with more consciousness of environmental issues. In Los Angeles, one experiment showed consumers willingly paid from two to twelve cents more per gallon for gasoline advertised as pollution reducing.[45] A study by Henion showed that when consumers were informed of the phosphate content in detergents, they tended to buy the lower phosphate alternatives.[46] Another study found that messages from a public service commission urging consumers to conserve energy were effective.[47]

What types of consumers are most likely to be environmentally conscious? Anderson et al. compared the characteristics of respondents who delivered materials to recycling sites to those who did not. They found "the ecologically responsible consumer [a user of the recycling centers] tends to be better educated, younger, of relatively higher socioeconomic and occupational status, and occupy an earlier stage in the family life cycle. . . ."[48] Users of recycling centers also considered themselves more personally competent, more alienated from existing institutions and less conservative, dogmatic, and status conscious than nonusers.

Webster developed an index of social (ecological) consciousness based on the purchase of a wide range of ecologically oriented products including lead-free gasoline, low phosphate detergents, beverages in returnable bottles, reuse of paper products, and use of recycling services.[49] He found that ecologically conscious consumers rely less on social values, are more influential and more tolerant. The environmentally conscious consumer is, therefore, insensitive to social pressures, likely to be better educated, and a self-actualizer. These consumers are more likely to be community leaders. As long as environmental issues continue to be relevant to consumer concerns in the 1980s, these individuals will ensure the link between environmentalists and consumerists.

The Right to Be in the Minority Without Disadvantage

The five consumer rights discussed above may have little relevance for low income consumers and minorities. Consumers living in inner-city ghettos:

- are more exposed to unsafe products;
- have less access to information;
- have fewer choices of alternative brands;
- are less likely to complain when dissatisfied and have less access to means of redress;
- are more exposed to pollution.

Therefore, being a low income or minority consumer is likely to result in fewer consumer rights. The right to be in the minority is not always without disadvantage.

Various studies have confirmed the fact that the poor pay more and shop less efficiently. Studies cited in Chapter 11 showed that blacks pay from 1 percent to 9 percent more on average for food products. The price differential for nonfood products is even greater. Sturdivant and Wilhelm found that prices for television sets in lower income areas in Los Angeles were 17 percent to 48 percent higher than in higher income areas.[50] Caplovitz found prices for appliances significantly higher in East Harlem.[51] The same study found ghetto merchants imposing extortionate finance charges. The inner-city poor are also victimized by other merchant practices such as products having no price marks, the bait of a low priced good to switch the customer to a higher priced item, and switching goods after the sale.

The consistent finding is that compared to other consumers, low income consumers do not always have the information which is necessary for a satisfactory choice or a knowledge of their rights as consumers. As a result, low income consumers:

- are unaware of the benefits of comparative shopping;
- lack the education and knowledge necessary to choose the best buy. Because of their low income, they have fewer opportunities to learn through experience;
- lack the freedom to go outside their local community to engage in comparative shopping;
- lack even a superficial appreciation of their rights and liabilities in post-sale legal conflicts;[52]
- lack the ability to budget incomes and plan purchases ahead.[53]

Consumerists identify the plight of the inner-city poor in particular because of their lack of consumer rights compared to others. This inequity has resulted in a feeling of alienation that can only have negative long-term consequences for a marketing economy.[54]

MARKETING'S RESPONSIBILITY TO THE CONSUMER

The foregoing discussion of consumerism and consumer rights considered the activities of only two of the three components of the consumer movement — consumerists and the government. The third component, the marketer, is equally important in advancing consumer rights. Marketing organizations have a responsibility to ensure each of the six rights which are described above. They must:

- test adequately for product safety;
- provide the consumer with adequate and reliable information;
- give the consumer an adequate choice of products that meet his or her needs;
- provide a means for consumers to register complaints;
- control pollution and be conscious of the use of scarce resources in production;
- try to protect the disadvantaged from higher prices, inadequate information, and poor distribution.

The question is whether marketing will accept these responsibilities in the interest of furthering self-regulation, or whether they will abdicate these responsibilities to government in the expectation of further legislation, more controls, and the establishment of more regulatory bodies. The preference in a marketing society, both from a pragmatic and ideological standpoint, is for self-regulation rather than additional government regulation. The history of the last twenty years is not encouraging. Failure of the automobile industry to restrain pollution and to encourage gas conservation, pollution of the waterways by the chemical industry, the failure of large companies to immediately recall unsafe products, the imposition of excessive credit charges by inner-city retailers are all indications of the need for some government controls.

However, marketing organizations have been moving toward self-regulation by the establishment of standards for children's advertising, labeling, and product safety. Of equal importance, many organizations have recently attempted to ensure consumer rights in two ways: by improving communications with consumers and by developing programs to educate consumers. This section will consider these more positive activities of marketing organizations in the area of consumerism.

Improving Communications Between Marketers and Consumers

Marketers can improve communications with consumers by establishing consumer advisory boards, ensuring adequate mechanisms for consumer complaints, and instituting corporate consumer affairs departments.[55]

Consumer Advisory Boards

A number of companies have developed boards of consumers who meet periodically with company executives. Executives explain corporate conditions and submit proposals to consumers. Consumers express their views of corporate policy and product offerings.

Stop and Shop, a Philadelphia-based food retailer, has instituted such a board to:

- make store personnel aware of what consumers are thinking;
- elicit the consumer's impression of store operations, merchandising and prices;
- give consumers an opportunity to voice their complaints;
- act as a sounding board for proposed products and policies;
- glean ideas to improve operations at all levels.[56]

Company executives state that board opinions can identify issues about four months before they are detected by marketing research surveys, but companies must be careful that board members do not become conditioned or begin to feel like "company people" and take a corporate view.

Hearing Consumer Complaints

Business firms are beginning to encourage communications regarding consumer complaints in a number of ways. Many airlines, hotels, and restaurants provide consumers with reply cards which solicit opinions about their service. General Electric conducted a continuous customer survey to determine level of satisfaction with appliances. Sears Roebuck conducts mail surveys of consumer feelings about fifty-two categories of general merchandise.[57] And, some companies have established organizational units to screen consumer complaint letters and send them to appropriate departments or executives. Such complaint letters "tipped off Pillsbury and General Foods to exploding pots, falling cakes, unjelled gelatin, and 'ground glass' in biscuits (actually crystallized sugar from excessive moisture during production)."[58]

Consumer Affairs Offices

The newest and most rapidly accepted form of corporate response to consumerism is the establishment of consumer affairs offices headed by a top level executive. One estimate is that over 600 corporations have formed units.[59] Among the firms that first established such units are J.C. Penney, Eastman Kodak, Giant Foods, and the automobile companies.

These departments are designed to:

- represent consumer interests in the company;
- formulate policy guidelines for handling customer complaints;
- receive and resolve customer complaints;
- review company messages to consumers to ensure clarity and completeness of information;
- maintain communications with other companies, consumer affairs groups and government agencies to keep informed of consumer issues and influence proposed regulatory or legislative activities;
- develop consumer education programs and disseminate information to consumers on the purchase and use of company products.[60]

A good example of the operation of a consumer affairs office is at Western Union. The department is headed by Mary Gardiner Jones, a former commissioner at the FTC. She established a complaint analysis program by computerizing consumer complaints in one central file, analyzing them, and disseminating them to appropriate areas within the organization.[61] But she also recognized that consumer complaint information is insufficient because "not all customers complain." Therefore, her office also conducts periodic surveys of the attitudes and concerns of customers, agents, and employees regarding company performance. In addition, company audits are performed to monitor performance in key areas such as message handling. Where required, corrective action programs will be instituted to ensure adequate customer service.

Consumer Education Programs

The second manner by which marketing companies can further consumer rights is through consumer education programs. There was a substantial growth in consumer education programs in the late 1970s because of inflation and the energy crisis. This growth has resulted in a "consumer education movement."[62]

The purpose of consumer education programs is not to inform but to educate. These programs "aim to teach people how to seek out, use and evaluate consumer information so that they can improve their ability to purchase or consume the products and services they deem most likely to enhance their well-being."[63] Therefore, the objective is to teach consumers how to make better choices. This objective is particularly pertinent for the poor and disadvantaged consumers since studies have shown that they are the least effective in searching for lower prices and brand alternatives.

A number of companies have established educational programs. J.C. Penney has one of the most comprehensive programs. They publish the *Forum,* a publication for teachers of consumer education; *Insights Into Consumerism,* a magazine providing teaching modules on consumer issues; and numerous buying guides containing factual product information.[64] They employ a staff of home economists who serve consumers by organizing educational programs such as sewing schools through local stores. They also participate in cooperative ventures in consumer education with a number of universities.[65] Other companies that have extensive consumer education programs are Procter and Gamble and Montgomery Ward. The success of these programs will result in the following benefits for consumers:

- A greater willingness to express their opinions to marketers about product performance and company policies.
- A desire to seek out more information to help make price, quality, and product comparisons.
- Less likelihood of purchasing products that are potentially harmful to health or to the environment.
- More of a tendency to become active in the debate on consumerist issues and environmental concerns.[66]

The advertising slogan of a discount retailer sums up the purpose of the consumer education movement and one objective of this book: "An educated consumer is our best customer."

SUMMARY

Our marketing economy does not always afford the consumer an environment for making an optimal or even an adequate choice. The necessity to promote consumer rights relative to the powers of big business has come to be known as the consumer movement or consumerism.

Consumerism is the set of activities of consumer organizations, government, and even business to promote the rights of the consumer. Although consumerism has not evolved into a national movement with substantial powers, certain consumer spokesmen such as Ralph Nader and organizations such as Consumers Union do represent consumers with a voice in government and industry.

The consumer movement is not new. Three distinct periods have been marked by increased activities to protect consumer rights: 1900–1915, 1935–1940, and 1965 to the present. Each of these periods was marked by increased prices and exposés of business practices leading to legislation protecting consumer rights. Current attitudes of consumers show a significant disparity from those of businesspersons. Consumers are more likely to feel that product quality and service are getting worse and that there are greater differences between manufacturers' claims and product performance. Whether these attitudes are a function of actual decreases in product quality or increasing consumer expectations coupled with inflation is an open question.

Of central concern to consumerists are four consumer rights spelled out by President Kennedy in the early 1960s and two additional rights that have become more apparent in the 1970s.

1. *The right to safety*   protects consumers against the marketing of goods which are hazardous. Central in this respect are the workings of the Consumer Product Safety Commission established in 1972.

2. *The right to be informed*   means protection from misleading information and the need for a sufficient amount of accurate information to make an informed choice. Of particular importance are regulations requiring more information on credit, nutritional labels, and prices.

3. *The right to choose*   requires access to a variety of products and services at competitive prices. The activities of the Federal Government in restraining monopoly powers and unfair trade practices has been important in ensuring this right.

4. *The right to be heard*   requires providing the channels of communication to permit consumers to register complaints to business. Although consumers do not generally voice such complaints, facilities such as hot lines to manufacturers or opinion cards may encourage consumers to express opinions about product performance.

5. *The right to a clean environment*   requires industry to protect the consumer from pollution and excessive use of scarce resources. This issue has become dominant in the 1970s with increased pollution and the advent of the energy crisis. The Environmental Protection Agency is active in ensuring this right and legislation has been passed to ensure clean air, clean water, and resource conservation.

6. *The right to be in the minority without disadvantage*   requires assurance that being a minority or low income consumer does not mean deprivation of the foregoing rights. Studies have found that the inner-city poor do pay more for products and are charged higher credit terms.

Marketing organizations have a role in ensuring these rights. Some organizations have accepted their responsibilities by establishing consumer advisory boards, the means for registering complaints, and consumer affairs offices. They have also furthered programs in consumer education to inform consumers how to make better choices in the marketplace.

QUESTIONS

1. Why has the consumer movement failed to establish power on a national level to represent the rights of consumers? Why has the labor movement been able to establish such power to represent the rights of workers?

2. The two previous periods in which consumer rights were an issue lasted fifteen years and five years respectively. The current period started in 1965 and promises to continue. Why will the current period of consumer rights activity most probably be longer than the two previous periods?

3. What were the similarities and differences between each of the three periods of the consumer movement?

4. Interpret the information in Table 23–2. What are the implications for
   - a pharmaceutical company considering the introduction of a new analgesic that is faster acting than anything now on the market;
   - an association of bicycle manufacturers considering the establishment of safety standards for bicycles?

5. Given the information provided in the chapter on past consumer rights legislation, develop a program for needed consumer rights legislation in the 1980s.

6. The Firestone radial 500 tire becomes damaged if it is driven for long periods in an underinflated condition. Should the company
   - recall the tires;
   - stop distribution without recall and inform current owners by mail;
   - continue marketing the tire and inform customers of the need to keep the tires inflated at a certain pressure?

7. Cite an example of a claims-fact discrepancy and of a claims-belief interaction. Should the FTC require the advertisers in either or both of these cases to cease using the claim?

8. What actions can (1) business people and (2) the federal government take to ensure the consumer rights of the inner-city poor?

9. Assume you are consumer affairs director for a large automobile company. What mechanisms would you establish for
   - ensuring consumer complaints are communicated?
   - interfacing with consumer rights organizations?

RESEARCH ASSIGNMENTS

1. Conduct a survey among forty to fifty consumers and identify those consumers who have taken some environmentally relevant action in the last month (e.g., purchased phosphate-free detergent, brought materials to a recycling center, purchased beverages in returnable bottles). Identify the demographic and life-style characteristics of these consumers and their media habits.
   - What are the differences in demographics, life-style, and media habits between the more environmentally conscious consumers and the rest of the sample?
   - What are the implications for a campaign by the federal government to influence people to purchase products that safeguard the environment?

2. Conduct a mail survey of 200 of the largest companies in the United States to determine:

(a) if they have a consumer affairs department;

(b) the organization and objectives of the department;

(c) if there are defined mechanisms for processing consumer complaints.

• What are the differences in organizational characteristics between companies that do and do not have consumer affairs departments?

NOTES

1. George S. Day and David A. Aaker, "A Guide to Consumerism," *Journal of Marketing* 34 (July 1970):13.

2. Robert O. Hermann, "Consumerism: Its Goals, Organizations and Future," *Journal of Marketing* 34 (October 1970): 56.

3. Jagdish N. Sheth and Nicholas J. Mammana, "Why Consumer Protection Efforts are Likely to Fail," faculty working paper, no. 104, College of Commerce and Business Administration, University of Illinois at Urbana-Champaign, April 11, 1973, p. 3.

4. Hermann, "Consumerism: Its Goals."

5. William M. Pride and O.C. Ferrell, *Marketing: Basic Concepts and Decisions* (Boston: Houghton Mifflin Co., 1977), p. 423.

6. Ralph M. Gaedeke, "What Business, Government and Consumer Spokesmen Think About Consumerism," *The Journal of Consumer Affairs* 4 (Summer 1970): 16.

7. James S. Hensel, *Strategies for Adapting to the Consumerism Movement* (Columbus, Ohio: Management Horizons, Inc., 1974).

8. Donald W. Hendon, "Toward a Theory of Consumerism," *Business Horizons* 18 (August 1975): 16–24.

9. Ibid., p. 17.

10. Gregory M. Gazda and David R. Gourley, "Attitudes of Businessmen, Consumers, and Consumerists Toward Consumerism," *The Journal of Consumer Affairs* 9 (Winter 1975): 176–186.

11. "Business Out of Sync With Public, Pollster Says," *Advertising Age,* May 23, 1977, p. 4.

12. "New Harris Consumer Study Causes Few Shocks in Adland," *Advertising Age,* May 30, 1977, p. 2.

13. *Advertising Age,* May 23, 1977, p. 102.

14. Hiram C. Barksdale, William R. Darden, and William D. Perreault, Jr., "Changes in Consumer Attitudes Toward Marketing, Consumerism and Government Regulation: 1971–1975," *The Journal of Consumer Affairs* 10 (Winter 1976): 117–139.

15. Executive Office of the President, *Consumer Advisory Council, First Report* (Washington, D.C.:

United States Government Printing Office, October, 1963), pp. 5–8.

16. Ibid.

17. Day and Aaker, "A Guide to Consumerism," p. 13.

18. *Consumer Product Safety Commission Annual Report, July 1, 1973–June 30, 1974* (Washington D.C.: United States Government Printing Office, 1975), p. 11.

19. Ibid.

20. Paul Busch, "A Review and Critical Evaluation of the Consumer Product Safety Commission: Marketing Management Implications," *Journal of Marketing* 40 (October 1976): 45.

21. Walter Guzzardi, Jr., "The Mindless Pursuit of Safety," *Fortune,* April 9, 1979, pp. 54–60.

22. David M. Gardner, "Deception in Advertising: A Conceptual Approach, *Journal of Marketing* 39 (January 1975): 40–46.

23. Boris W. Becker, "Consumerism: A Challenge or a Threat?" *Journal of Retailing* 48 (Summer 1972): 19.

24. Day and Aaker, "A Guide to Consumerism," p. 13.

25. George S. Day, "Assessing the Effects of Information Disclosure Requirements," *Journal of Marketing* 40 (April 1976): 43.

26. Ibid., p. 46.

27. Reed Moyer and Michael D. Hutt, *Macromarketing* (Santa Barbara, Calif.: John Wiley & Sons, 1978), Chapter 6, pp. 123–141.

28. Clive W. Granger and Andrew Billson, "Consumers' Attitudes Toward Package Size and Price," *Journal of Marketing Research* 9 (August 1972): 239–248; and J. Edward Russo, Gene Dreiser, and Sally Miyashita, "An Effective Display of Unit Price Information," *Journal of Marketing* 39 (April 1975): 11–19.

29. Day, "Assessing the Effects," p. 45.

30. Ibid., p. 46.

31. Becker, "Consumerism: A Challenge," p. 21.

32. Robert Moran, "Formulating Public Policy on Consumer Issues: Some Preliminary Findings," working paper P–57–A (Boston: Marketing Science Institute, September, 1971), p. 35.

33. John Kenneth Galbraith, *American Capitalism* (Boston: Houghton Mifflin Co., 1956), Chapter 7.
34. George S. Day, "The Mystery of the Dissatisfied Consumer," *The Wharton Magazine* (Fall 1977): 47.
35. Betty J. Diener and Stephen A. Greyser, "Consumer Views of Redress Needs," *Journal of Marketing* 42 (October 1978): 23.
36. Day, "The Mystery of the Dissatisfied Consumer," p. 45.
37. Diener and Greyser, "Consumer Views of Redress Needs," p. 25.
38. Day, "The Mystery of the Dissatisfied Consumer," p. 47.
39. Diener and Greyser, "Consumer Views of Redress Needs," p. 26.
40. Day, "The Mystery of the Dissatisfied Consumer," p. 59.
41. "Andreasen Reports Only 25% of Problems Consumers See Are Satisfactorily Resolved," *Marketing News,* July 16, 1976, p. 9.
42. "Business Responds to Consumerism," *Business Week,* September 6, 1969, p. 100.
43. "Earth Day '80 Dawns Tomorrow Amid Reflection and Plans for a New Decade," *The New York Times,* April 21, 1980, p. A16.
44. *New York Times,* April 21, 1980, p. A16.
45. George Fisk, "Product Planning and the Ecological Imperative," in Fred Allvine, ed., *Combined Proceedings of the American Marketing Association,* Series #35 (1973), pp. 243–257.
46. Karl E. Henion, "The Effect of Ecologically Relevant Information on Detergent Sales," *Journal of Marketing Research* 9 (February 1972): 10–14.
47. C. Samuel Craig and John M. McCann, "Assessing Communication Effects on Energy Conservation," *Journal of Consumer Research* 5 (September 1978): 82–88.
48. W. Thomas Anderson, Jr., Karl E. Henion, and Eli P. Cox III, "Socially vs. Ecologically Responsible Consumers," in Ronald C. Curhan, ed., *Combined Proceedings of the American Marketing Association,* Series #36 (1974), p. 308.
49. Frederick E. Webster, Jr., "Determining the Characteristics of the Socially Conscious Consumer," *Journal of Consumer Research* 2 (December 1975): 188–196.
50. Frederick D. Sturdivant and Walter T. Wilhelm, "Poverty, Minorities and Consumer Exploitation," in Frederick D. Sturdivant, ed., *The Ghetto Marketplace* (New York: The Free Press, 1969), pp. 108–117.
51. David Caplovitz, *The Poor Pay More* (New York: The Free Press, 1967).
52. Eric Schnapper, "Consumer Legislation and the Poor," *Yale Law Journal,* 76 (1967): 745–768.
53. Louise G. Richards, "Consumer Practices of the Poor," in Frederick D. Sturdivant, ed., *The Ghetto Marketplace* (New York: The Free Press, 1969), pp. 42–60.
54. Henry O. Pruden and Douglas S. Longman, "Race, Alienation and Consumerism," *Journal of Marketing* 36 (July 1972): 58–63.
55. Priscilla A. LaBarbera and Larry J. Rosenberg, "How Marketing Can Better Understand Consumers," *MSU Business Topics* 28 (Winter 1980): 29–36.
56. Dorothy Haase Kuper and Stephen A. Greyser, "The Stop and Shop Consumer Board of Directors," Intercollegiate Case Clearing House, No. 1–571–051, 1970, pp. 4–5.
57. Day, "The Mystery," p. 47.
58. La Barbera and Rosenberg, "How Marketing Can Better Understand Consumers," p. 31.
59. Richard T. Hise, Peter L. Gillett, and J. Patrick Kelly, "The Corporate Consumers Affairs Effort," *MSU Business Topics* 26 (Summer 1978): 17–26.
60. Leonard L. Berry, James S. Hensel, and Marian C. Burke, "Improving Retailer Capability for Effective Consumerism Response", *Journal of Retailing* 52 (Fall 1976): 5.
61. Mary Gardiner Jones, "The Consumer Affairs Office," *California Management Review* 20 (Summer 1978): 63–73.
62. Paul N. Bloom and Mark J. Silver, "Consumer Education: Marketers Take Heed," *Harvard Business Review* 54 (January–February 1976): 32–42; 149.
63. Ibid., p. 33.
64. Ibid., p. 40.
65. Ibid.
66. Ibid., pp. 40 and 42.

Glossary

Absolute threshold
Level below which the consumer cannot detect a stimulus. Minimal stimulus values capable of being sensed.

Acceptable price range
A price range the consumer views as realistic. If the product is priced below this range, quality is suspect. If the product is priced above, the consumer refuses to buy.

Acculturation
The process of learning a culture different from the one in which a person was raised. Learning the values of another culture (e.g., businessperson going abroad, immigrants moving to another country, foreign students).

Adaptation level
Point at which the consumer adjusts to a frequently repeated stimulus so that it is no longer noticed. Defined as the stimulus value (e.g., brightness, loudness) which is indifferent or neutral and with respect to which stimuli above or below it are relatively judged.

Adaptive strategy
Marketing approach whereby the needs and attitudes of consumers are determined and products are then developed to meet existing needs, with promotional policy guided by existing attitudes.

AIO inventories
A list of consumer activities, interests, and opinions constructed to empirically measure life-style components.

Anticipatory aspiration groups
Groups which an individual aspires to belong to and anticipates joining at some future time.

Aspiration group
Group which a consumer aspires to be associated with, but which he or she is not a member of.

Assimilation theory/effect

Theory in social psychology which focuses on a desire to maintain balance between experiences and expectations by selectively accepting information consistent with expectations. The tendency in perception for the highly similar parts of a whole to look as much alike as possible, that is, to assimilate. Assimilation occurs when the stimulus differences among the parts are sufficiently small; if the differences are sufficiently large, the opposite phenomenon of contrast tends to occur.

Assimilation-contrast effect

Combines the two views of assimilation and contrast theories in the belief that assimilation is more likely to occur if the disparity between experience and expectations is moderate; if it is extreme then a contrast effect is likely. States that when the consumer is only slightly disappointed, attitudes are likely to change in the direction of expectations and remain positive. When the consumer is very disappointed, a negative change in attitude is likely to occur after the purchase and may be exaggerated.

Attention span

The number and scope of stimuli that can be perceived at any given time.

Attitudes

Enduring systems of positive or negative evaluations, emotional feelings, and action tendencies with respect to an object. Consumer's overall liking or preference for an object. A learned predisposition to respond consistently with respect to a given object.

Attitudinal structure

The structure of attitudes contains three components directed to a single object: the beliefs about the object—the cognitive component; the affect connected with the object—the feeling component; and the disposition to take action with respect to the object—the action tendency component.

Attribution theory

States that a consumer attributes certain motives to his or her actions after the fact. A theoretical construct referring to cognitive processes through which an individual infers the cause of the behavior of others or of himself or herself.

Automatic Interaction Detector Analysis (AID)

A multivariate computer program used to develop segments by brand usage. This program selects those consumer characteristics that best distinguish one group from another (e.g., users versus nonusers of the brand).

Autonomic decisions

Product decisions made by either the husband or wife, either one of which is equally likely to make the decision.

Avoidance group

A group which an individual is not a member of and regards its members as examples of values and behavioral patterns to be avoided (e.g., social comparisons and prejudices that take the form of one social class or ethnic group being better than another).

Balance theory

A theory that asserts that unbalanced cognitive systems tend to shift toward a state of balance. Evaluation of an object is a function of consistently held beliefs about the object. When information about an object conflicts with the consumer's beliefs, balance will be achieved by either changing one's opinion about the object, about the source of information, or a combination of both. The result is a balance in beliefs about the information and the object.

Bargaining power

The consumer's influence on the salesperson to obtain price, delivery, or other concessions. This is distinct from the salesperson's influence on the consumer as represented by referent and expert power.

Behavioral segmentation

Identification of consumer groups by differences in behavior (e.g. users versus nonusers or heavy versus light users).

Behaviorists
Experimental psychologists who focus on the individual by seeking to determine the effects of variations in a stimulus on behavior, with emphasis on control over stimulus inputs and the environment.

Beliefs
Cognitive components of attitudes, representing the characteristics a brand is believed to have. Beliefs link a brand to a set of characteristics and specify the extent to which the brand possesses each characteristic.

Beliefs/evaluation models
States that an attitude toward a brand is a function of the probability that the brand has some attribute (e.g., What is the probability that Budweiser is a strong beer?) and the evaluative aspects of the attribute (Is strength a desirable characteristic in a beer?).

Beliefs/importance model
States that the overall evaluation of a brand (A_o) is a function of beliefs about the attributes possessed by a brand (b_{oi}) weighted by the importance of each attribute (I_i), so that $A_o = \sum_{i=1}^{N} b_{oi} I_i$

Beliefs only model
States that an attitude toward a brand is a function of belief about the brand's attributes with little relation to the importance assigned to each attribute.

Benefit segmentation
Identification of a group of consumers based on similarity in needs. Often marketing opportunities are discovered by analysis of consumers' benefit preferences. Frequently, one or more segments are identified that are not being adequately served by existing alternatives.

Brand image
Represents overall perception of the brand, formed from information about the brand and past experience. The set of beliefs that forms a complete picture of the brand.

Brand loyalty
Commitment to a certain brand because of prior reinforcement (satisfaction as a result of product usage). Brand loyalty is a result of two components: (1) a favorable attitude toward the brand, and (2) repurchase of the brand over time.

Buying center
The decision-making unit to select products and vendors in an organization.

Categorization
Tendency of consumers to place marketing information into logical categories in order to process information quickly and efficiently, and to classify new information.

Classical conditioning
A behaviorist concept in which behavior is conditioned by repetitive stimuli and the establishment of a close association (contiguity) between a secondary stimulus and the primary stimulus.

Closure
A principle of perceptual integration describing a perceiver's tendency to fill in the missing elements when a stimulus is incomplete. Experience tends to be organized into whole, continuous figures. If the stimulus pattern is incomplete, the perceiver fills in missing elements.

Cluster analysis
A computer program which groups respondents together by similarity so there is greatest similarity in ratings within groups and greatest difference between groups. (Statistically, the program minimizes within group variance and maximizes between group variance.)

Coercive power
The power of groups to express disapproval and even censure. Marketers have depicted

coercive power through the use of fear appeals.

Cognitive dissonance theory
Developed by Festinger, this theory asserts that an individual experiences discomfort when he or she holds logically inconsistent cognitions about an object or event, and that the consumer is thus motivated to reduce dissonance through cognitive and attitudinal changes. It states that when post purchase conflict arises, consumers will seek balance in the psychological set by seeking supporting information or by distorting contradictory information.

Cognitive school of psychology
Emphasizes the consumer's psychological set (formation of beliefs about brands, changes in attitudes, relation of brand attitudes to needs) in explaining purchasing behavior. The cognitive school describes learning within a framework of complex decision making and problem solving.

Comparative advertising
The naming of a competitive product in the marketer's ad. Advertisers use comparative advertising to point out weaknesses and to create a less favorable attitude toward the competitive brand, thus increasing the likelihood of buying the marketer's brand. It has become an important means of competitive positioning.

Comparative influence
The process of comparing oneself to other members of the group providing a basis for comparing one's attitudes and behavior to those of the group.

Compensatory model
When a compensatory model is used by the consumer, perceived strength of a given alternative on one or more evaluative criteria can compensate for weaknesses on other attributes. Generally, this process requires consumers to evaluate a brand by a number of criteria.

Competitive positioning
Communicates product benefits by establishing a distinctive postion for the product compared to competition. A classic example is 7-Up's positioning as the Un-Cola. Competitive positioning provides a clear frame of reference for the consumer by relating claims to other brands.

Complex or extensive decision making
Decisions in which the buyer is motivated to undertake a process of active search for information. Based on this information, alternative brands are evaluated on specific criteria. The cognitive process of evaluation involves consumer perceptions of brand characteristics and development of favorable or unfavorable attitudes toward a brand. The assumption is that consumer perceptions and attitudes will precede and influence behavior.

Compliance-aggressiveness-detachment (CAD) scale
Relying on social theories of personality to explain purchase behavior, this scale organizes traits into categories descriptive of a person's consistent means of relating to and coping with others. There are three basic types: compliant (moving toward people), aggressive (moving against people), or detached (moving away from people).

Conformity
The acceptance of group norms and values. Conformity is reflected by purchasing those brands and product categories purchased by the group leaders. Marketers are interested in such imitative behavior because it implies a "snowball effect" once products are accepted by the most influential members of a group. "Keeping up with the Joneses" is an example of conformity.

Conjoint analysis
A statistical technique which develops utilities for each attribute tested based on a rank order preference rating of alternative concepts. It is used to screen a large number of concepts and identify several candidates for further testing. A technique in which respondents' utilities or valuations of attributes are inferred from the preference they express for various combinations of these attributes.

Conjunctive decision rule
A consumer accepts a brand only if it is acceptable on key attributes. A brand that is seen as negative on one or two of the most important attributes would be eliminated, even if it is positive on all other attributes.

Consistency theory
The tendency in any given attitude system for the three components—beliefs, feelings, and actions—to be in agreement. States that information that is accepted is consistent with strongly held beliefs. Focuses on the balance between attitudes and behavior.

Constant sum scale
A scale in which values assigned to objects always add up to the same amount. (For example, assume you could select ten free soft drink bottles in a store, how many bottles of the following brands would you select?)

Consumer characteristics
The demographic, life-style, and personality characteristics of the consumer.

Consumer information processing
The nature of the consumer's search for and reactions to marketing communications. The process by which consumers perceive information in four steps—exposure to information, attention, comprehension, and retention of information.

Consumer panel data
Information obtained from a sample of consumers that record their purchases for a wide range of goods over time (brand purchased, store in which bought, price paid, whether bought on deal, etc.). Such data permits researchers to track brand purchases over time. It provides a behavioral measure of brand loyalty based on repeat purchases.

Consumer positioning
Positioning products based on the needs of the consumer. In positioning analysis, consumers are positioned on a perceptual map to identify target groups for product concepts. Consumers are positioned closest to the concepts they prefer most and furthest from those they prefer least.

Consumer socialization
The process by which consumers acquire the knowledge and skills necessary to operate in the marketplace. The two most important types of consumer socialization are the socialization of children and the socialization of new residents in a community.

Consumer thought variables
Represent the cognitive processes involved in decision making. They are of three types: needs or benefits sought by the consumer from the brand, perceptions of the brand's characteristics, and attitudes toward the brand.

Consumerism
The set of activities of independent consumer organizations and consumer activists designed to protect the consumer. Consumerism is concerned primarily with ensuring that the consumer's rights in the process of exchange are protected. A social movement seeking to augment the rights and power of buyers in relation to sellers.

Context
The setting or environment in which an object is presented.

Contiguity
Development of a close association between a secondary stimulus and the primary stimulus, generally through repetition.

Continuity
Principles of grouping which emerged from Gestalt psychology and which suggest that the basic flow of stimuli should be continuous and lead to a logical conclusion (e.g., the flow of a sales message).

Continuous innovation
An extension or modification of an existing product. Examples are fluoridated toothpaste, low-tar cigarettes, cook-in-the-bag vegetables. A continuous innovation has the least disrupting influence on established purchasing patterns.

Contrast effect
States that a disparity between expectations and experiences may lead the consumer to magnify the disparity. Implies that advertisers should moderate their claims so as not to increase consumer expectations to the point where dissatisfaction (e.g., a disparity between expectation and experience) is likely to result.

Cultural values
An especially important class of beliefs shared by the members of a society as to what is desirable or undesirable. Beliefs that some general state of existence is personally and socially worth striving for. Cultural values in the United States include achievement, independence, and youthfulness.

Culture
The implicit beliefs, norms, values, and customs which underlie and govern conduct in a society. The norms, beliefs, and customs learned from society. Culture leads to common patterns of behavior.

Decoding
The sequence of steps in consumer information processing from exposure to attention to comprehension of a message.

Demarketing
Using promotional tools to discourage consumption—a trend which has emerged recently due to realization that the availability of certain goods cannot be taken for granted.

Demographics
Objective characteristics of consumers such as age, income, or education. This information is characteristically used for media planning.

Depth interview
An unstructured, personal interview in which the interviewer attempts to get subjects to talk freely and to express their true feelings. Can be conducted individually, or in groups (focused group interviews). The latter have the advantage of eliciting more information because of group interaction.

Demonstration principle
Formulated by James Duesenberry, a Harvard economist, the demonstration principle states that due to increased mobility and purchasing power in America, consumers will come into increasing contact with new products and will be more likely to buy them. This demonstration effect is referred to as a social multiplier because ownership increases in multiples as a function of group influence and product visibility.

Determinant attributes
Referred to by Alpert as product attributes that "lead to the choice of that product . . ." since they determine preference and purchase behavior.

Deterministic model
Predicts a particular course of action based on such input variables as consumer characteristics, brand attitudes, consumer needs, etc. Deterministic models attempt to predict behavior in exact or nonprobabilistic terms (e.g., purchase versus no purchase).

Differential threshold
The minimum difference between two stimuli that can be detected. The minimal stimulus values capable of being told apart.

Diffusion theory
A theory which describes the process by which ideas and products are spread across groups through communications. Diffusion theory focuses on the time of adoption of the innovation or idea and on the environment provided by the social system, encouraging or discouraging adoption.

Disclaimant group
A group of which an individual is a member although rejecting its values.

Disconfirmation of expectations
Negative product evaluation resulting from consumption because expectations of prod-

uct performance are not met. In such cases, consumers may develop more negative attitudes toward the product after the purchase.

Discontinuous innovation
A major technological advance involving the establishment of a new product and new behavior patterns. Examples are solar energy, electric cars, and the video-disc. Such an innovation will significantly alter purchasing patterns.

Disjunctive decision rule
When following a disjunctive decision rule, the consumer establishes one or more attributes as being dominant. A brand will be evaluated as acceptable only if it exceeds the minimum specified level on these key attributes. The other attributes are of little significance.

Dissonance
A state of tension because information about a brand is not consistent with the consumer's expectations (e.g., negative information about a favored brand).

Dissonance theory
See *Cognitive dissonance theory.*

Downside elasticity
Sensitivity to price decreases. It is possible that a consumer will buy more if prices decrease, but will not buy substantially less if prices increase. This means the consumer is elastic on the downside.

Dynamically continuous innovation
A new product but not a major technological advance. It does not alter existing consumer behavior patterns. Examples are electric toothbrushes, touch-tone telephones.

Early adopter
Not the first consumer to adopt a product innovation, but adopts early in the product's life cycle. This group is distinct from innovators since it is much more reliant on group norms and values. It is also more oriented to the local community in contrast to the innovator's cosmopolitan outlook. Early adopters are most likely to be opinion leaders because of their closer affiliation to groups.

Encoding
The process of developing the marketing stimulus. The good advertising campaign is one in which the encoding process uses symbols and imagery which successfully communicate the product benefits to the consumer.

Environmental stimuli
Nonmarketing stimuli which generally reach the consumer through the mass media such as economic news, the energy crisis, attempts at pollution control, information on fashion trends.

Environmental variables
External forces which affect consumers' needs, attitudes, and perceptions; that is, face-to-face groups, situational factors, and social and cultural forces.

Expert influence
Influence due to the perception of an individual as a knowledgeable and objective source of information.

Expert power
Power based on the expertise of the individual or group derived from experience and knowledge. A salesperson has expert power if he or she is regarded as knowledgeable by the consumer.

Expressive roles
Family purchase roles related to the need for social and emotional support. Decisions regarding style, color, or design are examples.

Extended beliefs/evaluation model
An extension of the beliefs/evaluation model of attitudes. States that it is more relevant to measure attitudes toward the act of purchasing or consuming a brand than attitudes

toward the brand itself. The model also introduces social norms as a determinant of attitudes.

Extinction
Elimination of the link between stimulus and expected reward. If a consumer is no longer satisfied with a product, then a process of extinction takes place. Extinction leads to a rapid decrease in the probability that the same brand will be repurchased.

Factor analysis
A mathematical procedure for determining the intercorrelation between items and reducing the items into independent components or factors to eliminate redundancy. Typically, factor analysis is used to reduce a great amount of data into its more basic structure. An analytical technique which reduces purchasing motives to a smaller number of independent need criteria.

Figure and ground
Gestalt psychologists state that in organizing stimuli into wholes, individuals identify those stimuli that are prominent (the *figure*) and those stimuli that are less prominent (the *ground* or background). The figure appears well defined, at a definite location, solid, and in front of the ground. In contrast, the ground appears amorphous, indefinite and continuous behind the figure. A principle of advertising is that the product should appear as figure rather than ground.

Focused group interview
See *Depth interview.*

Follower
A consumer who is ordinarily influenced by others. An individual who actively solicits word-of-mouth information, but is not an influential.

Forgetting
Forgetting occurs when information stored in memory is lost or when new information interferes with retrieval of stored information. Occurs when the stimulus is no longer repeated or perceived. Lack of use of a product or elimination of an advertising campaign can cause forgetting.

Functions of attitudes
There are four functions served by attitudes: a utilitarian function, a knowledge function, a value-expressive function, and an ego-defensive function. Marketing strategies can attempt to influence attitudes serving each of these functions.

Gatekeeper
Information gatherer who may control the flow of information from the mass media to the group. The gatekeeper introduces ideas and information to the group but does not necessarily disseminate them.

Gestalt psychology
A German school of psychology which focuses on total configuration or whole patterns. Stimuli such as advertising messages are seen as an integrated whole. In short, the whole is greater than the sum of the parts.

Ground
See *Figure and ground.*

Grouping information
Collecting information into groups rather than perceiving separate units of information. Consumers evaluate one brand versus another over a variety of attributes such as taste, economy, convenience, nutrition, etc., and group various bits and pieces of information into organized wholes to form an overall brand image.

Habit
A connection between stimuli and/or responses that has become virtually automatic through experience, usually resulting in the purchase of the same brand. A limitation or absence of (1) information seeking and (2) evaluation of alternative brand choices.

Hierarchy of effects
Stipulates the sequence of cognitive stages the consumer goes through in reaching a

tendency to act. Needs are formulated, beliefs are formed about the brand, attitudes develop toward the brand, and the consumer then forms an action predisposition.

Hierarchy of motives
The basis for Abraham Maslow's theory specifying five levels of motives from lowest to highest order. An individual will satisfy the lowest motivational level first. Once satisfied, a new and higher order motive will emerge to generate behavior. Thus, it is the dissatisfied needs that lead to action.

High-involvement purchases
Purchases that are more important to the consumer, are related to the consumer's self-identify, and involve some risk. It is worth the consumer's time and energies to consider product alternatives more carefully in the high-involvement case. Therefore, a process of complex decision making is more likely to occur when the consumer is involved in the purchase.

Ideal point model
A multiattribute model which is an offshoot of the belief–importance model. A rating of the consumer's hypothetical ideal brand on various attributes represents the consumer's needs. The closer a brand is to the ideal on key attributes, the more positive the attitude toward the brand.

Impulse buying
A tendency to buy on whim with little preplanning.

Impulse shopping
Unplanned shopping trips—a spur-of-the-moment decision to enter a store.

Index of status characteristics (ISC)
A multiitem index combining several socioeconomic variables into one index of social class. The ISC measures four variables: occupation, source of income, house types, and dwelling area.

Inertia
A passive process of information processing, brand evaluation, and brand choice. The same brand is frequently purchased by inertia to save time and energy.

Information overload
The consumer's ability to process information has been surpassed because of excessive information. As a result, decision making becomes less effective.

Information processing
See *Consumer information processing.*

Innovative communicator
The innovator who is most likely to engage in word-of-mouth communication about an adopted innovation.

Innovativeness
The early adoption of a new product. Innovativeness is distinct from opinion leadership in that it is a behavioral variable (i.e., adoption). In contrast, opinion leadership is measured by the consumer's perception regarding his or her interpersonal influence on others.

Innovator
The earliest adopter of new products. The innovator (as distinct from the early adopter) obtains information from the mass media and is not likely to exert influence on others. This group is a small percentage of the population.

In-store stimuli
In-store marketing variables, that is, package, display, coupons, prices, salespersons, etc. In-store exposure to marketing stimuli are the most influential factors in unplanned purchases.

Instrumental conditioning
A learning theory that views behavior as a function of the consumer's past actions and assessment of the degree of satisfaction obtained from those actions. Exposure to a

stimulus is within the consumer's control and is instrumental in achieving satisfaction.
The development of brand loyalty is an illustration of learning through instrumental
conditioning.

Instrumental roles
Family purchasing roles related to task-oriented functions meant to provide direction
to the group. Decisions on budgets, timing, and product specifications are task oriented.

Integration
The tendency to perceive stimuli as an integrated whole, for example, a brand image.

Just noticeable differences (j.n.d.)
The minimal difference that can be detected between stimuli. The consumer will not
be able to detect any difference between stimuli below his or her differential threshold. The j.n.d. varies not only with (a) the sensitivity of the receptor and (b) the type
of stimuli, but also with (c) the absolute intensity of the stimuli being compared. (See
Differential threshold.)

Kelly Repertory Grid
A technique used to determine the relevant attributes consumers use to evaluate products
by asking consumers to verbalize why they see pairs of brands as similar or different.

Key informant method
Involves the use of informed individuals in a social system to identify opinion leaders
in a given situation.

Law of retail gravitation
Developed by William Reilly, the principle states that customers will be attracted to
a shopping facility in direct proportion to the population of the area and in inverse
proportion to the distance of the customer from the area.

Learning
The influence of past experience and information on future behavior.

Learning curve
Reflects changes in the probability of behavior as a result of past experiences. Initially,
a decision process takes place, but with continuous reinforcement the probability of
buying the same brand on repetitive purchase occasions increases until habit is
established.

Legitimation
A step in the adoption of an innovation whereby the decision is made that the purchase
of a new product should be given serious consideration.

Lexicographic decision rule
Requires consumers to rank product attributes from most important to least important.
The brand that dominates on the most important criterion is chosen. If two or more
brands tie, then the second attribute is examined and so on until the tie is broken. A
lexicographic rule follows a sequential approach.

Life style
An individual's mode of living as identified by his or her activities, interests, and
opinions. Life-style variables have been measured by identifying a consumer's day-to-
day activities and interests.

Low-involvement purchases
Purchases that are less important to the consumer. Identity with the product is low.
It may not be worth the consumer's time and effort to search for information about
brands and to consider a wide range of alternatives. Therefore, low-involvement purchases are associated with a more limited process of decision making.

Market segment
A group of consumers with similar needs or characteristics. Identification of a market
segment permits marketing resources to be directed to a well-defined group.

Market segmentation analysis
Involves identifying consumer groups by similarity in needs, usage, or characteristics

in order to direct marketing strategies to these groups.

Market segmentation strategy
Appealing to a market segment with a clearly differentiated product or service offering designed specifically for the target market. Allocating marketing resources to satisfy the needs of a well-defined group of consumers. The identification of market segments enables the manager to develop marketing strategies geared to consumer needs.

Market structure analysis
Positioning by product type, which provides a broad view of a market based on consumer perceptions (e.g., positioning various types of snack foods). Conducted to evaluate the positioning of alternative product categories by consumer needs, market structure analysis helps assess the potential for entry into a particular product category.

Marketing concept
The marketing concept states that all marketing strategies must be based on known consumer needs. Marketers must first define the benefits consumers seek from particular products and gear marketing strategies accordingly.

Marketing stimuli
Any component of a product's marketing plan. Price, package, advertising, the store that sells the brand, and the brand itself are all marketing stimuli. Most marketing stimuli are symbolic in nature. They are representations of the product, not the product itself.

Media effects
The message transmission component in the communication model, influenced by the image of the media selected and the environmental factors that distinguish media categories.

Membership group
A group of which an individual is a member and in which he or she has face-to-face communication with other members. Groups in which a person is recognized by others as belonging.

Memory
Represents information that is retained and stored by the consumer and that can be recalled for future use.

Message effects
The influence of the content of the message on consumer perceptions and behavior.

Motivational research
Research into consumer motives, particularly unconscious motives. These are determined through indirect assessment methods that include projective techniques and depth interviews. On this basis, hypotheses are developed regarding the motives for consumer behavior.

Motivation
An inner state that energizes, activates or moves, and that directs or channels behavior toward goals. A motive results in and can be inferred from purposive means-end behavior. General predispositions that direct behavior toward attaining certain desired objectives. Motives directly affect the specific need criteria used in evaluating brands.

Multiattribute models
Models that measure attitudes on a multidimensional basis by determining how consumers evaluate brands across product attributes. The sum of these ratings weighted by the value placed on each attribute represents the consumer's attitude toward the brand.

Multidimensional scaling
A set of computer programs which determine the relative position of brands and concepts in *n*-dimensional space based on consumer similarity or preference ratings of these brands.

Need criteria
The set of needs used to evaluate alternative brands.

Needs

Forces directed to specific goals that can be achieved by purchase behavior. The motive force for directing behavior to one brand or another.

Noise

Interference with message transmission which results as a natural outgrowth of the communications process.

Noncompensatory model

A model of attitude structure in which brands are evaluated on a few of the most important attributes. Weakness of a product or brand on one attribute cannot be compensated by its strength on another. The result is that the brand can be eliminated from consideration based on one or two attributes. Requires consumers to process information by attribute across brands.

Normative influence

The influence exerted on an individual to conform to group norms and expectations.

Norms

Rules of behavior in particular circumstances that specify actions which are proper and those which are improper. Beliefs held by a consensus of a group concerning the behavior rules for individual members. Rules and standards of conduct (generally undefined) established by the group. Group members are expected to conform to these norms.

Opinion leader

An individual who frequently exerts influence on others through word-of-mouth communication. One who exerts a disproportionately large amount of influence on others.

Organizational buyer

One who buys not for personal use but to satisfy some organizational need. Examples are industrial purchasers who buy products as input into manufacturing processes and institutional purchasers who buy for such organizations as hospitals and schools.

Outshopping

Shopping beyond a consumer's usual trading area. Greater mobility and the propensity of consumers to shop for alternatives have led to increased frequency of outshopping behavior.

Overprivilegedness/underprivilegedness

The use of relative income to define consumers in a certain social class. Those having above average income in their social class are overprivileged, those having below average income are underprivileged.

Passive learning

Occurs when consumers learn about brands with little involvement and purchase with little evaluation of alternative brands. Attitudes are more likely to be formed after rather than before a purchase.

Penetration strategy

A strategic option establishing a competitive price for a new product entry. A mass marketing approach would be followed. Most relevant for continuous innovation.

Perceived instrumentality

The degree to which a brand has the attributes allowing the consumer to achieve definite goals. (For example, the extent to which a certain brand of cereal is instrumental in achieving nutrition, weight control, or natural ingredients.)

Perceived risk

Degree of risk perceived in a purchase. It is composed of two elements, (1) uncertainty about the decision, and (2) potential consequences of the decision.

Perception

The process by which people select, organize, and interpret sensory stimuli into a meaningful and coherent picture. The way consumers view an object (e.g. their mental picture of a brand or the traits they attribute to a brand).

Perceptual defense

Distortion of information by consumers so that it conforms to their beliefs and attitudes.

This function operates to protect the individual from threatening or contradictory stimuli.

Perceptual equilibrium/disequilibrium

Consumers seek to maintain equilibrium in their psychological set by screening out information that does not conform to their predispositions. When consumers choose information consistent with prior beliefs or interpret information to conform to these beliefs, they are processing information to ensure perceptual equilibrium. Acceptance of contradictory information means the consumer is in a state of perceptual disequilibrium.

Perceptual mapping

A group of quantitative techniques which seeks to position various brands on a "map" based on the way they are perceived by the consumer. The closer one brand is to another on the map, the more similar it is to the other brand. The basic assumption is that if consumers see two brands as being similar, they will behave similarly toward the two brands.

Perceptual vigilance

A form of selective perception whereby the consumer's needs determine the information perceived. For example, words that connote important values often are perceived more readily. As a result, preferred brand names will be recognized more quickly than nonpreferred brand names. The tendency of consumers to select the information that helps them in evaluating brands to meet their needs.

Personality

Personality variables reflect consistent and enduring patterns of behavior. Represents a set of consumer characteristics that have been used to describe target segments.

Post-purchase dissonance

Perceptual disequilibrium whereby the consumer perceives conflicting information after the decision and seeks to change the information to conform to prior behavior.

Price elasticity

See *Response elasticity.*

Primary stimuli

Unconditioned stimuli. In marketing, the product and its components (package, contents, physical properties) are primary stimuli.

Product concept

A bundle of product benefits that can be directed to the needs of a defined group of consumers through symbolism and imagery. The product concept represents the organization of marketing stimuli into a coordinated product position that can be more easily directed to consumers.

Product concept test

Obtaining consumer reactions to a verbal description of the product generally before the product is manufactured. Usually tested against several alternative concepts.

Product positioning analysis

Requires determining how consumers perceive brands relative to their needs and developing product benefits to meet these needs. The purpose is to evaluate where a product should be positioned (normative analysis) or where it is currently positioned (descriptive analysis).

Product positioning strategy

Strategies to communicate product benefits to the consumer so as to achieve a distinctive position in the market.

Product use test

A test of the actual product. A sample of consumers are asked to use the product for a period of time, and state their reactions to it. Frequently, they are asked to use their regular brands as well for comparative purposes.

PROFIT (property fitting) program

A computer program used to associate a brand's position with evaluative attributes.

The program identifies the position of each attribute by determining a vector that provides the best fit between the attribute and the brands in a perceptual map.

Projective tests
Techniques used for detecting and measuring wants and attitudes not readily discernable through more direct methods. Consists of the presentation of ambiguous materials (e.g., ink blots, untitled pictures, etc.). In interpreting this material, the viewer "projects" tendencies of which he or she may be unaware or may wish to conceal. Diagnostic devices in which interpretation of ambiguous stimuli are taken to reveal something about the observer, based on previous experience and motives, needs, and interests in play at the time.

Proximity
The tendency to group stimuli by proximity means that one object will be associated with another based on its closeness to that object.

Psychoanalytic theory
Theory developed by Freud which emphasizes the conflict between id, ego, and superego in childhood, and the resolution of these conflicts in adult behavior. The dynamic interaction of these elements results in unconscious motivations that are manifested in observed human behavior.

Psychographics
Consumer psychological characteristics that can be quantified. They are represented by two classes of variables: life-styles and personality.

Psychological pricing
Pricing policies which rely on the consumer's perceptual sensitivity to certain price points, for example, odd-even pricing and multiple pricing.

Psychological set
The consumer's state of mind toward an object—that is, his or her needs, attitudes, and perceptions relative to various brands. The psychological set is represented at a given point in time prior to the decision process. It will change during the decision process as new information is processed, resulting in changes in needs, attitudes, and perceptions.

Random or unanchored learning
A situation in which messages are retained without a process of awareness and comprehension. Krugman regards the environment of television as encouraging random or unanchored learning.

Rank order of preference scale
A nonmetric scale in which objects are ranked by order of preference. Values have ordinal meaning only.

Rate of diffusion
A time-oriented measurement which reflects the cumulative level of adoption of a new product over time.

Reactance
When group pressures to conform become too intense, the consumer may be encouraged to reject group norms and to demonstrate independent behavior.

Reference group
Any group with which an individual identifies such that he or she tends to use the group as a standard for self-evaluation and as a source of personal values and goals. A group that serves as a reference point for the individual in the formation of beliefs, attitudes, and behavior. Such groups provide consumers with a means of comparing and evaluating their own brand attitudes and purchasing behavior.

Referent power
Power based on the identification of the individual with members of the group. The greater the similarity of the individual's beliefs and attitudes with those of group members, the greater the referent power of the group. A salesperson has referent power if he or she is seen as similar to the consumer.

Reinforcement
Satisfaction as a result of repeated product usage leading to an increased likelihood that the same brand will be purchased.

Response elasticity
Measures a consumer's sensitivity to a particular marketing stimulus by associating a percentage change in the stimulus with a percentage change in the quantity purchased. The most common example is price elasticity. Provides a basis for defining consumer segments by degree of sensitivity to marketing stimuli.

Reward power
Power based on the ability of the group to reward the individual.

Risky shift phenomenon
The hypothesis that joint decision making encourages the group to take riskier decisions because in this way, the failure of a wrong decision can be shared by all members of the group.

Rokeach Value Survey
The best known inventory of cultural values, developed by studying a particular culture, identifying the shared values of that culture, and then determining whether these values are in fact widely held.

Roles
Functions assumed by or assigned to individuals by the group in the attainment of group objectives.

Secondary stimulus
A stimulus that is repeatedly linked to a primary stimulus to produce a conditioned response. Communications designed to influence consumer behavior are secondary stimuli that represent the product or stimuli associated with the product (price, store in which purchased, effect of salesperson).

Selective attention
Being attentive to only certain portions of messages, resulting in greater awareness of supportive information and avoidance of contradictory information.

Selective comprehension
Interpreting discrepant information so that it is consistent with beliefs and attitudes.

Selective exposure
Avoiding contradictory information by not being in the audience or by ignoring such information. Consumers engage in selective exposure by choosing those sources of information they are most likely to agree with.

Selective perception
Consumers perceive marketing stimuli selectively to reinforce their needs, attitudes, past experiences, and personal characteristics. Selective perception means that the identical ad, package, or product can be perceived very differently by two consumers.

Selective retention
Consumers remember those messages or portions of messages most relevant to the decision and most likely to conform to their beliefs and attitudes.

Self-concept theory
A person's self-concept causes the individual to see herself or himself through the eyes of other persons. In doing so, an individual takes into account the other person's behavior, feelings, and attitudes. This evaluation is closely related to the perceptions of whether other persons in the reference group will approve or disapprove the "self" presented to the reference group.

Self-designating techniques
A set of techniques used to measure opinion leadership, innovativeness, perceived risk, or other marketing constructs. The method requires the consumer to categorize himself or herself in a given topic area.

Self-image theory
An individual has an image of self measured on such criteria as happy, careful, dependable, confident, social, etc., and an image of the ideal self. The self image measures who consumers think they are, the ideal image who consumers think they would like to be.

Semantic differential
A seven-point metric scale anchored by bipolar adjectives and used in marketing to measure beliefs about brands.

Similarity
A principle of grouping which suggests that stimuli will be grouped together by similarity in their characteristics.

Situational variables
The definition of a purchase or consumption situation; for instance, buying a car for business versus family use.

Skimming policy
A strategic option establishing a high price for a new product entry and "skimming the cream of the market" by aiming at the most price inelastic consumer. Advertising and sales promotion would be limited to specific targets, and distribution would be selective. The most relevant strategy for discontinuous innovations.

Social class
A division of society made up of persons possessing certain common social and economic characteristics which are taken to qualify them for equal-status relations with one another, and which restricts their interaction with members of other social classes.

Social judgment theory
A theory which describes an individual's position on an issue based on the individual's involvement with the issue. Sherif identifies a latitude of acceptance, a latitude of rejection, and a latitude of noncommitment to operationalize this concept of involvement. The greater the involvement, the narrower the latitude of acceptance and the wider the latitude of rejection on various positions.

Social multiplier effect
As a result of the demonstration principle, ownership increases in multiples as consumers come into contact with and acquire new products. The social multiplier effect illustrates the volatility of group influence in the American economy. (See *Demonstration principle*.)

Social stimuli
Communications from face-to-face groups. Sometimes referred to as word-of-mouth advertising, social stimuli frequently have more influence on purchase behavior than marketing stimuli. The opinion of friends and neighbors, the judgments of one's peers, or the influence of the family are all social stimuli.

Social stratification
The ranking of people in a society by other members of the society into higher and lower social positions so as to produce a hierarchy of respect, status, and power. Such rankings categorize people into higher, middle and lower social class groups.

Socialization
The process by which an individual learns the norms and values of the group and of society.

Socially dependent consumer
A consumer who scores low on opinion leadership but high on information seeking. This consumer represents the traditional view of a follower—an individaul who is socially active in soliciting word-of-mouth information, but is not an influential.

Socially independent consumer
A consumer who scores high on opinion leadership but low on information seeking.

This consumer represents the traditional view of opinion leadership—a consumer who transmits information and influence but does not solicit it.

Socially integrated consumer
One who scores high on both opinion leadership and information seeking. This consumer is the most socially active in both transmitting and receiving word-of-mouth communications.

Socially isolated consumer
One who scores low on opinion leadership and information seeking. This consumer is a passive individual who may receive but does not actively seek information. He or she is not socially active and may avoid personal influence.

Sociometric technique
A method developed to describe the patterns of communication and influence between members of a group. Members of a group are asked from whom they get advice and to whom they go to seek advice or information in making a decision. Specific individuals are identifed and can in turn be interviewed to trace the network of communication. Individuals with the most frequent communication links are identified as opinion leaders.

Source effects
The impact of the source on consumer information processing, determined by the nature and credibility of the source.

Standard price
What consumers regard as a fair price which serves as a basis for judging other prices. There is a range around a standard price that is not likely to produce any change in behavior such as a change in quantity consumed or a switch to another brand. But outside this range, price elasticity is greater, producing significant changes in behavior.

Status
The rank or position of an individual in the prestige hierarchy of a group or community. The position the individual occupies within the group. High status implies greater power and influence within the group.

Stimulus discrimination
The ability of the consumer to perceive differences in stimuli. Discrimination allows customers to judge brands selectively and to make evaluative judgments about preferences of one brand or another.

Stimulus generalization
Once a conditioned response has been established, it will be elicited not only by the conditioned stimulus but also by similar stimuli. When two stimuli are seen as similar, the effects of one can be substituted for the effects of the other. Generalization allows consumers to simplify the process of evaluation.

Stochastic models
Models that treat the response of consumers in the marketplace as the outcome of a probabilistic process over time. They attempt to explain brand loyalty and switching behavior based on past purchases.

Subculture
That part of the total culture of a society which is distinct from society in certain respects; for example, an ethnic group, a social class group, a regional group. The ways of behaving that distinguish a particular group from a larger one.

Subliminal perception
The threshold for awareness of conscious recognition may be higher than the threshold for perception. If the stimulus is beneath the threshold of awareness, but above the absolute threshold of perception, it is known as subliminal perception. It is perception of a stimulus below the conscious level. (The conscious level is referred to as the limen; thus perception below the conscious level is subliminal or below the absolute threshold.)

Symbolic aspiration group
A group in which an individual does not expect to receive membership, despite the acceptance of the group's norms and beliefs.

Syncratic decisions
Decisions made jointly by husband and wife.

Test market
A market in which the product is tested prior to national introduction. The last step in the process of testing new products, permitting the marketer to evaluate all components of marketing strategy.

Threshold level
Level of sensory discrimination. Ability to discriminate stimuli.

Trade-off analysis
A technique that provides a basis for determining the consumer's optimal combination of product characteristics. A limited number of concepts representing combinations of characteristics are presented to consumers. Consumers are asked their preference, and on this basis, an ideal combination of characteristics is identified.

Trait theory
A quantitative approach to the study of personality which postulates that an individual's personality is composed of definite predispositional attributes called traits. The most empirical basis for measuring personality, it states that personality is composed of a set of traits that describe a general response predisposition.

Trickle across effect
The process of diffusion occurring across groups regardless of socioeconomic status. A horizontal pattern of diffusion.

Trickle down effect
The process of information and influence traveling from higher to lower socioeconomic groupings. A vertical pattern of diffusion.

Unit pricing
The expression of the price of an item in terms of the cost per unit of measure (ounce, gram, etc.). The posting of the price for an item in a common unit such as an ounce, even though the actual size of the item may be more than an ounce. Unit pricing permits comparisons of various items in common units.

Unplanned purchasing
A buying action undertaken without buying intention prior to entering the store. Four types of unplanned purchases are (1) pure impulse, (2) reminder effect, (3) suggestion effect, and (4) planned impulse purchases.

Upside elasticity
Sensitivity to increases in price. It is possible that a consumer will buy less if prices increase, but will not buy substantially more if prices decrease. This consumer is therefore elastic on the upside.

Variety-seeking behavior
The motivation for brand switching is sometimes a desire for change, a search for novelty. It is the result of routinized choice and is a logical expression of consumer boredom.

Vocabulary of product attributes and benefits
A set of adjectives to describe a product's characteristics and benefits generally obtained from consumer in-depth interviews. For example, a vocabulary for soft drink brands might include terms like mild, sweet, carbonated, refreshing.

Weber's law
A law of psychological relativity: subjective discriminations are not bound to absolute characteristics of stimuli but to relations between them. The size of the least detectable change or increment in intensity is a function of the initial intensity: the stronger the initial stimulus, the greater the difference needs to be. For example, the higher the price of a product, the greater the price difference between two brands of that product must be in order for it to be detected.

Yielding
Message acceptance, measured by its impact on some behavioral measure such as brand attitudes or purchase intent.

Name Index

Subject Index